KEYGuide

KT-503-805

On the Move

The Sights

What to Do

Walks and Tours

Eating and Staying

Planning

Maps

The AA KEYGuide
Barcelona

Contents

Understanding Barcelona   **4–10**

Living Barcelona   **11–24**
Barcelona: Capital of Catalonia   12–13
Architecture: Geniuses and Saints   14–15
Art and Design   16–17
A Modern City of Traditions   18–19
A Melting Pot   20–21
Waterfront Barcelona   22–23
More than a Club   24

The Story of Barcelona   **25–38**
200BC–1153: The Beginnings   26–27
1153–1410: Medieval Barcelona   28–29
1410–1714: Spanish Unity and Decline   30–31
1714–1898: Barça Bounces Back   32–33
1898–1939: From Rebirth to Civil War   34–35
1939–2000: Postwar Barcelona   36–37
2000 onwards: The City Today   38

On the Move   **39–52**
Arriving   40–42
  By Air   40–41
  By Train, Bus, Car and Boat   42
Getting Around   43–50
  The Metro   44–45
  Buses   46–48
  Train, Taxis, Bicyles and Other Services   49
  Driving   50
Leaving Barcelona   51
Visitors with a Disability   52

The Sights   **53–130**
Sights Locator Maps   54–57
Sightseeing Areas   58–61
  Montjüic   58
  The Port   59
  Barri Gòtic   60
  La Ribera   61
A–Z of Sights   62–130

What to Do   **131–180**
Shopping   132–154
  Shopping Locator Maps   132–135
  Shopping Introduction   136
  Shopping Areas   137–140
  Shopping Directory   141–154
  Chain Stores Chart   152–153
Performance   155–164
  Performance Introduction   155
  Performance Locator Maps   156–159
  Performance Directory   160–164
Nightlife   165–170
  Bars and Cafés   166–169
  Clubs   169–170
Sports and Activities   171–176
Children's Barcelona   177–178
Festivals and Events   179–180

KEY TO SYMBOLS

✚ Map reference
☎ Telephone number
🕐 Opening times
💶 Admission prices
Ⓜ Underground station
🚌 Bus or tram number
🚆 Train station
🎫 Tours
📖 Guidebook
🍴 Restaurant
☕ Café
🏬 Shop
🚻 Toilets
🛏 Number of rooms
🅿 Parking
🚭 No smoking
❄ Air conditioning
🏊 Swimming pool
🏋 Gym

Out and About   181–204
Walks   182–193
Excursions   194–203
City Tours   204

Eating   205–234
Locator Maps   206–209
Eating Out in Barcelona   210–211
Menu Reader   212–213
Restaurants by Cuisine   214–215
A–Z of Restaurants   216–234

Staying   235–254
Locator Maps   236–239
Staying in Barcelona   240–241
A–Z of Hotels   242–253
Hotel Groups   254

Planning   255–276
Before You Go   256–257
Practicalities   258–259
Money Matters   260–261
Health   262–263
Finding Help   264
Opening Times and Tickets   265
Communication   266–267
Media   268
Books, Maps and Films   269
Tourist Offices and Useful Websites 270
Words and Phrases   271–276

Maps   277–291
Street Atlas   277–291
Sightseeing and Shopping Areas   Inside Front Cover
City Locator   4
Greater Barcelona   6–7
Airport Locator Map   40
Sights Locator Maps   54–57
Sightseeing Areas   58–61
Shopping Locator Maps   132–135
Shopping Areas   137–140
Performance Locator Maps   156–159
Walks   182–193
Excursions   194
Eating Locator Maps   206–209
Staying Locator Maps   236–239
Metro   Inside Back Cover

Indexes
Street Index   292–297
Book Index   298–307

Acknowledgments and Credits   308–310

UNDERSTANDING BARCELONA

Barcelona, the chic Catalan capital, barely feels like a Spanish city.
The classic tourist images of Spain are almost totally absent in this city of
wide boulevards and striking modern architecture. This is a confident,
prosperous, youthful, energetic, fun-loving city, with a passion for style and
design and an obsession with its own image. The reinvention of Barcelona
began in the early 1990s as it prepared to host the Olympic Games, but the
rebuilding and the rebranding have been going on ever since. The Modernista
architects have been rediscovered and the eccentric genius Antoni Gaudí
(1852–1926) has become an icon for the city. The seafront has been revived as
a busy urban entertainment area, with new beaches and promenades taking
the place of dilapidated warehouses and wharves. The warm climate, vibrant
nightlife and designer shopping are drawing increasing numbers of visitors,
and Barcelona has become one of the cultural hotspots of Europe.

BARCELONA

LAYOUT OF THE CITY

The oldest parts of Barcelona are eminently walkable. Most visitors head straight for Las Ramblas, the avenue that runs down from Plaça de Catalunya to the port. To one side is the Barri Gòtic, a warren of dark, narrow, medieval streets clustered around the cathedral; to the other side is the up-and-coming, multicultural district of El Raval. Heading north from the monument to Columbus at the foot of Las Ramblas are the beaches and promenades of Port Vell, Barceloneta and the Port Olímpic. The commercial heart of modern Barcelona is found in L'Eixample, which heads inland from Plaça de Catalunya towards the outlying district of Gràcia and the mountain of Tibidabo. At the turn of the 20th century, L'Eixample became the outdoor studio of the Modernistas and a number of their creations can be seen on the main boulevard, Passeig de Gràcia. This street, which is virtually an extension of Las Ramblas, makes an easy walk but despite its rigid street plan L'Eixample is not conducive to strolling and for the more outlying attractions, such as Gaudí's La Sagrada Família (see pages 124–129), it is better to take the metro or bus.

PEOPLE AND LANGUAGE

Barcelona is usually classed as Spain's second city, after the capital Madrid, but this status is most definitely not the opinion of the locals. The majority of the population of around 2 million are Catalan and are loyal first to their region. They do not consider themselves as Spanish. But other residents, who are foreigners or immigrants from other regions of Spain, speak Spanish (also called Castilian), which has led to linguistic conflict. In recent years there has been a strong push towards making Catalan, and not Castilian, the language of government and education. This has resulted in all children now being taught principally in Catalan at school, yet many will still speak Castilian. This bi-lingual attitude is also reflected in the media. The Catalan-language television channel, TV3, has the highest viewing figures, yet most people still read Spanish books and newspapers (see pages 268–269). But one thing that unites just about everyone in the city, Catalans and immi-grants alike, is their love of the soccer team FC Barcelona and a desire to see them get one over their old adversary, Real Madrid, the captial's own soccer team.

Barceloneta
The former fishing village now lies at the start of a series of beaches that stretch north to the Port Olímpic and beyond.

Barri Gòtic
Heading east off Las Ramblas, the medieval maze of the Barri Gòtic (Gothic Quarter) is the oldest part of the city and is a district of churches, intimate cafés and quirky shops.

L'Eixample
Created in the 19th century, the grid system of L'Eixample (extension) is the business and commercial hub of the city and home to some of the best Modernista architecture.

The Plaça d'Espanya, Montjuïc (left); Passeig de Colóm in Barceloneta (middle); L'Eixample (right)

Gràcia
This former township, which stretches across Avinguda Diagonal, retains a radical streak and a villagey, alternative feel.

El Raval
On the opposite side of Las Ramblas, the former red-light district is becoming a chic place to be, thanks to the arrival of the Museu d'Art Contemporani de Barcelona (MACBA).

La Ribera
This is also known as El Born after the main street Passeig del Born. The medieval mercantile area to the east of the Barri Gòtic is now a hip hangout of wine and tapas bars.

Montjuïc
This green mountain overlooking the port houses some of Barcelona's best museums, plus the sports facilities built for the 1992 Olympics.

Catalan in this book
The use of Catalan has been guided by what you will find on the spot; where a Catalan name predominates, and it usually does, we have used it. Examples of this are Museu and Plaça (Catalan) not Museo and Plaza (Castilian).

ECONOMY AND SOCIETY
Barcelona was the driving force of Spain's 19th-century industrial revolution and Catalonia is the most economically active region in Spain. Although manufacturing is still important, traditional industries like shipbuilding, textiles, chemicals and cork are being replaced by service industries such as banking, finance, fashion, design and tourism. The number of visitors has doubled since the 1992 Olympics and now stands at more than 3.5 million per year, making Barcelona one of the most visited cities in Europe. Tourism is thought to provide at least one in ten jobs, bringing financial benefits, but it has also created pressures as more and more people move into the city in search of jobs. Unemployment, homelessness and crime are all problems as in any major European city. Despite the outward appearance of prosperity, there are still pockets of poverty, especially in the outlying districts of the city that few visitors see.

MODERNISME
Modernisme is the Catalan version of the art and design movement that swept through Europe at the turn of 20th century, also known as art nouveau or Jugendstil. It was also part of the wider Catalan Renaixença (Renaissance) that celebrated all things Catalan. The designs of this movement emulated nature with soft, fluid forms and often using plants and flowers as the basis for an idea. The artists embraced new technology, which gave them the means to create these ideas. You won't want to miss the vast number of beautiful Modernista buildings in Barcelona, many of which still have a practical use and are why the city is so architecturally significant.

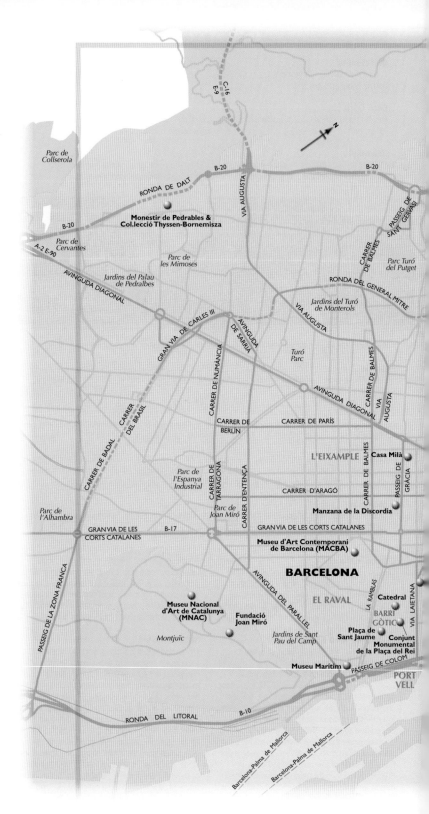

Parc de
Collserola

C-16
E-9

B-20

RONDA DE DALT

VIA AUGUSTA

B-20

B-20

**Monestir de Pedrables &
Col.lecció Thyssen-Bornemisza**

PASSEIG DE
SANT GERVASI

A-2 E-90

Parc de
Cervantes

Parc de
les Mimoses

CARRER
DE BALMES

Parc Turó
del Putget

AVINGUDA DIAGONAL

Jardins del Palau
de Pedralbes

RONDA DEL GENERAL MITRE

GRAN VIA DE CARLES III

AVINGUDA
DE SARRIA

Jardins del Turó
de Monterols

VIA AUGUSTA

CARRER DE NUMÀNCIA

Turó
Parc

CARRER DE BALMES

CARRER DEL BRASIL

AVINGUDA DIAGONAL

VIA AUGUSTA

CARRER DE BADAL

CARRER DE
BERLÍN

CARRER DE PARÍS

L'EIXAMPLE

CARRER DE BALMES

Casa Milà

PASSEIG DE GRACIA

Parc de
l'Espanya
Industrial

CARRER DE
TARRAGONA

CARRER D'ENTENÇA

CARRER D'ARAGÓ

Parc de
Joan Miró

Manzana de la Discordia

Parc de
l'Alhambra

GRAN VIA DE LES
CORTS CATALANES

B-17

GRAN VIA DE LES CORTS CATALANES

**Museu d'Art Contemporani
de Barcelona (MACBA)**

BARCELONA

PASSEIG DE LA ZONA FRANCA

AVINGUDA DEL PARAL·LEL

LA RAMBLAS

EL RAVAL

Catedral

VIA LAIETANA

**Museu Nacional
d'Art de Catalunya
(MNAC)**

**Fundació
Joan Miró**

**BARRI
GÒTIC**

Montjuïc

Jardins de Sant
Pau del Camp

**Plaça de
Sant Jaume**

**Conjunt
Monumental
de la Plaça del Rei**

Museu Marítim

PASSEIG DE COLOM

**PORT
VELL**

RONDA   DEL   LITORAL

B-10

Barcelona-Palma de Mallorca

Barcelona-Palma de Mallorca

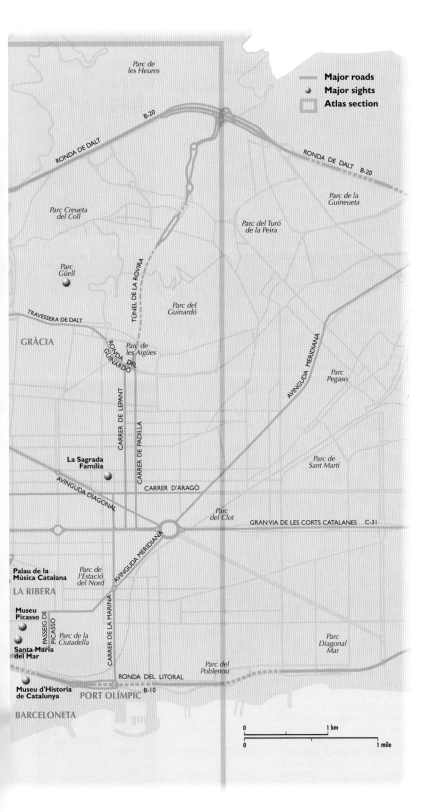

Major roads

Major sights

Atlas section

Parc de
les Heures

B-20

RONDA DE DALT

RONDA DE DALT B-20

Parc de la
Guineueta

Parc Creueta
del Coll

Parc del Turó
de la Peira

Parc
Güell

TÚNEL DE LA ROVIRA

Parc del
Guinardó

TRAVESSERA DE DALT

AVINGUDA MERIDIANA

GRÀCIA

RONDA DEL GUINARDÓ

Parc de
les Aigües

Parc
Pegaso

CARRER DE LEPANT

CARRER DE PADILLA

La Sagrada
Família

Parc de
Sant Martí

AVINGUDA DIAGONAL

CARRER D'ARAGÓ

Parc
del Clot

GRAN VIA DE LES CORTS CATALANES C-31

AVINGUDA MERIDIANA

Palau de la
Música Catalana

Parc de
l'Estació
del Nord

LA RIBERA

Museu
Picasso

PASSEIG DE PICASSO

CARRER DE LA MARINA

Parc de la
Ciutadella

Parc
Diagonal
Mar

Santa Maria
del Mar

Parc del
Poblenou

RONDA DEL LITORAL

Museu d'Historia
de Catalunya

PORT OLÍMPIC B-10

BARCELONETA

| 0 | | 1 km |
| 0 | | 1 mile |

BEST MODERNISTA ARCHITECTURE

Casa Milà (see pages 66–69): Gaudí's wavy apartment block with a stunning roof terrace.

Manzana de la Discordia (see pages 82–83): Three very different houses on Passeig de Gràcia by the holy trinity of Modernista architects.

Palau de la Música Catalana (see pages 104–107): Spectacular concert hall with a riot of mosaics and stained glass.

Park Güell (see pages 110–113): Fairy tale park overlooking the city, complete with a mosaic dragon by Antoni Gaudí.

La Sagrada Família (see pages 124–129): Gaudí's masterpiece has become the symbol of Barcelona.

BEST MUSEUMS AND GALLERIES

La Sagrada Família (above) and Park Güell (left) are two of Gaudí's most impressive buildings

Fundació Joan Miró (see pages 78–79): Playful paintings and sculptures in bright primary tones by an artist who sums up the spirit of Barcelona.

Museu d'Art Contemporani de Barcelona (see pages 90–91): Stylish modern art museum at the heart of El Raval.

Museu Marítim (see pages 94–95): The beautiful old building of the royal shipyards almost outdoes the collection.

Museu Nacional d'Art de Catalunya (see pages 96–99): Collection of medieval art housed in a palace on Montjuïc.

Museu Picasso (see pages 100–101): A homage to one of the great Spanish artists who spent his formative years in Barcelona.

Plaça de Catalunya is home to a number of fountains and statues

BEST OUTDOOR SCULPTURES

Barcelona Head (see page 119): Vast sculpture by Roy Lichtenstein on the waterfront at Port Vell.

Deessa (see page 115): Josep Clarà's nude goddess among the fountains of Plaça de Catalunya.

Dona i Ocell (see page 109): Huge sculpture by Joan Miró, fashioned out of concrete and mosaic and completed shortly before his death.

Fish (see page 118): Glistening golden fish sculpture by Frank Gehry and the symbol of the Port Olímpic.

Homage to Barceloneta (see page 63): Rebecca Horn's tribute to the *chiringuitos* (beach bars) on the beach.

BEST SHOPS

Rope-soled shoes from La Manual Alpargatera

Antonio Miró (see page 145): The leading name among Barcelona's contemporary fashion designers is best known for his casual but stylish men's suits.

Mercat de la Boqueria

Colmado Murria (see page 144): A sumptuous array of food and wine behind a stunning Modernista shopfront.

El Corte Inglés (see page 151): The huge department store on Plaça de Catalunya.

Escribà (see page 144): Heavenly chocolates and pastries.

La Manual Alpargatera (see page 148): An old-style Barri Gòtic workshop selling rope-soled shoes.

Loewe (see page 145): Classic leather goods in a Modernista mansion on Passeig de Gràcia.

Mercat de la Boqueria (see page 152): The city's wonderful central market, just off Las Ramblas.

Vinçon (see page 151): An illustration of Barcelona's obsession with design, with rare views of Casa Milà from the terrace.

The view from the poolside at the Arts Barcelona includes Frank Gehry's Fish, one of the best outdoor sculptures

BEST PLACES TO STAY

Arts Barcelona (see page 243): The ultimate in luxury in a skyscraper overlooking the beach and the marina of the Port Olímpic.
Claris (see page 244): Excellent service and style in a Modernista palace with a rooftop swimming pool and a private collection ranging from Andy Warhol to ancient Egyptian art.
España (see page 246): Modernista landmark by Lluís Domènech i Montaner (1850–1923), with dazzling details and extravagant murals.
Grand Marina (see page 247): Striking modern hotel on the waterfront with views over the harbour.
Mesón Castilla (see page 250): Old-style Spanish character in the trendy Raval.

BEST CAFÉS AND BARS

Café de l'Opera (see page 166): Mirrors, wooden panels and tables on the street at this coffee house on Las Ramblas.
Marsella (see page 168): Drink absinthe at wrought-iron tables in this old El Raval bar, a hangover from the days when this was the city's red-light district.
Mirablau (see page 168): Great views over the city from this terrace bar on the way up to Tibidabo.

BEST PLACES TO EAT

Agut (see page 216): Catalan classics and serious steaks in the heart of the Barri Gòtic.
Asador de Aranda (see page 217): Roast lamb from a wood-burning oven in a Castilian roasthouse on Tibidabo.
La Bombeta (see page 219): Delicious seafood and generous tapas, ideal for those on a budget.
Can Majó (see page 220): You won't get better or fresher seafood than at this Barceloneta beachfront restaurant.

Quim at the Boqueria market feeds visitors and stallholders alike (above)

Can Majó restaurant (right)

The restaurants along the waterfront pride themselves on serving the best quality seafood

Estrella de Plata (see page 222): The bar that started the trend towards designer tapas in Barcelona.
La Flauta Mágica (see page 222): Trendy restaurant in La Ribera, serving organic, vegetarian cuisine.
Els Pescadors (see page 228): Catalan fish dishes in an old fisherman's tavern on a pretty square in the district of Poble Nou.
Quim (see page 229): Stand-up bar in the Boqueria market serving no-nonsense classics like *callos* (tripe).
Set Portes (see page 232): The oldest restaurant in Barcelona still serves the best paella in town.
Sol Soler (see page 232): Vegetarian tapas, served up at a lively square in Gràcia.

TOP EXPERIENCES

Wander down Las Ramblas, enjoying the street entertainment and the flower stands at the heart of the city (see pages 120–121).

A classical guitar player is just one of the many performers that you will meet along Las Ramblas (left)

Dance the sardana, the Catalan national dance, in front of the cathedral on Sundays (see page 173).

Join the locals for an afternoon on the beach at Barceloneta or Port Olímpic (see page 173).

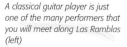

Hit the tapas trail in the bars of La Ribera, nibbling *pintxos* (Basque-style snacks) and drinking cava, a sparkling Catalan wine (see pages 214–215).

Move heaven and earth to get tickets to a concert at the Palau de la Música Catalana (see page 161).

All the ingredients for a picnic are readily available in the city's food stores

Join the crowds to watch FC Barcelona play soccer, or at the very least, take a stadium tour (see pages 92 and 172).

Climb one of the towers at La Sagrada Família for close up views of the intricate tile work (see pages 124–129).

Relax in the cool green corners of Parc de la Ciutadella, with its boating lake and ornamental gardens (see page 108).

The Cascada in the Parc de la Ciutadella by Josep Fonsere, assisted by Gaudí, and used as a boating lake

Go ballroom dancing at La Paloma, one of the last vestiges of the pre-makeover Raval (see page 173).

Fire breathing dragon at La Mercè festival

Take in a traditional Catalan festival, with its *dimonis* (devils), *correfoc* (fire-running) and *castells* (human towers, see page 179).

Go shopping, or window shopping depending on your budget, along Passeig de Gràcia and spoil yourself in the luxury stores (see page 139).

Take in the whole of the city at once from the peak of Tibidabo, which has views out over the sea and of Montjuïc (see page 130).

Living Barcelona

Barcelona: Capital of
  Catalonia   12–13
Architecture: Geniuses
  and Saints   14–15
Art and Design   16–17
A Modern City of Traditions   18–19
A Melting Pot   20–21
Waterfront Barcelona   22–23
More than a Club   24

Cheerful earthenware pots for sale at La Bisbal, heart of the Catalan ceramics industry

Tempting fresh vegetables (below); the Catalan flag (below left)

Catalonia's festivals celebrate its rich culture: Callela de Palafrugell even has one to sing sea shanties brought back from Cuba by local sailors (above)

The Parliament building in its pleasant garden setting (right)

Barcelona: Capital of **Catalonia**

Politically Catalonia has formed part of Spain for more than 500 years, but the firm belief that their land is a nation apart is still ingrained in many Catalans. Understanding this country within a country mentality is essential to understanding Catalonia. The Generalitat, the region's autonomous government, has its own police, hospitals and schools, though it is ever fighting for more rights. The use of Catalan is a constant battle, with the Generalitat pushing for greater recognition in the European Union and for the right to use the language in more government documents. On the streets Catalan is thriving after being brutally outlawed during Franco's dictatorship, as is a strong sense of national identity, a backlash to the repressions of those years.

Catalan politics today are dominated by the constant bickering between the rival nationalist and socialist parties. Both parties support Catalan autonomy and fall to the left of the Partido Popular that controls Spain. Since 1980 Jordi Pujol has ruled the nationalist Convergència i Unió (Convergence and Union), but his reign has come to an end. Pujol's hand-picked successor, Artur Mas, faced Pascual Maragall, the former Barcelona mayor, but neither won outright (see page 38).

Statue of Sant Jordi in a niche behind the balustrades of the Generalitat

An Economic Capital

Catalans have always had a reputation for being thrifty and business minded, a trait the rest of Spain loves to mock, as in the joke that wire was invented by two Catalans pulling on a coin. Yet the region is an important economic engine in Spain, responsible for nearly a quarter of the country's exports and a fifth of its gross national product. The Catalan Institute of Statistics reports that Catalans earn more, spend more and save more than most Spaniards. And as the Generalitat complains, they also contribute more heavily to the rest of the country through the main industries of chemicals, textiles and metals.

Fishing is still important in Catalonia, and the boats are lovingly maintained (right)

The *castell* (human tower) is a symbol of Catalan community spirit—a group of people co-operating to attain a common goal

Poster advertising the many facets of Forum 2004 (right)

Casting off Franco's Shadow

Franco seemed to make a special effort to punish Catalonia for opposing him throughout the Civil War (1936–39). He was brutal with dissenters here, taking thousands to work camps and executing others. In November 2002 the Spanish government officially condemned Franco's dictatorship for the first time ever and opened some previously undisclosed archives to the public. This move has encouraged people to talk more about the dictatorship and to come forward with information about that dark time. Until now, few details about the fates of Franco dissenters were known, but since that November, nine mass graves have been found in Catalonia alone. The graves hold the still-unidentified bodies of just some of the approximately 150,000 who died in the repressions.

The Widest Plaça

At first glance, the Plaça de Sant Jaume is a simple sunny square, an open space between the Casa de la Ciutat (House of the City, or Town Hall) and the Palau de la Generalitat (regional government headquarters). It's the perfect place for city celebrations and civic demonstrations. But there is as much distance ideologically as there is physically between the two buildings staring each other down across the square. The town hall is traditionally socialist, focusing on projects of urban renewal and city improvement. The nationalist Generalitat is bent on gaining Catalan autonomy. Plaça de Sant Jaume is the barrier between these proud entities, creating an eternal standoff and a constant reminder of the rivalry between the two.

Growing Pains

According to the town hall, growth is great, but it is making the city prohibitively expensive for residents, especially the younger ones. The average age at which a person moves out of the family house to get married is 29 (according to the Catalan Institute of Statistics). This is either a case of true family devotion or a reflection of the soaring housing prices that have rocketed by 87 per cent since 1997, calculated by the Municipal Housing Board, while salaries have only risen 15 per cent. Even by the age of 29 many haven't saved enough to start buying an apartment, so they either look outside Barcelona (the closest suburb, L'Hospitalet, is now Spain's seventh-largest city) or try to take advantage of the city's growing number of government-run housing options, which have lower rents.

Thematic Tourism

Barcelona learned its lesson from the 1992 Olympics, namely that a big-name international event does wonders for a city's image both at home and abroad. So these days the city, already Spain's most visited, is hard at work creating international events for every year. The Year of Gaudí was 2002, when dozens of exhibits, conferences and projects celebrated the architect's work. The plan worked, tourism shot up 11 per cent, and 2003 was declared both the Year of Design and the Year of Sports. But the event that comes closest to matching the scope of the Olympics is the 2004 Universal Forum of Cultures, when Barcelona plans to bring the world's leaders to a year-long debate about religion, education and globalism.

Artist's impression of the
bullring development on
Plaça d'Espanya (above)

A balcony at Casa Batlló (above)
and a Casa Milà chimney (left),
both buildings by Gaudí

Architecture: Geniuses
and Saints

Saint Gaudí

When you visit Gaudí's La Sagrada Família, take note of the small cards in the crypt asking visitors to describe miracles such as healings or conversions, that happened after a visit to the church. This is not simple curiosity, it's an effort to prove that Barcelona's most famous denizen was not only a brilliant designer, but a saint as well. The Catholic Church is investigating Gaudí's life to see whether his work is capable of provoking miracles and whether he should be made an example of holiness for Catholics worldwide. Gaudí was devoted to the project and dedicated his final years to La Sagrada Família, living like a hermit inside its unfinished shell and giving up all worldly pleasures.

Boom periods in Barcelona's history have always been accompanied by spurts of architectural development. The region's 13th-century Golden Age saw the birth of Catalan Gothic, a simple and elegant version of the classic Gothic. The Catalan Renaixença (Renaissance) of the late 19th century brought Modernisme and all its glory, and post-Franco prosperity has ushered in a host of modern projects. But the best-known buildings are those of architect and designer Antoni Gaudí i Cornet (1852–1926). Gaudí took his inspiration from the natural world, creating ceiling beams shaped like tree branches, spiral staircases like snail shells, and tile mosaics that shimmer like water. His methods were radical even by today's standards and it should be no surprise that his work was hated as often as it was adored. Although Gaudí is often called a Modernista, his style defies classification. The real Modernistas were contemporaries like Josep Puig i Cadafalch and Lluís Domènech i Montaner, architects who, like Gaudí, were financed by the new Catalan bourgeoisie. Bold tones, lots of ornamentation and natural light were important elements of their style and can be seen to dizzying effect across the city. Barcelona's rich architectural legacy is still alive, and international architects like Richard Rogers and Jean Nouvel have given the city its newest emblematic structures.

Sant Jordi slaying the dragon is a common image in Barcelona—this statue is on Passeig de Gràcia (right)

Candles in front of the illuminated altar in Catalan Gothic Santa Maria del Pí (left)

Cast iron house number at Casa Vicens, Gaudí's first major work

The modern Amrey Diagonal Hotel in the Glòries business district (left)

Plaça de Catalunya divides the medieval city from L'Eixample

The Expansion that Almost Wasn't

If Barcelona city planners had had their way, the checkerboard grid of streets that makes up Barcelona's huge L'Eixample (Expansion) district would never have existed. When in 1859 the town hall called for design proposals to expand the cramped city, they chose a plan comprising of a network of wide boulevards fanning out from the central Plaça de Catalunya. It was only after the last-minute intervention of Madrid bureaucrats that the job was given to Ildefons Cerdà, the engineer who thought up the utopic grid design that makes today's Barcelona so easy to navigate. His dream of wide streets and grassy squares, however, is a far cry from the dense urban space the Eixample has become.

The Indian Legacy

Gaudí's patron, Eusebi Güell, was one of many Catalan bourgeoisie who owed part of his fortune to trading with the New World. These businessmen-adventurers were dubbed *indianos* by Catalans as, after all, Columbus did believe he'd discovered India. *Indianos* traded Spanish wine and textiles for sugar and spices throughout the 19th century. Regrettably, from a modern perspective, the trade route often included a stop in Africa to pick up slaves to be sold in the Americas. This money funded large amounts of the Renaixença, paying for the Modernista creations as well as railways and water pipes, forming the basis of the city around you today.

The Legendary Modernistas

Pay attention to the ornate streetlights lining Passeig de Gràcia. Perched atop them are small iron bats with wings spread. The bats show up again on Gaudí's Palau Güell. What seems like a homage to Batman is really a reminder of Catalonia's medieval glory, when the bat was a symbol of powerful King Jaume I (see page 28). Jaume claimed that a bat once alerted him to an enemy presence, and he included it in his coat of arms. Other symbols of Catalan identity pop up in Modernista design. One of the most common is the dragon, which refers to the legend of Sant Jordi (St. George), who saved Catalonia by slaying a dragon, used at Casa Amatller and as a theme in Gaudí's Casa Batlló.

New Kids on the Block

On an endless quest of urban renewal, the city has a host of projects under way. By the end of 2004, a soaring bullet-shaped tower, known as La Torre Agbor and built by French architect Jean Nouvel, will mark the Plaça de Glòries in northern Barcelona. Locals had a hard time accepting the fact that the strikingly modern skyscraper, which has been compared to most things, including a large cigar, will become synonymous with the city. Other soon-to-be landmarks are a triangle-shaped conference building with water running down its sides, built for the Forum 2004, and the bullring on Plaça d'Espanya, converted into a shopping arcade by architect Richard Rogers.

Street performers along Las Ramblas (left) and stylized graffiti (above left) have been embraced as an extension to the outdoor museum

Picasso (left) was a regular at Els Quatre Gats (below)

Miró's *Dona i Ocell* dominates the area at 22m (72ft)

Art and Design

Blame it on the inspirational Mediterranean Sea or the abundance of sunny days here, but Barcelona is undeniably a hotspot for today's artists and designers. Areas like La Ribera and El Raval are filling up fast with studios, and a stroll through Barcelona's old quarter reveals an impressive number of shops selling locally designed jewellery, fashion and glassworks. Museums, galleries and expositions abound, and a great number of these are focused on contemporary art. One of the most important is Barcelona's modern art museum, the Museu d'Art Contemporari de Barcelona (MACBA, see pages 90–91). The Fundació Antoni Tàpies, a foundation in the name of one of Catalonia's greatest living artists, and the Fundació Joan Miró on Montjuïc are also important stops on Barcelona's museum route. Modern Catalan society has embraced art so strongly largely because of the lasting effects of the Modernista movement, whose heritage is everywhere and originally included painters and writers as well as architects. They helped to revive the city's artistic climate, paving the way for 20th-century artists like Picasso, Miró and Tàpies.

Custo creations are another example of the city's design taking the world by storm

Four Cats

On Carrer de Montsió, hidden in a corner of the old town, is the Quatre Gats (Four Cats) Café, and its draw is the dark little tavern's history. In 1897, the painters Ramon Casas, Santiago Rusiyñol, Miquel Utrillo and Pere Romeu established an artistic society where they could promote and discuss their bohemian ideas about life and culture. Their meeting place, which soon turned into a friendly tavern with art on the walls, was set up in this building, designed by Puig i Cadalfalch, and artists and free-thinkers streamed through the tavern. Famously, it was here that a young unknown painter, Pablo Picasso, had his first-ever exhibition at the turn of the 20th century. Today the interior is filled with paintings and photographs of the period.

MACBA is the home of modern art (left); *Barcelona Head* in Plaça d'Antoni Lopez (below)

Striking outfit at Pasarela Gaudí fashion show (left); Vinçon is the epitome of style (below)

An Outdoor Museum

One of Franco's most visible legacies in Barcelona is the prison-style architecture he let sprout up in the 1950s and 60s. After the dictator's death in 1975, innovative urban planners, led by architect Oriol Bohigas, set out to create visual distractions from these brick eyesores. The result was a wave of outdoor art, making Barcelona one of the best open-air museums in the world. Joan Miró's *Dona i Cell* (Woman and Bird), a bright piece with a bovine influence, is at the Parc de Joan Miró, and along the waterfront is the equally vibrant *Barcelona Head* by pop artist Roy Lichtenstein. Other world-famous artists brought in to liven up urban spaces, and only paid a fraction of their usual fees, were Antoni Tàpies, Josep Subirachs and Richard Serra.

Fashion Wars

Watch out Paris, Barcelona is on its way to becoming the latest thing in the world fashion scene. Barcelona has run the Pasarela Gaudí fashion show since 1985, and local designers like Antonio Miró, Lydia Delgado and Josep Font are finally becoming internationally known. Their success has convinced fashion promoters that the Pasarela Gaudí is destined for greatness. The industry agrees, as each year the fashion show draws more attention for the quality of its designers and their collections. The only fly in the ointment is the competition of Madrid's fashion industry. The two cities are historic rivals, fighting over soccer, the economy and now fashion. An effort in 2001 to combine Barcelona and Madrid's runway shows failed—no one is giving up the fight for fashion glory.

Custo Barcelona

Chances are you've seen and maybe even own a T-shirt by the fashion label Custo Barcelona. The brand was started here by two brothers (Custo and David Dalmau) but it's long gone global, and now their trademark tops hang in the closets of celebrities like Julia Roberts and Drew Barrymore. The look is based on wild mixes of shades, fabric and texture. A typical Custo may be described as green knit sleeves with flapping cuffs hung off a cotton body with a big red swirl painted on the back and a close-up of a coy girl staring at you from the front. A Custo original can cost €180, but less scrupulous manufacturers have been creating fakes as fast as they can.

The Chair of the Decade

Barcelona is perhaps the only city to have a guidebook, the *Design Guide*, covering its best-designed bars, hotels and restaurants. The fact that it exists is an indicator of the city's obsession with designer goods, and designer furniture is especially coveted. Minimalist, functional designs are ever changing at stores like Pilma and Vinçon, two of Barcelona's best spots for cutting-edge furniture, but once in a while a more emblematic piece makes an appearance. Óscar Tusquet's 1984 office chair Varius was dubbed the chair of the decade, and it was widely sold throughout Spain and abroad. Simple, clean, comfortable and versatile, the chair is all Barcelona designers claim themselves to be. Varius' shape imitates the body of a violin and it's gentle curves have made it a classic.

People work hard on their costumes for summer fiestas

The giants Jaume and Violant make regular appearances at fiestas (above); the city's trade halls, among the busiest in Spain, reflect the tradition of hard work (right)

A Modern City of
Traditions

Barcelona is cosmopolitan and undeniably modern, yet it grips the reins of tradition as though its life depended on it. But it's easy to see why. Much of Barcelona's charm is found in the combination of its old Roman ruins, Gothic buildings and sunny stone squares, skyscrapers, international eateries and bold modern architecture. An important part of this mix is Barcelona's folklore, especially the traditional festivals still thriving here. Throughout the summer, Barcelona's districts (many of which were once independent towns) go all-out for their respective *fiestas mayors* (major festivals). Celebrations are held in the streets with parades of giant statues, fire-breathing dragons and monsters. The party can last for several days, with bands filling the nights with music and fireworks lighting up the sky. Barcelona is equally proud of religious celebrations, like Corpus Cristi, when church fountains throughout the city are adorned with flowers and hollowed eggs are placed on them, left there to dance in the stream of water throughout the feast. These old traditions co-exist with the customs Barcelona is creating today, like the annual film and music festivals and the car rallies that have almost become fiestas in their own right.

The Essence of a Catalan

How to explain a culture that claims itself to be both a serious economic power and the creative capital of Spain? The Catalans know the answer—*seny* and *rauxa*. These two concepts explain the two faces of the traditional Catalan character and show up constantly in literature, folk phrases and every-day talk. *Seny* is a combination of common sense, self-control and practicality, and explains why Catalans are so frugal and logical. Its ideological opposite is *rauxa*, meaning emotion, passion and expression, seen in the wildly decorated Modernista buildings and summer festivals. It's been said that *rauxa* and *seny* are like the opposite sides of the same coin: different but totally inseparable.

Dragons at La Mercè highlight the connection with Sant Jordi and the dragon (above and right); La sardana statue on Montjuïc (below)

Eating out has long been a tradition in the city (above); garlic is an essential ingredient in traditional Catalan cuisine (below)

A Scatological Mindset

If someone toasts you saying, 'Eat well and crap hard', don't be offended. It's just a sign of Catalonia's curious fascination with defecation. A symbol of the life cycle, it appears repeatedly in Catalan art and folk culture, such as in Joan Miró's *Man and Woman in Front of a Pile of Excrement* at the Fundació Joan Miró (see page 78–79). Scatological traditions are most evident at Christmas. The *caganer*, a figurine of a red-capped peasant squatting with his pants down, is hidden in the manger scene. It may seem scandalous, but here it is considered harmless. The *caga tio*, another tradition that carries on the theme, is a piece of firewood children beat until it releases its gifts.

The World's Most Democratic Dance

Come to the square in front of Barcelona's cathedral any Sunday morning and the sight there may surprise you. The people holding hands in a circle aren't saying a prayer or having a seance. They're dancing that most revered dance, la sardana. La sardana seems simple from afar—dancers bob up and down, moving now and then to the left or right—but the dance is actually a complicated set of precise steps. The egalitarian circle is a symbol of social co-operation, and the dancers' positioning (an arms' length apart, with only the hands touching) is a visual symbol of Catalan restraint: a style that is far removed from the sensual flamenco dancing of southern Spain.

Playing with Fire

If tossing firecrackers, running from fire-breathing dragons and getting sprayed with sparks sounds like fun, the festival of La Mercè in September is for you. Barcelona's biggest fiesta is, like many Catalan celebrations, filled with flames. Catalans' love of fire is rooted in pagan festivals and can seem dangerous to outsiders, but few here seem to be worried about getting burned. The highlight of La Mercè is the fire run, or *correfoc*, when a parade of devils, monsters and dragons, who carry firecrackers in their mouths, makes its way through the Barri Gòtic, surrounded by people also carrying sparklers and firecrackers. Onlookers play a game of cat and mouse with the monsters, getting as close as possible to the danger then running away.

The Business of Eating Well

Miguel Sanchez Romera is one of a new breed of Catalan chefs: an artist in the kitchen of his L'Esguard restaurant, just north of Barcelona in Sant Andreu de Llavaneres. He uses local ingredients to create international fare, and has become well-respected for mixing the old with the new. Sanchez Romera is a self-taught chef with a Michelin star to his credit, but he can outdo most other chefs in another way: He trained first as a doctor and is a part-time neurologist, and head of the neurology department at the local hospital.

After many centuries of homogeneity, Barcelona has opened itself up to immigration and the cultural influences this brings (right)

Modern glass and steel buildings abound in Barcelona's burgeoning business district, thanks to the international firms that are moving in (top right and right)

The influx of students into the city has helped to give Barcelona its youthful reputation (top left and above)

A Melting Pot

Barcelona, and Catalonia, has been largely homogeneous for most of its existence. The first large waves of immigrants didn't arrive until the 20th century (first in the 1920s, later in the 1940s and 50s), when workers from southern Spain came searching for better jobs and a better life. Barcelona is still relatively ethnically homogeneous when compared to metropolises like New York, London or Paris, but newcomers from around the globe may be changing that, opening up the city to new influences. Since 1997, the number of resident foreigners in Catalonia has shot up by more than 250 per cent, the government reports, and two-thirds of the 300,000 foreigners now in the region are living in Barcelona. Nearly a quarter are from the European Union, and the others are largely from North Africa, South America and Asia. Barcelona is a popular destination for immigrants looking for work because it is accessible, with good transportation to and from other European countries, and is close to agricultural regions in need of workers. The city is also a magnet for European students because of the fabulous climate and relatively low cost of living. Big business is changing too, with an influx of foreign companies moving in, taking advantage of the new workforce.

El Raval

According to studies undertaken by Barcelona's most prominent newspaper, La Vanguardia, the world's most ethnically and culturally diverse urban space is El Raval district, a corner of the city off Las Ramblas of little more than one square kilometre. Some 40,000 people, half of them born outside Catalonia, live squashed together in this dense barri. The interaction this produces is an inspiration for artists, many of whom display their talent on the district's walls, and free-thinkers. Bars, second-hand clothes shops and art studios abound. On the not-so-positive side, it's a breeding ground for ethnic rivalries and gangs, which has created the first stirrings of racial tension in what is a traditionally tolerant society.

The varied faces of El Raval, one of the world's most ethnically diverse areas (right)

The Rita Blue restaurant in El Raval (above); marriages in Catalonia are now far more likely to have at least one partner that is not from the region (below)

Country is another outside influence on the city

Big Business

A survey of 500 European companies rated Barcelona as the best city in Europe in terms of employee quality of life. Companies like Renault, Volvo and Volkswagen, all of which have set up design workshops in Barcelona, are just a few of those enjoying the lifestyle here. Company directors say the sun, sea and creative vibe give their designers an edge. Other businesses, particularly chemical and pharmaceutical companies, have set up shop too, drawn as much by the climate as by the solid transportation system, infrastructure and economy. Today more than 3,000 foreign businesses are established in Barcelona, most of whom have arrived in the years since the city hosted the 1992 Olympics, all adding to the mix of nationalities found in the region.

The Guiri Culture

It's not much of a compliment to be called a *guiri*, or foreigner, but the European and North American immigrants who've adopted Barcelona out of love for its mild winters and active nightlife have accepted the nickname with a smile. *Guiri* likely has its root in the word *guirigay*, which means gibberish or language that's hard to understand and was meant as an insult by the resident Catalans. But the *guiris* have a very large presence in the city. Many are students in the Erasmus scheme, which enables university students to spend time studying at another university, or they work as teachers, bartenders or translators, living in the old flats of the Barri Gòtic or La Ribera.

Latin Lovers

The Catalan Statistics Institute's newest figures about marriages between Catalans and foreigners reveal an interesting trend. From 1997 to 2002, the number of Catalan men marrying foreign women, particularly those from Columbia, Russia and Brazil, doubled. This means that now more than 8 per cent of all weddings here have at least one fiancé saying I do in a language other than Catalan. Some see this as a positive step towards cultural integration, but there is one curious factor about these statistics: the numbers of Catalan women marrying foreign men has been pretty much stagnant. Obviously the irresistible charm of the Latin lover is unabated.

Catalan Country

Stopping in at the El Sutton bar on Wednesday nights is like hopping on a jet plane to Oklahoma, USA. Cowboy boots, jeans and wide-brimmed hats are the norm here, and the only music you'll hear is the twang of country. The confidence of the line dancers, who hook their thumbs in their belt loops and stomp and turn like professionals, proves that they are no newcomers to the scene. Country music has been gaining a steady following in Catalonia since American folk songs, most of them protesting against the establishment, became popular in the 1970s. These days bars throughout Barcelona, and the rest of Catalonia, have line dancing and local groups singing country tunes. A real crowd pleaser is the Spanish translation of the classic *Achy Breaky Heart* (*No Rompas Mi Corazon*, literally Don't Break My Heart).

A wooden walkway was built over the sea to the Maremagnum complex (left and right)

The improved waterfront attracts all generations (below left and right)

Waterfront Barcelona

Until the 1980s, Barcelona was pretty indifferent to its waterfront. The city's port was shallow and not very interesting, and anyway, coastal areas were traditionally reserved for fishermen and industry. The heart of the city was (and is) well inland, completely ignoring the presence of the Mediterranean. All of that changed when Barcelona renovated its coast in preparation for the 1992 Olympics. Port Vell (Old Port) was transformed from a commercial eyesore into one of the city's liveliest nightspots, with clubs, restaurants and even an IMAX cinema. The utilitarian containers of the commercial port were moved south, out of sight behind the mountain of Montjuïc. The highway that had long separated Barcelona from the sea was re-directed underground, new seaside walkways were put in and a whole new port, the Port Olímpic, was created. These days the waterfront improvement continues, with major urban renewal going on in the northern fringe of Barcelona in districts like Poblenou. According to visionaries, this is the Barcelona of tomorrow, and serious amounts of money have been invested. By the end of 2004, a well-groomed waterfront will extend from the base of Las Ramblas to the northern rim of the city.

Rooms with a View

Until the area around the Port Olímpic was developed in the early 1990s, the only way to get a home with a view of the sea in Barcelona was to die. The New Cemetery, built in 1883, looks like a miniature city on the slope of Montjuïc and has a perfect view of the glistening Mediterranean. The fact that it, and not homes or other buildings, was put here shows Barcelona's old indifference to the sea. The regular layout of the cemetery—coffins are neatly stacked one on top of the other like apartments in a block—imitates the order of L'Eixample, which was still new when this cemetery was founded. Locals joke that they're condemned to live in flats in both life and death.

The towers at Port Olímpic (right)

Cafés line Port Olímpic (above); a ship taking part in the Festival of the Sea (below left)

The City that Ate the Sea

Barcelona's shipyards, now the Museu Marítim (see pages 94–95), are one of the world's most splendid examples of medieval industrial architecture. How is it possible then, you may ask, that it is landlocked and not the least bit accessible from the sea? The answer is that Barcelona, blocked on two of its borders by the mountain of Montjuïc and hills of Collserola, has grown into the Mediterranean by the manual filling in of huge areas of sea with roads and buildings. The same thing happened along other parts of the coast. The Santa Maria del Mar church, in La Ribera, was once practically on the beach; now it's a good 10-minute walk from the water.

Cruisin' Right Along

Some 850,000 cruise-ship visitors docked in Barcelona in 2002, making the city the cruising capital of Europe, second only to Miami in the number of cruise ships (630) that dock here annually. The cruises account for only about three per cent of the port's business, but they bring eager spenders to Barcelona's shops and restaurants to the tune of €900 million a year. The success of the port, in terms of both cruises and container traffic, has led to plans to double its size by the year 2010. The huge under-taking will cost an estimated €1.7 billion and will give the port a surface area of 786ha (1,940 acres).

Superstitious Sailors

Traditionally, fishermen are a superstitious lot, and those working the waters off Barcelona's coast weren't much different. It was bad luck for women to set foot on board a fishing boat, but even worse was if they urinated in the sea, which would surely bring a mighty storm. A woman exposing her private parts to the sea, however, calmed the waters. If that didn't work, each boat carried a wind rope, made by witches to control the breeze, and a manatee skin to keep lightning away. If a sailor drowned, bread blessed by a priest was thrown into the water and would supposedly float to his body. Today, pollution and marine traffic have greatly reduced the number of fishermen here, but until the mid-1800s many of these rituals were closely observed.

La Ferralla sculpture (above)

The New Icária?

You'll sometimes hear the Vila Olímpica, or Olympic Village, referred to as Nova Icária. It was the original name for the *barri* and refers to Icária, a 19th-century French concept of a utopian, egalitarian city and was the inspiration for Cerdà's L'Eixample. A group of French and Catalan Icárians set off in 1848 to found their ideal city in America, but the expedition failed only a year later with the suicide of one of the Catalan leaders. Why exactly Barcelona city planners wanted to resurrect the name is unclear, but happily residents never did adopt it, insisting on calling the area Vila Olímpica. Interestingly, Icária Avenue has man-aged to hold onto its name and is the avenue leading directly to the old cemetery.

More than a club

The War Years

The first soccer martyr was Josep Sunyol, president of the club at the outbreak of the Spanish Civil War (1936–39). Sunyol was paying a visit to the front line in his new car, when he inadvertently ended up driving down the wrong road and straight into Fascist troops. When his captors executed him, they were well aware of the significance of the act and the effect it would have on the morale of a people who used their team as a focus for Catalan nationalism and opposition to the new regime. But despite Franco's best efforts, Barça survived thanks to the club secretary Rosendo Calvet, who spirited away the club's money to a Swiss bank account, and to Patrick O'Connell, the Irish coach who escaped to America with his best players, many of whom stayed in the US for the rest of the war.

When Barça fans declare that their team is more than a soccer club, there is some truth in their assertion. With over 105,000 paid-up members, FC Barcelona is the biggest soccer club in the world, yet it is its social dimension that makes Barça more than a sporting institution. The *socis* (members) regard membership as an essential sign of their Catalan identity, an inalienable right to be cherished and handed down through generations. From the newly born baby presented with a *carnet* (club card) days after baptism, to the grandparents who proudly sport the gold insignias given to those who surpass 50 years membership, Barça's support base cuts across class, political allegiance, age and gender. As a focus for regional pride and identity, symbolism is an important issue, which is one of the reasons Barça is the last remaining team in Europe to keep their kit free of commercial sponsorship, but along with all other teams, the maker's mark of the Nike swoosh is visible.

Know your Enemy

The rivalry between Real Madrid, the capital's team, and Barça stems from a number of complex reasons—some of them political, some sporting—but is so intense that sometimes it is unclear whether the two teams are seen as part of a historical struggle, so when Madrid come to town the stadium is packed with 115,000 screaming fans reminding the players that, in this match, they are playing for more than just three league points.

Barça fans derive more pleasure from Madrid's failures or from their own team's successes. Supporters grow up on stories of injustices from Franco's time onwards, and so the capital's team is linked with the curse of central government. Matches between

The Story of Barcelona

200BC–1153:
The Beginnings   26–27

1153–1410:
Medieval Barcelona   28–29

1410–1714:
Spanish Unity and Decline   30–31

1714–1898:
Barça Bounces Back   32–33

1898–1939:
From Rebirth to Civil War   34–35

1939–2000:
Postwar Barcelona   36–37

2000 onwards:
The City Today   38

The Beginnings

Lovers of legends like to think Hercules founded Barcelona but the reality is more prosaic. Neolithic tribes lived around Montjuïc and it is possible that a Carthaginian village existed, named after their general Hamilcar Barca (died 228BC), but this has never been proved. The Romans established a base here after their invasion of Spain in 218BC and in 15BC named it Barcino, but it remained a minor port in the shadow of Tarraco (Tarragona), Rome's provincial capital.

The fall of Rome opened the gates to a succession of invaders but greater turmoil washed over Spain with the arrival of the Moors in AD711. They swept all before them and by AD717 had subdued Barcelona. An invasion by the Franks (a western Germanic tribe) in the 9th century meant Louis the Pious, Charlemagne's son, conquered the city. The Franks established local nobles as their lieutenants, and of these, Guifré el Pelós (Wilfred the Hairy, AD840–97) rose to be Count of Barcelona and the most powerful Catalan lord. However, the vassalage of the Catalan lords evaporated in AD985 when the Franks failed to help defend the city in the face of a Moorish assault. The Counts, now on their own, spent the 11th and 12th centuries reconquering Catalonia and the last Moorish outpost surrendered in 1153.

200 BC

Life in Roman Barcino

By the time the final set of stout walls was raised around Barcino in the 4th century AD, still in evidence today, it had become a modest but prosperous place. Citizens inevitably gathered in the central forum, roughly where Plaça de Sant Jaume is, and worshipped at the nearby Temple to Augustus (four columns of which remain, see page 182), on a small rise known as Mont Tàber. Just east of the temple was a busy commercial area, whose paved streets were lined with *tabernae* (shops), warehouses for storing *garum*—a rather ghastly fish paste staple extremely popular around the Mediterranean in Roman times—and wine stores.

Santa Eulàlia is patron saint of sailors and of Barcelona

The Roman aqueduct at Tarragona is about 1km (0.5 mile) long (above); a 12th-century bridge at Sant Joan de les Abadesses in the north of the region (far right)

The archaeological museum has finds from Catalonia (right)

The Martyrdom of Santa Eulàlia

A splendid alabaster tomb in Barcelona's cathedral houses the remains of Santa Eulàlia, the city's co-patron saint and martyr. In the early 4th century the Roman emperor Diocletian launched a final and ultimately fruitless campaign to stamp out Christianity in the empire. The fearless virgin Eulàlia chose this rather inauspicious moment to publicly decry the wayward pagan lifestyle of Barcelona's townsfolk. For her trouble she was cruelly tortured with hot irons, pincers and other horrible instruments, and rolled down a hill in a barrel filled with nails. She was crucified and finally died at the stake in AD304. But some sceptics claim that Santa Eulàlia is a figment of medieval biographers' imagination.

Wilfred and the Birth of Catalonia

Covered with hair in the most unlikely places, some say even on the soles of his feet, Guifré el Pelós (Wilfred the Hairy) is considered Catalonia's founder. From AD870 to AD878 he conquered and cajoled his way around the north of the region that was not under Moorish rule and southern France, keeping his fellow nobles in check. Centuries later his chroniclers even attributed the creation of the Catalan flag to him. Louis the Pious, they say, walked into wounded Wilfred's war tent to find his shimmering gold shield bore no heraldry. So Louis dipped his fingers in Guifré's blood and traced four stripes down the shield. It's a nice story, except for one detail: Guifré was born the year Louis died.

The Blitz and Barcelona's Revenge

Al-Mansur (the Victorious) was the Vizier to the Caliph of Córdoba from AD978. He was virtual ruler of late 10th-century Moorish Spain and he tirelessly harried the Christian kingdoms in the north. In AD985 he fell upon Barcelona with a fury and ruled for three years, after which the Catalan Count Borrell II retook the city. The Count's Frankish overlords had left him to face Al-Mansur alone, for which he repaid them by officially confirming his autonomy. Then he mounted a blitz on Córdoba, a spectacular operation by the day's standards, as no Christian ruler had yet attempted to strike so deeply into the Moorish heartland. No lasting damage was done but the propaganda value was considerable.

A Medieval Code of Law

By the middle of the 12th century, Catalonia's judges were implementing new laws known as the Usatges de Barcelona. A complex mix of Roman and Visigothic law and local custom, the Usatges were designed to consolidate the rule of the Counts of Barcelona by depriving rival nobles of the right to take the law into their own hands. They also aimed to reduce general lawlessness and give peasants very basic protection. The Usatges remained at the heart of Catalan jurisprudence until 1716 but hopefully some of its clauses were modified over time: 'Let the rulers render justice as it seems fit…by cutting off hands and feet, putting out eyes, keeping men in prison for a long time'.

The Museu d'Arqueologia has collections from the Palaeolithic to the Visigothic eras (left and right)

1153

An illustration from a manuscript of the Usatges by Pere Albert (1291–1327; below)

Streets in Tarragona are proud to fly the Catalan flag (above)

Medieval Barcelona

The Counts of Barcelona ruled most of Catalonia and swathes of southern France when Count Berenguer IV married the heiress to the throne of Aragón in 1137. The new rulers of this merged Crown of Aragón came to be known as *comtes-reis* (count-kings). But disaster struck when the French defeated another member of the dynasty, Pere I, in 1213 at the Battle of Muret. Catalonia lost much of its French territory but Pere's successor, Jaume I, El Conqueridor (The Conqueror, 1208–76), turned matters around. In 1229 he wrested Mallorca from the Moors and by 1245 occupied Valencia. When the last count-king, Martí I, died heirless in 1410, the Crown's territories also included Murcia in southern Spain, Roussillon and Montpellier in France, Sicily and Sardinia. Conquest brought boom to Barcelona and the city walls were expanded in the 13th and 14th centuries. This was the golden age of Gothic building, from the Reials Drassanes (royal shipyards, see pages 94–95) to the powerful Santa Maria del Mar church (see page 123). The importance of the business class led to the creation of the Corts Catalanes (parliament) and Consell de Cent (city council). It was also a very harsh time as plague, anti-Jewish pogroms and riots rocked the city.

A statue of Jaume I presides over Plaça d'Espanya

Blood-Red Robes

Jaume I formed a citizens' committee in 1249 as he recognized the need for a burgeoning Barcelona to have decent administration. By 1274 this had become the Consell de Cent (Council of One Hundred). The council of well-to-do citizens and a handful of tradesmen elected five of their number to run the city's day-to-day affairs. The five also nominated the following year's council members. They wore flowing tunics of red or purple, symbolizing their own blood which they would willingly shed in the service of their city, and took off their hats before no man, not even the count-king. Its successor, the Ajuntament (town hall), still operates in the same building on Plaça de Sant Jaume.

1153

The banquet at which the conquest of the Balearic Islands was agreed in 1228

The Quests of Ramon Llull

Ramon Llull (1232–1316) was born in Mallorca three years after Jaume I conquered the island. He was the first notable writer to pen much of his opus in Catalan, with touches of Latin and Arabic. A rake in his young years, Llull changed path radically after claiming to see visions of Christ crucified. He then spent his life writing 250 religious and philosophical works, visiting north Africa and Asia Minor to spread the faith. He constantly sought backing for missions at royal courts all around the Mediterranean, but was politely turned away on many occasions. His most lasting works were the *Ars* (Art of) series, a compendium of contemporary knowledge. He still carried out missionary work in Tunis as late as 1315, where it is thought he died.

A memorial to Jaume I's arrival in Mallorca in 1229 (left)

Barcelona's Wall Street

As Barcelona boomed, the hub of its commercial life shifted to La Ribera, also known as El Born, and especially the area around Passeig del Born. The scene of medieval pageants, jousts and executions, the Born was also the heart of Barcelona's medieval financial district. Side streets were the preserve of money-changers and banks and in the late 14th century the Llotja (see page 192), Spain's first stock exchange, opened. Carrer de Montcada, in the Born, became one of the wealthiest streets in town and it is still lined with the Gothic-era mansions built by the city's then leading entrepreneurs.

Plague and Pogrom

In May 1348, plague infested rats began to spread their bubonic payload around the city and almost half the population succumbed. Some thought this disease a divine punishment, while others sought terrestrial scapegoats, including Jews who were accused of poisoning water wells. Mostly crowded into Barcelona's ghetto, the Call, the Jewish community held an ambivalent but often privileged position. Many of the city's north African and near East trade was in Jewish hands and their finances were key to Catalonia's well-being. But bigotry was rife. In 1391 a mob rampaged through the Call murdering and pillaging in a horrendous pogrom. Ten years later the Call was abolished and its residents were allowed to live where they chose.

Sardinia's Last Stand

When Catalan and Aragonese troops disembarked at Sardinia in 1323, the island had known centuries of foreign interference. This latest conquest proved gruelling and the newcomers were none too polite. When the port town of Alghero rebelled in 1354, Pere III retook it and replaced its population with Catalans, whose descendants still speak old Catalan. This ethnic cleansing was tried less successfully in other towns. The western region of Arborea remained independent and its ruler, Eleonora, reopened hostilities in 1391. She defied the Crown of Aragón until her death in 1404 but five years later resistance collapsed and Arborea became a Catalan duchy. But Eleonora had one last act of defiance up her sleeve—her law code, the Carta de Logu, so impressed the occupiers that they adopted it throughout Sardinia.

A stained-glass window in Santa Maria del Mar, begun in 1329 (left); the celestial ladder from *De Nova Logica* by Llull (far left)

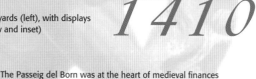

The Gothic royal shipyards (left), with displays of figureheads (below and inset)

1410

The Passeig del Born was at the heart of medieval finances and is still at the hub of the Ribera district

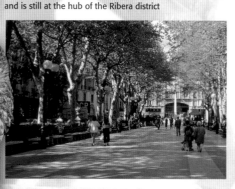

Spanish Unity and Decline

Barcelona's fortunes nosedived in the 15th century. Trade declined and the Crown of Aragón passed from Catalan hands to Fernando of Antequera in 1412. Years of civil disorder ensued and Catalonia was sucked into Castile's orbit when the Catholic Monarchs, Ferdinand II and Isabella I, united Spain in 1479. They finished the *Reconquista* (the Reconquest, capturing lands for the Christian Crown), defeating Granada's Moors in 1492. In that same year the Jewish community was expelled from Spain and Christopher Columbus discovered the Americas for their majesties.

Castile asserted its mastery in the 16th century, dominating South American gold and transatlantic trade. Shut out, Barcelona slipped into torpor and the increasingly impoverished Catalan countryside was devastated by uprisings like the Guerra dels Segadors (Reapers' War) in 1640–52. Charles II died in 1700 without an heir and this event unleashed the War of the Spanish Succession in 1702. Barcelona joined Austria and Britain against the French-backed Philip V but was left alone after the 1713 Treaty of Utrecht, when these two allies made separate peace deals with France. Philip kept his throne but lost all of Spain's European territories. And Barcelona lost its historic freedoms after falling to a vengeful Philip in 1714.

The Compromise of Caspe in 1412 by Salvador Viniegra y Lasso de la Vega, depicting the selection of Fernando of Antequera as king

The Inquisition

Four years after uniting Spain, the Catholic Monarchs introduced the Spanish Inquisition to Barcelona. This feared institution had been set up in 1478 to keep an eye on Jews and *conversos* (Jews who had converted to Catholicism), and during this time thousands of Jews were burned at the stake. These executions were grand, ghoulish, public spectacles, torture was used and no defence was allowed. In 1492 the first Grand Inquisitor, Tomás de Torquemada (1420–98), himself a *converso*, convinced the Catholic Monarchs to expel all Jews who refused baptism. This bigoted decision was also incredibly short-sighted and cost Barcelona (and Spain) its most dynamic business class at a stroke.

1410

The Museu d'Art Modern is housed in the only surviving part of the Ciutadella

Columbus' Caribbean Cruise

In 1493 the Catholic Monarchs were in Barcelona when their daring Genoese navigator, Christopher Columbus, returned to report on his first voyage to what he thought was China and the Indies. Europeans hoped a direct sea route westwards might lead to the riches of India and the Far East, which were increasingly difficult to reach by land east of Europe. But Columbus refused to believe that one year previously he had found a new world. Whether he liked it or not, he had bumped in to the Caribbean islands. At the Spanish royals' behest, he undertook three more voyages to the area and so Spain's South American adventure began.

Don John and a Fast Moving Christ

On 7 October 1571 Don John of Austria led a Christian armada against the Ottoman Turkish fleet off Lepanto in Greece. Don John's ornate galley was one of the finest vessels to come off the slipways of Barcelona's royal shipyards. The muscle power was provided by prisoners and conscripts. Chained to their oars, they ate, slept and relieved themselves where they sat—you could smell a fleet of galleys from some distance. As the fleets closed, Don John led his flagship into the fray and the wooden figurehead of Christ is said to have miraculously dodged a Turkish cannon ball. The curiously bending sculpture is now in Barcelona's cathedral, see pages 70–73. It was a good omen as the Christians went on to route the Turks.

A Grim Reapers' War

Fighting losing wars on several fronts, Spain needed extra troops and cash from the regions. Barcelona refused. So Madrid decided to invade France from Catalonia in 1639, creating an excuse to base troops in the area and get a tighter grip on the still largely autonomous region. The rural populace, already pressed by poverty and taxes, rose up in 1640 and overwhelmed the soldiers. Reapers armed with scythes converged on Barcelona and assassinated the viceroy. So started the Guerra dels Segadors (Reapers' War). As Madrid sent more troops, Barcelona appealed for French aid. By 1641, Paris had unseated Madrid as master of Catalonia, but Madrid finally retook Barcelona in 1652.

The Siege of Barcelona

By 1714, Barcelona stood hopelessly alone against Philip V as its allies in the War of the Spanish Succession had left the field. Armed with whatever came to hand, and assisted by a few thousand weary troops, the townspeople fought on doggedly. And in a moment of desperate inspiration, the city rulers declared the Virgin of La Mercè, the city's co-patron saint, commander-in-chief. After all, she had saved the city from plague the previous century. It was to no avail and on 11 September (now Catalonia's national day) the city fell. Philip stripped Catalonia of its privileges. He banned Catalan, closed the universities and built a huge fortress, the Ciutadella, in the park of the same name, to watch over his reluctant subjects.

The Archduke of Austria was declared King of Spain in September 1702

1714

Queen Isabella interviews her explorer Columbus (far left), and the top of the monument in his honour at the port end of Las Ramblas (left)

An engraving of the siege of the city by an unknown artist (above); the Christ of Lepanto crucifix (top left)

Barça Bounces Back

Barcelona slowly picked itself up by the bootstraps after being cowed by Philip V in 1714. In 1778 it was allowed trading access to Spain's American colonies, exporting brandy and textiles. The growth of the latter business spawned other industries and by the end of the 18th century Catalans were manufacturing everything from artillery to farm implements. Yet these industries suffered a setback as Spain became embroiled in Napoleon's maelstrom, first as reluctant ally in 1800 and then, from 1808, as occupied territory under Joseph Bonaparte. Insurgents joined Wellington's British army, who trounced the French in 1813.

Barcelona's factories recovered from this violent interlude in the 1830s and more growth took place. In 1848 Spain's first railway, between Barcelona and Mataró, opened and industrialization gathered pace. Iron, cotton, shipbuilding, cork and wine production grew, but so did an abject under-class. A soaring population led to the removal of Barcelona's city walls in 1854 and, in 1869, an ambitious grid plan enlargement began. The 1888 Universal Exhibition marked a high point, but glee turned to gloom when Spain lost Cuba, Puerto Rico and the Philippines in a clash with the US in 1898, hitting the city's economy hard.

Years after thousands of people in La Ribera had lost their homes to make way for the huge Ciutadella fortress, Spanish military engineers cooked up a plan to rehouse them. Juan Martín Cermeño drew up diagrams for Barceloneta (Little Barcelona), a triangle of reclaimed land upon which tight rows of cheap, uniform housing along narrow, claustrophobic lanes were to be raised. Work began in 1753 and some of the original family houses can still be seen. Most, however, were later replaced or swallowed up by much taller, often squalid and always overcrowded buildings. Barceloneta became a congested, fetid workers' and fishermen's quarter that even today, despite creeping gentrification, retains a whiff of its lively waterfront past.

1714

LA RAMB

The cork industry was vital to the economy (top) and helped finance the city's grand palaces (above)

The Building of a Boulevard

In the Middle Ages Barcelona's most famous street, Las Ramblas, was little more than a stinking open air sewer. By 1775, the rivulet had become a dusty, irregular roadway. That year, it was decided to tear down the long irrelevant 13th-century walls built by Jaume I that lined the road, and a new look, tree-lined avenue was laid out in the late 1770s. Jaume's defences had come to serve as a structural wall for slum hovels that were built against the side of it. These were all swept away with the walls and almost immediately the great and the good started to erect grand town houses along the revitalized boulevard, and many of these neoclassical caprices, like the Palau de la Virreina (see page 108), still stand.

Las Ramblas is excellent for walking and people-watching (left and bottom left)

The Burning of the Churches

On 26 July 1835 a bull-fight ended in a riot as spectators burst on to the arena incensed by the poor quality of the bulls. It was not really anything to do with the bulls, but they acted as a catalyst in an already volatile situation. The mob spilled into central Barcelona, where soap-box orators urged an assault on churches and convents. The Catalans had long considered the clergy a reactionary ally of the Spanish ruling class and a wave of anti-clerical violence had swept the region days earlier after the assassi-nation of some Catalan liberals. An orgy of arson ensued. Some of Madrid's politicians shared these sentiments and in 1837 Spain's finance minister, Juan Álvarez Mendizábal, ordered the divestment of Church land to stim-ulate the economy. Around 80 per cent of Church property in Barcelona was sold at auction.

Dive, Dive, Dive!

Driven by an obsessive curiosity with the depths of the oceans, Narcís Monturiol, a Barcelona socialist and editor, became a submarine inventor. In 1859 he launched his *Ictineo*, a fish-shaped contraption powered by human muscle. Monturiol made repeated short dives but could find no one to fund further research, so he plunged himself into debt to produce a better model. The 17m (56ft) *Ictineo II*, launched in 1864, has a revolution-ary system for providing oxygen and a steam driven motor. It was far more advanced than anything else thus far created, including sub-marines built by the Confederates during the American Civil War (1860–61). Monturiol could still find no back-ers and, crushed by debt, had to watch as his creation was scrapped in 1872.

The Fiasco of 1898

By the mid-19th century the only South American colonies left belonging to Spain were Cuba and Puerto Rico, but both provided Barcelona with a healthy living from cot-ton plantations and as export markets. In the 1890s demands in the islands for self-govern-ment, and then outright independence, grew. Spain met the challenge with repression that triggered an insurgency and the US came to the rebels' aid. A hopelessly ill-equipped Spanish fleet despatched to challenge the Americans was sent to the bottom of the sea in 1898 and the islands passed to US control. Soon the main import on Barcelona's docks were half-starved returning Spanish soldiers. And all that remained were the nostalgic *havaneres*, sea shanties sung on the Barcelona to Havana trade routes.

Joseph Bonaparte (1768–1844) by Jean Baptiste Joseph Wicar

1898

Factories such as the Isaura Metalworks helped the city's industrial growth (above); a statue of Joaquim Vara de Rey, who died defending Cuba on behalf of Spain in 1898 (left)

From Rebirth to Civil War

Even before the 20th century dawned, Barcelona revelled in its Renaixença (Renaissance), a sparking of renewed interest in all things Catalan. The language and its literature were revived and Catalan nationalism flourished. The greatest expression of this rebirth came in architecture. Modernisme (the Catalan version of art nouveau) began in the 1880s and reached its apogee in the early 1900s. Above all, Antoni Gaudí (1852–1926) dazzled with his uniquely weird and wonderful buildings.

Barcelona's population doubled to 1 million from 1900 to 1930 and, as elsewhere in Spain, worker unrest led to strikes, riots and the rise of the radical Left. In 1931 a republic was proclaimed in Spain to replace the monarchy. Catalan nationalists exploited this by reinstating the Generalitat (the regional government) and declaring Catalonia an autonomous republic, drawing an artillery bombardment for their trouble in 1934. In Madrid the Leftwing Popular Front's 1936 election victory enraged the Right and in July General Franco (1892–1975) rose against the Republic and launched the Spanish Civil War. In Barcelona a coalition of anarchists and Trotskyists (supporters of social revolution) took control, later replaced by the Communists. In 1937 the national republican government moved here, then fled to France shortly before the city's fall to Franco on 25 January 1939. The war ended in March that year.

1898

A statue of the sardana, the Catalan dance (above) and a detail from the Modernisme Casa Quadros (below), both part of the Renaixença

A Sacred Project

An enormous, sinewy church is being built in Barcelona. They have been at it since 1882 and La Sagrada Família (see pages 124–129) may be finished in around 2026. Antoni Gaudí, king of eccentric architecture and the soul of Modernisme, dedicated much of his life to this incredible house of God. But Barcelona's well-to-do tired of it and funds became scarce. Gaudí, believing his cause sacred, gave it all he had and lived like a pauper on site. When he died in 1926, only one tower, portal and the apse were complete. But Barcelona has carried on, even after anarchists destroyed many of Gaudí's on-site plans and models in 1936.

The sheer height of the spires of La Sagrada Família were designed to draw your eyes heavenward (below)

Barcelona Blues

In 1900 a precocious artist called Pablo Picasso (1881–1973) put on an exhibition in the Els Quatre Gats tavern, a bohemian haunt run by Barcelona's artistic avant-garde. Born in southern Spain, the fiery-eyed youth had been brought to Barcelona by his art teacher father in 1895. Pablo was already a fine academic painter in his teens but became bored with conventions and began experimenting. In his Blue Period, inspired by the death of a friend, all his works, whether portraits, cityscapes or snapshots of street life, were literally tinged with a forlorn, mournful blue. For Picasso, the end of this, one of many artistic phases to come, coincided with his definitive move from Barcelona to Paris in 1904.

Soccer Comes to Barcelona

In the dying years of the 19th century northern European expatriates in Barcelona and elsewhere around Spain began forming teams to kick a ball around a field. In 1899 the FC Barcelona soccer team was formed, mostly of English, German and Swiss players, along with several other squads that started playing friendly competitions. Intrigued by this odd sport, locals joined in and by late 1900 a Catalan league of 12 teams had been formed. Two years later at the first national championships, FC Barcelona lost 2–1 to Biscaia. By 1910 the side was the strongest in Catalonia and its clashes with Real Madrid were already a national event, frequently rigged in favour of the capital's team, reckon Barcelona fans even today.

The City of Bombs

During the 1890s, the anarchist movement gained ground among discontented workers, and bomb attacks against the rich became a fact of city life. By 1907 the anarchists had switched to strikes and founded the powerful Confederación Nacional de Trabajo trade union. The bombs kept coming in the 1900s, mostly from agents provocateurs aiming to discredit independent-minded Catalans and anarchists. In this volatile atmosphere, Madrid called up Catalan troops to fight a miserable colonial war in Morocco in July 1909. As the conscripts departed, the city rose. A general strike was accompanied by an anti-clerical rampage. Enraged citizens burned and looted 80 churches in what came to be known as the Setmana Tràgica (Tragic Week).

An Englishman Abroad

In December 1936 George Orwell found himself in Barcelona ruled by anarchist, with a 'notion of writing newspaper articles'. Instead, he joined the Trotskyist POUM militia and was sent to the front line. His return to Barcelona coincided with the brief civil war that broke out on 1 May with a communist assault on the anarchist-held telephone exchange on Plaça de Catalunya. Trouble had been brewing for some time. The Soviet-backed communists wanted to eliminate potential opposition and the anarchists seemed more preoccupied with social revolution than defeating Franco. The communists won and disarmed the anarchists and the POUM, throwing many into jail. Orwell described the events in *Homage to Catalonia*.

General Franco in 1936 (above left);
George Orwell (1903–50, above right)

1939

Memorabilia at FC Barça (below and left); the Museu Picasso was opened in 1963 (far left)

Museu
Picasso

Postwar Barcelona

After the war came repression. The castle on Montjuïc became the scene of torture and execution for many thousands of Franco's opponents. Lluís Companys, former president of the short-lived Generalitat, was handed over by the Gestapo and shot here. Franco banned Catalan and set about making the region much more Castilian.

The 1940s and 1950s were known as the Years of Hunger in Spain and massive migration from its poorer regions to Barcelona and other cities continued well into the 1960s. Up to 1.5 million converged on Barcelona, creating whole non-Catalan quarters for the first time. Anti-Franco activity continued in the form of protests and strikes but he clung to power until his death in 1975. The monarchy, under King Juan Carlos, and parliamentary democracy were restored. Under the new constitution, Catalonia and other regions were granted a generous degree of self-rule. In 1980, the pragmatic Catalan nationalist Jordi Pujol was elected president of the Generalitat, a post he retained until 2003.

One of the most significant events of this era was the 1992 Olympics. The city's popular mayor, Pascual Maragall, launched an ambitious project in the late 1980s to regenerate the city and the waterfront for the Games. They were a hit and the impetus to clean up the city continued in their wake.

The use of Catalan is vital to the identity of those born here, even on menus

POLLASTRE CUIT AMB LLENYA

1939

Catalonia Recovers Self-Rule

Few in Barcelona mourned the death of Franco in November 1975. The restoration of parliamentary democracy was good news for Catalonia, which awaited self-rule under the new constitution, and in 1979, King Juan Carlos gave the region's Autonomy Statute his approval. Josep Taradellas, head of the Catalan government-in-exile in Mexico, arrived in Barcelona in 1978 and declared simply: *Ja soc aquí* (loosely meaning 'I am back'). Taradellas was succeeded by Jordi Pujol, who had once been imprisoned in 1960 for singing a banned Catalan anthem in front of Franco, as the head of the new Generalitat after regional elections in 1980.

The re-built Liceu is the region's main classical concert venue (above)

Homage to Barceloneta by Rebecca Horne (1992) is part of the new waterfront (inset)

The Olympics Come to Town

Awarded the 1992 Olympic Games over rivals ranging from Belgrade to Brisbane, Barcelona did not disappoint, much to the relief of Juan Samaranch, then president of the International Olympic Committee and local boy. The Games prompted a campaign to revitalize the city, notably the derelict Port Vell (Old Port) waterfront and Montjuïc, where most of the events were held. The city also got a new marina around the seaside Olympic village, whose flats were later sold off to locals. King Juan Carlos opened the Games on 25 July, and for the first time in 20 years all nations were present with more than 9,000 athletes. The former USSR romped home with 45 gold medals, ahead of the USA on 37 and Germany on 33; Spain came in eighth with 13 gold.

The city now gives free reign to its Catalan, especially after the repression of Franco

Speaking in Tongues

In 1998 the Generalitat caused a storm with its latest law on linguistic normalization, that is the restoration of Catalan as the prime language of daily discourse. Already it is the main language of public administration and education, and many primarily Spanish-speaking residents of Barcelona feel discriminated against. The 1998 law allowed the Generalitat to demand that up to half of dubbed and subtitled foreign films shown in Catalonia be in Catalan, and the Generalitat announced it would impose quotas to that effect. The cinema industry denounced the move as folly, saying the pointless extra cost (virtually all Catalans speak Spanish too) would mean that many films simply did not screen in Catalonia. In the end the Generalitat backed off.

PLATS PER EMPORTAR
Croquetes
Canelons
Macarrons
Paella
Arròs negre
Arrossejat
Patates fregides
Botifarres sal i pebre
Truites de patates.

Phoenix from the Ashes

In January 1994, flames and a thick pall of smoke filled the air above Las Ramblas as fire consumed the city's premier opera house, the Gran Teatre del Liceu. All that remained standing was the main vestibule—the same as was left by a similarly destructive blaze in 1861. A foundation was quickly set up to organize funding for its reconstruction and plans were soon put in place. Architects decided to incorporate what had survived of the original opera house and to re-create faithfully the main auditorium. The latest techniques would be used to improve acoustics and comfort. They wasted no time and in September 1999, the new-look Liceu opened its doors to the city's opera lovers.

ETA Strikes in Barcelona

Barcelona was left in a state of shock when a respected Socialist politician and historian Ernest Lluch was shot dead by ETA (the Basque separatist terror group) outside his home on 21 November 2000. Since breaking a cease-fire earlier in the year, ETA had mounted several attacks in Barcelona. But the assassination of Lluch struck a particular chord, as he had a long history of promoting dialogue and a peaceful solution to the Basque problem. The three assassins were caught and each condemned to 33 years in prison.

2000

An activist of ETA talks on Basque television (top); the Palau Sant Jordi stadium was designed by Japanese architect, Arata Isozaki, for the 1992 Olympics Games (left); the closing ceremony on 9 August 1992 (above)

The City Today

Barcelona has entered the 21st century at once optimistic and forward-looking but equally conscious that it is losing ground to eternal rival Madrid. The port city remains in a building and renewal frenzy that began with the Olympics, and to many outsiders it appears inward-looking and too caught up in chip-on-shoulder questions of offended Catalan identity. Barcelona, with its reputation for business sense and hard work, and long the country's economic powerhouse, is watching with a sense of almost helpless dismay as the political capital, Madrid, scoots ahead as Spain's undisputed financial hub.

The New Face of Catalan Nationalism

After more than 20 years at the helm, conservative Catalan nationalist Jordi Pujol finally opted not to stand for re-election as president of the Generalitat (the Catalan regional government) in 2003, making way for his successor Artur Mas. Campaigning on a vigorous nationalist platform, Mas declared he would push for more self-rule and direct representation of Catalonia in European and international organizations. Against him was the Catalan Socialist Party (PSC), led by the popular former Barcelona mayor Pascual Maragall. However neither won a clear majority and both have to rely on the ERC, a party on the side of total indepence from Spain, to form a government.

Publicity for the Forum 2004 (right)

Forum 2004 and Urban Revolution

Ever anxious to bestride the world stage, Barcelona is host of the World Cultural Forum 2004. Whatever else the forum is, it has prompted a bout of urban development unparalleled since the Olympics. La Diagonal, one of Barcelona's grand boulevards, is being extended to the long neglected north coast of the city, which is being transformed into a luxury belt of apartments, hotels and offices. Change is in store for the cargo port and run-down districts like El Raval and Poble Nou are getting attention, the former with an ambitious hotel complex and the latter with the 22@ project, aimed at creating a high-rise, high-tech business district.

Artur Mas was born in Barcelona on 31 January 1956

2000–

A radical building designed for the Forum (top); Spanish prime minister José María Aznar, middle, discussing plans for Forum 2004 (below); an aerial view of the Forum's territory (right)

MAJOR AIRLINES	
American Airlines	www.aa.com
British Airways	www.britishairways.com
Easyjet	www.easyjet.com
Iberia	www.iberia.com
KLM	www.klm.com
Lufthansa	www.lufthansa.com
Virgin	www.virgin.com

TIPS
● If you are getting the train from the airport, and staying in the older part of town, you may find the connection at the Plaça Catalunya more useful than getting off at Sants. It also provides greater access to the metro system.
● Most of the car rental firms have desks in both main terminals, but only one may deal with reservations. If you want to rent on the spot, be prepared to walk to another terminal—not too much of a hardship as they are close together.

Barcelona's airport is light and spacious

shorten to Sants. Other stopping points on the route are the Plaça Catalunya (journey time 25 min), Arc de Triomf (27 min) and Clot-Aragó (31 min).

By bus
The Aerobús service runs every 15 minutes from 6am–midnight, and takes about 30 minutes, but this will be longer if the traffic is heavy. The service picks up from outside each terminal and stops at Plaça d'Espanya, Gran Vía, Plaça de Universitat and Plaça de Catalunya. You can buy single tickets from the driver. The Aerobús can get very busy at peak periods and you may find that you cannot get onto the first bus that arrives. The bus has limited space for luggage, considering that it is an airport bus, so if you have lots of bags and find there is a long queue, you might prefer to catch the train or a taxi.

If you arrive during the night, you can catch a local bus, number 106, from terminal B to Plaça d'Espanya. It departs from the airport at 10.15pm, 11.35pm, 0.50am, 2.05am and 3.20am.

By car
Several of the major car rental companies have rental desks at the airport, but you are likely to get better deals if you book, and pay, before you arrive. Another way of getting a good deal is to use a Spanish firm who will be able to offer very competitive rates—ATESA is the main one (*tel 93 298 34 33*). Ask at the tourist information desks at the airport.

To rent a car you will need your driver's licence and money for a deposit, preferably in the form of a credit card. Licences from major countries, such as Canada, the US, the UK and other EU countries will suffice. It is compulsory to carry your licence with you at all times.

The minimum age required for car rental is 21, but this can often be higher, and you will need to have been driving for at least a year.

The road for Barcelona from the airport is the C-246, known as the Autovía de Castelldefels, and the journey should take about 20 minutes, but will depend on traffic.

By taxi
Taxis are available from directly outside the terminal buildings A and C; the rank outside terminal B is to the right. Journey time to central Barcelona is 20 minutes, depending on traffic, and the fare should cost around €18. See page 49 for more information.

CAR RENTAL COMPANIES			
Company	Terminal A	Terminal B	Website
Avis	93 298 36 00	93 298 36 00	www.avis.com
Budget	As Avis	As Avis	www.budget.es
Europcar	93 298 33 00	93 298 33 00	www.europcar.com
Hertz	93 298 36 37	93 298 36 37	www.hertz.com

TRANSFERS			
	Time	Price	Frequency
Train	24 min	€2.50	Every 30 min
Aerobús	25–30 min	€3.45	Every 15 min
Car	20 min	–	–
Taxi	20 min	€15–€20	–

ON THE MOVE

By Train

The Spanish national railway company, RENFE, operates services throughout the country and runs some suburban lines within Barcelona. Sants Estació is the terminal for all international and national train journeys in the city and has its own tourist office, hotel booking office, banks and taxi ranks. Estació de Franca, near Barceloneta, has train connections to some regional lines, and other possible points of entry are Plaça Catalunya, Plaça d'Espanya and Passeig de Gràcia, which are on the suburban and metro lines.

The international Talgo trains, which are faster and more luxurious than most, run a service that connects Paris, Zurich, Milan and Montpellier to Barcelona. If you want to travel overnight from Paris there is a direct service on the Hotel trains, taking about 12 hours.

For information on RENFE's international routes call 93 490 11 22, for national routes call 90 224 02 02, or visit the website at www.renfe.es.

By Bus

Long-distance bus services run from Portugal, France, the UK and other western European countries to Barcelona. These services provide comfortable conditions on modern buses and can be less expensive than other forms of international travel. But the journey times are long. For example, Paris to Barcelona is 15 hours and London to Barcelona is 25 hours.

Eurolines (www.eurolines.com) is one of the biggest operators of buses, and their multi-day passes cover travel to up to 31 countries. Visitors from outside the UK can use this site or use the contact details below.

EUROLINES SERVICES

US: 800/327 6097 (toll free)
www.britishtravel.com
France: 892 89 90 91
www.eurolines.fr
Italy: 055 35 71 10
www.eurolines.it
Germany: 069 790 350
www.deutsche-touring.com

There are two main terminals. Estació del Nord (*tel 902 260 606*) is on the eastern side of the city, which is also served by local suburban trains. The nearest metro station to here is Arc de Triomf, five minutes walk away. The Estació Autobuses de Sants (*tel 93 490 40 00*), to the west of the city, is just around the corner from the main rail station, which has connections to the metro.

The city's main thoroughfares will help you find your way

By Car

The A7 is one of the country's main toll *autopista* (motorways or expressways). It connects France to Barcelona, and you can access the rest of Spain's road network via the A2 and A7. The website www.autopistas.com has a good range of useful information, including current road toll charges.

Once in the city, signs for Port Vell will take you to the main exit for the old town. If you don't want to have to drive around the city itself, there is a park and ride scheme that uses Plaça de las Glories car park. Buying a ticket here allows you unlimited travel by bus and metro for a day or a week (see page 50).

An alternative to driving all the way across mainland Europe is to use the motor rail system. You can take your car through the Channel Tunnel from Folkestone in England to Calais, France and then pick up the car sleeper trains. These are operated by French National Railways (SNCF), and run from northern France via Paris to the Spanish border. Visit the website www.eurotunnel.com for more information on the Tunnel, and for more detail on getting around by car see page 50.

By Boat

Car ferry services from Britain to Spain are operated by Brittany Ferries, running from Plymouth to Santander (*tel 08703 665 333*), and by P&O European Ferries, running from Portsmouth to Bilbao (*tel 08705 202 020*). There is a luxury car ferry between Genova in Italy and Barcelona, run by Grandi Navi Veloci; journey time is 18 hours. For details contact the agent Condeminas (*tel 934 43 98 98*). Ferry services also operate to the Moll de Barcelona, at the bottom of Las Ramblas, from the Balearic Islands. The largest company is Trasmediterranea; book online at www.trasmediterranea.es (*tel national: 902 45 46 45; international 93 295 91 00/07*).

GETTING AROUND

The best way to get a feel for any city is to walk its streets and Barcelona is no exception. Most of the southern areas, particularly around the pedestrianized Barri Gòtic, demand leg-work. But some of the city's best sights are not in the main part of town, so you are likely to need the excellent local transport system.

Barcelona's urban transport system consists of buses, metro, Ferrocarrils de la Generalitat (FGC) suburban trains and the Cercanías trains. You are most likely to use the metro (underground or subway) and the bus system.

The metro is an efficient system and very useful for moving longer distances than you may feel like walking. The bus network complements the metro with a huge array of routes, most of which pass through Plaça de Catalunya, Plaça d'Espanya or Universitat. The pedestrianized area around the Barri Gòtic makes it difficult to catch a bus across the city, so be prepared to walk for some of your journey, or use the metro.

The transport system is divided into zones, with One being the most central. However, Zone Two and the outer zones start a long way out and cover smaller towns and the suburbs. As a visitor, you are very unlikely to need anything other than Zone One.

TMB

● Transports Metropolitans de Barcelona (TMB) runs both the metro and the main bus service.
● Pick up a network map from tourist information offices (see page 270) or at one of the TMB information offices.
● TMB's website at www.tmb.net is a great interactive site in English, Spanish and Catalan. It is full of information on getting about the city, and it will tell you what bus number or line you need to catch.
● If you need more details, or wish to speak to someone, about TBM and its services, you can call 010 or 012, which is the city council's information line. The advisors speak a number of languages.

TMB OFFICES
Plaça de la Universitat:
Mon–Fri 8–8
Sagrada Família:
Mon–Fri 7am–9pm
Diagonal:
Mon–Fri 8–8
Sants:
Mon–Sat 7am–9pm, Sun 10–2, 3–6

DISCOUNT PASSES

A single ticket can be bought for any journey, but this is likely to become expensive. Passes are available in a number of combinations that provide different access to the metro, buses and the FGC. Buy them from ticket offices and automatic machines at all metro and train stations, kiosks and tobacconists. The most useful ones are:
● T-Dia provides unlimited 24-hour travel for one person. It becomes valid from the time that it is first used.
● T-10 is valid for 10 journeys and can be shared, so it just needs to be validated for each person using it.
● T-50/30 is good for larger groups, or those staying in the city for a while, as it allows travel for 50 journeys over 30 days and can be shared.
● A Bus+Metro+Ferrocarrils de la Generalitat (FGC, surburban train line) pass provides unlimited travel on the metro, buses and FGC, including the train to and from the airport. You can buy these for two (€8), three (€11.30), four (€14.50) or five (€17.30) days.
● If you forget how many trips you have left on a transport pass, look on the back of your ticket. When you validate a journey (see page 46), the machine prints the date and time of each journey here.

TRANSFERS

● You can not transfer on a single ticket; it must be a pass.
● Once you have activated your pass on boarding a bus or entering a metro station, you have 75 minutes in which you can transfer to another of the urban transport methods: bus, metro, FGC or the Cercanías.
● In this way, you will not be charged for a second journey—it counts as part of the first.
● You cannot take the bus, get off, then back on the same route, or leave the metro and go straight back on that line on a single trip.

BARCELONA CARD

This pass entitles you to free and unlimited travel on the metro and buses and reductions on admission charges at a large number of places of interest, some restaurants and shops, plus money off the Aerobús, the TombBus, the funicular and Telefèric de Montjuïc (see page 49).

The cards can be bought as one-, two- or three-day passes, costing €16.25, €19.25 or €22.25 for adults respectively, with reductions for children between 4 and 12 years, and free for children under 4. They are available at tourist information offices (see page 270) and the bus station, Estació de Nord.

TIPS
● Smoking is not allowed anywhere on the metro (trains, platforms and stations) or on buses. If you are caught, there is a €30 fine.

● Children under 4 travel for free on both the buses and metro.

The Metro

The city's metro is relatively small by other European city standards, with 85km (58 miles) of track. But it is a fast and frequent service that is used by 300 million people per year.

ON THE MOVE

The metro was begun in 1921 and was inaugurated in 1924 as the Gran Metropolitano de Barcelona. The first line to open was between Lesseps and Catalunya. Now, five lines make up the metro network, which covers much of the city.

● Some ticket machines use a touch screen method, which allows you to choose Spanish, Catalan or English as the language of the display.
● The machine will display a list of all the ticket types.

example if you want to go from Liceu to Tarragona on the green line 3, you need a train heading for Zona Universitària.
● The signs for the platforms are clour-coded to match the metro lines.
● Once you reach the platform there will be a board showing which line you are on and all the stops that will be called at.
● Inside the trains, on some lines only, there is a list of all the stops with lights above them—those already lit have been passed, the flashing light indicates the next stop, and those unlit are still to come.
● Some trains have signs at the end of the carriages to show which side of the carriage the doors will open on—very useful in a crowded train.
● Not all the doors on the train open automatically at each stop. If there is a lever on the door it must be pushed before the door will open.
● Exit signs in metro stations are grey and marked *Sortida*. The sign will also list the street name that you are about to exit onto.
● You don't need your ticket again on the way out, just push through the gate.

There are a number of zones that fan out from the city, but it is unlikely that you will venture beyond the central Zone One, as all metro stops are within Zone One; it's the local suburban trains that go beyond this. Zone maps can be found inside stations.

BUYING TICKETS

● All ticket types can be bought before you travel and not just on the day of travel. This is because your first journey will be counted from the first time you push it through the turnstile.
● Single tickets and passes can be bought from the ticket office or the ticket vending machines, which accept cash or credit cards.
● The T-10 pass (see page 43) can be bought from tobacconists around the city.
● Ticket offices are open the same hours as the metro.

Plaça d'Espanya metro station is one of the busiest in the city

Select the one you want by touching it, insert money or credit card and then wait for it to print your ticket and give you change, or in the case of a card, a receipt.

FINDING YOUR WAY

● To enter the system, push your ticket through the slot on the turnstile and walk through the turnstile to the right of that, remembering to retrieve your ticket. This activates your ticket.
● There are regular ticket checks, so keep yor ticket handy. The fine for not producing your ticket is €40.
● Each metro line is colour-coded and identified by a number. The direction in which the train travels is identified by the last stop on the line, so for

USEFUL LINES FOR REACHING THE SIGHTS

● Line 3 (green) probably covers the most amount of sights that you will want to see, even if the station stop is not directly at the attractions. See the line chart opposite for a guide of where you can visit.
● Line 5 (blue) runs through from Sants station across the city to La Sagrada Família and the Hospital de Sant Pau.

METRO INFORMATION

- Metro stations are recognized by the red diamond and white M sign outside.
- There is a map of the metro on the inside back cover of this book.
- Free maps of the system are available from metro stations and most tourist information points.

- Try to avoid the rush hours, around 7.30–9am and 6–8pm. Longer lunchtimes mean the metro and buses are busy around 1pm too.
- The metro runs Mon–Thu 5am–midnight; Fri–Sat 5am–2am; Sun 6am–midnight.
- After 10pm you may find that a station with several entrances

has only one open. This should be signposted at the station.
- Avoid changing lines if possible, as most interchanges, particularly at the Passeig de Gràcia, have a long walk between lines.
- Lost items found on a TMB metro or bus are sent to the Information Office at Universitat station (see page 43). Wait until the following day to contact them, and if it's there you will need some form of ID.
- If you have any difficulties at the stations, an internal phone that connects directly to the station manager is available.

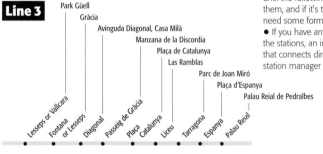

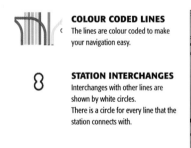

UNDERSTANDING THE METRO MAP

COLOUR CODED LINES
The lines are colour coded to make your navigation easy.

STATION INTERCHANGES
Interchanges with other lines are shown by white circles.
There is a circle for every line that the station connects with.

CONNECTION AT STREET LEVEL ONLY
Some connections can only be made at street level.

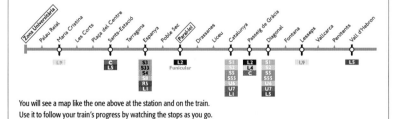

You will see a map like the one above at the station and on the train.
Use it to follow your train's progress by watching the stops as you go.

Buses

Buses are the most prractical way of reaching the sights that are further away from the main part of town, for example Park Güell or Monestir de Pedralbes. They are air-conditioned single-deckers and give a comfortable ride, but traffic can slow your journey time down.

Blue Route

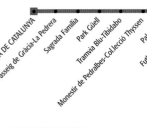

PLAÇA DE CATALUNYA · Passeig de Gràcia-La Pedrera · Francesc Macià-Diagonal · Estació de Sants · Plaça d'Espanya · Poble Espanol · L'Anella Olimpic-MNAC · Teleféric de Montjuïc-Fundació Joan Miró · Miramar-Jardins Costa I Llobera · Colom-Las Ramblas · Port Vell · Port Olimpic · Parc de la Ciutadella-Zoo · Pla de Palau · Barri Gòtic · PLAÇA DE CATALUNYA

PLAÇA DE CATALUNYA · Passeig de Gràcia-La Pedrera · Sagrada Familia · Park Güell · Tramvia Blu-Tibidabo · Monestir de Pedralbes-Col.lecció Thyssen · Palau Reial · Futbol Club Barcelona · Francesc Macià-Diagonal · MACBA-CCCB · PLAÇA DE CATALUNYA

Red Route

USING THE BUSES

● Free maps showing all routes are available from tourist offices (see page 270) and TMB offices (see page 43).

● Once you have decided on your route, you can check that you are catching the bus in the right direction by looking for the arrow on the timetable at each bus stop.

● Place names are displayed on the front of the bus. The top name shows where the bus has come from, the bottom name where it's going to.

● Board the bus through the front doors by the driver, who will sell you single tickets only, not passes.

● If you have a pass, remember that it will need to be validated. Place it vertically into the white on-board machines behind the driver (not the grey ones in front of the driver) for stamping.

● When you want to get off, press the button on the handrails, which will light up a sign to say the bus is stopping (*parada solicitada*). Exit via the back doors.

● If the bus is busy and you are standing nearer the front doors, you can get off this way.

Casa Milà is on the Passeig de Gràcia, a busy bus route

BUS TURÍSTIC

This bus provides a hop-on, hop-off service. Open-topped double-deckers serve two interlinked circular routes (the red route and the blue route; see above) that take in 27 of the city's main sights. You can get on and off as many times as you like on the one ticket, and each stop is announced by the on-board information officer in Spanish, English, German and French. The guides will also provide small bits of commentary as you pass other sights that aren't on the route, plus information on the approaching sight.

Tickets cost €15 for one day, €19 for two consecutive days, with a reduction for children: €9 and €12, respectively and is free for children under 4. They can be bought at tourist offices or on the bus. Your ticket also comes with discounts on admission charges to a number of major sights around the city. Frequency of the service depends on whether you go during the summer or the winter, and the wait ranges from six minutes up to 30 or 40 at very busy times, with long lines for the mid-morning buses from the Plaça de Catalunya.

To make the most of this service, be realistic about what you can see in one day, as it would be impossible to fit in all the sights on both routes. Buses only travel in one direction around the route, so it can be difficult to get back to somewhere, unless you are prepared to sit all the way around the loop. The two-day pass enables you to use the service as a city bus tour and orientate yourself on the first day. Then on the second day you can pick out the sights you want to visit.

NIGHT BUSES

Once the TMB buses have finished for the day, special night buses (Nitbus) take over. They run regularly from 11pm to 4.30am on selected routes. Most routes start at the Plaça de Catalunya, with route numbers starting with N.

TOMBBUS

This royal-blue single-decker plies the Shopping Line, a route between Plaça de Catalunya and Avinguda Diagonal via Passeig de Gràcia. It is designed to take you past some of the best shops in the city in the greatest comfort, with leather seats, magazines and piped music. A single trip costs €1.25, or pay €5 for an all-day pass called the T-Shopping Card (targeta T-shopping in Catalan). Note that you can't use any of the local transport passes on this route, as it's privately owned. The first departure from the Plaça de Catalunya is Mon–Fri 8am, Sat 10am, with buses running every six minutes.

BUS BUSTER CHART

Use this chart to find out which buses you'll need to catch to travel from one destination to another. Follow the rows of squares horizontally and vertically from the name of the destinations until they meet. This square contains the number(s) of the bus(es) you'll need to catch. Only the most frequent buses have been included. Bus numbers on a white square are direct. Numbers in coloured squares show that you have to change buses. Start out on the first bus listed, then change to the second bus. Look at the key to find out where you must change.

CHANGE AT:
- Pla de Palau
- Plaça d'Espanya
- Universitat
- Av. Diagonal
- Plaça Tetuan
- Plaça de Catalunya
- Ronda St Antoni
- Pla Portal de la Pau
- * Stay on in that direction, no need to change
- \+ Change at Urquinaona in that direction
- M Easier to use metro
- W Easier to walk

Routes change regularly, so check an up-to-date timetable or bus map before setting out.

Bus Buster Chart — triangular matrix of bus routes between destinations: Casa Milà, Catedral, Conjunt Monumental, Fundació Joan Miró, Manzana de la Discòrdia, Monestir de Pedralbes, Montjuïc, MACBA, M. d'Història Catalunya, M. Marítim, MNAC, M. Picasso, Palau Güell, Palau de la Música, Park Güell, Plaça de Sant Jaume, Las Ramblas, Santa Maria del Mar, Sagrada Família.

MAIN BUS ROUTES

Certain routes link key attractions, which are given below. The routes shown are stops in one particular direction, which are not always the same in both. The black stops in the graphic below denote stops nearest to places of interest.

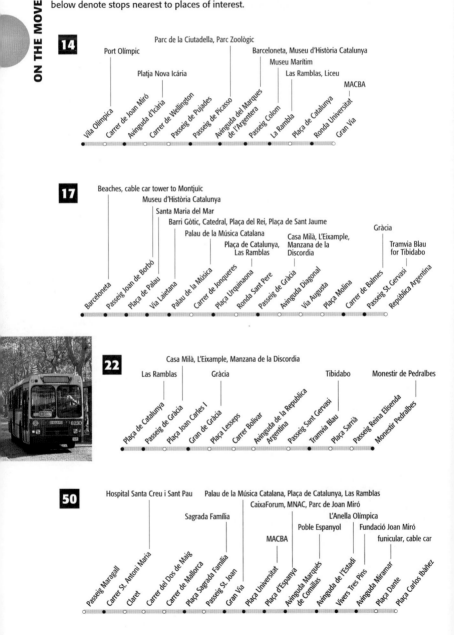

14

Parc de la Ciutadella, Parc Zoològic
Port Olímpic
Barceloneta, Museu d'Història Catalunya
Museu Marítim
Platja Nova Icária
Las Ramblas, Liceu
MACBA

Vila Olímpica · Carrer de Joan Miró · Avinguda d'Icária · Carrer de Wellington · Passeig de Pujades · Passeig de Picasso · Avinguda del Marques de l'Argentera · Passeig Colom · La Rambla · Plaça de Catalunya · Ronda Universitat · Gran Via

17

Beaches, cable car tower to Montjuïc
Museu d'Història Catalunya
Santa Maria del Mar
Barri Gòtic, Catedral, Plaça del Rei, Plaça de Sant Jaume
Palau de la Música Catalana
Plaça de Catalunya, Las Ramblas
Casa Milà, L'Eixample, Manzana de la Discordia
Gràcia
Tramvia Blau for Tibidabo

Barceloneta · Passeig Joan de Borbó · Plaça de Palau · Via Laietana · Palau de la Música · Carrer de Jonqueres · Plaça Urquinaona · Ronda Sant Pere · Passeig de Gràcia · Avinguda Diagonal · Via Augusta · Plaça Molina · Carrer de Balmes · Passeig St. Gervasi · República Argentina

22

Casa Milà, L'Eixample, Manzana de la Discordia
Las Ramblas
Gràcia
Tibidabo
Monestir de Pedralbes

Plaça de Catalunya · Passeig de Gràcia · Plaça Joan Carles I · Gran de Gràcia · Plaça Lesseps · Carrer Bolívar · Avinguda de la República Argentina · Passeig Sant Gervasi · Tramvia Blau · Plaça Sarrià · Passeig Reina Elisenda · Monestir Pedralbes

50

Hospital Santa Creu i Sant Pau
Palau de la Música Catalana, Plaça de Catalunya, Las Ramblas
CaixaForum, MNAC, Parc de Joan Miró
Sagrada Família
L'Anella Olímpica
Poble Espanyol
Fundació Joan Miró
MACBA
funicular, cable car

Passeig Maragall · Carrer St. Antoni Maria Claret · Carrer del Dos de Maig · Carrer de Mallorca · Plaça Sagrada Família · Passeig St. Joan · Gran Via · Plaça Universitat · Plaça d'Espanya · Avinguda Marqués de Comillas · Avinguda de l'Estadi · Vivers Tres Pins · Avinguda Miramar · Plaça Dante · Plaça Carlos Ibáñez

Train

The metro is supplemented by the Ferrocarrils de la Generalitat de Catalunya (FGC), a local train service run by the Catalan government. It is integrated with the metro and will take you out into the suburbs. There is also a regional service run by RENFE, the national train operator, which is signposted as Rodalies (Cercanías in Spanish) RENFE. This covers the province of Barcelona as well as taking you to the coast.

● The suburban and regional lines are colour-coded and numbered, but prefixed by a letter. For getting around the city it's unlikely you will make much use of these lines, but the FGC line from Plaça Catalunya to Tibidabo (line U7) is a quick way to reach the foot of the mountain, and the airport station is on Rodalies line C1.

● The same pricing and ticketing system as the metro applies, as long as you stay within Zone One. Check maps at stations.

● Both Plaça Catalunya and Plaça d'Espanya are main hubs for these local routes. You can get further rail information at www.renfe.es, or call 902 24 02 02 for national travel and 934 90 11 22 for international travel.

Taxis

There are around 11,000 black-and-yellow taxis in the city. They are privately owned, but licensed by the city council.

● Smoking is not allowed.

● Guide dogs are allowed but pets are at the driver's discretion.

● There is a schedule of approved fares for around the

city, but fares are not expensive: Between 6am–10pm: €1.15 minimum fare; €2.79 minimum fare when you order by phone; €0.69 per km.
Between 10pm–6am and Sun: €1.30 minimum fare; €3.48 minimum fare when ordering by phone; €0.88 per km.
Surcharges:
Luggage: €0.85
Pets: €1
To/from airport: €2.10
To/from port: €1.85
● If the green light on top of the taxi is lit, then it's available.
● For more information contact Institut Metropolità del Taxi, www.taxibarcelona.com (*tel 93 223 51 51*).

Bicycles

● You can get information on bicycle routes from the tourist office (see page 270), or the information line 010.
● Un Cotxe Menys rent bicycles by the hour, day or week. Their offices are at Carrer de Esparteria 3 (*tel 93 268 21 05; open Mon–Fri 10–2*) or visit www.bicicletabarcelona.com.
● Biciclot (*Verneda 16, tel 93 307 74 75; open*

Tue–Sun 10–2, 5–8, Mon 5–8) also rents out bikes; visit them at www.biciclot.net. Don't forget to take some ID with you.
● Amics de la Bici (*tel 93 339 40 60*) has a good website, www.amicsdelabici.org, listing more companies and routes.

Other Services

● The **Tramvia Blau** is an old-fashioned tramway that runs through the suburb of Tibidabo, from Avinguda Tibidabo to Plaça Doctor Andreu. It joins up with the funicular that takes you to the top of the mountain.
● The **funicular** to Montjuïc runs from the Paral.lel metro station to Avinguda de Miramar in about two minutes. It is probably the easiest way up onto Montjuïc, but as it runs inside the mountain for much of the journey, there isn't much to see.

The Tramvia Blau to Tibidabo

● The **Telefèric de Montjuïc** (cable car) also goes to Montjuïc, running from Avinguda de Miramar to the fortress. There is one stop in-between at a viewing point and the whole route runs for 815m (2,670ft). The views over the city are fantastic and can save you a steep walk up the hill.
● If you are looking for something different, Autoantic rent out vintage and classic cars with a driver (*tel 93 723 81 01*), or horse-drawn carriages can be rented at Portal de la Pau, Carrer de Maria Victòria 14 and Carrer de Rossend Arús 25 (*tel 93 421 15 49*).

MOTORCYCLE RENTAL

There are number of companies in the city to rent from, and the same laws apply as car rental (see page 41).

	Address	Telephone	Fax
Motorent	Portbou 14–28	93 490 84 01	93 490 84 01
Over-Rent	Av. Josep Tarradellas 42	93 405 26 60	93 419 96 30
Piaggio	Brasil 19	93 330 95 00	93 330 96 97
Vanguard	Viladomat 297	93 439 38 80	93 410 82 71

Driving

If you are planning to stay within the city, then it really isn't worth driving as it's just too busy, but if you want to explore the surrounding country, a car may be useful.

THE LAW
- You will need to be at least 18 years old and have with you the vehicle registration document, motor insurance and a valid driving licence.
- Licences from major countries, such as the United States, Canada, the United Kingdom and other EU countries will cover you.
- If in your own vehicle, it is essential to have a bail bond from your vehicle insurers.
- Seat belts are compulsory for drivers, front seat passengers, and for rear passengers if the vehicle is fitted with them. It is illegal to carry children under the age of 12 in the front passenger seat unless they are big enough to use the seat belts safely.
- The drink-driving limit is 0.5 grams per 1,000 cubic cm (0.3 grams for new drivers) and if you are stopped it is compulsory to comply with the alcohol tests.

PARKING
The main car parking company within the city is SMASSA, which operates around 30 underground car parks. To get into these you need to drive off the road and down a ramp—they are signed with a white P on a blue square. SMASSA car parks are at Plaça dels Ángels, near to the MACBA, Moll de la Fusta at Port Vell and Avinguda de

INFORMATION FOR ROAD USERS

It is compulsory for all drivers to carry the following equipment in their vehicle at all times. If you have rented a car, ensure that this equipment is provided and is functioning before you leave the rental office.

2 x self-standing warning triangles
1 x set of spare headlight and rear light bulbs
1 x set of spare fuses
1 x spare wheel

Speed limits
Motorway (expressway): 120kph (75mph), 80kph (50mph) for vehicles with trailers
Roads with overtaking lanes: 100kph (62mph), 80kph (50mph) for vehicles with trailers
Other roads outside built up areas: 90kph (60mph), 70kph (44mph) for vehicles with trailers
Towns/built-up areas: 50kph (31mph)

Road names
Autopistas: motorways (expressways) prefixed by A or E and followed by a route number
Autovías: non-toll dual carriageway (separated highway)
Peaje: toll roads
Carreteras nacionales: main roads, prefixed N or CN
Carreteras comarcales: local roads, prefix C

Francesc Combó, near the cathedral. It costs around €1.70 per hour, but you pay to the nearest five minutes. Another option is to buy a discount card, giving 25, 50 or 100 hours of parking with a discount of up to 30 per cent.

SABA run a number of car parks that can be found at Plaça de Catalunya, Plaça d'Urquinaona, Arc de Triomf, Avinguda Catedral and Passeig de Gràcia.

ON-STREET PARKING
This is a nightmare in the city and expensive. Four zones have been created (A, B, C and D) and are differentiated by price and the maximum length of time you are allowed to park. Zones A and B are the most central and therefore have high parking charges and shorter parking times than zones C and D. Visit www.smassa.es for details.

PARK AND RIDE
The Plaça de las Glóries forms the parking arm of the city's park and ride system. Leave your car here and then use public transport. Your ticket entitles you to use public transport for the day (€4.65)—weekly tickets are also available (€19.10 for Mon–Sat). The car park is open for 18 hours and you can pay using most major credit cards.

SPANISH ROAD SIGNS

No parking (clearway)	Maximum speed	No overtaking	No half-turns	Minimum speed limit	Pedestrian lane
Road narrows	Two-way traffic	Motorway (Expressway)	Two-lane highway	All vehicles prohibited	Parking

LEAVING BARCELONA

Catalonia has a whole host of places to visit, just two or three hours away from the main city. A good network of connections will help you to enjoy the rest of the region.

TRAINS

Sants Estaciò is the station to use for national travel. There are direct trains to Malaga, Granada, Seville, Valencia, Zaragoza, Pamplona, Vigo, La Coruña, Madrid and most main cities in Spain.

● Grandes Lineas is the umbrella term for trains that cover long distances and under this name there are different types of trains: Euromed, Alaris, Tren Estrella, Diurnos, Intercity, Trenhotel, Talgo, Arco and Altaria.

● AVE are high speed trains that travel up to 300kph and operate between Barcelona-Zaragoza-Madrid. They are more expensive than the Grandes Lineas.

● Regional trains in Catalonia are the Catalunya Express or Delta.

● First (*preferente*) and second (*turista*) class travel is available; first class is about 40 per cent more expensive.

● There is little difference between first and second class on day trains.

● The difference is most obvious on the overnight trains. You can travel in *asiento turista* (a seat, not reclining), in *cama turista* (a berth for 4 or 6 people in the same compartment), or *cama preferente* (couchettes for one or two people) with private shower and washbasin and complimentary breakfast.

● Overnight trains go from Barcelona to major cities in Andalucía, Madrid, Galicia, the Basque Country, Cantabria and Asturias.

TICKETS

● It is best to book your tickets in advance, especially for travel at busy times such as July, August, Christmas, New Year or Easter.

● Contact RENFE on 902 240 202 or www.renfe.es, where you can you can buy tickets on-line.

● Tickets can be also be bought from travel agencies and RENFE

First class (preferente) rail travel is available on a number of train services, including to Madrid

ticket offices at Estació de França, Estació de Passeig de Gràcia and Sants Estació.

DISCOUNTS ON TRAINS

● If you have an International Youth Card (for ages 14–26) you can get 20 per cent discount.

● Children under 4 travel for free if they don't use a seat, and children 4–13 are entitled to a 40 per cent discount.

● If you book a 4-couchette berth in the same compartment you get a 10 per cent discount.

LONG DISTANCE BUSES

The biggest national company is Alsa Enatcar, tel 902 422 242, www.alsa.es.

● They have two types of buses on every route: normal or Eurobus; the latter is more expensive but makes fewer stops and is more comfortable.

● Most buses leave from Estació del Nord. A few leave from outside Sants train station.

● For more destinations and companies the Estació del Nord has its own booking service: Estació del Nord, tel 902 260 606, open 7am–9pm, www.barcelonanord.com.

COMPARISONS

The table below outlines train and long-distance bus journey times and prices. A range is given where there are a number of different types of train or bus that you can catch. The general rule is that the faster the service the more expensive the ticket price.

TRAIN VERSUS BUS				
	Train		**Bus**	
Figueres	€7.20–€8.25	1hr 45 min–2 hr	€12.50	2hr 20 min
Girona	€5–€5.75	1hr 15 min	€8.80	1hr 20 min
Madrid	€40–€59	5–9hr	€23	7hr 30 min
Seville	€49–€76	8–12hr	€64–€75	14–16hr
Sitges	€2.20	40 min	–	–
Tarragona	€4.25–€4.90	1hr–1hr 30 min	€5.65–€8	1hr 30min
Valencia	€18.50–€34	3hr–5hr	€21	5hr
Vilafranca del Penedès	€2.70	1hr	–	–
Zaragoza	€18.50 –€34	3hr–5hr 20 min	€12	3hr 45 min

VISITORS WITH A DISABILITY

ARRIVING

By air
Barcelona airport is modern and is well-equipped for those with disabilities: look for adapted toilets, reserved parking spaces, elevators and ramps.
● The distances from the gates to the main terminal buildings and between terminals themselves are not very large, which is helpful to those with impaired movement.
● If you need particular assistance, you should let the airline know in advance, as they can arrange to help you.
● For more details call the information line at the airport (*tel 93 298 38 38*).

By train
● The RENFE station Sants is a good station to arrive at, and use when you are in the city, as there are lifts to every platform and no stairs to access the building.
● Other accessible stations (but not totally adapted) are: Plaça Catalunya, Provença, Sant Gervasi, Muntaner, Bonanova, Avinguda Tibidabo, Plaça Espanya, Mogoria and Campana.

TRANSFERS
● The Aerobús has not been adapted for use by those with a disability.
● The trains are more useful for transfers, changing at Sants or Catalunya, which have lifts. Be careful, however, as there is a gap between the train and the platform edge.

GETTING AROUND
● The Taxi Amic service has minivans which can fit wheelchairs easily, but it is a very popular service and you will need to book at least 24 hours ahead (*tel 93 420 80 88, www.taximic.cjb.net*).
● Some—but not all—TMB buses have been adapted for wheelchair access using lowered ramps. Look out for the wheelchair symbol.
● The metro line 2 (purple) is the only one that has been adapted, along with Fontana, Mundet, Valldaura and Canyelles on line 3. The rest are inaccessible to wheelchairs.
● Some metro stations have screens that indicate when the next train is arriving, and all have announcements.
● There is a dedicated TMB helpline for visitors with a disability (*tel 93 486 07 52, fax 93 486 07 53*), or use their webite www.tmb.net.
● TMB transport maps indicate all bus lines and metro stations that have been adpated for wheelchair use.
● RENFE has wheelchairs available for transfers at their main stations.
● Facilities at museums are limited, but newer museums, such as the MACBA, have a better range of amenities. If you have specific needs, it is advisable to phone ahead.

ACCESSOS FÀCILS I SEGURS
ACCESOS FÁCILES Y SEGUROS
SAFE AND EASY ACCESS

Access varies considerably across the city, so look out for signs

The Sights

This section is divided into two parts: Sightseeing Areas, consisting of four areas (shown on the map inside the front cover) highlighting what to see; and A–Z of Sights, an alphabetical listing of places to visit in Barcelona, all marked on the maps on pages 54–57.

Sights Locator Maps   **54–57**

Sightseeing Areas   **58–61**
Montjuïc   **58**
The Port   **59**
Barri Gòtic   **60**
La Ribera   **61**

A–Z of Sights   **62–130**
For quick reference, the major sights are listed below, with the key places highlighted in bold type.

Barceloneta   **63**
Barri Gòtic   **64**
Casa Milà   **66–69**
Catedral de la Seu   **70–73**

Conjunt Monumental de
la Plaça del Rei   **75**
Fundació Joan Miró   **78–79**
Manzana de la Discordia   **82–83**
Monestir de Pedralbes   **84–85**
Montjuïc   **86–87**
Museu d'Art Contemporani
de Barcelona   **90–91**
Museu d'Història
de Catalunya   **93**
Museu Marítim   **94–95**
**Museu Nacional d'Art
de Catalunya**   **96–99**
Museu Picasso   **100–101**
Palau Güell   **103**
**Palau de la Música
Catalana**   **104–107**
Park Güell   **110–113**
Plaça de Sant Jaume   **116–117**
Las Ramblas   **120–121**
La Ribera   **122**
Santa Maria del Mar   **123**
La Sagrada Família   **124–129**

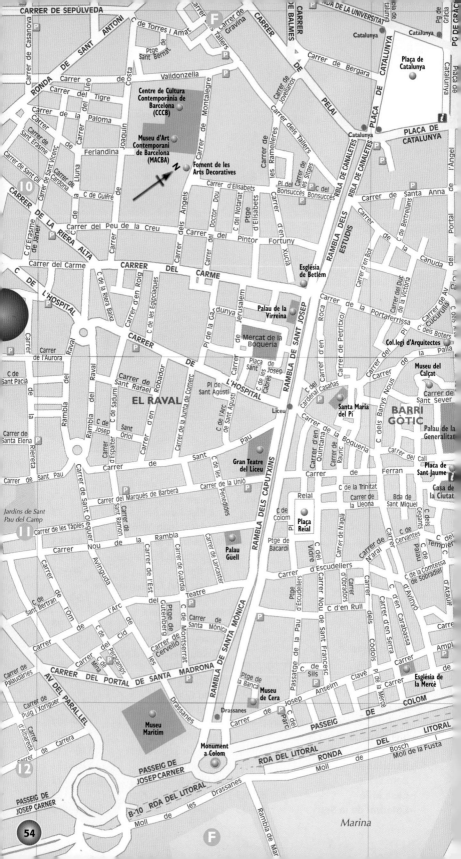

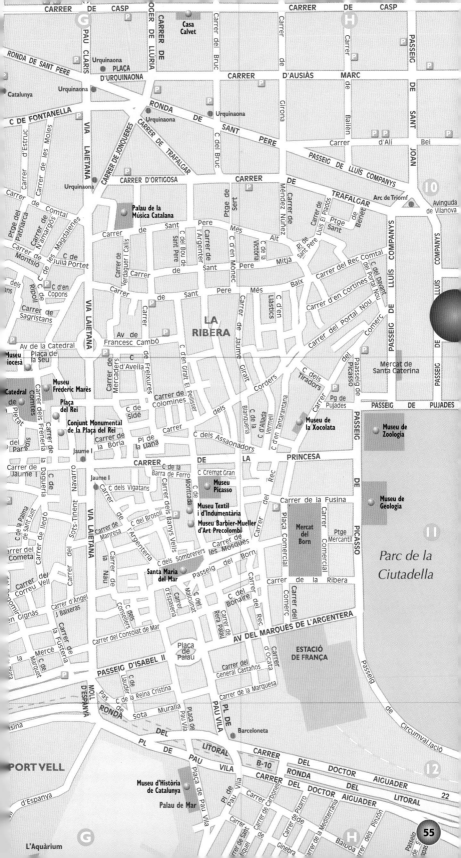

Montjuïc

HOW TO GET THERE

🚇 Espanya; Paral.lel, then Funicular de Montjuïc

🚌 50 to Montjuïc; 30, 37, 61 to Plaça d'Espanya

Montjuïc could well be nicknamed the mount of museums. You will find a dense concentration of them here, including the Fundació Joan Miró and the MNAC. It was also the focal point of the 1992 Olympic Games.

This steep mountain, with the mountains of the Collserola (see page 130), has historically isolated Barcelona from the world. The word Montjuïc translates as Jewish mountain, possibly earning its name from the tombstones found here and thought to have been a Jewish cemetery. It was also the first part of the city to be colonized by the Romans—a shrine to Jupiter was found on the site.

Its lack of a water supply meant that it was unsuitable for residential development for a long time. In 1929, however, the southern face was chosen as the site of the Universal Fair, which led to a regeneration of the area.

These exhibition traditions have continued with the massive exhibition and trade halls, Fira de Barcelona, that now flank either side of the Avinguda de la Reina Maria Cristina. This avenue stretches up from the Plaça d'Espanya, which is the best point to access all the sights from. Its sheer size, if not the traffic, is impressive as Montjuïc opens up before you, with the Museu Nacional d'Art de Catalunya (MNAC)—one of the city's best art collections—dominating the view.

Barcelona is rightly proud of its achievements in staging the 1992 Olympic Games, which created another major push to regenerate the area, and brought the city to the world's attention. The stadium and the swimming pools are still in use, and the hard landscaping of the Anella Olímpica (Olympic Ring) draws architectural contrasts with the neo-baroque MNAC and the greenery on much of the rest of the mountain. This open space attracts visitors and residents alike who want to take a breather from the old city. There are a number of gardens to explore, but the less developed face of the mountain, up past the Castell de Montjuïc, has a wilder side.

The one other, single reason to visit is the view. Glimpses of the city can be had from all over Montjuïc, but if you catch the cable car, from where the funicular drops you off, up to the Castell the panoramic views over the port and back towards the Barri Gòtic, La Sagrada Família and Tibidabo are amazing. For more information on Montjuïc, see pages 86–87.

THE MAIN SIGHTS

Take the whole day, or more, to explore the museums here. The range of art and architecture, from Roman to Miró, is a lesson in Catalan development. The only thing missing is the wealth of Modernista buildings found elsewhere in the city.

A forest of pillars outside the Olympic staduim

L'Anella Olímpica

Home to the sporting events of the Games (see page 62).

Fundació Joan Miró

An unrivalled collection set in a beautifully designed gallery (see pages 78–79).

Jardí Botànic

A relaxing space among all the museums (see page 81).

MNAC

Outstanding Romanesque and Gothic art (see pages 96–99).

Poble Espanyol

Architecture from all over Spain, with craft workshops thrown in (see page 118).

Other places to visit

The **Pavelló Mies van der Rohe** adds yet another architectural dimension to the area (see page 114) and the **Museu d'Arqueologia de Catalunya** has a good collection of local Roman finds (see page 88). The Plaça d'Espanya is the mountain's entry point and home of the **Magic Fountain** (see page 115). **CaixaForum** is a vibrant art gallery (see page 65).

WHERE TO EAT

There are few restaurants on Montjuïc, but the one at the Fundació Joan Miró is a good place to stop. Or picnic at a number of spots, including the Jardí Botànic, that have great views over the city.

The Port

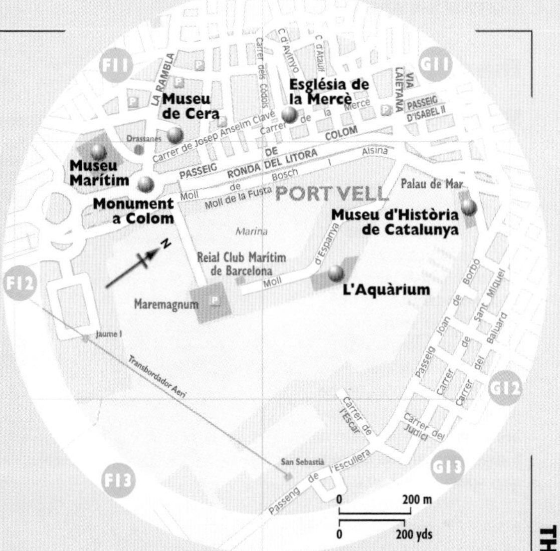

HOW TO GET THERE

🚇 Drassanes; Barceloneta

🚌 17, 19, 40

The Moll de Barcelona and the small peninsula of Barceloneta border this section of the port. It is the area of the city that most benefited from the regeneration project of the early 1990s and brings you face to face with Barcelona's maritime history.

This area of the port can be credited with renewing the city's interest in the sea. The container port used to confront you once you reached the bottom of Las Ramblas and the whole area was shabby and rather ignored. But the container port was moved, giving the area much more light and space. The wooden bridge, the Rambla del Mar, allows you to cross the sea and takes you to the IMAX cinema, the indoor entertainment complex Maremagnum and the aquarium.

It is edged on the opposite side by the Passeig Joan de Borbó that runs from the Plaça del Palau down to the sea. This avenue acts as the intersection between the glitz of Port Vell and the old *barri* (district) of Barceloneta. If you explore these streets you will reach the first of the urban beaches, Platja de la Barceloneta. The beaches, which stretch along the coast, were part of an overall clean up prior to the Olympic Games hitting town.

The Museu Marítim, housed in the beautiful former royal shipyards, is the place to visit for documentary evidence of all these changes. The museum tells the history of Catalan shipbuilding and trading routes, and gives you the chance to visit a tall ship. If you want to witness all these changes for yourself, walk to the end of the Passeig Joan de Borbó to the Torre de Sant Sebastià for great views of the whole port. You can pick

up the *transbordador*, or cable car, from this tower that will carry you over the Moll de Barceloneta to a lookout point at the top of Montjuïc. For more information see page 49 and pages 86–87.

THE MAIN SIGHTS

This area is good for children, with its wide variety of activities from the commercial Port Vell to more traditional museums. It is also a great spot to relax in, with cafés, bars and the beach all within easy reach.

L'Aquàrium
State-of-the-art aquarium (see page 62).

Museu d'Història de Catalunya
Take a tour through the history of the city at the Palau del Mar (see page 93).

Museu Marítim
Learn about the nautical history of the area at one of the city's best museums (see pages 94–95).

Platja de la Barceloneta
With beaches on the doorstep, make sure you visit (see page 173).

A figurehead at the Museu Marítim

Other places to visit
Església de La Mercè is dedicated to the patron saint of the city and is symbolically important to Barcelona (see page 76).

The cable car from the port gives views across the city

Maremagnum is the shopping complex (see page 152), next to the IMAX cinema (see page 160). **Museu de Cera** (see page 89), the waxworks, is along Las Ramblas, as is the **Monument a Colom** (see page 88).

WHERE TO EAT
Try the seafood in one of the many restaurants along the Passeig Joan de Borbó.

Julius
A seafood restaurant with friendly staff (see page 224).

Nou Can Tipa
A busy tapas bar (see page 227).

THE SIGHTS

Map labels: F11, G11, F12, G12, F13, G13, Museu de Cera, Església de la Mercè, Museu Marítim, Monument a Colom, PORT VELL, Palau de Mar, Museu d'Història de Catalunya, Reial Club Marítim de Barcelona, L'Aquàrium, Maremagnum, Transbordador Aeri, San Sebastià, RONDA DEL LITORA, PASSEIG, VIA LAIETANA, PASSEIG D'ISABEL II, COLOM, Marina, Jaume I, 0 200 m, 0 200 yds

Barri Gòtic

HOW TO GET THERE

🚇 Jaume I

🚌 14, 38, 59, 91

The Gothic quarter lies between Las Ramblas and the Via Laietana, much of which is pedestrianized. The 13th- to 15th-century buildings, still amazingly intact, are splendid examples of the period's architecture, and are now a combination of museums, private homes and specialist shops.

One of the best ways to explore this area is just to head off into the maze of lanes. There is a vast amount to see and the best way to discover the Barri Gòtic's is simply by trial and error. But if you want something more structured, think of the area as a

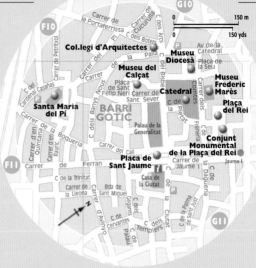

The Catalan Gothic church of Santa Maria del Pí

number of plaças, taking in the sights surrounding each one.

It is impossible to miss the Plaça de la Seu, dominated by the Catedral de la Seu. It is a wide, open square with lots of good shopping streets and cafés branching off it. If you want a quieter spot seek out the pretty Plaça de Sant Felip Neri, which is just behind the cathedral. You can move on from this religious stronghold to the old base of the monarchy: the Plaça del Rei, or Square of Kings. The Saló del Tinell (banqueting chamber) was once the headquarters of the Catholic Monarchs Ferdinand and Isabella. Also here is the Royal Palace, now the Conjunt Monumental de la Plaça del Rei, complete with Roman ruins.

The Plaça de Sant Jaume is the political arm of this trio of squares: home to the city's town hall, Ajuntament, (associated with central government) and the Generalitat (the seat of the autonomous government). These two have been battling for hundreds of years, each pushing forward its own political stance.

Strolling through the Barri Gòtic gives you some idea of what life must have been like for its medieval inhabitants, as little has changed. Yet some of the modern buildings are of no less merit. The most famous of these is the Bridge of Sighs (nothing like the Venetian original) in Carrer del Bisbe, which was built during the city's Gothic revival in the 1920s.

THE MAIN SIGHTS

There is a lot to see here, but as the type of museum varies, you can focus on what interests you.

Catedral de la Seu

An impressive example of Catalan Gothic architecture (see pages 70–73).

Conjunt Monumental de la Plaça del Rei

A run through the history of the city, with the most extensive underground Roman ruins in Europe (see page 75).

Museu Frederic Marès

An eclectic mix, focusing mainly on religious art and everyday objects (see page 92).

Plaça del Rei

One of the city's best medieval squares (see page 115).

Shop fronts blend in well with the medieval Plaça del Rei

Plaça de Sant Jaume

A grand square in the heart of the city (see pages 116–117).

Other places to visit

Museu del Calçat, a shoe museum (see page 89); the Museu Diocesà displays religious art (see page 92); Santa Maria del Pí, with its intricate rose window and simple style, is on the Plaça del Pí (see page 130).

WHERE TO EAT

Living

Impressive vegetarian food (see page 224).

Venus Delicatessen

Inexpensive lunchtime menu (see page 234).

La Ribera

HOW TO GET THERE

🚇 Jaume I or Barceloneta

🚌 14, 39, 51 along the Passeig de Picasso

La Ribera, which includes the Parc de la Ciutadella, is one of the city's oldest *barris* (districts) and is split from the Barri Gòtic by the Via Laietana. The rich Gothic mansions on the Carrer de Montcada, home to the Museu Picasso, stand as a testament to the city's mercantile history and show only a fraction of the wealth that it generated.

La Ribera translates as The Shore and one of the main sights here is the Basílica de Santa Maria del Mar: the Church of St. Mary of the Sea. In medieval times the Mediterranean cut much further inland than it does today. Santa Maria was almost on the water's edge and this close contact with the sea meant that much of the medieval maritime trade passed through La Ribera. It was connected with the Barri Gòtic by the Plaça del Blat, the wheat square, through which passed all the grain traded in the city. This occupied the space now known as the Plaça de l'Angel, right by the Jaume I metro station on the Via Laietana, the main road that was built in early 1900s. And so La Ribera was once an integral part of the main medieval city complex, and the heart of Barcelona's commercial area, its streets lined with warehouses and workshops supplying the needs of the traders.

As the merchants got richer, they built wonderful mansions designed to reflect their wealth, and the address of choice became the Carrer de Montcada. This dark, narrow street is home to an extraordinary procession of superb medieval palaces, which today house some compelling museums. One of these is the Museu Picasso.

From Carrer de Montcada it's a few minutes walk to Santa Maria del Mar to the west and, to the east, the Mercat del Born, built in the 1870s and once the city's main wholesale market. From these two focal points, a maze of tiny streets and arches lead to the Llotja (Exchange), once the oldest continuously functioning stock exchange in Europe—it was built in the 1380s and finally moved away in 1994.

East of the Born lies the Parc de la Ciutadella, a huge green space once occupied by a fortress and created after the 1714 siege. Today it's one of the city's most beguiling oases of cool greenery, and is home to several museums and the zoo.

THE MAIN SIGHTS

There are lots of famous places to see in this area, but they form a manageable group, helped by many of them being based around the Parc de la Ciutadella, which instils a much slower pace to your sightseeing.

Mercat del Born

Superb 19th-century wrought-iron structure fronted by a lovely square (see page 122).

Museu d'Art Modern

Homage to Catalan art from the mid-19th century to the 1930s (see page 88).

Museu Picasso

One of the best art collections in the city, started by the artist himself (see pages 100–101).

Parc de la Ciutadella

The largest green space in this part of town, with lots to see and do for everyone (see page 108).

Parc Zoològic

Barcelona's zoo (see page 114) occupies a large area of the Parc de la Ciutadella

Taking time to enjoy a drink on the Plaça del Santa Maria

and, with its range of animals, is great for children.

Santa Maria del Mar

Barcelona's loveliest Gothic church, in one of the city's best squares (see page 123).

Other places to visit

Museu Tèxtil i d'Indumentària (see page 102) is an exhibition of clothing and accessories, plus the Museu de Zoologia (see page 102) and Museu de Geologia (see page 92).

WHERE TO EAT

Hivernacle

This café—the name means Winter Garden—serves a good assortment of refreshments (see page 168).

THE SIGHTS

Map labels:
- Mercat de Santa Caterina
- PASSEIG DE PUJADES
- Museu de la Xocolata
- Museu Textil i d'Indumentària
- C DE LA PRINCESA
- Museu Picasso
- Carrer de la Fusina
- Museu de Zoologia
- Museu de Geologia
- Museu Barbier-Mueller d'Art Precolombi
- Mercat del Born
- PASSEIG DE PICASSO
- Parc de la Ciutadella
- Santa Maria del Mar
- Carrer de la Ribera
- La Llotja
- VIA LAIETANA
- AVINGUDA DEL MARQUES DE L'ARGENTERA
- Museu d'Art Modern
- PASSEIG D'ISABEL II
- ESTACIÓ DE FRANÇA
- Parc Zoològic
- Barceloneta
- CARRER DEL DOCTOR AIGUADER
- Museu d'Història de Catalunya
- RONDA DEL LITORAL
- CARRER DEL DOCTOR AIGUADER
- Carrer de Balboa
- Passeig de Circumval·lacio
- 0 200 m / 0 200 yds

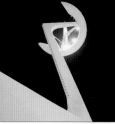

The communication tower is part of L'Anella's landscape

L'ANELLA OLÍMPICA

⊞ 56 C11 • Avinguda de L'Estadi
Ⓜ Espanya
www.fundaciobarcelonaolimpica.es

The eyes of the world were on Spanish archer Antonio Rebollo when he shot his fiery arrow to ignite the Olympic torch at the opening ceremony of the 1992 Games. The focus of the athletic action was here at the Estadi Olímpic (Olympic stadium), which forms part of L'Anella Olímpica—the Olympic Ring—on Montjuïc, along with the daring Palau Sant Jordi and the Picornell outdoor swimming pools.

The stadium was originally designed in 1929 by the architect Pere Domènech i Roura to house the alternative to the Berlin Olympic Games, but these games were cancelled on the outbreak of the Spanish Civil War (1936–39). The original façade was retained for the 1992 Games and the stadium refitted to hold 77,000 people. You can also visit the Galeria Olímpica (*Mon–Fri 10–2, 4–7, Apr–Sep*), a small exhibition space inside the Estadi Olímpic, which is principally dedicated to the Barcelona Games with photographs and memorabilia.

The Picornell swimming pools, designed by the world-renowned local architect Ricardo Bofill, are open to the public (see page 174) and hold open-air cinema screenings in July and August. But the grandest legacy of the trio is the stunning Palau Sant Jordi, designed by Japanese architect Arata Isozaki. The domed roof was actually assembled on the ground then raised into position, and the surrounding portico, gives the structure space and dynamism. The Palau is now the city's main venue for big-name music stars and large-scale meetings and conventions.

L'AQUÀRIUM DE BARCELONA

One of the finest aquariums in Europe, with interactive displays for children.

⊞ 57 G12 • Moll d'Espanya s/n, 08039 ☎ 93 221 74 74 Ⓒ Daily 9.30–9.30, Jun and Sep; daily 9.30am–11pm, Jul–end Aug; Mon–Fri 9.30–9, Sat–Sun 9.30–9.30, rest of year ⓦ Adult €13, child (4–12) €7.70 Ⓜ Drassanes 🚌 14, 17, 19, 36, 38, 40, 45, 57, 59, 64 🚻
www.aquariumbcn.com

RATINGS					
Good for kids	●	●	●	●	●
Shopping	●	●	●		
Value for money	●	●	●		

Barcelona's state-of-the-art aquarium is set in Port Vell. There are 21 tanks in all, with creatures ranging from poisonous and tropical fish to everyday varieties whose names you will recognize from local restaurant menus.

THE DEEP BLUE SEA

The first section focuses on the Mediterranean. Here you will find communities of cave and crevice dwellers from the rocky coasts, as well as eels and octopuses. The next section on tropical waters and the Red Sea is much brighter. Reef sharks, vivid yellow butterfly fish and the luminous marine life of the Caribbean, Hawaii and Australia are all found among their natural vegetation, which has fully developed since the aquarium opened in the mid-1990s.

The biggest crowd-pleaser is the close encounter with the sharks and stingrays in the huge Oceanarium. A wide glass tunnel lets you see these sleek creatures from all angles while being moved along by a conveyor belt. Grey sharks, marble rays and guitar fish are just some of the majestic creatures in this incredible show. The terrapin tank on your way out is also impressive, with dozens of caimans, turtles and other amphibians.

Upstairs the Explora! section lets children become familiar with three different Mediterranean seascapes: the marshland of the Ebro Delta, the underwater caves of the Medes Islands and the Costa Brava. With more than 50 interactive games and activities, there is plenty to keep them happy while adults can take in the spectacular views of the sea and surrounding port from the glass-enclosed terrace.

Close encounters at the aquarium (top); the Explora! section (right) makes learning about the oceans a fun activity

BARCELONETA

A fine beach, a fishing village with a strong maritime history and a great place to sample the local seafood.

Barceloneta (Little Barcelona) is the city's best-loved playground. Even before the area was smartened up for the Olympics, it was always packed at weekends. Post-Olympics, the beach is cleaner and the restaurants are more chic, but the same people who always came make their way down here in droves on a sunny Sunday.

Barceloneta was the city's first stab at contemporary urban planning. Originally it was meant to house the displaced residents of La Ribera in the 1750s after the Ciutadella was constructed—the fortress was built in the park of the same name and was loathed by Catalans as a symbol of central government oppression. The original idea was to make the cheap housing low-rise, but this was ignored and attics and other extensions were added, giving the area its congested feel.

FIESTAS

The local Fiestas de la Barceloneta are the most lively and least touristy in the city. The Diadeta, held in mid-September, is when the local clubs or *penyas* dress up in traditional costume and celebrate the area's maritime history. The Festa Major (Big Festival) in late September to early October is a week-long riot of local pride when dancing, outdoor feasts and other forms of revelry take place in its brightly decorated streets. Much of this activity is based around the Plaça de la Barceloneta, a picturesque square in the heart of Barceloneta with a fountain, a couple of cafés and the Església de Sant Miquel del Port, built in 1755. Its façade is its most interesting element, but it is home to a giant figure of St. Michael himself.

The main boulevard of Barceloneta is the Passeig Joan de Borbó, stretching from the Plaça Palau all the way down to the sea. Rows of warehouses were torn down to make way for the marina and the concrete pedestrian area that runs its entire length. With its dozens of seafood restaurants, and hawkers outside, it's easy to dismiss the street as a tourist trap until you realize that there are more locals than foreigners eating here. A paella amid the sea air of Barceloneta on Sunday is as traditional as *monas* (a type of cake) at Easter, and one to add to your list of culinary experiences.

The Arts hotel dominates the skyline (top); Homage to Barceloneta *by Rebecca Horne (middle, right); soaking up the sun (below, right)*

RATINGS			
Good for kids	●	●	●
Photo stops		●	●
Walkability	●	●	●

BASICS

✚ 57 H12

Tourist information office
Plaça de Sant Jaume, Carrer Ciutat 2 (in the town hall), 08002 ☎ 90 630 12 82
🕐 Mon–Fri 9–8, Sat 10–8, Sun and holidays 10–2
www.barcelonaturisme.com

Ⓜ Barceloneta

RATINGS	
Historic interest	●●●●○
Photo stops	●●●○○
Shopping	●●●○○

BASICS
✚ 54 G11

Tourist information office

Plaça de Sant Jaume, Carrer de Ciutat 2 (in the town hall), 08002 ☎ 90 630 12 82 🕐 Mon–Fri 9–8, Sat 10–8, Sun and holidays 10–2
www.barcelonaturisme.com

🚇 Jaume I or Liceu

BARRI GÒTIC

The most complete Gothic quarter on the Continent.

The Gothic period is Barcelona's other great contribution to the world of architecture, after Modernisme. Despite the famine, plague and social unrest that dogged the epoch, the city grew rapidly in medieval times, so much so that its expansion could no longer be contained within the old Roman walls. Not much is left of these walls, but the ensemble of 13th- to 15th-century buildings and narrow lanes of the Barri Gòtic (Gothic quarter) should be on every visitor's itinerary.

BACKGROUND

Guilds (or *gremis* in Catalan) were the backbone of Barcelona's medieval life and economic activity, and a forerunner of trade unions. Many of their shields can be seen on buildings dotted around the Barri Gòtic, denoting the headquarters of each particular trade. The tiny workshops were also here and many streets still bear the name of the activity that went on there for centuries, such as Escudellers (shield makers) or Brocaters (brocade makers).

El Call, the original Jewish ghetto, is also in the Barri Gòtic. A tiny area around the Carrer del Call and l'Arc de Sant Ramon del Call was the scene of the sacking of the Jews by Christian mobs in the late 1400s (see page 30). Little visual evidence remains of medieval Jewish culture, but there is a plaque from 1314 at Carrer de Marlet with a passage in Hebrew commemorating past inhabitants.

One of the prettiest and least visited squares in the Barri Gòtic is Sant Felip Neri. It can be tricky to find as it's tucked away to the right of the cathedral (see pages 70–73), but your effort will be rewarded as it is truly an oasis in an area sometimes overrun with visitors. The

Markets are held at the Plaça del Pí (above)

The Bridge of Sighs dates from the 1920s revival in Gothic architecture (right)

Plaça del Pí, home of the Gothic masterpiece the Església Santa Maria del Pí (see page 130), is another good place to take a break on your wanderings. It is filled with cafés, musicians and holds two regular markets. Carrer Petritxol, just off the Plaça del Pí, had its foundations laid in 1465 and now houses some of the most celebrated *granjas* (see page 211) in Barcelona.

Don't miss The tranquil square of Sant Just with its fountainheads and fine Gothic church of the same name.

The exterior of Casa Calvet is rich in stylish details

CASA CALVET

🏠 55 G10 • Carrer de Casp 48, 08010
☎ Restaurant: 93 412 40 12
🚇 Urquinaona 🚌 19, 39, 41, 45, 47, 55, 62
www.rutamodernisme.com

The Casa Calvet was the first of the three houses that Antoni Gaudí (1852–1926) built in L'Eixample, and has now been converted into apartments. The interior and the rear façade are not open to the public, but it is worth admiring from the outside.

It was built for the textile manufacturer Pere Calvet at the turn of the 20th century and the monochrome façade is probably Gaudí's most restrained work. Its undulating, three-tiered crown is reminiscent of rococo churches, but the main interest lies in the symbolism of the decorative elements. Gaudí placed a flamboyant C, the owner's initial, over the door and there are various mushroom reliefs on the main exterior, a reference to Calvet's interest in the study of mushrooms and fungi. The three heads of the crown represent St. Peter the Martyr, whom Calvet was named after, St. Genesius of Arles and St. Genesius of Rome, patrons of Vilassar, the family's home town.

The balustrades of the balconies and the *trencadís* work (surfaces covered with pieces of broken ceramics) of the rear façade can only be seen in photographs. The many pieces of furniture Gaudí designed for the residence are more accessible, being on display at Casa-Museu Gaudí at the Park Güell (see pages 110–113). But the best way to get a taste of Casa Calvet is to eat at the restaurant on the ground floor. It has one of the original, fluid wooden benches and some of the stained glass of the rear façade, and has retained many Gaudían touches.

CAIXAFORUM

This is one of the city's newest and most vibrant art spaces.

🏠 56 C10 • Avinguda del Marquès de Comillas 6–8, 08038 ☎ 93 476 86 00 🕐 Tue–Sun 10–8 💳 Free 🚇 Espanya 🚌 9, 27, 30, 56, 57, 65, 79 and all routes to Plaça d'Espanya 🍴 🏧
www.fundacio.lacaixa.es

RATINGS	
Good for kids	●●
Shopping	●●●●
Value for money	●●●

The museum is funded by La Caixa, Catalonia's largest bank, and has been praised by both the art world and residents since its opening in 2002. The CaixaForum is housed in the disused textile factory known as the Casaramona, one of the jewels of Spanish industrial architecture by the Modernista master Josep Puig i Cadafalch (1867–1957). The labyrinth-like, red-brick building with its high turret was faithfully restored to hold the Forum's exhibition spaces, an auditorium and a research centre. Its patio and entrance were added by Japanese architect Arata Isozaki, who also designed the Palau Sant Jordi (see page 62).

Contemporary art in all its forms, including plastic, architecture, photography, sculpture and installation, is the Forum's main agenda. The collection of 800 pieces was first started in 1985 and has grown into the most important of its type in Spain. The permanent collection is shown on a rotating basis, changing three times during the year.

THE EXHIBITS

After crossing the patio embedded with lights, you are greeted at the entrance by a huge abstract mural in primary shades by Sol LeWitt. From here, elevators take you up to the three exhibition spaces; one for the permanent collection and two dedicated to works on loan. The rooms lead onto a sunny, central interior patio, the setting for music recitals.

The startling *Room of Pain* by the German conceptual artist Joseph Beuys is often hailed as the collection's most powerful work. But there are also pieces by artists of the calibre of Tàpies, Julian Schnabel, Susana Solano and other international and national names covering the full gamut of modern and contemporary art from the 1970s to the present day.

The quality of the temporary exhibitions has been equally high, with names like Picasso, Renoir and Matisse, while a homage to architect Mies van der Rohe (whose Pavilion is across the road from the Forum, see page 114) has also won praise.

Don't miss Elya Kabakov's installation *For Sale*, an eerie room of everyday objects frozen in time

The entrance to the CaixaForum was designed by Arata Isozaki, who also designed the Palau Sant Jordi at L'Anella Olímpica

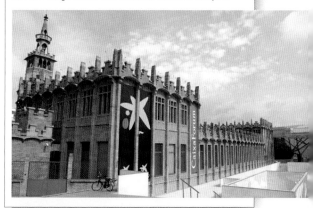

Casa Milà

**One of Gaudí's secular masterpieces, completed in 1912.
Eccentric, fantastical roof terrace with views over Barcelona.
Introductory exhibition on Gaudí provides an insight
into his life and work.**

*The roof terrace is one of
Gaudí's most striking works*

*One of the curvaceous chimeys
on the roof*

*The interior still sees residents
climbing its stairways*

SEEING CASA MILÀ

Casa Milà, standing like some giant, curving cliff face on the corner of Passeig de Gràcia and Carrer de Provença, was designed by Antoni Gaudí i Cornet (1852–1926). With its wavy lines and undulating façade, the building deliberately sets out to challenge the strict uniformity and grid plan of the Eixample. Most of the eight floors still serve as private apartments, but other parts are administered as a cultural centre by the Fundació Caixa Catalunya. The main entrance on Passeig de Gràcia leads to an inner courtyard, with a staircase to the first-floor art gallery. To see the sixth-floor apartments, Espai Gaudí and the spectacular roof terrace, you need to buy a ticket from the booth on Carrer de Provença and take the side entrance into the building.

HIGHLIGHTS

THE EXTERIOR

The creamy limestone façade has been likened to everything from an abandoned stone quarry to the rippling waves of the sea. Gaudí was frequently inspired by marine life forms, and it is easy to imagine the twisting wrought-iron balustrades on the balconies, designed by Gaudí's collaborator Josep Maria Jujol (1879–1949), as a mass of seaweed. Perhaps the most remarkable feature of Casa Milà is that it is said to contain not a single straight line or right angle in its construction. It may have been designed with a highly practical purpose, but this is a supreme example of architecture turned into sculpture.

ESPAI GAUDÍ

The tour of the upper floors begins by taking the elevator to the attic, where the former laundry has been turned into an exhibition of Gaudí's life and work. This is an unexpectedly special space, its 270 brick arches lending it the feel of a Gothic cathedral. It is the best place in Barcelona to get an overview of Gaudí's architectural techniques, with scale drawings and models of his buildings as well as audiovisual displays. Of particular interest are the interior photographs of some of the Gaudí buildings that are not normally open to the public, including Casa Vicens (see page 74).

RATINGS	
Good for kids	●●●
Photo stops	●●●●●
Specialist shopping	●●●●
Cultural interest	●●●●●

TIPS

● During June, July and August jazz, flamenco and Latin music performances are held on the roof. The entrance fee includes a glass of cava and a visit to the Espai Gaudí. Its setting on the roof under the stars is very special.

● For a view of the north side of the building, go next door to the furniture/design store Vinçon (see page 151). The back terrace of the building affords the only glimpse of this façade.

● Make time to visit the ground-floor gift shop (separate entrance) which, as well as having a superb range of gifts, is also part of the original structure.

Natural light is cleverly filtered into the Casa Milà to create a rich glow (left)

57 G8 • Passeig de Gràcia 92, 08027

☎ 93 484 59 00; 902 101 212 for night visits

🕐 Daily 10–8

💶 Adult €6 (€10 for night visits), child (under 12) free

Ⓜ Diagonal

🚌 7, 16, 17, 22, 24, 28

🎧 Audiotours in Catalan, English, French, Spanish, Italian and German for €3; tours by arrangement, tel 93 484 55 30

📖 Excellent guidebook available at both bookshops for €12

🎁 Two gift shops: one on the ground floor of the building with a fabulous collection of books and objects by local designers inspired by the Gaudían motif; the second shop in the apartment also sells books and faux Modernisme objects such as accessories and reproduction period toys

🚻 In the reception area and in the apartments

www.rutamodernisme.com
A good introduction to Modernisme, the key players and the buildings, but needs a bit of hunting around on. No official site dedicated to the Casa Milà.

The roof at night (top); Modernista furniture is displayed in the apartments (above)

THE APARTMENTS

Stairs lead down from the attic to Pis de la Pedrera, a pair of sixth-floor apartments which have been carefully restored to give a feel of early 20th-century Barcelona. A series of historical photographs is shown in the first, along with a display about the rapid technological changes that accompanied the Modernista architectural movement, such as the introduction of electricity and telephones, the opening of the metro, the arrival of cinemas and department stores. The second apartment, which is surprisingly spacious, is a reconstruction of the furnishings of a typical Modernista

apartment, and gives an insight into the lives of the early inhabitants of Casa Milà. A cabinet and bedroom suite by the Mallorcan furniture designer Gaspar Homar (1870–1953) are among the items on display, together with everyday objects of kitchen, bathroom and nursery equipment, which have been laid out in situ. From the apartment there are good views of the interior patio.

THE ROOF TERRACE

The high point of any visit to Casa Milà is the remarkable roof terrace, with its chimneys and ventilation shafts in the shape of owls, warriors, helmeted centurions and others fashioned out of broken pottery, marble and glass. This must be one of the best examples anywhere in Barcelona of Gaudí's ability to take something functional and imbue it with a sense of fun. One of the chimneys is made up of broken champagne bottles, apparently left over after a housewarming party. Like the rest of the building, the rooftop is not flat but undulating, with a series of curves and stairways giving varying views over the interior patios and across the skyline, in which Gaudí's Sagrada Família (see pages 124–129) is dominant. In keeping with Gaudí's religious and nationalist leanings, the central chimney is based on the cross of

FUNDACIÓ CAIXA CATALUNYA

In 1986, Casa Milà was acquired by the Fundació Caixa Catalunya, the cultural arm of a leading Catalan savings bank that has invested heavily in its restoration. Among the projects they have financed is the recovery of the first-floor apartments, where the Milà family lived. The partitions dividing some of the original rooms have been removed to reveal a fine example of a Gaudí interior, with trademark organic curves and blue-green marine motifs. This is now used as an exhibition hall with free exhibitions of contemporary painting and sculpture. You can get there by climbing the staircase from the entrance lobby.

The whole building has no load-bearing interior walls as it's all supported by concrete steel webbing (below left); the entrance hall (below right)

St. George, the patron saint of Catalonia. Gaudí's original plans included a huge bronze figure of the Virgin Mary for the roof, but he was forced to revise his ideas following the Tragic Week of 1909 (see page 35), when a number of churches were attacked in anarchist riots. Señor Milà told Gaudí that he feared such overt religious imagery might attract a similar fate.

BACKGROUND

Casa Milà was commissioned in 1906 by the businessman Pere Milà i Camps at a time when Passeig de Gràcia was the most fashionable address in town. Wealthy industrialists were attempting to outdo one another by building ever more fanciful Modernista houses, and Gaudí's brief was to surpass both the Casa Amatller and his own Casa Batlló (see pages 82–83) on the same street. Although it is now seen as perhaps the climax of Gaudí's creative genius, Casa Milà was ridiculed at the time and nicknamed La Pedrera (the quarry) because of its use of vast amounts of stone. This was Gaudí's last major secular commission—he spent the rest of his life working on the Sagrada Família.

SNAKES AND DRAGONS

Casa Milà has always aroused strong reactions. The Modernista artist Santiago Rusinyol joked that the people who lived in the apartments would not have cats and dogs for pets, but would have to keep snakes instead—presumably a reference to the sinuous, curvy lines of the building. And it was the French prime minister Georges Clemenceau, after a visit to Barcelona in the 1920s, who said that Catalans were so obsessed with the legend of St. George that they even built houses for dragons.

Catedral de la Seu

**The religious heart of the old town, with spectacular views
over the Barri Gòtic from its high roof.
One of the finest examples of Catalan Gothic
architecture in the region.**

SEEING THE CATEDRAL DE LA SEU

You are likely to find the cathedral easily if you spend any time
in the Barri Gòtic, as many of the area's narrow lanes seem to
channel you in this direction. The main entrance to the cathedral
is at the Plaça de la Seu, and you are free to roam around the
building. There is also a side entrance along the Carrer del Bisbe
that brings you into the cloister.

HIGHLIGHTS

THE FAÇADE

The money for the building project ran out before the façade could
be completed, so you might be surprised to learn that the front-facing
façade and spires were finished in 1913. The design was based on
the plain brick and stone front that had been in place since the 15th
century, and was paid for by Manuel Girona, a local businessman who
had made his fortunes in the Americas. Don't let this architectural
sleight of hand put you off. Entering the cathedral from the main
steps is a grand experience whatever its age. Flanked by two towering

spires and embellished with
hundreds of carvings of angels,
saints and other religious
imagery, as well as some fine
stained-glass windows, its detail
is almost as dizzying as its
dimensions. The structure
measures 93m (305ft) long,
40m (131ft) wide and 28m
(92ft) high. The cathedral's
bell towers are 53m (174ft)
high, while the main tower is
70m (230ft).

*The cathedral steps are used
for social gatherings (above);
the Christ of Lepanto crucifix is
said to have brought good luck
to John of Austria's fleet
(middle); soaring pillars are
typical of Catalan Gothic (right)*

CAPELLA DEL SANTÍSSIM SAGRAMENT

This is the first of the chapels
to your right as you come
through the main entrance. It
was designed and built while
Arnau Bargués was in charge
of construction, the third of the four architects to be so, having just
completed the original façade of the Ajuntament (town hall) on the
Plaça de Sant Jaume. The Capella's vaulted roof soars to more than
20m (66ft) and its treasure is the 16th-century figurine of the Christ
of Lepanto. This life-size icon is believed to have been on board the
flagship of John of Austria, who led a Christian fleet against the Turks
in the Gulf of Lepanto in 1571 (see page 31).

THE CRYPT

The crypt is one of the cathedral's more intimate corners. The
alabaster tomb of Santa Eulàlia is set into the wall at the back and
dates from the 14th century. Eulàlia was martyred at 13 under

RATINGS	
Good for kids	● ● ●
Historic interest	● ● ● ●
Value for money	● ● ● ●
Photo stops	● ● ● ●

TIP

● Even though the interior is
closed, a view of the cathedral
at night is breathtaking—subtly
lit up, with seagulls circling
its majestic spires. Take a few
minutes to sit on one of the
benches outside in the empty
square for some nocturnal
contemplation.

BASICS

✚ 55 G11 • Plaça de la Seu 3, 08002
☎ 93 315 15 54
🕐 Daily 9–1.30, 4–7
💶 Free; elevator €2; choir €1
Ⓜ Liceu
🚌 16, 17, 19, 45
🎧 Daily 1.30–4 for €4; advanced
booking required
🎧 Various available at €2 and €9
🏪 Two shops on site selling guide-
books, postcards, key rings and other
souvenirs
🅿 Underground car park in square in
front of cathedral
🚻 Public toilet in the cloister, but not
very comfortable

www.catedralbcn.org
Not a very useful site and the design
leaves a lot to be desired.

gruesome circumstances by the Romans. It is thought her remains were brought here in 1339 from Santa Maria del Mar in La Ribera (see page 27). The front face of the sarcophagus represents the solemn act of transferring her relics to their present resting place. The crypt often has a handful of people kneeling in devotion in front of it.

THE CHOIR

The central choir has beautifully carved 14th-century stalls. The coats of arms represent members of the chapter of the Order of the Golden Fleece, a meeting of which was organized by the Holy Roman Emperor Charles V in 1519 and attended by a host of European monarchs. Peek under the *misericordias* (stone seats) to see the sculptures of hunting scenes and games.

THE CLOISTER

A few minutes spent among the cloister's orange and medlar trees and shady palms, coupled with the tranquil pond, is an effective battery charger. This cool oasis has close ties to the area's medieval working life as key members of the various guilds (see page 64) are buried underneath its stone slabs. Its mossy, central fountain once provided fresh water for the clergy. During Corpus Christi in early June, an empty eggshell is placed on top of the fountain's jet and left to bob away for an entire week. Known as the *L'ou com balla* (how the egg dances), the tradition is not found elsewhere in Spain and its origins have been lost in time. The surrounding pond is home to a gaggle of white geese who are said to represent the purity of Santa Eulàlia, Barcelona's patron saint. The Chapel of Santa Llúcia leads off the cloister and it provides a quiet place for worship.

THE VIEW

The elevator on the opposite side to the cloister takes you to the roof from where magnificent panoramic views of the city and the cathedral's spires can be enjoyed from a platform placed over the central nave. The statue you see perched on top of the highest, central spire is of St. Helen and the two bell towers are also named after saints: Eulàlia and Honorata. There is a riot of sculptural detail on both, depicting saints, crucifixes and animal life.

The main façade kept to 14th-century plans, but was built in the late 19th century, with hundreds of intricate carvings (opposite)

BACKGROUND

This site has always been important to the city because of its prime position on a hill. A Roman temple and a Moorish mosque were both here, as was an earlier cathedral from the 6th century. The plans for the interior of the current cathedral were laid down in 1298. The bishops ordered a single nave, 28 side chapels and an apse with an ambulatory behind a high altar. For the next 150 years four different architects worked on the edifice and produced beautiful Catalan Gothic cloisters and chapels.

The cathedral is illuminated at night

Angels serenade you as you step inside

Candles burn in the cloister as an act of worship

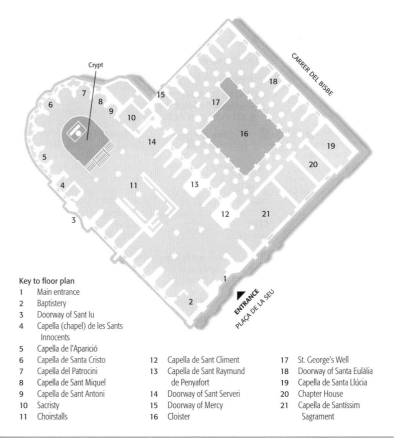

Key to floor plan
1   Main entrance
2   Baptistery
3   Doorway of Sant Iu
4   Capella (chapel) de les Sants Innocents
5   Capella de l'Aparició
6   Capella de Santa Cristo
7   Capella del Patrocini
8   Capella de Sant Miquel
9   Capella de Sant Antoni
10 Sacristy
11 Choirstalls
12 Capella de Sant Climent
13 Capella de Sant Raymund de Penyafort
14 Doorway of Sant Serveri
15 Doorway of Mercy
16 Cloister
17 St. George's Well
18 Doorway of Santa Eulàlia
19 Capella de Santa Llúcia
20 Chapter House
21 Capella de Santíssim Sagrament

Moorish influences displayed on the tiles on Casa Vicens

The mural on the exterior of Col.legi d'Arquitectes uses simple lines to allow the power of the subject, the Nativity, to come through

CASA-MUSEU VERDAGUER

✚ off 281 D1 • Vil.la Joana, Carretera de Vallvidrera, 08017 ☎ 93 204 78 05; 93 319 02 22 for weekday appointments ⏰ Tue–Fri by appointment only; Sat–Sun and public holidays 10–2, no appointment needed 🚻 Free 🚉 Baixador de Vallvidrera 🎫 Adult €3, child (under 7) free ♿
www.museuhistoria.bcn.es

This 18th-century house, in the middle of the Sierra de Collserola, was where Jacint Verdaguer (1845–1902) spent his last days. He was Catalonia's most famous poet and a key figure of the renaissance of Catalan culture known as the Renaixença. His last 24 days were spent here before his death on 10 June. Already a literary hero, Verdaguer's passing deeply moved the emerging Catalan nation and thousands attended his funeral. The exhibition shows the personal objects and some original writings of this man of letters, and the rooms have been preserved as they were before his death. Many of the explanations are only available in Catalan, so you would be wise to read up on the poet's life and heritage before you go, or take one of the special tours that explain the contents of the house and surrounding countryside in relation to the writer's work.

CASA VICENS

✚ 57 G6 • Carrer de les Carolines 18–24, 08006 🚇 Fontana 🚌 22, 24, 25, 27, 28, 31, 32 and all routes to Plaza Lesseps
www.rutamodernisme.com

This bright and eccentric house was the first work of Modernisme to be built in the city. It was conceived as a holiday home for the tile manufacturer Manuel Vicens i Montaner and his descendants still live here. It was one of Gaudí's first architectural projects and the year he signed the contract (1883) coincided with the beginning of La Sagrada Família (see pages 124–129).

Nearly all of the enigmatic façade is covered in tiles and the form of the building was inspired by the East. The result is an exotic impression of a series of desert pavilions complete with minaret-style turrets. This influence extended to the interior, particularly in the eccentric smoking room with a giant lamp decorated with characters from the Koran and an ornate, sculptured ceiling. The Casa Vicens is not open to the public, but photographs of the interior regularly appear in books about Gaudí.

CATEDRAL DE LA SEU

See pages 70–73.

CENTRE DE CULTURA CONTEMPORÀNIA DE BARCELONA (CCCB)

✚ 54 F10 • Carrer de Montalegre 5, 08001 ☎ 93 306 41 00 ⏰ Tue–Sat 11–8, Sun and holidays 11–3, Jun–early Sep; Tue, Thu–Fri 11–2, 4–8, Wed 11–8, Sat 11–8, Sun and holidays 11–7, rest of year 🚻 Adult €4, student/senior €3, child (under 16) free 🚇 Catalunya 🚌 120 or change at Plaça de Catalunya ♿ 🚻
www.cccb.org

Stunning modern architecture is one of the highlights of a visit to the CCCB. It is behind the MACBA (see pages 90–91), and was transformed from the 19th-century workhouse, the Casa de la Caritat. The entrance is through an elegant courtyard and its key feature is the mural on the wall in front of you, which has a floral and harp motif that has survived from the original building. On the left the restructuring work of the CCCB takes shape in an impressive steel and glass structure topped by an exterior mirror that lets you see the cityscape behind. There is no permanent collection on display, as the CCCB is a bustling arts centre for all sorts of cutting-edge shows and events. The annual independent short film festival is held here, and the CCCB is taken over every June by thousands of fans of modern music for the international techno and multimedia festival Sonar (see page 180). During the summer months there is a DJ and bar in the courtyard, making it a pleasant spot to enjoy an evening drink.

COL.LEGI D'ARQUITECTES

✚ 54 G10 • Plaça Nova 5, 08002 ☎ 93 301 50 00 ⏰ Mon–Fri 10–9, Sat 10–2; closed Aug 🚻 Free 🚇 Liceu 🚌 16, 17, 19, 45
www.coac.net

This is the hub of Barcelona's architectural world, with regular debates and workshops as well as exhibitions about architecture and urban planning. A modern structure in the old part of town, its most outstanding feature is its exterior mural, a simple line drawing of a nativity scene. It was designed by Picasso in the 1950s but carried out by Carl Nesjar, at a time when Picasso was in self-exile from Spain for his political beliefs. There is a bookshop in the basement and an extensive library about national and international architecture in the building opposite. The Col.legi d'Arquitectes also organizes half-day and full-day tours of different aspects of the city's architecture, from Modernisme to contemporary buildings to town planning. They are directed at professionals in the field, but interested parties are welcome. Information can be obtained from the Col.legi during the mornings.

CONJUNT MONUMENTAL DE LA PLAÇA DEL REI

Essential to understanding Barcelona's Roman history.

The relics of two millennia of Barcelona's history are on vibrant display at this museum, previously known as Museu d'Història de la Ciutat. The entrance is through the 15th-century Casa Pedellas, which was moved here stone by stone in the 1930s. It was during this move that the Roman remains were found. The visit consists of two parts. Firstly you descend underneath its foundations to visit the Roman city, which at 4,000sq m (43,000sq ft), is the most extensive found underground in Europe. Once you have explored this Roman world, you are brought back upstairs to Gothic Barcelona and the palace-complex of the Plaça del Rei (see page 115).

ROMAN BARCELONA

After seeing a small collection of Iberian and Roman objects found at Montjuïc, such as sandstone columns and busts, you are ushered to a elevator, which pronounces that you are about to be whisked back 2,000 years. The beautifully preserved streets and alleys contain houses, wineries, shops, dye works, laundries, fish-preserving factories, a chapel and pretty much everything else you would expect to find in a functioning town of the era. Cleverly lit, it is viewed from an intricate series of walkways perched above the remains, and explanatory leaflets take you through the workings of a Roman home. There are a couple of stunning mosaics that were once the floors of the *triclinium* (dining room) of a wealthy Roman home.

GOTHIC BARCELONA

The museum continues above ground with a visit to the Mirador del Rei, or watchtower of King Martin, who was the last of the direct line of Barcelona's count-kings. The Saló del Tinell (banqueting chamber) is a key architectural work of the era. Its six semicircular arches are the largest stone arches ever to be erected in Europe. It was used for parliament meetings in the late 14th century and in 1493 Ferdinand and Isabella are said to have received Christopher Columbus here after his return from the New World. This grand hall is often used for classical music recitals.

Don't miss The *garum* (fish sauce) and fish-preserving tanks, one of the most well-preserved sections of Roman Barcelona; the series of *bodegas* (wineries) towards the end of the visit.

RATINGS	
Historic interest	◕◕◕◕
Specialist shopping	◕◕◕◕
Value for money	◕◕◕◕

BASICS

55 G11 • Plaça del Rei s/n, 08002

93 315 11 11

Tue–Sat 10–8, Sun 10–3, Jun–end Sep; Tue–Sat 10–2, 4–8, Sun 10–2, rest of year

Adult €4, child €2; first Sat of every month free after 4pm; admission allows free entry to the Museu-Casa Verdaguer and Monestir de Pedralbes

Jaume I

16, 17, 19, 40, 45

In Catalan or Spanish Wed 6pm Jul–Aug; Sun 11.30 rest of year; adult €5, child (under 7) free; tours in English by appointment

Large format, beautifully produced guidebook available in Spanish, Catalan and English for €24 at the ticket office and gift shop

Very good gift shop on the corner of Carrer Llibreteria sells books and objects related to Roman and Gothic Barcelona, including some wonderful reproductions of tiles and figurines

At the main entrance

www.museuhistoria.bcn.es

Entrance to the museum is through the Casa Pedellas (top); the Mirador del Rei has views over the city (above)

Much of the Església de Betlem is from 1671, restored after a fire

L'EIXAMPLE

A district containing the highest concentration of Modernista architecture in the world.

⊕ 57 F8 ℹ Centre del Modernisme, Passeig de Gràcia 41, tel 93 488 01 39; Mon–Sat 10–7, Sun 10–2 Ⓜ Passeig de Gràcia 🚌 17, 20, 22, 24, 28, 39, 44, 45 (to the Quadrat d'Or) www.rutamodernisme.com

RATINGS	
Photo stops	●●●●
Cultural interest	●●●●
Walkability	●●●

The socialist engineer Ildefons Cerdà (1815–76) designed L'Eixample (extension) in 1859 to have perfectly symmetrical blocks. Divided into the left (esquerra) and right (dreta), L'Eixample fans out on either side of the main boulevard, the elegant Passeig de Gràcia. This is the home of the Manzana de la Discordia (Block of Discord, see pages 82–83), with its trio of buildings from three of Modernisme's key figures: Lluís Domènech i Montaner (1850–1923), Josep Puig i Cadafalch (1867–1957) and Gaudí.

The famed Quadrat d'Or (Golden Square, the hundred or so blocks edged by Carrers del Bruc and Aragó, the Passeig de Gràcia and the Diagonal) has been named the world's greatest living museum of late 19th-century architecture. The Quadrat has dozens of Modernista works, ranging from public buildings to private homes, such as Gaudí's Casa Milà (see pages 66–69), Casa Tomas at Carrer de Mallorca 293 by Domènech i Montaner and the Casa Terrades by Puig i Cadafalch. This casa is popularly known as the Casa de les Punxes (the House of Spikes) for its spires and weathervanes.

There are so many smaller charms in L'Eixample—a wrought-iron pharmacy sign, an ornate elevator in the entrance of an apartment block or a ceramic plaque bearing a street number—that they are best discovered by chance as you stroll around. Before you set off, visit the Centre del Modernisme at the Casa Amatller in the Manzana de la Discordia. The centre has comprehensive maps and informative packs about the great architects as well as information about tours of the area (see page 265).

ESGLÉSIA DE BETLEM

⊕ 54 F10 • Carrer d'en Xuclà 2, 08027 ☎ 93 318 38 23 🕐 Daily 7.30–2, 5.30–9.30, mid-Jun–mid-Sep; 7.30–2, 4.30–8, rest of year 🎟 Free Ⓜ Liceu 🚌 14, 38, 59

This vast, imposing church looms up over Las Ramblas like a behemoth. The church dates from the late 17th century and was an addition to a Jesuit compound that was built in 1553. A rose window tops its lofty entrance but this, as with many of its features, was added after the interior of the church was destroyed during the Spanish Civil War in 1936. The interior never regained its richness, but is still an excellent example of baroque architecture. Every December, in the basement of the church, there is an exhibition of pessebres—Christmas nativity dioramas. It's also home to the caganer (see page 19).

ESGLÉSIA DE LA MERCÈ

⊕ 54 G11 • Plaça de la Mercè 1, 08002 ☎ 93 315 27 56 🕐 Daily 10–1, 6–8 🎟 Free Ⓜ Drassanes 🚌 14, 20, 36, 38, 57, 59, 64

A visit to this church is important for what it represents. According to legend, La Mercè, Our Lady of Mercy, appeared in the dreams of Jaume I (1208–1276), instructing him to start a monastic order that would protect Barcelona from North African pirates. The first church of the Order of Mercy was built here in 1267. The saint is said to have freed the city from a plague of locusts in 1637 and was subsequently named the patron of Barcelona by a grateful city council. The church is topped by an elegant sculpture of the saint herself, which has become a feature of the skyline. Barcelona's main fiesta is also dedicated to La Mercè.

L'Eixample is full of Modernista architecture, such as at Casa Tomas, which is now BD, one of the city's top stores (right)

A wrought-iron work of art, in the form of a dragon, protects Finca Güell

Cloud and Chair *sculpture on the roof of the Fundació Antoni Tàpies*

THE SIGHTS

FINCA GÜELL

⊞ 280 B5 • Avinguda de Pedralbes 7, 08034 ☎ 93 204 52 50 ⊙ Not open to the public, enquire for private visits; library: Mon–Fri 9–2 🚇 Palau Reial 🚌 7, 63, 67, 68, 74, 75 www.rutamodernisme.com

The Finca Güell was the first of many commissions Gaudí received from Eusebi Güell. Started in 1884, Gaudí was put in charge of the gatekeeper's building, the coach house, a fountain and the main gate, the latter being the most dramatic element of the project. The hissing dragon jumps out at you from this spectacular example of wrought-iron design. The work was carried out by a local smith but the image is purely Gaudían, and dragons and lizards were to make regular appearances in his later work. This beast comes from the epic Catalan poem *L'Atlàntida* by Verdaguer (see page 74) and is a reference to the voyage of Hercules and his battle with the dragon to enter the garden of Hespérides, a metaphor for the citrus gardens of the *finca* (estate) itself.

The mosaic-covered pavilions with their exotic turrets held the gatekeeper's lodge and the coach house. The latter is now the Reial Càtedra Gaudí, a place for study and research about the man and his work. Only the library is open to the public, but you get a good view of all the buildings from the gate, which is the highlight of the *finca*.

Iron citrus trees at Finca Güell refer to L'Atlàntida

FORMENT DE LES ARTS DECORATIVES

⊞ 54 F10 • Plaça dels Àngels 5–6, 08001 ☎ 93 443 75 20 ⊙ Mon–Fri 11–8, Sat 11–8, Jul–end Aug; Mon–Fri 11–8, Sat–Sun 11–3, rest of year 🚇 Free 🚇 Catalunya or Liceu 🚌 14, 18, 38, 59 and all routes to Plaça de Catalunya 🍴 🏛 www.fadweb.com

Barcelona is a reference point for professionals working in all fields of design. From a park bench to a paint can, many of the city's home-grown objects and products have received the *disseny* (design) touch. Forment de les Arts Decoratives (FAD) is the body much credited with consolidating this tradition. Founded more than a hundred years ago, the headquarters is now in a renovated Gothic convent. The organization's principal aim is to bring the general public and design worlds closer together through a full calendar of exhibitions and events. These include MerkaFad, where young fashion designers are given space within the FAD to market their wares, and the enormously popular *Tallers Oberts* (Open Workshops), an annual week-long event where artists give free lessons in their crafts all over El Raval. Exhibitions act as a showcase for both national and international designers in all fields, whether it be jewellery textiles or graphic design, and change on a regular basis.

FUNDACIÓ ANTONI TÀPIES

⊞ 57 G9 • Carrer d'Aragó 255, 08007 ☎ 93 487 03 15 ⊙ Tue–Sun 10–8 💷 Adult €4.20, child (under 16) free 🚇 Passeig de Gràcia 🚌 7, 16, 17, 20, 22, 24, 28, 43 🚻 🏛 www.fundaciotapies.org

Antoni Tàpies is Catalonia's most prolific living artist. Born in 1923, he first trained as a lawyer but this direction soon changed and his work as a painter, draughtsman, printmaker and sculptor often defies definition. He is known for mixing two or more mediums and for challenging works that nearly always include the letter T. This recurring motif has been interpreted as having religious or sexual references, or perhaps it was used because it's the artist's initial. The Tàpies Foundation is in a former Modernista publishing house built by Lluís Domènech i Montaner (1850–1923) and was started in 1984 by the artist himself.

The foundation has always helped to promote art, and as well as housing the most extensive collection of Tàpies' enormous output, it also puts on regular shows from known and not-so-known contemporary artists. The library, which is open to the general public, is probably one of the best of its type in the country, with an impressive collection of 20th-century art documents and a large section on Asian art. Be warned though, with its extreme designs, this foundation is for die-hard contemporary art fans only.

Cloud and Chair, the bizarre sculpture that sits on the roof, is what the foundation is most known for, and is also by Tàpies. It was a symbolic gift to the city of Barcelona, executed in 1990, and has become an integral part of L'Eixample landscape.

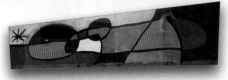

Fundació Joan Miró

**A collection of more than 11,000 pieces, with more than 200 paintings,
by this most prolific and iconic of Catalan artists.
One of the best gallery spaces of the world.
Miró's work is a great introduction to modern art,**

GALLERY GUIDE

BASEMENT
Room 13: Espai 13, dedicated to young artists
Rooms 14–15: Homage a Miró, works donated by other artists
GROUND FLOOR
Rooms 1–10: temporary exhibitions
Rooms 11–12: works to mid-1930s
Room 16: Sala Joan Prats
FIRST FLOOR
Room 17: Sala Pilar Juncosa
Rooms 18–21: mid-life development, 1960–1970s.
Rooms 22–23: Sala K, works on long-term loan

Visitors relax outside the Fundació (above left); temporary exhibitions by international and national contemporary artists are held at the foundation (above right)

SEEING THE FUNDACIÓ JOAN MIRÓ

The Fundació Joan Miró, housed in a gleaming white building on the hilltop of Montjuïc with panoramic views across the city, is the perfect setting in which to appreciate the work of this extraordinary Catalan artist. The simple white walls, terracotta flagstones and arched roofs neatly complement the vibrancy of Miró's work, symbolized by its childlike shapes and bold use of primary tones. Much of the collection is displayed in 10 purpose-built galleries and bathed in natural light. You can wander around at will, but for a greater understanding of Miró's work you should take the audiotour which helps to explain the motivation and political statements behind some of the paintings and sculptures.

HIGHLIGHTS

FOUNDATION TAPESTRY
This monumental tapestry was designed especially for the Fundació Joan Miró in 1979. It was produced in collaboration with Josep Royo, who had worked with Miró on a series of textiles which also incorporated aspects of painting and collage. The tapestry is all reds, greens, blues and yellows, with a star and crescent moon in the background. For the best views, you need to look at it from the upstairs gallery.

PORTRAIT OF A YOUNG GIRL
This charming portrait, dating from 1919, is full of lyrical expression and clearly shows the influence of Van Gogh as well as the medieval masters. It is in the Sala Joan Prats, named after Miró's friend, patron and art dealer who donated many of these works. The room has several examples of Miró's early style.

MAN AND WOMAN IN FRONT OF A PILE OF EXCREMENT
Despite the playful nature of much of his work, Miró was deeply political and this work from 1935 is an expression both of his Catalan identity and his anguish and foreboding at the approaching Spanish Civil War (1936–39). The bright tones of this painting are set off by powerful imagery, with apocalyptic scenes of darkness and broken limbs. It is displayed in the Sala Pilar Juncosa, named after Miró's wife, which contains items donated by her.

MORNING STAR

Several paintings in the Sala Pilar Juncosa reveal the familiar themes which were starting to characterize Miró's style by the 1940s, with repeated images of women, stars, moon and birds. His fascination with the night sky is particularly evident in this painting from 1940, which forms one of a series known as *Constellations*.

THE ROOF-TERRACE

The rooftop terrace makes a good place to unwind, with quirky sculptures and dreamy views over the city. Among the items on display is *Caress of a Bird* (1967), a bronze sculpture covered in red, blue, green and yellow.

BACKGROUND

Joan Miró (1893–1983) was born into a family of artisans. He moved to the town of Mong-roig in his early twenties, where he decided to take up painting. Miró was sometimes described as a visual poet, whose work could be enjoyed simply for its vivid tones and animated forms. Instantly recognizable and symbols of the city itself, Miró's trademark figures include birds, women, Catalan peasants (a metaphor for his deep-rooted sense of Catalan identity) and above all heavenly stars, all portrayed with sweeping brushstrokes in his famed palette of red, yellow, blue and green. The Fundació Joan Miró was established by Miró himself not just as a permanent setting for his works but also as a focus for modern art in Barcelona, with a library, bookshop and auditorium as well as gallery spaces. The building was designed for Miró in 1972 by his friend Josep Lluís Sert, a Catalan architect who had also designed Miró's studio on Mallorca. The extensive collection, much of it donated by Miró, covers a wide range of styles, allowing you to trace his development from youthful realism to later experiments with surrealism and abstract art, all in his own uniquely Miróesque style.

BASICS

⊞ 56 D11 • Parc de Montjuïc, 08038

☎ 93 443 94 70

⏱ Tue–Sun 10–8 (also Thu 10–9.30pm), Jul–end Sep; 10–7 (also Thu 10–9.30pm), rest of year

💶 Adult €7.20, child (under 14) free. Temporary exhibitions only: adult €3.60, child (under 14) free

🚇 Paral.lel then Funicular de Montjuïc

🚌 50, 55

🎧 Audiotour included in admission price, in English, French, Catalan, Spanish, German, Japanese and Italian. Guided tours in Catalan and Spanish only, Sat and Sun at 12.30pm, free

📖 Very good, pocket-size guide book available in Spanish, Catalan, English, French and Japanese for €10

🍴 Smart café-restaurant with summer terrace

🛒 Two shops, one with an excellent selection of books about Miró and his contemporaries and the other selling gifts and gadgets

🚻 On the ground floor in the reception area

www.bcn.fjmiro.es
An excellent site, easy to navigate, with detailed information about specific works and on-line shopping.

The Foundation Tapestry *is the first major work that you see in the collection (above); the roof terrace has a number of bright and unusual pieces (left)*

GRÀCIA

One of the city's most picturesque suburbs.

Gràcia, once an outlying village, was annexed to the main city by the elegant Passeig de Gràcia. Yet this suburb still retains a strong sense of independence and many of the city's underground and alternative movements have their roots here. During the day, Gràcia's charm lies in strolling around its series of squares, including the Plaça del Sol, which is a relaxed place to have coffee. The majestic Plaça de la Virreina and the Plaça de Rius i Taulet with its stately watchtower are some of the oldest squares, but Gràcia also has new hard squares, made mostly from concrete, such as the Plaça John Lennon.

Gràcia is not without a few Modernista buildings. The neo-Moorish Casa Vicens (see page 74), still a private home, is an early work of Gaudí's and the beautiful Casa Fuster by Domènech i Montaner, at the beginning of Gran de Gràcia, is being converted into a five-star hotel. The cultural life of the area is very strong and includes the Verdi Cinema Complex that shows original language films, and dozens of galleries, shops, bars and restaurants. The Carrer Verdi is a great place to shop for funky clothing.

A visit to the annual Fiestas de Gràcia will give you a sense of the pride the locals have for their beloved *barri*. All year long, neighbourhood associations work on the elaborate decorations that are hung in the streets in mid-August. Each street chooses a different theme, from marine life to moonscapes, and competes for the prize of best-dressed street. The *barri* (district) then becomes a giant stage for ten days of no-holding-back frolicking and fun.

THE SIGHTS

RATINGS	
Good for kids	● ● ●
Shopping	● ● ● ●
Walkability	● ● ●

🔢 57 G7 ℹ️ Plaça de Catalunya 17, 08002, tel 90 630 12 82; daily 9–9 Ⓜ️ Diagonal or Fontana 🚌 16, 17, 22, 24, 25, 27, 28
www.barcelonaturisme.com

Ornate balconies decorate the buildings around the Plaça del Sol (left); the square is a good place to take a break and a popular spot by night (below)

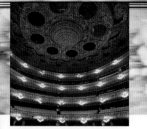

The dramatic interior of the Liceu was rebuilt after a fire

GRAN TEATRE DEL LICEU

🔢 54 F11 • La Rambla 51–59, 08001 ☎️ 93 485 99 00 🕐 Daily 10–1, Sep–end Jul 💷 Adult €5, child (under 10) free 🎫 Compulsory 1-hour guided tour in Spanish and English, other languages by arrangement, for the admission fee Ⓜ️ Liceu 🚌 14, 18, 38, 59 💻 🏛️
www.liceubarcelona.com

The residents of Barcelona mourned when a fire swept through their beloved opera house in 1994, but after six years of careful renovation it was returned to its former glory. Now its lush interior and superb acoustics make it one of the best in Europe.

A trip to the Liceu represented social prestige for the city's bourgeoisie during the mid-1800s. From its inauguration in 1847, the institution became a metaphor for good taste and social display. But then El Liceu was never intended to be a people's theatre. The original funding for the project did not come from the government of the time but from donations from the mercantile classes. At the time the Liceu was being built, a craze for the German composer Robert Wagner (1813–83) was sweeping across Europe. This heavily influenced the architectural style, which was bold and grandiose.

After the fire little of the original structure remained and a complete change of direction was needed to attract the funds to resurrect the building. After private and corporate donors were found, a new wing was built to house rehearsal and administration rooms and the interior was meticulously restored. The new building also ushered in a new musical direction with the staging of works by more avant-garde and lesser-known composers.

Strelitzia, or Bird of Paradise flower, is from South Africa

JARDÍ BOTÀNIC

🏛 56 C12 • Doctor Font i Quer s/n, Parque de Montjuïc, 08038 ☎ 93 426 49 35 🕐 Mon–Sat 10–5, Sun 10–3, Oct–end Jun; Mon–Sat 10–8, Sun 10–3, rest of year 💶 Adult €3, child (under 16) free, last Sat of every month free 🚇 Espanya 🚌 50 🍴
www.jardibotanic.bcn.es

Opened in 1999, the Jardí Botànic is a superb example of contemporary landscape gardening. Geometric paths and staircases run throughout the inclined terrain, creating a modern topography. The garden focuses on Mediterranean vegetation and there are various sections devoted to countries with a Mediterranean climate. In the Australian section, for example, you can see indigenous species such as eucalyptus, while the California section is replete with various strains of cacti.

The garden supplies you with an imaginatively designed map that colour-codes the different countries. Each colour takes you on a walk through that country. The Iberian species occupy the large perimeter of the garden and the other countries' fauna are laid out within this. Although the site will take a few more years to develop fully, try to visit in spring when the native flowers are in bloom. The garden itself is already being praised by park and garden experts all over the world and sets the standard for future projects of this type.

Cacti from Tenerife, just one of the many species on display

HOSPITAL DE LA SANTA CREU I SANT PAU

A UNESCO World Heritage Site, this building challenges your notions of hospital design.

The hospital is the largest work by Modernista Lluís Domènech i Montaner, who produced a beautiful, detail-rich building that is still a working hospital. The complex is 13.5ha (33 acres) and was conceived as a garden infirmary according to the wishes of its patron, the Paris-based banker Pau Gil i Serra. He had been impressed by the French trend of hospital villages. The complex consists of 48 mosaic-covered pavilions, serving the same purpose as wards in modern hospitals. All are distinctive and highly ornate and are spread over various streets and leafy avenues. Heavy with symbolism, the hospital is almost a metaphor for the Modernista creed itself: Catalan nationalism, exuberant use of colour and an abundance of references to mother nature. There are many details, but watch out for the dainty, sculptured heads on the wooden doors of the individual pavilions and the elegant figures of Faith, Hope and Charity that flank the windows of the main building.

Domènech i Montaner was also a practical man: He built an enlightened series of underground walkways so that patients and staff were protected from bad weather when commuting from one pavilion to another. If you are not taking the guided tour, the hospital is not strictly open to the general public. However, nobody seems to mind if you take a discreet walk around the gardens and view the pavilions from the outside.

The hospital is at the opposite end of the same road as La Sagrada Família

RATINGS			
Good for kids	●	●	●
Cultural interest	●	●	●
Walkability	●	●	●

🏛 287 K7 • Carrer de Sant Antoni Maria Claret 167–171, 08025 ☎ 93 488 20 78 🕐 By guided tour, in Catalan, Spanish, French and English, starting every half-hour, Sat–Sun 10–2; by appointment only, Thu 10–2 💶 Adult €4.60, child (under 15) free; grounds free 🚇 Hospital Sant Pau 🚌 15, 19, 20, 25, 35, 45, 47, 50, 51
www.hspau.com

Manzana de la Discordia

**Three emblematic buildings standing side by side
on the elegant Passeig de Gràcia.
They provide an outstanding insight into the
Modernisme movement in the city.**

*Rich stained-glass windows at
the Casa Batlló*

*Start your tour of Casa Batlló at
the sinuous stairway*

*The wedding cake on top of
Casa Lleó Morera*

RATINGS	
Good for kids	● ● ●
Historic interest	● ● ● ●
Photo stops	● ● ●
Value for money	● ● ● ●

TIPS

● The Casa Batlló is beautifully lit at night and its façade glistens magically under the artificial light. Don't try to view the building at noon when it is very sunny as the reflected sunlight can be dazzling.

● Look for the Modernista maidens holding a camera and a lightbulb by sculptor Eusebi Arnau. They are among the few remaining features of the original Casa Lleó Morera.

● The sculpture of St. George and the Dragon by the entrance of the Casa Amatller serves as a neat contrast between the styles of Gaudí and Arnau.

SEEING THE MANZANA DE LA DISCORDIA

These adjacent buildings, built when Modernisme was in full swing, are by the three undisputed masters of the movement. They are quite disparate in style and serve as an insight to the consistently differing approaches of the architects themselves. The interior of the Casa Batlló and the ground floor of the Casa Amatller, which holds the Centre del Modernisme, are open to the public, while the Casa Lleó Morera is not. But the exteriors alone are well worth the visit.

CASA BATLLÓ

Passeig de Gràcia 43, 08007 ☎ 93 216 03 06 🕐 Mon–Sun 9–8 🎫 Adult €10, child (under 6) free 🚇

This is the most famous of the trio, completed in 1906 for a local textile baron, Josep Batlló i Casanovas, and designed by Gaudí. The rippling effect of the façade is achieved through *trencadís*, covering surfaces with pieces of broken ceramic. Its depth of tone and movement are equal to that of an Impressionist painting and it glitters like a giant jewel. Casa Batlló is said to represent the legend of St. George, Catalonia's patron saint, and the dragon. The spectacular fairy-tale outline of the upper façade is the humped back of the dragon and the tiles are its scales. The sinuous bones and tendons of the victims are seen in the framing of the windows, while the wrought-iron balconies are their skulls. A tour of the interior gives you an insight into Gaudí's amazing design. Its richness is further revealed and the close-up view of the stained-glass windows in the living room is stunning, as is the terrace. Try to go on a sunny day when the whole place will glow with natural light.

CASA AMATLLER

Passeig de Gràcia 41, 08007 ℹ️ Centre del Modernisme, tel 93 488 01 39; Mon–Sat 10–7, Sun 10–2 🎫 Free

In contrast to Gaudí's nationalist overtones, the architect Josep Puig i Cadafalch (1876-1956) didn't shy away from northern European influences. This is very much in evidence at his Casa Amatller, the first building on the block. It was built in 1900, and Dutch and Flemish architectural influences can be seen, as well as a number of Gothic details. The façade is dotted with eccentric stone carvings of animals blowing glass and taking photographs, two of the architect's hobbies. These were executed by Eusebi Arnau, a decorative sculptor much in vogue at the time who also used his talent on the Casa Lleó Morera next door. To discover the rest of the works of Puig i Cadafalch and other Modernistas, visit the Centre del Modernisme on the ground floor of the Casa Amatller. It provides visitors with information and a walking map showing the city's Modernista masterpieces.

CASA LLEÓ MORERA
Passeig de Gràcia 35, 08007
The third of the Manzana's structures was adapted in 1905 from an existing building. Its style is what most people will relate to as the more typical international form of art nouveau, and not the Catalan

The uniform lines of the roof on Casa Amatller, on the right are in sharp contrast to the curves of Casa Batlló in the middle

version. Lluís Domènech i Montaner (1850–1923) was a politician and craftsman who lent a hand to every facet of his projects. He fully embraced the new materials of his field, which he then applied to building design, including this one. Although greatly modernized in 1943, the building still has a riot of detail: rounded corner balconies, female figures holding up innovations of the period, such as the light-bulb and telephone, and a wedding cake dome crowning the roof. To please the commissioner of the building, the local tycoon Albert Lleó i Morera, Domènech i Montaner included within the symbolism the recurring themes of the lion (*lleó*) and mulberry bush (*morera*). The upper floors of the building are now private offices and the ground floor houses a top leatherwear shop, which does not have much in the way of period detail. But some of the original furniture and objects especially designed for the home can be seen at the Museu d'Art Modern at Parc de la Ciutadella (see page 88).

WHAT'S IN A NAME?
A play on words, as well as mythology, gives the Manzana de la Discordia its name. The title translates as both the block of discord and the apple of discord in Castilian. The latter term relates to the Greek goddess Eris who was known as Discordia to the Romans. She threw an apple onto Mount Olympus and declared it should be given 'to the fairest'. The resulting mayhem led to the Judgement of Paris and the Trojan War. This word play doesn't translate into Catalan, so you are likely to see its other name of Illa de la Discòrdia, block of discord.

BASICS

➕ 57 G9 • Passeig de Gràcia 35, 41 and 43, 08007

Ⓜ Passeig de Gràcia

🚌 7, 16, 17, 22, 24, 28

🎫 Tours conducted by the Centre del Modernisme by arrangement of the exteriors of the Manzana in Catalan, Spanish and English: adult €3, child €2

📖 Small bookshop in the Centre del Modernisme has books about the Manzana de la Discòrdia and other Modernista buildings; well-stocked shop in Casa Batlló sells Gaudí and Barcelona-related books and souvenirs

www.rutamodernisme.com
A good introduction, with a bit of hunting, to the three key players and the buildings, but not much about the Manzana collectively.

The balconies of Casa Batlló form victims' skulls which continue the dragon theme of the building

Monestir de Pedralbes

This well-preserved 14th-century stone monastery is
a serene oasis in a busy city.
A chance to see Old Masters in an environment
dominated by modern art.

SEEING THE MONESTIR

Barcelona's oldest surviving monastery is hidden
away in the northern district of Pedralbes, a
wealthy suburb which still retains the feel of
a country town. It is one of the finest examples
of Catalan Gothic architecture, and since 1993
it has also housed the Thyssen-Bornemisza
collection of mostly religious art from the 14th
to 18th centuries. You can buy a ticket for just
the art collection which also allows you to see
the cloister. But having come all this way, it is
worth buying a combined ticket and exploring
the interior of the monastery.

HIGHLIGHTS

THE CLOISTER

The three-tiered Gothic cloister, with ornate well,
herb garden and cypress trees, exudes a sense of
calm, helped by the gentle trickle of the fountains. A
few quiet moments here will give you a taste of the
peaceful life of the nuns. For the best views, stroll
around the upper gallery, which meanders its way
around the building's exterior. Just off the cloisters
are little prayer cells, some of which contain original
objects. The Pietat chamber has a 16th-century
retable of the Virgin Mary as a child.

CAPELLA DE SANT MIQUEL

The artistic highlight of the monastery is this magnificent chapel,
which is found off the cloister. It is vividly decorated with paintings
by Ferrer Bassa, a student of the Florentine painter Giotto who is
credited with introducing the Italian-Gothic style to Catalonia. The
murals, depicting scenes of Christ's Passion on the upper level and
the life of the Virgin Mary on the lower level, were completed in
1346, two years before Bassa's death from the plague.

MONASTIC LIFE

A permanent exhibition depicts 14th-century monastic life through
the original infirmary, kitchen and refectory, where the Mother
Superior would break her vow of silence with Bible readings from the
pulpit while the nuns ate in silence around her. Descend into the
basement, where a cell has intricate dioramas of the life of Christ.

THE THYSSEN COLLECTION

The works are displayed on the restored, stucco-white walls of
the old dormitory. There are five sections: Medieval Art, the Early
German Renaissance, the Italian Renaissance, baroque and late
Venetian baroque, which are arranged in chronological order. Among
the Old Masters whose works are exhibited here are Rubens, Tiepolo,
Tintoretto, Titian and Zurbarán. The Spanish painter Diego Velázquez
(1599–1660) is represented with one of his many court paintings.

RATINGS	
Good for kids	● ● ●
Historic interest	● ● ● ●
Photo stops	● ● ●
Value for money	● ● ● ●

TIPS

● Look into the Gothic church
next door, used for prayer and
song by the nuns, before you
leave. It is beautiful, to be
particularly enjoyed if you
manage to find the place near
empty (closed 1pm–5pm).

● Large items, such as bags
and umbrellas, will need to
be left at reception to prevent
damage to the art works.

*Queen Elisenda, who founded
the monastery, is buried in an
alabaster tomb in the church
(above)*

The cloister is a peaceful retreat from the bustle of the modern city (above); the narrow, cobbled street, Baixada del Monestir leads to the complex (left)

A small room off the main dormitory contains works from the 17th century, including a splendid waterscape of Venice, *Il Bucintoro*, by Canaletto (1697–1768), depicting feast day celebrations on the Grand Canal.

Madonna of Humility

This beautiful painting by the Italian artist Fra Angelico, which dates from around 1435, marks a high point in Florentine art and it justifiably takes pride of place in the collection. The intimate portrait of the Virgin and the baby Jesus offering his mother a lily, the symbol of purity, in his left hand reveals a conscious attempt by the artist to lend religious art a more human touch.

BACKGROUND

The monastery was founded in 1326 by Elisenda de Montcada, wife of Jaume II of Aragón, for the nuns of the Order of St. Clare. Following the king's death, Queen Elisenda retired to the convent and lived here until she died. A small community of nuns still lives in the convent, but now in separate modern quarters. In 1993 the priceless art collection of Baron Hans-Heinrich von Thyssen-Bornemisza was given to the Spanish state. Most of it went to Madrid but a small selection of paintings was bequeathed to Barcelona and a dormitory at the monastery was converted to house it. This was an inspired choice, for these medieval religious art works are perfectly at home among the Gothic stone walls.

BASICS

✚ 281 C4 • Baixada del Monestir 9, 08034
☎ 93 280 14 34
🕐 Tue–Sun 10–2 for both the collection and the monastery
💶 The Thyssen Collection: adult €3.50, child (under 16) free. The monastery: adult €4, child (under 16) free. Combined ticket: adult €5.50, child (under 16) free; first Sun of every month free to all
🚌 22, 63, 64, 75, 114
🚇 FGC Reina Elisenda, then 10-minute walk
🎫 First Sun of the month, in Spanish and Catalan, €2; Catalan only rest of the time €5. No audiotours
📖 Illustrated pocket-size guidebook in Catalan, Spanish and English, €7.50
☕ Coffee, drink and snack machines only
🏬 Small shop sells postcards and books about both the Madrid and Barcelona collections
🛈 In reception area

www.museothyssen.org
Based solely around the Madrid collection.

Montjuïc

The greenery of this mountain acts as the city's lungs and is the largest recreational area in Barcelona. Spectacular views across the city. Home to the stadium of the 1992 Olympic Games.

SEEING MONTJUÏC

This mountain juts out into the Mediterranean and is the first thing you notice if arriving by sea or air. A series of avenues winds through its woodland, drawing hundreds of joggers, cyclists and day trippers on weekends. Some of the city's top museums are here, such as MNAC and Fundació Joan Miró, as well as the Olympic Ring. Much of this is concentrated on the lower slopes, while the previously neglected higher sections are undergoing renewal. You can access the bottom of Montjuïc via the Plaça d'Espanya and Avinguda de la Reina Maria Cristina. Take the funicular from Paral.lel station to the higher slopes. The only practical way to reach the Museu Miliar is by the *telefèric*, a cable car that you can pick up from the funicular. It makes a stop at the *mirador* (lookout point) and then carries on uphill.

HIGHLIGHTS

MUSEU MILITAR

✚ 56 D12 • Parc de Montjuïc, 08004 ☎ 93 329 86 13 ◷ Daily 9.30–7.30, Jul–end Sep; Tue–Sun 9.30–7.30, rest of year 💷 Adult €2.50, child (under 14) free

The huge castle perched on Montjuïc's highest point is an old 18th-century fortress, now the military museum. The views from the upper terrace seem endless, stretching from the sea to Tibidabo. This contrasts with the rather sinister fortress where Republicans were confined and tortured in its gloomy cells throughout the Civil War (1936–39). However the museum doesn't recognize these events. It

RATINGS	
Good for kids	●●●○
Historic interest	●●○○
Photo stops	●●●○
Walkability	●●●●

TIPS

● Some parts are still affected by petty crime, so keep your wits about you and make sure you are in more public areas by dark.

● The slopes of Montjuïc are quite steep, so catch either the No. 50 or 61 buses from the Plaça d'Espanya that visit the lower slopes. Or catch the Parc de Montjuïc (PM) bus that visits all the main sights, plus those on the upper slopes.

Montjuïc is full of landscaped gardens (top); the terraces of Jardins de Mossèn Costa i Llobera are a useful for making your way downhill (above)

holds an extensive collection of period arms and armoury, dating from 1900 to 1970 and displayed in the echoing chambers of the fortress' ground floor. The Marès collection of swords and suits of armour from Europe and Asia holds some incredibly intricate pieces.

THE HIGHER SLOPES

Much of the area surrounding the fortress is either being dug up for an overhaul or has been neglected. The site is home to a couple of sculptures, the *Sardana*—a ring of young women performing Catalonia's traditional dance—being the most famous. The Jardins de Mossèn Costa i Llobera (*daily 10–dusk*) is a little-visited cacti garden with species from Europe and Africa, and has views of the port at every turn. The Jardins can be reached via a cable car from Barceloneta to the nearby *mirador*.

THE LOWER SLOPES

This part of the mountain is much more accessible, reached via the ceremonial Avinguda de la Reina Maria Cristina that houses two huge trade-fair buildings on either side. At the end of the avenue, the MNAC (see pages 96–99), the Mies van der Rohe Pavilion (see page 114) and the CaixaForum (see page 65) are within easy reach, and the rest of the landscaped gardens and sights can be navigated via a series of escalators. The outdoor Teatre Grec, used during the festival of the same name only (see page 163), its picturesque gardens and La Font del Gat (the fountain of the cat) can be found slightly further up the mountain. The latter, between the Teatre Grec and the Fundació Joan Miró, is a curious work, replete with feline details— hence the name. It is attributed to Puig i Cadafalch and was once a fashionable outdoor restaurant. It is now an information office. Only the baroque façade and square remain but its charm is intact.

BACKGROUND

Although it was the first part of the city to be colonized by the Romans—a shrine to Jupiter was found on the site—Montjuïc's lack of any substantial water source meant that it was unsuitable for residential development. The site was ignored for a long period, but it did become the city's cemetery. In 1929 its lower slopes were chosen as the site of the Universal Fair. In 1992, the main events of the Olympic Games took place here and now the local government is to spruce up neglected pockets, turning Montjuïc into the city's own Central Park.

BASICS

✚ 56 C11

Tourist information office
Plaça de Catalunya 17, 08002
☎ 90 630 12 82 ⏰ Daily 9–9
www.barcelonaturisme.com

🚇 Espanya then No. 50 bus; Paral.lel then Funicular de Montjuïc; a cable car from Barceloneta

THE SIGHTS

The telefèric *cable car will carry you to the Museu Militar (top); the view from the Museu Militar stretches along the coast (left); the stunning shots of the city from the Olympic swimming pool helped bring Barcelona to the world's attention (above)*

Palm trees on Passeig de Colóm lead to the Monument a Colom

Finds from the Bronze Age and the Greco-Roman empire are displayed at the Museu d'Arqueologia de Catalunya

MONUMENT A COLOM

✚ 54 F12 • Plaça del Portal de la Pau s/n, 08001 ☎ 93 302 52 24 🕒 Daily 9–8.30, Jun–end Sep; Mon–Fri 10–1.30, 3.30–6.30, Sat–Sun 10–6.30, Oct–end Mar (to 7.30 Apr–end May) 🎫 *Mirador*: adult €1.80, child (4–12) €1.20, child (under 4) free 🚇 Drassanes 🚌 14, 36, 38, 57, 59, 64

A statue of Christopher Columbus (1451–1506) is at the port end of Las Ramblas, perched on top of a column more than 60m (197ft) high. He supposedly points at the Americas, but because of the uneven coastline of Barcelona, he has his eyes firmly fixed on North Africa. The four imposing lions on the elaborate base are a homage to Catalonia's role in the colonization of the Americas and its subsequent economic independence from the region of Castile. The monument contains a tiny elevator, from which visitors ascend to the *mirador*, a glass-enclosed lookout tower. The view is 360 degrees and gives new arrivals a quick orientation to the layout of the city. But be warned, the windows are relatively small and it is not for those who suffer from claustrophobia.

Its sheer size makes the Monument a Colom a good meeting point

EL MONUMENTAL

✚ 57 J9 • Gran Vía de les Corts Catalanes 749, 08013 ☎ 93 245 58 04 🕒 Museum: Mon–Sat 11–2, 4–8, Sun 11–1, Apr–end Sep 🎫 Museum: adult €4, child €3 🚇 Monumental 🚌 6, 75, 56, 62

This mock-Moorish bullring and museum is in L'Eixample, near to the Plaça de les Glories. It is one of two bullrings in Barcelona, the second being Las Arenas in the Plaça d'Espanya (see page 115). El Monumental was built in 1915 and is heady in Arabic influences, perhaps a homage to the spectacle itself, which has its roots in Andalucía. It also houses a small museum focusing on the art of bullfighting, *tauromaquia*, with photographs and memorabilia of the matadors who have entered the ring's doors over the decades. Entrance to the museum also allows you into the ring itself, providing there is no performance taking place. The perfect proportions of the space are breathtaking. For details on bulfights see page 172.

MUSEU D'ARQUEOLOGIA DE CATALUNYA

✚ 56 D11 • Passeig de Santa Madrona 39–41, Parc de Montjuïc, 08038 ☎ 93 424 65 77 🕒 Tue–Sat 9.30–7, Sun 10–2.30 🎫 Adult €2.40, child (under 16) free 🚇 Espanya 🚌 55 ♿ www.mac.es

The city's archaeological museum displays finds of predominantly Catalan origin and focuses on the Greco-Roman settlement of L'Empúries in the north of Spain. Objects date from as far back as 40,000BC, and there are exhibits from the Bronze Age, plus finds relating to the Greeks, Phoenicians and Estruscans. In particular, look out for the collection of Punic jewellery and terracotta goddesses found at a dig in Ibiza in room 8.

The Romans arrived in 218BC, using Empúries as an entry point. The collection of Roman glassware, kitchen utensils and other everyday items in the museum is outstanding, as are the extensive mosaics that have been laid in the floors of the last rooms. The curators believe that the pieces are better preserved if trodden upon. The serene and beautifully intact bronze head in room 6 should not be missed. The museum's Roman section makes it a cut above others in this genre, but the exhibits are let down by unsatisfactory explanations which are only in Catalan.

MUSEU D'ART MODERN

✚ 57 H11 • Plaça d'Armes s/n, Parc de la Ciutadella, 08003 ☎ 93 319 57 28 🕒 Tue–Sat 10–7, Sun 10–2.30 🎫 Adult €3, child (7–14) €2.10, child (under 7) free; first Thu of every month free 🚇 Arc de Triomf, Barceloneta 🚌 14, 36, 39, 40, 41, 42, 51 ♿ www.mnac.es

This modern art museum contains pieces from 1800 to the 1930s. The exhibits include examples from the Olot school, painters from the rural town of the same name who focused on landscapes and light. The collection's main jewel, though, is its Moderisme works. Ramon Casas (1866–1932) was often criticized for his monotone palette. But the beige-toned portrait of Casas himself and Pere Romeau on a tandem (1897) is considered a key work of the movement. Catalan art nouveau also excelled in the decorative arts and there are fabulous pieces of inlaid wood by the master carpenter Gaspar Homar, as well as furniture by Gaudí and Puig i Cadafalch that once graced the interiors of houses on the Manzana de la Discordia. The collection is due to move to the MNAC (see pages 96–99).

Join a host of famous faces for a drink at the Museu de Cera

The city's new Science Museum will be four times larger than the old one

MUSEU BARBIER-MUELLER D'ART PRECOLOMBI

⊞ 55 G11 • Carrer de Montcada 12–14, 08003 ☎ 93 310 45 16 ◉ Tue–Sat 10–6, Sun 10–3 ◍ Adult €3, child (under 16) free ◉ Jaume I ⊟ 14, 17, 19, 39, 40, 45, 51 www.bcn.es/icub

The magnificent medieval mansion of the Palau Nadal houses this outstanding collection of pieces from the indigenous cultures of Mexico, Central America, the Andes and the lower Amazon. It is a smaller version of the museum of the same name in Geneva, Switzerland, widely recognized to be one of the finest collections of anthropological art in the world. The collection in Barcelona starts with a room of gold adornments of the various deities of northern Peru from 1000BC. From there, three more rooms display Mayan pottery figures and Aztec sculptures, the focal point of which are some highly naïve but seductive statues of squat figures used in death rituals in pre-Christian Mexico. The darkened rooms add to the lost treasure feel of the museum, and—unusually for Barcelona—the exhibits are explained in French and English as well as Spanish.
Don't miss The two austere, 3000BC stone owls from Ecuador found at the far end of the exhibition.

MUSEU DEL CALÇAT

⊞ 54 G11 • Plaça de Sant Felip Neri 5, 08002 ☎ 93 301 45 33 ◉ Tue–Sun 11–2 ◍ Adult €2, child (under 12) free ◉ Jaume I ⊟ 14, 17, 19, 40, 45

The Museu del Calçat is a small shoe museum with a highly fascinating history. It is the fruit of the Catalan order of the Cofradía de Sant Marc, a religious fraternity dedicated to the patron saint of cobblers (St. Mark) and the oldest *cofradía* in Europe. The building itself, set on the oval-shaped square of Sant Felip Neri, dates back to 1565 and was the original headquarters of the *cofradía*. The examples of Roman sandals and medieval footwear are reproductions, but still remarkable. These oversized slippers hung outside the cobblers' workshops in the Barri Gòtic, announcing their trade during a time when their customers could not read or write. The rest of the collection is based around the 18th to 20th centuries, from the dainty satin boots of the 1700s to the 1930s boots of classical musician Pau (Pablo) Casals (1876–1973), who was from Catalonia. The collection also has a dozen or so pairs of sports shoes from the 1970s, which are now highly covetable items.

MUSEU DE CERA

⊞ 54 F11 • Passatge de la Banca 7, 08002 ☎ 93 317 26 49 ◉ Mon–Fri 10–1.30, 4–7.30, Sat–Sun 11–2, 4.30–8.30, Oct–end Jun; daily 10–10, rest of year ◍ Adult €6.65, child (5–11) €3.75, child (under 5) free ◉ Drassanes ⊟ 14, 36, 57, 59 ◻ ⊞ www.museocerabcn.com

Barcelona's waxworks museum may not rank alongside London's Madame Tassaud's, but the mannequins—who at times look amusingly unlike their models—give an insight into who is considered famous in Catalonia and Spain. This ranges from political figures such as Jordi Pujol (see page 38), General Franco, Bill Clinton and Yasser Arafat to Gaudí, Bonnie and Clyde and Dracula. The curators have added some cunning special-effect lighting and music that enhance many of the exhibits. The setting for the Museu de Cera is a late 19th-century building, with a winding staircase, period rooms and frescoed ceilings that are attractions in themselves.
Don't miss A visit to El Bosc de les Fades (the Fairy Forest), the café outside in the adjoining lane, embellished with running brooks and magic mirrors.

MUSEU DE LA CIÈNCIA

⊞ 282 F3 • Passeig de Sant Joan 108, 08037 (temporary address); Teodor Roviralta 55, 08022 (permanent address) ☎ 93 212 60 50 ◉ Mon–Fri 9.30–8, Sat 10.30–7.30, Sun 10.30–2.30 ◍ Free ◉ Verdaguer ⊟ 6, 15, 19, 20, 21, 33, 34, 43, 50, 55 www.noumuseudelaciencia.com

The city's Science Museum is currently undergoing a major overhaul. Due to be finished in 2004, it will have more of the same of its excellent predecessor: exhibits, mostly interactive, about the laws of nature, the evolution of mankind, technology and the power of the mind. While the building work is going on, a provisional Science Museum has been set up in the Fundació La Caixa, a beautiful building by the Modernista master Puig i Cadafalch, found in L'Eixample, that mixes Moorish and Gothic styles.

The exhibition space is divided into two sections. The first, Rastros y Restos (Evidence and Remains), shows a small but pretty impressive collection of fossils from all over the planet, including an enormous prehistoric fish that died in the act of digestion and a fragment of a meteorite. The second section is devoted to the solar system, with paintings of the various planets, moons and major stars with layman term explanations (in Spanish only) of their functions and characteristics.
Don't miss Exhibit 11, the dainty skeleton of a tiny bear from 42,000BC.

Museu d'Art Contemporani de Barcelona

A stunning building with a permanent collection that is fast becoming one of the strongest in the country.

Swathes of white and glass greet you at the façade of the MACBA

The MACBA is part of the regeneration project of El Raval, intent on including the ethnically diverse community

RATINGS

Good for kids	●●
Shopping	●●●●
Value for money	●●●

BASICS

✚ 54 F10 • Plaça dels Àngels 1, 08001

☎ 93 412 08 10

🕐 Mon, Wed–Fri 11–8, Sat 10–8, Sun 10–3, late-Jun–late-Sep; Mon, Wed–Fri 11–7.30, rest of year

💶 Adult €6, child (under 14) free. Temporary exhibitions: adult €4, child (under 14) free. Wed (except hols) €3

🌐 Catalunya

🚌 9, 14, 16, 17, 22, 24, 38, and all routes to Plaça de Catalunya

🎧 Wed and Sat 6pm; Sun 12pm only during the winter; audiotour included in admission price

📕 Large format catalogue of the permanent collection for €30

☕ Café is shared with the CCCB next door; there are a number to pick from outside

🏢 Very good gift and bookshop selling books about contemporary art, catalogues from past exhibitions and designer objects and accessories

♿ Available on all floors

www.macba.es
An excellent site, providing useful background information and easy to navigate.

SEEING THE MACBA

This dramatic structure, one of the most architecturally ambitious museums in Spain, opened in 1995. What you see will depend almost entirely on when you go. Although there is a permanent collection focusing on modern art of the late 20th century to the present day, with works by Catalan and Spanish artists including Antoni Tàpies, Miquel Barceló and Eduardo Chillida, a system of rotation means that only a small amount is on display at any one time. Much of the gallery space is given over to temporary and frequently challenging exhibitions of contemporary and avant-garde painting, sculpture, photography, video and conceptual art. Use the audioguide to help explain what's there.

HIGHLIGHTS

THE BUILDING

The luminous white façade of Richard Meier's contemporary art museum dominates Plaça dels Àngels, the large open square on which it stands in the northern half of El Raval. Natural light floods into the building through swathes of glass, designed to create a dialogue between the museum and its surroundings. Inside the museum, the overwhelming impression is of space and light, with gentle ramps carrying you up to the different floors and creating a sense of fluid movement through the galleries.

DAU AL SET

This Catalan surrealist movement, whose name means dead at seven, was founded in the late 1940s by Joan Brossa (1919–98), Barcelona's celebrated visual poet. Typical of Brossa's style is his *Poema-Objecte* (1956), a straw broom with a handle fashioned out of dominoes. The aim of such pieces was to provoke a reaction through the medium of everyday items, using a juxtaposition between two apparently unrelated items to set off a chain of associations.

HIA

The Spanish painter Antonio Saura was born in the Pyrenean town of Huesca in 1930. In 1957 he helped to form the El Paso avant-garde

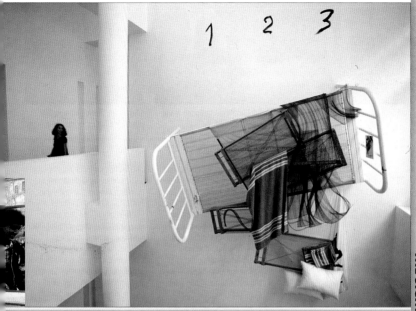

Antoni Tàpies' exploded bed (1992) hangs near the entrance

movement whose first exhibition in Barcelona brought him into contact with Tàpies and other members of Dau Al Set. _Hia_ (1958) is one of his most powerful works, a monochrome portrait of the female body which was heavily influenced by Goya and his black paintings series, which are on display at the Prado in Madrid.

BACKGROUND

The basic floor space at the MACBA measures 120m (394ft) by 35m (115ft)

MACBA was conceived as the focus of an ambitious project of urban renewal encompassing the entire district of El Raval. Once a byword for poverty and social decay, by the 1990s El Raval was in desperate need of reform. Tenement blocks in cramped, narrow streets were torn down almost overnight in an attempt to let in the light and create airy, open spaces. At the same time, Barcelona was looking for a suitable spot for a first-class museum of contemporary art. Richard Meier's stunning museum has succeeded on both counts. Visitors and locals now flock to El Raval and the area around MACBA, with its new restaurants, cafés, galleries and boutiques.

At Museu FC Barcelona

Ornamental trees and an arched loggia form the entrance to Museu Frederic Marès

Museu de Geologia—the first purpose built museum in the city

MUSEU DIOCESÀ

➕ 55 G11 • Avinguda de Catedral 4, 08002 ☎ 93 315 22 13 🕐 Tue–Sat 10–2, 5–8, Sun 11–2 💵 Adult €2, child (under 10) free 🚇 Jaume I 🚌 17, 18, 40, 45 ♿

The Diocesan Museum, inaugurated in 1982, is a small collection of religious art in a restored early-Gothic building, and sections of the rear wall are actually part of the original Roman wall. The collection starts on the ground floor with pieces of Roman funerary art found at Montjuïc, but quickly passes into the world of Catalan religious objects on the first and second floors. On the second floor, the series of triptychs, retables and panels portraying saints and martyrs is the most interesting. The 15th-century retable of Sant Quinze and Santa Julita is particularly gruesome, showing how the unfortunate duo had their throats cut by court guards before being dismembered. You can also ride to the top of the building in the glass elevator for a view across the cathedral's roof.

MUSEU FC BARCELONA

➕ 284 A6 • Carrer d'Aristides Maillol, entrance 7 or 9, 08028 ☎ 93 496 36 08 🕐 Mon–Sat 10–6.30, Sun 10–2 💵 Adult €5, child (5–13) €3.50 🚇 Collblanc 🚌 15, 52, 53, 54, 56, 57, 75 🚋 Mon–Sat 10–5.30, Sun 10–1; adult €9, child (5–13) €6.20 ♿ www.fcbarcelona.es

The city's soccer club is an obsession for many and its motto *més que un club* (more than a club) bears this out. Camp Nou is the largest stadium in Europe, and despite its seating capacity of nearly 100,000,

tickets for important games are very rare to come by. The next best thing is to visit the museum, which allows access to the empty stadium. The plush exhibition space sports a three-part collection: El·Museu Històric tells the history of the club through posters, photographs, trophies and other memorabilia; El Fons d'Art displays works from such artists as Dalí and Miró; and there is the world's largest collection of objects and curios from the 19th century to the present day all relating to the beautiful game. A treat for die-hard soccer fans is the tour of the dressing rooms, the tunnel, the field and the press and club rooms.

MUSEU FREDERIC MARÈS

➕ 55 G11 • Plaça de Sant Iu 5–6, 08002 ☎ 93 310 58 00 🕐 Tue–Sat 10–7, Sun 10–3 💵 Adult €3, child (under 16) free; first Sun of every month and Wed after 3pm free 🚇 Liceu, Jaume I 🚌 17, 19, 40, 45 📷 Apr–end Sep only ♿ www.museumares.bcn.es

Sculptor and teacher Federic Marès i Deuloval (1893–1991) was probably Spain's most prolific and varied collector. The museum that bears his name displays sublime Gothic religious imagery and paraphernalia from the Modernista epoch. Marès' areas of interest fell into two basic categories: religious art, particularly figurines from the Romanesque to Renaissance periods, and household curios from the late 19th century.

Soccer memorabilia at Museu FC Barcelona

The first category is impressive, but it can be overwhelming in number. One of the highlights is the relief *Appearance of Jesus to His Disciples at Sea* taken from the monastery of Sant Pere de Rodes near Cadaqués. The second part, called The Collector's Cabinet, is the fruit of determined flea-market searching, with such items as snuff boxes, cigarette papers and perfume bottles

The museum occupies a huge palace next to the cathedral, and the entrance is probably the prettiest in Barcelona. The Verger, the garden of the building that was once the Royal Palace of the Counts of Barcelona, has a calming central fountain and is dotted with orange trees and benches to sit on, providing a cooling city oasis whether you plan to head inside or not.

MUSEU DE GEOLOGIA

➕ 55 H11 • Passeig de Picasso s/n, Parc de la Ciutadella, 08003 ☎ 93 319 68 95 🕐 Tue–Sun 10–2 (also Thu 2–6.30pm) 💵 Adult €3, child (under 16) free; first Sun of each month free to all; includes entry to the Museu de Zoologia 🚇 Arc de Triomf 🚌 14, 39, 40, 41, 42, 51, 141 www.museugeologia.bcn.es

The Geology Museum is next to the greenhouse in the beautiful Parc de la Ciutadella (see page 108), in a late 19th-century building designed by Antonio Rovira i Trias, the city's municipal architect of the time. It was designed as part of the Universal Exhibition of 1888. This is the largest geology collection in Spain with more than 100,000 examples, only a tiny proportion of which is on show. Divided into two wings, there are displays of granites, quartzes and naturally radioactive rocks from all corners of the globe, plus a more interesting fossil section.

MUSEU D'HISTÒRIA DE CATALUNYA

**A tour of Catalonia's history
from the Iberians to the post-Fascist period.**

The Museu d'Història de Catalunya's slogan is a 'stroll through history', and that pretty much sums up what it is. The huge museum is in a restored brick warehouse in Port Vell, often referred to as the Palau del Mar, and spans over four floors. The ground and first floors are dedicated to temporary shows; a moving photographic portrait of the Mauthausen concentration camp and a homage to Josep Tarradellas, the first president of the Generalitat, are two examples. The second and third floors are where the main exhibition is held. Because of the sheer expanse of it, you would be wise to follow it numerically as it takes you through the different periods and key events in Catalonia's history, such as the peasants' revolt, the Civil War and the first autonomous government of the modern age.

THE DISPLAYS
Starting with the Iberians, the exhibits consist of re-created scenes, reproduction maps and documents, historical sound recordings and footage, and interactive gadgets. Some of these are ingenious. The recreated medieval chapel complete with chanting monks is likely to make the hairs on the back of your neck stand up, and there is a suit of amour for the children to try on. Some exhibits rely on verbal communication and as the majority of the text is in Catalan you may need to refer to the handbook you are given at the entrance.

THE THIRD FLOOR
This section, starting with the Industrial Revolution, is a lot easier to digest, mainly because of the photographic and cinematic material available. The re-created cinema showing a propaganda film of Franco and his family is fabulous, as is the 1950s bar interior next door which celebrates the coming of television and Catalan mass media.

*Palau del Mar is home to the
museum and seafood restaurants*

RATINGS

Good for kids	●●
Historic interest	●●●
Value for money	●●●

BASICS

✚ 55 G12 • Palau del Mar, Plaça de Pau Vila 3, 08003

☎ 93 225 47 00

🕐 Tue–Sat 10–7 (also Wed 7–8pm), Sun 10–2.30

💶 Adult €3, child (7–18) €2.10, child (under 7) free; first Sun of every month free to all

🚇 Barceloneta

🚌 14, 17, 39, 40, 45, 57, 59, 64

🍴 Lunchtime snacks and à la carte in the evenings, on the fourth floor with sweeping views over Port Vell

🎁 Sells gifts made by local designers, and stocks a good range of books on a number of subjects, including Catalan history

🚻 On the fourth floor

http://cultura.gencat.es/museus/mhc

Museu Marítim

The royal shipyards are the finest example of their kind in the world.
Learn more about Barcelona's maritime history in one of the city's most
impressive museums, in terms of both its setting and contents.
Admire a spectular replica of a 16th-century galley ship.

Different eras of maritime history are brought to life

Works of art on a nautical theme are on display

Exhibitions allow a close look at shipbuilding techniques

RATINGS	
Good for kids	● ● ● ●
Historic interest	● ● ●
Specialist shopping	● ●
Value for money	● ● ●

TIPS

● Arrive after lunch to avoid school groups.

● Once you have finished your visit, take a stroll around the outside of the shipyards in order to appreciate their sheer grandeur.

GALLERY GUIDE

Section 1: Temporary exhibitions
Section 2: Traditional fishing in Catalonia
Section 3: Shipbuilding
Section 4: Maps and navigational instruments
Section 5: *La Galera Real*
Section 6: Figureheads
Section 7: Maritime Barcelona 1750–1850
Section 8: Steamships

SEEING THE MUSEU MARÍTIM

The soaring arches and columns of the former Drassanes Reials (royal shipyards) make an elegant and highly appropriate setting for one of Barcelona's most visited museums, devoted to the city's long relationship with the sea. Beneath the Gothic naves of this secular cathedral is an impressive collection of fishing boats, yachts, seafaring memorabilia and a full-scale replica of a royal galley. The visit is made more enjoyable by an entertaining audiotour, refered to as The Great Sea Adventure, with everything from a simulated storm at sea to the conversations of emigrants leaving Barcelona by steamer for a new life in South America. Although the entire museum is under a single roof, the exhibits are arranged in a logical order and it's easy to follow the floor plan that you can pick up.

HIGHLIGHTS

FIGUREHEADS

Figureheads served a variety of functions. On warships they acted as a deterrent, using symbolism such as lions, warriors and sea monsters to strike fear into the hearts of the enemy and prey on man's deep fears of the sea. At other times they served a religious or decorative purpose. The figureheads on display were mostly retrieved from Catalan sailing vessels of the 19th century. Among the most impressive is the Negre de la Riba, a figure of a Native American warrior.

LA GALERA REAL

The focal point of the museum is this spectacular replica of the royal galley built in these shipyards for Don Juan of Austria in 1568. This was the flagship of the squadron formed by Spain, Venice, Malta and the Papal States, which defeated the Turkish fleet at Lepanto in 1571 (see page 31). It was this victory that ended Ottoman dominance throughout the Mediterranean. The replica was built in 1971 to celebrate the fourth centenary of the battle and its dimensions follow the original. It is 60m (197ft) in length and more than 6m (20ft) wide, with 59 oars rowed by 236 oarsmen, four to an oar, many of whom were chained to the benches as slaves. The boat

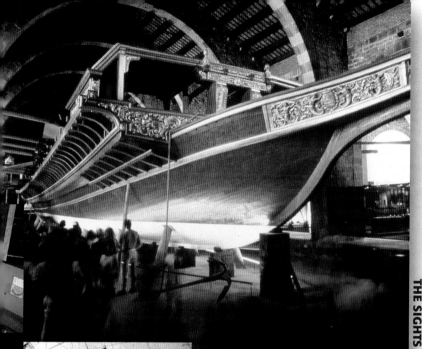

occupies the central aisle of the museum and you can walk right around its entire gilt and red lacquer hull, peeking into the hold and up onto the deck. It is worth taking a close-up look at the spectacular prow, with its lavish gilt carvings and figurehead of Neptune riding a dolphin.

SANTA EULÀLIA

The adventure does not end when you leave the magnificent shipyards. Across the road in the old port is the three-masted schooner *Santa Eulàlia*. Launched in 1918 as *Carmen Flores*, it has been used for a whole host of tasks, such as a trading ship and tourist boat. It was acquired by auction by the museum in 1997 and named after one of the city's patron saints. The masts and rigging have been rebuilt and restored to working order and the tall ship is once again fully seaworthy.

BACKGROUND

The Drassanes Reials were built between 1283 and 1390, replacing the smaller Arab-built shipyards that occupied the same site. They provided warships for the Catalan Crown at a time when Catalonia was a major power in the Mediterranean, with conquests including the Balearic Islands, Sardinia, Sicily and Naples. Originally standing on the water's edge so that vessels could be pulled up for repair, the shipyards consisted of a series of long parallel aisles facing the sea. All of the great European seafaring cities, such as Venice, had their own covered shipyards, but Barcelona is the only city to have conserved the original layout and these are the finest example of their kind in the world. They continued to be used for shipbuilding until the 17th century.

BASICS
✚ 52 F12 • Avinguda de les Drassanes s/n, 08001
☎ 93 342 99 20
◷ Mon–Sun 10–7
💷 The shipyards: adult €5.40, child (7–16) €2.70, child (under 7) free; first Sat of every month free to all after 3pm. The *Santa Eulàlia*: adult €2.40, child (7–16) €1.20, child (under 7) free
Ⓜ Drassanes
🚌 14, 18, 36, 38, 57, 59, 64, 91
🎧 Audiotours in Spanish, Catalan, English, French, German, Italian and Japanese included in admission price
📖 Pocket guidebook available in Spanish, Catalan and English, €3.90
☕ Full café service available with a terrace overlooking the gardens
📚 Sells nautical-related books and souvenirs
🚻 At the beginning and end of the exhibition

www.diba.es/mmaritim
A good site, with lots of information and clearly laid out.

La Galera Real *was rowed by slaves and a screen with simulated footage depicts their suffering (top); maps were highly embellished items (above)*

Museu Nacional d'Art de Catalunya

Bringing together a thousand years of Catalan art in one place.
Magnificent frescoes salvaged from remote Pyrenean churches.

From the cathedral of La Seu d'Urgell, c1495

The neo-baroque palace of MNAC

Still Life with Four Vessels by Francisco de Zurbaràn in the Cambó Collection

SEEING THE MUSEU NACIONAL D'ART DE CATALUNYA (MNAC)

The museum is housed in the Palau Nacional, the neo-baroque palace on Montjuïc conceived by Josep Puig i Cadafalch (1876–1956) as the centrepiece of the 1929 International Exhibition. This grandiose domed building is visible from across the city and dominates the views of Montjuïc from Plaça d'Espanya (see page 115). The museum itself is divided into two main sections on the ground floor, which are devoted to Romanesque and Gothic art. After passing through the main entrance, you'll find the Romanesque galleries are on the left and the Gothic the right, separated by a central hallway. The Romanesque collection is divided into 21 rooms or ambits, with the frescoes displayed in faithful reproductions of their original settings. Each of the ambits, in addition to full-size works, displays explanatory photographs and scale models of the original churches. The Gothic gallery is 19 ambits, and both are broadly laid out in chronological order. The MNAC is also home to the Cambó Collection, a small but significant bequest of Renaissance and baroque art from financier Francesc Cambó, including pieces by Rubens, Goya, Velázquez, Tintoretto and Gainsborough.

TIPS

● The trek up the hill from the Espanya metro stop to the MNAC entrance can be exhausting. Take the bus option to conserve your energy for this wonderful museum.

● Don't forget to take in the stunning view of the city and Tibidabo from the MNAC's front steps.

HIGHLIGHTS

CHRIST IN MAJESTY

Christ in Majesty (Romanesque gallery, room V) was painstakingly removed from its original home in the remote Pyrenean church of Sant Climent de Taüll at the beginning of the 20th century. This magnificent fresco, painted c1123, is from the apse of the church and is considered a masterpiece of Catalan Romanesque art. It depicts Christ with wide eyes and flowing hair, looking down upon humanity and holding up a book inscribed with the Latin words *Ego Sum Lux Mundi* (I am the light of the world). The portrait of Christ is set off by the intense blue pigment of a lapis lazuli background. The anonymous artist was influenced by French, Italian and Byzantine styles but managed to create a personal vision through his use of colour and geometric form, giving the work an unrealistic but striking feel.

Frescoes from the central apse at the church of Sant Climent de Taüll, more commonly known as Christ in Majesty, *were sensitively remounted to show how they would originally have been seen (left)*

Altarpiece of St. Michael and St. Stephen, *c1455, from Santa Maria del Pí, showing St. Michael (above left); the* Apostles Frontal *from La Seu d'Urgell, dated early 12th-century (above right);* Batlló Majesty *is one of the finest pieces on display (right)*

BASICS

✠ 56 C10 • Palau Nacional, Parc de Montjuïc, 08038

☎ 93 622 03 75

🕐 Tue–Sat 10–7, Sun 10–2.30

💶 Adult €4.80, child (under 7) €2.40; first Thu of every month free

Ⓜ Espanya

🚌 9, 13, 27, 30, 50, 55, 57, 91

🚶 Free guided tour Sat and Sun at 12.30pm in Spanish; no audiotours available

📖 Small guidebooks about the Gothic and Romanesque periods €12; large format €15

🚪 Open as part of the renovations

🏪 Selling mainly books about the Gothic and Romanesque periods, art catalogues and reproductions

🚻 In entrance hall, plus in both main galleries

www.mnac.es

A very detailed site that breaks down each of the sections, with lots of information, but menus are not always easy to follow.

BATLLÓ MAJESTY

This extraordinarily well-preserved wooden sculpture from the mid-12th century (found in the Romanesque gallery, room VIII) depicts Christ on the Cross in royal robes, triumphant at the moment of death. His expression transcends suffering, as he looks downwards impassively, already detached from the world of men. This extremely rare piece is noted for its delicate craftsmanship and for the fact that it still has most of its original colours. This styling also betrays a Syrian influence.

CONQUEST OF MALLORCA

Works of art with a civil theme are also on display at MNAC. The powerful merchant class of the Middle Ages used the Gothic form to celebrate their achievements and display their wealth. The fragments of this painting (c1285–90), in the Gothic gallery room I, formed part of an epic depiction of different episodes of the conquest of Mallorca by Jaume I in 1229. It once decorated the Palau d'Aguilar, now in the Museu Picasso (see pages 100–101). Its vibrant dynamism and the artist's singular use of narrative give this work a comic-book feel.

MADONNA OF THE COUNCILLORS

This painting by Luís Dalmau, in the Gothic gallery room XI, is rich in political symbolism and dates from the mid-1440s. It was commissioned by the Barcelona city council to show the power and sanctity of the city's rulers by cleverly blending secular and religious imagery. The picture shows the Madonna and Child sitting upon a throne resting on four lions surrounded by several portraits of prophets. The five councillors who commissioned the work are kneeling piously at her feet. The contract for the painting, which stipulates that a faithful and holy representation of the donors be made, still exists.

ALTARPIECE OF ST. MICHAEL AND ST. STEPHEN

Among the many important Catalan Gothic artists represented in these galleries is Jaume Huguet, one of the most brilliant and innovative artists of the age. The central compartment of this grand altarpiece (c1455–60) is in the Gothic gallery room XII, and was originally in the church of Santa Maria del Pí (see page 130). It depicts St. Michael holding a cross in his right hand and a sword in his left hand, having slain the apocalyptic dragon. He daringly challenges the viewer by looking directly out of the painting.

BACKGROUND

Romanesque art was the first great artistic movement to spread across western Europe, between AD900–1200, reaching Catalonia through pilgrims who crossed the Pyrenees on the medieval route to Santiago de Compostela. It was designed for a community that was largely illiterate and so is characterized by bright tones, vivid expressions and graphic imagery to explain religious notions and biblical texts. However until the late 19th century, Romanesque art was largely ignored by art historians who considered it unsophisticated in comparison with the richness of the Gothic and Renaissance periods that followed. It was only in the early 20th century, when collectors began to strip bare Catalonia's isolated and crumbling Pyrenean churches, that the nation woke up to the value of its Romanesque heritage. At the same time, new techniques for stripping frescoes from walls were being developed in Italy, allowing experts to remove the frescoes intact in order to protect them from disintegration, vandalism and theft. In 1934 these treasures found a home in the Palau Nacional. The Italian architect Gae Aulenti was employed to restore the elegant arches and columns of the palace to create a suitable home for a comprehensive museum of Catalan art and it opened in its current form in 1995.

MNAC 2004

The new galleries focus on Renaissance and baroque art, along with modern art from the 19th and 20th centuries from the Museu d'Art Modern (see page 88). There are also separate collections of photography, prints and coins, gathered in from various locations across the city. Each of the four main sections exits into the Sala Oval, a central domed space with frescoes. This was designed as an official function room for the International Exhibition and is now set to be the focal point of the museum with its café and shops.

Grand Ballerina *by Pablo Gargallo (1881–1934), made in 1929 from cut iron*

There are great views from the Palau National to the foothills of Tibidabo and the Plaça d'Espanya, so make sure you take time to enjoy them (left and above)

Museu Picasso

A collection that traces the development of one of
the 20th century's great artists.
The most visited museum in Barcelona.

RATINGS

Good for kids	●●
Cultural interest	●●●●
Specialist shopping	●●●
Value for money	●●●●

TIPS

● Late afternoon is the best
time to go to avoid the crowds.
Even if it's busy you shouldn't
have to wait for long as crowds
are moved through the ticket
office surprisingly quickly.

● Some may be disappointed
by the absence of one of
Picasso's most celebrated
works, *Guernica* (1937), which
is on display in Madrid.

*Pablo Picasso stayed in Carrer
d'Avinyó in the Barri Gòtic during
his time in Barcelona (above)*

SEEING THE MUSEU PICASSO

The Museu Picasso is in five separate medieval mansions along
Carrer de Montcada, the beautiful street at the heart of the
La Ribera district. After years of restoration work the palaces
have been carefully joined together, but you can still see traces
of their original majesty in the Italianate courtyards, baroque
salons and painted ceilings. The main entrance is through the
15th-century Gothic Palau Berenguer d'Aguilar. Arrows guide you
around the permanent collection and you must follow this route,
spread out over the first and second floors. Inevitably there is a
focus on Picasso's early work, reflecting the time that he spent in
Barcelona, which included his famous Blue Period (1901–04).

HIGHLIGHTS

MAN WITH HAT (1895)

The small-scale oil paintings that line the walls of the opening galleries
were the product of Picasso's childhood in Malaga and his adoles-
cence in La Coruña and Barcelona, where his father taught at their
school of fine art. This famous portrait marks perhaps the first time
that the young Picasso moved from a straightforward realism towards
an attempt to create something more expressive.

BEACH AT LA BARCELONETA (1896)

This painting comes from the same period as *Man with Hat* and its
subject matter makes it a popular choice within the city. It is a splendid exercise in perspective, and the free brushwork continues the
move towards a more abstract way of perceiving the world.

CARRER DE LA RIERA DE SANT JOAN (1900)

At the end of the 19th century Picasso was living in Barcelona and
making friends with the Catalan artists Ramón Casas and Santiago
Rusinyol. There are several paintings from this time, a number using
Els Quatre Gats café (see page 229) as a subject. One of the best is
this view from his studio window, revealing his first hint of abstraction.

THE MADMAN (1904)

Picasso spent much of his Blue Period in Barcelona, producing haunt-
ing studies of poverty and despair. This classic of the period skilfully
conveys the depth of human suffering.

THE HARLEQUIN (1917)

Picasso was fascinated by the world of the theatre, with dancers and
pantomime characters a recurring theme in his work. This painting
was produced on one of his visits to Barcelona, with Diaghilev's
Russian ballet. The model for the portrait was the Russian dancer
Léonide Messine. Picasso donated this work to the city of Barcelona
in 1919 and it was displayed in the Museu d'Art Modern until being
transferred to the Museu Picasso on its opening.

LAS MENINAS (1957)

The high point of the collection is this series of 58 paintings hung
together in the Great Hall. During the 1950s, Picasso began looking to

the great artists for inspiration and in particular to Diego Velázquez (1599–1660). The result was a series of canvases on the theme of the Velázquez masterpiece *Las Meninas* (The Maids of Honour), depicting the women of the Spanish court, and executed in a hermitic period in his studio in 1957. Picasso's Cubist reinterpretations of the paintings reveal this work by Velázquez in a completely new light.

BACKGROUND

Pablo Picasso was born in Málaga in 1881. His family moved to Barcelona in 1895 and it was here that he spent his formative years as an artist. He moved to Paris in 1904 and settled permanently in France. The first donation to the collection was made by the artist himself. He gave *The Harlequin* to the local council in 1919, and a further 22 paintings donated by a private collector enabled the museum to open its doors in 1934. The Museu Picasso, in its current form, was founded in 1963 by Jaume Sabartés, Picasso's lifelong friend and secretary, who is featured in a number of portraits on display. In 1968, Sabartés died, leaving his entire private collection to the museum, a move which required expansion from the original Palau Berenguer d'Aguilar into the adjoining mansion. As a tribute to his friend, Picasso took an interest in the museum, bequeathing his entire *Las Meninas* series and many other works. Following Picasso's death in 1973, the museum acquired a large body of his graphic work as well as a collection of ceramics donated by his widow Jacqueline.

BASICS

✚ 55 G11 • Carrer de Montcada 15–23, 08003

☎ 93 319 63 10

🕐 Tue–Sat 10–8, Sun 10–3

💶 Adult €5, child (under 16) free; first Sun every month free to all; extra fee for temporary exhibitions

Ⓜ Jaume I

🚌 16, 17, 19, 22, 39, 40, 45, 51, 59

📖 Comprehensive, well-laid-out guidebook available in all major European languages and Japanese for €9.10

☕ Pleasant enough, with an outside terrace, although the café at the Textile Museum across the road is a better option for a post-visit break

🎁 Two gift shops on site, selling postcards, a good selection of catalogues from both past and present exhibitions, and assorted Picasso paraphernalia; both can get very busy

🚻 Although on every floor, they can be tricky to find, so make use of the ones on the ground floor

www.museupicasso.bcn.es
Plenty of information in Catalan, with clear menus, but the sections in other languages are too small to be of much use.

GALLERY GUIDE

Rooms 1–10: Picasso's early drawings
Room 9: The Embrace
Rooms 11–14: The Blue Period
Rooms 15–17: *Las Meninas* series
Rooms 18–19: Late years and ceramics

Portrait of Jacqueline *(above)* and The Pianist *(left) date from 1957, the same year Picasso painted his* Las Meninas *series*

The interior of Museu de la Xocolata, from where you can buy chocolates to take home

Museu de Zoologia was established in 1906 and set up home in the Castle of Three Dragons

MUSEU DEL PERFUM

🚩 57 G9 • Passeig de Gràcia 39, 08007 ☎ 93 216 01 21 🕐 Mon–Fri 10.30–1, 5–8, Sat 11–1.30 💰 Free 🚇 Passeig de Gràcia 🚌 7, 16, 17, 22, 24, 28 🏛 www.museodelperfume.com

Regia is one of the city's top perfumeries, and to its rear is the Museu del Perfum, with more than 5,000 examples of perfume bottles, flasks, distillers and all sorts of vessels from Grecian times to the present day. All the big French names are represented—Gallet, Lubin, Worth, D'Orsay—and there is also a section devoted to Eastern European perfumes, like the flaming-red bottles of Kremlin from the Soviet Union. Spain's own Myrurgia is given an entire section and the spectacular bottle by Salvador Dalí, Le Roi Soleil, has pride of place. More historic pieces are found in the Roman glass and Greek pottery sections and there is also a showcase of highly decorated, Victorian bottles that were the height of fashion among the genteel set of their day. The museum also shows you how a brand's image can change over the decades, or how it stays the same—for example, the shape of the Chanel No. 5 bottle has retained its classic lines since the 1930s.

MUSEU PICASSO

See pages 100–101.

MUSEU TÈXTIL I D'INDUMENTÀRIA

🚩 55 G11 • Carrer de Montcada 12, 08003 ☎ 93 319 76 03 🕐 Tue–Sat 10–6, Sun 10–3 💰 Adult €3.50, child (under 16) free 🚇 Jaume I 🚌 14, 17, 45, 39, 40, 51 🅿 🏛 www.museutextil.bcn.es

Textiles were Catalonia's principal industry during the Industrial Revolution and the Museu Tèxtil i d'Indumentària is a satisfying collection of period costumes and accessories. Spread over two floors, it starts with the Gothic period and then moves through the Renaissance, baroque and Elizabethan periods and on to Regency. Also present in this section are ladies' gloves that would only fit a present-day 10-year-old and some wonderfully ornate fans and opera glasses. The second floor deals with 20th-century attire, and Spain's most celebrated couturier, the Basque-born Cristóbal Balenciaga, is well represented with more than 100 items he designed between 1934–72. The chain mail mini dress by Paco Rabanne would still stop traffic on any street in the world. The museum's shop stocks a range of clothing, gifts and accessories, and the pretty café is in the Gothic courtyard.
Don't miss The collection of Catalan lacework on the ground floor includes some beautiful *mantillas* (scarves).

MUSEU DE LA XOCOLATA

🚩 55 H11 • Carrer del Comerç 36, 08003 ☎ 93 268 78 78 🕐 Mon, Wed–Sat 10–7, Sun 10–3 💰 Adult €3.80, child (under 7) free 🚇 Arc de Triomf 🚌 14, 16, 17, 19, 36, 39, 40, 45, 51, 57, 59 🅿 🏛 www.museudelaxocolata.com

Wandering through the clever, well-laid-out exhibits (a loose term, as the museum is structured as a giant textbook as opposed to a series of objects), you learn that it was the Spanish who brought cocoa from the New World to Europe and that the first industrialized chocolate-making machine was invented in Barcelona in 1780. The first section relates many other anecdotes, such as Native Americans using cocoa as a primitive form of money. The second half of the exhibition is dedicated to the thoroughly Catalan invention, the *mona*. Originally a humble, egg-laden yeast cake, *monas* have evolved into extravagant chocolate sculptures that appear in cake shop windows at Easter. This is a particularly good time to visit the museum as it hosts the annual *mona* competition.

MUSEU DE ZOOLOGIA

🚩 57 H12 • Passeig de Picasso s/n, Parc de la Ciutadella, 08003 ☎ 93 319 69 12 🕐 Tue–Sun 10–2 (also Thu 2–6.30) 💰 Adult €3.50, child (12–25) €2, child (under 12) free; first Sun of each month free to all; includes entry to the Museu de Geologia 🚇 Arc de Triomf 🚌 14, 39, 40, 41, 42, 51, 141 www.museuzoologia.bcn.es

Set in the Parc de la Ciutadella, this is one of the city's older museums, and together with the Museu de Geologia (see page 92), goes under the rather formal name of Museu de Ciències Naturals de la Ciutadella. One of the main reasons to visit is to see the fairy-tale mock fortress in which it is housed. The Castle of Three Dragons was designed as a café-restaurant by Lluís Domènech i Montaner (1850–1923) for the 1888 Universal Exhibition. The ceramic plates of flora and fauna under the building's battlements are a particularly relevant detail, reflecting the content of the museum itself.
The theory that the bigger the better dominates some of the displays, as shown by the 5m (16ft) Nile crocodile and the gigantic Japanese crab. The museum also holds temporary exhibitions every three months on related subjects. Apart from anyhting else, the museum gives you the feeling that you are stepping back into a Victorian-era research laboratory.

PALAU GÜELL

An early form of Gaudí's style, with a dramatic roof terrace.

Gaudí received carte blanche from his patron Eusebi Güell for this project, a plot was chosen for the palace in the old city and work began in 1886. The detail is astonishing and everything that could be has been dressed, painted, polished or embellished with decorative touches. To visit the Palau, you must take the designated tour.

THE LOWER FLOORS
The first room is the reception area that was once the concierge's office. The rest of the floor, with two marble-embellished halls, was used as the coach house. The floor here is made of wood, even though it looks like marble, presumably to muffle the sounds of the horses and carriages that came and went. The basement stables, which you enter by a rear stairway, consist of a series of red-brick columns and mushroom capitals, a well-known Gaudían motif.

THE UPPER FLOORS
The first room upstairs is the anteroom. Really four salons in one, there is a magnificent gallery that sweeps the length of the first three. The latticed windows filter the bright Mediterranean light and a series of pristine marble columns define the area. In the first room, the oak and bulletwood ceiling is decorated with seeds, which bud and grow, until finally they bloom into full foliage in the third room. The fourth, more discreet room, was for female visitors and is complete with a screen, dressing table and mirror. These rooms lead to the grand salon, used for parties and music recitals. Its domed roof shoots up to the very roof of the palace itself. Light is ingenuously filtered through windows from the two floors above and through perforations in the roof of the dome. The tour also takes in the dining room, smoking rooms and private apartments.

THE ROOF
Stepping out onto the roof gives you a close-up view of Gaudí's handiwork. The masterful architectural landscape that he produced is dominated by 14 chimneys and ventilators and the central dome of the palace. The chimneys are covered in forms of *trencadís* (broken pieces of pottery) using a plethora of materials such as marble, earthenware and tiles. There is even an all-white chimney bearing the hallmark of Limoges, the porcelain makers. The shapes of the chimneys also vary, creating another of Gaudí's trademarks: using an everyday item, such as a chimney, to produce fanciful imagery.

RATINGS	
Photo stops	● ● ● ●
Shopping	● ● ●
Value for money	● ● ●

TIP
● If you speak anything other than Spanish, Catalan or English, pick up a guide book in the foyer before you start your visit, as these are the only languages used on the tour.

BASICS
✚ 54 F11 • Nou de la Rambla 3–5, 08001
☎ 93 317 39 74
🕐 Mon–Sat 10–6.15
💶 Adult €3, child (under 7) free
Ⓜ Drassanes
🚌 14, 38, 59, 64, 91
🎫 Admission by tour only, starting every 15 minutes and lasting one hour
📖 Large format, highly graphic guidebook €18; smaller pocketbook €4
🏬 Good selection of books about Gaudí and Modernisme, plus souvenirs
🚻 On the ground floor

The roof, with its myriad of shapes, gives impressive views over El Raval (left); a detail of trencadís from one of the chimneys (above)

Palau de la Música Catalana

**A superb example of Modernista architecture.
The spiritual home of Catalan music and culture.**

The foyer of the Palau　　　　*Lluís Domènech i Montaner*　　*The façade at night*　　*A detail*

SEEING THE PALAU DE LA MÚSICA CATALANA

Lluís Domènech i Montaner (1850–1923) was one of the best Modernista architects, and this outrageously over-the-top concert hall is perhaps the most emblematic Modernista building of all. It is in the narrow streets of the Sant Pere district, which frustratingly means that it is difficult to get an overall view of the outside without craning your neck from the street. If at all possible, you should come to a concert here, as this is much the best way to appreciate the building—the music and the architecture were designed to be enjoyed together. Otherwise you will have to take one of the regular guided tours to gain access to the building.

HIGHLIGHTS

THE FAÇADE

Before you go in, spend some time admiring the façade. The first thing you notice is the forest of bright floral mosaic columns, each one different, adorning the first-floor balcony. On the corner of Carrer d'Amadeu Vives and Carrer de Sant Pere Més Alt, beneath the shield of the Palau, is an extravagant sculptural ensemble entitled *La cançó popular catalana*. It has numerous references to Catalan folk song and includes the figures of St. George, Catalonia's patron saint, and a beautiful maiden bursting out of the stone. Higher up are the busts of the great composers Bach, Beethoven, Palestrina and Wagner, a deliberate statement by Domènech i Montaner that Catalan folk art could sit comfortably with the classics. At the summit of the façade, beneath a mosaic dome, is a fine allegorical mosaic of the Orfeó Català (Catalan Choral Society). Although this is very difficult to see from street level, the mosaic is rich in symbolism, from the jagged peaks of the mountain of Montserrat to the use of yellow and red from the Catalan flag and the shield of St. George.

THE FOYER

The entrance foyer is a series of elaborate arches and columns adorned with floral capitals and motifs. Domènech i Montaner conceived this building as a garden of music, open to the outside world, and the predominant material is glass in order to let in the

TIPS

● Although booking in advance is not a requirement, it is unlikely you will be able to buy a ticket for a tour if you just turn up on the day. If you can, try to book tickets a couple of days ahead from the box office in the foyer or from the gift shop, where tickets can be bought up to 7 days in advance.

● No photographs or videos are allowed to be taken anywhere inside the building, and this includes the foyer. Instead, visit the shop for posters and postcards.

The tour of the Palau ends at the Lluís Millet Hall, from where there is close-up view of the balcony (left)

✚ 55 G10 • Carrer de Sant Francesc de Paula 2, 08003

☎ 93 295 72 00

🕐 Daily 10–3.30

🎟 Adult €7, child (under 12) free

Ⓜ Urquinaona

🚌 16, 17, 19, 45 and all routes to Plaça d'Urquinaona

📷 Guided tours every half-hour, held alternately in Catalan, Spanish and English; tours may be cancelled at short notice because of rehearsals

📖 Small pocket guidebooks for €3, larger coffee table book about the Palau for €21 (both available at the shop)

🏪 Les Muses del Palau gift shop sells tour tickets, books and other gifts with the Palau's motif, and assorted objects such as pottery

🚻 In the main entrance hall, but behind the roped-off section from where the tour starts, so access is only allowed once the tour has begun

www.palaumusica.org
Very easy to navigate with good information, but strangely lacking in pictures of this beautiful building.

THE SIGHTS

The Palau lit up at night, with an allegorical mosaic visible at the top (right); the magnificent skylight in the main hall (far right); the auditorium has capacity to seat 1,970 people (below)

light. This theme is furthered by a deliberate lack of clear division between the interior and the exterior, for example by the use of street lamps within the foyer.

THE HALL

Because of the limited amount of space available, the main concert hall was built directly above the entrance. With more than 2,000 seats in stalls (orchestra seats) and two circles, this is a magnificent setting for a concert. Light pours in through the stained-glass windows garlanded with flowers and through the huge central skylight, an extraordinary multicoloured inverted dome surrounded by 40 female heads which are said to represent a heavenly choir. The ceiling is dotted with ceramic rose heads, and the enormous winged horses by the sculptor Eusebi Arnau seem to fly overhead. A concert here is an unforgettable experience.

THE STAGE

The apse-shaped stage area is seen through an arch set with sculptures. On the left is a bust of Josep Anselm Clavé (1824–75), a key figure in the revival of Catalan folk music, beneath a tree of life representing the song *Les Flors de Maig* (The Flowers of May). On the right, a bust of Beethoven peers through the winged horses from Wagner's 'Ride of the Valkyries' from *The Valkyrie*. This pair of sculptures is clearly designed to reinforce the message that the Palau was a temple to all kinds of music, from Catalan folk song to more traditional European tastes. At the back of the stage, a mosaic panel

with the Catalan shield is flanked by 18 female figures, their upper bodies sculpted in terracotta and their costumes fashioned out of mosaics by artist Lluís Bru. These are Les Muses de Palau, a group of muses each holding a different musical instrument in her hands, apart from one who is singing to represent the human voice. The muses, their flowing costumes linked by garlands of flowers, form a permanent backdrop to the performers on the stage.

BACKGROUND

The Palau de la Música Catalana was built between 1905 and 1908 as a headquarters for the Orfeó Català. This choral society, founded in 1891, had played a leading role in La Renaixença, the revival of Catalan art, language and political thought which had a direct influence on the Modernista architectural movement. The choice of Domènech i Montaner was significant—he had a background as a Catalan nationalist politician and as the chairman of the Jocs Florals, the literary arm of La Renaixença. All of the main themes of Modernisme were employed in the design, from the extravagant use of floral decoration and themes from nature to the *trencadís* (mosaics of broken tiles) and the repeated use of Catalan nationalist symbols including the shield of St. George. In 1960 it was the setting for a patriotic protest when Catalan nationalists sang their unofficial anthem during a concert for the dictator General Franco. Declared a UNESCO World Heritage Site in 1997, the Palau is being extended by contemporary architect Òscar Tusquets onto the site of an already demolished church. The extension will provide an additional underground concert hall as well as an outdoor plaza for summer recitals.

The 50-minute tour begins in the foyer and continues in the rehearsal room with a 20-minute film about the history of the building. Next, a double staircase with white marble handrails leads to the first floor and the entrance to the grand concert hall. You are taken into the upper circle for a closer look before ending in the Lluís Millet Hall, a two-floor lounge and reception room named after one of the founders of the Orfeó Català. This hall fills the entire area behind the main façade of the Palau, and from its stained-glass windows there are close-up views of the mosaic-covered columns that you will have seen outside. The rest of the hall is subdued when compared to the richness of the auditorium, though there are sculptures and paintings of various figures associated with the history of the Palau.

Palau Reial de Pedralbes has a pond outside the main entrance

The Cascada, a hugh water fountain, at the Parc de la Ciutadella

Old and new design interact at Parc del Clot

THE SIGHTS

PALAU REIAL DE PEDRALBES

✚ 280 B5 • Avinguda Diagonal 686, 08034 ☎ 93 280 50 24 ⊙ Tue–Sat 10–6, Sun 10–3 💷 Adult €3.50, child (under 16) free; first Sun of every month free to all (entry is to both museums and Museu Textil) 🚇 Palau Reial 🚌 7, 33, 63, 67, 68, 69, 74, 75, 78 📷
www.museuceramica.bcn.es;
www.museuartsdecoratives.bcn.es

Viewed as a double act, the Museu de Ceramica and the Museu de les Arts Decoratives are in landscaped gardens that once belonged to the Finca Güell (see page 77) next door, now called the Parc de Pedralbes. The handsome palau was built in 1924 as a residence for the royal family. The Ceramics Museum collection stretches from the 11th century to the present day. Medieval, Arabic-influenced Mudéjar, plus other elaborate baroque and Renaissance pieces are among the highlights. There is a huge collection of simpler forms of clay pottery from all over Catalonia laid out in chronological order, and one-off pieces from artists like Picasso and Miró take pride of place. The Decorative Arts Museum is smaller and falls short of covering Catalonia's important design heritage. The objects and furniture from the Middle Ages to the present day, unsurprisingly, has its high point in the Modernisme glassware section.

PALAU DE LA VIRREINA

✚ 54 F10 • La Rambla 99, 08001 ☎ 93 316 10 00 ⊙ Tue–Sat 11–8.30, Sun 11–3 💷 Exhibition Room 1 free; Exhibition Room 2: adult €3, child (under 16) free 🚇 Liceu or Catalunya 🚌 14, 18, 39, 59 and all routes to Plaça de Catalunya ⛯ Free guided tours Tue 6pm
www.bcn.es/virreinaexposicions

The Palau de la Virreina was built in the 1770s for Manuel d'Amat, a viceroy returning from a long stint in Peru. It is a good place to find out what's going on in the city, as it is home to the information office of ICUB, the local government's events and culture department. Upstairs are the administrative offices, downstairs on the ground floor is the office that issues information and tickets to the city's main events such as the Grec summer festival (see page 180). The Palau also puts on frequent free exhibitions, ranging from contemporary art and photography to profiles of prominent local personalities. Every year in September FotoMerce showcases the entries from the previous year's competition for best snap of Barcelona's local week-long fiesta La Mercè (see page 180).
Don't miss The *gigants* (giants; see page 179) Jaume and Violant are usually in the main entrance and make appearances at carnival and other city fiestas.

PARC DE LA CIUTADELLA

✚ 55 H11 • Passeig de Picasso 15, 08003 ⊙ Daily 10–dusk 💷 Free 🚇 Arc de Triomf 🚌 14, 17, 36, 39, 51, 57, 59 📷

This is the largest and greenest park in the city, and at one time it was the only park in Barcelona. It was created when the fortress was demolished (see page 31) and was used as the setting for the Universal Exhibition of 1888, for which the Arc de Triomf at the northern end of the park served as the main entry point. Its formal, leafy avenues, central boating lake and shady, hidden corners are very enticing, and it is home to various museums and the city zoo (see page 114).

The park is noted for its sculpture. Roig i Soler's pert and proper *Lady with the Parasol*,

also known as *Pepita* (1885), has become a well-recognized image in the city, and the over-the-top fountain-sculpture *The Cascade* is the combined effort of seven sculptors and emulates Rome's Trevi Fountain. The Umbracle (the Shade House) and the Hivernacle (Winter Garden, also a café-restaurant) were both designed by Josep Fontseré, the park's original architect, and should not be missed. There are a number of play areas for children, a fish-filled boating lake and bicycles for rent. It is a great place to visit on Sunday afternoons to relax and people-watch.

PARC DEL CLOT

✚ 287 L9 • Carrer de Rosend Nobas s/n, 08018 (access: Carrer de Escultors Claperós and Plaça de Valentí Almirall) ⊙ 24 hours 💷 Free 🚇 Clot 🚌 56, 62, 92
www.bcn.es/parcsijardins

The Parc del Clot is a good example of the type of urbanization projects that Barcelona is known for all over the world. In the suburb of Clot, it draws on industry for its inspiration, in this case the national train company RENFE, the former occupants of the land. The park is laid out over three shrub-covered levels, with the remains of the original walls of the 19th-century warehouse interwoven throughout. An ingenious touch is the series of flights of stairs that act as acoustic barriers and as protection from flying tennis or basket balls, as most of the games areas are tucked away behind them. But perhaps more than any architectural merits, the Parc del Clot is an opportunity to experience *barri* life. It is always buzzing with parents and children, spontaneous soccer matches and people playing boules.

A very modern interpretation of public Roman baths at the Parc de l'Espanya Industrial

The Parc de L'Estació has sculptures by Beverly Pepper

PARC DE LA CREUETA DEL COLL

🎫 282 H4 • Carrer de Castellterçol 24, 08023 🕐 Daily 10–dusk 💲 Free
🚇 Penitents 🚌 25, 28, 87 ♿
www.bcn.es/parcsijardins

Perhaps only in Barcelona would you find an abandoned stone quarry turned into a park by the design team that re-built the waterfront for the Olympics. And perhaps only in this design-conscious city would it be complete with a swimming pool and a work by the country's most eminent sculptors. The shallow artificial lake, used as the pool, and the *Elogio del Agua*, a huge work of oxidized metal by Basque sculptor Eduardo Chillida (1924–2002) is typical of the sort of imaginative design Barcelona is renowned for in the creation of its public spaces. Summer is the best time to visit, when the local children are splashing around in the lake. At other times, try and go just before the sun sets, pull up a seat at the outdoor bar and enjoy the serenity of this truly unique oasis.

PARC DE L'ESPANYA INDUSTRIAL

🎫 56 C8 • Carrer de Watt 24, 08014 (access: Plaça dels Països Catalans and Carrer de Muntadas) 🕐 Daily 10–dusk
💲 Free 🚇 Sants Estació or Hostafrancs 🚌 27, 30, 43, 44, 52, 53, 56, 57, 78,109
www.bcn.es/parcijardins

In the run-up to the Olympic Games, Barcelona underwent a frenzied urbanization renewal that resulted in the building of new public places and squares. The Parc de l'Espanya Industrial, directly behind Sants station, is the largest and most ambitious of these very Catalan hard squares. You are first struck by the park's odd-shaped boating lake, complete with rowing boats for rent. It is flanked by an amphitheatre-type seating area and 10 futuristic, lighthouse-style watchtowers. The rest of the park is also dotted with public sculptures, predominantly of the post-modern school, and towards the southern end of the park there is a more urban woodland feel.

PARC DE L'ESTACIÓ DEL NORD

🎫 57 J10 • Carrer de Napoles 70, 08018 🕐 Daily 10–dusk 💲 Free
🚇 Arc de Triomf or Marina 🚌 6, 10, 19, 39, 40, 41, 42, 51, 54, 55, 141
www.bcn.es/parcijardins

The Parc de l'Estació del Nord, completed in 1999, is one of Barcelona prettiest parks. It is a very busy place not just because of this, but also as it is beside the Estació del Nord, the city's main terminal for national and international bus services. Travel links are also maintained through the land's original use as a railway station. The entire park is covered in lawn, which is unusual for Barcelona. Various undulating levels give the space a fluid air, heightened by two works by the US-born sculptress Beverly Pepper. The ceramic works *Fallen Sky* and *Wooded Spiral* have been placed into the lawns, forming an integral part of the landscape. The only other vegetation is a small group of trees and this restraint, seen in all the park's elements, has made this one of the most delicate public spaces in the city.

PARC DE JOAN MIRÓ

🎫 56 D9 • Carrer d'Aragó 1, 08026 🕐 Daily 10–dusk 💲 Free 🚇 Espanya
🚌 9, 13, 27, 30, 38 and all routes to Plaça d'Espanya
www.bcn.es/parcijardins

The Parc de L'Escorxador, more commonly known as the Parc Joan Miró, was the first of a series of public parks to be built in locations made obsolete by their previous use, in this case the city's slaughterhouse or *escorxador*. Designed by a group of local architects, the park looks decidedly barren on first approach. The towering sculpture *Dona i Ocell* (Woman and Bird) by Miró (1893–1983) is its focal point, and for many is the only thing worth closer inspection. But a change of mindset is needed here. The main purpose of these areas is to provide light and space for a population that lives in the second-most condensed city in the world. Palm trees are used to create avenues on the hard concrete surface, and glimpses of the adjoining bullring, Las Arenas, through the vegetation lend the space a Mediterranean air. It's one of the few city parks where dog-walking is encouraged, and the children's play area makes it very appealing to its immediate neighbours seeking out a tranquil spot at the end of a busy day.

The sculpture Dona i Ocell *at the Parc de Joan Miró*

Park Güell

**One of Gaudí's best-loved contributions to Barcelona, contrasting natural forms with his trademark tile work.
A playful, whimsical, fairy-tale park covering 15ha (37 acres).
Fresh air, woodland walks and views over the city.**

The serpentine bench is the focal point of the park

One of the gatehouses at the main entrance

Porticoed walkways made of material found at the site

RATINGS	
Good for kids	●●●●●
Photo stops	●●●●●
Value for money	●●●●●
Walkability	●●●●○

TIPS

● If there is a line of people outside the Casa-Museu Gaudí, don't even attempt to go inside. The rooms are too small to get a good view of the contents if the place is crowded.

● Visit the organic interior of the gatehouse on the right, which is occasionally open for temporary exhibitions.

● After your visit, take a walk along the wall on Carrer d'Olot—it has a fabulous ceramic frieze with shields bearing the park's name.

● Remember that the bus No. 24 is the only bus that drops you directly outside at the side entrance. The others, plus the nearest metro station, are about a 10- to 15-minute walk to the park.

Sala Hipóstila is also known as the Hall of 100 Columns, even though there are only 86 (right)

SEEING PARK GÜELL

The park is laid out on the slopes of the unpromisingly named Mont Pelat (bare mountain). The best approach is via the main entrance on Carrer d'Olot, though this does involve a steep walk up from the nearest bus stops on Carrer Mare de Déu de la Salut. Alternatively, bus No. 24 drops you outside the side entrance to the park on Carretera de Carmel. Although the main sights can be easily seen in a visit of one to two hours, it is best to allow at least half a day. Take a picnic and take your time exploring the network of paths, soaking up the sun or sitting in the shade. The park tends to get very crowded in summer and at weekends.

HIGHLIGHTS

THE ENTRANCE

The entrance gate on Carrer d'Olot sets the tone for the entire park. Here is a wrought-iron gate vaguely reminiscent of palm leaves, flanked by a pair of gatehouses that come straight out of a children's fairy tale. In fact they were based on Antoni Gaudí's (1852–1926) designs and were inspired by the story of Hansel and Gretel. The one on the right, topped by a mushroom, is the house of the witch; on the left, surmounted by a double cross on the roof, is the children's house. Both houses are almost totally covered in *trencadís* (see page 113). From here, a double stairway leads past a fountain adorned with the Catalan shield towards a large salamander, also covered in *trencadís*. This well-loved creature has become an instantly recognizable symbol of the park and there is usually a line to have your photograph taken alongside it. Behind the salamander is a covered bench in the form of an open mouth. The staircase continues to the Sala Hipóstila (hypostyle, where a roof is supported by pillars). It was designed as a covered market place with kaleidoscopic patterns of glass and mosaic set into the ceiling in the shape of suns and moons.

THE SQUARE

Two further flights of steps on either side of the hall lead up to the focal point of the park, the main square surrounded by a serpentine bench. This wave-like, sinuous bench, attributed to Gaudí's assistant

The main staircase, overlooked by the market place, is a good photo stop (top); the spire at one of the gatehouses is 16m (52ft) and is said to represent the childrens' house in the Hansel and Gretel story (above); the boundary wall carries mosaics of the words Park and Güell (right)

Josep Maria Jujol, is both a riot of colour and a giant jigsaw puzzle pieced together out of shards of broken ceramics. Its shape is thought to resemble a protective dragon watching over the park. With its palm trees and terrace café, this is undoubtedly the most social area of the park, and the ceramic bench is an attractive spot to soak up the afternoon sun and the sweeping views over the city. As with so much of Gaudí's work, the square combines fantasy with function. The surface of covered sand was designed to filter the rainwater into an underground reservoir through the columns of the market place below.

CASA MUSEU GAUDÍ

The house in which Gaudí lived between 1906–26, leaving just before his death, has been turned into a museum. Designed by Gaudí's assistant Francesc Berenguer, this was the first home to be built on the site and it was used as a show home to attract prospective investors (see Background). Among the exhibits are furniture and mirrors from the Gaudí-designed houses of Casa Batlló (see page 82), Casa Milà (see pages 66–69) and Palau Güell (see page 103), along with Gaudí's wardrobe, bed and personal possessions.

THE WALKS

Park Güell contains more than 3km (2 miles) of woodland paths, together with viaducts and porticoes weaving their way through plantations of palm trees and Mediterranean pines. There are arches and slanting columns leaning into the hillside, giving the impression of a series of natural caves. In contrast to the bright gatehouses and

BASICS

✚ 282 H5 • Carrer d'Olot s/n, 08014

☎ Casa-Museu Gaudí: 93 219 38 11

🕐 Park: daily 10–dusk; Casa-Museu Gaudí: daily 10–8, Apr–end Sep; 10–6, rest of year

💶 Park free. Casa-Museu Gaudí: adult €4, child (under 10) free

Ⓜ Lesseps

🚌 24, 25, 28, 31, 32, 74, 87

🎧 Guided tours by appointment (tel 93 319 02 22) in Spanish, Catalan, French and English for €75 (price for the tour). Mobile phone tours in English on 629 003999 (mobile phones for rent at the information points €3, or use your own mobile phone; calls cost €0.18 per minute)

📙 Very pretty pictorial guidebook available at the main gift shop, in Dutch, German, Japanese, French, Italian, Spanish, Catalan and English for €10

🍴 Terrace restaurant overlooking the main square

🍫 At the entrance, selling a basic range of snacks

🏬 Shop at main entrance selling post-cards, slides and guidebooks; smaller shop selling the same in the Casa-Museu Gaudí

🚻 At the main entrance

www.rutamodernisme.com
It is unfortunate that such an important place doesn't have its own official website, but this one has some useful background.

ceramic bench, these effects were deliberately designed by Gaudí in monochrome stone, so that without looking carefully it is sometimes difficult to tell what is natural and what is man-made. For an energetic walk, take the path to the group of three crosses that marks the summit of the park.

BACKGROUND

Park Güell was commissioned in 1900 by Gaudí's patron, Count Eusebi Güell. It was originally conceived as an English-style garden city (hence the use of the English spelling of park), a residential estate surrounded by gardens, which would provide a retreat for the wealthy. In the event, the project was not a success. The plan was to build 60 houses, but only three appeared before work was interrupted by the outbreak of World War I in 1914: One is now the Museu Gaudí, one a school and the third is still a private residence. Güell died in 1918, and four years later the unfinished estate was taken over by the city of Barcelona as a municipal park. The Count's loss was undoubtedly Barcelona's gain as this has become one of the most attractive places for the people of Barcelona to spend their spare time.

TRENCADÍS

The method of piecing together broken pieces of pottery and glass to form an abstract mosaic is known in Catalan as *trencadís*, a technique thought to be the earliest example of collage. *Trencadís* can be found in many of Gaudí's works; it was here at Park Güell that the technique achieved its fullest expression. Nobody knows whether Gaudí discovered the technique by accident or if it was planned, but while working on Park Güell he became so obsessed with the idea that he ordered his workmen to scour local building sites in order to salvage any broken bottles, plates or tiles. There are also reports of bemused passers-by watching as workmen took delivery of brand-new tiles and smashed them up in front of their eyes.

The maze at the Parc del Laberint

You'll see a host of unusual animals at Parc Zoològic

Pavelló Mies van der Rohe has become a modern classic

PARC DEL LABERINT

⊞ 283 L2 • Passeig dels Castanyers s/n, 08035 ☎ 93 428 39 34 ⏰ Daily 10–dusk 💶 Adult €1.85, child (under 6) free; Wed and Sun free to all 🚇 Mundet 🚌 27, 60, 73, 76, 85

The park is the oldest in the city and gets its name from the maze at its heart. Cultivated in the 18th century and fully restored 200 years later when it was acquired by the local council, it is laid out over three levels in 9ha (22 acres) with swooping terraces in the style of grand Italian gardens such as Rome's Villa Borghese. On the upper terrace there is an elegant pond that acts as the park's watering system and the lower terrace holds the small cypress labyrinth, the park's main attraction. The foliage itself is less formal, consisting mainly of natural pine forest, and the garden is replete with nooks and crannies, statues, Italianate balustrades and pagodas, making it one of the more private—and therefore romantic—parks in the city. Families have a great time here too, as children love the maze and there are a couple of play areas, allowing the adults the opportunity to sit back and breathe in the pine-scented air.

PARC ZOOLÒGIC

⊞ 57 H12 • Parc de la Ciutadella s/n, 08003 ☎ 93 225 67 80 ⏰ Daily 9.30–7.30, May–end Aug; 10–7, Apr and Sep; 10–6, Mar and Oct; 10–5, rest of year 💶 Adult €12.50, child (3–12) €8, child (under 3) free 🚇 Arc de Triomf, Barceloneta 🚌 14, 39, 41, 42 🍴 🚻 www.zoobarcelona.com

The Parc Zoològic is set over 13ha (32 acres) of parkland on the eastern side of Parc de la Ciutadella. More than 400 species live at the zoo, but without a doubt its reputation lies in the primates section. Most of the primates here are in danger of extinction, most notably the Bornean orangutans and the mangabeys, the world's smallest monkey. Other fast-disappearing forms of animal life found at the zoo include the Iberian wolf and various big cats like the magnificent snow leopard from Central Asia. The Doñana Aviary is helping to repopulate Spain's diminishing bird life by breeding night herons, spoonbills and ducks from the southern marshlands of the same name. The zoo is due to move to a larger site in 2005, so this could be your last chance to see it in its historic setting, which was inaugurated for the Universal Exhibition of 1888.

PARK GÜELL

See pages 110–113.

PASSEIG DE GRÀCIA

⊞ 57 G8 🚇 Passeig de Gràcia or Diagonal

Two of Gaudí's most famous buildings and the city's most exclusive shops are to be found along the Passeig de Gràcia, the most well-known road in Barcelona after Las Ramblas. Originally a dirt road that connected the nearby village of Gràcia, it immediately became a popular strolling boulevard for the city's chattering classes who enjoyed the open-air café on the corner of the Gran Via. At that time here were fields and stretches of country on either side, but as the Modernista movement got under way it became a showcase for the architects of the period. It is home to Gaudí's Casa Milà (see pages 66–69) and the Manzana de la Discordia (see pages 82–83). The dozens of city blocks surrounding the Passeig are collectively known as the Quadrat d'Or (Golden Square, see page 76) after the large number of Modernista apartments here, which is the highest concentration of this period of architecture anywhere in the world.

PAVELLÓ MIES VAN DER ROHE

⊞ 56 C10 • Avinguda del Marquès de Comillas s/n, 08038 ☎ 93 423 40 16 ⏰ Daily 10–8 💶 Adult €3.40, child (under 18) free 🚇 Espanya 🚌 13, 27, 30, 37, 50, 56, 57, 61 and all routes to Plaça d'Espanya 🚉 www.miesbcn.com

This pavilion was built by Ludwig Mies van der Rohe (1886–1969), one of the masters of modern architecture. While other architects were busy imitating Spanish baroque and Renaissance styles for the 1929 World Exhibition at Montjuïc, Mies van der Rohe built what was to become a classic of the international style. It is a key work in the development of functional architecture, with clean lines and austere interiors, using a diverse range of materials: travertine, marble, onyx, chrome and glass. This was one of Mies van der Rohe's last works before he emigrated to the United States and most critics consider it to be one of his best, remaining as a point of reference in 20th-century European architecture. Mies van der Rohe also designed a chair for his project, the Barcelona Chair, reproductions of which are sold in the city's top designer stores. The pavilion was dismantled after the exhibition and spent some time occupying an outer suburban plot. In the early 1980s, prominent architect and urban planner Oriol Bohigas started a campaign to have it moved back to its original site, which is where it now stands, exuding a tranquillity that brings relief from the exuberance of the city's Modernista buildings.

Plaça d'Espanya, seen through the lights of the Magic Fountain

Shop fronts in the Plaça del Rei take on the style of the square

The pretty central fountain at Plaça Reial

PLAÇA DE CATALUNYA

➕ 54 G10 🅜 Catalunya

This is the hub of the city, the equivalent of London's Piccadilly Circus or New York's Times Square. Even if you don't plan on going there, chances are you'll cross its paved surface at some point, possibly to have a drink at its celebrated Café Zurich (see page 167). In addition to holding the largest of the El Corte Inglés department stores in Barcelona, the shopping complex El Triangle, and the largest tourist office, it is also the principal transport stop-off. You can catch a bus or train connection to anywhere in town, including the airport.

Architecturally the square has lost a lot over the years through alterations to accommodate traffic and public transport. Built in 1927 by architect Francesc Nabot, its original 50,000sq m (538,213sq ft) have been somewhat reduced and are now populated by balloon and pigeon-seed sellers, students relaxing on its lawns in front of the fountain and shoppers taking a breather on one of its many benches. The statue on the Las Ramblas side is a homage to Francesc Macià, the first president of Catalonia's autonomous government, the Generalitat.

PLAÇA D'ESPANYA

➕ 56 C9 🅜 Magic Fountain displays: Thu–Sun every half-hour from 9.30pm–midnight, Jun–end Sep; Fri–Sun every half-hour from 7pm–9pm, rest of year 🎟 Free 🅜 Espanya 🚌 27, 30, 37, 50, 56, 57, 62, 65 and all routes to Plaça d'Espanya

The Plaça d'Espanya is another of Barcelona's principal thoroughfares and landmarks. Originally the access point for the 1929 Universal Exhibition, the square is now a busy roundabout (traffic circle). The Plaça d'Espanya is

the best way to approach Montjuïc, and its museums all lie within a short walk. The two mock-Venetian bell towers mark the entrance of the two trade-show halls, the biggest and busiest in Spain. On the opposite side, the now-disused bullring Las Arenas, where the Beatles played in 1966, awaits its fate, but it seems likely to be a shopping arcade. In the middle of the roundabout (traffic circle), a classical Italianate fountain by Gaudí's protégé Josep Maria Jujol watches over the constant stream of traffic.

The main attraction in the immediate area itself is undoubtedly the Font Màgica (Magic Fountain): a sound, light and water spectacle. The spouting, illuminated water dances to a mixture of pop and opera classics, but almost always including the Olympic tune Barcelona, belted out by the late Freddie Mercury and the Catalan opera diva Montserrat Caballé. The Magic Fountain also co-stars with gigantic fireworks displays in the city's festivals of luz y agua (light and water) put on for grand occasions and events.

PLAÇA DEL REI

➕ 55 G11 🅜 Jaume I 🚌 17, 19, 45

Flanked by the Palau Reial (Royal Palace), which houses the fascinating Conjunt Monumental de la Plaça del Rei (see page 75), this is one of the most architecturally complete of Barcelona's medieval squares, and has one of the most interesting histories. The 14th- to 16th-century buildings, with the palace and magnificent Saló del Tinell (banqueting chamber), were once the headquarters of the Catholic Monarchs Ferdinand and Isabella. The mid-16th-century Mirador del Rei on the left was used as a watchtower, and Palau de

Lloctinent in front of it was the official home of the viceroy after Catalonia lost its independence in the 16th century. The Basque sculptor Eduardo Chillida's (1924–2002) 1986 work Topo is the square's only reference to modernity. The severe half-cube in metal, with arches protruding from one side, somehow manages to blend in beautifully with the rich stone of the palaces.

The paved square once rang with the comings and goings of official visitors as well as buyers and sellers of flour and hay. It is now frequently used as an open-air stage for music concerts during the Grec and La Mercè festivals, and there is no nicer place in the city to enjoy a drink alfresco.

PLAÇA REIAL

➕ 54 F11 🅜 Liceu or Drassanes
🚌 14, 17, 19, 38, 40, 45, 59, 91

The bars that line the Plaça Reial's generous diameter are a magnet for both locals and visitors on balmy summer nights. During the day, however, the square has a slower pace, which means its architecture can be more easily appreciated. A Capuchin convent was demolished to make way for the square that was designed in the 1840s by Daniel Molina, who was also responsible for the city's market La Boqueria. It was one of the larger projects in Barcelona's urban renewal project of the 1880s and it is still the only one in Barcelona that was designed as a complete unit, including the housing, the porticoes and the central fountain, inspired by the Three Graces, and the Gaudí-designed lampposts. The overall feel is one of tranquillity and elegance. Because of concerns about petty crime, it is best to have your wits about you when visiting in the evening.

Plaça de Sant Jaume

The political hub of Barcelona, where all major decisions about
the running of Barcelona and Catalonia are made.
A grand square in the heart of the city,
used for social and political gatherings.

SEEING THE PLAÇA DE SANT JAUME

This generous square, halfway between Las Ramblas and Via
Laietana, is flanked on either side by the Casa de la Ciutat
(the city's town hall, or Ajuntament) and the Palau de la
Generalitat (the seat of the autonomous government). Public
entry to both is restricted, but the expanse of flagstones between
the two is a major stage for many public-participation events.
The Barça soccer team greets ecstatic crowds from the Casa
de la Ciutat's balcony after a major win, and two great Catalan
folk traditions—*castellers* (human towers) and the sardana
(a group dance)—are played out here on weekends and public
holidays. Whenever there is a demonstration, people generally
start off or finish at the Plaça de Sant Jaume to make their
voices heard by the politicians who can make a difference to
their cause.

HIGHLIGHTS

PALAU DE LA GENERALITAT
☎ 93 402 46 17 ◷ 10.30–1.30, second and fourth Sun of each month, and
23 Apr, 11 and 24 Sep ▣ Free
The Generalitat is both the name of Catalonia's autonomous government and the building from which it governs. One hundred and
fifteen presidents of Catalonia have so far ruled from its beautiful
Gothic interior, making it one of the few medieval buildings in Europe
that has been continually used for the same purpose for which it was
built. Its rather austere façade hides a wealth of interior lushness, only
a minor part of which is accessible to the public, but visit if you can.
When the president of the Generalitat is in town, he stays at the Casa
dels Canonges, a set of 14th-century canons' houses next door to the
Palau. The hanging enclosed walkway, which joins the two buildings,
was modelled on Venice's Bridge of Sighs, but dates from the 1920s.

The Courtyard
The main highlight comes as soon as you enter: the spectacular Pati
de Tarongers (Courtyard of the Oranges), a luscious interior stone
courtyard dotted with orange trees, with a central sculpture of St.
George (or Jordi in Catalan), the region's patron saint and a recurring
image throughout the Generalitat. The pink marble columns are
topped with gargoyles, each of them with special significance to the
history of Catalonia: The Turk's head is a reminder of the scourge of
pirates that once roamed the Mediterranean, and the Macer was in
charge of keeping the peace during rowdy parliamentary sessions.

The Interior
The flamboyant Capella de Sant Jordi, a private chapel with a mainly
red interior and embellished with 15th-century Gothic details, follows
on from the courtyard. It has a giant stained-glass window and a silver
embossed altar both showing St. George and his fearful dragon. The
magnificent Flemish tapestries were woven in the mid-17th century
and tell the story of Noah and the Ark. The splendid Saló de Sant
Jordi, glimpses of which are possible from the Generalitat's main

RATINGS	
Good for kids	●●
Historic interest	●●●
Photo stops	●●
Value for money	●●●●

BASICS

✚ 54 G11

Tourist office information
Carrer Ciutat 2 (inside the town hall),
08002 ☎ 90 630 12 82 ◷ Mon–Fri
9–8, Sat 10–8, Sun 10–2
www.barcelonaturisme.com

◉ Jaume I ▣ 16, 17, 19, 45

*A statue of St. George (Sant
Jordi) sits in a niche above the
entrance to the Generalitat
(above)*

The classical façade of the Casa de la Ciutat was added in the 1840s (above)

entrance, has a sumptuous domed ceiling. It has three naves separated by giant pillars, and the walls are covered in modern murals of key historical events. A huge chandelier crowns the room, giving this rather solemn civil space a touch of grandeur.

CASA DE LA CIUTAT

☎ 93 402 73 64 🕐 Sun 10–2 💶 Free

Across the road the Ajuntament (meaning both city hall and local council) also has its roots in the Middle Ages. The institution started out as the Consell de Cent, a representative council of 100 guild leaders and ordinary citizens that was one of the first truly democratic political bodies in the world. Although not as spectacular as the Generalitat, the classic early-1900s façade hides a Gothic interior with recent additions. The highlight is the Saló de les Croniques with murals by painter Josep Maria Sert, carried out in 1928. Sert went on to decorate New York's Rockefeller Center.

The square is used as a gathering place for political rallies (above) and more social ones, such as to dance the sardana (right)

Visitors can sit and relax in the archways of Poble Espanyol

Port Olímpic is part of Barceloneta, which was rejuvenated by the new marina and Hotel Arts

POBLE ESPANYOL

🏛 56 C10 • Avinguda del Marquès de Comillas s/n, 08038 ☎ 93 508 63 30 🕐 Mon 9–8, Tue–Thu 9–2, Fri–Sat 9am–4am, Sun 9–noon 💶 Adult €7, child (7–12) €3.60, child (under 7) free 🚇 Espanya 🚌 9, 13, 38, 50, 91, 100, 109 🍴 🛍 ♿
www.poble-espanyol.com

Where else would you get 115 examples of Spanish architecture in one place? The Poble Espanyol (Spanish Village) lying at the foot of Montjuïc was constructed for the 1929 International Exhibition and, curiously enough, its fake vintage buildings have now had enough time to look properly aged. The Poble also has its own community of artisans—both traditional and innovative—working away on textile painting, toy making, ceramics and other disciplines. Their goods are sold at the large, central craft market. The prestigious Massana design school also has its jewellery and engraving department inside the Poble Espanyol, further adding to its claim to be the City of Artisans.

Once you enter through the replica of the grand gateway to the walled city of Ávila and its huge Plaza Major, you'll find dozens of tiny streets laid out with architecture that includes white-washed Andalucían homes and the high-Gothic style of Burgos. From the typical hanging balconies of Galicia to the mansions of Castile, all of the 17 regional Spanish vernaculars are crammed into its 23,000sq m (247,578sq ft). At night the place is buzzing with dozens of bars, a couple of cabaret-restaurants (including one of the best flamenco shows in the city) and some of Barcelona's top clubs. During the Grec Festival, over the summer, the Poble's main square is used for outdoor concerts and every June it is overrun with modern music fans for the weekend-long rock festival Primavera Sound. Despite its obvious kitsch value, the Poble Espanyol is a pleasant way to spend an afternoon in the city. It's also a great place for children, with lots of wide spaces to let them loose in.
Don't miss The Monestir de Sant Miquel del Poble Espanyol, a mock-Romanesque monastery often chosen for weddings in the city.

PORT OLÍMPIC

🏛 57 J12 🚇 Ciutadella-Vila Olímpica 🚌 6, 14, 36, 41, 92, 141

The Port Olímpic and Vila Olímpica (Olympic Port and Village) are part of the heritage of the 1992 Games, and are the most visitor-friendly. The area also has one of the city's best beaches at Nova Icària. Dozens of old factories and warehouses were bulldozed to make way for the apartments used as athletes' accommodation during the Games, and before 1992 neither the marina nor the esplanade—nor even the sand on the beach itself—existed. The Olympic area now serves as both a smart residential district and a lively entertainment place. The port is the biggest attraction here, and the esplanade heading past the luxurious Hotel Arts complex is buzzing with seafood restaurants, bars and cafés and holds an outdoor market at the weekend. The development is very popular with residents and is largely credited with reversing the city's old reputation that it ignored the sea.
Don't miss The stunning metallic *Fish* by Frank Gehry, the architect responsible for Bilbao's Guggenheim Museum, in front of the Hotel Arts.

PORT VELL

🏛 55 G12 🚇 Barceloneta or Drassanes 🚌 14, 17, 19, 20, 36, 39, 40, 45, 51, 57, 59, 64

Port Vell is the perfect place for a stroll or to while away a couple of hours. A cross between a pleasure playground and a port, all sorts of indoor pursuits are available at the nearby entertainment mecca Maremagnum.
Port Vell is the second of Barcelona's two Olympic ports and perhaps no other single project changed the face of the city so

The Fish, *as seen from the Hotel Arts' swimming pool*

One of the many restaurants at Maremagnum, Port Vell

dramatically. Officially, it is the marina that sweeps along the length of the Passeig de Joan de Borbó from the end of Via Laietana all the way down to Barceloneta beach. It's here you will see the expensive boats and yachts moored. Colloquially the name also encompasses the vast pedestrianized Molls (wharves) d'Espanya and de Barcelona.

The wooden swing bridge Rambla del Mar, an extension of Las Ramblas, leads you to Maremagnum (see page 152), a vast entertainment complex with the city's aquarium (see page 62), an IMAX cinema and a conglomeration of bars, eateries and shops. To the right of this is the World Trade Center, or the wedding cake as it is locally known because of its huge white, round shape, and the terminal for the Balearic Ferries.

All these facilities mean that the place is constantly busy. Especially on the weekends, Port Vell is a hive of activity with people riding their bikes, dogwalkers and families going for a stroll. On Sundays there is a craft market on the northern side of Palau del Mar, a restored series of brick warehouses that now accommodates the Museu d'Història de Catalunya (see page 93). The area is also known for two of the city's most famous pieces of public art. The first is the unmissable *Barcelona Head*, carried out by US artist Roy Lichtenstein (1923–97), standing at the entrance of the marina. The second is the rather more subdued full-scale replica of the world's first steam-powered submarine invented by Catalan Narcís Monturiol (see page 33), on the Maremagnum side of the port.

LAS RAMBLAS

See pages 120–121.

EL RAVAL

Essential to get a true feel for inner-city life.

✚ 54 F11 ℹ Plaça de Catalunya 17, 08002, tel 90 630 12 82; daily 9–9 🚇 Catalunya or Liceu 🚌 24, 120 www.barcelonaturisme.com

RATINGS		
Photo stops	●●	
Shopping	●●●	
Walkability	●●●	

The largest district of Barcelona's old town is El Raval, the suburb, and many say it's the true Barcelona. It is divided into two distinct areas. North of the Carrer de L'Hospital is the somewhat gentrified *barri* that contains the MACBA (see pages 90–91). South of here, in the direction of the port, lies the Barri Chino, a warren of tiny streets whose fame is of a less salubrious kind.

THE BARRI'S DEVELOPMENT

The 1920s American journalist, Francesc Madrid, dubbed the area El Chino, or Chinatown, because it reminded him of the ganglands of San Francisco. These days the local council is tearing down entire apartment blocks to make a series of squares and to widen its dank streets. But its reputation still lingers, so if you are exploring this part of El Raval, keep an eye on your wallet. Farther north the ambitious townplanning projects for the area have borne fruit, particularly around the MACBA and the enormous Plaça dels Àngels. After its completion, it wasn't long before the surrounding streets started sprouting new bars, restaurants and galleries alongside the more traditional establishments selling *bacalao* (cod fish) and bed linen.

El Raval's major historic buildings include the Gothic Antic Hospital de la Santa Creu. The old chapel is now used as an occasional exhibition space, while the hospital itself houses the Catalan National Library. The latter is not open to the public, but the colonnaded cloister and garden is accessible to all. To complete your tour of the *barri*, stop for a drink at the Plaça Martorell, a lively meeting place for locals.

Urban renewal in El Raval incorporates street art (top, above right); Plaça dels Àngels is used for skateboarding (right)

Las Ramblas

No trip to the city is complete without seeing
Las Ramblas, considered to be its very heart.
The avenue, 1km (0.5 mile) long, is ideal for people-watching,
as it is a giant stage for anyone with a story to tell or a song to sing.

An aerial view of Las Ramblas from the port end

A detail from the Casa dels Paraigües

Living statues and mime artists perform along Las Ramblas

RATINGS	
Photo stops	● ● ●
Shopping	● ●
Value for money	● ● ● ● ●
Walkability	● ● ● ●

TIPS

● Watch your wallet and other belongings on Las Ramblas, as it is pickpocketing territory, and avoid the scams pulled on tourists with the balls under the cup and card tricks.

● Don't even try to drive down Las Ramblas in your car (the road runs either side of the pedestrianized walkway), as the traffic during the day is horrendous.

● There are plenty of places to eat on the central avenue, but they are aimed at tourists and it is likely to be more expensive to take a table outside rather than eating inside the establishment—check prices beforehand.

SEEING LAS RAMBLAS

It was described by the writer Somerset Maugham (1874–1965) as the most beautiful street in the world. Souvenir shops and fast-food joints are appearing along this tree-lined promenade at a worrying rate, but that has done nothing to deter its popularity among the city's residents. Las Ramblas is actually five streets in one, hence the plural vernacular, with Canaletes at the Plaça de Catalunya end stretching down to the port at the other.

HIGHLIGHTS

LA RAMBLA DE CANALETES

Die-hard Barça soccer fans gather here after a big win and sometimes there are thousands of wave-flagging, hymn-singing supporters. Canaletes is the 19th-century fountain here and legend has it that anyone who drinks from this water source will return to the city. There

Las Ramblas is a great place to people-watch

are ample public chairs to sit on at this part of the Ramblas, but they are not free. This is the only form of paid public seating in Barcelona and once you take a seat a ticket seller will come around and ask for a modest fee. Living statues are also seen along this stretch and are a good photo opportunity, as long as you remember to tip them.

LA RAMBLA DELS ESTUDIS

This section is named after the university that once stood here. It is also known as the Rambla dels Ocells (of the birds) because of the birds and other animals that are locked in cages and sold here. The Teatro Poliorama at No. 115, once the home of Catalonia's National Theatre Company, was the place where writer George Orwell (1903–50) took refuge from gunfire during the Spanish Civil War while in the service of the International Brigade.

A Modernista shopfront along the promenade

Flowers on display on La Rambla de les Flors

You can buy international newspapers from stands

LA RAMBLA DE LES FLORS

This is the prettiest part of the avenue, with dozens of flower sellers and their blazing displays. This is its colloquial name, as it is officially the Rambla de Sant Josep after the 16th-century convent that once stood here. The convent was torn down to make room for the Boqueria (see page 153), still the city's principal market. Opposite this is the bizarre Casa dels Paraigües (House of Umbrellas), on the site of an old umbrella shop, and with an umbrella-decorated façade. A giant mural laid on the street in 1976 by Joan Miró marks the Plaça de la Boqueria, the halfway point of the Rambla.

LA RAMBLA DELS CAPUTXINS

This is home to the city's opera house, the Liceu (see page 80). Opposite here is the Café de l'Opera (see page 166), one of the oldest cafés in the city, which still serves the post-performance opera crowd during the season with their wonderful hot chocolate.

LA RAMBLA DE SANTA MÒNICA

The next stretch is the threshold of Barcelona's port. There are dozens of portrait artists, advertising their talents through pictures pinned around their stands. The Teatre Principal (see page 164), on the right, is the oldest theatre in the city—it started out in 1603 as a modest wooden building for the theatrical arts.

BACKGROUND

The word *rambla* itself comes from the Arabic term *raml*, which means riverbed, and that is where Las Ramblas' origins lie. A filthy gully that ran along the medieval city walls was filled in at the end of the 1700s, and soon after cash-rich Catalans started to build their mansions along the city's newest and most fashionable address (see page 33). Since 1994 people have been able to continue their stroll across the sea. The wooden walkway, the Rambla del Mar, starts from the Passeig de Colóm and continues to the Maremagnum entertainment complex. It is dotted with benches from where you can admire the port, and it's the perfect way to finish a visit to the city's most famous street.

BASICS

✚ 54 F10

Tourist information office
Plaça de Catalunya 17, 08002
☎ 90 630 12 82 🕐 Daily 9–9
www.barcelonaturisme.com

🚇 Catalunya, Liceu or Drassanes

The drinking fountain on La Rambla de Canaletes; people from other parts of Spain refer to the residents of Barcelona as those who drink from Canaletes

LA RIBERA

One of the city's most fashionable areas.

BASICS

✚ 55 G10

Tourist information office
Plaça de Sant Jaume, Carre Ciutat 2
(inside the town hall), 08002
☎ 90 630 12 82 🕐 Mon–Fri 9–8,
Sat 10–8, Sun 10–2
www.barcelonaturisme.com

Ⓜ Jaume I or Barceloneta

La Ribera is more commonly known as El Born after the *barri's* market, the Mercat del Born. It is a small district between the Via Laietana and Parc de la Ciutadella and it has changed dramatically in the past few years. It has been home to some of the larger museums, such as the Museu Picasso, for years, but fashion and design boutiques are springing up on an almost daily basis and it has a good number of the city's best private art galleries. Window shopping or having coffee at one of the many cafés has become the new Sunday pastime of the city's *gente guapa* (beautiful people).

A MERCANTILE PAST

Catalonia's trading history can be seen in a stroll around El Born. This was the city's trading area thanks to the old Mercat del Born, Barcelona's steel-and-glass ode to the industrial age, which was inspired by the former market at Les Halles in Paris. It was on the main thoroughfare, the Passeig del Born, and was the wholesale market until 1971. You will find that the street names around it proclaim the commercial activity that once went on there: Argenteria (silver) was lined with silversmiths, Flassaders (blanket) was were you popped in to get a woven-to-order blanket and Vidrieria (glassworks) was once lit up with glass-blowers' torches and ovens. Near the Plaça de Palau and La Llotja (the stock exchange), Canvis Vells would have once rung with the sound of nimble fingers weighing foreign coins on scales. The market is still the area's landmark, and the Passeig del Born connects it at the other end with the Gothic Santa Maria del Mar (see page 123): the Passeig was once the scene of public jousts.

The Estació de França near the Parc de la Ciutadella was built in 1848 to accommodate the first train line in Spain, to the outlying town of Mataró. With the trains now mostly using Sants station, the beautiful wrought-iron and marble structure has become more of a showpiece, where you can appreciate a time when train travel was a more elegant affair. But the area's charm lies in finding its small, hidden architectural gems. Its series of squares and streets, and the smell of freshly ground coffee and spices from the few wholesale outlets that remain in the area, are the true jewels of this *barri*.

THE SIGHTS

Inside the Casa Antigua, owned by the city's most celebrated of pastry-makers (below); Plaça de Santa Maria makes a great place for a drink (bottom); narrow streets in La Ribera will turn up hidden gems (right)

SANTA MARIA DEL MAR

The most beautiful church in Barcelona, as well as the most complete example of Catalan Gothic architecture in the city.

The Basílica de Santa Maria del Mar, to give it its full name, is in the heart of La Ribera. The funding for the building work came from the rich merchants of the area, collected in order to celebrate Catalonia's conquest of Sardinia, and the site was chosen as it was believed that Santa Eulàlia (the patron saint of Barcelona) was originally buried there. It is said that most of the able-bodied male workers in Barcelona were employed on the building work at one time or another over its 54-year construction period. The church was attacked during the Spanish Civil War (1936–39) and it was relieved of the adornments added over the years. Ironically, this act of vandalism has only added to the purity of style.

THE INTERIOR

The entrance remains the most highly embellished part of the church, but still in keeping within the formal aesthetic of the Catalan Gothic style, characterized by austerity, as well as sheer size. Inside, the central nave is 26m (85ft), the widest in Europe, and is flanked on either side by two aisles and the building's supporting columns. These soar up to a series of fan vaults—typical of the period—with a further set of eight at the far end of the church in a semicircle to define the presbytery. One decorative element that survived the attacks on the church during the war are the glorious stained-glass windows from the 15th to 19th centuries, which are placed on either side of its main walls, and in particular the enormous, opaque 15th-century rose window above the entrance.

The church's acoustics make it perfect for concerts and recitals, mainly of classical and religious music, which are held here during the year—ask at the tourist office for details. Santa Maria del Mar is also a popular place in Barcelona in which to get married. Pull up a chair in the square outside and watch the stream of petal-throwing wedding parties on Saturdays.

RATINGS

Historic interest	●●●○
Photo stops	●●●○
Value for money	●●●●●

TIPS

● Santa Maria del Mar is a functioning place of worship and it's not uncommon for the clergy to reprimand visitors whom they think are talking too loudly or showing disrespect. Silence is required, especially during Mass.

● The best days to move freely around the church are Monday to Thursday, when there are fewer ceremonies.

BASICS

✚ 55 G11 • Plaça de Santa Maria del Mar, 08003 ☎ 93 310 23 90
🕐 Daily 9–1.30, 4.30–8
💶 Free
Ⓜ Jaume I
🚌 16, 17, 19, 22, 39, 40, 45, 51, 59
📖 Small booklet available in Catalan, Spanish and English for €3
🍴 None, but a handful of cafés and restaurants outside the church

The elegant central nave of the Santa Maria del Mar (top left); stained-glass windows from the 15th century (top right)

La Sagrada Família

**Gaudí's extraordinary unfinished church is the symbol of Barcelona.
The culmination of Gaudí's eccentric genius, but still creating controversy
with an on-going building schedule using modern designs.
The highest of the dramatic towers is 112m (367ft).**

A small bridge links two of the towers

A Passion façade figure, inspired by the centurions of Casa Milà

A detail from the Nativity façade

SEEING LA SAGRADA FAMÍLIA

Love it or loathe it, you cannot ignore the Temple Expiatori de la Sagrada Família (Expiatory, or Atonement, Temple of the Holy Family). Its towers and cranes are visible from all over Barcelona and it is the one must-see sight on every itinerary. The drawback of this is that it can get very crowded, so it is best to come early or late in the day. Work on the Sagrada Família is progressing continually and what you see will depend on when you go. Entry to the interior is at the Passion façade on Carrer de Sardenya. After passing the gift shop on your left and the elevator to the towers on your right, you reach the central nave. This is still under construction and the whole area resembles a building site—the constant noise can act as a barrier to any notions of spirituality. Yet the sheer scale of the work will take your breath away. At first glance, the entire church looks like the work of a fevered imagination, but every detail of every spire, tower and column has its own precise religious symbolism, which is why the Sagrada Família has been called a catechism in stone.

HIGHLIGHTS

PASSION FAÇADE

The figures on the Passion façade, the first sight that confronts you, are harsh and angular, evoking the pain and humiliation of Christ's crucifixion and death. The Catalan sculptor Josep M. Subirachs (born 1927), who completed these figures in 1990 and still has a workshop on the site, has come in for much criticism, but Gaudí (1852–1926) always intended that this should be a bleak and barren counterpart to the joyful scenes of the Nativity. Six huge, leaning columns, like the trunks of uprooted trees, support a portico containing a series of sculptural groups depicting Christ's Passion and death, beginning with the Last Supper and ending with Christ on the Cross. The figures of Roman centurions are clearly influenced by Gaudí's chimneys on the roof of Casa Milà (see pages 66–69). Look for the Kiss of Death, a

TIPS

● Before you go in, take a walk around the exterior of the building and cross Carrer de la Marina to reach Plaça Gaudí, as the best views of the Nativity façade are from this small park.

● A five-minute walk up the Avinguda de Gaudí, towards the Hospital de Sant Pau, gives you a better view of the overall dimensions of the church.

● If you decide to use the audioguides, you will be asked to leave some identification (such as passport or driver's licence) as a deposit. If you don't have these on you, you may be asked for something of value instead, such as a credit card.

The main towers of the church, on which a prayer is spelled out, dominate views of the city (far left); a detail from the stark Passion façade (left)

The severe lines of the Passion façade face the setting sun,
reflecting the façade's theme (above); Judas' kiss in stone (right)

BASICS

✚ 57 J8 • Carrer de Mallorca 401,
08013

☎ 93 207 30 31

🕐 Daily 9–8, Apr–end Sep; daily 9–6,
Oct–end Mar; 9–2, 25–26 Dec, 1 and
6 Jan

💶 Adult €8, child (under 10) free;
combined ticket for entry to the Sagrada
Família and Casa-Museu Gaudí at Park
Güell, valid for one month €9; elevator
€2

🚇 Sagrada Família

🚌 19, 33, 34, 43, 44, 50, 51, 54

📻 Audiotours €3 in English, French,
Spanish or Catalan. Guided tours €3,
held daily in alternating languages
(some languages once a day only,
phone for details)

🛍 A large selection available in the gift
shop, ranging from €4 to €45

🍴 Food and snack machines only

🏛 Selling books about the church and
Gaudí, plus the usual assortment of gift
items with Sagrada Família imagery

🚻 At the entrance, with more throughout the site

www.sagradafamilia.org
An easy to follow site, in English, French
and Spanish, but much of it still under
construction.

sculpture showing Jesus' betrayal
by Judas, complete with a biblical
reference in stone (Mark 14:45).
The magic square next to it has
rows, columns, diagonals and
corners that all add up to 33. The
significance of this, according to
Subirachs, is that this was Christ's
age at the time of his death.

NATIVITY FAÇADE
This is the sculptural high point of the church that was begun in 1891
and completed during Gaudí's lifetime in 1904. The stone carvings on
the façade just drip with detail, so that at times it resembles a fairy
grotto, a hermit's cave or a jumble of molten wax. The theme of the
façade is the joy of creation at the birth of Jesus, and it deliberately
faces east to receive the first rays of the rising sun. The focal point is
the Nativity scene, and above the Holy Family are angels playing
trumpets and singing to celebrate Christ's birth. Three doorways,
dedicated to Faith, Hope and Charity, depict other biblical scenes,
from the marriage of Mary and Joseph to the presentation of Jesus
in the temple. At least 30 species of plants, native to both Catalonia
and the Holy Land, have been identified on the façade, along with
36 different species of birds, echoing the theme that all creation
worships Jesus. This theme reaches its climax in the Tree of Life, a
ceramic green cypress tree swarming with doves, which sits atop the
façade, nestling between the tall towers.

THE TOWERS
By the time Gaudí died, only one bell-tower had been completed,
but there are now four towers above each of the Nativity and Passion
façades. The final plans envisage a total of 18 towers, dedicated to
the 12 apostles, the four evangelists (or Gospel writers), Christ and
the Virgin Mary. The vast spires are clad in ceramic mosaics and have
been likened to everything from wine bottles to cigars, as well as to
the *castellets* (human towers) that are a feature of Catalan festivals.
Gaudí maintained that by looking at the towers, your gaze would be

Apse
(Crypt below)

Altar

CARRER DE PROVENÇA

CARRER DE MARINA

The Lady
Chapel

10

B

9

8

7

A 3
1 2
4

6

5

MAIN ENTRANCE

CARRER DE SARDENYA

CARRER DE MALLORCA

C

Key to floor plan

1   Main entrance
2   Information
3   Shop
4   Lift 1
5   Baptistery
6   Chapel of the Sacrament
7   Models
8   Lift 2
9   Stairs
10   Portal of the Rosary
A   Passion Façade
B   Nativity Façade
C   Glory Façade

Floor plan of La Sagrada Família (above left); building work in progress (above right); the joy of creation on the Nativity façade mixes with Modernista themes of nature (left); go a long way back to take in the whole building (below)

The central nave is filled with columns, intended to act as a forest, and each group has its own symbolic meaning

drawn upwards to heaven, transmitting the words of the prayer *Sanctus Sanctus Sanctus, Hosanna in Excelsis* (Holy, Holy, Holy, Glory to God in the Highest) which is spelled out in broken ceramic tiles at the top. Spiral staircases give access to the towers, and there is also an elevator at each end of the building that will take you most of the way—a good option is to take the elevator up and then descend by the stairs. Climbing the towers gives close-up views of the spires and also allows you to look down over the central nave. Another good vantage point is the footbridge linking two towers above the doorway of the Nativity façade.

THE CRYPT

The crypt, designed in neo-Gothic style by the original architect Francesc de Villar, is reached by an entrance to the right of the Passion façade and now contains a museum. Among the items on display are some of Gaudí's scale models and drawings—though most were destroyed during the Civil War—along with sketches and casts for the Passion façade by Subirachs. There is also a confessional box and a tenebrarium (a candleholder used during Holy Week), both designed by Gaudí. You can look into the workshop where artists are preparing plaster casts for the Glory façade. One of the chapels, dedicated to Our Lady of Carmen, contains Gaudí's simple stone tomb, inscribed in Latin *Antonius Gaudí Cornet, Reusensis*, a reference to his home town of Reus.

The museum in the crypt is an essential part of any visit, as the drawings and models help explain the church's history

BACKGROUND

It is something of an irony that a building widely perceived as a triumph of Moderisme, with all its extravagance, should have been conceived as a way of atoning for the sins of the modern city. The original idea for the temple came from Josep Bocabella, a bookseller and conservative Catholic who had founded the Associació Josefina, an organization that was dedicated to St. Joseph. The first architect, Francesc de Paula del Villar, envisaged a conventional Gothic-style church, but when Gaudí took over the project at the age of 32 he was given free rein and his fantasies were let loose. Despite the playfulness of his architecture,

A SAD END

On 7 June 1926, Gaudí was run down by a tram. He was taken to hospital but nobody recognized him because of his shabby clothes. When friends eventually discovered him in an iron cot in the public ward, they tried to arrange a private clinic, but Gaudí is reported to have refused, saying shortly before he died: 'My place is here with the poor'.

Gaudí was a deeply religious man. In his later years, he devoted himself totally to the Sagrada Família, living like a recluse in a hut on the site, refusing to draw a salary, wearing simple clothes, eating little food and begging passers-by and rich businessmen alike for money to allow work on the church to continue. In 1936, 10 years after Gaudí's death, his plans for the Sagrada Família were destroyed in an anarchist riot, so it is impossible to be certain what the finished building would have looked like. However, despite widespread opposition, work on the church resumed in 1952 and it has now taken on an unstoppable momentum, fuelled by massive worldwide interest and financed by public subscription and the money from entrance fees. The current plan is to complete the temple by 2026 in time for the centenary of Gaudí's death.

BAD TASTE

Not everyone is impressed by the Sagrada Família. 'I think the anarchists showed bad taste in not blowing it up when they had the chance,' wrote the English novelist George Orwell in *Homage to Catalonia* (1938), his account of the Spanish Civil War.

The cloister is dedicated to the Virgin Mary (below)

La Sagrada Família forms a stunning backdrop to a drink

A CHANGING CHURCH

It is envisaged that the nave will have five aisles, divided by a forest of pillars. Work has already begun on four massive stone columns designed to support the central spire, which will be 170m (558ft) high and topped by a cross, making the Sagrada Família the tallest building in Barcelona. Around the spire will be four more towers, dedicated to the evangelists and topped with the symbols of an angel, an ox, an eagle and a lion. Standing in the nave, look left to see Gaudí's altar canopy and the neo-Gothic wall of the apse; to the right, work has begun on the Glory façade, which will eventually be the church's main entrance, together with four more towers. Straight ahead, across the transept, a doorway leads outside for a close-up look at the Nativity façade. The plans envisage that the entire church will one day be surrounded by an ambulatory, or external cloister. Despite all the construction work, the completion of the church seems a long way off, but as Gaudí himself said: 'My client is in no hurry'.

The exterior of the church of Sant Pau del Camp

The Ferris wheel at the Parc d'Atraccions on Tibidabo

The torre, watched over by a rooftop statue

SANTA MARIA DEL PÍ

⊞ 54 F11 • Plaça del Pí 7, 08002
☎ 93 318 47 43 ⏰ Daily 9–1, 4–9
🎫 Free 🚇 Liceu 🚌 14, 18, 38, 59

The squat and imposing Santa Maria del Pí is a fine example of the single nave church, typical of the austere Catalan Gothic style from around the 1300s. The nave spans 16m (54ft) or roughly one third of its entire length and, like other churches of the period, there are no aisles, rather one giant space that unfolds around you. There are 14 chapels in all, set between the buttresses, but even these do nothing to deter from the dominating spatial clarity. A rose window sits over the entrance to the church, filling it with light, and an ingenious stone arch spanning the church's entire width has supported its choir stalls for centuries. The church's surroundings are perfect for a pit stop or to while away a lazy hour or so people-watching, as it is in one of the most picturesque pockets of the Barri Gòtic.

SANT PAU DEL CAMP

⊞ 56 E11 • Carrer de Sant Pau 99, 08001 ☎ 93 441 00 01 ⏰ Mon–Fri 6pm–7.45pm; Sun Mass: 10.30, 12.30, 8
🎫 Free 🚇 Paral.lel 🚌 36, 57, 64, 91

This is Barcelona's oldest church, founded in AD911, and the only example of Romanesque architecture that remains in the city. Its name (St. Paul of the Countryside) came from its location, as this site, now part of the inner city, was in fields outside the city walls. Sant Pau del Camp is smaller than other churches from the same era, but its period details are remarkably intact. Inside, the layout imitates a Latin cross with three apses, a dome and the delicious 12th-century cloister. The western door has some Visigothic columns and a serene arch showing Christ surrounded by St. Peter and St. Paul. Guifré Borrell, the church's founder and the son of Wilfred the Hairy (see page 26), is buried here.

TIBIDABO

⊞ 282 F1 • Plaça del Tibidabo, 08035
☎ 93 211 79 42 ⏰ Mon–Thu noon–10, Fri–Sun noon–11, Jul–end Aug; Mon–Fri noon–8, Sat–Sun noon–9, Jun and Sep; Sat–Sun 12–7, Mar–end May, Oct; Sat–Sun 12–6, Nov–end Feb 🎫 Adult €22, child under 1.10m (3.6ft) €9, ticket for 6 rides €10 🚇 FGC to Peu de Funicular, then funicular; bus or FGC to Avenida Tibidabo, then Tramvia Blau, then funicular (only operates opening days of fun park) 🚌 17, 60, 73, T2 🍴

Tibidabo, the highest point of the Collserola hills, dominates the city's backdrop and also serves as a handy geographic indicator: Locals often refer to a building being on the sea or mountain side of the street. At night, the church, the Sagrado Corazón, and the statue of Christ by Frederic Marès (1893–1991) are lit up and can be seen from around the city. Most people, however, wind up its steep ascent for more earthly pleasures. The Parc d'Atraccions is the only amusement park in the city and has spectacular views. Some of its rides and attractions date back to the beginnings of the 20th century and one of the oldest is the charming L'Avio, a replica of the first plane that flew the Barcelona–Madrid route. Visitors are treated to a whisk over the peak of Tibidabo while being safely suspended from a central axis. More hair-raising fun is to be had from the Krüeger Hotel and the roller-coaster. The journey to Tibidabo is part of the attraction—the 100-year-old Tramvia Blau (blue tram) rattles up from the train station to the beginning of the summit, and from there you make the rest of the trip in a high-speed funicular.

TORRE DE COLLSEROLA

⊞ 281 E1 • Carretera de Vallvidrera al Tibidabo s/n, 08017 ☎ 93 406 93 54; park 93 280 35 52 ⏰ Daily 11–8 Jun–end Sep; daily 11–7 Apr–end May, Oct; Wed–Sun 11–6, Nov–end Mar 🎫 Adult €4.40, child (7–14) €3.10, child (under 7) free 🚇 FGC to Peu de Funicular, then funicular de Vallvidrera, then No. 211 bus 🚌 www.torredecollserola.com

The British architect Sir Norman Foster has left his mark on Barcelona in the form of a telecommunications tower, which stands at 288m (945ft), on the Collserola hills, 488m (1600ft) above sea level. The main attraction of the tower (torre) lies in the mirador, the lookout point that has some fantastic views of the city, Montserrat and, on a clear day, the Pyrenees. After passing through a tunnel and café-restaurant, the space-age glass lift whisks you up to the top in less than two minutes, leaving you free to contemplate the amazing 360-degree vista.

The tower itself is set in the Collserola National Park, a rambling 8,000ha (19,760 acres) of Mediterranean forest abundant in bird and animal life. Its close proximity to the city centre and its easy walking and bicycle tracks make it a top Sunday destination for those looking for an alternative to the beach. The best way to take your bicycle up to Collserola is by train, hopping off at the station Baixador de Vallvidrera where there is an Information Office with maps and other information about the park. There is also a large number of picnic areas, some complete with barbecues to rent.

This chapter gives information on things to do in Barcelona, other than sightseeing. Shops and performance venues are shown on the maps at the beginning of each section.

What to Do

Shopping   132–154
Locator maps   132–135

Barcelona Shopping Areas
  Barri Gòtic   137
  La Ribera   138
  L'Eixample   139
  La Diagonal   140
Shopping Directory   141–154
Chain Store Chart   152–153

Performance   155–164
Locator maps   156–159

Cinemas   160
Classical Music,
  Dance and Opera   161
Contemporary Live Music   161–162
Theatres   162–164

Nightlife   165–170
Bars and Cafés   166–169
Clubs   169–170

Sports and Activities   171–176
Children's Barcelona   177–178
Festivals and Events   179–180

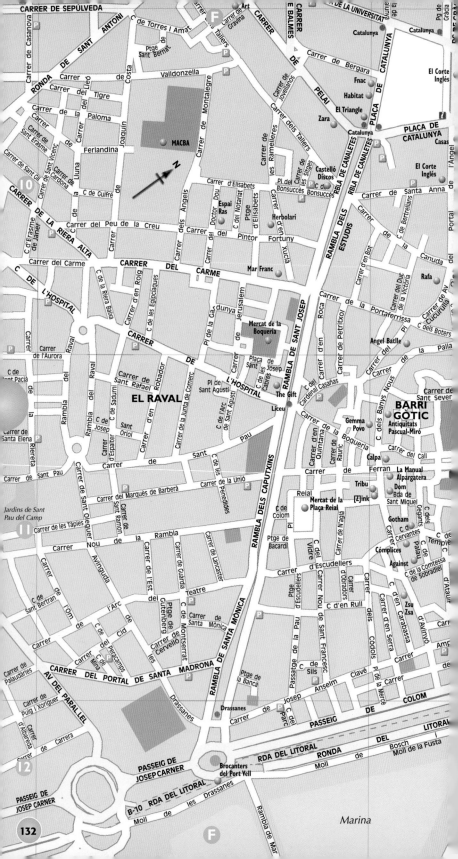

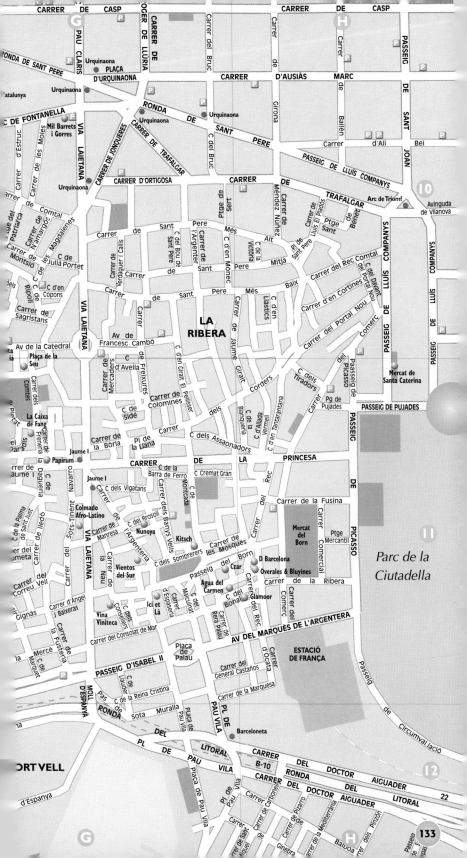

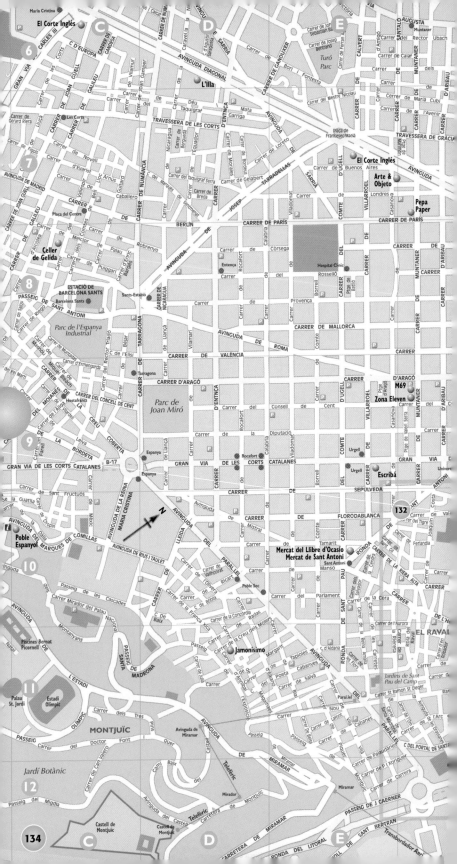

SHOPPING

Spain is good value for money, even if it's not as cheap as it used to be, and Barcelona is the country's top shopping destination. The city's retail make-up has changed dramatically over the past five years, with more and more stores selling imported and regional goods, which is a reflection of the city's budding multi-culturalism. But there are still plenty of home-grown products to hunt down.

shops are also good places to pick up trendy objets d'art and no true design junkie should miss out on Vinçon: the emporium that has launched many local designers (see page 151).

While it may be tempting to head to the malls and depart-ment stores, nothing compares to the experience of seeking out small, local establish-ments. Catalonia was once known as a nation of shop-keepers and this is how most residents still shop: small outlets with personal service. Nobody seems to mind

vacuum-packed (*envolver al vacío*) and once sealed they will keep for months. Most visitors reach for a Rioja, but wine from the Catalan regions of Penedès (the home of cava—a sparkling wine) and Priorat are gaining a good reputation among vinicultural-ists. Some of the larger stores (such as El Corte Inglés, see page 151) can arrange to have larger purchases shipped home. If you are planning to take your food item home with you, you should check customs regulations.

LEATHER
Spanish leatherwear is world famous and a bargain compared to Italian price tags. Shoes—many of them made on the Balearic island of Mallorca— are fabulous, both in

Many fashion stores are at the cutting edge of design

waiting for just the right cut of ham off the bone or a perfectly matching button. This sort of one to one contact is part of the experience for the visitor and all it takes is confidence in your communication skills.

FOOD
One of the best choices, either for yourself or as a gift, is food. Catalonia's cured pork travels and keeps extremely well. *Butifarras* (rich pork sausages), *fuet* (a type of salami) and other varieties are produced throughout the region but are particularly good from the city of Vic. Have your selections

terms of design and quality, particularly the Camper brand which is available everywhere. Leather coats and jackets are sold along Las Ramblas and while the selling technique may be a bit aggressive, a luxurious leather jacket at a bargain price is worth it.

DESIGN
Barcelona shines in the field of fashion and design. Young designers display their wares in tiny shops in the La Ribera district, in the streets around the MACBA (see pages 90–91) in El Raval and to a lesser extent in Gràcia. Museum

CRAFTS
Many objects can be picked up for a couple of euros. Basic beige and yellow ceramics from Catalonia's Costa Brava are inexpensive and plentiful, especially the everyday, fired terracotta *sarténs* (pans) that you will probably spot on your tapas bar visits. Reproduction Modernista tiles are a stunning

The wide range of food that is available in the city will making choosing difficult

asset to bathrooms and kitchens. The *alpargatara*, the Catalan espadrille (rope san-dal) usually have two-toned ribbons that wrap around the ankle, making stylish summer shoes. Most of these items can be picked up in souvenir shops, but they are likely to be mass produced, so try and seek them out in *barri* stores and markets.

SHOPPING AREAS
Pages 137–140 highlight areas in the city that are particularly good for shopping. The maps show stores that are in the shopping directory.

Barri Gòtic

HOW TO GET THERE
🚇 Liceu or Catalunya
🚌 14, 38, 59, 91

Barcelona's Barri Gòtic, the oldest part of the city, is a dense maze of shops, cafés and squares. You'll find antiques dealers, galleries and gourmet food stores side by side with boutiques and chains.

NORTH OF PLAÇA DEL PÍ

The tour begins at the corner of Las Ramblas and Carrer de la Portaferrisa. Portaferrisa is one of the city's busiest shopping streets, with its trendy stores, and you'll find a few originals, like El Mercadillo (No. 17), marked by a life-size camel statue and dedicated to punk fashion. Casa Colomina (No. 8), a family-owned store, serves creamy ice cream and *torrons*, the fudge-like treats

It's hard to miss the entrance to El Mercadillo

eaten at Christmas. Turn right on to Carrer de Petritxol, where you'll find more chocolatey temptations and several chic art galleries, like the sprawling Sala Parés (No. 5). The collections have a local feel and often sell landscapes of Catalonia and Barcelona. At the corner is the bookshop Llibreria Quera (No. 2), perfect for planning a camping or hiking trip in the region.

At the end of the street Carrer de Petritxol joins the picturesque Plaça del Pí. Try to come the first or third weekend of the month, when a mouth-watering artisan food

fair is set up in the square with tempting honeys, cheeses and home-made goodies. Antiga Pasamaneria J. Soler (No. 2) has been selling ribbons, tassels and cords since 1898, and the adjoining Plaça de Sant Josep Oriol has an art market every Saturday.

Several good shopping streets branch off the square and you can take a number routes. But take the Carrer de la Palla from the Plaça de Sant Josep Oriol, and next door to the Plaça del Pí you will come across an enticing concentration of antiques and curio shops. The oldest of these is at Galeria F. Cervera (No. 9), an archaeological gallery where an authentic headless Roman statue will cost you €70,000.

SOUTH OF PLAÇA DEL PÍ

Alternatively, take Carrer de l'Ave Maria out of the Plaça de Sant Josep Oriol. You'll meet up with Carrer dels Banys Nous, devoted to fashion and furniture shops. Gemma Povo (No. 5) sells chairs, beds, tables and lamps made with iron and Germanes Garcia (No. 15) has everything from furniture to hammocks made of wicker. At L'Arca de L'Àvia (No. 20), which translates as Granny's Treasure Chest, you will find lovely textiles including traditional Spanish shawls.

Carrer dels Banys Nous has an intersection with the Carrer del Call. On this corner is the old-fashioned hat shop Sombreria Obach (No. 2), the best place to find sombreros. There are other quirky shops

here, like Antiga Casa Sala (No. 8), selling beads, and La Celestial (No. 6), a fashion boutique on the site of the old Jewish synagogue. This street then turns into Carrer d'Avinyó, with lots of designer fashion, such as at [Z]ink (No. 14), Sita Murt (No. 18) and SO_DA (No. 24).

Antiga Pasamaneria is the place to go to for ribbon

WHERE TO EAT

BAR DEL PÍ
Plaça de Sant Josep Oriol 1, 08002
Tel 93 302 21 23
One of the oldest bars in town, with stunning views and tapas on the menu (see page 166).
🕐 Wed–Mon 9am–11pm

LA VERÓNICA
Carrer d'Avinyó 30, 08002
Tel 93 412 11 22
This pizzeria has good, well-priced food, making it an ideal spot for a salad and a pizza (see page 234).
🕐 Tue–Fri 7pm–1.30am, Sat–Sun 1pm–2am

La Ribera

HOW TO GET THERE

🚇 Jaume I

🚌 14, 39, 51 along Avinugda del Marquès de L'Argentera or 17 along Via Laietana

Chic shops abound in La Ribera. Designer objects, fashion and jewellery are the staples, but it's also a great place to pick up ceramics and foodstuffs.

The Plaça de Santa Maria del Mar is an obvious starting point. The eclectic design shop Ici Et Là (No. 2) is a vivid mix of highly unusual homeware and furniture from young, local designers. Next door La Botifarreria de Santa Maria (No. 4) is a well-known ham, sausage and cheese store that will pack your edibles for travel home. Further round on the Carrer de Santa Maria is Candela con Burundanga

La Botifarreria

(No. 6). Its stock of women's wear by young local designers is top class, with matching price tags.

On the Passeig del Born Rafa Teja Atelier (No. 18) is home to a sublime collection of wool and silk scarves and accessories from India, Asia and Spain. Across the road 37°C (No. 11) displays fine gold and silver jewellery and watches.

RIGHT OF PASSEIG DEL BORN

To your right off the Passeig del Born, the Carrer de Vidreria holds lots of surprises. Origins 99,9% (No. 6–8) stocks cava, cheese, olive oils and other food items from all over Catalonia and is good place to stop for a drink and snack. Anna Povo (No. 11) makes her own elegant and beautifully tailored women's clothes and knitwear. Vialis (No. 15) is one of the city's cult shoe brands, but the big draw is at the end of Carrer de Vidreria on Plaça de les Olles. Here you will find Custo's flagship store (No. 6) and their seriously cool printed T-shirts (see page 17).

From the Carrer de Vidreria, you can access a number of interesting shopping streets. Follow your nose down the tiny Carrer de l'Espaseria to the divine La Galeria de Santa Maria Novella (No. 4–8). These famed Florentine soaps, perfumes and body products in their 16th-century styled packaging will seduce your senses. This street, along with Bonaire and Rec, is a real fashion hub. Agua del Carmen (C. Bonaire, 5) is an own-label collection of fresh, young women's wear noted for unusual fabrics. Mechén Tomàs (C. Rec, 46) has a decidedly French look to its beautifully tailored coats, trousers and tops. MTX (C. Rec, 32) is more on the extravagant side with one-off, daring pieces suitable for that special evening. Giménez & Zuazo (C. Rec, 42) makes funky urban wear for Barcelona's bright young things and La Comercial Woman (C. Rec, 52) stocks beautifully detailed and highly feminine clothing and accessories from the likes of Cacharel, Paul&Joe and

Scooter, as well as Spain's own Jocomomola.

LEFT OF THE PASSEIG DEL BORN

This side of the Passeig is more concerned with dressing your home. Daaz (C. Flassaders, 27) is the brainchild of a French

Olives on sale in La Ribera

and Japanese pair of designers, with bright modular furniture and lamps. Re-Born (C. Flassaders, 23) is a mix of Cuban crafts and Venetian glass, with other flea market finds thrown in. The stunning Vitra (Pl. Comercial, 5) is hard to miss. The city's branch of this Swiss showroom has unique pieces of furniture by top names.

WHERE TO EAT

LITTLE ITALY
Carrer del Rec 30, 08003
Tel 93 319 79 73
A range of pasta, meat and fish dishes (see page 224).
🕐 Mon–Sat 1–4, 9pm–12.30am

The Plaça de Santa Maria del Mar area map showing:
- CARRER DE LA PRINCESA
- Barra de Ferro, C Cremat Gran
- Carrer de Flassaders
- Carrer de Rec
- Museu Picasso
- Museu Textil i d'Indumentària
- Museu Barbier-Mueller d'Art Precolombi
- Carrer de la Fusina
- Plaça Comercial
- Carrer Comercial
- C del Brosoli
- C dels Banys Vells
- Nunoya, Kitsch
- Carrer de les Mosques
- Vientos del Sur
- Santa Maria del Mar, Czar, D Barcelona Overales & Bluyines
- Agua del Carmen
- Glamoor
- Ici et Là
- Carrer de la Ribera
- AV DEL MARQUES DE L'ARGENTERA
- Plaça de Palau
- 0 100 m / 0 100 yds

L'Eixample

HOW TO GET THERE

🔲 Diagonal

🚌 7, 16, 17, 22, 24, 28

The Passeig de Gràcia, the area's main road, is often called Barcelona's Fifth Avenue and is home to the likes of Hermés (No. 33), Chanel (No. 70), Armani Collezioni (No. 68–72) and Carolina Herrera (No. 87). The streets around the Passeig are a shopper's paradise and even if you don't have much to spend, you are bound to find something to suit—or just enjoy the window shopping.

THE NORTHERN END
One of the city's most emblematic stores is right next to one of its most emblematic sights: Vinçon (No. 96, see page 151), selling the most chic of all designer household

Zara is one of the country's most popular clothing chains

gadgets, is beside the Casa Milà (see pages 66–69). For a little male pampering, visit Santa Eulalia (No. 93), a shop selling elegant tailor-made suits since 1843, and Iranzo (No. 100), an exclusive men's hair salon.

At the intersection with Carrer de Provença, take a left for Josep Font's opulent signature store (No. 304). He is one of Barcelona's most gifted designers and his creations are noted for their rich mix of fabrics.

Further down the Passeig de Gràcia, Roberto Verino (No. 68) sells his simple suits and

classic elegance at this tiny boutique beside the Hotel Majèstic. For even more Spanish design, turn right onto Carrer de València where you'll find the comfortable yet chic style of Camper (No. 249, see page 148) and Miró Jeans (No. 272), the informal branch of this well-known Catalan designer's line.

Bulevard Rosa (No. 55) is found off the Passeig de Gràcia, where there are lots of distinctive shops under one roof, like the gadget-filled Casa Claramunt (shop 51) and Zas Two (shop 55), whose motto, dress young, is borne out in its funky jeans, tops and international labels. Beside the Bulevard is the Centre Català d'Artesania (No. 55), selling glasswork, textiles and jewellery.

THE SOUTHERN END
For more jewellery designs, stop at Bagués Joieria (No. 41), housed in the Casa Amatller. This fine jeweller is known for avant-garde and elegant designs. Next door is Regia (No. 39), a perfume and cosmetics shop with a museum dedicated to perfume (see page 102).

Take another detour onto Carrer del Consell de Cent, the hub of Barcelona's art gallery district. Contemporary art reigns in most galleries, such as at Jordi Barnadas (No. 347), but you can find something older at Gothsland Galeria d'Art (No. 331), dealing in Catalan Modernista art.

Back on the Passeig de Gràcia the fashion continues, with Diesel (No. 19), plus the trend-following giants at Mango (No. 8–10) and Zara (No. 16).

PLAÇA DE CATALUNYA
If your feet and your wallet can handle it, head into Plaça de Catalunya, where you'll find branches of several of Spain's most important chains such as El Corte Inglés (No. 14). They sell everything: buy a blender, a wedding gown and an apartment all in the same mammoth store. El Triangle, a small mall, is also here. Inside, FNAC (No. 4) is the first stop

Bright shirts on sale in M69 in L'Eixample

for books and CDs. The chic perfume and cosmetics megastore Sephora (No. 13–39) is the place to match your face to your new outfit.

WHERE TO EAT

CERVECERIA CATALANA

Carrer de Mallorca 236, 08008

Tel 93 216 03 68

Great for a superb, hassle-free meal, as this *cerveceria* has the most spectacular tapas (see page 221).

🕐 Daily 9am–1.30am

Map labels:

AVINGUDA / DIAGONAL
Pilma
Rambla de Catalunya
Agatha
Them
Carrer del Rosselló
Passatge de la Concepció
Diagonal
Vinçon
F8
Riera
Carrer de Provença
G8
Hipótesis
Gastón y Daniela
CARRER DE MALLORCA
Joaquín Berao
Mango
El Bulevard dels Antiquaris
Camper
Bulevard Rosa
CARRER DE VALÈNCIA
Casa del Libro
Gaia
Passeig de Gràcia
CARRER D'ARAGÓ
Centre Català d'Artesania
Armand Basi
Antonio Miró
Loewe
Carrer del Consell de Cent
Adolfo Domínguez
Antonio Pernas
F9
Carrer de la Diputació
G9
Señor
Rambla de Catalunya
Passeig de Gràcia
Carrer de Pau Claris
GRAN VIA DE LES CORTS CATALANES
Altair
Laie
Carrer de Casp
Catalunya
El Corte Inglés
F10
Plaça de Catalunya
G10
FNAC
Habitat
Mil Barrets i Gorres
CARRER DE FONTANELLA
El Triangle
Casas
0   200 m
0   200 yds

WHAT TO DO

La Diagonal

HOW TO GET THERE

🚇 Diagonal

🚌 7, 16, 17, 22, 24, 28, or the Tombus from Plaça de Catalunya

Avinguda Diagonal, the commercial heart of Barcelona, is home to as many smart shops as it is to towering office buildings. It's both a fashionable avenue and a place of

Barcelona has become famous for its shopping culture

serious business, and that combination is reflected in the mix of stores and services, for example Gucci (No. 415) shares a block with several bank headquarters.

Starting from the intersection with the other fashion boulevard, Passeig de Gràcia, head left. Farga (No. 391) is one of the most elegant delicatessens in the city, selling sumptuous cakes, cookies and yummy gifts all in creative packages. If you want to find this season's clothing fashions, you should visit the likes of Calvin Klein (No. 484), Emporio Armani

(No. 490) and Adolfo Dominguez (No. 490).

The block between Rambla de Catalunya and Carrer de Balmes has become a focal point for home furnishings, with several shops catering to the design conscious. The best of the lot is Pilma (No. 403), with minimalist furniture and cool kitchenware. MDM (No. 405) is next door and has a similar style. Another big, international name is Habitat (No. 514), just a few blocks up. Natura Casa (No. 472) is a sprawling store, but because of the amount of space it is also calming. It sells textiles and furniture from India and Asia.

After shopping for your home, you can then shop for gifts. Riera (No. 421) is one of the most refined gift shops in Barcelona, and it's a great place to find presents for those back home. Crystal vases and Lladro figurines (famous as a Spanish product) all sit delicately in the display window. Turning left at Carrer d'Enric Granados, you'll find a few quality antiques shops and another fine gift store, Victor Caparros (No. 124) selling objects, such as Modernista-inspired candlesticks.

Just two blocks down Diagonal, you can take another detour onto Carrer de Muntaner. Several adorable children's shops, including a kids'-only shoe store, are on this steep, uphill street. Stylish babies clothes are at Neck and Neck (No. 235), while Sarri (No. 244) is the place to find exquisite christening gowns and elegant infant wear.

Trendy chain stores fill the horizon from here to the

traffic-clogged Plaça Francesc Macià. Shop at Zara, Mango, Benetton, Massimo Dutti and Promod, all with a similar range of fashionable clothes.

Yet just around the corner, on Avinguda de Pau Casals, the story changes. Chic boutiques sell designer handbags and one-of-a-kind necklaces. Toscana (No. 5) is one of the best places in the city to find outrageously priced, but oh-so-stylish,

Gucci is one of the most famous names along La Diagonal

purses and accessories. Men are catered for at Conti (No. 7), selling classy sportswear, linen suits and elegant underwear.

WHERE TO EAT

DAPS

Avinguda Diagonal 469

Tel 93 410 90 89

Creative Mediterranean cusine.

🕐 Daily 1pm–4.30pm, 8.30pm–1am

CROS DIAGONAL

Avinguda Diagonal 433

Tel 93 414 37 48

Mediterranean and international cusine.

🕐 Daily 8am-2am

Shopping Directory

This selection of shops, arranged by theme, covers some of Barcelona's top fashion and design stores, plus shops selling art, gifts and books.
See pages 132–135 for shopping locator maps.
See pages 152–153 for chain store chart.
See page 258 for clothing sizes.

BOOKS

ALTAÏR
Map 135 F9
Gran Vía de les Corts Catalanes 616, 08007
Tel 93 342 71 71
www.altair.es
Al-taïr is an Arabic word meaning the one that flies, and from the moment it opened in 1979 this bookshop has sourced and sold reliable travel literature. The number of countries and cultures covered makes this the first, and perhaps, only, stop if you are researching a trip. Altair's website is just as good, helping you get your hands on specific travel material or even find somebody to travel with.
🕐 Mon–Sat 10–2, 4.30–8.30
🚇 Universitat

CASA DEL LIBRO
Map 135 G9
Passeig de Gràcia 62, 08007
Tel 93 272 34 80
www.casadellibro.com
It would be a rare thing not to find what you're looking for in this vast bookshop. It is part of a group of shops which sells books on all imaginable subject matter, and this includes a good foreign language section. Book presentations and academic gatherings are held here from time to time, as in a number of other bookshops in the city.
🕐 Mon–Sat 9.30–9.30 🚇 Passeig de Gràcia

CÓMPLICES
Map 132 G11
Carrer de Cervantes 2, 08002
Tel 93 412 72 83
This bookshop, near the town hall in the heart of the Barri Gòtic, focuses on gay and lesbian literature. Art and photography titles, novels, poetry, essays and videos are available here. The bookshop is also a good meeting point and source of information if you want to find out more about the gay scene in Barcelona.
🕐 Mon–Fri 10.30–8, Sat 12–8
🚇 Jaume I

ESPAI RAS
Map 132 F10
Carrer del Doctor Dou 10, 08001
Tel 93 412 71 99
This store is part bookseller and part exhibition space. The first area you come to is the bookshop dealing in national and international contemporary architecture and design publications. The exhibitions give young designers in the city valuable exposure, and recurring themes are urbanism and landscape design.
🕐 Tue–Sat 11–9 🚇 Catalunya

LAIE
Map 135 G9
Carrer de Pau Claris 85, 08010
Tel 93 318 17 39
www.laie.es
A bookshop with a magnificent stock of titles, Laie is also a venue for book presentations, exhibitions and literary discussion groups. Some of

these events take place in the shop's café, where customers can sit, read, relax and, if they time it right, engage in a little academic debate.
🕐 Mon–Fri 10–9, Sat 10.30–9
🚇 Urquinaona

LORING ART
Map 132 F9
Carrer de Gravina 8, 08001
Tel 93 412 01 08
This shop stocks more than 3,000 design and contemporary art titles, including classics and rare finds. In addition, enthusiasts will find a range of specialist magazines and books by independent publishers. Loring Art supports contemporary art festivals in Barcelona, which is often reflected in their creative window displays.
🕐 Mon–Fri 10–8.30 🚇 Universitat

MUSIC

CASTELLÓ DISCOS
Map 132 F10
Carrer dels Tallers 3, 08001
Tel 93 318 20 41
www.discoscastello.com
The first Castelló Discos opened its doors in 1934 and the company now owns eight shops in the Raval area (based around Nou de la Rambla and Sant Pau). Its success is partly down to its departure from the mainstream: you'll find some rare and interesting imports in the way of records and CDs.
🕐 Mon–Sat 10–2, 4.30–8.30
🚇 Catalunya

FNAC
Map 132 F10
Plaça de Catalunya 4, 08002
Tel 93 344 18 00
www.fnac.es
FNAC has three branches in Barcelona, all within shopping centres. This one is in the El Triangle, and the other two are at L'Illa and Diagonal Mar. These stores sell so much more than CDs and there will be plenty to keep you amused: music, books, hi-fi systems, video and photographic

supplies and an IT department covering everything from hardware to mouse mats and printer paper. Everything has a

lowest price guarantee, so if you find something less expensive somewhere else, FNAC will refund the difference.
🕐 Mon–Sat 10–10 🚇 Catalunya

ANTIQUES

ANGEL BATLLE
Map 132 G10
Tel 93 301 58 84
Carrer de la Palla 23, 08002
This street has many antiques shops, which is fitting for one of the oldest parts of town that also formed The Call, or Jewish ghetto of the Middle Ages. Angel Batlle stocks beautiful old engravings, maps, fashion plates and prints as well as intriguing old texts in Spanish and Catalan. Credit cards are not accepted.
🕐 Mon–Fri 9–1.30, 4–7.30 🚇 Liceu

EL BULEVARD DELS ANTIQUARIS
Map 135 G9
Passeig de Gràcia 55–57, 08007
Tel 93 215 44 99
www.bulevarddelsantiquaris.com
This boulevard, or shopping centre, on the Passeig de Gràcia has the largest selection of antiques in Barcelona. Just about everything you could want is here, from the unusual to the more usual large or small items of furniture, jewellery and china. A committee of experts oversees all of the stores, giving buyers a guarantee of authenticity on their buys. In addition to the many

antiques shops, there is a restoration service along with very good art galleries.
🕐 Mon–Sat 10.30–2, 5–8.30 🚇 Passeig de Gràcia

CASA USHER
Off map 135 J9
Carrer d'Aragó 533, 08026
Tel 93 232 38 15
If you are a collector of nostalgia, then this is the place for you. The theme of Casa Usher's stock is pure, unadulterated pop culture: there are Dinky toys, Madelman, Michelin and Coca

Cola merchandising, as well as movie posters. There are also interior design and home decoration pieces from the 1950s, 60s and 70s.
🕐 Mon–Fri 10.30–2, 5–8, Sat 10.30–2 🚇 Glories

OTRANTO
Map 135 H8
Passeig de Sant Joan 142, 08037
Tel 93 207 26 97
This company sources its antiques when houses and businesses turn out their contents. Its warehouse is full of interesting items; you might find art nouveau radiators, a

1950s bar counter or early 20th-century bathroom fittings. There are certainly some great finds, so determined searching and patience pays off.
🕐 Mon–Fri 10–2, 4–8 🚇 Verdaguer

PASCUAL MIRÓ
Map 132 G11
Carrer dels Banys Nous 140, 08002
Tel 93 301 53 65
Pascual Miró is at one of the the narrow streets of the Barri Gòtic; an apt setting for the large selection of Spanish colonial furniture, decorative objects and paintings displayed here. If you are more daring in your purchases, and you can get them home, be sure to look out for the brightly painted wooden sculptures of religious subjects from the Spanish baroque period.
🕐 Mon–Fri 11–1.30, 5–7.45, Sat 11–1.30 🚇 Liceu

URBANA
Map 135 G7
Carrer de Séneca 13, 08006
Tel 93 237 36 44
Urbana salvages architectural features from demolitions and restores them to their original glory. Traditional American furniture, balustrades, chimneys and stairs are a staple of what you might find. This branch of Urbana deals with smaller items such as furniture, while its other branch on Carrer de Còrsega sells mainly fireplaces, mirrors and hardware.
🕐 Mon–Fri 10.30–2, 3–8 🚇 Diagonal

ARTS, CRAFTS AND GIFTS

LA CAIXA DE FANG
Map 133 G11
Carrer de Frenería 1, 08002
Tel 93 315 17 04
Marcelí Garreta has been in business since 1977 and sells wooden and clay kitchen utensils from this shop. Although he insists that all items serve a practical purpose, most of his customers buy his wares (of which many are pots and spoons) for decoration. You'll

also find pieces from all over Spain.

🕐 Mon–Sat 10–8 🚇 Jaume I

CENTRE CATALÁ D'ARTESANIA

Map 135 G9
Passeig de Gràcia 55, 08007
Tel 93 467 46 60
www.artesania-catalunya.com

The Catalan Crafts Centre was set up in 1985 by the Government of Catalonia to promote Catalan crafts and the exchange of knowledge. You'll be able to browse some of the best handmade products from the region, including glass, pottery, textiles, nativity scenes and other religious figures. There are two rooms on site, where themed exhibitions take place annually.

🕐 Mon–Sat 10–8 🚇 Passeig de Gràcia

KITSCH

Map 133 G11
Tel 93 319 57 68
Placeta de Montcada 10, 08003

This shop is an outrageous and vibrant display of what can be done with some paper, paste, paint and a bit of dexterity. Kitsch isn't actually all that kitsch but it is certainly curious. One of its most impressive lines is the papier mâché figurines. You can't miss the particularly startling flamenco figure in the doorway, to be found near the Santa Maria del Mar church.

🕐 Mon–Sat 11.30am–8pm, Sun 11.30am–3.30pm 🚇 Jaume I

MACBA

Map 132 F10
Tel 93 412 59 08
Plaça dels Àngels 1, 08001
www.macba.es

The gift shop attached to the MACBA modern art museum (see pages 90–91) is a great source for unusual and amusing gifts, such as hand-crafted jewellery, toys, novelty stationery and kitchenware designed by the Italian team Alessi. It's also a wonderful place for books on art and design. Although it has a

separate entrance from the museum, it shares its sleek modern architecture.

🕐 Mon, Wed–Sat 11–8, Sun 10.30–3 🚇 Universitat

NUNOYA

Map 133 G11
Tel 93 310 02 55
Carrer de Mirallers 7, 08003

Nunoya is a pretty little shop in the rambling back streets of the La Ribera. It sells Japanese and Asian-influenced clothing, accessories and items for the home such as cushions, candle holders and dining ware. The bright cotton kimonos are good value at about €60. Credit cards are not accepted.

🕐 Tue–Sat 11–2, 5–9, Mon 5–9pm 🚇 Jaume I

PAPIRUM

Map 133 G11
Baixada de la Llibreteria 2, 08002
Tel 93 310 52 42

Lovers of elegant stationery won't be able to resist the Barri Gòtic's Papirum, a tiny shop dealing in exquisite hand-printed paper, marbled blank books and writing implements. Desk accessories such as pencil cases are also stocked, some of which are even made out of paper. Credit cards are not accepted.

🕐 Mon–Fri 10–8.30, Sat 10–2, 5–8.30 🚇 Jaume I

PEPA PAPER

Map 134 F7
Carrer de París 167, 08036
Tel 93 494 84 20

Paper is taken extremely seriously here. This fashionable stationer stands out for its

letterhead designs and range of fun items, including pencils, bright paper and fascinating presents. A personalized card service allows customers to emerge original and organized.

🕐 Mon–Fri 10–8.30, Sat 10–2, 5–8.30 🚇 Hospital Clinic

POBLE ESPANYOL

See page 118.

FOOD AND DRINK

BOTIGA DEL TE I CAFÈS

Map 135 F9
Plaça del Doctor Letamendi 30–33, 08007
Tel 93 454 16 75

This shop stocks more than 40 different teas, including Hawaii Flower and Pina Colada among other herbal and fruit infusions. Coffee is by no means ignored, with eight blends of organic coffee, including Puerto Rico Yauco select. Botiga del Te i Cafès also sells accessories to aid in the preparation and serving of the perfect cup of either. Credit cards are not accepted.

🕐 Mon–Sat 9–8.30 🚇 Universitat

SPECIAL
COLMADO MURRIA
Map 135 G9
Carrer de Roger de Llúria 85, 08009
Tel 93 215 57 89

This delicatessen is in an art nouveau building with tiled art by the designer Ramón Casas (1866–1932). The fine products available here come from all over the world. Try some of the finest Iberian cold meat or take home some delicious Norwegian salmon. As far as wines, cavas and spirits are concerned, the range is large and expertly selected.
🕐 Mon–Fri 10–1, 4.30–8.30
🚇 Passeig de Gràcia

CELLER DE GELIDA
Map 134 C8
Carrer del Vallespir 65, 08014
Tel 93 339 26 41
This shop opened its doors as early as 1885 and has been in the same family for four generations. There are more than 3,500 different wines and spirits from Spain and beyond for you to choose from. The expert customer service is an integral part of the house philosophy. It's a chance to practise you langauge skills so ask, listen and learn.
🕐 Mon–Sat 9–2, 5–8.30, Oct–mid-Jun; Mon–Fri 9–2, 5–8.30, Sat 9–2 rest of year 🚇 Sants

SPECIAL
ESCRIBÁ
Map 134 E9
Avinguda de Gran Vía 546, 08011
Tel 93 301 60 27

You can buy arguably the most divine chocolates and pastries in the city at this beautiful Modernista building. The owner, Antoni Escribá, is the many times winner of Champion Patisser of Barcelona. He is famous for his *rambla*, which is a combination of biscuit, truffle and chocolate.
🕐 Daily 8.30am–9pm 🚇 Urgell

COLMADO AFRO-LATINO
Map 133 G11
Via Laietana 15, 08003
Tel 93 268 27 43
An exotic supermarket selling products from far-off lands: brandy, beer and fried doughnuts from Colombia; noodles and sauces from the Philippines; *chimichurri* (a spicy garlic sauce for grilled meat) from Argentina; all sorts of spicy African produce; Brazilian cheese and bread; rum and *guandules* (pigeon peas) from the Dominican Republic; Peruvian turkey and yellow chilli peppers. Credit cards are not accepted.
🕐 Mon–Sat 9am–10pm 🚇 Jaume I

HERBOLARI
Map 132 F10
Carrer d'en Xuclà 23, 08001
Tel 93 301 14 44
Established in 1927, this shop is dedicated to healing herbs from all over the world and its staff are experts with many years' experience. Follow their advice on the most suitable herbs for any complaint, and how best to prepare them, even if it's just a soothing drink. Credit cards are not accepted.
🕐 Mon–Sat 9–2, 4–8; 9–2 only in Aug
🚇 Catalunya

JAMONÍSIMO
Map 134 D11
Carrer de Radas 55, 08004
Tel 93 439 08 47
This is the ideal destination for purchasing Spanish ham, alongside other delicacies. There are many different varieties to choose from, and you can even be picky about how it's sliced, demanding the thickness or thinness required.
🕐 Mon–Fri 9.30–2.30, 5–9, Sat 9.30–2.30, 5.30–9
🚇 Poble Sec

QUILEZ
Map 135 F9
Rambla de Catalunya 63, 08007
Tel 93 215 23 56
One of the city's institutions at the heart of the Eixample. Try the house blend of Colombian coffee Café Quilez, or a bottle of La Fuente cava. National and imported beers number about 300 and there are selected wines from more than 100 different cellars. You'll be able to find all you need in food shopping too. Credit cards are not accepted.
🕐 Daily 9–2, 4.30–8.30 🚇 Passeig de Gràcia

VINA VINITECA
Map 133 G11
Carrer dels Agullers 7 & 9, 08003
Tel 93 310 19 56
Vina Viniteca carries about 4,500 different wines and spirits, many of which are exclusive to the shop. All of Spain's wine regions are represented, alongside a solid selection sourced from the world's most significant wine-producing countries. If you are not sure which one to choose

for a particular occasion, ask the knowledgeable staff.
🕐 Mon–Sat 8.30–2.30, 4.30–8.30; 8.30–2.30 only in Aug 🚇 Jaume I

ADOLFO DOMÍNQUEZ
Map 135 G9
Passeig de Gràcia 32, 08007
Tel 93 487 41 70
www.adolfodominguez.com
Adolfo Domínguez is one of Spain's top designers. His linen suits were responsible for a fundamental shift in Spanish men's fashion, but he does do ladieswear and sportswear. The target audience is chic urban professionals seeking something a little sophisticated. A cornerstone of his philosophy is that creases are aesthetic.
🕐 Mon–Sat 10–8.30 🚇 Passeig de Gràcia

ANTONIO MIRÓ
Map 135 G9
Carrer del Consell de Cent 349, 08007
Tel 93 487 06 70
www.antoniomiro.es

This shop is popular with the city's young professionals. Local designer Toni Miró is best known for his superbly tailored men's suits. Both his ladies' and men's collections are excellent value for money and the style is modern and simple, with a focus on quality trousers, soft cotton and classic accessories.
🕐 Mon–Sat 10–8.30 🚇 Passeig de Gràcia

AGUA DEL CARMEN
Map 133 G11
Carrer del Bonaire 5, 08003
Tel 93 268 77 99
A shop in which attention to detail is fundamental. This is a collection of one-off and limited edition designs in natural fabrics, mostly silk, cotton and linen. The patterns are inspired by a fantasy world of goblins, elves and fairies. The shop also stocks accessories by Claudia d'Anca, Herrietta and Vibes.
🕐 Mon–Sat 11–2.30, 5–9 🚇 Barceloneta

ANTONIO PERNAS
Map 135 G9
Carrer del Consell de Cent 314–316, 08007
Tel 93 487 16 67
Antonio Pernas, a Galician designer, is known for his understated, stylish jackets and suits. There's a great collection of modern and effortlessly

sophisticated clothes and accessories, designed with the dynamic urban woman in mind.
🕐 Mon–Sat 10.30–8 🚇 Universitat

ARMAND BASI
Map 135 G9
Passeig de Gràcia 49, 08007
Tel 93 215 14 21
www.armandbasi.com
This is the flagship store of this ultra-cool Spanish designer and is the only place in town that stocks his complete men's and women's collections. He began his career in the 1980s and his experience shows. Choose from soft leather jackets, timeless suits, classic

LOEWE
Map 135 G9
Passeig de Gràcia 35, 08007
Tel 93 216 04 00
www.loewe.es
Top-quality leather goods, clothes and accessories, all classic and all stylish. Loewe was started in 1846, and has always been the ultimate Spanish luxury fashion and accessory label. Its international reputation is formed by the ladies' ready-to-wear collection. The flagship store, in a beautiful 19th-century mansion, reflects this reputation.
🕐 Mon–Sat 10–8.30 🚇 Passeig de Gràcia

knitwear, evening dress and a wide variety of accessories.
🕐 Mon–Sat 10–8.30 🚇 Passeig de Gràcia

CAMISERÍA PONS
Map 135 G7
Carrer Gran de Gràcia 49, 08012
Tel 93 217 72 92
Established in 1909, this chic store occupies an impressive building with a dark wooden façade and vast windows. The sign outside follows the same theme, with glorious 1900s lettering on a black background. This is a stockist of the local designer Josep Abril, as well as some international names, such as DKNY. Camisería Pons' own label clothes have baggy shapes and old-fashioned fabrics.
🕐 Mon–Sat 10–2, 5–8.30 🚇 Fontana

GABRIEL TORRES
Map 135 G7
Carrer Lluís Antúnez 8, 08006
Tel 93 217 16 61
The young designer Gabriel Torres presents his own collection here, which is inspired by bold Japanese style. The designs are clean cut and aimed at professional men. Itxaso Lecumberri handbags

are stocked as well, and this small shop also doubles as the designer's workshop.
🕐 Mon–Fri 4–9, Sat 11–9; closed Aug 🚇 Diagonal

M69
Map 134 F9
Carrer de Muntaner 69, 08011
Tel 93 453 62 69
A multifunctional store selling mainly fashion, but also books, music and graphic design items. The elegant, modern setting forms a backdrop to collections by most of the

famous Spanish designers, such as Amaya Arzuaga, who produces wearable, creative, sexy pieces, and Antoni Miró. International designers, such as Dirk Bikkembergs and Paul Smith, are also stocked.
🕐 Mon–Fri 10–2, 4.30–8.30, Sat 9.30–2.30, 5–9 🚇 Universitat

MANGO
Map 135 G8
Passeig de Gràcia 65, 08007
Tel 93 215 75 30
www.mango.es
Selling innovative and trendy clothes at fair prices, Mango joins the ranks of Spain's internationally known stores. Since

1985, it has blossomed from five shops in its hometown of Barcelona to more than 700 worldwide. The designers like to use a basic palette mixed with the latest styles, ranging from casual to formal evening-wear and fun accessories.
🕐 Mon–Sat 10–9 🚇 Passeig de Gràcia

MASSIMO DUTTI
Map 135 F7
Vía Augusta 33, 08006
Tel 93 217 73 06
www.massimodutti.com
Massimo Dutti has retail space in 12 different countries and has a complete range of lines, covering sophisticated fashion, urban chic and the sporty look. The basic, modern styles on the rails here are created using contemporary fabrics, but are good quality and always remain practical and attractive.
🕐 Mon–Sat 10–9 🚇 Diagonal

ON LAND
Map 135 G8
Carrer de València 273, 08009
Tel 93 215 56 25
www.on-land.com
On Land has an extensive collection of women's and men's clothing. Check out the house label or go for something by one of the featured new designers. Stylish seasonal outfits here include modern, angular tailoring from Catalans Josep Abril and Gabriel Torres, and the more romantic, feminine styles of womenswear designer Josep Font.
🕐 Mon–Sat 11–2, 5–8.30 🚇 Passeig de Gràcia

OVERALES & BLUYINES
Map 133 H11
Carrer del Rec 65, 08003
Tel 93 319 29 76
This outlet concentrates on denim, as well as stocking Pringle clothes and Paul Smith shoes. On top of the house collection, you'll find top brands such as Levi's Red, Duffer of St. George, Seal Kay, Rare and Red Ear Shoes. There are some second-hand items

for sale in the shop, although the majority are new. If you want something exclusive a customized design service is available.
🕐 Mon–Sat 10.30–8.30 🚇 Barceloneta

SEÑOR
Map 135 G9
Passeig de Gràcia 26, 08007
Tel 93 317 69 67
In a late 19th-century building, Señor has successfully combined traditional tailoring with the latest leather fashions for men. It stocks a number of prestigious international labels including Boss, Canali, Versace, Trussardi, Armani and Caramelo. A delivery service is available, either to your hotel or shipped back home.
🕐 Mon–Sat 10–8.30 🚇 Passeig de Gràcia

THEM
Map 135 G8
Avinguda Diagonal 379, 08008
Tel 93 218 77 50
www.them-barcelona.com
Both men and women will find well-cut clothes here. Spanish designers are represented in the work of Josep Abril, Josep Font and Gimenez & Zuazo. The latter label is known for its starkly cut retro-look clothes in muted tones and heavy fabrics. International labels include the club chic of W&LT, and the avant-garde creations of British designer Vivienne Westwood.
🕐 Mon–Sat 10–2.30, 5–9 🚇 Verdaguer

TRIBU
Map 132 G11
Carrer d'Avinyó 12, 08002
Tel 93 318 65 10
When you first enter this shop, you'd be forgiven for thinking it only carries a sparse collection of clubbing fashion. But a great collection of designer clothing awaits. There are pieces by a.t.shirt, Michiko Koshino, Fake London, E.Play, Jocomomola, No.L.Ita, Rare, Diesel, Impasse de la Défense

and Rice and W&LT. The staff update the impressive window displays every six weeks.
◎ Mon–Sat 11–2.30, 4.30–8.30
Ⓜ Drassanes

ZARA
Map 132 F10
Carrer de Pelai 58, 08001
Tel 93 301 09 78
www.zara.com
This Galician fashion chain has expanded its empire in the last few years to cover 30 countries. Zara is modern and trendy, producing quality

clothes at palatable prices. The fashions here may not last until next year, but at these prices it doesn't really matter.
◎ Mon–Sat 10–9 Ⓜ Catalunya

[Z]INK
Map 132 G11
Tel 93 342 62 88
Carrer d'Avinyó 14, 08002
This small shop on one of Barcelona's coolest fashion streets doubles as an art gallery, with local artists making over the interior every few months. The limited stock consists mainly of Levi's Red, Vintage labels and accessories from cutting-edge designers. Such coolness don't come cheaply, but the gallery theme means you can just browse.
◎ Tue–Sat 10.30–2.30, 4.30–9, Mon 4.30–8.30pm Ⓜ Jaume I or Liceu

ZONA ELEVEN
Map 134 F9
Carrer de Muntaner 61, 08011
Tel 93 453 71 45
A modern, trend-conscious shop selling designer labels

for men. You'll find a good collection of clothes and accessories by the likes of Kenzo, Just Cavalli, Dolce & Gabbana, Frederic Homs and Versace, as well as underwear and swimwear by Moschino, Calvin Klein, Emporio Armani and Amadeus.
◎ Mon–Sat 10.30–2, 5–8.30
Ⓜ Universitat

ZSU ZSA
Map 132 G11
Carrer d'Avinyó 50, 08002
Tel 93 412 49 65
This is a small shop that sells selected stock, but what is here is retro and trendy. Zsu Zsa has its own label, floaty and feminine, yet with unusual shapes and details, presented alongside the designs of Norma Álvarez, Bad Habits, Andrea B, Ricardo Ramos and Ixio. Choose your accessories from collections by Guilty, Pequeño poder, Opa Loka and Locking Shocking.
◎ Mon–Sat 11–2, 5–8.30; closed Sat 5–8.30, Jul–Aug Ⓜ Drassanes

JEWELLERY AND ACCESSORIES

AGATHA
Map 135 G8
Rambla de Catalunya 112, 08008
Tel 93 415 59 98
Agatha jewellery is known beyond Spain's borders and this store has a sizeable collection of pieces. It's best known for its cultured pearl necklaces, available in a range of tones and selectively designed for conservative clients. You'll also find gloves, handbags and sunglasses, as

well as perfumes presented in beautiful bottles.
◎ Mon–Sat 10.30–2, 5–8.30
Ⓜ Diagonal

CARLES GALINDO
Map 135 G6
Carrer de Verdi 56, 08012
Tel 93 416 07 04
This is an imaginative range of costume jewellery, fashioned using unconventional materials such as vinyl, plastic and nylon. The shop also sells black leather accessories with studs, well-worn leather belts, cashmere and vintage denim. These pieces combine to create a punk look accented by artfully tarnished metals.
◎ Mon–Sat 10–2, 4.30–9 Ⓜ Fontana

GEMMA PICHOT
Map 135 G6
Carrer d'Asturies 4, 08012
Tel 93 237 59 23
Gemma Pichot's jewellery shop, which doubles as a studio, is in a former medal factory in the old Gràcia area. She has created an interesting setting, retaining the factory's original interior and furniture. The pieces on sale incorporate a lot of wood and glass, with designs inspired by nature. Credit cards are not accepted.
◎ Mon–Fri 10–2, 5–8.30, Sat 10.30–2; closed Aug Ⓜ Fontana

THE GIFT
Map 132 F11
Tel 93 302 5002
La Rambla 83, 08002
This tiny narrow slit of a shop on Las Ramblas is easily missed, but that would mean missing out on some handmade jewellery, ceramics and other craftworks. The jewellery is simple and elegant, as well as reasonably priced. The helpful owner claims this is one of the few shops in town where the local handicrafts aren't made in China. Find it between Carrers de Petxina and de l'Hospital.
◎ Mon–Fri 9–1.30, 4–7.30
Ⓜ Liceu

GLAMOOR

Map 133 H11

Carrer de Calders 10, 08003

Tel 93 310 39 92

This optician brings a touch of glamour to La Ribera. It stocks exclusive designs and limited edition glasses, sunglasses and accessories, and even has a minibar at which to deliberate your purchases. The innovative designs make this shop one to consider if you're looking for something a little bit different.

Ⓒ Mon–Sat 10–2.30, 4.30-8.30 Ⓜ Barceloneta

HIPÓTESIS

Map 135 F8

Rambla de Catalunya 105, 08008

Tel 93 215 02 98

North of Plaça de Catalunya, this shop stocks all manner of jewellery by a number of different artists. There are pieces to suit all types of budget, and the collection is notable for its rich shades, interesting shapes and unusual textures. It's also a good place for hand-painted silk scarves and other garments.

Ⓒ Mon–Fri 10–8.30, Sat 11.30–2, 5-8.30 Ⓜ Diagonal

JOAQUÍN BERAO

Map 135 G8

Rambla de Catalunya 74, 08037

Tel 93 215 00 91

Berao has designed jewellery for over 30 years. His artistic pieces are inspired by shells and sea creatures such as sea horses and starfish. His innovative work is well respected and is often exhibited at the Zurich Museum of Contemporary Art.

Ⓒ Mon–Fri 10–8, Sat 10–2 Ⓜ Diagonal

MIL BARRETS I GORRES

Map 133 G10

Carrer de Fontanella 20, 08010

Tel 93 301 84 91

This hat shop has been a supplier of headgear to a discerning, wealthy clientele since 1850. It stocks a fine collection of traditional hats, a handful of modern, urban labels such

as Kangol, and even a few Stetsons from the USA.

Ⓒ Mon–Sat 9.30–1.30, 4.15–8, Sat 10–2, 4.30–8 Ⓜ Urquinaona

CALPA

Map 132 G11

Carrer de Ferran 53, 08002

Tel 93 318 40 30

www.bossesdepellcalpa.com

Creative and increasingly exclusive, Calpa is a friendly, busy store that can overwhelm customers with its jumble of bags, belts and other leather accessories. All shapes, styles and sizes are piled high in every available space. Prices are reasonable and you can find some very distinct and unusual designs here as many of the bags are made by young local designers.

Ⓒ Mon–Fri 9.30–2, 4.30–8, Sat 10–2, 5-8.30 Ⓜ Liceu

CAMPER

Map 135 G8

Carrer de València 249, 08007

Tel 93 215 63 90

www.camper.es

The Camper label was conceived in Mallorca, but has a high profile in Barcelona. You'll

LA MANUAL ALPARGATERA

Map 132 G11

Carrer d'Avinyó 7, 08002

Tel 93 301 01 72

You'll find this shop, selling handmade espadrilles and sandals, in the Barri Gòtic, where the open workshop enables customers to view the skilled craftswomen. In addition to footwear, there's also a good collection of walking sticks and hats. The company has been trading in Barcelona since 1910, and former clients allegedly include the Pope.

Ⓒ Mon–Sat 9.30–1.30, 4.30–8 Ⓜ Jaume I

find comfortable, stylishly quirky shoes, made from durable, high-quality leather. It is known around the world for its distinctive bowling shoe designs. The informal style of the shop reflects the concept of the label itself.

Ⓒ Mon–Sat 10–9 Ⓜ Diagonal

CASAS

Map 132 G10

Avinguda del Portal de l'Angel 40, 08002

Tel 93 317 90 36

This is probably the most comprehensive of the city's shoe shops, where you'll find all the most prominent labels under one roof. Dr. Martens and Caterpillar for the young (or young at heart) and Début, Pura López, Mare, Rodolfo

WHAT TO DO

Zengarini and Robert Clergerie for the seriously trend conscious. The house collection, Camilla Casas, will suit more conventional shoppers.
⊕ Mon–Sat 10–9 ⊗ Catalunya

CZAR
Map 133 G11
Passeig del Born 20, 08003
Tel 93 310 72 22
Choose sports shoes for men and women by the likes of Merrell, Asics, Converse, Adidas and Diesel. If you want something a little dressier try Paul Smith, Sessura, Fly London and W&LT. Watch and bag labels include Diesel, Le Coq Sportif and Levi's; for costume jewellery try Takeshi.
⊕ Mon–Fri 10.30–2.30, 5–9, Sat 11–9
⊗ Barceloneta

GALA
Map 135 G9
Bulevard Rosa 9–12, Passeig de Gràcia 55, 08007
Tel 93 215 01 61
www.bolsosgala.com
There's no shortage of bag shops in the gleaming Bulevard Rosa shopping centre, off the Passeig de Gràcia. Gala has one of the best selections of high fashion, creative, designer bags and purses, stocking national and international labels such as Calvin Klein and Donna Karan.
⊕ Mon–Sat 10.30–8.30 ⊗ Passeig de Gràcia

MAR FRANC
Map 132 F10
Carrer del Carme 10, 08001
Tel 93 317 5535
www.marfranc.es
Part of a chain of leather clothing stores, Barcelona's Mar Franc is on the edge of Las Ramblas, just in El Raval. The sleek blonde-wood store stocks classic designs in leather, suede and sheepskin, including coats, jackets and accessories for men and women.
⊕ Mon–Sat 10–8; closed Aug
⊗ Liceu

RAFA
Map 132 G10
Avinguda del Portal de l'Angel 3–5, 08002
Tel 93 318 33 45
This small, smart boutique sits at the heart of the shopping

zone in Barcelona's old town. In the chic and sleek shop, you can find an interesting range of bags from top brands such as Furla and Mandarina Duck.
⊕ Mon–Sat 10–8.30 ⊗ Liceu

INTERIOR DESIGN AND HOME FURNISHINGS

AGAINST
Map 132 G11
Tel 93 301 54 52
Carrer de Palau 6, 08002
www.againstbcn.com
A funky shop in the streets of the Barri Gòtic, which is cluttered with superb examples of retro furniture from the 1960s and 70s. Prices may seem a little high for stuff you may remember throwing out, but are great examples of design.
⊕ Mon–Fri 4.30–8.30pm, Sat 11–2, 5–8.30 ⊗ Jaume I

ARTE & OBJETO
Map 134 F7
Passatge Lluis Pellicer 5–7, 08036
Tel 93 321 61 80
This showroom is a mix of shop and exhibition space, demonstrating that art can be integrated happily into your home. The items are renditions of traditional furniture, showcased as objets d'art, and are mostly one-offs.
⊕ Mon–Fri 10–7.30, Sat 10.30–2.30
⊗ Diagonal

BD EDICIONES DE DISEÑO
Map 135 G8
Carrer de Mallorca 291, 08037
Tel 93 458 69 09
Established in 1972, avant-garde BD Ediciones de Diseño pulls together the highlights of 20th-century design in a vast and remarkable art nouveau interior. You will find furniture and accessories from internationally established labels such as Driade, Poliform, Vitra and Alessi. There's also an in-house interior design consultancy and project team if you want some one-to-one advice.
⊕ Daily 10–2, 4–8, May–end Sep; 10–8 rest of year ⊗ Passeig de Gràcia

CORIUMCASA
Map 135 F8
Carrer de Provença 268, 08008
Tel 93 272 12 24
This shop sets out a clear identity in its style and stock: fine, elegant and seriously chic. The setting, in a Modernista building in the Eixample, is countered by a modern approach to design, making use of rich materials like wood, velvet, linen and leather in the furniture and homewares it sells. The company is happy to custom-make items of furniture if you wish.
⊕ Mon–Fri 10–2, 4.30–8.30
⊗ Diagonal

D BARCELONA
Map 133 H11
Carrer del Rec 61, 08003
Tel 93 315 07 70
Unusual, trendy design pieces for the home, as well as a range of imaginatively designed fashion accessories and playful gifts. D Barcelona stocks (among other brands) Storm watches, Mathmos lava lamps, household utensils by Koziol and Pylones, inflatable armchairs and painted cows by Cow Parade.
⊕ Mon–Thu noon–10, Fri–Sat noon–midnight, Sun 5–10
⊗ Barceloneta

DOM

Map 132 G11
Carrer d'Avinyó 7, 08002
Tel 93 487 11 81
www.id-dom.com
DOM is a perfect shopping spot for those who like to hunt for unconventional home accessories for themselves or for gifts. The style is epitomized by plastic furniture and funky lamps, all tending toward the world of kitsch.
🕐 Mon–Sat 10.30–8.30 🚇 Drassanes

GASTÓN Y DANIELA

Map 135 G8
Carrer de Pau Claris 171, 08037
Tel 93 215 32 17
www.gastonydaniela.com
Tradition and quality have served Gastón y Daniela well in the face of mounting competition from companies using modern fabrics and techniques. The first branch opened in Bilbao 125 years ago, and throughout its lifetime the shop's clients have loved the great range of luxurious patterns and textiles available. Perfect for prints, fitted carpets, upholstery, mats and bedspreads.
🕐 Mon–Fri 10–2, 5–8, Sat 10.30–2 🚇 Diagonal

GOTHAM

Map 132 G11
Carrer de Cervantes 7, 08002
Tel 93 412 46 47
www.gotham-bcn.com
Gotham is run by professional interior designers and stocks fabulous accessories, furniture and design pieces dating from the 1950s, 60s and 70s, alongside some reproductions of

modern interior design classics. This collection is often the source of props for film, TV and advertising productions, and the company has collaborated with such well-known publications as *Wallpaper*.
🕐 Mon–Sat 10.30–2, 5–8.30
🚇 Liceu

GEMMA POVO

Map 132 G11
Tel 93 301 37 76
Carrer dels Banys Nous 5–7, 08002
This cosily cluttered shop resembles a country farm-house kitchen, so it's the perfect place to shop if you want to re-create that Catalan *masia* (country house) look in your own home. Gemma Povo sells original ironwork lamps and furniture made in its own workshop, and complements these with antique Spanish furniture and local crafts.
🕐 Mon–Sat 10.30–9.30 🚇 Liceu

HABITAT

Map 132 F10
Plaça de Catalunya 4, 08002
Tel 93 301 74 84
www.habitat.net/spain
Minimalist style, top-quality materials and great value for money have been responsible for Habitat's worldwide success. Tom Dixon's furniture

has found a target market in Barcelona's trend-conscious buyers who are looking for modern style in their homes. All bases are covered when it comes to items for home furnishing, ranging from glasses, kitchen utensils, sofas,

beds, linen and bathroom accessories.
🕐 Mon–Sat 10–9 🚇 Catalunya

ICI ET LÀ

Map 133 G11
Plaça de Santa María 2, 08003
Tel 93 268 11 67
www.icietla.com
A gift-hunter's paradise, this design gallery sells furniture, lamps and accessories for the home, as well as pieces by specially selected designers. Every item is a limited edition, using vivid shades and shapes. If you don't want to buy, sit in the pretty square and look at the window display.
🕐 Tue–Sat 10.30–8.30, Mon 4.30–8.30 🚇 Barceloneta

MDM

Map 135 F8
Avinguda Diagonal 405 bis, 08037
Tel 93 238 67 67
In the last few years, this store has become one of Barcelona's most important players in furniture and interior

decoration. MDM commands a two-floor, minimalist retail space housing the collections of many a famous label. It's a good place to hunt for garden and terrace furniture.
🕐 Mon–Fri 10–8.30, Sat 10–9 🚇 Diagonal

PILMA

Map 135 F8
Avinguda Diagonal 403, 08008
Tel 93 416 13 99
www.pilma.com
Pilma sells modular furniture, tables and chairs, upholstery, garden and terrace furniture,

WHAT TO DO

VINÇON

Map 135 G8
Passeig de Gràcia 96, 08008
Tel 93 215 60 50
www.vincon.com

Modern European design in an enormous old palatial setting. The retail space here is vast, but the stock includes small items such as Filofaxes alongside smart kitchenware. A must-see in Vinçon is one of Barcelona's most elaborate Modernista fireplaces. Vinçon is next door to one of Barcelona's most famous buildings, Casa Milà (see pages 66–69) and the two help trace the history of design in the city.
🕐 Mon–Sat 10–8.30 🚇 Diagonal

carpets, curtains, artwork, kitchen goods and accessories. The two buzzwords when it comes to design are simplicity and practicality, influencing the shapes and materials used. The shop itself is spacious, modern and airy.
🕐 Mon–Sat 10–2, 4.30–8.30 🚇 Diagonal

RIERA

Map 135 G8
Passeig de Gràcia 91, 08008
Tel 93 215 14 13
Established at the beginning of the 20th century, this is one of the city's best known shops dealing in household accessories. Luxury and quality are the main themes, with an

ample collection of glassware, cutlery and china. The Swedish Kosta-Boda glasswork is particularly attractive.
🕐 Mon–Sat 10am–8.15pm; 7–1.30, 4.30–8, Aug 🚇 Diagonal

VIENTOS DEL SUR

Map 133 G11
Tel 93 268 25 25
Carrer de l'Argenteria 78, 08003
This is a journey to exotic climes via furniture. Vientos del Sur stocks items that reflect Asian, African and South American ethnic design. Richly coloured rugs and cushions, dark wood tables and beaded lamps are piled together with ethnic clothing and jewellery, as incense (also on sale) perfumes the air.
🕐 Mon–Sun 11–8.45 🚇 Jaume I

BULEVARD ROSA

Map 135 G9
Passeig de Gràcia 55, 08007
Tel 93 215 83 31
www.bulevardrosa.com
This shopping centre has two branches; the first was opened in Passeig de Gràcia, and the second sprang up in Diagonal Avinguda. Both have a mixture of well-known label boutiques and outlets, as well as a handful of small local shops. It has a reputation for good quality clothes and shoes.
🕐 Mon–Sat 10am–11pm 🚇 Passeig de Gràcia

EL CORTE INGLÉS

Map 132 G10
Plaça de Catalunya 14, 08002
Tel 93 306 38 00
www.elcorteingles.es
This is Spain's most prominent and popular department store. With branches all over the country, El Corte Inglés

showcases clothes, food, shoes, electrical appliances, sports gear and more. Perfect if you are short on time and aren't able to trawl separate specialist shops. The rooftop café is a handy place for a break with great views over the city.
🕐 Mon–Sat 10–10 🚇 Catalunya

DIAGONAL MAR

Off map 135 J9
Avinguda Diagonal Mar 3, 08019
Tel 900 900 955
www.diagonalmar.com
This is in one of Barcelona's most recently developed districts. Diagonal Mar is part of a major regeneration project encompassing residential, retail, office, hotel and leisure facilities. The shopping centre itself brings together shops selling books, fashion, shoes, household items, groceries and plenty more besides.
🕐 Mon–Sat 10–10 🚇 Selva de Mar

L'ILLA

Map 134 D6
Avinguda Diagonal 545–557, 08029
Tel 93 444 00 00
www.lilla.com
The main focus is on fashion and accessories. Famous labels here include FNAC, Decathlon, Corte Fiel, Benetton, Massimo

Dutti, Caprabo, Bang & Olufsen, Mandarina Duck and Zara. It's right next to one of Barcelona's most significant business centres, so it is often busy with professionals looking for the latest purchase.
🕙 Mon–Sat 10–9.30 Ⓜ María Cristina

MAREMAGNUM
Map 135 F12
Moll d'Espanya, 08039
Tel 93 225 81 00
www.maremagnum.es
The shops mostly sell gifts, accessories, casual clothes and souvenirs. There's a typical mall-style food court, plus bars and clubs open in the evenings. It's approached across the wooden footbridge from Las Ramblas, with a good view of the harbour—though you may have to wait for up to 15 minutes if it's raised for boats to go through.
🕙 Daily 11–11 Ⓜ Drassanes

EL TRIANGLE
Map 132 F10
Plaça de Catalunya, 08002
Tel 93 318 01 08
This is one of the busiest shopping centres in Barcelona, set

right at the top of Las Ramblas. You'll find branches of all the major chains, including FNAC, Habitat, Massimi Dutti, Camper, Shéphora and Dockers. The opening of this shopping centre prompted the renovation of the famous Café Zurich, which is next door and a great stop-off after some retail therapy.
🕙 Mon–Sat 10–10 Ⓜ Catalunya

MARKETS
LA BARCELONETA
Map 135 G12
Plaça del Poeta Boscà s/n, 08003
Tel 93 221 64 71
One of the city's oldest indoor markets, Mercat la Barceloneta is currently in a temporary home while its old one is rebuilt. Its proximity to the water lends it a maritime

CHAIN STORES CHART

NAME	Womenswear	Menswear	For children	Shoes	Jewellery and accessories	Souvenirs and gifts	Books, music and magazines	Sports and outdoor kit	Household goods	Toiletries	CONTACT NUMBER
Adolfo Domínguez	✔	✔	✔								93 487 41 70
Benetton	✔	✔	✔								93 216 09 83
Bershka	✔	✔									93 302 01 04
Camper				✔							93 302 41 24
Castelló							✔				93 442 34 97
Cortefiel	✔	✔									93 301 07 00
Decathlon								✔			93 444 01 65
CDom						✔	✔				93 487 11 81
FNAC							✔				93 344 18 00
H&M	✔	✔	✔		✔						901 12 00 84
Habitat									✔		93 415 44 55
Ikea									✔		93 497 00 10.
Mango	✔										93 412 15 99
M et F Girbaud	✔	✔									93 301 67 75
Massimo Dutti	✔	✔									93 412 28 28
Natura									✔		93 444 91 20
La Perla Gris									✔		93 415 34 52
Platamundi					✔						93 317 42 99
Prénatal			✔								93 302 05 25
Pull and Bear			✔					✔			93 302 08 76
Querol				✔							93 304 02 05
Stradivarius	✔				✔						902 11 57 19
Women's Secret	✔										93 318 92 42
Yves Rocher										✔	93 342 45 99
Zara	✔	✔	✔						✔		93 318 76 75

atmosphere, and the products you can buy here range from fresh fish, meat and vegetables to cold meat, beans and tinned foods.

🕐 Mon–Thu, Sat 7–3, Fri 7–3, 5–8
🚇 Barceloneta

ELS ENCANTES
Off map 135 J9
Plaça de les Glories Catalanes s/n, 08013
Tel 93 246 30 30
There's a definite early 20th-century feel to this flea market, with no end of marvellous reminders of the past: old toys, fading photographs, old-fashioned wedding gowns and hats, as well as all sorts of antiquated kitchen accessories.

🕐 Mon, Wed, Fri, Sat 9–7 (also 8pm in summer) 🚇 Glories

LA BOQUERÍA
Map 132 F10
La Rambla 91–101, 08002
Tel 93 318 25 84
Barcelona is not short of markets, but La Boqueria (also called Mercat de Sant Josep) is the most popular. Right at the heart of Las Ramblas, this covered market is an eruption of noise, colour and aroma, and is great for fresh produce. Once you've done your shopping, stop at one of the bars to rest your feet.

🕐 Mon–Sat 8–8 🚇 Liceu

LA LLIBERTAT
Map 135 G7
Plaça de Llibertat 27, 08012
Tel 93 217 09 95
Built at the end of the 19th century, this market is found in the Gràcia area. It's a free-standing building covering about 2,500sq m (27,000sq ft) of space, where you'll find top quality fresh food, most notably fish and meat. The facilities are good; there's parking and an ATM nearby, as well as a customer service office.

🕐 Tue–Thu 8–3, 5–8, Fri 7am–8pm, Sat 7–3, Mon 8–3
🚇 Fontana

With so many stores, it can be a time-consuming business finding those that sell exactly what you are looking for. Barcelona does not have the abundance that some cities do, but there are a few key chains that you will come across. This chart tells you what to expect in many of the stores that can be found throughout the city. Call the contact number to find your nearest branch or visit the website.

DESCRIPTION	WEBSITE
Sophisticated, contemporary clothing for professional men and women	www.adolfodominguez.es
Quality Italian sportswear at inexpensive prices	www.benetton.com
Trend setting styles for bright young things	www.bershka.com
Shoes and boots from Mallorca that have achieved cult status	www.camper.com
The oldest music chain in Barcelona, selling pop, funk, flamenco, classical and jazz	www.discoscastello.com
Contemporary clothing using quality fabrics	www.cortefiel.es
Budget-priced sportswear and equipment for all ages and pastimes	www.decathlon.es
Kitsch objects, plus a range of design bibles and magazines	www.id-dom.com
All types of music sold, as well as cameras and audio/visual equipment	www.fnac.com
Cut-price evening and daywear plus accessories	www.hm.com
Stylish textiles, kitchenware, furniture and gadgets for the home	www.habitat.net
The homeware phenomenon continues	www.ikea.es
Young day, evening and work wear for women	www.mango.es
An avant-garde French label, selling designs in denim	www.girbaud.com
Well-cut business suits and smart weekend outfits	www.massimodutti.com
Ethnic-influenced furniture, objects and textiles	www.naturaselection.com
Long-established chain selling luxurious bed linen and towels	www.laperlagris.com
Affordable silver, enamel and semiprecious stone pieces from local designers	n/a
Selling toys, clothing and accessories for young children and pregnant mums	www.prenatal.es
Sports and office wear for the modern man at inexpensive prices	www.pullbear.com
The best of local and imported shoes, selling sandals, sports shoes and stilettos	n/a
Throw-away fashion for trendy teens and young women	www.e-stradivarius.co
Stylish underwear and slumber garments for women at great prices	n/a
Complete range of good value, botanical skincare and cosmetics	www.yves-rocher.com
The latest fashions at unbeatable prices	www.zara.com

LLIBRE D'OCASIÓ

Map 134 E10
Carrer del Comte d'Urgell 1, 08011
Tel 93 423 42 87

Mercat del Llibre d'Ocasió attracts a diverse crowd outside the old Mercat de Sant Antonio every Sunday. The main theme here is books (*libre*) and even if old books aren't your thing, it's pleasant to stroll around and there are numerous places to grab a bite to eat before lunch.

🔘 Sun 9–2 🚇 Sant Antoni

PLAÇA DEL PÍ

Map 132 F11
Plaça del Pí, 08002

The regular outdoor market held here sells artwork and homemade cheeses, honey, chocolate and other products from rural Catalonia.

🔘 First and third Fri, Sat and Sun of the month 11–2, 5–9 🚇 Liceu

PLAÇA REIAL

Map 132 F11
Plaça Reial, 08002

Anything and everything can be bought or exchanged here. Old coins and stamps from all over the world are traded at

Plaça Reial on a Sunday morning. This street market also has some miscellaneous stalls brimming with objects of interest such as telephone cards and antique pins.

🔘 Sun 9–2 🚇 Liceu

PLAÇA DE LA SEU

Map 133 G11
Plaça Nova

If you find yourself in the Barri Gòtic on a Thursday, take some time to check out this antiques fair. It is central, right on the same square as the cathedral, and the crowds mean you can't miss it. Wares include furniture, novels and comics, second-hand clothes, clocks and general bric-à-brac. Don't be shy in donning your bargaining hat to make sure that you get the price you want.

🔘 Thu 10–10; closed Aug 🚇 Jaume I

POBLE NOU

Off map 135 J11
Rambla del Poble Nou, 08018

This market takes place once a month, and it's almost a social event in this old neighbourhood. You can buy all sorts of items ranging from handmade jewellery and crafts to local food delicacies, sweets and oil.

🔘 First Sat of the month 9–9
🚇 Poble Nou

PORT VELL

Map 132 F12
Plaça de les Drassanes s/n, 08002

If you stroll down Las Ramblas on a Sunday morning you'll encounter a whole host of antiques stands. This market is full of books, watches, bright tin boxes, unusual and dated electrical appliances, glass ornaments, small items of furniture and plenty of fascinating bric-à-brac. It is the place to hunt to your heart's content.

🔘 Sat–Sun 10–8 🚇 Drassanes

SANT ANTONI

Map 134 E10
Carrer del Comte d'Urgell 1, 08011
Tel 93 423 42 87

This market's association with the best quality seafood, meat, fresh fruit, vegetables, dried fruit and nuts extends back into the 19th century. Nowadays, it's almost three markets in one; there's the food market inside, a fashion and general market four days

a week outside and a second-hand book market in the street on Sunday mornings.

🔘 Food market: Mon–Sat 8–2, 5–8; clothes market: Mon, Wed, Fri–Sat 8–8
🚇 Sant Antoni

SANT JOSEP ORIOL

Map 132 F11
Plaça de Sant Josep Oriol, 08002

This picture market, said to be the equivalent of Paris' Montmartre art market, is a great place to browse on a weekend, where you can enjoy the pretty setting.

🔘 Sat–Sun 10–2 🚇 Liceu

SANTA CATERINA

Map 133 H11
Passeig de Lluís Companys, 08003
Tel 93 319 21 35

Established in 1848, this food market's namesake is the convent that once stood on

the site. The original building has been renovated by the prestigious Enric Miralles Benedetta Tagliablue architecture studio.

🔘 Mon, Wed, Sat 7–3, Tue, Thu–Fri 7–3, 5–8.30 🚇 Arc de Triomf

SANTA LLÚCIA

Map 133 G11
Plaça Nova

This art and craft market is held every year around Christmas. All the items sold here are handmade, and you can choose from a range of Christmas tree decorations and imaginative jewellery fashioned from unusual materials.

🔘 8–23 Dec 10–10 🚇 Jaume I

WHAT TO DO

PERFORMANCE

With Barcelona's wide choice of performances, you can hear every type of music, watch cutting-edge modern dance, opera or classical ballet, go to the theatre, take in the latest Hollywood blockbuster or a thought-provoking arthouse production at the cinema.

Barcelona has a well established reputation for modern music and is home to the Sónar festival (see page 180)

CINEMA

Barcelona has plenty of venues, ranging from single-screens to multi-complexes. Some will show movies in the original language with Spanish subtitles.

● First showings are usually 4pm to 4.30pm, and the most popular is at 10pm–10.30pm.
● Many cinemas have a reduced-price day, the *día del espectador*, usually on Monday or Wednesday.
● Cinema listings are in the *Guía del Ocio* and the papers.
● Smoking is not permitted in the city's cinemas.

CLASSICAL MUSIC, DANCE AND OPERA

The star venues are L'Auditori, home to the city's symphony orchestra, the OBC, and the Palau de la Música Catalana. The city's churches make wonderful settings for occasional concerts. The tourist office will be able to provide information.

Barcelona is Spain's most vibrant city for contemporary dance, and particularly for performances by groups such as the Gelabert-Azzopardi Companyia de Dansa and Metros who appear during

festivals. You can catch visiting ballet companies at the Liceu, as well as flamenco companies. The city has its own *tablaos*, places where you can see flamenco, such as Poble Espanyol (see page 118).

● The season runs from September to the end of June.
● Buy tickets from the box offices, by phone or via Servi-Caixa or Caixa de Catalunya (see below).
● Get information in the monthly *Informatiu Musical* from tourist offices, *Guía del Ocio* and the daily press.
● Smoking is not permitted in the auditoria of these venues.

CONTEMPORARY LIVE MUSIC

Rock, jazz, *rumba catalana* and Catalan music thrive alongside the vibrant DJ-based scene, and the city is famous for its live music and summer festivals. Latin, Cuban and the sounds of Africa also have strong followings.

● Listings magazines include the *Guía del Ocio*, *Barcelona Metropolitan*, *AB*, *Go BCN* and *Mondo Sonoro*; all available at news-stands, bars and shops.
● Friday's edition of *El País*

carries the excellent *Tentaciones* magazine.
● Note that many smaller music venues close in August, but outdoor concerts are often held during the summer.
● Tickets are usually bought at the door.

THEATRE

Catalan theatre, with its blend of music, dance and spectacular production, seamlessly crosses the language barrier, making theatre a far more accessible experience than elsewhere in Spain. Look out for companies such as Els Comedians, whose productions are based on mime, folklore, circus and music; La Cubana, popular for its mix of glitz and audience participation; and the mainstream Lliure. Els Comedians and La Cubana have no fixed base, but Lliure, the city's most prestigious company, is based at Teatre Lliure.

● The main season runs from September to the end of June.
● Performances start between 9pm and 10.30pm. Some theatres have 6pm–7pm performances on Wednesday, Saturday and Sunday; most theatres close on Monday.
● Buy tickets at box offices (some are cash only).
● The magazine *Guía del Ocio* has listings.

TICKETING IN BARCELONA

Services run by two savings banks, known as Servi-Caixa and Tel-Entrada, allow you to book tickets on the internet, over the counter in some branches, by telephone or via the ticketing machines found next to the cash machines in bigger branches.

● Servi-Caixa, La Caixa
Tel 902 33 22 11
www.serviticket.com.
● Tel-Entrada, Caixa Catalunya
Tel 902 10 12 12
www.telentrada.com.

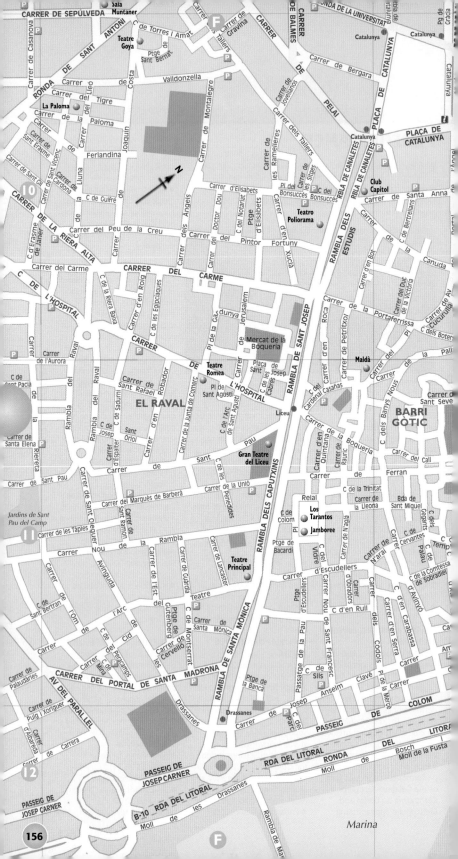

CARRER DE SEPÚLVEDA

Sala Muntaner

CARRER DE SANT ANTONI

Teatre Goya

Ptge. Sant Bernat

de Torres i Amat

Carrer de Gravina

CARRER DE BALMES

CARRER

Carrer dels Tallers

RONDA DE LA UNIVERSITAT

Catalunya

Catalunya

Pg de Gràcia

RONDA DE SANT ANTONI

Carrer del Lleó

Carrer del Tigre

de Costa

Valldonzella

PL de Montalegre

Carrer de Jovellanos

CARRER DE PELAI

Carrer de Bergara

PLAÇA DE CATALUNYA

La Paloma

Carrer de la Paloma

Joaquim

Carrer dels Tallers

Catalunya

PLAÇA DE CATALUNYA

Carrer de Sant Erasme

Carrer de Sant Vicenç

Carrer de Cardona

Ferlandina

de Lluna

C de Guifre

N

Carrer de les Ramelleres

Pl de Bonsuccés

Carrer de les Sitges

C del Bonsuccés

Club Capitol

Carrer de Santa Anna

10

CARRER DE LA RIERA ALTA

C d'Erasme de Janer

Carrer del Peu de la Creu

dels Àngels

Carrer d'Elisabets

Carrer del Doctor Dou

Ptge d'Elisabets

C del Notariat

Teatro Poliorama

Carrer d'en Bot

C de Betrellans

de Santa Anna

Canuda

C de Sant Gil

Carrer del Pintor Fortuny

Xucla

RAMBLA DELS ESTUDIS

Carrer del Duc de la Victòria

Carrer de la Portaferrissa

Pl

C dels Boters

CARRER DEL CARME

C de la Riera Baixa

Carrer d'en Roig

Carrer de les Egipcíaques

Jerusalem

Pl de la Gardunya

Mercat de la Boqueria

Plaça de Sant Josep

RAMBLA DE SANT JOSEP

Roca

Carrer d'en

Carrer de Petritxol

Maldà

Carrer del

BARRI GÒTIC

CARRER DE L'HOSPITAL

Carrer de Sant Pacià

CARRER DEL CARME

CARRER DE L'HOSPITAL

Carrer de Sadurní

Teatre Romea

Carrer de Sant Rafael

Carrer de Robador

Carrer de la Junta de Comerç

Pl de Sant Agustí

C de l'Arc de Sant Agustí

Cabres

Liceu

Cardenal Casañas

Carrer de la Boqueria

C dels Banys Nous

Carrer de Sant Seve

EL RAVAL

Rambla del Raval

C de Josep

Sant Oriol

C d'en

Pau

Gran Teatre del Liceu

Carrer d'en Quintana

Carrer d'en Rauric

C dels Gegants

Carrer del Call

Carrer de Santa Elena

Carrer de l'Aurora

Carrer de l'Espater

Sant

Carrer de les Penedides

Carrer Reial

Ferran

C de la Trinitat

Carrer de la Leona

Bda de Sant Miquel

C de N'agla

Carrer de N'aral

Cervantes

C de

Temp

11

Jardins de Sant Pau del Camp

Carrer de les Tàpies

Carrer de Sant Pau

Carrer del Marquès de Barberà

Carrer de Sant Oleguer

Carrer de Sant Ramon

Carrer de la Unió

Rambla

RAMBLA DELS CAPUTXINS

C de Colom

Los Tarantos

Jamboree

Ptge de Bacardi

Pl

C del Vidre

Carrer d'en Rull

Carrer de Palau

C de la Comtessa de Sobradiel

d'Avinyó

Ca

Carrer

Avinguda

Carrer de Guàrdia

Carrer de Lancàster

Teatre Principal

Teatre

del

Ptge de la Pau

Passatge d'Escudellers

d'Escudellers

Carrer Nou de Sant Francesc

Carrer dels Codols

Carrer d'en Carabassa

Carrer d'en Serra

Carrer

Ptge de la Banca

Am

Carrer de Sant Bertran

C de l'Om

l'Arc

C de la Cid

C de Guttenberg

C de Montserrat

Cervelló

C de Santa Mònica

RAMBLA DE SANTA MÒNICA

C del Pelaions

C de la Mina

Ptge de Gutenberg

C de

Sils

Anselm

Clavé

Pl de la Merè

COLOM

CARRER DEL PORTAL DE SANTA MADRONA

Drassanes

Drassanes

PASSEIG DE COLOM

12

Carrer de Palaudàries

Carrer de Puig i Xoriguer

Carrer d'Albareda

Carrer

Carrera

PASSEIG DE JOSEP CARNER

RDA DEL LITORAL

PASSEIG

DEL

LITORAL

Moll de la Fusta

Bosch

RDA DEL LITORAL

RONDA

Moll

PASSEIG DE JOSEP CARNER

B-10 RDA DEL LITORAL

Moll de les Drassanes

Rambla de Mar

Marina

F

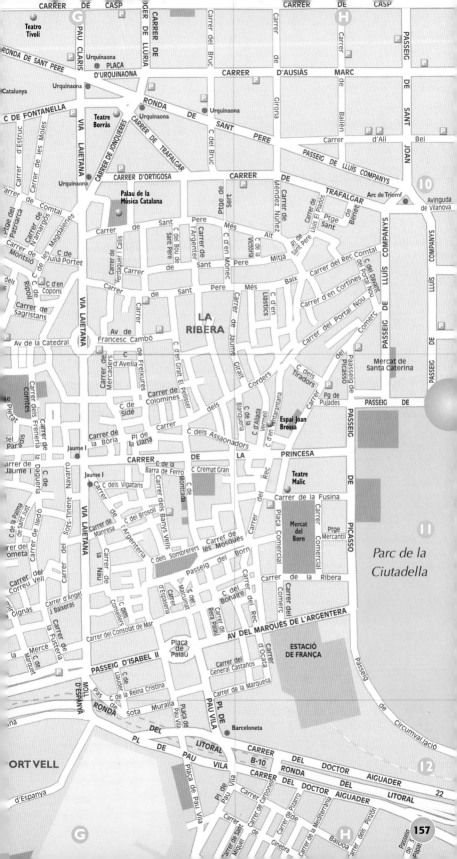

Cinema

COLISEUM

Map 159 F9
Gran Vía de les Cortes Catalanes 595, 08007
Tel 902 42 42 43
This neo-baroque cinema was built in the 1920s with the intention of lending Barcelona a touch of the splendour that America's first cinemas had.

It seats 1,689 people and has the latest developments in cinematic technology, but doesn't show original language films. Snacks are available.
🎞 €7 🚇 Universitat

COMEDIA

Map 159 G9
Passeig de Gràcia 13, 08007
Tel 902 15 84 54
Formerly a theatre, Comedia has been converted into a small multiplex cinema with the capability of running five movies at a time. It shows mostly international mainstream films, which are often dubbed into Spanish. There are late performances at weekends and snacks are available.
🎞 From €4 🚇 Passeig de Gràcia

FILMOTECA DE CATALUNYA

Map 158 E7
Avinguda de Sarria 33, 08029
Tel 93 410 75 90
www.cultura.gencat.net/filmo
The Catalan film archive shows movies as part of season dedicated to particular directors. Many of these directors are not household names, yet have a rich collection of work. Films are shown in their original languages, sometimes with Catalan subtitles. Unusually, smoking is allowed and there is a café open on nights when there are screenings.
🎞 From €2 🚇 Hospital Clinic

IMAX

Map 159 F12
Moll d'Espanya s/n, 08039
Tel 93 225 11 11
www.imaxintegral.com
One of the few IMAX cinemas that has three projection systems: Imax, Omnimax and 3D. The screen is 27m (90ft), which means that the movies prove to be spectacular. You'll find it in Maremagnum shopping complex at Port Vell.
🎞 €6.60–€9.60 🚇 Drassanes

MALDÀ

Map 156 F11
Carrer del Pi 5, 08002
Tel 93 317 85 29
This small cinema retains a timeless feel in the manner of old-fashioned cinemas, showing original language films with subtitles. From time to time, customers can buy two tickets for the price of one. Snacks are available.
🎞 From €5 🚇 Liceu

MÈLIES

Map 158 E9
Carrer de Villarroel 102, 08011
Tel 93 451 00 51
This two-screen cinema shows both classic and modern arthouse movies in their original language, with Spanish subtitles. Contrary to cinema-going habits the world over, Mèlies does not allow food and drink on the premises.
🎞 From €6 🚇 Urgell

RENOIR LES CORTS

Map 158 C6
Carrer d'Eugeni d'Ors 12, 08028
Tel 93 490 55 10
www.cinesrenoir.com
Multiplex with six screens on which to watch original language films with Spanish subtitles. It is very popular place, and particularly among young cinema enthusiasts. Snacks are available.
🎞 From €4 🚇 Les Corts

RENOIR FLORIDABLANCA

Map 158 E10
Carrer de Floridablanca 135, 08011
Tel 93 228 93 93
www.cinesrenoir.com
This is part of the same chain as the Renoir Les Corts. It usually has a choice of seven different original-language movies, all subtitled in Spanish. One particular plus is that it's very central, close to the old town and lively El Raval area. Snacks are available.
🎞 From €4 🚇 Sant Antoni

VERDI

Map 159 G7
Carrer de Verdi 32, 08012
Tel 93 238 78 00
This was one of the first cinemas in Barcelona to break the mould of screening mainstream blockbusters. It shows non-commercial, original-language films, all subtitled in Spanish. Snacks are available.
🎞 From €5 🚇 Fontana

VERDI PARK

Map 159 H7
Carrer de Torrijos 49, 08012
Tel 93 238 79 90
Due to the overwhelming success of its first cinema, Verdi opened a second multiplex, which also shows quality original language films. This second Verdi is set behind the first. Snacks are available.
🎞 From €5 🚇 Fontana

YELMO CINEPLEX ICARIA

Map 159 J12
Carrer de Salvador Espriu 61, 08005
Tel 93 221 75 85
www.yelmocineplex.com
This multiplex commands no fewer than 15 screens, all showing subtitled original language films. As it's in a shopping centre, it is often busy, despite its considerable capacity. Snacks are available.
🎞 From €5 🚇 Ciutadella-Villa Olímpica

WHAT TO DO

Classical Music, Dance and Opera

L'AUDITORI
Map 159 J10
Carrer de Lepant 150, 08013
Tel 93 247 93 00
www.auditori.com
L'Auditori is a comparatively recent addition to Barcelona's cultural landscape. It was designed by the Spanish architect Rafael Moneo and opened in 1999. The hall is the venue for contemporary, classical, jazz and folk music concerts.
From €6 Glories

GRAN TEATRE DEL LICEU
Map 156 F11
La Rambla 51–59, 08002
Tel 93 485 99 13
www.liceubarcelona.com
One of the most prestigious opera houses in Europe, the Liceu underwent a comprehensive restoration following a fire in 1992 (see page 80).

The opera is first class; classical music concerts and ballet productions are also held here. Bar on premises.
€6–€150 Liceu

PALAU DE LA MÚSICA CATALANA
Map 157 G10
Carrer de Sant Francesc de Paula 2, 08003
Tel 93 295 72 00
www.palaumusica.org
Attending a concert in this Modernista hall is an unforgettable experience. The building was designed by Lluís Domènech i Montaner (1850–1923) and was con-

ceived for the Orfeó Catalán (see pages 104–107). The type of concert does vary, although classical is most prominent, but there is also some jazz and folk. Bar on premises.
From €5 Urquinaona

TEATRE MUSICAL
Map 158 C10
Carrer de Lleida 40, 08004
Tel 93 423 15 41
This large hall occupies Barcelona's former sports arena and is now devoted to huge productions for which only a larger stage will do. Shows typically include national and international touring musicals and a variety of other remarkable stage events. Bar on premises.
From €18 Espanya

Contemporary Live Music

BIKINI
Map 158 D7
Carrer de Deu i Mata 105, 08029
Tel 93 322 08 00
www.bikinibcn.com
This is a well-known spot for nightlife and music in Barcelona and it has been at

the forefront of the scene since 1953. There are three halls in all, each staging different styles of music and each attracting its own crowd. The live music includes Latin jazz, pop, rock and DJ sessions. Light snacks are available, including a Bikini sandwich.
From €9 Les Corts

LA BOÎTE
Map 158 E7
Avinguda Diagonal 477, 08036
Tel 93 319 17 89
www.masimas.com
This is one of Barcelona's oldest concert halls. It focuses on funk, soul, rock, hip-hop, flamenco fusion and plenty more besides. Jam sessions are organized on Mondays and Tuesdays.
From €7 Hospital Clinic

CAIXAFORUM
Map 158 C10
Avinguda del Marquès de Comillas 6–8, 08038
Tel 93 476 86 00
www.fundacio.lacaixa.es/caixaforum
This arts centre has several art galleries, a magnificent restaurant, a café and a shop. It also has a large, modern

auditorium that plays host to a range of music events, most notably world music concerts. The building is one of the newest art spaces in the city (see page 65).
From €9 Espanya

LA COVA DEL DRAC
Off map 158 F6
Carrer de Vallmajor 33, 08021
Tel 93 200 70 32
The Dragon's Cave is dimly lit and smoky, making it an ambient venue for live music and entertainment, with jazz, Latin jazz and fusion booked here regularly. Jam sessions and comedians are also here from time to time.
From €8 Lesseps

L'ESPAI
Map 158 F7
Travessera de Gràcia 63, 08021
Tel 93 414 31 33
www.cultura.gencat.es/espai
This public space belongs to the Catalan autonomous government's Department of Culture. All sorts of cultural events are held here, which include folk, cabaret and Catalan music nights, as well as modern and alternative music and dance.
From €7 Diagonal

JAMBOREE
Map 156 F11
Plaça Reial 17, 08002
Tel 93 301 75 64
Jamboree opened in 1959 and its popularity has grown so much that it is today one of the busiest jazz clubs in town. It can be found just off Las Ramblas, and this spot makes it a popular club for visitors. Live jazz and blues are played here and the later the evening, the funkier the music. Credit cards are not accepted.
From €6.50 Liceu

LUZ DE GAS
Map 158 F7
Carrer de Muntaner 246, 08021
Tel 93 209 77 11
www.luzdegas.com
This old music hall is one the city's prime concert venues. Enjoy some great live music, ranging from blues to cover bands. Arrive early to avoid a long wait outside.
From €8 Diagonal

LA PALOMA
Map 156 F10
Carrer del Tigre 27, 08001
Tel 93 301 68 97
www.lapaloma-bcn.com
On weeknights, La Paloma becomes a salsa dance hall. After midnight, the clientele changes dramatically; younger

people flock to the venue for its excellent house music. The live music varies on different nights of the week.
€6 Sant Antoni

RAZZMATAZZ
Off map 159 J10
Carrer dels Almogavers 122, 08018
Tel 93 320 82 00
www.salarazzmatazz.com
This former steel factory has three different halls hosting music events of all kinds. The larger hall provides a venue for live music concerts, lounge, techno, pop and Brazilian nights. The other two are set up for DJ use. Credit cards are not accepted.
From €12 Marina

LOS TARANTOS
Map 156 F11
Plaça Reial 17, 08002
Tel 93 318 30 67
Other Spanish cities are more closely associated with flamenco, but you'll find many a fan among the region's Andalucían residents. Los Tarantos gives you a taste of Seville in the heart of the Barri Gòtic. You'll also dance to tango, salsa and other Latin rhythms.
€25 Liceu

Theatre

ARTENBRUT
Map 159 G8
Carrer del Perill 9–11, 08012
Tel 93 457 97 05
www.artenbrutteatre.com
Artenbrut is not the sort of theatre to churn out the same play week after week; it changes around every two weeks. It provides a stage for national and international productions, mostly the work of smaller theatre companies. Bar on the premises.
From €8 Diagonal

CLUB CAPITOL
Map 156 F10
La Rambla 138, 08002
Tel 93 412 20 38
www.teatral.net/clubcapitol
This is a modern theatre, with two auditoria in use simultaneously. You'll find comedy, recitals and cabaret, as well as other dramatic works here, at the top of La Rambla. Bar on the premises.
From €15 Catalunya

ESPAI JOAN BROSSA
Map 157 H11
Carrer d'Allada Vermell 13, 08003
Tel 93 310 13 64
www.espaibrossa.com
The shows staged at Espai Joan Brossa include flamenco, contemporary ballet, French cabaret, magic, poetry and a handful of avant-garde productions, which may not be suitable for every audience.
From €6 Arc de Triomf

INSTITUT DEL TEATRE
Map 158 D11
Plaça Margarida Xirgú, Montjuïc
Tel 93 227 39 00
www.diba.es/iteatre
This is Barcelona's main theatre and dance school which hosts performances in three auditoria. These shows have often been developed with leading choreographers and can showcase some of the best of cutting-edge dance.
Free Espanya

MERCAT DE LES FLORS

Map 158 D10

Carrer de Lleida 59, 08004

Tel 93 426 18 75

This theatre space, host to many disciplines of the dramatic arts, was once a flower market—hence the name—and part of the 1929 International Exhibition complex. The building holds two performing areas, staging avant-garde theatre, dance and electronic music.

From €10 Espanya

SALA BECKETT

Map 159 H6

Carrer de l'Alegre de Dalt 55 bis, 08024

Tel 93 284 53 12

www.salabeckett.com

The Sala Beckett organization was founded in 1989 for the purpose of researching avant-garde theatre and emerging dramatic language. It has since developed and this small place has bold shows, including contemporary dance and other performance arts. There are occasional productions in English.

From €17 Joanic

SALA MUNTANER

Map 156 F9

Carrer de Muntaner 4, 08011

Tel 93 451 57 52

www.salamuntaner.com

Sala Muntaner is the scene of alternative productions, recitals, cabaret, music concerts and dance shows. Late performances at weekends.

From €6 Universitat

TEATRE BORRÀS

Map 157 G10

Plaça d'Urquinaona 9, 08010

Tel 93 412 15 82

www.teatral.net/borras

This theatre is known for its drama by British playwrights, with Catalan interpretations of works by Shakespeare, Wilde and Noel Coward, to name but a few. The intimate stage is used to full effect during the shows, and the theatre

is easy to find, opposite the metro station.

From €8 Urquinaona

TEATRE GOYA

Map 156 F10

Carrer de Joaquín Costa 68, 08001

Tel 93 318 19 84

www.teatral.net/goya

Teatre Goya has stood the test of time: It opened in 1917 and the art nouveau auditorium has been well preserved. It stages a variety of theatre, ballet and musicals from a diverse range of companies.

From €8 Universitat

TEATRE GREC

Map 158 D11

Passeig de Santa Madrona 36, 08038

Tel 93 301 7775/90 210 1212 (tickets)

www.bcn.es/grec

This faux ancient-Greek amphitheatre, carved out of an old stone quarry in 1929, is found through the Jardins Amargós on Montjuïc. It's home to many of the concerts performed under the umbrella of the Grec summer music festival in late June and July every year. There's an outdoor café open in the evenings in July.

From €15 Espanya, then bus 55 or 50 to Montjuïc

TEATRE LLIURE

Map 158 D11

Passeig de Santa Madrona 3, 08034

Tel 93 289 27 70

www.teatrelliure.com

The old Agriculture Palace is now the headquarters of the forward-thinking Lliure Theatre. Two halls exist, where you'll see diverse plays, music events, dance performances and other shows. There is also a good restaurant and café. Credit cards are not accepted.

From €10 Espanya

TEATRE LLIURE DE GRÀCIA

Map 159 G7

Carrer del Montseny 47, 08012

Tel 93 218 92 51

www.teatrelliure.com

This was the only place in the city to stage plays in Catalan

during Franco's era. It's name means freedom and it is well known for alternative theatre, contemporary dance, cabaret and music, primarily jazz.

From €8 Fontana

TEATRE MALIC

Map 157 H11

Carrer de la Fusina 3, 08003

Tel 93 310 70 35

www.teatremalic.com

La Fanfarra, a local theatre company, opened the tiny 60-seat Teatre Malic in 1984. Since then it has staged an eclectic range of productions, including jazz, cabaret, magic shows and shadow theatre. Every two years this company takes part in the Butxaca opera festival, which concentrates on new works and the revival of little-know or neglected works. The last one was held in 2004. Credit cards are not accepted.

From €5 Jaume I

TEATRE NACIONAL DE CATALUNYA

Map 159 K9

Plaça de les Arts 1, 08013

Tel 93 306 57 00

www.tnc.es

Catalonia's official public theatre was completed in 1997 and has its own resident company. It is a modern building and in keeping with a number of other buildings in the city it uses lots of glass and

columns. Famous Spanish and international productions are staged here. There is a bar on the premises.

From €16 Glòries

TEATRE PRINCIPAL
Map 156 F11
La Rambla 27, 08002
Tel 93 301 47 50
www.teatreprincipal.com
Teatre Principal was built on the site of Barcelona's first theatre, which opened at the end of the 16th century as an opera house. It was a charitable affair, as all the money it made was donated to the nearby Santa Creu hospital. The shows here are rich and varied, ranging from comedy to opera.
🎭 From €8 🚇 Drassanes

TEATRE ROMEA
Map 156 F11
Carrer de l'Hospital 51, 08001
Tel 93 301 55 04
www.teatral.net/romea
This is one of Barcelona's most popular theatres. Teatre Romea has preserved its original structure and interior, including the magnificent entrance. All kinds of theatre and performance can be seen here, often by well-known Spanish and international playwrights.
🎭 From €12 🚇 Liceu

TEATRENEU TEATRE
Map 159 G7
Carrer de Terol 26–28, 08012
Tel 93 285 79 00
Gràcia is becoming well known as provider of lively year-round entertainment in the heart of the city. Theatres such as Teatreneu, which puts on contemporary plays, musicals and dance, are springing up alongside good restaurants and cafés.
🎭 From €5 🚇 Fontana

TEATRO APOLO
Map 158 E11
Avinguda del Paral.lel 57, 08004
Tel 93 441 90 07
www.teatreapolo.com
The old Apolo theatre building was pulled down some years ago and transformed into a smart hotel. The theatre itself lived on, though, and now occupies the ground floor of the same building. This is an accessible theatre company that caters for all tastes: Commercial drama is performed, alongside *zarzuela* (Spanish light opera), ballet and a range of other events. There is a bar on the premises, but credit cards are not accepted.
🎭 From €10 🚇 Paral.lel

TEATRO POLIORAMA
Map 156 F10
La Rambla 115, 08002
Tel 93 317 75 99
www.teatrepoliorama.com
This is one of the oldest theatres in the region of Catalonia. You will find it in the former building of the Academy of Sciences and Arts and nestling behind an art nouveau façade. It is the headquarters of the Catalan company Dagoll Dagom and you'll find mainly comedies and musicals here.
🎭 From €16 🚇 Catalunya

TEATRO TÍVOLI
Map 157 G10
Carrer de Casp 8, 08010
Tel 93 412 20 63
www.teatral.net/tivoli
Tívoli's façade and entrance hall are both original architectural features dating from the late 19th century when the

theatre was built. Commercial theatre is the preference and the famous Catalan theatre company La Cubana (see page 155) is a regular collaborator in these productions.
🎭 From €10 🚇 Urquinaona

TEATRO VICTORIA
Map 158 E11
Avinguda del Paral.lel 67, 08004
Tel 93 441 39 79
www.teatrevictoria.com
This area housed a proud cluster of theatres and concert halls in the early 20th century. Sadly, only a few remain as reminders of those glorious days: The Victoria is one of the original set, showing comedies, classical dance and flamenco. Bar on the premises.
🎭 From €18 🚇 Paral.lel

TEATRO VILLARROEL
Map 158 E9
Carrer de Villarroel 87, 08011
Tel 93 451 12 34
www.teatral.net/villarroel
This is a relatively new theatre, with a varied and often commercial slant. In the past, it has caused a furore for staging productions with scandalous content. The auditorium seats just over 500 and there's a small bar in the foyer.
🎭 From €10 🚇 Urgell

VERSUS TEATRE
Map 159 K9
Carrer de los Castillejos 179, 08013
Tel 93 232 31 84
www.versusteatre.com
Founded in 1995, Versus Teatre puts on a range of dramatic works and leans

greatly towards fringe theatre. The poetry sessions regularly held here, entitled Poets and Prophets, are becoming particularly popular. Credit cards are not accepted.
🎭 From €8 🚇 Glories

NIGHTLIFE

There's some of the country's best nightlife in Barcelona, where club culture is taken seriously and top DJs make regular appearances. The scene evolves constantly, with bars and clubs opening, closing and changing management all the time, and city's resident DJs skipping from one venue to another.

Make a point of collecting flyers when you arrive and pick up free listings magazines, such as *Punto H, Mes & Mes* and *Barcelona Metropolitan*. Things get going late, so set out to hit the bar scene around 11pm or later and be prepared to wait in line before partying at the clubs until 5am or 6am. Weekends are particularly frenetic, when locals, weekenders from all over Europe and huge numbers of UK bachelor parties come face to face at popular night-time venues. Entry to bars and cafés is usually free, but expect to pay to get into the clubs.

Barcelona's nightlife attracts visitors from all over Europe, who come with the intention of sampling as much as they can

The summer scene is a different beast. Some outdoor clubs only operate from June to the end of September and there's the bonus that others, normally weekend-only venues, will be pulling in the huge crowds. This is when Barcelona's waterfront setting comes into its own, with beach bars spilling onto the sand.

Don't miss the final part of nights out in the city: breakfast at one of the all-night bars where you can finish the evening with fresh pastries and chocolate, or boost your energy for more clubbing. This stop has become an institution of its own.

GAY AND LESBIAN

Barcelona's gay and lesbian scene is among the best in Europe, with hundreds of establishments supplying everything from gym access to more staple needs such as food and accommodation, as well as some of the best party nights. Nightlife brings many types of people together, so you'll have a great time even at places that are not strictly gay—*el ambiente* (the atmosphere) is all. Head for the Eixample, known as the 'Gayxample' with the largest concentration of gay venues in the city, to start your explorations.

Remember that Barcelona is close to Sitges (see pages 196–197), just down the coast, which is also known for its gay nightlife.

● The group Coordinadora Gai-Lesbiana is your best source of information for what's happening. This umbrella organization works with the Ajuntamant (town hall) on all issues of concern to the gay community in the city, and should be your first stop. You can drop by during the evening (*Mon–Fri 7pm–9pm, Sat 6pm–8pm*) to pick up literature and information, or call the free information line (*tel 900 601 601*) from anywhere in Spain between 6pm–10pm. You can find Coordinadora Gai-Lesbiana at Carrer de Finlàndia 45, 08014 (*tel 93 298 00 29, fax 93 298 06 18*) or visit www.cogailes.org.
● There are two publications that you should look out for. The *Gay Barcelona* map, which is updated annually, and the *Nois* magazine, which is comprehensive and accurate; visit www.revistanois.com for more details. You'll find both of these at the shop Sestienda on the Carrer de Rauric 11, Barri Gòtic (*tel/fax 93 318 86 76*).

WHAT'S WHERE

● Maremagnum and the Port Olímpic for salsa, mainstream rock and house clubs.
● Plaça Reial and the Barri Gòtic for pop, rock, funk and soul.
● El Raval for old-established bars and clubs.
● La Riberia for designer bars and clubs.
● Montjuïc for non-stop all-night clubbing.
● Eixample and Gràcia for trendy clubs, salsa, samba and tango.
● Zona Alta (including Sarrià, Puxet, Sant Gervasi and Tibidabo) for serious poseurs and spending serious money.

Bars and Cafés

AL LIMÓN NEGRO
Carrer de Escudellers Blancs 8, 08002
Tel 93 318 97 70
This bar is more than just a place for a drink: art exhibitions, shows, performances and inspired music are all part of the entertainment. A limited no-fuss menu is available.
🕐 Tue–Sun 6pm–3am 🚇 Jaume I

L'ASCENSOR
Carrer de Bellafila 3, 08002
Tel 93 318 53 47
A Frankenstein of the drinking world, this bar has been created using parts of other, older bars. L'Ascensor certainly has character. The major feature is an old elevator from which the bar gains its name. Latin-American cocktails set the mood and it's invariably busy at the weekends. Credit cards are not accepted.
🕐 Mon–Thu, Sun 6.30pm–2.30am, Fri–Sat 6.30pm–3am 🚇 Jaume I

EL BAR DEL MAJESTIC
Passeig de Gràcia 68, 08008
Tel 93 488 17 17
Chic, discreet and peaceful, this café is in the grounds of the Majestic Hotel (see page 250). The clientele is mostly VIPs, businessmen and young trendsetters, relaxing after a busy day. In the evenings, it's transformed into a piano bar. Sandwiches are available.
🕐 Daily 10am–2am 🚇 Passeig de Gràcia

BAR DEL PÍ
Plaça de Sant Josep Oriol 1, 08002
Tel 93 302 21 23
One of the oldest bars in town, where the drinking space is split over three levels. The clientele love a good discussion of the political, cultural or intellectual kind. If you don't want to talk, there's a stunning view over the church Santa Maria del Pí and the Barri Gòtic, with basic tapas on the menu. Credit cards are not accepted.
🕐 Mon, Wed–Sat 9am–11pm, Sun 10am–10pm 🚇 Liceu

BCN ROUGE
Carrer del Poeta Cabanyes 21, 08004
Tel 93 442 49 85
Ring the doorbell to gain entry here. Its rooms are not vast, but have dark velvet walls bathed in candlelight. A perfect place for that romantic date,

especially as the barstaff serve creative cocktails.
🕐 Thu 11pm–3am, Fri–Sat 11pm–4.30am 🚇 Paral.lel

BENIDORM
Carrer de Joaquín Costa 39, 08001
Tel 93 317 80 52
With its shrewd 1960s interior, Benidorm brings new life to the term kitsch. The interesting design theme extends into the smaller details, with retro gadgets placed throughout the bar. It is a light-hearted place for a drink to start the evening. You'll find fellow drinkers are from all over the world. Credit cards are not accepted.
🕐 Mon–Thu 7pm–2am, Fri–Sat 7pm–3am 🚇 San Antoni

CAFÉ DE L'ÒPERA
La Rambla 74, 08002
Tel 93 317 75 85

This fin de siècle café is popular with opera enthusiasts as the Gran Teatre de Liceu is just across the road. Chocolate with typical Spanish *churros* is a must. The terrace looks out over the lively Rambla.
🕐 Daily 8.30am–2.30am 🚇 Liceu

BERIMBAU
Passeig del Born 17, 08003
Tel 646 005 514
This bar opened 25 years ago and was originally a Brazilian dance hall. Today the colonial air remains, as does the samba and salsa music. A great place to begin an evening—sampling some delicious Brazilian cocktails made with fresh fruit juices. No credit cards.
🕐 Daily 6pm–2.30am 🚇 Jaume I

BOADAS COCKTAIL BAR
Carrer dels Tallers 1, 08001
Tel 93 318 95 92
Picasso and Hemingway were regulars here. It was opened in 1933 by a barman who used to work at the famous La Floridita of La Habana in Cuba, one of Hemingway's much-loved watering holes. The cocktails served here count among the best in town and it is also a perfect place to stop for an aperitif. Credit cards are not accepted.
🕐 Mon–Thu noon–2am, Fri–Sat noon–3am 🚇 Catalunya

WHAT TO DO

EL BOSQUE DE LES FADES

Passatge de la Banca 7, 08002
Tel 93 317 26 49
www.museocerabcn.com

This bar is reminiscent of a fairy tale, complete with an enchanted forest, fairies and waterfalls. El Bosque de les Fades takes you back to your childhood and is positively dreamlike. Storytellers perform here and it's also a venue for live music.

🕔 Mon–Thu 10.30am–1.30am, Fri–Sat 10.30am–2.30am 🚇 Drassanes

BUDA BARCELONA

Tel 93 318 42 52
Carrer de Pau Claris 92, 08010

The fashionista set have been flocking to this bar/restaurant since it opened in the summer of 2003. Faux rococo furniture and Persian-style rugs contrast with its airy spaces. Come after 12.30am at the weekend to avoid having to wait outside.

🕔 Daily 9.30pm–3am 🚇 Diagonal

CAFÉ D'ESTIU

Plaça Sant lu 5–6, 08002
Tel 93 310 30 14

Café d'Estiu is part of Museu Frederic Marès, in an old courtyard with a fountain. The café is hidden away from the bustling activity of the nearby cathedral square and is a great spot for a rest. Sandwiches and a simple menu are available. Credit cards are not accepted.

🕔 Daily 10–10, Apr–end Sep 🚇 Jaume I

CAFÉ ROYALE

Carrer Nou de Zurbarano 3, 08002
Tel 93 317 61 24

Made popular by the film director, Pedro Almodóvar, and his crowd, Café Royale is sophisticated, making good use of modern lighting and a split-level venue. Style-conscious customers frequent the bar and dance to soul, funk, bossa nova and Latin jazz. Credit cards are not accepted.

🕔 Daily 11pm–2.30am 🚇 Liceu

CAFÉ ZURICH

Plaça de Catalunya
Tel 93 317 75 86

This café is so well known, and in such an obvious position at the top of Las Ramblas, that you are very likely to come across it at some point. And it's a good place to meet up with

people. It has lots of tables outside, so you can catch the sun and you're away from the road. But due to the position you can get lots of hassle from buskers and beggars.

🕔 Mon–Sat 8am–2pm, Sun 8am–11pm, Jun–end Oct; Mon–Thu, Sun 8am–11pm, Fri–Sat 8am–midnight, rest of year 🚇 Catalunya

CAPUTXES

Carrer de les Caputxes 4, 08003
Tel 93 319 77 57

This café was once just a flower shop. The flora has remained and refreshments such as coffees, teas, cakes and natural juices have been added to the formula. The food is simple but appetizing and substantial.

🕔 Tue–Sun 1.30–4, 8.30–11.30 🚇 Jaume I

ESPAI BARROC

Carrer de Montcada 20, 08003
Tel 93 310 06 73

Espai Barroc can be found on the ground floor of the Gothic Palau Dalmases: Flowers, chandeliers, candles, sculptures and paintings dominate the interior. Stop here for a glass of cava or a juice and let the music drift over you.

🕔 Tue–Sat 8pm–2am, Sun 6–10pm 🚇 Jaume I

SPECIAL

HOTEL RITZ

Gran Vía de les Corts Catalanes 668, 08010
Tel 93 318 52 00

This is about as luxurious and stylish as it gets. Service is faultless and the prices suit the name and surroundings. Breakfast is served in the flamboyant greenhouse-style dining room. In the evenings, listen to piano music while sipping your drink.

🕔 Daily 7am–11pm 🚇 Urquinaona

LA FIRA

Carrer de Provença 171, 08036

Fira means fairground, and this bar is so packed with items based on this theme that it looks rather like a museum. It's popular with larger groups and a lively, boisterous place to spend your evening. Credit cards are not accepted.

🕔 Tue–Thu 10pm–3am, Fri–Sat 7pm–4.30am, Sun 7pm–1am 🚇 Hospital Clinic

LES GENS QUE J'AIME

Carrer de València 286, 08008
Tel 93 215 68 79

You'll find baroque surroundings here, with comfortable sofas on which to spend intimate and peaceful evenings. You might even encounter a palm reader to reveal your future. The present will certainly be relaxed, comfortable and a little bohemian. Credit cards are not accepted.

🕔 Sun–Thu 6pm–2.30am, Fri–Sat 7pm–3am 🚇 Passeig de Gràcia

WHAT TO DO

MARSELLA

Carrer de Sant Pau 65, 08001
Tel 93 442 72 63

The interior of this bar was inspired by Toulouse-Lautrec, but dates back to the beginning of the 19th century. In keeping with its history, there are period mirrors on the walls and absinthe behind the bar.

Ⓒ Mon–Thu 10pm–2.30am, Fri–Sat 10pm–3.30am Ⓜ Liceu

GLACIAR

Plaça Reial 3, 08002
Tel 93 302 11 63

Thanks to its impressive selection of beers, Glaciar has become popular with visitors. It has a fantastic terrace on which to contemplate the comings and goings in Plaça Reial. Credit cards are not accepted.

Ⓒ Mon–Sat 4pm–2.30am, Sun 8am–2.15pm Ⓜ Liceu

GRANJA DE GAVÀ

Carrer de Joaquín Costa 37, 08001
Tel 93 317 58 83

This café was once an old dairy that now serves juices, coffees and other drinks. The interior has plenty of candles, flowers and plants, with regular poetry readings, exhibitions and live music. Credit cards are not accepted.

Ⓒ Mon–Thu 8am–1am, Fri–Sat 8am–3am Ⓜ San Antoni

HARLEM JAZZ CLUB

Carrer de la Comtessa de Sobradiel 8, 08002
Tel 93 310 07 55

Harlem was the very first jazz club to open in Barcelona. Live music is a way of life for the owners and the regulars come for the tango, flamenco, Celtic music, bossa nova and, of course, the jazz. Credit cards are not accepted.

Ⓒ Tue–Thu 8pm–4am, Fri–Sat 8pm–5am Ⓜ Drassanes

MIRABLAU

Plaça del Doctor Andreu, 08035
Tel 93 418 58 79

Coffee and snacks form the main focus in the morning and afternoon, but the evening brings drinks, cocktails and a fabulous view of the city. A perfect place for relaxing under the light of a summer sunset.

Ⓒ Sun–Thu 11am–4.30am, Fri–Sat 11am–5am Ⓜ Tramvia Blau

HIVERNACLE

Passeig de Picasso s/n, 08003
Tel 93 295 40 17

Hivernacle is in an old conservatory in Parc de la Ciutadella. Coffee and refreshments are served amid exotic plants. Occasionally live jazz and classical music concerts are held here. It's also a good place to eat in the evening.

Ⓒ Mon–Sat 9am–midnight, Sun 10am–4pm Ⓜ Arc de Triomf

IDEAL

Carrer d'Aribau 89, 08036
Tel 93 453 10 28

A British pub through and through, with a roaring fire, good beer and a range of whiskeys. It's relatively quiet so you might be surprised to find that it's where businessmen often bring their clients. There is a simple menu available, but credit cards are not accepted.

Ⓒ Mon–Sat 12.30pm–2.30am Ⓜ Passeig de Gràcia

LOS JUANELE

Carrer d'Aldana 4, 08015
Tel 93 454 06 49

This tapas bar comes with traditional Andalucían decoration: there's a bull's head on the wall and fairy lights hanging from the ceiling. The Juanele family, who run the bar, even teach customers how to dance sevillanas. Groups only on Tuesdays; credit cards are not accepted.

Ⓒ Thu–Sat 10pm–5.30am Ⓜ Paral.lel

KENTUCKY

Carrer de l'Arc del Teatre 11, 08001
Tel 93 3182878

This bar, with its late opening times, is a good choice for those times when you don't feel like heading home just yet. Sit back and marvel at the 1960s decorations. Credit cards are not accepted.

Ⓒ Tue–Sat 8pm–3am Ⓜ Drassanes

LONDON BAR

Carrer Nou de la Rambla 34, 08001
Tel 93 318 52 61

The art nouveau London Bar has long been popular in intellectual circles. Nowadays, the crowd is a mix of locals and visitors, who all enjoy the live music that is sometimes put on here. Credit cards are not accepted.

Ⓒ Tue–Thu, Sun 7.30pm–4.30am, Fri–Sat 7pm–5am Ⓜ Liceu

MIRAMELINDO

Passeig del Born 15, 08003
Tel 93 310 37 27

A wood-panelled, Colonial-style, intimate space where weekday nights are relaxing. The cocktails should not be missed here; try the Cuban mojitos (fresh mint, sugar, lime juice, rum and soda water) or caipirinhas (lime juice, sugar, brandy and ice) and then a coffee to help you regain a grasp on sobriety before leaving. Credit cards are not accepted.

Ⓒ Mon–Thu 8pm–2.30am, Fri–Sat 8pm–3.30am, Sun 7.30pm–2.30am Ⓜ Jaume I

MOND

Plaça del Sol 29, 08012
Tel 93 272 09 10

The motto of this pub is 'pop will make us free', plus the management employ some very talented DJs. If you don't manage to get in before it fills up, there's always space to mingle outside on the Plaça del Sol. Credit cards are not accepted.

Ⓒ Sun–Thu 9pm–2.30am, Fri–Sat 9pm–3am Ⓜ Fontana

WHAT TO DO

MUEBLES NAVARRO

Carrer de Riera Alta 4–6, 08001

This café gained its wealth of 1960s and 70s furniture when the old furniture shop that used to occupy the site closed down. Three long rooms lead off a central bar, and the presence of sofas gives a more relaxed atmosphere in one of the rooms. Coffee and cakes are on the menu. Credit cards are not accepted.

🕐 Tue–Thu 6pm–midnight, Fri–Sat 6pm–3am; closed Aug 🚇 Sant Antoni

PILÉ 43

Carrer d'Aglà 4, 08002
Tel 93 317 39 02

Pilé 43's bar stocks a wide range of beers, cocktails and teas. It is dotted with furniture and ornaments from the 1950s, 60s and 70s, all of which are available to purchase. Both vegetarian and non-vegetarian food is served.

🕐 Mon–Thu 8.30pm–2am, Fri–Sat 8.30pm–3am 🚇 Liceu

PUNTO BCN

Carrer de Muntaner 63–65, 08011
Tel 93 453 61 23

Punto BCN is right in the middle of Barcelona's gay area, the 'Gayxample'. This is an ideal choice for a quiet drink to start an evening out, with lounge music playing in the background. It is popular with students and visitors. Credit cards are not accepted.

🕐 Sun–Thu 6pm–2am, Fri–Sat 6.30pm–2.30am 🚇 Universitat

SCHILLING

Carrer de Ferran 23, 08002
Tel 93 317 67 87

This café maintains a traditional look. Breakfast is served in the morning, coffee and cakes in the afternoon and alcoholic drinks and cocktails in the evening.

🕐 Mon–Sat 10am–2.30am, Sun noon–2am 🚇 Liceu

EL TACO DE MARGARITA

Plaça del Duc de Medinaceli 1, 08002
Tel 93 331 86 32

A Mexican bar full of lively colours and plastic flowers. Breakfast is served, along with Mexican tacos in the afternoon and drinks in the evenings. There's also Mexican tapas in case you are peckish.

🕐 Mon–Fri 8am–3am, Sat–Sun 7pm–3am 🚇 Drassanes

TETERÍA JAZMÍN

Carrer de Maspons 11, 08012
Tel 93 218 71 84

Expect a rush on the senses with the aromas and colours at Moroccan-themed Tetería Jazmín. You can order from a large range of standard and herbal teas, and tuck into some wonderfully exotic cakes. Credit cards are not accepted.

🕐 Tue–Sun 6pm–2am 🚇 Fontana

ELS TRES TOMBS

Ronda de Sant Antoni 2, 08001
Tel 93 443 41 11

Great for an early breakfast after a night out and before going home: The ratio of locals to clubbers is surprisingly even. If the weather is good, sit out on the terrace, opposite Sant Antoni's book market. Credit cards are not accepted.

🕐 Daily 6am–2am 🚇 Sant Antoni

Clubs

ARENA

Carrer de Balmes 32, 08007
Tel 93 487 83 42

Barcelona has five Arena clubs and this is the longest established of the lot. House and techno fills the dance floor; the crowd is mixed and of all sexual orientations. It is not the place for a quiet night out. Credit cards are not accepted.

🕐 Tue–Sun midnight–5.30am 💶 From €7 🚇 Universitat

DANZATORIA

Carrer de Ramón Trias Fargas s/n, Marina Village, 08005
Tel 93 268 74 30
www.clubdanzatoria.com

The club has two fashionable and elaborate halls. You'll find the beautiful people here, all dressed in cutting-edge designer wear. Upstairs, the DJs choose lounge music, while downstairs house and techno create a more energetic atmosphere. A number of different music nights are held here throughout the week.

🕐 Hall 1: daily midnight–6am; Hall 2: Thu–Sun midnight–6am 💶 €15 including a drink 🚇 Ciutadella-Vila Olímpica

DIETRICH

Carrer del Consell de Cent 255, 08011
Tel 93 451 77 07

At Dietrich you'll find house music filling the dance floor. One of the two large bars looks out onto a garden. There's also a stage, which is well-loved by the drag queen regulars. All in all, a fun gay and lesbian venue where anything goes.

🕐 Daily 10.30pm–3am 💶 Free 🚇 Universitat

DISCOTHÈQUE

Avinguda del Marquès de Comillas s/n (at Poble Espanyol), 08004
Tel 93 272 49 80
www.nightsungroup.com

Discothèque is one of Barcelona's most famous clubs, presenting house and techno by leading Spanish and international DJs. The revellers are always ready for a great night out.

🕐 Fri–Sat midnight–6am, Oct–end Apr 💶 €15 🚇 Espanya

DOSTRECE

Carrer del Carme 40, 08001
Tel 93 301 73 06
www.dostrece.net

This club combines music, food and cocktails, right in the heart of the Raval. DosTrece's music displays Latin influences with bossa nova, tango and flamenco played alongside an occasional spot of deep house.

🕐 Tue–Sun 11am–3am 💰 Free
🚇 Liceu

DOT

Carrer Nou de Sant Francesc 7, 08002
Tel 93 302 70 26
www.dotlightclub.com

This dance bar is divided into two main areas that are smart and minimalist. It's busy almost every night, with dancing to deep house, garage and Latin music. Scenes from cult movies are projected onto the dance floor, adding quirky visuals to the upbeat mood. Credit cards are not accepted.

🕐 Sun–Thu 10pm–2.30am, Fri–Sat 10pm–3am 💰 Free 🚇 Drassanes

LEKASBAH

Plaça de Pau Vila, Palau del Mar s/n 08003
Tel 626 561 309

Walking into this informal club is like entering a scene from The Arabian Nights. Rugs and heavy cushions cover the floor, perfect for relaxing and starting the evening. Later on, there's some excellent house music to tempt you from your blissful lethargy. There's also live music from time to time. Credit cards are not accepted.

🕐 Tue–Sun 10pm–3am 💰 Free
🚇 Barceloneta

METRO

Carrer de Sepúlveda 185, 08001
Tel 93 323 52 27

One of the largest and busiest gay discos in Barcelona. There are two dance floors, one playing Spanish music, while the other plays international house. Metro is a very popular choice with visitors, especially in summertime.

🕐 Sun–Thu midnight–5am, Fri–Sat midnight–6am 💰 From €6
🚇 Universitat

MOOG

Carrer de l'Arc del Teatre 3, 08002
Tel 93 301 72 82
www.masimas.com

Moog, although relatively small, is known to stage some of the city's best DJ sets. There are two different spaces; the music varies from room to room but the crowd is the same—young electronic music fans with the energy to dance. Credit cards are not accepted.

🕐 Daily 11.30pm–5am 💰 From €6
🚇 Drassanes

OTTO ZUTZ

Carrer de Lincoln 15, 08006
Tel 93 238 07 22

This is a popular spot in the Gràcia area and, in keeping with that area, you will need to dress smartly to get in. But once inside you can choose to join the dance floor, which mostly has house music playing, or join the beautiful people looking cool at the bar.

🕐 Tue–Sat 11pm–6am 💰 From €7
🚇 Fontana

REPÚBLICA

Avinguda del Marquès de l'Argentera, 08003
Tel 93 319 65 62

You'll find this club in the grounds of Estació de França. It's a large spot, popular with locals and with three separate areas that cater for a range of different musical tastes. Resident DJs share the decks with selected guest DJs. Credit cards are not accepted.

🕐 Fri–Sat midnight–7am 💰 From €15
🚇 Barceloneta

SWEET CAFÉ

Carrer de Casanova 75, 08002
Tel 93 454 10 30

A gently lit, minimalist club playing house music to a less minimalist, often gay and lesbian crowd. It's certainly a

place to see and be seen in. Credit cards are not accepted.

🕐 Tue–Sat 10pm–3am, Sun 6.30pm–2.30am 💰 Free 🚇 Urgell

LA TERRAZA

Avinguda del Marquès de Comillas, 08004
Tel 93 272 49 80

When the warm weather comes to the city, Discothèque (see page 169) closes and its summer sister-club opens its doors. All elements of the winter version move here to this open-air venue, with the same music, the same outrageous atmosphere and the same faithful crowd. It doesn't really heat up until 3 in the morning, so don't turn up until very late—or very early. Credit cards not accepted.

🕐 Fri–Sat midnight–6am, May–end Sep 💰 €15 🚇 Espanya

VIP

Avinguda del Marquès de Comillas 23 (at Poble Espanyol), 08004
Tel 93 424 93 09
www.viptorresdeavila.com

This club was incorporated by the Spanish designer Xavier Mariscal into one of the exhibitions at Poble Espanyol—the Avila Towers. It is frequented by all the A-list partygoers in the Barcelona club scene. The music is great and it's an ideal place to enjoy a drink outside on the terrace under the stars.

🕐 Thu–Sat 11pm–5am 💰 From €8
🚇 Espanya

SPORTS AND ACTIVITIES

You will find plenty of options for sports all over the city, whether you want to experience the buzz of a live match, or work off some of those delicious Catalan meals. As a general rule, tickets for the major venues are available via the Servi-Caixa or Tel-Entrada booking services (see page 155).

SOCCER

Barcelona has some superb facilities in the shape of the Olympic complex on Montjuïc, which are regularly used for soccer and American football, as well as for international sporting events. Soccer is top of the list for locals, and many visitors too. The city's main clubs are FC Barcelona and RCD Espanyol. The season runs from September to the end of May and most league matches take place on Saturday and Sunday evenings.

The FC Barcelona badge found at the club's musuem

You shoudn't have much trouble getting hold of a ticket for a RCD Espanyol game, but Barça, which has more season ticket holders than there are seats in the stadium, is another matter. However, some 4,000 tickets go up for sale a week before matches, so phone the club to find out the time and line up at the ticket office on the Travessera de les Corts at least an hour before the box-office opens. You'll find up-to-the-minute information for both clubs at www.fcbarcelona.com and www.rcdespanyol.com.

OTHER SPORTS

After soccer, basketball is Spain's best-loved spectator sport, and Barcelona has two major teams competing in the league, FC Barcelona (run and financed by the soccer team) and Club Juventut Badalona. Their season runs from September to the end of May and matches are played mainly on Saturday and Sunday evenings. If tennis is your thing, Barcelona's Reial Club de Tenis hosts an important 10-day tournament in April as part of the ATP circuit. Find out more on www.rctb1899.es.

Unlike other areas of Spain, support for bullfighting in Catalonia has never been particularly strong, and the Catalan government dislikes it. The season runs from April to the end of September, and the minimum age to attend a bullfight is 14.

Bridging the gap between watching and doing is Barcelona's Marathon, established in 1977 and attracting huge crowds of runners and spectators alike. If you want to take part, visit the website at www.marathoncatalunya.com, or call Marató de Catalunya-Barcelona (*tel 93 268 01 14*).

There are a host of different sporting activities that you can get involved in on your holiday to the city

GETTING INVOLVED

For exercise gentler than the marathon, consider using one of the many *poliesportius* (sports halls), run by the town hall. These range from basic to superbly equipped gyms with pools; they welcome visitors and charges are low. Hot weather may make cooling off a priority, which is not a problem with more than 25 municipally run, inexpensive pools and a choice of beaches on the edge of the city. Head further out and you'll find golf, riding and watersports galore. Above all, remember that Barcelona is blessed with some lovely green spaces, where you can walk, stroll, jog or simply relax. Tibidabo and Montjuïc are biggest, but don't neglect Park Güell, Pedralbes or Parc Miró.

You can get information on city sporting facilities from: Servei d'Informació Esportiva, Avinguda de l'Estadi 30–40, Montjuïc (*tel 93 402 30 00*).

Spectator Sports

BASKETBALL

PALAU BLAUGRANA
Carrer d'Aristides Maillol s/n, 08028
Tel 93 496 36 00
www.fcbarcelona.com
The 8,000 capacity Palau Blaugrana is part of Barcelona soccer club's complex, and its name comes from the Barça team's strip: blue *(blau)* and deep red *(grana)*. This particular pavilion hosts Barcelona's basketball matches—the team even has the same name as the soccer team: FC Barcelona.
Season: Sep–early Jun €10–€25 Les Corts

PALAU SANT JORDI
Passeig Olimpic 5–7, 08038
Tel 93 426 20 89
www.agendabcn.com
This steel and glass stadium was built for the Olympic Games by the Japanese architect Arata Isozaki (see page 62). It's now a multifunctional hall used as a venue for

all kinds of events, including rock and pop concerts and occasional sports fixtures, mainly basketball.

Dependant on what competitions are held From €11 Espanya

BULLFIGHTING
PLAZA DE TOROS MONUMENTAL
Gran Vía de les Corts Catalanes 749, 08013
Tel 93 245 5804
Bullfighting isn't really that popular among the Catalans, but *corridas* (fights) still take place here weekly during the

season. There's also a museum if you would prefer to see bullfighting in a less vivid format (see page 88).
Bullfights: Sun 5–7, Apr–end Sep. Museum: daily 10.30–2, 4–7 Bullfights €18–€97. Museum €4 Monumental

MOTORSPORT
CIRCUIT DE CATALUNYA–MONTMELÓ
Montmeló, 08160
Tel 93 571 97 00
www.circuitcat.com
This is the most modern racing circuit in Spain and is the venue for the Spanish Formula One Grand Prix, as well as the Catalonia Motorcycling Grand Prix. Both take place once a year.
RENFE Cercanias train (line 2, direction Maçanet) from Sants station to Montmeló. Trains leave about every 30 min. Journey takes 40 min Take the A7 towards Girona to exit 17, then head to Granollers–Montmeló

SOCCER
CAMP NOU (FC BARCELONA)
Carrer d'Aristides Maillol s/n, 08028
Tel 93 496 36 00
www.fcbarcelona.com

Camp Nou is among Europe's biggest soccer stadiums, with a capacity of about 100,000. The importance of the game will dictate the atmosphere, but if you can get hold of tickets then any game is worth going to (see page 171).
Season: Sep–mid-Jun; league matches usually Sat or Sun evenings; cup matches usually midweek evenings From €25 Mariá Cristina

ESTADI OLÍMPIC DE MONTJUÏC
Passeig Olímpic 17–19, 08038
Tel 93 426 20 89
www.agendabcn.com
This old stadium was originally built for the 1936 Olympic Games. It missed its chance to find fame, as the games were cancelled as a result of the Spanish Civil War. It was

revamped for the 1992 Olympics and now hosts the matches of Real Club Deportivo Espanyol, who are the city rivals of FC Barcelona.
Season: Sep–mid-Jun; league matches usually Sat or Sun evenings; cup matches usually midweek evenings From €25 Espanya

Activities

ATHLETICS

MARATÓ DE BARCELONA
Carrer de Jonqueres 16, 08003
Tel 93 268 0114
www.redestb.es/marathon_cat
The Barcelona Marathon takes place once a year, usually in March. The route starts and finishes next to the Plaça d'Espanya. If you want to enter, call or check out the website within 4 weeks of the marathon date.
🎫 €35, €45 entry fee 🚇 Espanya

BEACHES

BARCELONETA
Barcelona's large seafront is separated into several beaches. Bordering the seafront in the Barceloneta area, this beach is a popular choice with families and

couples. One of its main attractions is the good range of playing facilities for children, a rich selection of restaurants and bars, deckchair rental and water sports.
🚇 Barceloneta

MAR BELLA
At the far end of the sea promenade is the city's official nudist beach, which is a relaxed and peaceful spot.
🚇 Poblenou

SANT SEBASTIÀ
This beach is the first you reach, if you approach the sea from the old city, and is very busy in summer. Just about all members of the community use the beach, so you won't

feel out of place or too like a tourist. It has showers, plus you can rent umbrellas and sunloungers. In summer time there is a lively open-air bar.
🚇 Barceloneta

CYCLING

BICICLETA CLUB CATALUNYA
Carrer de la Vermeda 18, 08018
Tel 93 307 71 00
www.bacc.info
This bicycle club has quite a high profile in promoting cycling around Barcelona and organizing cultural and art-inspired rides within the city. It also runs workshops throughout the region. You can rent bicycles here and find everything you'll need for your ride in the shop.
🕐 Mon–Fri 9–3 🎫 From €2 per hour 🚇 Clot

DANCING

LA PALOMA
Carrer del Tigre 27, 08001
Tel 93 301 6897
Line up with the mostly middle-aged couples to get into this wonderfully decorated 1900s dance hall. The band plays tunes from the Latin end of the ballroom dance spectrum, such as the mambo and the tango. Credit cards are not accepted.
🕐 Thu–Sat 6.30pm–9.30pm, Sun 6.30pm–10pm (also Thu–Sat 11.30pm–5am, Aug) 🎫 From €7 🚇 Universitat

LA SARDANA
Plaça de la Seu or Plaça de Sant Jaume 08002
Tel 93 319 7637
If you've ever wanted to try the sardana, the Catalan

national dance, you can, outside the cathedral on Sunday afternoon or Plaça de Sant Jaume on weekend evenings. These gatherings, organized by the Federació Sardanista, allow groups of varying abilities from beginners to the more advanced, to dance in a circle.
🕐 Cathedral: Sun noon–2. Plaça Sant Jaume: Sat 6.30pm–8.30pm, Sun 6pm–8pm 🚇 Liceu or Jaume I

FOUNTAIN DISPLAY

LA FONT MÁGICA
Avinguda de la Reina María Cristina s/n, 08004
The Avinguda de la Reina María Cristina leads up to the enormous illuminated magic fountain in front of the Museu Nacional d'Art de Catalunya (MNAC). This is a popular

attraction where the fountain dances in time to the music and light show.
🕐 Shows every 30 min between the following times: Thu–Sun 9.30–11.30pm, Jun–end Sep; Fri–Sat 7–8.30pm, rest of year 🎫 Free 🚇 Espanya

GOLF

CLUB DE GOLF SANT CUGAT
Carrer de Villa s/n, Sant Cugat del Vallés, 08190
Tel 93 674 39 58
www.koncepto.com/santcugat
This is one of Spain's oldest golf clubs, founded in 1914, and 20km (12 miles) outside Barcelona. There's an 18-hole course and three executive holes; other facilities include electric trolley rental, a putting green and a driving range. It is expensive, but the entrance

fee gives you access to the club's restaurant, bar and pool.

🕐 Tue–Fri 7.30am–8.30pm, Sat–Sun 7am–9pm, Mon 8am–8.15pm

💶 Non-members: Mon €50, Tue–Fri €65, Sat–Sun €130, club rental €19

🚆 FGC train from Catalunya to Sant Cugat, then 5-min walk from station

🚌 Take Tunel de Vallvidrera (C16) to Valldoreix

HORSE RIDING
ESCOLA MUNICIPAL D'HÍPICA LA FOIXARDA
Avinguda Muntayans 14–16, 08026
Tel 93 426 10 66

This is a riding school with an enviable setting, right in the middle of Montjuïc, and half hidden in a pine forest. This establishment gives horse-riding lessons to children and adults, and also has a good restaurant. Courses are held every day, but single lessons are available only at weekends. Credit cards are not accepted.

🕐 Mon–Fri 4.30–10.30, Sat–Sun 9–9

💶 One-hour class: €14.40 🚇 Espanya

ICE-SKATING
PISTA DE GEL
Carrer de Roger de Flor 168, 08013
Tel 93 245 28 00
www.skatingbcn.com

This large, modern rink is very central, making it easy to find and useful for visitors. There is

a café-bar from where you can watch skaters, and there are babysitters at weekends and holidays so the young ones can be looked after while parents skate with older children.

🕐 Wed–Thu 10.30–1.30, 5–9, Fri 10–1.30, 5–midnight, Sat 10.30–2,

4.30–midnight, Sun 10.30–2, 4.30–10, Tue 10.30–1.30 💶 €6.20; skate rental: €9.50; glove rental (compulsory): €1.30 🚇 Tetuán

SPORTS COMPLEXES
POLIESPORTIU MUNICIPAL EUROPOLIS
Carrer de Sardenya 553, 08024
Tel 93 210 07 66
www.europolis.es

This is under the Europa soccer arena. You'll find a range of sports including a gym, squash courts, a swimming pool, a restaurant, bar and shop. Medically trained staff are on hand, and those who prefer not to break into a sweat can simply book one of the beauty treatments.

🕐 Mon–Fri 7am–11pm, Sat 8–8, Sun 9–3 💶 Non-members €7 entry, allows use of all facilities 🚇 Alfons X

SWIMMING
BERNAT PICORNELL
Avinguda de l'Estadi 30–40, 08038
Tel 93 423 40 41
www.picornell.com

This swimming pool was renovated as part of the preparation for the 1992 Olympic Games and as a result is one of the best in the city. The building also contains a public

gym with a complete range of sporting facilities. Suitable for families. Credit cards are not accepted.

🕐 Mon–Fri 7am–midnight, Sat 7am–9pm, Sun 7.30–8 (until 4, Oct–end May) 💶 Adult €8, child €4 🚇 Espanya

TENNIS

CENTRE MUNICIPAL DE TENNIS
Passeig de la Vall d'Hebron 178–196, 08035
Tel 93 427 65 00
www.fctennis.org

This was once the former training environment for several Spanish tennis champions. It is now open to the public, with 17 clay and seven grass courts. Centre Municipal de Tennis also has beautiful grounds, a pleasant café and a good restaurant.

🕐 Mon–Fri 8am–11pm, Sat 8am–9pm, Sun 8am–7pm 💶 From €12 per hour 🚇 Montbau

TENPIN BOWLING
BOWLING PEDRALBES
Avinguda del Doctor Marañón 11, 08028
Tel 93 333 0352
www.bowlingpedralbes.com

If all 14 bowling lanes are full, put your name down and the staff will page you. Have a drink in the bar, or play snooker or darts while you're waiting. Shoe rental available.

🕐 Mon–Thu 10am–2am, Fri–Sat 10am–4am, Sun 10am–midnight

💶 €3–€5 🚇 Collblanc

TOURS AND TRIPS
LAS GOLONDRINAS
Plaça del Portal de la Pau 1, 08001
Tel 93 442 31 06
www.servicom.es/lasgolondrinas

One of the best ways to see the port is to take a boat ride. It's a 35-minute trip to the breakwater sea wall, and two hours to reach the Olympic Port. This is a good way to get a closer look at the old boats and yachts moored here. Credit cards are not accepted.

🕐 Mon–Fri 11–2, Sat–Sun 11.45–5, Jan–end Mar, Nov–end Dec; Mon–Fri 11–6, Sat–Sun 11.45–7, Apr–end Jun; Mon–Sun 11.45–7.30, Jul–end Sep; Mon–Fri 11–6, Sat–Sun 11.45–7, Oct 💶 Adult €3.50, child €1.75 🚇 Drassanes

SABOROSO

Carrer del Comte d'Urgell 45, 08011
Tel 93 451 5010
www.saboroso.com

This tour company, dedicated to food and wine, helps visitors explore Barcelona's culinary

delights. Choose from a number of tours that cover everything from a circuit of tapas bars to a tour of a cava vineyard in Penedès followed by lunch. Credit cards are not accepted.

🕐 Tue–Sat, times by appointment 💶 From €45

WATER SPORTS

BASE NÀUTICA DE LA MAR BELLA

Avinguda del Litoral, 08038
Tel 93 221 0432
www.basenautica.org

This sailing club, on one of the farthest city beaches, rents out catamarans, windsurfing boards and kayaks, but you have to take a proficiency test first (€12 if you fail). Courses for all levels are available.

🕐 Daily 10–8, Jun–end Sep; 10–5, rest of year 💶 10-hour windsurf course €120; 16-hour catamaran course €150; windsurf rental €15/hour 🚇 Poblenou

Health and Beauty

AGUAS DE VIDA

Carrer de Gran de Gràcia 7, 08012
Tel 93 238 41 60

The day spa craze has hit Barcelona in a big way. Aguas de Vida goes one step farther by providing specialized water-based treatments for poor circulation, skin conditions and cellulite, as well as a Turkish steam bath, Roman bath, small mineral water pools and spas and pressure showers of various degrees. All just the trick to relax aching limbs after a hard day seeing the sights.

🕐 Mon–Fri 8.30am–9.30pm, Sat 9.30am–8.30pm 💶 75-min treatment €51 🚇 Diagonal

A.K.A. PERRUQUERS

Carrer d'Avinyó 34, 08002
Tel 93 301 45 13

A.K.A. Perruquers is in trendy Carrer d'Avinyó, famous for its alternative shopping. This hairdresser follows new styles, revives great classics or develops one to reflect your character; a formula that keeps the clients coming back. Making an appointment is advisable.

🕐 Tue–Sat 10.30–8 💶 Women €25, men €15 🚇 Liceu

BASIC

Carrer de Muntaner 77, 08011
Tel 93 451 44 32

This hairdresser can be found in L'Eixample's commercial area. It maintains a relaxed atmosphere through a friendly approach and good music. Go

for a classic haircut or have your hair coloured using the most advanced and innovative techniques. Hair styling, extensions, highlights and a make-up service are available. Call for an appointment.

🕐 Mon noon–8.30, Tue–Fri 11–8.30, Sat 10–7 💶 Women €30, men €15 🚇 Universitat

GUITART GEM HOTEL

Carrer de Josep Maria Sert 38, Lloret de Mar, 17310
Tel 97 234 70 04

This old fashioned, 56-roomed hotel is in the middle of the popular coastal town of Lloret de Mar, which is outside Girona. It provides massage and has a sauna, a swimming pool and a special health-food restaurant. Cycling, walking, tennis and outdoor bowling in the surrounding parkland complete the package and there are medical staff on hand for detox advice and treatments.

💶 €63–€89 per person in a double room full board 🚗 A7 to Girona, leaving at the exit Lloret de Mar, taking one hour; also see page 51 for information on getting to Girona

HOTEL BALNEARI BROQUETAS

Plaça de la Font del Lleó 1, 08140
Caldes de Montbui
Tel 93 865 01 00
www.grupbroquetas.com

This little town outside Barcelona has been known for its hot springs and the medicinal quality of its water since Roman times. It was the focus of investment by the Catalan bourgeoisie at the turn of the 20th century, and is still very smart today. The hotel has a variety of hydro treatments, plus special packages for weekend breaks.

💶 Weekend pass, with accommodation and all treatment from €240 🚌 12 Sagalés buses a day between Barcelona and Caldes de Montbui, taking about 45 min 🚗 N152 towards Vic, exit Caldes de Montbui

INSTITUTO FRANCIS
Ronda de Sant Pere 18, 08010
Tel 93 317 78 08
This salon, near to Barcelona's main shopping district, has basic beauty treatments such as body and face peeling, waxing and massage. It's a particularly handy place because it remains open at noon when most of the nearby beauty salons close. Booking ahead is recommended.
🕐 Mon–Fri 9.30–8, Sat 9–2 💆 Face peeling €33, depilation from €21
🚇 Urquinaona

KORE
Gran Vía de les Corts Catalanes 433, Principal 1, 08015
Tel 93 425 44 40
Should you find yourself in the commercial area around the Plaça de Catalunya and Carrer de Pelai and in need of a break, Kore is a good stop. The experts here provide

reflexology, chiropody, chiropractic therapy, aromatherapy, kinesiology and natural beauty treatments. All the staff are personable and professional.
🕐 Mon–Fri 10–2, 3–9 💆 Reflexology: from €45, massage from €30
🚇 Urquinaona

MANITAS
Carrer de Calabria 272, 08029
Tel 93 410 56 04
The name of this beauty salon means little hands, as it specializes in hand and nail care. You can have all kinds of manicures or have false nails applied. Conventional beauty treatments, such as body and

face peeling, are also available. Book for an appointment.
🕐 Mon–Fri 10–8, Sat 9–2 💆 Manicure from €9, face peeling from €27
🚇 Entença

MASAJES A 1000
Carrer de Mallorca 233, 08008
Tel 93 215 85 85
This quick fix, walk-in massage and beauty salon can soothe those stressed out shoulders with a 10-minute siesta massage. You are then allowed to sleep off the effect in the ergonomic massage chair for 20 minutes afterwards. Other pampering services include manicures and pedicures and the full range of skin treatments.
🕐 Daily 7am–1pm 💆 Massage from €4 🚇 Diagonal

MEMORÁNDUM
Carrer de Sicilia 236, 08013
Tel 93 231 94 37
After a visit to Gaudi's Sagrada Família, treat yourself to something relaxing at this beauty shop. The shop is well known for its aromatherapy and the salon uses plants and aromatic oils that have been part of beauty remedies for over 5,000 years. Also available is refined techniques used by Egyptians and other ancient cultures.
🕐 Mon–Fri 9.30–2, 4.30–8.15, Sat 10–2 💆 Body massage from €30
🚇 Sagrada Família

LA PELU
Carrer dels Tallers 35, 08001
Tel 93 301 97 73
This hair salon is in the busy shopping area close to Carrer de Pelai. Not many hairdressers in Barcelona give you a view of a Romanesque (c10th–12th century) wall, or the opportunity to get online and surf the net while you wait. Booking is advisable.
🕐 Tue–Sat 10.30–8, Fri–Sat 10.30–9 💆 Women €30, men €18
🚇 Catalunya

SAGNA SAURINA
Avinguda Diagonal 611, 3rd Floor, 08028
Tel 93 419 4516
With branches in Barcelona, Madrid and Andorra, the Saurina sisters' treatments have a nationwide reputation among Spain's jet set. Their services range from a one and a half hour oxigizing facial to sophisticated treatments before and after plastic surgery, all in the comfort of their salons' luxury interiors.
🕐 Mon–Fri 8.30am–7pm 💆 Oxigizing facial €55 🚇 Maria Cristina

EL TALLER DE ALQUIMIA
Carrer de Pau Claris 104, 08009
Tel 93 302 74 23
El Taller de Alquimia is a perfume shop in the middle of Eixample. All the products here are made using natural materials, such as herbs, fruits, plants and flowers, and no chemicals are used. In addition, clients can enjoy shiatsu massage, Bach flower remedies and many other alternative beauty treatments.
🕐 Mon–Fri 10–8, Sat 10–2
💆 Swimming pool with massage jets from €73 🚇 Passeig de Gràcia

TERMES LA GARRIGA
Banys 23, 08530 Garriga
Tel 93 871 70 86
www.termes.com
The little town of Garriga is just 35km (22 miles) outside Barcelona. The hotel has a range of spa facilities: a swimming pool with massage jets, a sauna-steam bath and treatments such as facials, body peeling, body moisturizing and wraps; the list goes on. You'll also be able to get special deals for weekend breaks.
💆 Weekend pass, with accommodation and all treatment from €240
🚍 From Plaza Urquinaona, 13 a day (five on Sat and Sun), taking about 1 hour 🚆 Six a day, leaving from Sants station, taking about 50 min 🚗 N152 towards Vic, exit La Garriga

CHILDREN'S BARCELONA

Barcelona has lots going on for children. The city itself, with its quirky Modernista buildings, picturesque cobbled streets and bustling waterfront, has a high entertainment factor, and there's a good choice of museums, parks and attractions.

If your children need to let off steam, head for the parks, hills or beaches, or consider a day out at one of the nearby coastal resorts. Within the city, children's attractions are focused around Montjuïc, Tibidabo and the Port Vell. Even getting there will be fun by way of the trams, funiculars, cable cars and *golondrines*, the harbour swallow boats. If you want to throw in a bit of education, children enjoy watching the craft demonstrations at the Poble Espanyol, while the hands-on exhibits in museums such as the Museu de la Ciència and the Museu de l'Història de Catalunya are big draws.

Children will love the street entertainers on Las Ramblas

- In July and August, many museums stage fun activities for kids as part of the Estiu als Museus (Summer in the Museums). Find out more at tourist information offices and La Virreina (see page 108).
- The Ajuntament puts on regular children's entertainment, including concerts, puppet and magic shows, mainly held in local civic halls. La Virreina can fill you in on these.

PORT AVENTURA
Theme park fans will love Port Aventura, one of Europe's biggest and best parks. It's an hour and 15 minutes by train from Barcelona, with its own railway station, making it an easy option if your children are cultured out by the charms of

the city. The main park's divided into five zones: Mediterranean, Polynesia, the Far West, Mexico and China, and all five have a selection of themed rides and entertainment, with plenty for small children as well as teenagers and adults. The admission price gives you unlimited rides; a supplement gets you admission to the adjoining Costa Caribe park. The park has plenty of food outlets and buggy rental.
Port Aventura at Salou (*tel 977 77 91 10; ticket information 902 20 20 41; RENFE train information 902 24 02 02*); www.portaventura.es; prices from €17–€49. By car: Take A7 (La Jonquera to Valencia) and come off at exit 35.

Attractions

L'AQUÀRIUM
See page 62.

CASA MILÀ
See pages 66–69.

CASTELL DE MONTJUÏC
Passeig de Montjuïc 66, 08038
Tel 93 329 86 13
The view from the top of Montjuïc is splendid, and you can enjoy it before visiting this fascinating castle, complete

with 18th-century fortresses and a collection of canons and ancient weaponry, all of which should keep the kids entertained (see pages 86–87).
Credit cards are not accepted.
🕐 Tue–Fri 9.30–5, Sat–Sun 9.30–8
🎫 Adult €2.50, child €1 🚇 Para.lel, then funicular and Telefèric de Montjuïc

FUNDACIÓ JOAN MIRÓ
See pages 78–79.

MUSEU DE CERA
See page 89.

MUSEU DE LA CIÈNCIA
See page 89.

MUSEU EGIPCI DE BARCELONA
Carrer de València 284, 08007
Tel 93 488 01 88
www.fundclos.com
This well laid-out museum is dedicated to all things Egyptian. The fascinating displays include a number of sarcophagi and a whole section devoted to pharaohs. The shop is a good place to part with your euros, with an excellent selection of books, games and gifts.
🕐 Mon–Sat 10–8, Sun 10–2 💶 Adult €5.50 🚇 Passeig de Gràcia

MUSEU DEL FC BARCELONA
See page 92.

MUSEU MARÍTIM
See pages 94–95.

PARC ZOOLÒGIC
See page 114.

POBLE ESPANYOL
Avinguda del Marquès de Comillas s/n, 08038
Tel 93 325 78 66
www.poble-espanyol.com
The Spanish Village holds workshops for families, where you can try your hand

at a number of crafts like engraving. There are also demonstrations of traditional local customs such as folk dances and fiesta celebrations (see page 118).
🕐 Fri–Sat 9am–4am, Sun 9am–midnight, Mon 9–8, Tue–Thu 9am–2am
💶 Adult €7, child €3.70, under 6 free 🚇 Espanya

Film and Theatre

IMAX
See page 160.

JOVE TEATRE REGINA
Carrer de Sèneca 22, 08006
Tel 93 218 15 12
Jove Teatre Regina, aimed at children, was established at the beginning of the 1990s. Puppet-based shows are often staged here, for example with interpretations of traditional Catalan poems or folktales. Previous shows have included a musical based on the works of Shakespeare, and another based on The Three Little Pigs.
🕐 Weekends; closed Aug–end Sep
💶 From €6.50 🚇 Diagonal

Parks

PARC D'ATRACCIONS
Plaça Tibidabo, 08035
Tel 93 211 79 42
www.achus.net/tibidabo
This park, renovated in the 1980s, was opened in 1908 and is therefore one of the world's oldest funfairs. There are a number of rides you can take, such as the replica of the first plane to fly from Barcelona to Madrid and the Aeromàgic, dating from 1935 that gives you great views of the city below. There is also a fascinating display of old fairground automatons. The

biggest attraction of all, however, is the Ferris wheel (see page 130).
🕐 Noon–10, summer; noon–6, winter
💶 Adult €22, child under 1.10m €9, 6 attractions €10 🚇 Funicular Tibidabo

PARC DE LA CIUTADELLA
Passeig de Picasso 15, 08003
This is the largest green space in the city with lots of room for the kids to run around in. They can take advantage of the play areas and boating lake, while parents can take a seat and watch (see page 108).

🕐 Daily 10–dusk 💶 Free 🚇 Arc de Triomf

PARC DE LA CREUETA DEL COLL
See page 109.

PARC DEL LABERINT
Passeig de les Castanyers s/n, 08035
Tel 93 424 38 09
The Parc del Laberint is certainly a labyrinth, thanks to its maze of well-kept cypress

hedges, the largest in Spain. The huge garden is a beautiful example of 18th-century, neoclassical landscape gardening (see page 114). Credit cards are not accepted.
🕐 Daily 10–sunset 💶 Adult €3, child €1.50 🚇 Mundet

PARK GÜELL
See pages 110–113.

FESTIVALS AND EVENTS

Barcelona's cultural department runs a comprehensive information office with details of cultural events and festivals. It also sells tickets and has an excellent bookshop: Centre d'Informacío de la Virreina, Palau de la Virreina, La Rambla 99 (tel 93 301 77 75, Mon–Fri 10–2, 4–8). The 010 city information phone line has details of festivals, as does the cultural section on www.bcn.es.

There are a number of elements that have become part of Barcelona's festivals, and you will see some or all of them at the major events, especially at those held in the *barris.*

● *Castellers* are human towers, formed by up to nine levels of people balancing on the shoulders of the level below. It is a superb illustration of balance and communal collaboration.

● *Gegants* and *Capsgrossos*: *Gegants* (giants) are huge papier-mâché and wooden figures, often representing historical and folkloric characters. They are accompanied by the *capsgrossos* (bigheads), capering characters wearing huge mask heads.

● *Correfoc* means fire-running, when a parade of dragons run through the streets spitting fire and showering onlookers with sparks from the firecrackers they carry, all accompanied by a compelling drumbeat.

SETMANA SANTA
Week before Easter
A number of religious processions held on Palm Sunday and throughout the week leading up to Good Friday. Churches around Barcelona participate, but the principal processions take place in Barri Gòtic.

SANT JORDI
23 April
This is St. George's Day, the patron saint of Catalonia. Traditionally, men give women a rose and receive a book in exchange. As a consequence, book stands and rose sellers will be out and about in the city.

CAVALCAVA DELS REIS
6 January
Moll de la Fusta to Plaça Sant Jaume
This is the procession of the three kings through the city, celebrating the Epiphany. They throw sweets for the children who traditionally receive their Christmas presents today.
🚇 Drassanes for Moll de la Fusta

CARNESTOLTES
End February
This 10-day pre-Lent carnival takes place all over the city, with processions, dancing, street markets and concerts, culminating in the Enterrament de la Sardina (Burial of the Sardine) on Montjuïc to mark the Lenten fasting to come.

SANT MEDIR DE GRÀCIA
Early February
Collserola
A procession of traditionally dressed men, mounted on horses, who ride to the hermitage of Sant Medir for a bean feast: something residents of Catalonia are known for.

There's no escaping the dragons at the festival of La Mercè

FERIA DE ABRIL
Late April
Diagonal-Mar
There is a large Andalucían population in Barcelona, and

they started this 10-day festival, celebrating all things Andalucían, with flamenco and food.
🚇 Besòs-Mar

FESTIVAL DE MÚSICA ANTIGA
Late April
Barri Gòtic
Indoor and outdoor concerts are performed by ensembles from all over Europe.
🚇 Jaume I

FESTA DE LA DIVERSITAT
May
Moll de la Fusta
This three-day festival is part of a wider one across Spain. It aims to bring together Barcelona's huge ethnic diversity, with concerts, stands and food from different parts of the community.
🚇 Drassanes

SÓNAR
Mid-June
www.sonar.es
Barcelona likes to be at the

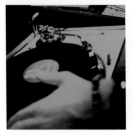

cutting edge of everything, including music. This three-day electronic music festival includes exhibitions, concerts and chilled-out dance.

SANT JOAN
23 June
The eve of the feast of St. John is La Nit del Foc (night of fire) with spectacular firecracker displays, processions and dancing all over the city.

FESTIVAL DEL GREC
June to end July
Barcelona's main performing arts festival gets it name from the Teatre Grec, the faux Greek amphitheatre on Montjuïc. This is where a good many of the performances take place.

FESTA MAJOR DE GRÀCIA
Mid-August
Gràcia
A huge district festival with decorated streets, entertainment and feasting (see page 80). Here you will see *gegants*, *castells* and *correfoc*.

DIADA DE CATALUNYA
11 September
This is the region's national day, which actually commenorates the day the city was taken by Philip V in 1715 (see page 31). It is a serious day by comparison to other festivals, and you are likely to see political demonstrations.

FESTES DE LA MERCÈ
Late September
Held in the name of the Lady of Mercy, this week-long celebration marks the end of summer with music, procession, *gegants*, *castells*, *correfoc*, concerts, firecrackers, dancing and music everywhere. It is one of the best festivals in the city.

MOSTRA DE VINS I CAVES DE CATALUNYA
Late September
Maremagnum
Tel 93 487 6738

This fair coincides with La Mercè festival and gives you the chance to sample Catalonia's wines and cavas. Join the line to buy tasting tickets, which includes a tasting glass. Local cheeses and other good are also sold.
🚇 Drassanes

FESTIVAL INTERNATIONAL DE JAZZ DE BARCELONA
October to end December
Palau de la Música
One of the key festivals in this

jazz-loving city, attracting a wide range of national and international names.
🚇 Urquinaona

TOTS SANTS
1 November
All Saints' Day is the day when people traditionally visit the graves of their loved ones—and to eat *castanyas* (sweet chestnuts) and *panellets* (small sweet cakes) from food stands.

FIRA DE SANTA LLÚCIA
1–23 December
Plaça de la Seu
A Christmas market selling all you could need, including trees, decorations and gifts. There are traditional crib figures and a life-size crib in Plaça de Sant Jaume.
🚇 Jaume I

CAP D'ANY
31 December
New Year's Eve is celebrated with parties and public celebrations—eat 12 grapes while midnight chimes to ensure good luck for the year ahead.

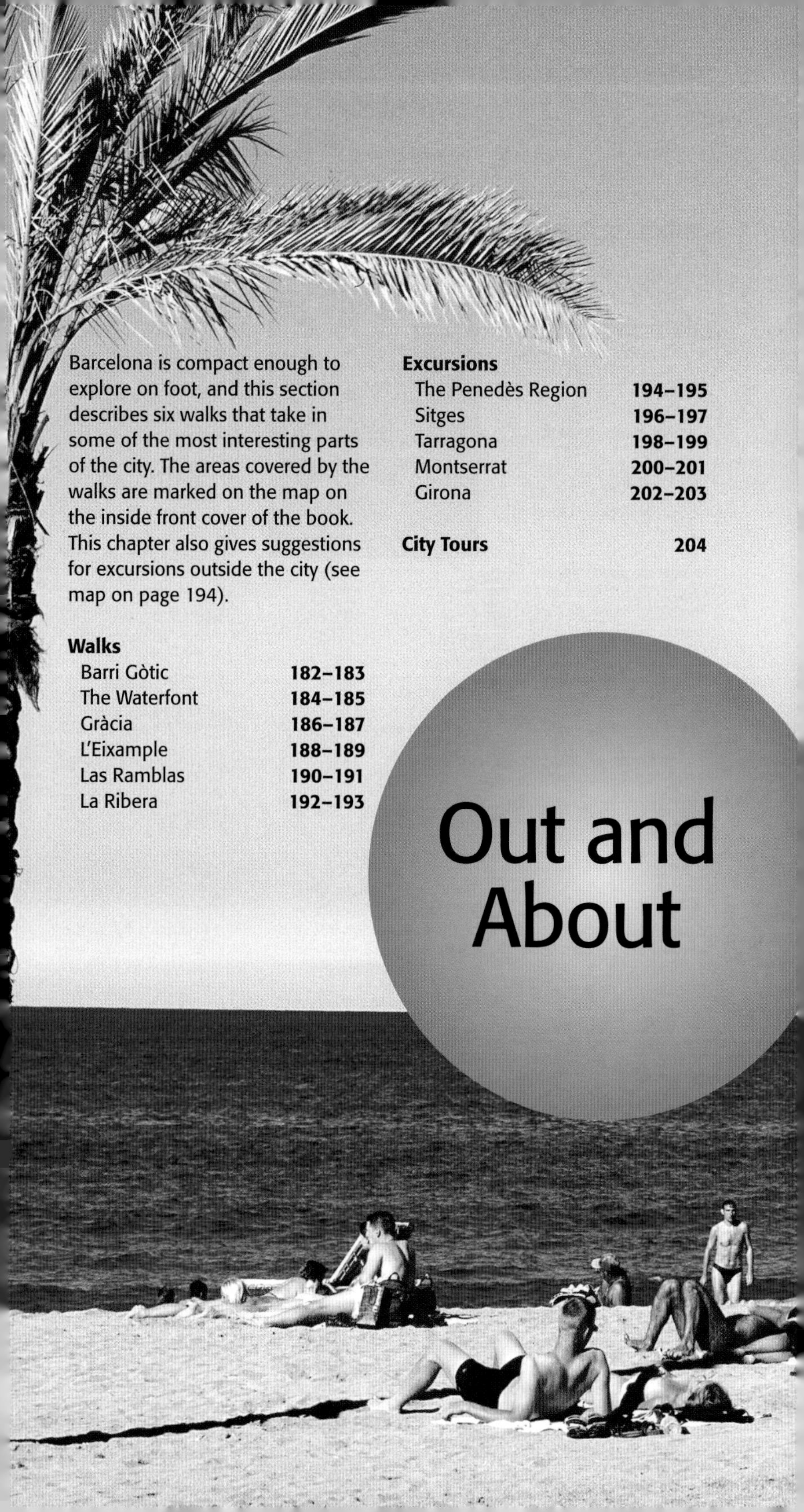

Barcelona is compact enough to explore on foot, and this section describes six walks that take in some of the most interesting parts of the city. The areas covered by the walks are marked on the map on the inside front cover of the book. This chapter also gives suggestions for excursions outside the city (see map on page 194).

Walks

Barri Gòtic	182–183
The Waterfont	184–185
Gràcia	186–187
L'Eixample	188–189
Las Ramblas	190–191
La Ribera	192–193

Excursions

The Penedès Region	194–195
Sitges	196–197
Tarragona	198–199
Montserrat	200–201
Girona	202–203

City Tours	**204**

Out and About

BARRI GÒTIC

Bars and restaurants have replaced many of the workshops that once dotted the narrow streets of Barcelona's medieval hub, but an afternoon spent here is richly rewarding, and essential to understanding Barcelona's Gothic architecture.

THE WALK

Distance: 1.5km (1 mile)	
Allow: 1 to 1.5 hours	
Start at/end at: Plaça de l'Àngel	

HOW TO GET THERE

Metro: The closest station to the Plaça de l'Àngel is Jaume I on the yellow line 4

Start the walk once you have exited the metro station onto the Plaça de l'Àngel. With your back to the large thoroughfare, Vía Laietana, look for the road to your right, Baixada Llibreteria, and start walking along it.

The Cereria Subira ❶, at Baixada de la Llibreteria 7, is notable for being the oldest shop in the city and for the pair of elegant statues at the base of its staircase. The premises date from 1761 and started life by selling ladies' apparel long before the handmade candles you see on display today.

Continue walking up Baixada de la Llibreteria to the intersection with Carrer de Veguer and turn right, walking right to the end.

This will bring you to the Plaça del Rei ❷ (see page 115), the very heart of the Barri Gòtic and home of the Conjunt Monumental de la Plaça del Rei (see page 75). The 14th- to 16th-century complex was once used to rule Catalonia and it is said that Ferdinand and Isabella received Columbus here after his voyage to the New World.

With your back to the Plaça, take the right-hand exit onto Baixada de Santa Clara. You will then come to the rear of the city's cathedral (see pages 70–73). Turn right along Carrer dels Comtes, with the cathedral running parallel to your left. Immediately to your right is the baroque Palau del Lloctinent, which forms part of the medieval palace-complex of the Plaça del Rei. It was built as the home of the Viceroy of Catalonia.

The columns of the Temple d'Augustus built to worship Caesar Augustus (63BC–AD14)

Continuing along the same street you also pass the Museu Frederic Marès (see page 92) and its courtyard, with a fountain and citrus trees. Walk to the end of Carrer dels Comtes to the Plaça de la Seu. Take an immediate left onto Carrer de Santa Llùcia, which leads past the cathedral's main entrance.

The Casa de l'Ardiaca ❸ is just before this intersection, on the right. It dates from the 16th century and was once the residence of the city's archdeacon. Today it stores the city's archives, but its exquisite patio, with a century-old palm tree, is open to the public.

Turn left onto Carrer del Bisbe and then turn hard right onto the winding Montjuïc del Bisbe.

This leads to one of the most charming squares in the *barri*: Sant Felip Neri ❹. Apart from its baroque church, central fountain and the Museu del Calçat (Shoe Museum, see page 89), set in the oldest guild headquarters in the city, this tranquil spot is testimony to a dark past. The holes on the church's façade were caused by a bombardment by fascist troops during the Civil

War (1936–39) in which 20 children, pupils from the school next door, were killed.

Take the furthest exit out of the square onto Carrer de Sant Felip Neri and then left onto Carrer de Sant Domenec del Call. You are now in the heart of El Call, the city's old Jewish ghetto. Turn left onto Carrer del Call and continue to the immense Plaça de Sant Jaume (see pages 116–117). Flanked on either side by the seats of Catalonia's regional governments, spend some time taking a tour of the façades of the Generalitat and Casa de la Ciutat.

For a short detour, take Carrer del Paradís, to your right as you look at the Generalitat. This brings you to the four remarkably intact Corinthian columns that are the remains of the Temple d'Augustus, a Roman temple.

Once back in the Plaça de Sant Jaume, take Carrer de la Ciutat, the road to your left as you face the Casa de la Ciutat. After a minute or so of walking, the street changes its name to Carrer del Regomir and contains vestiges of Roman Barcelona.

The Pati Llimona ❺, on the left at No. 3, is used for lively community events and has part of the old Roman water and sewerage system, which are visible from street level. Next door is the tiny Chapel of St. Christopher, dating from the 16th century.

Continue down Carrer del Regomir and then turn left onto Carrer del Correu Vell, named after the old post office in its immediate vicinity, and left again up the steep incline, Baixada Viladecols. Immediately on your right is the most complete section of the city's original Roman walls. After a few steps the street changes its name to Carrer de Lledó and will bring you to the Plaça de Sant Just, another pretty square with a Gothic church of the same name

OUT AND ABOUT

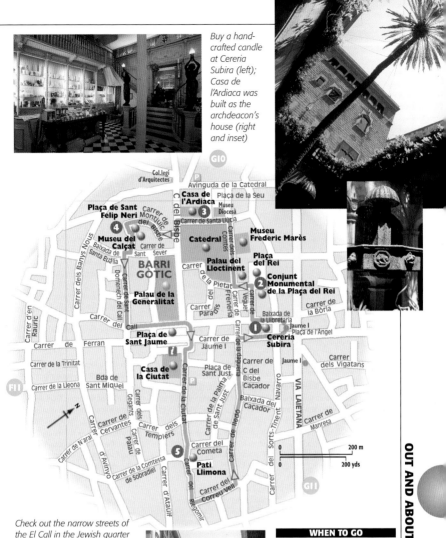

Buy a hand-crafted candle at Cereria Subira (left); Casa de l'Ardiaca was built as the archdeacon's house (right and inset)

Check out the narrow streets of the El Call in the Jewish quarter

as well as the oldest water source in the city. A market selling artisan foodstuffs is set up here on the first Thursday of every month.

If you exit the Plaça the same way you entered, onto Carrer de Lledó, the entrance to a tiny lane, Bisbe Caçador, is opposite. Here you will see the threshold of the Academia de les Bones Lletrès, one of the best-conserved historic palaces in the vicinity, which is not open to the public.

Back on Carrer de Lledó, turn right, where the road name changes to Carrer Dagueria. At the intersection with Carrer de Jaume I, turn right, and the Plaça de l'Àngel, where you started, is on the left. The metro station, Jaume I, is also to be found here.

WHEN TO GO

After lunch is the best time to avoid the tour groups.

WHERE TO EAT

The outdoor café at the Museu Frederic Marès is accessible to all, and has great views of Gothic architecture and Roman ruins.

PLACES TO VISIT

Casa de l'Ardiaca
Carrer de Santa Llùcia s/n
Tel 93 318 11 95
🕐 Mon–Fri 9–7.30, Sat 9–1
🎫 Free

Temple d'Augustus
Carrer del Paradís 10
Tel 93 315 11 11
🕐 Tue–Sat 10–8, Sun 10–2, Jun–Sep; Tue–Sat 10–2, 4–8, Sun 10–2, rest of year
🎫 Free

THE WATERFRONT

Before the 1992 Olympics, the coastline north of Barceloneta consisted of mud pools backing onto industrial estates. Now you can't keep people away from the shore, whether for a ramble along the boardwalks or to relax on the sandy beaches.

THE WALK

Distance:	5km (3 miles)
Allow:	2 hours
Start at:	Monument a Colom
End at:	Ciutadella-Vila Olímpica metro station

HOW TO GET THERE

Metro: Drassanes station is on the green line 3

Bus: Any of the following take you to Monument a Colom: 14, 36, 38, 57, 59, 64

Start your walk outside the towering Monument a Colom (Columbus Monument, see page 88), which is at the port end of Las Ramblas, a few steps from the Drassanes metro. Cross over to the port, and with your back to the Monument, turn left.

This stretch of wide, well-paved walkway is known as the Moll de la Fusta ❶ (Wooden Quay). From here you get a splendid view of the Maremagnum entertainment complex (see page 152) and the aquarium (see page 62), both of which are accessible from the Rambla de Mar, the bridge to your right. Outside the aquarium there are vast stretches of grass to laze on and a full-scale replica of the world's first steam-powered submarine invented by Catalan Narcís Monturiol.

Continue to the end of the Moll de la Fusta, where it intersects with the Moll d'Espanya. Directly to your left is the eye-catching *Barcelona Head* by pop artist Roy Lichtenstein (1923–97). To the right, a small craft market takes place at the weekends. Walk to your right along the Moll del Dipósit, following the water's edge.

The large building you see on your left is the Palau del Mar, an old warehouse that is now home to the Museu d'Història de Catalunya (see page 93). Outside, there is a cluster of cafés and restaurants, a great place to soak up the sun. Continue walking with the water's edge to your right—you are now on the Moll de Barceloneta.

On your right-hand side is Port Vell ❷ (see pages 118–119), the city's most exclusive marina where millionaires in their yachts drop anchor on a regular basis. On your left, Passeig Joan de Borbó is flanked by outdoor seafood restaurants, a traditional place for a Sunday *paella*.

Now turn left, so that you cross over the Moll onto Passeig Joan de Borbó, and continue walking right. On the corner of Carrer de l'Almirall Cervera stands a stunning example of 1950s Catalan architecture, La Casa de la Marina, built as public housing in the early 1950s. Walk to the end of Passeig Joan de Borbó. To your left is the large open space of the Plaça del Mar. Face the beach and turn left. Follow the shoreline via the ample wooden boardwalk laid out in front of you.

After about 2km (1.5 miles) you will see the crown of a water tower on your left. Dating from the late 1800s, it was the first in Spain and now resides in the Parc de la Barceloneta. Carry on along the boardwalk, which then changes its name to become the Passeig Marítim de la Barceloneta.

Roy Lichtenstein's Barcelona Head, in comic strip style, was an instant hit

As you reach the end of the Passeig, on your left-hand side you will pass the unmistakable form of Frank Gehry's celebrated *Fish* sculpture ❸, a symbol of the city since it was installed in 1992. The twin skyscrapers behind it are the tallest in the city—the one on the left is the Hotel Arts (see page 243), the city's most exclusive hotel. The multi-level gardens in front of it are open to the public.

At the end of the Passeig, turn right, then left and left again, walking around the Moll de la Marina to the marina on the opposite side.

The glitzy Port Olímpic ❹ (see page 118) is on your right, with more millionaires' boats and dozens of outdoor bars and restaurants lined up along the Passeig Marítim del Port Olímpic. This is the road that stretches away to your left as you look at the marina. It is also one of the city's hottest spots after dark.

Continue walking away from the sea. To your left, the Plaça dels Voluntaris, with its huge central

Gehry's Fish *completes views of Barceloneta (top); expensive yachts at Port Olímpic (left); the Palau del Mar is often busy with visitors (right)*

fountain, was named after the thousands of volunteers who helped out during the 1992 Olympic Games.

A few paces more bring you to the corner of Carrer de Salvador Espriu and the heart of the former Olympic Village, housing that was built especially for the visiting athletes. On the left, in the Jardins d'Atlanta, is the quirky *Tallavents* (Windbreaker) sculpture by Francesc Fornells-Pla (1921–99). Walk to the next intersection with Avinguda d'Icaria, turn left and walk for two blocks to the Ciutadella-Vila Olímpica metro station.

WHEN TO GO

On a bright sunny day! But if you can't organize that, take a jacket, as it gets windy along Barcelona's coast.

WHERE TO EAT

One of the many *chiringuitos* (beach bars) on the shore at the end of Passeig Joan de Borbó.

PLACES TO VISIT

Parc de la Barceloneta
Passeig Marítim s/n
🕓 24 hours

Parc de les Cascades
Salvador Espriu s/n
🕓 24 hours

[Map: The Waterfront area showing Barcelona Head, Palau de Mar, Museu d'Història de Catalunya, PORT VELL, L'Aquàrium, Casa de la Marina, BARCELONETA, Parc Zoològic, Ciutadella Vila Olímpica, Talavents, Hotel Arts, Peix, Port Olímpic, with street names including Passeig Joan de Borbó, Carrer del Doctor Aiguader, Ronda del Litoral, Avinguda Litoral Mar, Carrer de la Marina]

0 200 m
0 200 yds

G13   H13   J13

GRÀCIA

Small workshops and factories still dot Gràcia's narrow streets and squares, as it is an area with a strong industrial history, and the architectural heritage of Francesc Berenguer graces it with a few Modernista works.

THE WALK

Distance:	3.5km (2 miles)
Allow:	1.5 hours
Start at:	Gràcia FGC station
End at:	Fontana metro station

HOW TO GET THERE

Train: Gràcia station is on a number of the suburban lines run by the FGC. They are linked with various metro stations, the main one being at Catalunya.

Bus: 16, 17, 22, 24, 25, 27 and 28 will all take you to Gràcia

Walk out of the FGC station, following the exit marked Plaça de l'Oreneta. Walk a few steps and turn left onto Carrer de l'Oreneta which soon reaches the Plaça de la Llibertat **1**.

The square is occupied by the first of two markets in Gràcia, Mercat de la Llibertat (1893), a pretty wrought-iron affair designed by Fransesc Berenguer (1866–1914). Food sellers line the square's perimeters on market day (*closed Sun and Aug*) and it brings the whole area to life.

Walk down the right side of the square and exit along Carrer de la Riera de Sant Miguel. At the intersection with Carrer de Seneca turn left.

You will find yourself in an open space in the middle of Gràcia's main street, Gran de Gràcia. Known as Jardins de Salvador Espriu **2**, or more commonly the Jardinets (Little Gardens), they are the backdrop for various community activities throughout the year. Directly opposite is the area's best-known Modernista building, the Casa Fuster, designed by Lluís Domènech i Montaner (1850–1923). Directly behind you, at No. 15, is the elegant Casa Francesc Cama Escurra, designed by Francesc Berenguer, with ornate stained-glass

Fresh vegetables are abundant at the Mercat Abaceria, one of two main markets in Gràcia

glorietas (oriels) jutting out onto the street.

With your back to the gardens, walk a few steps up Gran de Gràcia and turn right onto the narrow street, Carrer de Gràcia, which runs beside the Casa Fuster. The austere Santa Maria de Gràcia, originally a Carmelite convent, is on your left. Many of its stones were laid in 1835, although the building was expanded more than a century later, and it is the oldest church in the area. Continue to the end of Carrer de Gràcia, and when the road intersects with Carrer de Sant Pere Martir, take the road almost directly in front of you, Carrer de Domènech. Turn left onto Carrer de Mozart and keep walking until you reach the Plaça de Rius i Taulet **3**.

This is one of Gràcia's most appealing squares. With its fine clock tower and the quaint blue and white façade of Gràcia's turn-of-the-20th-century town hall (also by Francesc Berenguer), it is an ideal place to stop for coffee and watch the comings and goings of life in the *barri*.

Walk through the square to Carrer del Penedès, the northern exit, then turn right and walk to the end of the street, until it meets Carrer de la Mare de Deu dels Desemparats.

The Mercat Abaceria **4** is to you left. It's a lot larger than the Mercat de la Llibertat, but what it lacks in architectural merit it makes up for as a hive of activity. It is also worth exploring the

streets that fan out from it for basketware, ceramics and other local crafts.

Turn left onto Carrer de la Mare de Deu dels Desemparats and then left again onto the busy axis of Travessera de Gràcia. After a minute or so you will come to Carrer de Torrent de l'Olla; turn right, then take the first left onto Carrer Maspons.

Here you will find the Plaça del Sol **5**, a Gràcia institution. Restrained by day, it comes alive at night as a vibrant meeting and drinking place. As the name suggests, it is also a great place for a spot of sunbathing.

Exit the square in the opposite direction to which you entered—onto Carrer del Planeta. Turn right and walk until you meet Carrer de Torrent de l'Olla again. Turn left, then take the first right onto Carrer de Terol. This tiny street will bring you to Carrer de Verdi, Gràcia's fashionable hub. It is home to a number of fashion, book and art shops and Middle Eastern cafés, and to the cinemas of the same name that show the latest releases. Turn left to walk up Carrer de Verdi to Carrer d'Astúries. Turn right and walk to the next intersection.

The Plaça de la Virreina **6** is Gràcia's most spacious square. It is dominated by the squat Església de Sant Joan with a chapel designed by Berenguer. The first service was held here in 1884, six years after the Plaça itself was completed.

OUT AND ABOUT

The Casa Fuster, completed in 1911, was one of Domènech i Montaner's last residential projects

Plaça del Sol is one of the focal points of Gràcia

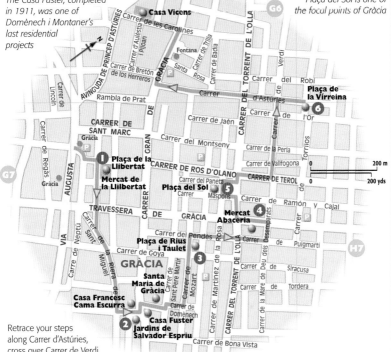

Retrace your steps along Carrer d'Astúries, cross over Carrer de Verdi, and continue along this road. After a few minutes you will hit Gran de Gràcia and the Fontana metro station. Either end the walk here, or turn right along Gran de Gràcia and left onto Carrer de les Carolines to see an early work by Antonio Gaudí (1852–1926)—the Casa Vicens (see page 74) at No. 18.

WHEN TO GO

Anytime, but take advantage of Gràcia's bars and restaurants at lunch or for a snack.

The splendid clock tower on Plaça Rius i Taulet dates from 1862 (left); local produce is tasty and inexpensive (above)

WHERE TO EAT

Bar Canigó
Carrer de Verdí 2
Tel 93 213 30 49
An old-style, wood-lined bar frequented by students and locals. The giant-sized sandwiches are hearty enough to satisfy even the largest of lunch-time cravings.
Mon–Fri, Sun 4pm–1am, Sat 8pm–2am

PLACES TO VISIT

Santa Maria de Jesús de Gràcia
Carrer de Sant Pere Màrtir 5
Tel 93 218 75 72
Daily 10–1pm

Església de Sant Joan
Plaça de la Virreina s/n
Tel 93 237 73 58
Daily 8.30am–12.30pm

L'EIXAMPLE

L'Eixample (the Extension) was designed in 1859 and became a canvas for Barcelona's budding Modernista movement. The result is an abundance of work from most of its key figures, all found within a short distance of each other.

THE WALK

Distance: 2.5km (1.5 miles)
Allow: 1–1.5 hours
Start at/end at: Manzana de la Discordia

HOW TO GET THERE

Metro: Passeig de Gràcia station is on lines 3 and 4
Bus: 7, 16, 17, 22, 24 or 28 will drop you nearby

Start the walk at the intersection of Passeig de Gràcia and Carrer del Consell de Cent. The building on the corner is the Casa Lleó Morera, the first of the trio of the Manzana de la Discordia (Block of Discord, see pages 82–83). The other two on the block are the Casa Amatller and the Casa Batlló, a shimmering, sinuous building that takes its inspiration from the legend of St. George, Catalonia's patron saint, and his battle with the dragon. The Manzana should be on your left. Walk a few more steps north to Carrer d'Aragó, cross the road and turn left.

The Fundació Antoni Tàpies ❶ (see page 77) appears on your right, easily recognizable by the swirling wire cloud sculpture on the roof. The building itself was an old publishing house designed by Domènech i Montaner (1850–1923) in 1885. With a pronounced Arabic influence, it was considered a breakthrough work that ushered in the beginnings of the Modernista movement.

Continue along Carrer d'Aragó, with the Foundation on your right, to the next intersection, Rambla de Catalunya, and turn right. Walk up to the intersection with Carrer de Valencia. Here you will find the Farmàcia Bolós (No. 77), a prime example of the dozens of functioning Modernista pharmacies around L'Eixample. Its florid wooden façade dates from 1902. Carry on up Rambla de Catalunya and turn right onto Carrer del Rosselló. Walk until you reach the intersection with Carrer del Bruc.

Rambla de Catalunya runs parallel to the Passeig de Gràcia

The Casa de les Punxes ❷ (House of Spikes) was designed in 1906 by Josep Puig i Cadafalch (1867–1957), and is on your right. It is another key example of how Modernista architects hailed past eras and cultures in their work, in this case the Central European castles of the Middle Ages. St. George is also paid homage to in a huge ceramic panel that declares 'Holy Patron of Catalunya, give us back our freedom'.

Turn right onto Carrer del Bruc as far as the intersection of Carrer de Mallorca and then turn right again.

Casa Tomas ❸, on the right-hand side of the road, was designed by Domènech i Montaner, but is better known as BD, Barcelona's most exclusive designer furniture and gift store. Take advantage of the public access to admire the reptilian entrance and upper floors, with a view down into the interior of the block.

Continue walking along Carrer de Mallorca to Carrer de Roger de Llúria. Turn left and walk down to Carrer de Valencia. Here you are at the centre of the Quadrat d'Or (Golden Square), considered the most exclusive part of the L'Eixample when the area started to take shape in the late 1800s. This particular intersection has three superb examples of Modernista apartment blocks. Walk a little farther down Carrer de Roger de Llúria to No. 85, on your right.

Colmados Murria ❹ is the best-conserved Modernista shop in the area. It originally supplied coffee, and the glass and ceramic exterior panels have elegant turn-of-the-20th-century advertising. The best known is the Anis de Monos girl, a languid maiden who was the symbol of a celebrated anise-based liquor that you can buy inside.

Walk down Carrer de Roger de Llúria to Carrer d'Aragó and turn right. Continue for two blocks and you will return to the starting point.

WHEN TO GO

Try to avoid early afternoon (2–4pm), as many main entrances to the Modernista apartment buildings are closed at this time. Outside these hours you may be allowed a peek at the detailed lobbies and lifts, depending on the mood of the concierge.

Even the pharmacies have elegant entrances

OUT AND ABOUT

La Bodegueta

Rambla de Catalunya 100
Tel 93 215 48 94

L'Eixample has been taken over by franchise cafés. La Bodegueta is an exception, with its wood-lined tapas bar, barrelled wine, a great lunch-time menu and buzzing atmosphere.

⏰ Mon–Sat 8am–2am, Sun 6.30pm–1am

BD

See page 149.
Carrer de Mallorca 291
Tel 93 458 69 09
⏰ Mon–Sat 10–2, 4–8

Colmados Murria

See page 144.
Carrer de Roger de Llúria 85
Tel 93 215 57 89
⏰ Daily 10–2, 4–8, May–end Sep; 10–8, rest of year

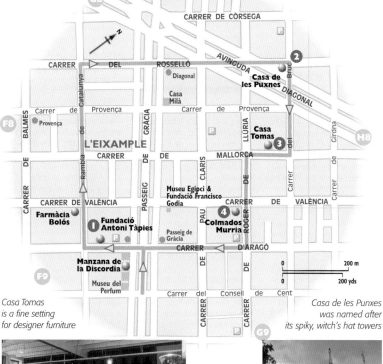

Casa Tomas is a fine setting for designer furniture

Casa de les Punxes was named after its spiky, witch's hat towers

Pretty ceramics adorn the walls of Colmados Murria (below)

OUT AND ABOUT

L'EIXAMPLE **189**

LAS RAMBLAS

No trip to the city is complete without a stroll along Las Ramblas. It is the sum of five different *ramblas* (pedestrian avenues), which together form one of the best-known images of the Catalan capital.

THE WALK

Distance: 2km (1 mile)
Allow: 1 hour
Start at: Catalunya metro station, Las Ramblas entrance
End at: Plaça Portal de la Pau

HOW TO GET THERE

Metro: Catalunya station is on the red line 1
Bus: A large number of buses run to or through the Plaça de Catalunya, including 14, 16, 17, 22, 24, 28, 39, 41, 45, 47 and 58

Start your walk at the northern end of Las Ramblas, outside the main entrance of the Catalunya metro station, with your back to Plaça de Catalunya. This first section is known as Rambla de Canaletes, after the wrought-iron drinking fountain you see as soon as you hit the street. On the right, at No. 10, is the Farmàcia Nadal, an example of the elegant Noucentista style that followed Modernisme. Turn left onto Carrer de la Canuda.

The Ateneu Barcelonès **1** is on the right at Carrer de la Canuda 6, where the street meets Plaça Vila de Madrid. It is the Modernista home of the city's elite literary and cultural association. It has a charming indoor patio and garden that is not strictly open to the public, but nobody seems to mind if you have a discreet look around. After a few paces you reach Plaça Vila de Madrid itself, which has remains of the necropolis of Roman Barcelona.

Return along Carrer de la Canuda to Las Ramblas. Turn left and continue for a minute or so until you reach the pedestrianized Carrer de Portaferrisa **2**, also on your left. Turn down this road.

This is one the main shopping streets and is marked by a pretty ceramic drinking fountain at its entrance. Carrer de Petritxol, the second street along on your right, is known for its *granjas*, cafés serving cakes and cream-laden hot chocolate. If you continue to the end of Carrer de Petritxol, you reach Plaça del Pi, one of the Barri Gòtic's most attractive squares.

Retrace your steps along Carrer de Petritxol and Portaferrisa to Las Ramblas and turn left. You are now in La Rambla de les Flors, named after the numerous flower-sellers who trade here.

On your right, at No. 91, is La Boqueria **3** (see page 153), Barcelona's food market. It is famous for its masterful Modernista wrought-iron entrance, but it's worth taking a look at the quality of the local produce inside, even if you don't plan to buy anything. The noise and the energy of the place is exhilarating.

Continue along the same side of Las Ramblas for a short while to the corner of the tiny Carrer de Petxina on your right.

The Casa Antiga Figueres **4** is a glittering example of a Modernista ceramic façade. The shop is owned by the most celebrated families of pastry-makers in the city and is a haven for lovers of chocolates and confectionery.

Return to Las Ramblas, turn right and continue along the same side to the next intersection with Carrer de l'Hospital. You are now outside El Liceu (see page 80), Barcelona's celebrated opera house. Directly opposite is the Café de l'Opera, a city institution, and a few doors down, at No. 45 on the opera-house side, is the Hotel Oriente, where many famous opera stars, including Maria Callas, have stayed while performing at El Liceu. With your back to the hotel, turn right and continue along Las Ramblas until you are just past the intersection with Carrer de Ferran.

The large square you see to the left is the Plaça Reial **5** (see page 118). With lamp-posts designed by Gaudí and a central fountain, it is a popular place to hang out during the day and to have a drink at night. There are a few porticoed streets and small shops that flank its edges.

Return to Las Ramblas and turn left, continuing towards the port. The Centre d'Art Santa Mònica, the modern building on the right at No. 7, puts on mainly free exhibitions of contemporary artists from Spain and abroad. Just a few steps farther along Las Ramblas bring you to the tiny Passatge de la Banca, on the left. This is a pretty walkway that leads to the Museu de Cera (see page 89). The Bosque de les Fades (Fairy Forest) next door is the museum's café, which also has some whimsical installations, including magic mirrors and a running brook.

Return to Las Ramblas, turn left and walk toward the vast Monument a Colom (see page 88). This marks the official end of Las Ramblas. But if you have the energy you can walk across the suspended bridge, the Rambla de Mar, directly in front, to cross to the shopping and entertainment complex of Maremagnum (see page 152).

Plaques mounted on the side of buildings tell you which of the five ramblas you're on (above)

OUT AND ABOUT

Las Ramblas is a great place for people watching (above); it's also good for postcards (below)

PLACES TO VISIT

**Casa Antiga Figueres
(Pastelería Escribá)**
Rambla de les Flors 83
Tel 93 301 60 27
🕐 Mon–Sun 8.30am–9pm

Centre d'Art Santa Monica
Rambla de Santa Mònica 7
93 316 28 10
🕐 Mon–Fri 11–2, 5–8, Sat 11–3
🎟 Free

WHEN TO GO

Anytime, but be aware of your personal belongings in crowded parts of Las Ramblas and in the streets around the Plaça Reial at night.

WHERE TO EAT

Xocoa
Carrer de Petritxol 11
Tel 93 301 11 97
Without doubt the best *granja* (pastry shop) along a street that is renowned for them. Try their *ventall*, a scrumptious concoction of almond pastry and chocolate truffle.
🕐 Mon–Sun 9–9

Café de l'Opera
See page 166.
La Rambla 74, 08002
Tel 93 317 7585
🕐 Fri–Sat 8am–3am, Mon–Thu, Sun 8am–2.15am

It is said that if you drink from the fountain in Rambla de Canaletes (left) you will be sure to return to Barcelona

LAS RAMBLAS 191

LA RIBERA

The tiny La Ribera district is a living testament to the fact that Catalans were noted as a nation of shopkeepers, and the Mercat del Born was once the city's wholesale market. These days the area is undergoing a new retail renaissance, as cutting-edge fashion and design shops take over traditional food premises.

OUT AND ABOUT

THE WALK

Distance: 1.5km (1 mile)

Allow: 45 minutes to 1 hour

Start at/end at: Plaça de Santa Maria del Mar

HOW TO GET THERE

Metro: Line 4 goes to Jaume I. Leave the station, cross Via Laietana, then walk down Carrer de l'Argenteria, following the sign for Basílica de Santa Maria del Mar.

The square in front of the Gothic masterpiece of the Basílica de Santa Maria del Mar ❶ (see page 123) is a good starting point for a walk around La Ribera. Take advantage of the abundant outdoor cafés from which you can admire its grand entrance and magnificent rose window. Don't miss the quaint Fuente de Santa Maria, one of the oldest water sources in the city, at the beginning of Carrer de l'Argenteria on the left-hand side of the church.

Walk to the right of the church and continue onto Carrer de Santa Maria.

A few steps up the road on the right is a plain, solemn-looking square that has a modern, arched column topped by an eternal flame. This is Fossar de les Moreres ❷ (Mulberry Graveyard), a deeply significant place in the hearts of the Catalan people. It was the site of a massacre of the last defenders of the city during the fall of Barcelona to the Spanish in the 1714 War of Succession. On 11 September every year hundreds gather here to commemorate the event and call for the independence of Catalonia from central Spanish rule.

Continue to the end of Carrer de Santa Maria, which brings you to the back of the church, and turn left, crossing over the Plaça de Montcada and Carrer de Montcada. This was where the city's noblemen once resided in their imposing mansions. Immediately to your right is the gated Carrer de les Mosques, a dank lane said to be the narrowest street in Barcelona and now closed off to the public.

Continue along Carrer de Montcada, looking out for the baroque courtyard of the Palau Dalmases, on the left at No. 20. At the end of Carrer de Montcada turn right onto Carrer de la Princesa. Of the old wholesale outlets selling olives, dried cod and other foodstuffs, only one remains—the enticing spice emporium Angel Jobal, at No. 38 on your right. Continue to the end of Carrer de la Princesa to the threshold of the Parc de la Ciutadella (see page 108) and the fanciful Museu de Zoologia (see page 102). Turn right onto Passeig de Picasso and follow the perimeter of the park.

You will walk under the elegant Porxes de Fosteré, a series of arches named after the architect responsible for the Parc de la Ciutadella, Josep Fosteré. On the opposite side of the Passeig de Picasso, near the intersection with Carrer de la Fusina, is the conceptual glass-and-water structure *Homenage a Picasso* ❸ by Antoni Tàpies (born 1923).

Turn right onto Carrer de la Fusina and then left onto Carrer del Comerç.

Here you walk around the façade of the former Mercat del Born ❹. Its vast amounts of ironwork looks like a homage the Industrial Age. In 2001 excavation work revealed the amazingly complete remains from the 18th century. After much debate—the authorities originally planned to turn it into a library—the market is now destined to be a museum and community hall, displaying the subterranean ruins through glass floors.

With your back to the market, keep left, following Carrer del Comerç to the intersection with Avinguda del Marquès de l'Argentera. Directly in front of you is the beautifully restored Estació de França, from where the first train in Spain made its inaugural trip in 1848. Turn right onto the Avinguda and then right again onto Carrer de Pescateria—so named after the fishmongers that once lined the street.

Turn left onto Carrer del Bonaire, which brings you to the charming Plaça de les Olles, a small square with outdoor cafés and apartment blocks with pretty façades. Carry on along Carrer del Bonaire, which farther on changes its name to Carrer del Consolat del Mar. Stop when you reach the intersection with Carrer dels Canvis Vells on your right.

This will bring you face to face with the imposing La Llotja ❺ (see page 122), formerly the city's stock exchange. Although its façade dates from 1802, it was originally built in the late 14th century and glimpses of the Gothic interior courtyard are possible from street level. The building has had a varied life. For most of the 19th century, its upper floors housed the art school where Picasso senior taught his young son, Pablo for a time in the mid-1890s.

Turn right onto Carrer dels Canvis Vells, named after the money-changers who worked their nimble fingers in the streets around La Llotja. Here you will see more examples of the district's picturesque arcades that once marked the water's edge. At the end of the road is the Plaça de Santa Maria del Mar.

Intricate wrought-ironwork characterizes many of the buildings along the walk

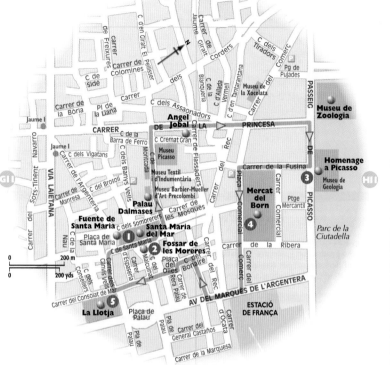

WHEN TO GO

During shop hours (remember to avoid the lunch closing hours 1–4pm). Many eccentric and esoteric shops are to be found in the streets around La Ribera.

WHERE TO EAT

Hivernacle
Passeig de Picasso s/n
Tel 93 295 40 17
This restaurant/bar, found in an old hothouse opposite the Museu de Zoologia in the Parc de la Ciutadella, is a tranquil, leafy place in which to gather your energy.
⊙ Mon–Sat 10am–midnight, Sun 10am–8pm

PLACES TO VISIT

Angel Jobal
Carrer de la Princesa 38
⊙ Daily 10–2, 4–7.30

Palau Dalmases (Bar Espai Barroc)
Carrer de Montcada 20
Tel 93 310 06 73
⊙ Tue–Sat 8pm–2am, Sun 6pm–10pm

Go along to Plaça de les Olles to be entertained by talented street performers (left)

Some of the smaller squares in La Ribera are ideal for a shady drink at lunch (right)

EXCURSIONS

Barcelona has a great deal for any visitor, but its exuberance may leave you feeling the need for something slower paced, or a change from the bright Modernista architecture. This is your chance to explore the different aspects of the region of Catalonia, whose cities and coastal areas provide an impressive variety of day trips, such as the coastal resort of Sitges or stepping back in time to see the Roman ruins at Tarragona and Girona. You are unlikely to be on your own at any of these places as they are popular with residents and visitors, but all have something special. For more travel details, see page 51.

For more travel details, see page 51.

EXCURSION 1

THE PENEDÈS REGION

Vineyards carpet the gently rolling valleys of Penedès, Catalonia's wine region, which is also the production epicentre of cava, the Catalan version of champagne. With a handful of period *bodegas* (wineries) open to the public, superb local cuisine and the bustling capital Vilafranca, the Penedès provides a welcome break from the city.

OUT AND ABOUT

BASICS

Tourist information office
Carrer de la Cort 14
Vilafranca del Penedès 08720
☎ 93 818 12 54
◉ Mon–Fri 9–1, 4–7, Sat 9–1, 5–8 Jul–end Aug; Mon–Sat 10–1, 4–7 rest of year
www.avilafranca.es

HOW TO GET THERE

By train: From Sants, trains run to Vilafranca and Sant Sadorní d'Anoia, taking around 50 minutes, departing hourly

By car: Leave the city by the B-20 (at Ronda de Dalt or Ronda Litoral) or C-16 and to the A2 (exit 8 Terrassa) and then the A7 to reach Sant Sadorní d'Anoia, then stay on the A7 for Vilafranca

VILAFRANCA

This is the most logical starting point when exploring the region. Try and arrive on a Saturday morning and head straight to the main square, Plaça de la Vila. The Saturday open-air market is busy with vendors selling home-grown produce and shops in the old town doing a brisk trade.

To find out about the Penedès' wine-making history, head to the Museu del Ví (*Tue–Sat 10–9, Sun 10–2, Jun–end Aug; Tue–Fri 10–2, 4–7, Sat 10–2, 4–8, Sun 10–2, rest of year*) on 12th-century Plaça Jaume I. The collection is housed in a former royal palace and is among the best in Europe. Its 11 halls show the history of the industry in the area through didactic dioramas and old production aids such as wine presses, with a wine-tasting in an 18th-century tavern at the end of the visit. Once your appetite is whet for more, the Museu de Vilafranca (in the Casa de la Festa Major, *Tue–Sat 10–9, Sun 10–2, Jun–end Aug; Tue–Fri 10–2, 4–7, Sat 10–2, 4–8, Sun*

10–2, rest of year) next door includes paintings by local artists on wine-related themes and a substantial collection of Spanish and Catalan ceramics from the 15th century onwards. Also on Plaça Jaume I is the Basílica de Santa Maria (*Tue–Sat 11–2, 5–9, Sun 11–2, Jun–end Sep; Sat 11–2, 5–8, Sun 11–2, rest of year*), a 15th-century Gothic church with a 52m (170ft) bell-tower that you can climb (*summer only*) for views of the town and the surrounding area.

The *castellers* (the human towers) of Vilafranca are generally considered to be the best in Catalonia. They normally perform outside the town hall, reaching incredible heights and wowing the crowd, but you are likely to see them only if your visit coincides with a local fiesta.

CODORNÍU

☎ 93 818 32 32 ◉ Mon–Fri 9–5, Sat–Sun 9–1, guided tours every hour
🎟 Free Mon–Fri; €2 Sat–Sun

You can learn all about cava production on a trip to the Codorníu *bodega*. Codorníu is a major manufacturer of the Catalan version of champagne and their winery is 10km (6 miles) from Vilafranca in Sant Sadorni d'Anoia, a pretty village where more than 85 per cent of cava is made.

This beautiful Modernista construction was designed by Josep Puig i Cadafalch (1867–1957), responsible for the Casa Amatller (see pages 82–83) and Casa de les Punxes (see page 76) in Barcelona, at the end of the 19th century. Even the caves where the wine is left to age are elegant—and the most extensive of their kind in the world, with more than 25km (15 miles) of underground cellars. The complex is replete with art nouveau touches and details and there is a museum of interesting advertising posters from the past. As it is too large to see the whole winery on foot, a mini train transports you around the complex, including the vast sums of Chardonnay, Macabeo, Parellada and Xarel.lo grapes (the principal cava varieties), with wine tasting to end your visit.

Take a look at the old wood and stone wine press at the Museu del Vi in Vilafranca (above), and then go out into the elegant courtyard

FURTHER TOURS
Freixenet, another big-name cava producer, also gives tours of its headquarters (*hourly Mon–Fri 9–5*), next to the Sant Sadorni d'Anoia train station. Its façade is one of the area's landmarks.

Torres (*Mon–Fri 9–5, Sat 9–6, Sun 9–1*), one of Spain's largest wine-makers, includes a train ride through a virtual reality tunnel where modern wine-making practices are explained.

VILLAGES AND TOWNS
Exploring the region's dozens of picturesque villages unearths pretty Gothic and Romanesque architecture. Gelida, a tiny, elevated village, has some Modernista chalets—the result of a time when it was a popular summer retreat—and the majestic Gothic church of Sant Pere del Castell. Olèrdola shows off a pair of Romanesque churches as well as an important archaeological site. The settlement, on the top of a craggy hill, was first an Iberian village, then later used by the Romans as a fort. There is a small archaeological museum (*Tue–Fri 10–2, 3–6, Sat–Sun 10–2, 4–6, mid-Sep–end Mar; Tue–Fri 10–2, 3–8, Sat–Sun 10–2, 4–8, rest of year*) next door to the site, belonging to the Museu d'Arqueologia de Catalunya and displaying finds from the area.

The old town of Sant Quintí de Mediona is a great place for a stroll, with fountains and grottoes and some of prettiest country-side in its immediate vicinity.

ACTIVITIES
The Penedès is perfect for lovers of outdoor sports. Cyclists fill the roads at the weekends, enjoying its gentle slopes and mild Mediterranean climate. Horse-riding is another popular pastime and the tourist office can supply information on the area's Hípicas ranches, with horses that you can ride out on for the day.

Most *domingueros* (day-trippers) are mainly concerned with satisfying a more basic need. The area's gastronomy is well respected, helped of course by the fine local wines, which are readily available. Pull up to even the tiniest village at the weekend and the smell of *botifarras* (sausages) being cooked on an open coal fire will fill the air. Other local delicacies include wild pigeon and duck (*pato*), and *calçots* (huge spring onions, or scallions) cooked on hot coals, which make a short appearance in February and March.

TIP
● If you possibly can, visit the region in September. This is when the harvest (*vendemia*) is gathered in the Penedès, a magical time when vineyards are alive with grape picking.

WHERE TO EAT
Fonda Neus
Marc Mir 14, Sant Sadurní d'Anoia
Tel 93 891 03 65
This restaurant was founded in 1929 and serves traditional dishes—*canelones* (cannelloni) is the most popular.
🕐 Daily 1–4, 9–10
🍽 L €40, D €60

Cal Blai
Josep Rovira 11, Sant Sadurní d'Anoia
Tel 93 891 23 00
Catalan cooking, with a number of modern innovations and a good wine list.
🕐 Daily 1.30–4, 9–11
🍽 L €30, D €48

SITGES

The seaside town of Sitges has everything for a great day, and night, out—nine sandy beaches, excellent bars, restaurants and nightlife, a couple of very good museums and an abundance of Modernista architecture.

OUT AND ABOUT

BASICS
Tourist Information Office
Sínia Morera 1, 08870 Sitges
☎ 93 894 50 04
⊙ Mon–Sat 9–9, Jun–end Sep;
Mon–Fri 9–2, 4–6.30, rest of year
www.sitges.org

HOW TO GET THERE
By train: Two or three trains every hour leave from Sants station, taking you along the coast in about 25 minutes
By car: Take the C-246 from the Plaça d'Espanya southwest to Sitges
By bus: A regular bus service runs from Sants bus station, next to the main rail station

OVERVIEW
Set on a cliff face overlooking the sea, Sitges' topography is the reason its small historic quarter has remained so intact. Hannibal had to bypass it on his way to Rome and the town has managed to avoid attack because of its fortress-like characteristics. Fishing and wine-making have always been the local industries, coupled with tourism, which took off at the beginning of the 20th century. Sitges is also home to a large gay community.

The long promenade, the Passeig de Marítim, curves along the shoreline and is crowded with people even in winter, although the water is generally only warm enough to swim in between June and October.

THE MUSEUMS
From the station, all streets lead down through the old town to the shore. Here your eyes will be drawn upward to the majestic, whitewashed, 17th-century Church of Sant Bartomeu i Santa Tecla (*Mass only, Mon–Fri 9am, 7.30pm, Sat 8pm, Sun 9am*). Most of Sitges' historic buildings are clustered around it, as it stands tall and defiant on a cliff. The most important of these is Museu Cau Ferrat (*Tue–Sun 10–2, 5–9, Jun–end Sep;*

Stroll along the promenade or worship the sun

Tue–Fri 10–1.30, 3–6.30, Sat 10–7, Sun 10–3, rest of year), the former home of Modernista artist Santiago Rusinyol (1861–1931). Rusinyol and his cohorts were largely responsible for making Sitges fashionable by forming an artists' colony at his out-of-town hideaway and weekend retreat in the 1890s.

Rusinyol was an avid collector of wrought-ironwork, particularly the pieces of the Modernista period, which are the highlights of this collection, as are paintings of the period by the artist himself, his artistic soulmate Ramon Casas (1866–1932) and other contemporaries. The windows frame some splendid views of the sea and it is a fascinating glimpse into the mind of one of the key figures of the movement. The home itself is built in the *Americano* style, the name given to the grand mansions of the returning merchants who had made their fortunes in the Americas. There are 88 examples of these in Sitges—a map of them is available at the tourist office.

Next door is the Palau Maricel, another elegant residence that is used for private functions. The Museu Maricel (open same times as Museu Cau Ferrat) has a small collection of Noucentista and Modernista paintings, sculpture and ceramics.

The Museu Romàntic (open same times as Museu Cau Ferrat), the third in Sitges' trio of museums, is found in the heart of the old town. Also known as the Casa Llopis, after the mansion's original owner, the collection is testimony to genteel, upper-class life at the end of the 18th century. Señor Llopis was another *Americano* who returned from the New World a very rich man, as this wide-ranging exhibition of everyday objects and curios shows. The whole second floor is taken up with a doll collection that once belonged to the Catalan children's book writer and illustrator Lola Anglada.

OTHER SIGHTS

Admirers of contemporary architecture should take the 20-minute stroll down the Passeig Marítim to the Hotel Terramar. The huge, white, nautical-looking building is a Sitges landmark, and was the first of the grand hotels on this stretch of coast. The public areas were refitted in the 1970s,

The Museu Maricel, originally a hospital, was restored for American millionaire Charles Deering and is now filled with an eclectic art collection

including the quirky, marine-themed foyer. The complex is surrounded by the Jardins del Terramar (*Fri–Wed 10.30–8.30, summer; Fri–Wed 10–5, winter*), which are a good place to cool off after the beach.

Sitges also stages a number of well-known festivals. It is the only place in Catalonia that takes Carnival in February seriously, with a week-long calendar of parties and parades, including a special Children's Day. The Sitges Festival International de Cinema in October draws top film makers and is a showcase for new home-grown talent. One of the prettiest local customs takes

place during the week of Corpus Christi in June when the streets of the old quarter are carpeted in flowers forming ornate patterns. The night of 23 June (St. Joan, or Midsummer's Eve) is one of the best times to be in Sitges, when there are beach bonfires and firework displays.

TIP

● If you take the train to Sitges, make sure you check the time of the last return train—those going back to Barcelona leave notoriously early.

WHERE TO EAT

Fragata
Passeig de la Ribera 1
Tel 938 94 10 86
Traditional Catalan dishes.
🕐 Daily 1.30–4.15, 8.30–11.15
💶 L €25, D €50

The mermaid statue on Passeig de Marítim is a fitting tribute to Sitges' association with the sea

TARRAGONA

Greek writers called Tarragona Callipolis the beautiful city, and it was founded in 218BC as a military camp by the Scipio brothers. It once outshone Barcelona, and remains open, airy and inviting, with some of the best Roman remains in Spain.

BASICS

Tourist Information Office
Carrer Major 39, 43003
☎ 977 25 07 95
🕔 Mon–Fri 9–9, Sat 9–2, 4–9, Sun 10–2, Jul–end Sep; Mon–Sat 10–2, 4–7, Sun 10–2, rest of year
www.costadaurada.info

HOW TO GET THERE

By train: Express trains run from Sants to Tarragona, taking about an hour

By car: Take the N-340, or the motorway A2 and then the A7 via Vilafranca

By bus: From outside metro station Maria Cristina, run by La Hispania (tel 97 775 41 47)

OVERVIEW

The city's cultural legacy was recognized by UNESCO when Tarragona was named a World Heritage City in 2000. The Roman ruins bear witness to a time when it was a principal port in the Roman-dominated Mediterranean. To get your bearings on the city and its coastline, head for the Balcó del Mediterrani (Balcony of the Mediterranean), a clifftop lookout at the sea end of the main boulevard, the Rambla Nova. On the way there are some remarkably fine Modernista mansions and some of the most fashionable cafés in which to take a short break.

Even the smaller streets are smart and attractive

From the lookout you can see Tarragona's most famous relic, the stunning amphitheatre (*Tue–Sat 9–9, Sun 9–3, Jun–end Sep; Tue–Sat 9–7, Sun 9–3, rest of year*) built in the second century AD. It is the most vivid reminder that Roman *Tarraco* was once the capital of the province and a powerful seat in the Empire.

ROMAN REMAINS

Take a stroll around the Passeig Arqueològic (*Tue–Sat 9–9, Sun 9–3, Jun–end Sep; Tue–Sat 9–7,*

Sun 9–3, rest of year), on Avinguda Catalunya, a walkway that was built along part of the city walls. Measuring 6m (20ft) in width at some points, the massive inner walls were built by the Romans, while the outer walls were erected by the British during the War of the Spanish Succession. The three towers that form part of the walls—the Torre del Arquebisbe, the Torre del Cabiscol and Torre de Minerva—were built in the Middle Ages. Fountains, statues, gardens and other adornments complete the site.

The Pont del Diable (Devil's Bridge), the aqueduct on the outskirts of Tarragona towards the town of Valls (4km/2.5 miles), was built in the second century. Its 217m (712ft) length is still in perfect condition.

THE OLD CITY

This is where the main sights, monuments and museums are concentrated. The highlight of medieval Tarragona is the cathedral (*daily 10–1, 4–7, Mar–end May; 10–7, Jun–end Sep; 10–5, Oct–end Nov; 10–2, Dec–end Feb*) in the Plaça de la Seu. It was begun in 1171, during the Romanesque period, but its architecture took on Gothic elements towards its completion in 1331. The mixture of styles is most evident upon entering, with the main door rich in Gothic sculptures and details while the two side doors are more sparse. Inside, the main altarpiece by 15th-century Catalan master Pere Joan (flourished 1418–55) illustrates the life and struggles of St. Tecla, Tarragona's patron saint. Other notable artworks consist of an elaborate chapel dedicated to St. Michael and various retables from the 15th century. The Gothic cloister is beautiful, with perfectly dimensioned arches and columns—look for one depicting a procession of mice.

The Roman aqueduct is to the north of the city

The cathedral cloister and garden (above)

Off the cloister, you will find the Museu Diocesà (*daily 10–1, 4–7, Mar–end May; 10–7, Jun–end Sep; 10–5, Oct–end Nov; 10–2, Dec–end Feb*), which has an extensive collection of religious relics, Renaissance paintings and tapestries, which is the most important exhibit.

The city's Archaeological Museum (*Tue–Sat 9–9, Sun 9–3, Jun–end Sep; Tue–Sat 9–7, Sun 9–3, rest of year*) was the first museum of its kind in Catalonia, with exhibits of everyday objects of old Tarraco. Mosaics are well represented, including the beautiful Medusa Head in Salon III. Next door the restored *praetorium* (governor's residence) is where Emperor Augustus lived, and it is believed that Pontius Pilate was born here. It now houses the Museu de la Romanitat (*Tue–Sat 9–9, Sun 9–3, Jun–end Sep; Tue–Sat 9–7, Sun 9–3, rest of year*) displaying medieval and Roman finds, and also lets you access the first-century Roman Circus through some immense passageways.

The 15th-century Casa Castellarnau was home to one of the city's most influential families until the 19th century, and in 1542 England's Charles I resided here during his stay in the city. Inside, its grand salons

house the Museu d'Historia (*Tue–Sat 9–9, Sun 9–3, Jun–end Sep; Tue–Sat 9–7, Sun 9–3, rest of year*), an eclectic sum of three high-calibre private collections and one-off donations that have been acquired by the council in the last few decades. The highlight is the Molas Collection, a disparate series of archaeological and ethnographic exhibits from prehistory to the present. Spanish contemporary painting is on display too, dating from the beginning of General Franco's dictatorship (1939) to the 1960s, and includes a piece by Salvador Dalí (1904–89) donated by the artist himself and one of Joan Miró's (1893–1983) rare tapestries, which hangs in the entrance.

Buy a painting as a memento from one of the stalls outside the cathedral (left)

TIP
● If it's hot, pack some swimwear as Tarragona has good beaches at Platjas del Miracle and del Cossis, as well as south of the city at Cambrils and Salou.

WHERE TO EAT

La Cantonada
Fortuny 23
Tel 977 213524
This is one of the oldest cafés in Tarragona. Having a coffee and a relaxed chat are not the only incentives to visit—you can also play pool or the piano, listen to live music or check out an art exhibition. Try *Ilesca*, Catalan bread with a wide variety of toppings.
🕐 Daily 9pm–1am
🍴 L €16, D €30, Wine €5

Lizarrán
Plaza de la Font 16
Tel 977 230062
An ideal place to taste a wide variety of local and regional dishes. You have a choice of about 500 tapas—help yourself from the counter—plus breakfast and traditional casseroles for lunch and dinner. The list of wines is long.
🕐 Daily 12.30pm–1am
🍴 L €18, D €27, Wine €5

MONTSERRAT

Catalonia's spiritual heart, the immense monastery at Montserrat has a spectacularly rugged mountain setting, one of Spain's most impressive natural sights. Reports of miracles make it an intriguing place for visitors and pilgrims.

BASICS

Tourist Information Office
Plaça de la Creu s/n
☎ 93 877 77 77
🕐 Daily 8.50–7.30
www.abadiamontserrat.net

HOW TO GET THERE

By train: FGC train from the Plaça d'Espanya to Aeri de Montserrat, leaving every 2 hours, taking about 1 hour; then cable car to the monastery, leaving every 15 mins, except between 1.45 and 2.20
By car: Leave Barcelona by the B-20, take the A2 (exit Martorell), or the autopista Barcelona–Terrassa via the Valvidriera tunnels (exit Montserrat)
By bus: Julià Bus Company departs 9am from Plaça dels Països Catalans in Barcelona (beside Sants rail station), returns 6pm summer, 5pm winter

OVERVIEW

Monsterrat's rocky peak rises to 1,236m (4,054ft) and its eerie formations can be seen for long distances. The main attraction is the Monastery of Montserrat and La Moreneta, the statue of the Black Virgin, inside the Basilica. Every weekend thousands of pilgrims line up to pay their respects. The first mention of the complex dates back to the 9th century, but in 1811 it was attacked by the French during the Napoleonic War and its clergy were killed. Rebuilt in 1844, it became a symbol of Catalan defiance, particularly during General Franco's reign

(1939–75) when a Sunday trip to Montserrat became akin to an expression of independence. Today the monastery is home to a community of more than 300 Benedictine monks.

Montserrat (literally meaning serrated mountain) is a fabulous place to walk around, with its lunar-like landscape, secretive chapels and hermits' caves, and some breathtaking views of the valley below.

LA MORENETA

Legend has it that the statue of the Virgin of Montserrat was actually carved by St. Luke and brought to Montserrat by St. Peter in AD50. She was found in one of Montserrat's caves in the 12th century and a cult was born. Her name comes from her blackened face and body, and by touching her hand one is said

to be touching the universe and showing the ultimate respect. She became the official Patroness of Catalonia in 1881. After this, Montserrat became the most popular name for girls born all over Catalonia, along with the name of 150 churches in Italy and even an island in the Caribbean.

THE MONASTERY

Plaça de la Creu is the main entry point to the monstery, and is named after a huge cross (*creu*) with the phrase Who is God engraved on it in various languages. It was designed by Joseph Subirachs (born 1927), the sculptor responsible for the Passion façade of La Sagrada Família (see pages 124–129). The square is surrounded by three buildings, used as accommodation for the pilgrims.

La Moreneta's face has been blackened over time by the lighting of countless candles (above); the statue of a monk and choirboys stands on the Plaça de Santa Maria (left)

The Plaça de Santa Maria, the long esplanade designed by architect Josep Puig i Cadafalch (1867–1957) is the huge focal point that leads you to the threshold of the monastery. The façade's three upper arcades are decorated with reliefs of Christ and the Apostles and are built on polished mountain stone. The ruins of the Gothic cloisters

OUT AND ABOUT

(designed by Abbot Giuliano della Rovere, who later became Pope Julius II, 1443–1513) are to the left of the façade, but most were designed by Puig i Cadafalch in 1925.

The grandiose Basilica was greatly damaged when Napoleon brought his army to Spain between 1808 and 1814, but it wasn't reconstructed until the end of the 19th century. As soon as you enter, your eyes are drawn upwards to the ceiling of the nave where the choir, the richly enamelled high altar and a small chapel with a silver throne are found. La Moreneta sits behind the altar in a glass case. Worshippers ascend a small staircase to touch her orb, which protrudes from the glass.

The nearby museum has a collection of gifts that have been bequeathed to the Black Virgin, including a couple of works by Picasso. Some of the other highlights of this diverse collection include important archaeological pieces from Mesopotamia and the Holy Land (including an Egyptian mummy) and liturgical objects connected with the monastery over the centuries. The collection of 13th- to 18th-century paintings includes works by El Greco and Caravaggio and the French Impressionist section includes artists such as Monet, Sisley and Degas.

EXPLORING

If the commercialization gets too much, escape to the splendid scenery. Commonly called a sea of stone, its unique, molten-wax-

The strangly eroded mountain encircles the huge monastery (above and below)

like peaks were formed by geological upheavals 10 million years ago and have been sculpted through erosion after the softer land that surrounded this mass sank into the ground.

The tourist office provides various walking maps, including the Camino de la Santa Cova (Route of the Holy Cave, where La Moreneta was found), along which you will see a couple of monuments by Puig i Cadafalch and Gaudí (1852–1926). There are 13 hermitages, all of which are signposted once you are at the top.

The mountain is also home to some fantastic bird- and animal life—such as wild pigs and goats—and the rocky terrain is scattered with evergreen oaks, pine and maple trees.

PLACES TO VISIT
Basilica
🕐 Mon–Fri 7.30–7.30, Sat–Sun 7.30am–8.30pm. Shrine of the Virgin: Daily 8.30–10.30, noon–6.15, 7.30–8.30, Jul–end Sep; 8.30–10.30, noon–6.15, rest of year 🎟 Free

Museum
🕐 Mon–Fri 10–6, Sat–Sun 9.30–6.30
🎟 Adult €4.50, child (6–12) €3

Audiovisual exhibition
🕐 Daily 9–7.45, Jul–mid-Sep; daily 9–6, rest of year 🎟 Adult €2, child (6–12) €1

GIRONA

Catalonia's second city, a mix of styles from its many inhabitants, is often called a miniature-size Venice. It's a striking place to come and soak up history and culture, not to mention really fine dining with a riverside setting.

Riverside residences characterize the city (above); Carrer de la Força was Girona's original road to Rome (left)

BASICS

Tourist Information Office
Rambla de la Libertat 1, 17004
☎ 972 226 575
🕐 Mon–Fri 8–8, Sat 8–2, 4–8, Sun 9–2
www.ajuntament.gi

HOW TO GET THERE

By train: Trains leave regularly from Sants and from Passeig de Gràcia, taking one hour
By car: Take the A7 at Ronda Litoral, head north via A7 or the N-11
By bus: Buses leave regularly from Estació del Nord

OVERVIEW

Girona is a prosperous city with a high standard of living. Its compact old quarter, with wonderful examples of Gothic and Romanesque churches and monasteries, the remains of a fascinating Jewish quarter and excellent local gastronomy make it a great place for a day trip or a long weekend. The original Roman walls that surround the city have remained remarkably intact given the regular sieges the town suffered over the centuries. As you wander around the top of the walls, views of the lush green countryside—nourished by a higher-than-average rainfall—are guaranteed, as are glimpses of the Onyar River, which runs through the city.

THE CATHEDRAL

The cathedral (*Tue–Sat 10–2, 4–7, Mar–end May; 10–8, Jun–end Sep; 10–2, 4–6, Oct–end Feb; Sun 10–2, all year*) stands on top of a hill that looks down over the winding streets of the old quarter, with a grand, 90-step stairway sweeping up to the entrance. The architecture is a mixture of styles, predominantly from the Gothic period with 18th century touches. Its nave, an incredible feat of engineering, is the widest

in Europe. The serene cloister is another highlight, where the capitals of its pillars depict biblical scenes and everyday life and legends. Pay the small entrance fee into the Chapter House, which contains the Museu Capitular and the cathedral's Treasury. By far the best item of this collection of religious objects is the breathtaking 12th-century *Tapestry of Creation*. It was probably originally double the size of the fragment on show. Its figures and icons represent chapters from the book of Genesis laid out in a circular design as if it in a mosaic.

THE CALL

At the base of the cathedral lies the Call, the remains of the Jewish quarter. The Jewish community left an indelible mark on Girona's culture, from the end of the 9th century—when many emigrated here after the destruction of Jerusalem—to the late 1400s, when they were evicted from Spain by order of the Catholic King Ferdinand and

Queen Isabella. Life for the Jewish people was hard and the area had turned into a ghetto by the beginning of the 15th century. In the heart of the quarter the excellent Centre Bonastruc Ca Porta (*Mon–Sat 10–8, Sun 10–3, May–end Oct; Mon–Sat 10–6, Sun 10–3, Nov–end Mar*) recreates what life was like for the Jewish people here through art exhibits, musical events, recitals and food tastings. The site was formally a synagogue, and the complex also houses the Institute for Sephardic and Kabalistic Studies and the Catalan Museum of Jewish Culture. Don't miss the library as it has an important collection of medieval Jewish manuscripts.

Muslims also settled in Girona and the most vivid evidence of this is at the 12th-century Arabic Bathhouse (Banys Àrabs, *Tue–Sat 10–7, Sun 10–2, Apr–end Sep; Tue–Sun 10–2,*

rest of year), a short walk from the Call. Found in one of the most atmospheric pockets of the old city, where vegetation seeps through the golden granite of the medieval buildings, the bathhouse is close to the Monastery of Sant Pere de Galligants and the church of Sant Nicolau, two fine examples of Romanesque architecture. The Museu Arqueològic (*Tue–Sat 10.30–1.30, 4–7, Sun 10–2, Jun–end Sep; Tue–Sat 10–2, 4–6, Sun 10–2, rest of year*) is in the monastery, with finds from the Paleolithic to Visigothic periods discovered at digs in northern Catalonia. The cloister was once the old Jewish cemetery, as witnessed by the inscriptions in Hebrew.

MUSEUMS

Other museums include the Museu d'Art (*Tue–Sat 10–2, 5–7, Sun 10–2*) and the Museu d'Historia (open same times as Museu d'Art). The latter is in an 18th-century Capuchin convent on Carrer de la Força, part of the old Roman city at an intersection with the Via Augusta. The area is dotted with antiques shops and workshops. The museum's collection has a mixture of exhibits from Catalonia's prehistoric times to the present day, and displays Spain's first street lamps (which made their debut in Girona), tools, shields, dioramas and objects documenting the changes in city life over the centuries.

The Museu d'Art is also in the old quarter, in the beautifully

restored Palau Episcopal. Most of the collection comes from the former Diocese Museum, including some 14th-century retables, baroque and Gothic tapestries, and items related to Catalonia's traditional dance, the sardana. A collection of paintings is on show from the renowned Olot School—19th-century landscape painters from the nearby town of the same name who were known for their use of light.

Lovers of more contemporary culture should visit the Museu del Cinema (*Tue–Sun 10–8, Apr–end Sep; Tue–Fri 10–6, Sat 10–8, Sun 11–3, rest of year*) near Plaça Independencia. In 1994 the local council acquired one of the best cinematography collections in the world from local film-maker Tomàs Mallol (born 1923) and have created a hands-on experience. The exhibition takes you through ancient Chinese shadow puppets to the arrival of commercial cinema through objects used in early film-making, footage, and informative displays.

TIPS
● Leave the car behind—trains to Girona are fast and frequent from Barcelona.

● Stay for at least one meal as the restaurants in the old quarter are good on hearty local cuisine.

● To access the walls of the city, head for the Passeig Arqueològic and the Museu Arqueològic (*Mon–Sat 10–2, 4–7, Sun 10–2*).

The walled village of Hostalric, on the A7 from Barcelona to Girona (below)

The rococo stairway leads up to Girona's cathedral and its rose window (left); L'Arcadia is one of many cafés along Rambla de la Libertat (middle)

WHERE TO EAT
Café-Café
Plaça d'Espanya s/n
Tel 972 214676
Inside the train station, this caféteria is proud to serve real coffee—hence its enthusiastic name. There's a wide choice of pastries, baguette sandwiches, omelettes and sausage dishes.
Mon–Fri 6am–10pm, Sat–Sun 7am–10pm
Breakfast or afternoon snack for two around €3 (coffee plus pastry)

Sala Gran
Barceloneta 44, Llofriu
Tel 972 301638
www.sala-gran.com
The perfect place to taste traditional Catalan food. Among the house dishes are chicken with Dublin Bay prawns and snails. Booking is advisable.
Mon–Sun 1–4, 8–11, 16 Jun–14 Sep; Mon 1–4, Wed–Sun 1–4, 8–11, 15 Sep–15 Jun
L €50, D €70, Wine €5

OUT AND ABOUT

There are lots of different ways to explore Barcelona and the towns and sights beyond. Take advantage of its coastal location with a boat trip or uncover a hidden history with a guided walk.

GUIDED WALKS

ASSOCIACIÓ CALL DE BARCELONA
Carrer de Marlet 5, 08006 Barcelona
Tel 93 317 07 90
www.calldebarcelona.org
This group promotes the history of the Jewish community within the city and there is a guided tour of the old synagogue.
🕐 By arrangment
🎫 €15

TOURISME DE BARCELONA
Plaça de Catalunya
Tel 93 368 97 30
www.barcelonaturisme.com
The tourist office has guided walks around the Barri Gòtic and a Picasso trail. Book in advance.

Barri Gòtic
🕐 Sat–Sun 10am in English (also Thu and Fri 10am, Apr–end Oct)
🎫 Adult €7.50, child (4–12) €3

Picasso
🕐 Sat–Sun 10.30am in English
🎫 Adult €10, child (4–12) €5, includes admission to Picasso Museum

Ruta del Modernisme
Self-guided walk (see page 265).

BICYCLE TOURS

UN COTXE MENYS
Carrer de Esparteria 3
Tel 93 268 21 05
www.bicicletabarcelona.com
Around the Barri Gòtic and the port area with a guide. Book in advance. Also tours in Catalonia.
🕐 Sat–Sun 10am, returning 12.30pm
🎫 €20 (including drink); bicycle rental for one hour €5, per day €10

BUS TOURS
A range of these tours go around Barcelona and into Catalonia. The tourist office gives advice.

JULIÀ TOURS
Ronda de la Universitat 5
Tel 93 317 64 54
www.juliatours.es

PULLMANTUR
Gran Via de les Corts Catalanes 645
Tel 93 317 12 97
www.pullmantur-spain.com

Half-day tours
Go through the main streets and see some of the major sights on a 3-hour tour. If you want to see specific sights, check which are on the morning and which on the afternoon tours.
🕐 Daily; morning 9.30, afternoon 3.30
🎫 €33.25

Full-day tours
These tours whisk you through the city's biggest attractions. If a museum is closed on the day you go, an alternative is provided. Check if there are specific sights you want to see.
🕐 Tue–Sun, leaving 9.30am
🎫 €86.50

Night-time tours
For a different perspective on the city, followed by *tapas* and a flamenco show.
🕐 Thu–Sat, departing 7.30pm and returning 12.30am
🎫 €86.50

BARCELONA TOURS
Tel 93 402 69 55
www.barcelonatours.es
These orange buses with blue stripes have 20 stops and 20 sights on their route. Get on and off as many times as you like. Commentary is via headphones. There is also a guide on board. Tickets can be bought from the guide, from travel agencies and at many hotels.

Take a tour bus; Barcelona is splendid at night, here looking towards Plaça d'Espanya from the MNAC

🕐 Daily 9–9, every 10–20 minutes (depends on season)
🎫 One day: adult €16, child €10. Two days: adult €20, child €13

BUS TURÍSTIC
See page 46.

CAR TOURS

LIVE BARCELONA
Frederica Montseny 12, 08980 Sant Feliu de Llobregat
Tel 93 632 72 59
www.livebarcelona.com
If you have reduced mobility or want an extra level of comfort, a guide will take you round the city in a large car, in groups of up to seven. They also have day excursions. Prices vary depending on numbers and are arranged at mutual convenience.

BESPOKE TOURS

BARCELONA GUIDE BUREAU
Via Laietana 54, 08003
Tel 93 268 24 22
www.bgb.es
The BGB offer a range of tailor-made walking or bus tours. Interpreters can be provided. Prices available on request.

HELICOPTER TOURS

HELIPISTAS
Tel 902 194 073
www.barcelonahelicopters.com
Take in the whole of the city in one go on a helicopter ride. Flights take around 30 minutes.
🕐 Daily 9–7
🎫 €460 for flight, maximum of 3

BOAT TOURS
See page 174.

OUT AND ABOUT

Eating

Locator Maps	**206–209**
Eating Out in Barcelona	**210–211**
Menu Reader	**212–213**
Restaurants by Cuisine	**214–215**
A–Z of Restaurants	**216–234**

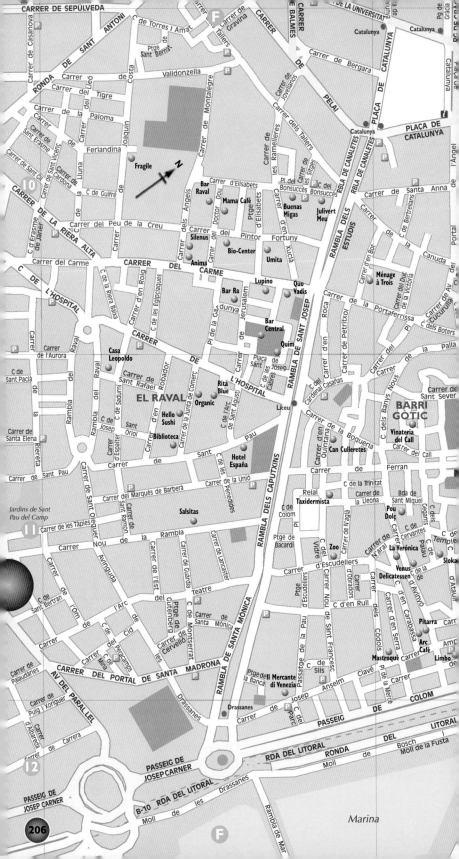

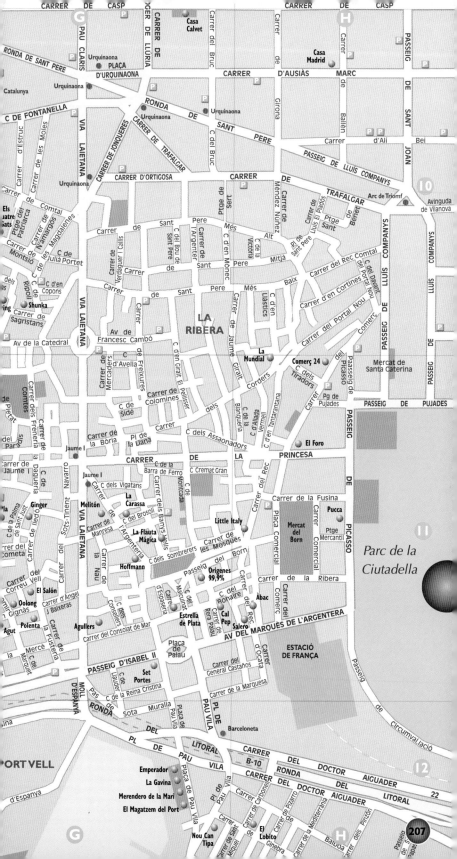

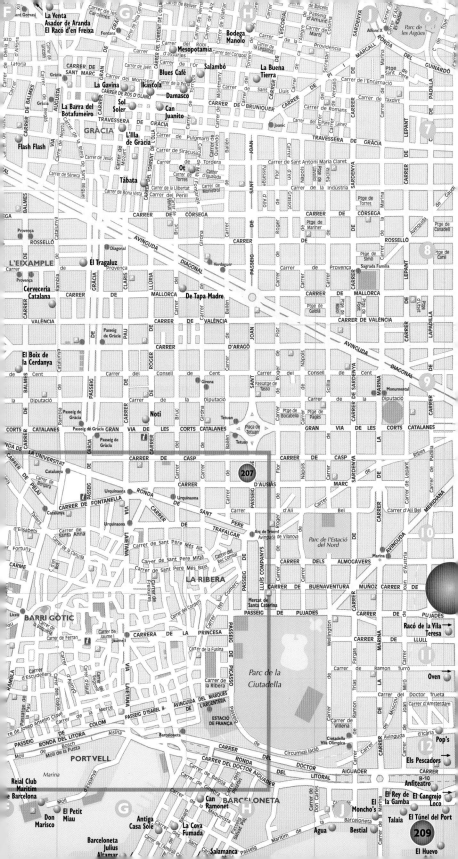

EATING OUT IN BARCELONA

Eating out in this city is a real pleasure, with the emphasis firmly on seasonal and fresh produce, and a huge range of restaurants, snack bars, tapas bars, cafés and *granjas* feeding residents and visitors throughout the day and night. Spain has no true national cuisine, apart from paella (saffron-flavoured rice, chicken and seafood), tortilla (omelette) and gazpacho (tomato- and pepper-based chilled soup), as cooking is firmly regional.

Tapas are at the heart of eating out in the city, many of which are served on toasted bread (left); larger portion of tapas, such as Russian salad, make a filling meal (middle); xocolata amb xurros *(right)*

Barcelona, however, has embraced mainstream Europe more wholeheartedly than anywhere else on the peninsula, and the city's cosmopolitan air shines through in its restaurants. Regional Catalan food is to the fore, but there is a good range of places serving food from other parts of Spain and from other countries—something not readily available in many other Spanish cities. But if you are dying for a fast food burger, you will find that too.

BREAKFAST
The first meal of the day (*desayuno* or *esmorzar* in Catalan) is usually eaten by city residents between 9 and 10, often after they've started work. In hotels, breakfast may be included in the room price, but if not, head for a bar or café. The quintessential breakfast is chocolate with churros (*xocolata amb xurros*), a thick sweet chocolate served with strips of deep-fried dough, which you dip in the chocolate. Toast with coffee is the other main choice.

LUNCH
The main meal (*almuerzo* or *dinar* in Catalan), is served between 2 and 4, and is traditionally the most important meal of the day. In Barcelona most restaurants serve a *menú del día*, a fixed-price menu with a choice of a starter, main course, dessert, bread and a drink. It's excellent value and a good way to sample some of the city's more expensive restaurants.

DINNER
Cena (*sopar* in Catalan) starts any time after 9pm, and continues until midnight, though visitor-orientated restaurants open as early as 8pm. It's traditionally a lighter meal than lunch, such as salads, soups and egg dishes.

VEGETARIAN FOOD
There are few vegetarian restaurants in Barcelona, but an increasing number of places serve good vegetable dishes. You may need to be on your guard, as some of the more traditional places may use meat stock, ham or pork fat, and still think they're serving meat-free dishes.

CHILDREN
Children's menus are non-existent, but they'll be welcome at all establishments, except the most expensive restaurants. If your children want smaller or plain meals, tapas are a good chocie, with options such as bread or tortilla.

RESERVATIONS
Booking is advised in mid- to upper price range restaurants, particularly for groups of four or more and at the weekends. For less formal establishments, such as tapas bars, you can walk in and secure a table, even if you have to wait at the bar for a space to become available. However, if there is an establishment that you really want to visit, check out whether booking is necessary.

MONEY
It's customary to leave a small tip at any bar or restaurant and 10 per cent of the bill is usual. More expensive restaurants will add a 7 per cent tax to the bill. The menu will state if this is the case. All major credit cards are accepted, except in the smallest of places, which is stated within the A–Z listings (see pages 216–234).

SMOKING
Smoking is usually permitted. If this is not the case, or a non-smoking section is available, this is stated within the listings (see pages 216–234).

EATING

A QUICK GUIDE TO CATALAN CUISINE

TASTES
Catalan cooking is related to Spanish cuisine and that of France, but is highly individual and uses combinations of textures and tastes to give it an extra twist. Signature elements that distinguish Catalan dishes include:

- *Sofregit*, onion and tomatoes gently sautéed in olive oil.
- *All i oli*, garlic and olive oil mayonnaise served with meat and seafood.
- *Samfaina*, an onion, garlic, peppers and aubergine (eggplant) mix served with grilled meat and fish.
- *Picada*, a sauce made with garlic, bread, chillies, nuts and parsley used to enrich and thicken stews and casseroles.
- *A la brasa*, meat, fish or sausage grilled over an open charcoal fire.

GRANJAS
These are very much part of the city refreshment scene and were originally outlets for fresh dairy products. They still concentrate on dairy-based goodies, and are great places to come for coffee, milkshakes (*batidos*) and thick hot chocolate topped with a mountain of whipped cream (*suizos*). They're also strong on cakes and pastries, and make good stops for weary sightseers in need of a sugar boost, but you won't be guaranteed a beer in many of them.

HORCHATERIAS
Another alternative is the *horchateria*, which sell the wonderfully refreshing hot drink *horchata*, made from crushed tiger nuts. This curdles once it's made, so has to be drunk on the spot while it's fresh.

When ordering in both *horchaterias* and *granjas* follow the general rule: pay as you leave. You can attract attention by a polite *oiga* (hear me), which should bring you the waiter. Tipping is discretionary here, but most people round up the bill to the nearest euro.

TAPAS
Tapas, snacks once traditionally served free with a drink, are Spain's great contribution to the European culinary scene, and you'll find a good range of tapas bars in Barcelona.

Tapas range from a few olives or almonds, to tortilla, chunks of meat and fish, cured ham, shellfish, anchovies, salads, meat croquettes and wonderful vegetable dishes laced with garlic and chilli. They can be either hot or cold, but don't just see them as a snack, or pre-dinner eat. Make a few selections and have them as your evening meal. If you are still hungry, you just order more.

TAPAS ETIQUETTE
When you enter a tapas bar, the food will be laid out on the counter for you to choose from (useful if your Spanish isn't great, as you can point at what you like the look of), listed on a blackboard behind the bar or, in some of the smarter bars, on menus. If you want more than a mouthful or two, ask for a *ración*, a larger serving. Don't worry about how many different dishes you order, as the barman will normally keep track of what you've had.

FAST FOOD
International burger chains, such as McDonalds, can be found in Barcelona. Two nationwide chains, Pans & Co and Bocatta, serve *bocadillos* (sandwiches) and other snacks and have branches throughout the city. Don't be confused though, as a sandwich in Barcelona is akin to a toasted sandwich, made using sliced white bread. The Spanish and Catalan version is a *bocadillo*, made with French bread or rolls.

ALCOHOLIC DRINKS
Beer is one of the most popular choices and comes in bottles or on draught; ask for a *caña* or *caña doble* for a larger glass. Estrella, Voll-Damm and Bock-Damm are the Catalonian specials and imported beers are widely available. However, wine is probably still first choice. House wines are more than acceptable, which is useful as good wines tend to be expensive. The sparkling wine cava makes a good aperitif. Spirits are inexpensive and served in hefty measures. Long drinks such as *gin-tonic*, *vodka-tónica* and *Cuba-libre* (rum and Coke) are popular.

SOFT DRINKS
Locals normally drink bottled water in restaurants; ask for *agua mineral con gas* (sparkling) or *sin gas* (still). The full range of international soft drinks is everywhere. Fresh fruit juice (*zumo*) and *granizado* (slush) are also widely available.

Coffee is served in bars, cafés and *granjas*. It's normally served as good, strong black espresso (*café sol/solo*). If you want milk, ask for a *café tallat/cortado*, a small cup with a drop of milk, or *café amb llet/café con leche*, made with lots of hot milk. Tea is hard to find; try an *infusione*, such as *manzanilla* (camomile) instead.

Fresh fish and shellfish are dishes that Barcelona excels at

EATING

Launching yourself into the city's vibrant restaurant culture can be a daunting experience if you don't speak Castilian, let alone Catalan, and working out what's on the menu something of a challenge. But don't be put off, as a few key words will help and the menu reader below will familiarize you with individual foods and dishes that you are likely to come across. Each is given in Catalan, followed by the Castilian in brackets, although some dishes are regional and are therefore not translated.

You will find a vast array of dishes on the city's menus and find something to suit your tastes, whether it's meat, fish or vegetables

Plats (Platos) Courses
els entrants (l'entrants) appetizers
el primer (el primero) first course
el segon (el segundo) main course
postres (postre) dessert

Carn (Carne) Meat
ànec (pato) duck
anyell (cordero) lamb
bistec (bistec) steak
botifarra negra (butifarra negra) blood sausage
carn (carne) beef
conill (conejo) rabbit
fetge (hígado) liver
gall dindi (pavo) turkey
llengua (lengua) tongue
perdiu (perdiz) partridge
pernil dolç (jamón cocido) cooked ham
pernil (jamón serrano) cured ham
peus (pies) trotters
pollastre (pollo) chicken
porc (cerdo) pork
vedella (ternera) veal
salsitxa (salchicha) sausage
xoriço (chorizo) spicy sausage

Peix (Pescado) Fish
anxoves (anchoas) anchovies
bacallà (bacalao) salt cod
llenguado (lenguado) sole
lluç (merluza) hake
llobarro (mero) sea bass
moll (salmonete) red mullet
rap (rape) monkfish
salmó (salmón) salmon
truita (trucha) trout
tonyina (atún) tuna

Marisc (Mariscos) Seafood
anguila (anguila) eel
calamars (calamares) squid
cranc (cangrejo) crab
gambes (gambas) prawns (shrimps)
llagosta (langosta) lobster
musclos (mejillone) mussels
ostres (ostras) oysters
pop (pulpo) octopus

Vedures (Verduras) Vegetables
albergínia (berenjena) aubergine (egg plant)
bròquil (brécol) broccoli
carabassó (calabacín) courgette (zucchini)
ceba (cebolla) onion
cogombre (pepino) cucumber
col (berza) cabbage
enciam (lechuga) lettuce
espàrrecs (espárragos) asparagus
faves (habas) broad beans
mongetes tendres (judías verdes) green beans
pastanagues (zanahorias) carrots
patates (patatas) potatoes
pebrots (pimientos) peppers
pèsols (guisantes) peas
xampinyons (champiñones) mushrooms

Mètode de cuina (Método de cocina) Cooking methods
al forn (al horno) baked, roasted
a la brasa (a la brasa) flame-grilled (broiled)
a la planxa (a la plancha) grilled
cru (crudo) raw
escumat (poché) poached
farcit (relleno) stuffed
fregit (frito) fried
rostit (asado) roast

EATING

Especialitats (Especialidades) Specials

ajo de la mano potatoes cooked with chillies, then dressed with pounded garlic, cumin, oil and vinegar

mandonguilles amb salsa (albóndigas en salsa) meatballs in sauce, usually tomato

allioli (alioli) mayonnaise with garlic

arroz (arròs) rice dishes, some cooked with fish, others with vegetables, meat or sausages

bacallà a la biscaïna (bacalao a la vizcaína) salted cod in a sauce of piquant peppers and sweet chillies

canelons similar to cannelloni, but stuffed with

postres de músic (postre de músico) dessert of dried fruit and nuts

el pastís de formatge (la tarta de queso) cheesecake

la cassoleta de fruites (la tartaleta de frutas) fruit tart

el pastís de xocolata (el pastel de chocolate) chocolate cake

amb nata (con nata) with cream

Fruita (Fruta) Fruit

albercoc (albaricoque) apricot

cirera (cereza) cherry

The lunchtime menú del dia, or menu of the day, will consist of three courses and often includes a choice of soup, fish and a dessert

tuna or spinach as well as meat and covered in white, rather than tomato, sauce

xurros (churros) circles of fried dough covered in sugar

amanida mixta (ensalada mixta) salad that can include a wide range of vegetables

ensalada russa (ensalada rusa) Russian or little salad made of potato, peas, carrots and mayonnaise

escalivada a dish of peppers, aubergine (eggplant) and courgette (zucchini)

escudella meat and vegetable stew

fideuà paella made with fine noodles

gaspatxo (gazpacho) chilled soup made from puréed bread and garlic, raw peppers, tomatoes and cucumber

pa amb tomàquet (pan con tomate) bread rubbed with tomato, sprinkled with salt and drizzled with olive oil

paella the most famous of the arròs, but saffron is less used than in the traditional Valencian dish

patates braves (patatas bravas) potatoes in a spicy tomato sauce

tortilla española Spanish omelette made with potatoes

tortilla francesa plain omelette

Postres (Postre) Cakes and Desserts

bunyols (buñuelos) warm, sugared, deep-fried doughnuts, sometimes cream-filled

crema catalana a creamy sweet custard, served cold with a crackling layer of caramelized sugar on top

flam (flan) crème caramel

gelat (helado) ice cream

pastís (pastel) cake

pijama (pijama) ice cream with fruit and syrup

gerd (frambuesa) raspberry

maduixa (fresa) strawberry

llimona (limón) lemon

poma (manzana) apple

préssec (melocotón) peach

meló (melón) melon

taronja (naranja) orange

pera (pera) pear

pinya (piña) pineapple

plàtan (platano) banana

raïm (uva) grape

Begudes (Bibidos) Drinks

aigua amb gas (agua con gas) sparking water

aigua sense gas (agua sin gas) still water

cafè (café) coffee

cervesa (cerveza) beer

gel (hielo) ice

llet (leche) milk

suc de taronja (zumo de naranja) orange juice

te (té) tea

vi blanc (vino blanco) white wine

vi negre (vino tinto) red wine

Entremesos (Entremés) Side Dishes

amanida (ensalada) salad

formatge (queso) cheese

mantega (mantequilla) butter

ou (huevo) egg

pa (pan) bread

patates fregides (patatas fritas) French fries

sopa (sopa) soup

Condiments (Adrezo de mesa) Condiments

pebre (pimienta) pepper

sal (sal) salt

sucre (azúcar) sugar

EATING

Areas at a glance
- **Barceloneta, Port Vell** and **Port Olímpic:** known for its fish and seafood.
- **Barri Gòtic:** Strong on traditional Catalan restaurants, with some Spanish regional food.
- **Eixample** and **Zona Alta:** Expect high prices with food and service to match.
- **Raval:** Plenty of Catalan choice.
- **Gràcia:** More Catalan eateries, and some international and regional food.
- **La Ribera:** The hot spot for the newest trends, with designer restaurants frequently opening.

The restaurants are listed alphabetically (excluding El or La) on pages 216–234. Here they are listed by cuisine.

CATALAN

	LOCATION
El Abrevadero	Poble Sec
Agut	Barri Gòtic
Antiga Casa Solé	Barceloneta
El Boix de la Cerdanya	L'Eixample
Ca l'Isidre	El Raval
Can Juanito	Gràcia
Can Culleretes	Barri Gòtic
Casa Calvet	L'Eixample
Casa Leopoldo	El Raval
Hotel España	Las Ramblas
Julivert Meu	El Raval
Orígenes 99,9%	La Ribera
Ot	Gràcia
El Petit Miau	Poble Sec
Pitarra	Barri Gòtic

	LOCATION
Arabian	
Damasco	Gràcia
Italian	
Buenas Migas	Las Ramblas
Little Italy	La Ribera
La Gavina	Gràcia
Il Mercante di Venezia	Barri Gòtic
Japanese	
Hello Sushi	El Raval
Shunka	Barri Gòtic
Latin-American	
Blues Café	Gràcia

	LOCATION
Mediterranean	
La Gavina	Port Vell
El Magatzem del Port	Port Vell
Merendero de la Mari	Port Vell
Pou Dolç	Barri Gòtic
Pucca	La Ribera
Taxidermista	Barri Gòtic

Enjoying the food at La Gavina, Port Vell

Nouvelle Cuisine	
Àbac	La Ribera
Altamar	Barceloneta
Anfiteatro	Port Olímpic
Bestial	Port Olímpic
Biblioteca	Las Ramblas
Limbo	Barri Gòtic
Lupino	Las Ramblas
Mastroqué	Barri Gòtic
Melitón	La Ribera
Negro	L'Eixample
Oven	Port Olímpic
El Racó d'en Freixa	Gràcia
Rúccula	Port Vell
Salsitas	Las Ramblas
Talaia	Port Olímpic
El Tragaluz	L'Eixample
La Verónica	Barri Gòtic
Oriental	
Mesopotamia	Gràcia
Regional Spanish	
Agua	Port Olímpic
Casa Madrid	L'Eixample
Ikastola	Gràcia
Mesón David	El Raval
Nervión	L'Eixample
Norbaltic	L'Eixample
Rías de Galicia	Poble Sec

EATING

Seafood	LOCATION
Barceloneta	Port Vell
El Cangrejo Loco	Port Olímpic
Don Marisco	Port Olímpic
Emperador	Port Vell
Julius	Barceloneta
El Lobito	Barceloneta
Reial Club Maritim	Port Vell
Fl Rey de la Gamba	Port Olímpic
Salamanca	Barceloneta
El Tunel del Port	Port Olímpic

Spanish
Agullers | La Ribera
Asador de Aranda | Tibidabo/Sarriá
La Barra del Botafumeiro | Gràcia
Bodega Manolo | Gràcia
Can Majó | Barceloneta
Can Ramonet | Barceloneta
Cerveceria Catalana | L'Eixample
La Cova Fumada | Barceloneta
El Huevo de Colón | Port Olímpic
Nou Can Tipa | Barceloneta
Quo Vadis | El Raval
Els Pescadors | Port Olímpic
Pop's | Port Olímpic
Racó de la Vila | Port Olímpic
Set Portes | Port Vell
El Vell de Sarriá | Tibidabo/Sarriá
La Venta | Tibidabo/Sarriá
Vía Veneto | Tibidabo/Sarriá

Swiss
La Carassa | La Ribera

Tapas Bars
Bar Central | Las Ramblas
Bar Raval | El Raval

	LOCATION
La Bombeta	Barceloneta
Cal Pep	La Ribera
Comerç 24	La Ribera
De Tapa Madre	L'Eixample
Estrella de Plata	Port Vell
Ginger	Barri Gòtic
El Moncho's	Port Olímpic
La Mundial	La Ribera

Staff will be happy to suggest dishes for you

Quim	Las Ramblas
Quimet, Quimet	Poble Sec
San Telmo	Poble Sec
Vinatería del Call	Barri Gòtic

Vegetarian
Bio-Center | El Raval
La Buena Tierra | Gràcia
La Flauta Mágica | La Ribera
L'Illa de Gràcia | Gràcia
Organic | El Raval
Salambó | Gràcia
Sésamo | El Raval
Sol Soler | Gràcia

International	LOCATION
Anima	El Raval
Arc Café	Barri Gòtic
Bar Ra	Las Ramblas

	LOCATION
Flash Flash	Gràcia
El Foro	La Ribera
Fragile	El Raval
Hoffmann	La Ribera
Living	Barri Gòtic
Mama Café	El Raval
Ménage à Trois	Barri Gòtic
Noti	L'Eixample
Oolong	Barri Gòtic
Pla	Barri Gòtic
Plats	El Raval
Polenta	Barri Gòtic
Rita Blue	El Raval
Salero	La Ribera
Silenus	El Raval
Slokai	Barri Gòtic
Tábata	Gràcia
Umita	El Raval
Venus Delicatessen	Barri Gòtic
Zoo	Barri Gòtic

Outdoor eating at Rita Blue in El Raval

EATING

Restaurants

The restaurants below are listed alphabetically, excluding El and La, and cover a range of prices. The prices given here are for a two-course lunch (L) for two people and a three-course dinner (D) for two people, without drinks, unless stated. The wine price is the starting price for a bottle of wine. For alternatives, see bars and cafés on pages 166–169.

ÀBAC

Map 207 H11
Carrer del Rec 79–89, 08003
Tel 93 319 66 00
The cuisine served here is the result of Xavier Pellicer's extensive experience as a chef in various prestigious restaurants.

Delicacies include squid with aromatic herbs, spicy partridge with date purée and sweet potato and Parmesan gnocchi with grape cream. This is a lavish choice, helped by the exquisite, minimalist setting.
🕐 Mon–Sat 1.30–3.30, 8.30–10.30; closed Aug and Mon in Sep
🍴 L €150, D €160, Wine €12
Ⓜ Barceloneta

EL ABREVADERO

Map 208 E11
Carrer de Vilá i Vilá 77, 08004
Tel 93 441 38 93
Jordi Vilà and Sònia Profitós have given El Abrevadero a creative and modern look and it has become well known in the city. Two of the main

attractions are the Norwegian garlic lobster with rice and parsley sauce and the ox stew. Traditional Catalan recipes are served with a twist or two; try

the delicious sardine pie with olives or the cannelloni and peppers.
🕐 Tue–Sat 1.30–3.30, 8.30–11; closed 9–18 Aug
🍴 L €25, D €36, Wine €8
Ⓜ Paral.lel

AGUA

Map 209 J12
Passeig Marítim de la Barceloneta 30, 08005
Tel 93 225 12 72
Agua has the most popular terrace in the Olympic Village; when you are seated at your table, you can even get sand in your shoes. It is famous for its risottos and fish, and very popular with locals. Sunday lunchtime is busy, with people stopping for a beer and a bite to eat.
🕐 Mon–Thu 1.30–4, 8.30pm–midnight, Fri–Sat 1.30–5, 8.30pm–1am, Sun 1.30–5
🍴 L €70, D €100, Wine €10
Ⓜ Barceloneta

AGULLERS

Map 207 G11
Carrer dels Agullers 8, 08003
Tel 93 268 03 61
People flock to this pint-sized place, but as there are just a handful of tables, it only has enough room to seat 15 lucky people. The dishes are wholesome and the portions generous. Mercè Rosselló prepares excellent casserole noodles and meat stew. This is not a place for leisurely sipping of coffee because, although nobody would actually show you the door, space is highly valued. Credit cards are not accepted.

AGUT

Map 207 G11
Carrer d'en Gignàs 16, 08002
Tel 93 315 17 09
This quiet, welcoming place was founded at the beginning of the 19th century and builds its menu on Catalan food. The Agut family, which has owned and managed the restaurant for the last three generations, has a menu reflecting seasonal availability as well as dishes that are popular all year round, such as *olla barrejada* (a typical Catalan stew with vegetables and meat) and *fideuà* (fish noodles), cod with red peppers and garlic mayonnaise.
🕐 Tue–Sat 1.30–4, 8–11; closed Aug
🍴 L €18, D €30, Wine €7
Ⓜ Jaume I

🕐 Mon–Fri 8.30–5.30, Sat 8.30–4; closed mid-Aug–mid-Sep
🍴 L €24, D €32, Wine €6
Ⓜ Jaume I

ALTAMAR

Off map 209 G12
Passeig de Joan de Borbó 88, 08003
Tel 93 221 00 07
Altamar is one of the best-placed restaurants in the city, as it is perched up in the Sant Sebastian tower (see page 59). It serves highbrow cuisine enhanced by the best quality produce, but mostly leans towards fish dishes. The huge restaurant is fitted out like a luxurious yacht: Try to get a seat at the Captain's Table, which has the best views, or in the private dining room.
🕐 Tue–Sat 1–3.30, 9–11.30, Mon 1–4
🍴 L €100, D €120, Wine €14
Ⓜ Barceloneta

ANFITEATRO

Map 209 J12
Avinguda del Litoral s/n, Parque del Port Olímpic, 08005
Tel 659 69 53 45
You'll find a very creative and elaborate menu here, with squid, lamb, liver and onion tapas, rabbit stuffed with prawn, tortellini with cuttlefish and cod with shellfish. The restaurant is set in gardens and overlooks the sea. As a result, there is plenty of light from dawn right through until sunset.

🕐 Mon–Sat 1–4, 8.30–midnight,
Sun 1–4
🍴 L €48, D €60, Wine €12
🅂 Section
Ⓜ Ciutadella-Vila Olímpica

ANIMA
Map 206 F10
Plaça dels Àngels 6, 08001
Tel 93 342 4912
Halfway between the MACBA
(see pages 90–91) and La
Boqueria food market, Anima
is a welcome addition to the
Raval's legion of small trendy
restaurants. The young staff
are friendly and efficient, the
dining room decorated with
avant-garde touches, but still
comfortable. The food bears
all the hallmarks of fashionable cooking trends, such as
balsamic ice cream, tuna in
sesame crust and pea foam,
and is incredibly tasty and
satisfying. You'll be safe
with any of the well-chosen
Spanish wines.
🕐 Mon–Sun 1–4, 9–midnight
🍴 L €34, D €50, Wine €9
Ⓜ Liceu

ANTIGA CASA SOLÉ
Map 209 G12
Carrer de Sant Carles 4, 08003
Tel 93 221 50 12
Established in 1903, this tavern
was frequented by harbour
workers during their breaks.
The news about its good food
and reasonable prices spread
quickly and, little by little, businessmen, cotton importers
and even celebrities such as
Joan Miró became regulars.

It's just as popular today, with
excellent rice dishes cooked
in a variety of ways, such as
in a casserole, in squid ink or
served with lobster.
🕐 Tue–Sat 1–4, 8.30–11pm, Sun 1–4;
closed Aug
🍴 L €70, D €90, Wine €9
Ⓜ Barceloneta

ASADOR DE ARANDA
Off map 209 F6
Avinguda del Tibidabo 31, 08022
Tel 93 417 01 15
www.asadoraranda.com
This fine example of a
Modernista building has
been declared part of the
national heritage and an
artistic monument. The
restaurant successfully
combines traditional Castilian
cooking with a typical interior,
as the huge dining room is
medieval Castilian in style.
The best dish is the wood
oven-cooked lamb, said by
some to be the best dish in
the world of Spanish cuisine.
There are some private dining
rooms available.
🕐 Mon–Sat 1–5, 9–midnight,
Sun 1–5
🍴 L with wine €65, D with wine €85
🚌 Avinguda del Tibidabo

ARC CAFÉ
Map 206 G11
Carrer de Carassa 19, 08002
Tel 93 302 52 04
This bar-restaurant serves
international cuisine that
should cover everyone's tastes.
The menu is not extensive but
the dishes are substantial and

vary from month to month. Arc
Café's Thai curries, which are
faithfully made to traditional
recipes and prepared with
coconut milk, are particularly
good, and a testament to the
many influences upon this
hardworking kitchen. After you
have finished your dinner, stay
for a cocktail and to listen to
some music.
🕐 Mon–Thu 9am–midnight, Fri
9am–3am; Sat 11am–3am, Sun
11am–1am
🍴 €15, D €22, Wine €6
Ⓜ Drassanes

BAR CENTRAL
Map 206 F10
Mercat de la Boqueria 494–496, 08001
Tel 93 301 10 98
Bar Central is not much
more than a food stand in
the art nouveau market La
Boquería, right in the heart of
Las Ramblas. As customers eat
standing up at the bar, it's neither romantic nor particularly
comfortable, but the food is
always fresh. Mario and Anna
conjure up delicious dishes
including grilled, stewed or
baked fish, and game such
as quail and partridge. Their
snail tapas are a well-loved
treat, enjoyed by those who
frequent the market. Credit
cards are not accepted.
🕐 Mon–Sat 6am–5pm
🍴 L €16, Wine €4
Ⓜ Liceu

BAR RA
Map 206 F10
Plaça de la Gardunya 3, 08001
Tel 93 301 41 63
Bar Ra, which is behind La
Boqueria, is so popular that
an extension has been added.
It is great for a late breakfast
or a health conscious lunch,
including Thai and West Indian
fare. Some of the clientele
return for the performance
art that also takes place, con-
sisting of circus, dance and
poetry pieces. Credit cards
are not accepted.
🕐 Mon–Sat 1.30–4.30, 9.30–midnight,
Sun noon–7
🍴 L €8, D €18, Wine €4
Ⓜ Liceu

BAR RAVAL
Map 206 F10
Carrer del Doctor Dou 19, 08001
Tel 93 302 41 33
Lucila and Rafa opened Bar
Raval 20 years ago when the
local area was a less salubrious
part of town. The district has
undergone a regneration and
this little restaurant remains
one of the highlights.

EATING

Bar Raval serves traditional tapas, including Iberian cold meats, cheeses, toast, salads and sandwiches. Non-profit-making exhibitions and book presentations are regularly organized. Credit cards are not accepted.

🕐 Daily 7.30pm–3am; closed Aug
🍽 D €24, Wine €5
🚇 Catalunya

BARCELONETA
Off map 209 G12
Carrer de l'Escar 22, 08039
Tel 93 221 21 11

Barceloneta nestles in one of the old harbour's most beautiful and sought-after corners. This is Mediterranean food at its best, with unmiss-able fresh fish and lobster casserole. The dining room is spacious and lined with windows, and the walls are hung with oars, fishing nets and barrels. There's a huge terrace with a full view of the harbour and seafront, and there's even valet parking. Booking is strongly advised, particularly if you would prefer to dine on the terrace.

🕐 Daily 1–4, 8.30pm–1am
🍽 L €35, D €45, Wine €10
🚇 Barceloneta

LA BARRA DEL BOTAFUMEIRO
Map 209 G7
Carrer Gran de Grácia 81, 080012
Tel 93 217 96 42

The first-class shellfish served here is a real attraction, even though this restaurant has built its reputation on *arroz caldoso* (casseroled rice) and its house lamb. The service is faultless and there are some very good wines to accompany your meal. There's usually space at the bar, where you can sit on

comfortable high stools. It is open late, so it's ideal for a post-cinema or concert bite to eat.

🕐 Daily 1.30pm–1am
🍽 L €80, D €100, Wine €12
🆂 Section
🚇 Fontana

BESTIAL
Map 209 J12
Carrer de Ramón Trias Fargas 2–4, 08005
Tel 93 224 04 07

Bestial is right by the beach and in the shade of the Arts Hotel (see page 243). The food served is primarily Italian, a variety of risottos (with barbe-cued Norwegian lobster, wild asparagus or mushrooms),

pastas (with basil, garlic and olive oil, or prawn and olives) and pizzas from the wood-fired oven. A huge glass façade makes one wall a frame for the beautiful sea views.

🕐 Mon–Thu 1.30–4, 8.30pm–midnight, Fri–Sat 1.30–4, 8.30pm–3am
🍽 L €30, D €50, Wine €8
🚇 Ciutadella-Vila Olímpica

BIBLIOTECA
Map 206 F11
Carrer de la Junta de Comerç 28, 08001
Tel 93 412 62 21

Biblioteca is a restaurant, even if its name means library, but it does come complete with its own collection of cookery books for guests to scrutinize.

The chef, who purchases all his ingredients fresh at the market La Boqueria (see page 153), constantly updates the menu. The different choices will encourage you to explore

a range of new tastes. The eclectic dishes include oysters with dark beer, marinated tomatoes with basil and cod with clams.

🕐 Tue–Sat 1–4, 9pm–midnight
🍽 L €19, D €25, Wine €6
🚇 Liceu

BIO-CENTER
Map 206 F10
Carrer del Pintor Fortuny 25, 08001
Tel 93 301 45 83

Bio-Center was one of the first vegetarian restaurants to appear in this part of town, and the scope of the menu has increased with demand. You will give the dishes top marks for imaginative presen-tation that makes good use of colour and texture, along with

high-quality ingredients, for example the extensive salad bar displays a plethora of dif-ferent leaves and vegetables. Other staple dishes are curries, couscous and pizza. Credit cards are not accepted.

🕐 Mon–Sat 1–4.30, 7–11
🍽 L €15, D €20, Wine €5
🆂 Section
🚇 Catalunya

BLUES CAFÉ
Map 209 H7
Carrer de la Perla 37, 08012
Tel 93 416 09 65

Blues Café caters to both vegetarians and carnivores, though only a few of the dishes contain meat. It serves excellent hot and cold toasts with your choice of topping, as well as excellent salads. The dishes are simple and tasty, and its relaxed atmos-phere makes it the perfect place to unwind.

🕐 Mon–Thu 7pm–1am, Fri–Sun 8pm–3am
🍽 L €15, D €20, Wine €6
🚇 Fontana

EATING

BODEGA MANOLO

Map 209 H6
Carrer del Torrent de les Flors 101, 08024
Tel 93 284 43 77

The excellent food that you find here makes up for the rather shabby appearance of this restaurant. Dishes include roasted aubergine (egg plant) with goat's cheese, grilled asparagus with anchovies and vinaigrette, pork liver with

apples and several variations on cod. It has gained some popularity among business people, who often head up to Gràcia for lunch. Credit cards are not accepted.
🕐 Tue–Wed 9am–7.30pm, Thu–Sat 9am–11.30pm, Sun 10.30am–3pm (tapas only); closed Aug
🍴 L €14, D €25, Wine €6
Ⓜ Joanic

EL BOIX DE LA CERDANYA

Map 209 F9
Carrer del Consell de Cent 303, 08007
Tel 93 451 50 75

Boix is a chain of restaurants and Boix de la Cerdanya faithfully adheres to the philosophies set down by its sister restaurant on Passeig de Gràcia. The menu consists

of Catalan food, as well as typical dishes from the Pyrenees, with an emphasis on fresh ingredients and elaborate food preparation. Other dishes include game, boar stew, mushrooms, chickpeas from

SPECIAL

LA BOMBETA

Map 209 H12
Carrer de la Maquinista 3, 08003
Tel 93 319 94 45

This old fishermen's bar is perfect for those on a budget who still want to enjoy delicious, fresh seafood. You can either settle at a table or simply stand at the bar and dig into some of the generous tapas. Choose from steamed mussels, *esqueixada* (cold cod with vegetables) or fried squid, to name just a few. Even better, if you are having trouble adjusting to Spanish eating times, it's open all day, even in the early afternoon when many others are shut. Credit cards are not accepted.
🕐 Thu–Tue 10am–midnight; closed Sep
🍴 L €16, D €25, Wine €5
Ⓜ Barceloneta

Castile with black sausage, and fresh fish, served either grilled or stewed.
🕐 Mon–Sat 1–4, 8.30–midnight
🍴 L €45, D €60, Wine €9
Ⓢ Section
Ⓜ Universitat

LA BUENA TIERRA

Map 209 H7
Carrer de l'Encarnació 56, 08024
Tel 93 219 82 13

A comfortable restaurant that is mainly frequented by young people seeking fairly priced, good food. The terrace at the back gets busy, especially in summer. Some of the vegetarian delicacies on offer are moussaka, tortellini with Roquefort and a range of quiches.
🕐 Mon–Sat noon–4, 8pm–1am
🍴 L €20, D €25, Wine €6
Ⓢ Section
Ⓜ Joanic

BUENAS MIGAS

Map 206 F10
Plaça del Bonsuccés 6, 08001
Tel 93 319 13 80

Buenas Migas is the perfect place if you don't have the time to linger or are on a budget. If you seek value, try one of the huge salads or a vegetable tart. The most popular dish is *focaccia*, a distant

relative of the pizza, the portions of which are reasonable and there's a sizeable list of toppings. Make sure that you leave space for dessert—try *la bomba* (a chocolate cake) or an apple and cinnamon tart.
🕐 Daily 9am–midnight
🍴 L €12, D €15 Wine €5
Ⓜ Catalunya

CA L'ISIDRE

Map 208 E11
Carrer de les Flors 120, 08002
Tel 93 441 11 39

Over the last 25 years, this family-owned restaurant has perfected a dynamic, varied menu. Delicacies fall into two main groups: market cuisine and confectionery. The menu can change on a daily basis according to seasonal availability of some ingredients; for example, duck liver might be served with plums, chestnuts, puréed grapes or Chinese mandarins. Montse, Isidre's daughter, is the driving force behind the desserts, such as chocolate soufflé with coconut ice cream and apricot tart with toasted cumin seeds.
🕐 Mon–Sat 1.30–4, 8.30–11, Oct–end Jun; Mon–Fri 1.30–4, 8.30–11, Jul–end Sep; closed public holidays and 1–18 Aug
🍴 L €110, D €140, Wine €11
Ⓜ Paral.lel

CAFÉ DE L'OPERA

See page 166.

EATING

CAL PEP

Map 207 G11
Plaça de les Olles 8, 08003
Tel 93 315 49 37

There are mountains of the freshest seafood to be had in this tiny, much-loved tapas bar. Once seated at the bar itself, choose from sardines, prawns or whatever else is in season and watch in wonder as it is prepared before your eyes at lightining speed. Cal Pep is supposedly the humbler version of the owner's restaurant Passadis del Pep (in the same square), but most people prefer this option.

🕒 Tue–Sat 1.30–4, 8–11.45; closed Aug
🍴 L €15, D €30, Wine €8
🚇 Barceloneta

EL CANGREJO LOCO

Off map 209 J12
Moll de Gregal 29–30, 08005
Tel 93 221 05 33
www.elcangrejoloco.com

This is about the biggest restaurant in the area and it is known for its grilled, stewed, fried or baked fish and shellfish. It is split into three sections: two ground floor dining rooms and another on an upper floor with a sea-view window and a huge terrace. Its sheer size lends itself well to parties, and the staff are always happy to tailor special menus according to preference and budget.

🕒 Daily 1pm–1am
🍴 L €80, D €120, Wine €12
🚇 Ciutadella-Vila Olímpica

CAN CULLERETES

Map 206 F11
Carrer d'en Quintana 5, 08002
Tel 93 317 30 22

This is one of the oldest restaurants in Barcelona, which was founded in 1786. The interior hasn't changed much since then, as the walls are lined with period paraphernalia, as well as photographs of Can Culleretes famous clients. There is a lengthy menu of all things Catalan: *suquet* (a seafood stew of fish, potatoes and saffron) or chicken with the classic *samfaina*, a rich vegetable and tomato sauce. The desserts are calorie-laden and creamy and they do a particularly good *crema catalana*, which is the local version of crème brûlée.

CAN MAJÓ

Off map 209 H12
Carrer del'Almirall Aixada 23, 08003
Tel 93 221 58 18

This restaurant, in the heart of La Barceloneta, serves excellent Mediterranean cuisine. Fresh fish and shellfish are used to enrich dishes such as lobster casserole, sautéed Norwegian lobster and baked hake. As it is right on the seafront, it's an idyllic place to dine out during the summer.

🕒 Tue–Sat 1–4.30, 8–11.30, Sun 1–4.30
🍴 L €70, D €90, Wine €7
🚇 Barceloneta

🕒 Mon–Sat 1.30–3.30, 9–11, Sun 1.30–3.30
🍴 L €11, D €18, Wine €7
🚇 Liceu

CAN JUANITO

Map 209 G7
Carrer de Ramón y Cajal 3, 08012
Tel 93 213 30 43

The building is more than 100 years old and was originally an inn. Some of the dining rooms were converted from stables, and the others were previously living quarters. The chef has always been faithful to Catalan recipes and uses the freshest market ingredients. Keep an eye out for the squid, the snail stew and the cod served with prawns and potatoes.

🕒 Tue–Sat 1–4, 8.30–midnight, Sun 1–4
🍴 L €60, D €70, Wine €6
🚇 Fontana

CAN RAMONET

Map 209 H12
Carrer de la Maquinista 17, 08003
Tel 93 319 30 64

Can Ramonet was established in 1763, and is arguably the oldest tavern in Barceloneta. The menu balances seafood, rice dishes and paellas, as well as black rice prepared with

squid ink. If your appetite extends only to tapas, sit at one of the barrel-top tables. Should you prefer a full meal, the terrace is ideal. The beach is only a few steps away—perfect for an after-dinner stroll.

🕒 Mon–Sat 10–4, 8–midnight, Sun 10–4
🍴 L €26, D €65, Wine €10
🚇 Barceloneta

LA CARASSA

Map 207 G11
Carrer del Brosolí 1, 08003
Tel 93 310 33 06

La Carassa's typically bohemian interior lends an elegant dimension to the dining experience. The cuisine is a mixture of Catalan, French and

even Swiss influences, reflected in the presence of delicious fondues on the menu. Try a chocolate fondue and dip pieces of apple, pear, strawberry, orange and banana into it.

🕐 Mon–Sat 8.30–11pm
🍽 D €40, Wine €7
🚇 Jaume I

CASA CALVET
Map 207 G10
Carrer de Casp 48, 08010
Tel 93 412 40 12
The art nouveau Casa Calvet (see page 65) was one of the first houses built by Gaudí in Barcelona. The structure was originally a textiles factory, but

now the building is made up of private flats on the upper levels with a ground floor restaurant. The chef Miguel Alija has a very modern take on Mediterranean cuisine and his menu includes pea and squid soup, prawns cooked in rosemary oil and duck liver with Seville oranges.
🕐 Mon–Sat 1–3.30, 8.30–11; closed Aug
🍽 L €80, D €100, Wine €14
🚇 Urquinaona

CASA LEOPOLDO
Map 206 F11
Carrer de Sant Rafael 24, 08001
Tel 93 441 69 42
This is a relatively unknown, yet outstanding culinary hotspot in the old town, close to the city's famous opera house, the Gran Teatre del Liceu. Casa Leopoldo is a mixture of Andalucían tavern,

French bistro and Italian trattoria. It opened in 1929 and is well known in Barcelona for serving traditional Catalan dishes, such as fried fresh fish and oxtail stew, with some dishes varying according to season.
🕐 Tue–Sat 1.30–4, 9–11, Sun 1–4; closed Easter and Aug
🍽 L €70, D €85, Wine €10
🚇 Liceu

CASA MADRID
Map 207 H10
Carrer d'Ausiàs Marc 37, 08010
Tel 93 265 67 23
This is the closest you'll get to Madrid while you're still in Barcelona. Two of the capital's most popular dishes are at

their best here: *callos* (tripe) and *cocido* (a combination of potatoes, vegetables, pork, veal and cold meat). There's also a garlic soup, great for cold days and a lighter choice to *cocido*.
🕐 Mon–Fri 1–4
🍽 L €18, Wine €7
🚇 Urquinaona

CERVECERIA CATALANA
Map 209 F8
Carrer de Mallorca 236, 08008
Tel 93 216 03 68
A great choice for a superb, hassle-free meal. This tavern (*cerveceria*) has the most spectacular tapas, ranging from Spanish omelettes to shrimps in garlic sauce, and sirloin canapés. Stop off here if you're shopping in the area; simply order a glass of wine and choose your tapas from the great display. Because of its popularity, it's also an ideal spot of people watching.
🕐 Daily 9am–1.30am
🍽 €20 for about 6 tapas, Wine €8
🚇 Diagonal

COMERÇ 24
Map 207 H11
Carrer del Comerç 24, 08003
Tel 93 319 21 02
This is the most talked about of Barcelona's wave of tapas bars run by chefs who aim to revolutionize Spain's bar food. Taking a leaf out of the cookbook of the renowned Catalan chef Ferran Adrià (see page 19), Comerç 24 serves up such exotic concoctions as truffle-filled eggs and asparagus with mandarin foam. This is a long way from your average slice of tortilla or bread rubbed with tomato, but you can wash the food down with a glass of old-fashioned wine.
🕐 Tue–Sat 1.30–3.30, 8.30–12.30
🍽 L €30, D €40, Wine €12
🚇 Arc de Triomf

LA COVA FUMADA
Map 209 G12
Carrer del Baluard 56, 08003
Tel 93 221 40 61
La Cova Fumada is a modest and noisy tavern with an open kitchen, boxes everywhere and marble tables shared by both harbour workers and business types. The food, however, is outstanding and the tapas, fish and meat in particular, are excellent. The menu, like the set up, never changes. Although the restaurant has been open since the 1940s, there's no sign on the door. Find it on the right-hand side of Passeig Joan de Borbó. Credit cards are not accepted.
🕐 Mon–Fri 8.30–3.30 (also Thu–Fri 6pm–9pm), Sat 8.30am–2pm; closed Sun and Aug
🍽 L €7, D €7, Wine €4
🚇 Barceloneta

DAMASCO
Map 209 G7
Carrer del Torrent de l'Olla 99, 08012
Tel 93 218 34 98
The chef Nasif created Damasco after gathering a wealth of experience in many of Barcelona's Arabic restaurants. Syrian cuisine is served here, bursting with aroma and rich in colour. Nasif insists that Lebanese wine must be drunk with all his dishes; he says it is the only wine that does not spoil the taste. At weekends, guests may be entertained over dinner by a belly dancer. Credit cards are not accepted.
🕐 Sun–Thu 8.30pm–midnight, Fri 8.30pm–1am, Sat 1–4, 8.30pm–1am
🍽 L €26, D €30, Wine €7
🚇 Fontana

EATING

DE TAPA MADRE
Map 209 G8
Carrer de Mallorca 301, 08037
Tel 93 459 31 34
After breakfast has been served, an extensive selection of tapas is available throughout the day: *morcilla mix* (black sausage), grilled meat, cold meats, fried fish and more, which can be rounded off with *crème catalana*. Guests can sit on the terrace if the weather is good, or simply settle at the bar. Excellent Iberian produce is available to buy, including oils and tinned goods.
🕐 Daily 8am–1am
🍴 L €34, D €45, Wine €7
Ⓜ Diagonal

DON MARISCO
Map 209 F12
Carrer Moll de Mestral 15–17, 08005
Tel 93 221 04 63
This is one of the few restaurants in the area with its own tank from which you can select your dinner. It's also known for serving prawns from Huelva in Andalucía. It's popular with locals and visitors, and the service is friendly and efficient, even when it's busy.
🕐 Daily noon–midnight
🍴 L €16, D €24, Wine €5
Ⓜ Ciutadella-Vila Olímpica

EMPERADOR
Map 207 G12
Palau del Mar, Pau Villa 1 08039
Tel 93 221 02 20
Right next to the Museu d'Història de Catalunya (see page 93), the spacious terrace has a fabulous view over the harbour. Not surprisingly, eating outside is a popular choice during the summer months. Don't miss the cod with honey, a fantastic union of savoury and sweet, combined with the texture of the fish. The cod croquettes and the octopus are also worth trying.
🕐 Daily 11.30–11.30
🍴 L €60, D €70, Wine €8
Ⓜ Drassanes

ESPAÑA
See page 246.

FLASH FLASH
Map 209 F7
La Granada del Penedès 25, 08006
Tel 93 237 0990
Excellent hamburgers, salads and tortillas in this uptown

SPECIAL

ESTRELLA DE PLATA
Map 207 G11
Plaça del Palau 9, 08003
Tel 93 268 06 35
Estrella de Plata is one of the area's most popular tapas bars, where friends meet for a glass of wine and some tapas after a hard day's work. This is quite an achievement because this area, between El Born, Barceloneta and Port Vell, has a high tally of fantastic bars and restaurants. Didac Lopez's creative tapas are well above the average sort with dishes such as artichoke hearts stuffed with quail eggs and caviar. Try to come in the middle of the week when it is quieter.
🕐 Tue–Sat 1.30–4, 8.30pm–midnight, Mon 8.30pm–midnight
🍴 L €40, D €45, Wine €7
Ⓜ Barceloneta

eatery where the 1970s interior attracts customers from all over the city. The murals of a snap-happy girl on the walls were created by Leonardo Pómes, a famous local photographer of the period (the model was his wife) and white leather sofas contrasting with red fittings complete the design. Tortillas come in all varieties and the bun-less hamburger is a treat.
🕐 Daily 1pm–1.30am
🍴 L €25, D €25, Wine €9
Ⓜ Diagonal

FRAGILE
Map 206 F10
Carrer de Ferlandina 27, 08001
Tel 93 442 18 47
If you're at the MACBA (see pages 90–91), stop in here for a bite to eat, as Fragile is across the square. The kitchen serves both Mediterranean and Japanese food, and weather permitting, guests can sit

SPECIAL
LA FLAUTA MÁGICA
Map 207 G11
Carrer dels Banys Vells 18, 08003
Tel 93 268 46 94
This minimally decorated restaurant, close to the site of the old Roman baths, serves top-of-the-range organic food, lovingly prepared. Both vegetarians and meat-eaters are catered for with dishes such as sushi, Sri Lankan rice and curry, and Venezuelan arepa corn fritters.
🕐 Sun–Thu 8.30–11.30, Fri–Sat 8.30–midnight
🍴 L €24, D €40, Wine €8
Ⓢ Section
Ⓜ Jaume I

outside in the shade of the museum, facing a tile mural by the Basque artist Chillida.
🕐 Daily 4pm–2am
🍴 L €20, D €30, Wine €6
Ⓜ Sant Antoni

EL FORO
Map 207 H11
Carrer de la Princesa 53, 08003
Tel 93 310 10 20
Succulent slabs of steak, pizzas, pastas, *botifarras* (Catalan sausages) and ribs *a la brasa* (barbecued) make up the menu of this split level, wood-lined restaurant. Its huge popularity means you may have to wait, but judging by the lines outside most think it's worth it. There is an intimate dance club in the basement at weekends.
🕐 Tue–Sun 1–4, 9–12.30
🍴 L €8.50, D €20, Wine €8
Ⓜ Arc de Triomf

LA GAVINA
Map 209 G7
Carrer de Ros d'Olano 17, 08012
Tel 93 415 74 50
This small pizzeria uses only the freshest ingredients from nearby Llibertat market, and this is the key to its success. It's a simple place, serving only pizzas, and there are just three options for dessert: tiramisu, chocolate cake or coffee with cream. Credit cards are not accepted.
🕐 Tue–Sun 1pm–2am; closed Aug
🍴 L €14, D €18, W €6
Ⓜ Fontana

LA GAVINA

Map 207 G12
Palau del Mar, Plaça de Pau Vila 1, 08003
Tel 93 221 05 95

La Gavina is a good choice for enjoying seafood cuisine. There are plenty of enticing starters and delicious Mediterranean dishes to choose from, including salt-baked *fideuas* (fish noodles) and various rice dishes. It is

right by the sea in the beautiful Palau del Mar and the generous terrace overlooks the harbour and the bustling activity of the seafront promenade.

🕐 Daily noon–11.30pm
🍽 L €40, D €60, Wine €8
🚇 Barceloneta

GINGER

Map 207 G11
Carrer de la Palma de Sant Just 1, 08002
Tel 93 310 53 09

Ginger is a cocktail/tapas bar that quickly became an immediate hit with the local ex-patriot community, particularly as it is run by an English chef. The plush 1970s interior matches the sophistication of the tapas: smoked salmon tartar, salad with grilled goat's cheese and fois gras. The cocktails and wine selection are also excellent and its one of the only a few places in the city to get a genuine Pimms, which is served with ginger, the bar's namesake.

🕐 Tue–Sat 7pm–3am; closed Aug
🍽 Tapas €4–6, Wine €12
🚇 Jaume I

HELLO SUSHI

Map 206 F11
Carrer de la Junta del Comerç 14, 08001
Tel 93 412 08 30

Hello Sushi is rather a hectic place known for its Japanese fast food. Enjoy a seaweed salad and the mixed tempura, or make use of the barbecue,

upon which guests can grill food to their own tastes. Sushi and sashimi are also on the menu. To round off your meal, order one of the chef's sake cocktails. From time to time circus-style performances or poetry readings are organized in the restaurant.

🕐 Tue–Sat 12.30–4.30, 8pm–1am, Sun 8pm–1am
🍽 L €16.50, D €30, Wine €5.60
🚇 Section
🚇 Liceu

HOFFMANN

Map 207 G11
Carrer de l'Argenteria 74–78, 08003
Tel 93 319 58 89

This is the restaurant of one of Europe's most prestigious cookery schools. The brains behind the concept, Mey Hoffman, wanted a property in medieval Barcelona, brimming with history and close to the

sea. The tempting menu has exquisite dishes such as sardine pie with tomato and onion, and mushroom-stuffed turbot dressed with a pine vinaigrette. Don't leave before you have had at least one dessert, as this establishment excels at them; try the house varieties of ice cream or the fresh cheese board.

🕐 Mon–Fri 1.30–5, 9–11.30pm; closed Aug
🍽 L €50, D €60, Wine €12
🚇 Section
🚇 Jaume I

EL HUEVO DE COLÓN

Map 209 J12
Moll de Gregal 31, 08005
Tel 93 221 78 64

This restaurant holds its own in the face of strong competition, as it is in the heart of the Vila Olímpica harbour area—an area known for its excellent maritime-baesd menu. Here you will find a wide selection

of seafood and rice dishes with cuttlefish, shrimps and paella. The tapas include squid, anchovies and caviar.

🕐 Tue–Sat 1–3.30, 8–11, Sun 1–3.30
🍽 L €60, D €70, Wine €8
🚇 Ciutadella-Vila Olímpica

IKASTOLA

Map 209 G7
Carrer de la Perla 22, 08012
Tel 647 71 91 96

Ikastola is made up of three very different spaces—a quiet bar, a small and comfortable restaurant and an interior terrace. A youthful crowd gathers in the evenings for simple

dishes such as sandwiches or salad, and excellent cocktails made with fresh juices. As an extra touch, there are blackboards everywhere for the clientele to write or draw whatever they like. Credit cards are not accepted.

🕐 Daily 6pm–1am
🍽 D €7, Wine €4
🚇 Fontana

L'ILLA DE GRÀCIA

Map 209 G7

Carrer de Sant Domènec 19, 08012

Tel 93 238 02 29

Healthy food is served at reasonable prices in this simple setting. Some of the menu's main highlights are the

garlic soup, stewed apples and the vegetable and potato pies. The food is nutritious and very generously portioned; one to remember if you ever want a quiet, inexpensive evening out.

🕐 Tue–Sun 2–4, 9–midnight

🍽 L €12, D €16, Wine €6

Ⓢ

Ⓜ Fontana

JULIUS

Off map 209 G12

Passeig Joan de Borbó 66, 08003

Tel 93 224 70 35

Julius was named after Julius Henry Marx, one of Spain's leading contemporary comedians. Andreu Buenafuente, the most popular showman on Catalan TV, and Toni Martin, a chef born in London, serve up

great fish and rice, and have created a friendly and relaxed atmosphere for their customers. The menu is constantly updated, but eight different types of rice are a standard feature: black, lobster, prawn, vegetable, casseroled, risotto, *a banda* (rice with mixed fish) and Julius (the week's special).

🕐 Wed–Sun 1.30–4, 8.30–11.30

🍽 L €60, D €70, Wine €9

Ⓜ Barceloneta

JULIVERT MEU

Map 206 F10

Carrer del Bonsuccés 7, 08001

Tel 93 318 03 43

This Catalan restaurant is close to Las Ramblas so much of its trade is passing customers. It lends itself well to accommodating larger groups of diners and can get a bit noisy in the evenings. That said, it does select the best elements of traditional Catalan cuisine: bread rubbed with tomatoes, garlic and olive oil; sausage served with white beans; and selections of cold meats, hams and cheeses.

🕐 Daily 1pm–1am; Mon–Sat 1–4, 8pm–1am, Sun 1–4, Aug

🍽 L €40, D €56, Wine €7

Ⓜ Catalunya

LIMBO

Map 206 G11

Carrer de la Mercè 13, 08002

Tel 93 310 76 99

This restaurant has an eclectic interior and a menu that successfully combines a number of cuisines. The most popular

dishes include the hot grilled prawns and the tuna tataki with goat's cheese, lime and figs. However, look out for new dishes as Carlos, the chef, works tirelessly at renewing the menu.

🕐 Tue–Sun 6–midnight

🍽 D €45, Wine €7

Ⓜ Jaume I

LITTLE ITALY

Map 207 H11

Carrer del Rec 30, 08003

Tel 93 319 79 73

This restaurant is named after New York's Italian quarter and, although the chef is American, the food is not. The menu includes a range of pasta, meat and fish dishes, and there's a comprehensive wine list. A number of informal, comfortable rooms make up the dining space, and there is live,

laid-back jazz on Wednesday and Thursday nights.

🕐 Mon–Sat 1–4, 9pm–12.30am

🍽 L €18, D €35, Wine €8

Ⓜ Barceloneta

LIVING

Map 207 G10

Carrer dels Capellans 9, 08002

Tel 93 412 31 37

This discreet restaurant is in one of the Barri Gòtic's smaller streets. Unusually for Barcelona (and Spain generally), Living has an impressive selection of inexpensive, creative vegetarian dishes such

as leek pancake and a range of salads; meat eaters should try duck with honey, green beans and sesame seeds. Portions are generous and jazz and house music are played in the background.

🕐 Mon–Sat 1–4.30, 9–midnight

🍽 L €18, D €20, Wine €6

Ⓜ Urquinaona

EL LOBITO

Map 207 H12

Carrer de Ginebra 9, 08003

Tel 93 319 91 64

A no-fuss restaurant that is perfect for good shellfish. There is no menu in the traditional sense—just a series of dishes made from the catch of the day, all for one set price. Speak up if you want to choose from what's on offer; otherwise, the staff will just bring you all manner of seafood, and the portions are generous. Don't expect to get a

EATING

table immediately upon arrival, as there's invariably a wait.
⏰ Mon–Sat 1–4.30, 9–midnight; closed Aug
🍴 L €100, D €100, Wine €9
🚇 Barceloneta

LUPINO
Map 206 F10
Carrer del Carme 33, 08001
Tel 93 412 36 97
Lupino serves a fixed-priced menu at lunchtime and an extensive à la carte menu in the evening, with precision-cooked steaks and succulent fish in the fashionable Asian-Catalan fusion style. Main courses include fillet of pork with mustard and roast apple sauce and monk fish in tamarind and mango sauce.

These are complemented by cocktails and music in the lounge area. The relaxing, soft yellow lighting provides welcome relief from the city's hectic lifestyle. Weather permitting, try to get a table on the terrace, facing the market La Boqueria.
⏰ Sun–Wed 1–4, 9–midnight, Thu–Sat 1.30–4.30, 9pm–1.30am
🍴 L €20, D €30, Wine €7
🚇 Catalunya

EL MAGATZEM DEL PORT
Map 207 G12
Palau del Mar, Plaça de Pau Vila 1, 08003
Tel 93 221 06 31
The grounds of Palau del Mar are home to five restaurants, all serving similar cuisine but

the small Harbour Warehouse is known for its paellas and rice dishes. The restaurant presents a creative twist on traditional recipes and the chef seeks out all his ingredients at

the market La Boqueria, ensuring his menu retains its extraordinary quality and freshness.
⏰ Tue–Sat 1.30–4, 8.30–11.30, Sun 1.30–4
🍴 L €60, D €70, Wine €8
🚇 Barceloneta

MAMA CAFÉ
Map 206 F10
Carrer del Doctor Dou 10, 08001
Tel 93 301 29 40
The relaxing Mama Café was designed in harmony with feng shui, and calm prevails even when it's packed. It is spacious, with the central kitchen painted in bright shades of red, blue, yellow and orange. The salads are delicious, and the vegetable creams, turkey with mustard, and grilled cuttlefish with basmati rice are all particularly good. It is also open as a café in the afternoon.
⏰ Mon–Sat 1–1
🍴 L €16, D €23, Wine €7
🚇 Catalunya

MASTROQUÉ
Map 206 G11
Carrer dels Còdols 29, 08002
Tel 93 301 79 42
You will find this chic restaurant, with its intellectual, bohemian clientele, in a street that runs towards the Església

de la Mercè. Portions here are not especially large, so if you are particularly hungry order more than you normally do, especially if dining in a group. The house wine is pleasant, and don't miss the surprising spinach with chocolate. Booking is essential.
⏰ Sun, Tue–Fri 1.30–3.30, 9–11.30, Sat 9–11.30, Oct–end May; Tue–Sun 9–11.30 Jun–end Sep; closed Aug
🍴 L €20, D €30, Wine €7
🚇 Drassanes

MELITÓN
Map 207 G11
Carrer de l'Argentería 6, 08003
Tel 93 319 31 71
Balanced, healthy and creative cuisine near Santa Maria del Mar, the most beautiful of Barcelona's Gothic churches. This is a stylish, reasonably priced restaurant serving hearty portions. Start with shellfish or cod croquettes followed by a honey vinaigrette

goat's cheese carpaccio with raisins and pine nuts, steak with garlic, or five-pepper fish. Save room for dessert as there are warm brownies and custard cream.
⏰ Mon–Fri 1–4, 9–midnight, Sat 9pm–12.30am
🍴 L €22, D €35, Wine €9
🚇 Jaume I

MÉNAGE À TROIS
Map 206 F10
Carrer d'en Bot 4, 08002
Tel 93 301 55 42
The interior of Ménage à Trois is kitsch and cool, with deep warm shades on the walls. It has a light menu: spinach volcano with stir-fried prawns and cream cheese, chicken with ginger, and sweet *alfajores* (a type of Argentinian sponge and toffee cake) for dessert. Vegetarians are catered for, and there's a selection of teas, including mallow and hibiscus or aniseed and liquorice.

© Mon–Sat 9.30am–11pm
🍴 L €16, D €22, Wine €6
🚇 Catalunya

IL MERCANTE DI VENEZIA
Map 206 F11
Carrer de Josep Anselm Clavé 11, 08002
Tel 93 317 18 28
Soft classical music, candlelight and luxurious curtains evoke Renaissance times in Venice, yet prices here remain reasonable. Fillet steak flavoured with lemon, a range of seasonal

carpaccio and fresh pasta form the highlights of the menu. Also try the delicious pesto sauce and don't forget the unmissable tiramisu.
© Tue–Sun 1.30–4, 8.30pm–midnight
🍴 L €16, D €30, Wine €7
🚇 Drassanes

MERENDERO DE LA MARI
Map 207 G12
Palau del Mar, Plaça de Pau Víla 1, 08003
Tel 93 221 31 41
www.merenderodelamari.com
This open-air restaurant is another based in the Palau del Mar. There's a wide selection of seafood and fish but the mussels, clams, snails and sea cucumber stew are particularly good. Panes of glass around the open kitchen allow customers to watch their food being prepared.
© Mon–Sat 12.30–4, 8.30–11.30, Sun 12.30–4
🍴 L €60, D €65, Wine €11
🚇 Barceloneta

MESÓN DAVID
Map 208 E11
Carrer de les Carretes 63, 08001
Tel 93 441 59 34
A riotous restaurant that is popular with large groups with events to celebrate. Mesón David dishes out hearty meals from all regions of Spain such as Galician steamed octopus, grilled trout stuffed with *jamón serrano* (cured ham) from Navarra or Castilian roast suckling pig. Spontaneous singing, visiting acts (it's not unusual to witness the odd singing telegram) and jovial waiters provide the entertainment.
© Mon–Tue, Thu–Sun 1–4, 8–11.30; closed Aug
🍴 L €6, D €18, Wine €3
🚇 Paral.lel

MESOPOTAMIA
Map 209 G6
Carrer de Verdi 65, 08012
Tel 93 237 15 63
This is a warm, peaceful and comfortable spot that was set up by Pius Hermés, a university professor of Semitic languages. A variety of meats, intensely seasoned with herbs and spices are a staple of the menu as is the leg of lamb and aubergines (egg plant) marinated in yoghurt sauce. Oil lamps and exposed brick dominate the interior, and at weekends guests can request a *narguilé*, a water pipe for smoking tobacco, fruits and honey. There are two sittings every evening, so booking is required.
© Tue–Sat 8.30pm–1am
🍴 D €35, Wine €6
🚇 Fontana

EL MONCHO'S
Map 209 J12
Platja Nova Icária 27, 08005
Tel 93 221 14 01
One of the seven restaurants in Barcelona owned by the Moncho's chain, this became popular during the Olympics because of its location next to the beach. Locally the chain is known as the house of fish and paella, and there is a good selection of cuttlefish, octopus, prawns, cod, hake and more, mostly served fried. Salads are huge and always dressed with excellent olive oil.
© Daily 11am–midnight
🍴 L €40, D €45, Wine €6.50
🚇 Ciutadella-Vila Olímpica

LA MUNDIAL
Map 207 H11
Plaça de Sant Agustí Vell 1, 08003
Tel 93 319 90 56
La Mundial's setting harks back to the early 20th century, and it is decorated with photographs of boxing champions and lion tamers who were regulars here in the past. You'll find a range of traditional tapas, such as peppers, squid, ham and cod croquettes. The staff here are very friendly and love talking to the clientele—if you ask them, they will be happy to tell you more about the lives of the characters in the photographs.
© Tue–Sun 10am–11pm, Sun noon–4pm
🍴 L €24, D €30, Wine €4
🚇 Arc de Triomf

NEGRO
Map 208 D6
Avinguda Diagonal 640, 08017
Tel 93 405 94 44
Negro boldly combines Oriental and Mediterranean influences; the menu is adventurous and you'll find sushi, rice with ginger, and enticing

desserts. The interior is creative and contemporary, with ample use of black and deep blue tones, with cool music to match.
© Sun–Wed 1.30–4, 8.30–midnight, Thu–Sat 1.30–4, 8.30pm–2am
🍴 L €34, D €40, Wine €8
🚇 Reina Cristina

NERVIÓN
Map 208 F8
Carrer de Còrsega 232, 08036
Tel 93 218 06 27
Spain's Basque region is famed for having one of the best food traditions in the country. Ingredients are always fresh, especially the fish and the meat, and the region's chefs have an excellent reputation. Nervión serves fine examples of this type of

cooking; it specializes in meat dishes and the chef Juan Sáiz sources the best cuts from the local market. There's also an excellent selection of wines.

⏰ Mon–Sat 1–4, 9–11; closed Easter and Aug
🍴 L €40, D €50, Wine €11
Ⓜ Diagonal

NORBALTIC

Map 208 F9
Carrer del Consell de Cent 239, 08011
Tel 93 451 42 71

Maite Garcés spends hours formulating the Basque menu, making use of knowledge learned from years of experience and, of course, the freshest ingredients. She is well known for her innovative seasonal dishes and delicious cod, cooked in a number of ways; the most prominent is the Basque dish *bacalao al pil pil*, cod simmered with garlic and parsley. The surroundings are calming and somewhat bohemian in style and you can trust the waiting staff to pick you something delicious.

⏰ Daily 12.30pm–2am
🍴 L €16, D €20, Wine €8
Ⓜ Urgell

NOTI

Map 209 G9
Carrer de Roger de Llúria 35, 08009
Tel 93 342 66 73

The sleek, urban interior as well as the Spanish/Italian dishes have made this restaurant a hit with the city's media set. It takes a great deal of its styling influences from New York—the seating consists of plush velvet sofas and the waiting staff come clad in black. Risottos, steaks and fish dishes are the highlights, as is the highly polished interior that even extends to the rest rooms.

⏰ Mon–Fri 1.30–4, 8.30–11.30, Sat 1.30–4
🍴 L €23, D €45, Wine €12
Ⓜ Urquinaona

NOU CAN TIPA

Map 207 G12
Passeig Joan de Borbó 6, 08003
Tel 93 310 13 62

This noisy bar on Barceloneta's main street is well-loved among locals, serving steamed mussels, fresh fish and all manner of shellfish. Over and above the tapas, the bar is well known for its cod dishes. *Estar*

tip in Catalan means to be full, so as the name indicates, portions are very generous. It does get quite busy so booking is advisable.

⏰ Tue–Sun 1–4, 8–midnight, summer; closed Sun pm in winter
🍴 L €18, D €28, Wine €6
Ⓜ Barceloneta

OOLONG

Map 207 G11
Carrer de Gignàs 25, 08002
Tel 93 315 12 59

This restaurant nestles behind Barcelona's neo-baroque post office building. The appealing menu displays much creativity

and imagination, and is updated on a weekly basis. You will find that Japanese vegetables are put to good use, and the orange and almond salad and Thai fried rice are both wise choices, if available. There's also a fine selection of wines to choose from.

⏰ Mon–Sat 8pm–2am, Sun 8pm–1am
🍴 L €25, D €40, Wine €7
Ⓢ Section
Ⓜ Jaume I

ORÍGENES 99,9%

Map 207 G11
Carrer de Vidreria 6–8, 08003
Tel 93 310 75 31

An inviting little piece of Catalonia nestled in the multicultural La Ribera area. Here you can buy or sample Catalan products carrying an official guarantee of quality. Each month the menu focuses on a

particular area of Catalonia. Snacks are served all day; try tapas of your choice with a cava aperitif. For lunch, choose

from *escudella i carn d'olla* (soup with meat), *fideuà* (fish noodles), toast with *escalivada* (roasted peppers, onions and eggplant), meatballs or cuttlefish.

⏰ Daily 12.30pm–1.30am
🍴 L €15, D €20, Wine €6
Ⓜ Barceloneta

ORGANIC

Map 206 F11
Carrer de la Junta de Comerç 11, 08001
Tel 93 301 09 02

This old warehouse, right in the heart of the Raval, has been transformed into a relaxed vegetarian shop and restaurant. Customers can

drop by to pick up good organic produce or stay a little longer to enjoy an affordable lunch in the restaurant. All the organic goods sold or served here come with a quality guarantee label. Credit cards are not accepted.

⏰ Mon–Sat 11–6
🍴 L €15, Wine €5
Ⓢ Section
Ⓜ Liceu

EATING

OT

Map 209 H7
Carrer de Torres 25, 08012
Tel 93 284 77 52

Ot has only a few tables but Oriol and Ferran, the owners, have turned this limited space into a successful restaurant.

Their skilled use of texture and taste hints at their combined experience. Typical highlights from the menu include artichoke soup with prawns and a lime-pepper ice cream. The wine list is varied and reasonably priced, but booking is essential.

🕐 Mon–Fri 2–3.30, 9–10.30, Sat 9pm–10.30pm; closed Aug
🍴 L €50, D €60, Wine €12
🚇 Diagonal

OVEN

Off map 209 J11
Carrer de Ramón Turró 126, 08005
Tel 93 221 06 02
www.oven.es

Oven is in an old industrial warehouse in the middle of the new, emerging Poblenou area. All aspects of your evening are catered for: This huge venue has a bar, a restaurant, a lounge area and a

garden. A varied selection of salads, pasta, fish and meat dishes are available, and the menu is tailored to each season. The cod with herbs and garlic, dressed with orange vinaigrette, is simply delicious. After dinner, stay to listen to the DJ.

SPECIAL

ELS PESCADORS

Off map 209 L12
Plaça de Prim 1, 08005
Tel 93 225 20 18

Els Pescadors' roots as a fisherman's tavern are still obvious—contemporary fashions and designs are of little significance here. Rafa Medrán's reputation is built on excellent fish and rice dishes and seasonal stews with mushrooms. The wine is exclusively Spanish and the desserts are made with seasonal fruits.

🕐 Daily 1–3.45, 8–midnight; closed Easter
🍴 L €30, D €35, Wine €8
🚇 Poblenou

🕐 Mon–Fri 1.30–4, 9.30–midnight, Sat 9.30–midnight
🍴 L €20, D €40, Wine €4.50
🚇 Bogatell

EL PETIT MIAU

Map 209 F12
Moll d'Espanya s/n, 08003
Tel 93 225 81 10

El Petit Miau is inside the Maremagnum shopping complex. Its art nouveau design and its furniture lend the restaurant a feeling of days gone by. Old recipes from Catalonia are the crux of the cuisine, but in some cases they have been modernized. Tapas are prepared here too; for example, you'll find Galician-style octopus and grilled squid.

🕐 Daily noon–2am
🍴 L €15, D €34, Wine €8
🚇 Barceloneta

PITARRA

Map 206 G11
Carrer d'Avinyó 56, 08002
Tel 93 301 16 47

Pitarra, a traditional Catalan restaurant, looks back over a century of history and has no shortage of character. It was named after Serafí Pitarra, a famous Catalan actor and former resident, and the rooms

are decorated with personal effects such as books and clocks. The cuisine is excellent, particularly the cannelloni and the seasonal highlights, notably the mushroom-based dishes. The service is attentive.

🕐 Mon–Sat 1–4, 8.30–11; closed Aug
🍴 L €35, D €45, Wine €10
🚇 Drassanes

PLA

Map 207 G11
Carrer de Bellafila 5, 08002
Tel 93 412 65 52

Pla is within walking distance of the town hall on Plaça de Sant Jaume. The chef, Jaume Pla, draws on the influences of Mediterranean, vegetarian and international cooking, and creates seasonal specials for his clientele. There's a wide selection of carpaccio: fish with prawns, beef with pineapple vinaigrette, and veal with liver.

The crêpes with nuts and the sautéed vegetables with chicken are good, but a house special is the tuna tataki with lime leaves in a citrus and coconut sauce, presented on a banana leaf.

🕐 Sun–Thu 9pm–midnight, Fri–Sat 9pm–1am
🍴 D €40, Wine €8
🚇 Jaume I

EATING

PLATS
Map 208 E10
Carrer de les Carretes 18, 08001
Tel 93 441 64 98
Mia showcases her passion for cooking in this restaurant, where she is owner and chef. The menu consists of 12 imaginative dishes; try fig salad with goat's cheese, Indian lentils and couscous. Mia never stops experimenting and presents unusual dishes, such as Brazilian *feijoao* (bean dish) with fresh fruit.
🕐 Mon–Sat 9pm–midnight
🍴 D €30, Wine €6
🚇 Sant Antoni

POLENTA
Map 207 G11
Carrer Ample 51, 08002
Tel 93 268 14 29
Bernardo and Patricio, two talented chefs and old friends, put their professional and international experience together to create Polenta.

They serve a careful mix of local, South American and Japanese food. Let the chefs advise you and you won't be disappointed. The kitchen has glass walls so that diners can watch them in action.
🕐 Daily 1–4, 7–midnight, Sep–end Jun; 7–midnight, rest of year
🍴 L €30, D €40, Wine €6
🚇 Jaume I

POP'S
Map 209 J12
Avinguda d'Icària 153, 08005
Tel 93 221 30 98
Pop's was originally a butcher's shop but the owner decided to transform it into a restaurant after a big shopping mall was built in the area. It's popular with nearby office workers, perhaps because of its reasonably priced lunches. There are all kinds of grilled fish, and once a week *trinxat de la Cerdanya* (cabbage, boiled potatoes, white and black

sausages and streaky bacon). Credit cards are not accepted.
🕐 Mon–Fri 1–4
🍴 L €12, Wine €6
🚇 Ciutadella-Vila Olímpica

POU DOLÇ
Map 206 G11
Baixada de Sant Miquel 6, 08002
Tel 93 412 05 79
Pou Dolç is an elegant, minimalist restaurant. Delicious Mediterranean fare is the order of the day, primarily from Sicily, France and Catalonia. The seasonal menu has prawn ravioli with sundried tomatoes; beef steak with mashed potato and truffle; and hake with tomato and Parmesan cheese. The wine list has quality wines, such as Rioja and Priorat, at reasonable prices, but the house wine is also fine. For dessert, sample the pineapple ice cream or indulge in a piece of strawberry cake.
🕐 Mon–Fri 1.30–4.30, 9–11, Sat 9–11
🍴 L €15, D €25, Wine €10
🚇 Liceu

PUCCA
Map 207 H11
Passeig de Picasso 32, 08003
Tel 93 268 72 36
Fernando Sancheschulz, who runs this establishment, was born in Mexico and studied architecture. On a trip to Thailand, Fernando discovered that the local tastes had a lot in common with his own country, and the imaginative, Eastern/Mexican-influenced Mediterranean cuisine of Pucca is the result: seared tuna sprinkled with fish flakes, Mediterranean prawns in coconut batter and avocado-laced guacamole. The cool, clean interior is typical of the new wave of Barcelona's restaurants.
🕐 Tue–Sat 1.30–4.30, 9–midnight, Sun 9–midnight
🍴 L €30, D €35, Wine €15
🚇 Arc de Triomf

ELS QUATRE GATS
Map 206 G10
Carrer de Montsió 3 bis, 08002
Tel 93 302 41 40
It's not just the food that draws people to this restaurant, although it is known for its good, traditional Catalan fare. It was here that avant garde artists of the early 20th century, such as Pablo Picasso

SPECIAL
QUIM
206 F10
Mercat de la Boquería, 585–606, 08001
Tel 93 301 98 10

This is one of many well known stands in the market La Boqueria. Even though it has a tiny space in which to operate, the tapas are excellent. The cook, Quim, prepares the best *callos* (tripe) in the market, and his cod with garlic, rice dishes and stews also pull in the clientele. Restaurant owners in Barcelona gather here to lunch and discuss their trade. The lengthy wait is an accolade, but that makes it tricky to secure one of the 17 high stools. Credit cards are not accepted.
🕐 Mon–Sat 6am–5pm
🍴 L €12, Wine €5
🚇 Liceu

and his contemporaries, used to meet. When you've finished absorbing the historical significance, tuck into some *botifarra i mongetes* (grilled black sausage with white beans) and *esqueixada* (salt cod salad with onion and peppers).
🕐 Daily 9am–2am
🍴 L €20, D €30, Wine €6
🚇 Catalunya

EATING

QUIMET, QUIMET

Map 208 E11
Carrer del Poeta Cabanyes 25, 08004
Tel 93 442 31 42

This is undoubtedly the best place to go for an early bite to eat in Poble Sec. There are just three high, chairless tables, so customers stand while drinking a glass of wine. Tapas are

prepared in full view at the bar, and include beans with cod, tuna with pepper, and anchovies with sundried tomatoes, plus there is a choice of some excellent cheeses.

ⓒ Mon–Sat noon–4, 7–10.30, Sun noon–4; closed Aug
🍽 L €10, D €20, Wine €6
Ⓜ Paral.lel

QUO VADIS

Map 206 F10
Carrer del Carme 7, 08001
Tel 93 302 40 72

This restaurant dates back to the 1950s, and it was always a prime option for dinner after the opera, as it's not far from the Liceu (see page 80). The choice of dishes is wide, among them examples of Spanish and French cuisine with a modern slant. The frogs' legs or roasted pork with apple purée are both fabulous. They also serve good seasonal fare, especially mushroom-based dishes. The wine and cava lists are excellent.

ⓒ Mon–Sat 1–4, 8.30–11.30
🍽 L €35, D €60, Wine €12
Ⓜ Liceu

EL RACÓ D'EN FREIXA

Off map 209 F6
Carrer de Sant Elies 22, 08006
Tel 93 209 75 59

Ramon Freixa is one of Spain's best contemporary chefs. He enjoys playing with textures; in his own words, his work is a mixture of the traditional and the classic, openly daring and creative. Winter is welcomed with a chestnut cream with

cheese and grapes, and Iberian pork steaks with potatoes and sausages; in summer, the focus is on delicious, refreshing salads. The white chocolate cake with mint is delectable.

ⓒ Tue–Sat 1–3, 9–11.30, Sun 1–3.30; closed Easter and Aug
🍽 L €100, D €120, Wine €15
Ⓜ Lesseps

RACÓ DE LA VILA

Off map 209 J11
Carrer de la Ciutat de Granada 33, 08005
Tel 93 485 47 72

You'd be forgiven for missing Racó de la Vila, as it's hidden away in a century-old building. Only first-class ingredients are used and some of the best dishes are stuffed oxtail, lentils, and noodles with prawns. The restaurant is bustling at

lunchtimes but drop by in the evenings to sample the wines on the extensive list. If you're a smoker, sample one of the cigars on offer.

ⓒ Daily 1–4, 9–midnight
🍽 L €40, D €60, Wine €8
Ⓜ Llacuna

REIAL CLUB MARITIM DE BARCELONA

Map 209 F12
Moll d'Espanya s/n, 08003
Tel 93 221 62 56

If you want to see a beautiful sunset, have an unbeatable view of the port, or if you simply wish to get away from the city, try Barcelona's yacht club. You'll be spoilt for choice when it comes to fish and seafood, with turbot, sea bass, sea bream, crab and lobster. For the less fish inclined, there are also traditional Catalan meat dishes on the menu. Because of its summer terrace, booking is essential.

ⓒ Mon–Sat 1.30–4, 9–11.30, Sun 1.30–4
🍽 L €40, D €55, Wine €12
Ⓜ Barceloneta

EL REY DE LA GAMBA

Map 209 J12
Moll de Mestral 23–25, 08005
Tel 93 221 00 12

An intimate family restaurant serving a range of seafood, mostly grilled, such as lobster, fish and all types of *gambas*: the name means king of the prawns. There are also several rice dishes, but the house is known for its black rice, made with squid ink. Plenty of room is available for larger groups, though booking is necessary. There is a good view over the harbour.

ⓒ Daily 11am–2am
🍽 L €40, D €60, Wine €6
Ⓜ Ciutadella-Vila Olímpica

RÍAS DE GALICIA

Map 208 D10
Carrer de Lleida 7, 08004
Tel 93 424 81 52

This Galician restaurant is the place to come for excellent shrimp, giant prawns and lobster, all brought straight from Galicia. The chef, Argelio Díaz,

is an expert in perfectly cooked fish, and counts mouthwatering hake among his many specials. Live music is played while you eat.

ⓒ Daily 1.30–4, 8.30–midnight
🍽 L €70, D €85, Wine €10
Ⓜ Espanya

RITA BLUE

Map 206 F11
Plaça de Sant Agustí 3, 08001
Tel 93 412 34 38

This is a restaurant, bar and club rolled into one but split over two spacious, diverse floors. Blue Rita is a trendy and bustling place where you may even rub shoulders with the stars. The restaurant serves Mediterranean, Greek, Moroccan and Lebanese cuisine, from fried fish to couscous. The more informal bar will serve you with a range of tapas.

EATING

🕐 Daily 6pm–1.30am
🍴 D €35, Wine €7
🚇 Liceu

RÚCCULA
Map 208 F12
Moll de Barcelona 1, 08039
Tel 93 508 82 68
Rúccula, in Barcelona's World Trade Center, has a splendid menu that includes rice (either black, with cod and mushrooms, or with partridge, black sausage and artichokes), vegetable minestrone soup with chilled coconut curry cream, sardines with basil oil, and salmon with spinach and ginger. The view is as inspiring as the food.
🕐 Mon–Sat 1.30–4, 8.30–midnight, Sun 1.30–4
🍴 L €50, D €70, Wine €9
🚇 Drassanes

SALAMANCA
Off map 209 H12
Carrer de l'Almirall Cervera 34, 08003
Tel 93 221 50 33
Silvestre and his staff meticulously take care of every detail to ensure that your meal is enjoyable. This restaurant serves outstanding seafood,

such as prawns from Huelva, oysters and clams, complemented by a broad list of wines and cavas. If you're not in the mood for fresh fish, try some of the many Iberian cold meats accompanied by tomato, garlic and olive oil-dressed bread. Eat al fresco on the terrace and enjoy the view.

🕐 Daily 1pm–1am
🍴 L €50, D €65, Wine €5
🚇 Barceloneta

SALAMBÓ
Map 209 H7
Carrer de Torrijos 51, 08012
Tel 93 218 69 66
Salambó mainly serves Catalan food but the menu also includes Hungarian dishes, such as *meleg* (beef or chicken with cheese). Pasta, stews, soups and burgers are

also available. Although the restaurant cleverly maximizes its space, it still gets very busy, so booking in advance is recommended.
🕐 Daily 1–4, 9–1
🍴 L €18, D €30, Wine €6
Ⓢ Section
🚇 Fontana

SALERO
Map 207 H11
Carrer del Rec 60, 08003
Tel 93 319 80 22
www.accua.com/salero
Creative cuisine based on Mediterranean and Asian influences. The relaxing, minimalist setting forms a striking contrast to the busy street outside. Franc, the chef and owner, prepares a delicious vegetable

tempura, and the choice of salads is extensive—try one with nuts and honey. If you prefer meat, the teriyaki chicken or steak with mango are both good choices. The spectacular desserts include German

cheese with hazelnuts and an impressive chocolate and orange concoction. Booking is essential.
🕐 Mon–Fri 1.30–4, 9–1, Sat 9–1
🍴 L €17, D €25, Wine €6
🚇 Barceloneta

EL SALÓN
Map 207 G11
Carrer Hostal d'en Sol 6–8, 08002
Tel 93 315 21 59
This restaurant has always nurtured its own individuality and charming character. The dining room is grand baroque with a bar tucked down one end while the food is sophisticated. Enjoy such taste-bud treats as goulash with clams and satay chicken with coconut spiked rice, followed by one the delicious desserts.
🕐 Mon–Sat 2–4, 9–midnight
🍴 L €22, D €28, Wine €10
🚇 Jaume I

SALSITAS
Map 206 F11
Carrer Nou de la Rambla 22, 08001
Tel 93 318 08 40
Salsitas is as versatile as it is innovative. Guests can stop for a drink or to dine, or if you arrive after midnight, you will find the tables replaced by a dance floor and the restaurant transformed into a nightclub. International cuisine is served at affordable prices and the menu has a good range of pasta, meat and fresh fish. The restaurant is popular with the gay crowd.
🕐 Tue–Sun 9pm–1am
🍴 D €30, Wine €7
🚇 Liceu

SAN TELMO
Map 208 E11
Carrer de Vilá i Vilá 53, 08004
Tel 93 441 30 78
The menu at San Telmo is heavily influenced by Basque, Italian and French cuisine. Fridays see many regulars coming in to enjoy home-cooked bean dishes, originating from Tolosa. Another well-known house dish is steak in red wine sauce, but you'll also find plenty of fish, salads and desserts, all presented with outstanding creativity. There's a solid wine list and attentive service.
🕐 Mon–Sat 1–4, 8pm–midnight
🍴 L €40, D €60, Wine €6
🚇 Paral.lel

EATING

SET PORTES

Map 207 G11
Passeig d'Isabel II 14, 08003
Tel 93 319 30 33
www.7puertas.com

Set Portes was established in 1836 and has always served high quality, traditional cuisine using fresh ingredients from the local market. Rice dishes are the main attraction, so don't miss the mixed fish and meat paella, or the *arròs negre* (rice cooked in squid ink). The stunning high-

ceilinged dining room has a black and white marble floor and more than its fair share of mirrors. It is not possible to make a reservation, so plan to come early or be prepared to wait outside.

🕐 Daily 1pm–1am
🍽 L €50, D €60, Wine €10
🚇 Barceloneta

SÉSAMO

Map 208 E10
Carrer de Sant Antoni Abat 52, 08001
Tel 93 441 64 11

The owners of Sésamo are so committed to the vegetarian cause that they have their own slogan: *comida sin bestias*, meaning food without animals. In this informal restaurant, you can sit down to a three-course set lunch or dine à la carte in the evenings. Sésamo functions as a café in the afternoon, serving fresh

juices, cakes, herbal teas and coffee. It's also one of the few vegetarian restaurants that do take out.

🕐 Wed–Sat 1pm–1am, Sun 7pm–1am
🍽 L €16, D €22, Wine €5
🚇 Sant Antoni

SHUNKA

Map 207 G10
Carrer de Sagristans 5, 08002
Tel 93 412 49 91

Shunka is in one of the city's narrow medieval streets and attracts an almost entirely Japanese customer base. The limited space has been put to good use, but if you prefer a bit more elbow room, eat at the bar. Try the salmon caviar, eel with rice, or the tuna, served in a variety of styles. The rice dishes and sake truffles are in a league of their own.

🕐 Mon–Sat 1–3.30, 8.30–11.30pm
🍽 L €24, D €28, Wine €8
🚇 Section
🚇 Urquinaona

SILENUS

Map 206 F10
Carrer dels Àngels 8, 08001
Tel 93 302 26 80

Silenus' modern style reflects its location near to the modern art museum, the MACBA (see pages 90–91), and it has become a meeting place for young artists. This style is even carried through into the way the time is shown: projected onto an interior wall. The food is creative and elaborate; for example, rabbit rice with

mushrooms and rosemary, and ravioli with chocolate and banana chutney. The exhibitions of paintings and photos change monthly.

🕐 Mon–Thu 1.30–4, 9–11.30, Fri–Sat 1.30–4, 9–midnight
🍽 L €20, D €26, Wine €10
🚇 Liceu

SOL SOLER

Map 209 G7
Plaça del Sol 13, 08012
Tel 93 217 44 40

Sol Soler breaks from Spanish tradition by serving exclusively vegetarian tapas. These include pies, quiches, salads, omelettes and cakes, and are set out on display for guests to select. There's no set price list, and like many of the bars in Gràcia, this tapas bar is also a tea room and restaurant. Customers are primarily students and film fans, as the Gràcia area is home to the best art-house cinema (see page 160) in Barcelona. Credit cards are not accepted.

🕐 Mon–Fri 1pm–2am, Sat–Sun 1.30pm–2.30am
🍽 L €18, D €20, Wine €5
🚇 Fontana

SLOKAI

Map 206 G11
Carrer de Palau 5, 08002
Tel 93 317 90 94

Gianfranco serves a fabulous combination of Basque, Italian, French and Chilean cuisines. The enticing dishes are imaginatively presented, bringing together a number of textures and irresistible aromas. Possible options might be avocado tartare with fresh tuna and soya sauce; watercress salad with green apple; saffron risotto with glazed onion and dried tomato, and tender sirloin prepared with a variety of different oils.

🕐 Mon–Fri 1.30–4.30, 9–midnight, Sat 1.30–4.30 Sep–end Jun; 9–midnight, rest of year
🍽 L €24, D €30, Wine €7
🚇 Liceu

TÁBATA

Map 209 G7
Carrer del Torrent de l'Olla 27, 08012
Tel 93 237 84 96

It couldn't be simpler: diners cook the food themselves, according to their own tastes. Order the raw meat, fish and vegetables, and a *taba*, a special Finnish stone, is delivered with the ingredients. When heated up, these stones keep their temperature for about three hours. Everything is served with salt and a range of specially prepared sauces. If

this is too much effort, there are salads and some pasta dishes. It's also popular with the rich and famous.

🕐 Tue–Fri 1–4, 9–midnight, Sat 9–midnight, Mon 1–4
🍴 L €16, D €30, Wine €7
Ⓢ Section
Ⓜ Diagonal

TALAIA

Map 209 J12
Carrer de Marina 16, 08005
Tel 93 221 90 90
www.talaia-mar.es

Talaia has a fantastic view of the Olympic Port and has a menu of mostly Mediterranean dishes, all well presented with

attention to detail. Choose from liver terrine with apple nougat, pine nuts and a Modena sauce, minted beans and roasted squid pasta. If you aren't very hungry, try a *pica pica*, a perfect compromise between a snack and lunch.

🕐 Tue–Sun 1–4, 8–midnight
🍴 L €90, D €100, Wine €12
Ⓢ Section
Ⓜ Ciutadella-Vila Olímpica

TAXIDERMISTA

Map 206 F11
Plaça Reial 8, 08002
Tel 93 412 45 36

Taxidermista is resident in the old natural science museum, overlooking the city's liveliest square. The interior is bright

and rather Parisian in style, and it has become a meeting spot for an international crowd. The menu is comprehensive, light and well presented, covering sandwiches and tapas such as squid and salmon.

🕐 Tue–Sun noon–4, 8.30pm–12.30am
🍴 L €20, D €24, Wine €7
Ⓜ Liceu

TERESA

Off map 209 J11
Carrer de Roc Boronat 70, 08005
Tel 93 309 14 84

If you're relaxed enough to order your food without seeing the prices, this is the restaurant for you. Teresa never shows you the menu unless you ask for it; rather, she tells you what is on offer that day. Teresa does everything herself—buys the ingredients, takes all the bookings and cooks. The salads are fantastic, as are the spinach croquettes, fish cannelloni and cheesecakes. It's a carefree and rewarding way to dine but be careful when ordering the wine: it can be more expensive than you expect.

🕐 Mon–Sat 1–4
🍴 L €40, Wine €7
Ⓜ Llacuna

EL TRAGALUZ

Map 209 G8
Passatge de la Concepció 5, 08007
Tel 93 487 01 96
www.grupotragaluz.com

Beneath a huge glass ceiling, this restaurant is split over two floors: the à la carte menu is served on the first floor, while the ground floor has a menu

consisting of tapas. The food is essentially the same but the portions vary in size—a great idea if you want to sample before committing to a sit-down meal. Try the salad with ginger or cod with roasted pepper and garlic.

🕐 Tue–Sun 1.30–4, 8.30–midnight
🍴 L €40, D €50, Wine €14
Ⓜ Diagonal

EL TÚNEL DEL PORT

Map 209 J12
Moll de Gregal 12, 08005
Tel 93 221 03 21

In another guise, El Túnel del Port has been around since 1923, but moved to the area when the Olympics were held. The cuisine is Mediterranean, and the seafood comes with all manner of vegetables. There are also *fideuas* (like paella but with noodles instead of rice), grilled meat and traditional paella on the menu. The restaurant can seat up to 300 diners and the large dining rooms have terraces overlooking the sea.

🕐 Mon–Sat 1–4, 9–midnight, Sun 1–4
🍴 L €40, D €50, Wine €10
Ⓜ Ciutadella-Vila Olímpica

UMITA

Map 206 F10
Carrer de Pintor Fortuny 15, 08001
Tel 93 301 23 22

An attractive and original meeting point of two contrasting cultures, as it successfully fuses Latin-American and Japanese flavours. Its name is Chilean: *humita* is a kind of maize and basil *tamale* (meat and maize flour steamed or baked in maize husks). Excellent sushi is also on the menu. The interior is imaginative and bold, with flowers emerging through a hole in each table.

🕐 Mon–Sat 9pm–12.30am; closed Mon in Aug
🍴 D €50, Wine €8
Ⓜ Catalunya

EL VELL DE SARRIÁ
Off map 208 D6
Carrer Major de Sarriá 93, 08017
Tel 93 204 57 10
In an elegant villa in the district of Sarriá, this restaurant's cuisine changes with the seasons. Tasty dishes include the prawn and mushroom paella, pig's trotters with cuttlefish, and warm mushroom salad. There are excellent rice dishes with a variety of accompaniments, a great Catalan meat soup, and some outstanding desserts. The staff are attentive.

🕐 Mon–Sat 1.30–3.30, 9–11.30, Sun 1.30–4
🍴 L €15, D €25, Wine €8
Ⓜ María Cristina

LA VENTA
Off map 209 F6
Plaça del Doctor Andreu s/n, 08035
Tel 93 212 64 55
This restaurant is on garden terraces at the foot of Tibidabo, so there's a fantastic view of the city, making La Venta a great place to eat if you are spending your day up on the mountain. It serves traditional Catalan cuisine and one of its delicacies is sea urchin sprinkled with cheese and then browned. Booking is advisable, especially if you want an evening meal.

🕐 Mon–Sat 1–3.30, 9–11pm
🍴 L €30, D €50, Wine €10
Ⓜ Tramvía Blau

VENUS DELICATESSEN
Map 206 G11
Carrer d'Avinyó 25, 08002
Tel 93 301 15 85
Venus is affordable, has a great value fixed price lunch menu and is a good choice if you're looking for more varied dishes

than the usual fare. Choices range from Greek moussaka and Arabic couscous to Mexican chilli con carne. Venus is in Carrer d'Avinyó, a street in the Barri Gòtic full of designer shops and frequented by the young and trendy. Credit cards are not accepted.

🕐 Mon–Sat noon–midnight
🍴 L €10, D €25, Wine €7
Ⓜ Liceu

LA VERÓNICA
Map 206 G11
Carrer d'Avinyó 30, 08002
Tel 93 412 11 22
At the cathedral end of Carrer d'Avinyó, in a sunny little square, this trendy pizzeria has good, well-priced food, making it an ideal spot for a salad and a pizza. The two dining areas, joined by a bar, are contrastingly lit, while the minimalist design benefits from vast windows that allow plenty of sunlight. If visiting in summer, however, make the most of the terrace.

🕐 Tue–Fri 7pm–1.30am, Sat–Sun 1pm–2am
🍴 L €20, D €22, Wine €6
Ⓜ Liceu

VÍA VENETO
Map 208 E6
Carrer de Ganduxer 10, 08021
Tel 93 200 72 44
Josep Monje's restaurant is a seamless combination of luxury, good taste and creativity. His experience and professionalism is reflected in his dishes, which include Montserrat tomatoes with meatballs, warm scallops with mousse, game, and seasonal dishes such as mushrooms and white truffles. Leave some room for dessert, though you might find it difficult to make a selection.

🕐 Mon–Fri 1–4, 8.45–11.30, Sat 8.45–11.30; closed Aug
🍴 L €80, D €100, Wine €11
Ⓜ María Cristina

VINATERÍA DEL CALL
Map 206 G11
Carrer de Sant Domènec del Call 9, 08002
Tel 93 302 60 92
www.lavinateria.com
You'll find one of Barcelona's most charming wine bars amid the Gothic streets of the old Jewish quarter. The food is simple but exquisite, and the tapas excel in both size and quality. The range of cheese and ham is served with typical

Catalan bread rubbed with tomato, salt and olive oil. The wine list is impressive and includes Rioja, Penedès and a good Somontano.

🕐 Mon–Sat 7pm–1am
🍴 L €14, D €22, Wine €7
Ⓜ Liceu

ZOO
Map 206 F11
Carrer d'Escudellers 33, 08002
Tel 93 302 77 28
Zoo attracts a youthful crowd keen on the good music; after 1am, it's a bar playing ambient, funky and ethnic music. Inside, bright tones, flowers and miniature animals are set

off by interesting recycled furniture, created by local design students. The dishes span Mexican enchiladas, Japanese noodles and Arabic stews.

🕐 Sun–Thu 6pm–2am, Fri–Sat 6pm–2.30am
🍴 D €20, Wine €6
Ⓜ Drassanes

EATING

Locator Maps   236–239
Staying in Barcelona   240–241
A–Z of Hotels   242–253
Hotel Groups   254

Staying

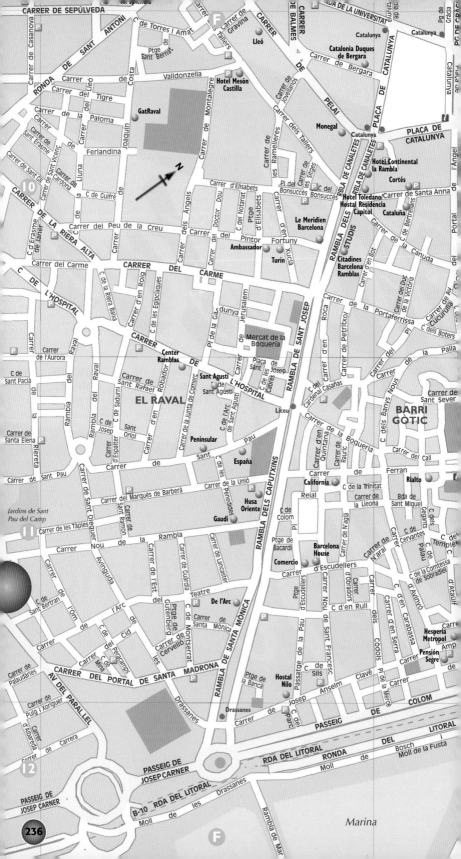

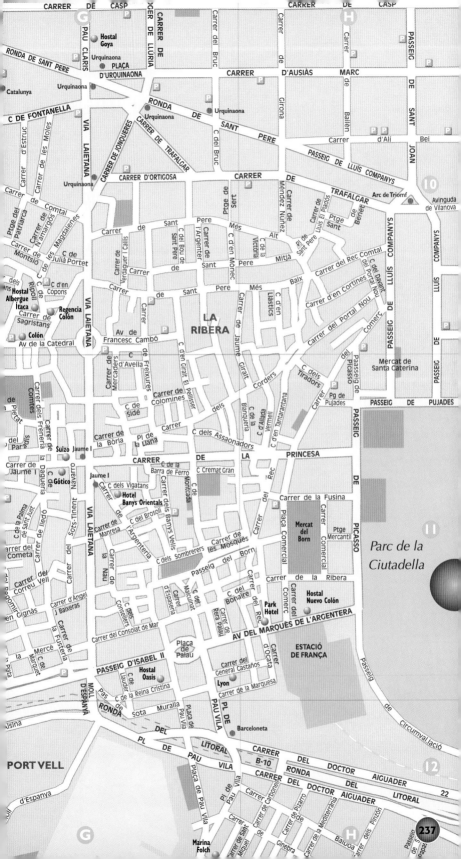

STAYING IN BARCELONA

Barcelona has hotels all over the city and, thanks to the excellent public transport system, none are more than 20 minutes or so from the heart of town. This is a real bonus, given the huge demand for hotel rooms in recent years, due to the growth in popularity of the city. Whether you aim for the ultimate luxury of the top end hotels or just want somewhere clean and simple to sleep, you'll find it.

The city prides itself on providing a full range of accommodation, especially in more unusual establishments that reflect Barcelona's architectural past

There are times when accommodation is hard to come by, particularly during the summer and the major trade fairs, which run at intervals all year. All accommodation in Catalonia is officially regulated by the Generalitat, the regional government, and is broken down into two categories.

HOTELS
These are denoted by (H) and rated on a scale of one to five stars. All rooms must have a private bathroom to qualify as a hotel and the number of stars is determined by the amenities each hotel provides. You can expect five-star hotels to be truly luxurious, with superb facilities and a high level of service. Four-star listings will be almost as good and the accommodation first-class, while a three-star hotel will cost appreciably less.

Rooms in these hotels will all have TV and air-conditioning, but the public areas will be less imposing. Hotels with one- or two-star ratings are relatively inexpensive, will be clean and comfortable, and rooms will almost always have private bathrooms in two-star places. Simpler hotels rarely have restaurants or provide breakfast.

Many hotels in Barcelona are built round an inner courtyard. Rooms overlooking this will be quiet but may be gloomy, ask for an outside room when booking to be sure of light or a view.

HOSTALS
Hostals (HS) sometimes classify themselves as *fondes, pensions* or *residències,* are rated on a scale of one to three stars and are normally less expensive than hotels. Many have been reno-vated over the past 15 years or so and will have a number of rooms with bathrooms. Hostals tend to be family-run, very few have restaurants and many do not serve breakfast. A three-star hostal is

generally on a par with a two-star hotel, but star ratings should not be taken as an automatic guide to facilities or cost.

INDEPENDENT TRAVEL
If you want total independence, or have young children, accommadation with a kitchen might be an attractive option. To set things up yourself, contact the tourist office (see page 270) well in advance or book in at one of the city's apartment hotels, which consist of small, self-contained flats. You can do this on the internet, at such sites as www.holidayrentals.com, and you can also find sites devoted to private house rentals.

FINDING A ROOM
If you haven't booked in advance, the tourist offices in the Plaça de Catalunya and the Plaça de Sant Jaume have hotel booking desks which will usually be able to find you something. They charge a deposit against the cost of the room. Once at the hotel, it's perfectly acceptable to ask to see the room before you make up your mind.

PRICING
Room rates vary according to the season, some-times by as much as 20 per cent. Other times when prices will soar are during national holidays or festival periods. The quietest time for hotels is January and February. Hotels will often quote their most expensive prices. If you know you want that hotel, ask if they have anything less expensive. All room costs are liable to 7 per cent tax on top of the basic price. This is normally annotated separately on bills, but may not have been included in the original quote. If you want the total price for your stay, ask when you make the booking.

• Check-out is normally noon, although at some hostals it may be 11am; so check.

• Hotels will often store your luggage until the end of the day if you have an afternoon or evening flight.

• Hotels are often willing to put an extra bed in a room for a small charge, which is ideal for families with children.

• If you want to use the hotel car park, if available, expect to pay extra and book a space when you reserve the room.

• Few Barcelona hotels have weekend or short-term discount rates, but it's worth asking when you book.

• If you have problems with charging, ask to see the *libro de reclamaciones*, the complaints book, which all establishments are legally required to keep and have inspected by tourist and hotel officials. Such a request generally produces instant results.

ON-LINE BOOKING

www.madeinspain.net
www.travelweb.com
www.all-hotels.com
www.hotelconnect.co.uk
www.bestbarcelonahotels.com
www.hotels-in-barcelona.net
www.interhotel.com/spain/es

WHERE TO STAY

Las Ramblas, El Raval and **Barri Gòtic**: Barcelona's first hotels were built here, and it's still the area with the widest choice of less expensive accommodation. Prices here may be steep for what you get, but it's a wonderful location, though it can be noisy, and street crime needs watching.

L'Eixample: Barcelona's other main hotel area, with a wide range of places to stay, and good choice of mid-range hotels and *hostals*.

STAYING BY AREA

The hotels are listed alphabetically (excluding El or La) on pages 242–253. Here they are listed by area.

Barceloneta
Marina Folch

Barri Gòtic
Ambassador
Barcelona House
California
Cataluña
Citadines Barcelona Ramblas
Colón
Comercio
Continental
Cortes
Gótico
Hesperia Metropol
Hostal Ítaca
Hostal Nilo
Husa Oriente
Le Meridien Barcelona
Peninsular
Regencia Colón
Rialto
Sant Agustí
Suizo
Turín
Toledano/Hostal Residencia Capitol

L'Eixample
AC Diplomatic
Actual
Alexandra
Catalonia Roma
Claris

Condado
Condestable
Continental Palacete
Gallery Hotel
Gran Hotel Havana
Granvia
Hilton Barcelona
Hostal Central
Hostal Goya
Hostal Oliva
Majestic
Princesa Sofía
Rey Juan Carlos I
Ritz
Ritz Roger de Lluria

Gràcia
Abalon
Confort
Rubens

Pedralbes
Relais d'Orsa
Turó de Vilana

Poblenou
Amrey Diagonal

Poble Sec
Barcelona Plaza
Ònix
Paral.lel

Port Olímpic
Arts Barcelona

Port Vell
Grand Marina Hotel
Hostal Oasis

El Raval
Best Western Hotel Millennium
Catalonia Duques de Bergara
Center Ramblas
De l'Arc
España
Gaudí
Gat-Raval
Lleó
Mesón Castilla
Monegal
Principal
Splendid

La Ribera
Banys Orientals
Hostal Nuevo Colón
Lyon
Park Hotel
Pensión Segre

Tibidabo
Gran Hotel La Florida

STAYING

Hotels

The hotels below are listed alphabetically, excluding El and La, and cover accommodation for a range of budgets. The prices given here are for a double room for one night including breakfast, or the entry states if breakfast is not included. All swimming pools are indoor, unless stated. Prices are quoted without tax (see page 240).

ABALON
Off map 239 J7
Travessera de Gràcia 380–384, 08025
Tel 93 450 04 60
www.hotelabalon.com
The Medium hotel chain has six hotels in Barcelona—the Abalon is the closest of them to the Sagrada Família and

Park Güell. There's a warm, family atmosphere, helped by the furnishings and design. Although a one-star hotel, it has parking and room service—and all the rooms have a bath, satellite TV, radio and direct telephone line.
🏨 €94–€124
🛏 40
♿
🚇 Joanic

AC DIPLOMATIC
Map 239 G9
Carrer de Pau Claris 122, 08009
Tel 93 272 38 10
www.ac-hoteles.com
A four-star hotel that is an excellent example of the city's love of contemporary design.

All the rooms are minimally decorated with wooden panelling that contrasts with white linen or darker furnishings.

There is a solarium, sauna, internet access, free minibar and parking.
🏨 €182, excluding breakfast
🛏 211 (15 non-smoking)
♿ 🏊 Outdoor 🐾
🚇 Passeig de Gràcia

ACTUAL
Map 239 G8
Carrer del Rosselló 238, 08008
Tel 93 552 05 50
www.hotelactual.com
This hotel is competitively priced and also claims an excellent spot, behind Casa Milà, one of Gaudi's masterpieces. Small, modern and

sleek, this is the place to stay if you want an intimate atmosphere in a sophisticated setting. All the rooms have a good range of facilities, such as cable TV, minibar and internet access.
🏨 €138–€180, excluding breakfast
🛏 29 (12 non-smoking)
♿
🚇 Diagonal

ALEXANDRA
Map 239 G8
Carrer de Mallorca 251, 08008
Tel 93 467 71 66
www.hotel-alexandra.com
The Alexandra is in the heart of L'Eixample, so it's near to just about everything. All rooms have strong interiors, with reds, blues, blacks, wooden floors and panels, and are equipped with TV and minibar. The more expensive rooms have Jacuzzis, and junior suites have a terrace. The hotel also has a restaurant and parking.

🏨 €185–€260
🛏 100
♿
🚇 Passeig de Gràcia

AMBASSADOR
Map 236 F10
Carrer del Pintor Fortuny 13, 08001
Tel 93 412 05 30
www.rivolihotels.com
The Ambassador is set in a beautiful contemporary building near to the Plaça de Catalunya, with a grey façade and modern metal balconies. The public areas and the guest rooms have purple and blue furnishings. But the best thing about the hotel is the rooftop,

where you can take in great views of the city and in the summer freshen up in the swimming pool. The hotel's Carmen restaurant serves local and international cuisine.
🏨 €187–€234
🛏 105 (50 non-smoking)
♿ 🏊 Outdoor 🐾
🚇 Catalunya

AMREY DIAGONAL
Off map 239 J9
Avinguda Diagonal 161–163, 08018
Tel 93 433 51 51
www.amrey-hotels.com
This was the first hotel to open in Poblenou and it has set the standard with its impeccable service. It has become a local landmark in District 22@, the name given to the regeneration project of this industrial area, and only steps away from the stores at Les Glòries, and

from Bogatell beach. Rooms have been soundproofed and come equipped with individual climate control, internet connection, safety deposit box, minibar, telephone with voice-mail and satellite TV. The café has daily fixed-price menus from €12 and à la carte orders from the restaurant menu.

€127–€160
92 (7 non-smoking)
Glories

BANYS ORIENTALS

Map 237 G11
Carrer de l'Argenteria 37, 08003
Tel 93 268 84 60
www.hotelbanysorientals.com
This cool hostel with generous accommodation and a soothing, Zen-like interior is one of the few in the La Ribera area. The sleek and spacious rooms are decked out in calm tones of white, beige and grape. The lack of amenities (there is no pool or gym) may be a drawback for some, but judging by its popularity this is not a problem for most guests.

€89–€95, excluding breakfast
43
Jaume I

BARCELONA HOUSE

Map 236 F11
Carrer d'Escudellers 19, 08002
Tel 93 301 82 95
This hotel is only 50m (55yd) from the heart of the Barri Gòtic, close to Plaça Reial. Its furnishings run through the

ARTS BARCELONA

Map 239 J12
Carrer de la Marina 19–21, 08005
Tel 93 221 10 00
www.ritzcarlton.com
The distinctive tower block of the top-class Arts Hotel rises beside the seafront in the Port Olímpic. All the rooms command spectacular views,

either over the city or out over the Mediterranean, and are lavishly decorated; all have a CD player, satellite TV and video. There is a huge range of services, including a babysitting and limo service, a beauty salon and a non-smoking floor. There is also a series of apartments, complete with kitchen and dining area, which were furbished by Catalan designer Jaime Tresserra.

€310–€400
482 (241 non-smoking)
Outdoor
Ciutadella-Vila Olímpica

whole rainbow—each room has its own individual interior but always reflects the dominant reds, blues, greens and purples. The breakfast room doubles as a chic café and is open all day. There's also a bar downstairs.

€56–€71
77
Drassanes

BARCELONA PLAZA

Map 238 C9
Plaça d'Espanya 6–8, 08014
Tel 93 426 26 00
www.hoteles-catalonia.es
Don't let the fortress-like exterior put you off this hotel, as although it is directly in front of Barcelona's trade fair buildings, it also has stunnings

view of Montjuïc. The Barcelona Plaza is an elegant place with facilities in the guest rooms well above its four-star category. The best of these is the rooftop pool terrace with its 360-degree view of the city. The restaurant and function room host a constant stream of events and weddings, which give the foyer a real buzz.

€199–€235
347
Outdoor
Espanya

CALIFORNIA

Map 236 F11
Carrer de Rauric 14, 08002
Tel 93 317 77 66
www.seker.es/hotel_california
If you want to be at the heart of everything, then this is the choice for you, as it is in the Barri Gòtic. The small but smart lobby is in black and ochre. The guest rooms are clean but rather

characterless, with dark linens and white tile floors. All have TVs and individual safety boxes, plus a laundry services is also available. Rather unusually for a city hotel, pets are permitted.

€80–€90
31
Liceu

CATALONIA DUQUES DE BERGARA

Map 236 F10
Carrer de Bergara 11, 08002
Tel 93 301 51 51
www.hoteles-catalonia.es
Bring a touch of sophistication to your visit by staying at this fin de siècle hotel. Built in 1898, it has preserved the original marble staircase and, on the first floor, the original moulded ceiling and dome. The façade has a magnificent neo-Gothic glass and iron

STAYING

★ ★ ★ ★

Hotel
Ducs de Bergara

balcony. The hotel comes
with a restaurant, coffee bar,
garden, solarium and business
facilities.
🛏 €150–€186, excluding breakfast
🛈 148
❄ 🏊 Outdoor
Ⓜ Catalunya

CATALONIA ROMA
Map 238 D8
Avinguda de Roma 31, 08029
Tel 93 410 66 33
www.hoteles-catalonia.es
This hotel makes a good base
for exploring as Sants, the city's

main railway station is near by.
The interior makes full use of
wood, creams and whites; the
rooms have a minibar, satellite
TV and room service. There
is also a restaurant, meeting
rooms and parking. It is part
of the same chain that runs
Catalonia Duques de Bergara
(see page 243).
🛏 €85–€120
🛈 49
❄
Ⓜ Tarragona

CATALUÑA
Map 236 G10
Carrer de Santa Anna 24, 08002
Tel 93 301 91 50
If you are looking for a budget
hotel, but still want to be in
the middle of everything,
Cataluña is right on target.
The rooms are basic but clean,
comfortable and equipped
with bathroom, telephone and
local TV. Breakfast is included
but unusually is not served on

the premises: you will need to
cross the street for this.
🛏 €90
🛈 40
Ⓜ Catalunya

CENTER RAMBLAS
Map 236 F11
Carrer de l'Hospital 63, 08001
Tel 93 412 40 69
www.center-ramblas.com
Housed in a century-old build-
ing, this youth hostel is in the
Raval district, next to Las
Ramblas. A member of Youth
Hostels International (YHI), the
hostel is open 24 hours a day,
and its multitude of facilities
include internet access, a bar,

lounge with satellite TV,
kitchen, laundry, luggage
storage, dining room, vending
machines, sheet and towel
rental, safety deposit lockers,
board games and a travel
library. The staff are helpful
and considerate, and eager to
advise guests on any aspect of
the city.
🛏 Over 26 years €20; under 26 years
€16
🛈 33 rooms, 200 beds
❄
Ⓜ Liceu

CITADINES BARCELONA RAMBLAS
Map 236 F10
La Rambla 122, 08002
Tel 93 270 11 11
www.citadines.com
If you want to have a bit more
freedom then this might be
the option for you. It consists
of self-contained apartments
with kitchen, satellite TV, hi-fi
system and telephone. It's a
good choice if you have
children, who are welcome,
as you can set your own
schedule. You are even
allowed to bring your pet.
There's also a laundry and dry-
cleaning service, meeting
rooms and parking. The
windows are soundproofed,

CLARIS
Map 239 G8
Carrer de Pau Claris 150, 08009
Tel 93 487 62 62
www.derbyhotels.es

This used to be the home of
the collection of Egyptian art
that forms the basis of the
Museu Egipci (see page 177).
Once these had been moved,
they were replaced with pre-
Columbian art, all part of
owner Jordi Clos' collection.
The restaurant East47 has
original Andy Warhols. The
Claris provides impeccable
service in a luxurious 19th-
century setting and is only
minutes away from some
of the most outstanding
Modernista buildings in town.
Facilities include 24-hour
room service and sauna.
🛏 €310–€354
🛈 120
❄ 🏊 Outdoor 📺
Ⓜ Passeig de Gràcia

so the noise of Las Ramblas
outside does not disturb a
good night's sleep.
🛏 €125–€152
🛈 131
❄
Ⓜ Catalunya

COLÓN
Map 237 G10
Avinguda de la Catedral 7, 08002
Tel 93 301 14 04
www.hotelcolon.es
This hotel's enviable position,
facing the cathedral, has drawn
a number of illustrious visitors
over the years, including Miró,
Hemingway, Tennessee
Williams and Francis Ford
Coppola. The furnishings are
neutral and red tones; guest
rooms are equipped with TV,
safe and minibar, and some
have balconies overlooking the
cathedral. There's a restaurant,

STAYING

La Carabela, and piano bar, plus parking is available.
🏨 €180–€220, excluding breakfast
ℹ 145
♿
🚇 Jaume I

COMERCIO
Map 236 F11
Carrer de Nou de Zurbano 7, 08002
Tel 93 318 73 74
The rooms in this hotel, close to Las Ramblas, are small and the furnishings basic. But they are clean and come with private bathroom, satellite TV, telephone and safety deposit box. Rooms facing the street

can be rather noisy, otherwise it is a good choice if you are on a budget. There is a café and bar on site.
🏨 €75–€80
ℹ 51
♿
🚇 Liceu

CONDADO
Map 238 F7
Carrer d'Aribau 201, 08021
Tel 93 200 23 11
www.hotelcondado.es
This comfortable hotel in the Eixample is close to the shopping streets of Rambla de Catalunya and Passeig de Gràcia. The public areas, decorated in whites and blues, are refreshing after a hard day's shopping. The guest rooms are functional with safety deposit boxes, satellite TV and minibar, and some have balconies.

🏨 €80–€110
ℹ 81 (8 non–smoking)
♿
🚇 Diagonal

CONDESTABLE
Map 239 F9
Ronda de la Universitat 1, 08007
Tel 93 318 62 68
www.hotelcondestable.com
A sensible choice for visitors on a modest budget. The rooms, while not luxurious, are comfortable and well equipped. They all have a

bathroom, satellite TV and safety deposit boxes. There is a café, a laundry service and there is parking very near by.
🏨 €70–€84, excluding breakfast
ℹ 78
♿
🚇 Universitat

CONFORT
Map 239 F7
Travessera de Gràcia 72, 08006
Tel 93 238 68 28
www.hotel-confort.com
The interior of this two-star hotel is a combination of warm and neutral shades. The

rooms all have a bathroom, direct-line telephone, satellite TV, internet connection, safety deposit box and minibar. There's a comfortable terrace garden, and all 36 rooms are found on one floor. The hotel also has parking facilities.
🏨 €102–€126, excluding breakfast
ℹ 36
♿
🚇 Fontana

CONTINENTAL
Map 236 F10
La Rambla 138, 08002
Tel 93 301 25 70
www.hotelcontinental.com
If you want to be at the very heart of everything, then stay here. This 100-year-old, three-star hotel, where the novelist George Orwell once stayed, is on Las Ramblas at the Plaça de Catalunya end of the promenade. The rooms are tidy and furnished in floral patterns; all have satellite TV, telephone, fridge, minibar and fan. There's

also room service and laundry service, internet access and a bar. It's smarter, sister hotel is the Continental Palacete.
🏨 €70–€75
ℹ 35
♿
🚇 Catalunya

CONTINENTAL PALACETE
Map 239 G9
Rambla de Catalunya 30, 08007
Tel 93 487 17 00
www.hotelpalacete.com
Enjoy the excellent service at this refurbished 19th-century palace, where you can dine under the glittering chandelier in sumptuous white and gold surroundings. This traditional elegance is combined with modern practicality in the guest rooms, some of which overlook Rambla de Catalunya. Room and laundry service, bar, internet access, car rental and money exchange

are available, plus a 24-hour light buffet.

€125–€145

19

Passeig de Gràcia

CORTES
Map 236 G10
Carrer de Santa Anna 25, 08002
Tel 93 317 91 12

Like many hotels in the heart of the city, Cortes was built at the beginning of the 20th century but completely refurbished before the 1992 Olympic Games. It is now a modern and functional two-

star hotel, with half the rooms overlooking a quiet courtyard. All are bright, clean and spacious, with a TV. There is also a restaurant and a bar.

€90–€100

44

Catalunya

DE L'ARC
Map 236 F11
La Rambla 19, 08002
Tel 93 301 97 98

This family hotel, at the port end of Las Ramblas, has clean, unpretentious accommodation. The rooms, some of which have balconies looking onto the street, are reasonably spacious with cable TV, telephone and hairdryer. Meeting rooms, a bar and laundry service are also available. De l'Arc is a good choice if you don't want to

ESPAÑA
Map 236 F11
Carrer de Sant Pau 9–11, 08001
Tel 93 318 17 58
www.hotelespanya.com

If you want to enter into the Modernista spirit, stay here at one of the city's best art nouveau hotels. Domènech i Montaner, the architect who built the Palau de la Música, designed the ground floor, and Ramon Casas was commissioned to decorate the dining room. All the public areas have retained their 19th-century glamour and elegance. The guest rooms have not survived so well and are more functional than Modernista, but are well equipped and meeting rooms are available. Don't miss the excellent restaurant, where there's a good assortment of salads, fish and meat dishes.

€80–€90

77

Liceu

spend a great deal on your accommodation and is close to the restaurants along the waterfront.

€77–€97, excluding breakfast

46

Drassanes

GALLERY
Map 239 G8
Carrer de Rosselló 249, 08008
Tel 93 415 99 11
www.galleryhotel.com

This hotel belongs to the Design Hotel Association, an international organization for hotels that cares about contemporary design. The modern, spacious rooms are neutral with strong accented tones in the soft furnishings.

All are equipped with TV, fax, soundproofed windows and minibar. The restaurant serves first-rate Mediterranean food and haute cuisine. Business rooms also available.

€118–€200

115 (22 non-smoking)

Diagonal

GAT-RAVAL
Map 236 F10
Carrer de Joaquin Costa 44, 08001
Tel 93 481 66 70
www.gataccommodation.com

Look out for the striking green and black cat (gat) logo if you're trying to find inexpensive accommodation.

It's ideal for backpackers who want a clean room, with TV and washbasin, at an affordable price. Museums, trendy bars, restaurants and shops are all within easy reach.

€37 (single), €61 (double), excluding breakfast

24

Universitat

GAUDÍ

Map 236 F11
Carrer Nou de la Rambla 12, 08001
Tel 93 317 90 32
www.hotelgaudi.es

The Gaudí hotel can be found opposite the Palau Güell, another of Gaudí's buildings. On entering the foyer, you'll be confronted with a sculpture of three chimneys made of bright

mosaics and resembling those at Casa Milà—to honour the man who gave the hotel its name. Rooms have satellite TV and a minibar; there are balconies on those higher up. The hotel has room service and 24-hour parking facilities.

💶 €120–€150
🛏 73
📶 📺
🚇 Liceu

GÒTICO

Map 237 G11
Carrer de la Jaume I 14, 08002
Tel 93 315 22 11
www.gargallo-hotels.com

This hotel is perfectly placed in the heart of the Barri Gòtic and thanks to a pre-millennium renovation, it's one of the most exceptional hotels in the area. The public areas make use of exposed, richly-toned brick work to create both warmth

and a sense of drama, but the height of the ceilings means that this is not overpowering. The guest rooms are less dramatic, but are fitted with soundproofed windows and

have safety boxes and minibar; some have their own balconies. There's also a snack bar and solarium.

💶 €127–€205, excluding breakfast
🛏 78
📶
🚇 Jaume I

GRAN HOTEL HAVANA

Map 239 G9
Gran Vía de les Cortes Catalanes 647, 08010
Tel 93 412 11 15
www.hoteles-silken.com

This hotel was built in 1872 and although two modern elements were added—a glass canopy and a round clock— the traditional elegance of the original façade was preserved.

The foyer, with its beautiful lamps and atrium, is particularly impressive. Rooms have cable TV, radio, minibar and Italian marble bathrooms. The restaurant serves excellent paella and Catalan cuisine, and there's a blues night on the first Thursday of the month. Parking is available and pets are welcome.

💶 €155–€175
🛏 145 (50 non-smoking)
📶
🚇 Girona

GRAN HOTEL LA FLORIDA

Off map 239 F5
Carretera de Tibidabo s/n, 08035
Tel 93 259 30 00
www.hotellaflorida.com

High up on the Tibidabo mountain (see page 130) to the north of the city, this five-star hotel is another addition to the city's growing list of luxury accommodation. It closed in 1979, before which La Florida was the haunt of distinguished guests such as Hemingway. Its new era promises to surpass its former glory. The suites and rooms, most with spectacular sweepings views of the city, have been

GRAND MARINA

Map 238 F12
Moll de Barcelona s/n, 08039
Tel 93 508 84 18
www.grandmarinahotel.com

The Grand Marina Hotel can be found at Barcelona's Port Vell. There are wonderful views over the Barri Gòtic,

Montjuïc and the shiny Maremagnum shopping arcade. Expensively furnished throughout, using relaxing shades and wood, this five-star hotel's top-class facilities include two restaurants, a buffet and a business services. The water massage baths are a wonderful bonus after a day's sightseeing.

💶 €200–€300
🛏 273
📶 🏊 Outdoor 📺
🚇 Drassanes

fitted out by a top set of international design talents.

💶 €350–€725
🛏 74
📶 🏊 📺
🚇 Peu del Funicular, then funicular to Tibidabo

GRANVIA

Map 239 G9
Gran Vía de les Cortes Catalanes 642, 08007
Tel 93 318 99 97
www.nnhotels.es

This hotel combines some excellent elements—it's right at the heart of town, just around the corner from the Plaça de Catalunya and the building was once a 19th-century palace. It has managed to retain the palace's splendour, containing furniture and works of art from that period and the wide, sweeping staircase with its elegant banister is the finishing touch. It has three meeting rooms, business

STAYING

facilities and a terrace garden. Room facilities include safe, minibar, satellite TV and internet access. Parking is also available.

🛏 €110–€120, excluding breakfast
🛏 53
❄
🚇 Urquianona

HESPERIA METROPOL
Map 236 G11
Carrer Ample 31, 08002
Tel 93 310 51 00
www.hesperia-metropol.com

The Hesperia Metropol prides itself on giving a personal, caring service to its guests. This welcoming theme is carried through into the warm tones, tempered with whites and blues, used in the furnishings.

Rooms come with balcony, minibar, safe and cable TV. Meeting rooms are also available. It's in the middle of the Barri Gòtic, close to the Museu Picasso (see pages 100–101).

🛏 €95–€110
🛏 71
❄
🚇 Drassanes

HILTON BARCELONA
Map 238 C6
Avinguda Diagonal 589–592, 08014
Tel 93 495 77 77
www.hilton.com

Although the outside of the Hilton Barcelona may look just like another of the office blocks along the Avinguda Diagonal, it's a world of modern lavishness within. The

furnishings are predominantly dark, with reds and purples, to give a sense of opulence, all highlighted by lighter pieces, such as the bed linen or sofas.

It has an exceptional range of amenities including a terrace, restaurant, bistro, meeting rooms, internet access and nightlights in the bathrooms.

🛏 €200–€320
🛏 286 (147 non-smoking)
❄ 📺
🚇 María Cristina

HOSTAL CENTRAL
Map 239 H9
Carrer de la Diputació 346, 08013
Tel 93 245 19 81
www.hostalcentralbarcelona.com

This hostel is set in a well-preserved art nouveau house, next to Plaça de Tetuán. The rooms are basic but clean and centrally heated, and most

have bathrooms. There is a theme of light, pastel shades that runs throughout the interior. Staff are friendly and attentive. Smoking is not allowed in the hostel.

🛏 €40–€62
🛏 14
❄
🚇 Girona

HOSTAL GOYA
Map 237 G10
Carrer de Pau Claris 74, 08010
Tel 93 302 25 65
www.hostalgoya.com

The Goya is great value for money in the heart of the city.

Ask for a room in the more modern part of the hostel, referred to as Hostal Goya Principal. Rooms here are well decorated, in whites, creams and browns, and have laundry and heating facilities, but are more expensive. Not all rooms have bathrooms.

🛏 €44–€83, excluding breakfast
🛏 19
❄
🚇 Urquinaona

HOSTAL ÍTACA
Map 237 G10
Carrer de Ripoll 21, 08001
Tel 93 301 97 51
www.itacahostel.com

This youth hostel has a great location close to the cathedral. Dormitories sleeping five, six or eight, and one double room, are available. Facilities include internet access, a cafeteria with great murals,

kitchen, lockers, sheets and towels for rent, parking and a book exchange service. It has a good website as well.

🛏 €19–€45, breakfast €2, sheet and towel rental €1.20
🛏 4 rooms, 24 beds
❄
🚇 Urquinaona

HOSTAL NILO
Map 236 F11
Carrer de Josep Anselm Clavé 17, 08002
Tel 93 317 90 44

Strategically placed at the heart of the Barri Gòtic, this is an area full of bars and

restaurants. It is perfect for visitors on a low budget, as it is clean but has a slightly faded edge about it. Credit cards are not accepted.

🎫 €36–€39
ℹ️ 57
🚇 Drassanes

HOSTAL NUEVO COLÓN
Map 237 H11
Avinguda del Marquès de l'Argentera 19, 08003
Tel 93 319 50 77
www.hostalnuevocolon.com
Nuevo Colón has a large public area where you can relax and watch TV; the guest rooms are clean and some have private bathrooms. The hostel also rents out apartments with kitchen facilities, in which six

people can easily be accommodated. Parking is available. It's a useful place if you are arriving in Barcelona by train, as it is near to the Estació de França.

🎫 €48–€62, excluding breakfast
ℹ️ 33
🚇 Barceloneta

HOSTAL OASIS
Map 237 G11
Carrer de la Reina Cristina 13, 08003
Tel 93 319 31 67
This hostel is well managed, if a bit basic. The reception area is a little dark but the large mirrors and marble tiled floors give it a lift. Rooms are clean and there is a pleasant café that is open all day. It's only a

short distance from the old harbour and not far from the Olympic Port. Credit cards are not accepted.

🎫 €40–€45, excluding breakfast
ℹ️ 11
🚇 Barceloneta

HOSTAL OLIVA
Map 239 G9
Passeig de Gràcia 32, 08007
Tel 93 488 01 62
www.lasguias.com/hostaloliva
This well-kept hostel was built in 1931, and it's one of the few to be found along the expensive Passeig de Gràcia. The old-fashioned lift, marbled

floors and mirrors create a wonderful art nouveau atmosphere. There are only 16 rooms, all of which have TVs. Some have bathrooms and a few overlook the beautiful buildings nearby. It's a great place if you're on your own, as the area is very safe; the only downside is the noise level, due in part to the wooden floorboards. Credit cards are not accepted.

🎫 €45–€55, excluding breakfast
ℹ️ 16
🚇 Catalunya

HUSA ORIENTE
Map 236 F11
La Rambla 45–47, 08002
Tel 93 302 25 58
www.husa.es
Built in 1842, this is the city's original grand hotel. It's in a great spot right on

Las Ramblas, just around the corner from the Gran Teatre de Liceu, which means it was once popular with visiting opera singers. You can marvel

at the amazing glass dome in the dining room as you eat your breakfast. The comfortable, if plain, rooms have TV, direct-dial telephone and safety deposit boxes, and many have views of Las Ramblas. Meeting rooms and parking facilities are available.

🎫 €100–€120
ℹ️ 142
🚇 Drassanes

LLEÓ
Map 236 F10
Carrer de Pelai 22–24, 08001
Tel 93 318 13 12
www.hotel-lleo.es
Lleó, a smart and functional hotel, is in the heart of Barcelona, next to Plaça de la Universitat. All rooms have a bathroom, satellite TV, minibar

and a safe. Other services include a buffet breakfast, cafeteria, snack bar and a non-smoking dining hall.

🎫 €138–€148, excluding breakfast
ℹ️ 89
🚇 Catalunya

LYON

Map 237 G11
Carrer del General Castaños 6, 08003
Tel 93 319 43 60
www.gargallo-hotels.com

This is the most modest of the seven Barcelona hotels belonging to the Gargallo hotel chain. It is found up a stairway, next to Estació de França railway station and close to the

Barri Gòtic and La Ribera, an area teeming with bars, restaurants and shops. Rooms are plain and basic, with telephone and TV.

€55–€60, excluding breakfast
20

Barceloneta

MAJESTIC

Map 239 G8
Passeig de Gràcia 68, 08007
Tel 93 488 17 17
www.hotelmajestic.es

The Majestic dates from the early 20th century and it lives up to its name in every conceivable way. Run by the Soldevila Casals family for the past three generations, it's

the epitome of quality service and hospitality. Every room has been carefully designed and contains a minibar, safe, cable TV, internet access and a PC connection. There's a restaurant, buffet and two bars, plus you can also enjoy a massage, or use the comprehensive health facilities, including sauna and steam room.

€165–€320, excluding breakfast
302 (50 non-smoking)
Outdoor
Passeig de Gràcia

MARINA FOLCH

Map 237 G12
Carrer del Mar 16, 08003
Tel 93 310 37 09

This small and efficient family-run hotel has everything you need for an inexpensive stay. It is just a short distance to the beaches and open-air bars of Barceloneta, and there's a

fabulous view of the old harbour from some rooms. Don't expect luxury, although one bonus is the reasonably-priced restaurant where you can tuck into good food. A few words of Catalan will be helpful and appreciated at this hotel.

€55–€60, excluding breakfast
10

Barceloneta

LE MERIDIEN BARCELONA

Map 236 F10
La Rambla 111, 08002
Tel 93 318 62 00
www.lemeridien-barcelona.com

Walk through this hotel's beautiful entrance in Las Ramblas and you might find

yourself thinking you're in early 20th-century France. Despite revamps, this hotel has retained its fin de siècle look. All rooms have been fitted out with every conceivable comfort and this top-level

SPECIAL

MESÓN CASTILLA

Map 236 F10
Carrer de Valldonzella 5, 08001
Tel 93 318 21 82
www.mesoncastilla.com

The neo-Gothic Mesón Castilla is decorated with gilt mirrors, ornate dark wood fittings and its furniture is in keeping with the style. All rooms have minibars and TVs, and some at the rear have balconies. A good buffet breakfast, with a selection of cheese, meats and eggs, is served on a beautiful terrace in the summer. The service is warm and efficient and the hotel is well-placed both for nightlife and sights in the increasingly fashionable El Raval.

€117–€130
60

Universitat

luxury attracts celebrities who are visiting the city. Try to get a room overlooking Las Ramblas—the double-glazing filters out a lot of the noise—or enjoy the view while having breakfast on the roof terrace. The hotel has its own parking.

€350–€380
212 (20 non-smoking)

Catalunya

MILLENNIUM

Map 238 E11
Ronda de Sant Pau 14, 08001
Tel 93 441 41 77
www.hotel-millennium.com

This is a Best Western hotel but it is managed by Apsis, a company based in the city. Although it occupies a

19th-century building, the façade and interior are fine examples of modern design. Rooms are spacious with a

STAYING

contemporary look, wooden floors and marble in the bathrooms. Excellent buffet breakfasts are served at the bar. There is childcare available and the hotel has several meeting rooms.

🛏 €160–€198
🛈 46 (24 non-smoking)
🔗 🖾
🚇 Liceu

MONEGAL
Map 236 F10
Carrer de Pelai 62, 08001
Tel 93 302 65 66
www.mediumhoteles.com
Walk out of this hotel and you will find yourself directly across from the legendary Café Zurich (see page 167), which gives

you a fabulous spot for breakfast. A practical hotel, which is reflected in the interior scheme of browns and pinks and white walls. There are some nice touches such as stylish floor lamps and the leafy ferns in the public areas. The rooms have telephone and satellite TV.

🛏 €85–€120, excluding breakfast
🛈 54
🔗
🚇 Catalunya

ÒNIX
Map 238 D9
Carrer de Llança 30, 08015
Tel 93 426 00 87
This three-star hotel is a real find, in a quiet street near Plaça d'Espanya and Montjuïc. The front rooms have a view of the disused Las Arenas bullring, but the real attraction is the intimate rooftop pool and terrace which looks out onto the Parc de Joan Miró (see page 109).

🛏 €109–€150, excluding breakfast
🛈 80
🔗 🏊
🚇 Espanya

PARAL.LEL
Map 238 E11
Carrer del Poeta Cabanyes 5, 08004
Tel 93 329 11 04
www.hotelparalel.com
This two-star hotel has good access to the Metro and buses, and only a short distance from Montjuïc. Whites and creams are used to give the rooms a

clean, airy look. They have a bathroom, direct dial telephone, minibar, satellite TV and a safe. Twenty-four hour parking and a laundry service are also available.

🛏 €100–€125, excluding breakfast
🛈 66
🔗
🚇 Paral.lel

PARK HOTEL
Map 237 H11
Avinguda del Marquès de l'Argentera 11, 08003
Tel 93 319 60 00
www.parkhotelbarcelona.com
Built in the 1950s, but carefully renovated in 1990, this hotel received the Ciutat de Barcelona prize for being the best refurbished hotel. The top four floors have parquet flooring, wood fittings and are

decorated in neutral tones with dark red splashes. All rooms have satellite TV, minibar, safety box and terrace.

🛏 €135–€140
🛈 91
🔗
🚇 Barceloneta

PENINSULAR
Map 236 F11
Carrer de Sant Pau 34, 08001
Tel 93 302 31 38
The Peninsular is a little oasis away from the bustling El Raval. It was built at the end of the 19th century and has retained the original features of an art nouveau house, such as the impressive high ceiling found in the dining room. Rooms are basic but spacious and clean; each has a bathroom, telephone and safety

deposit box, and most overlook family apartments. An additional benefit is the beautiful tiled inner courtyard, surrounded by hanging plants.

🛏 €50–€70
🛈 59
🔗
🚇 Liceu

PENSIÓN SEGRE
Map 236 G11
Carrer de Simó Oller 1, 08002
Tel 93 315 07 09
This discreet *pension* is often overlooked, despite being a few minutes walk from the port, beach and the galleries of La Ribera. Only about half the rooms have private bathrooms, but all are spacious and have balconies facing a quiet street. Furniture and fittings are far more functional than flash, but the Segre is a good option for budget accommodation in the old city. Credit cards are not accepted.

🛏 €35–€45, excluding breakfast
🛈 24
🚇 Drassanes

PRINCESA SOFÍA
Off map 238 C6
Plaça Pío XII 4, 08028
Tel 93 330 71 11
www.barcelona.interconti.com
The Princesa Sofia, part of the InterContinental chain, enjoys an international reputation that predates the plethora of

STAYING

five-star hotels built for the Olympics. The interior is light and spacious, with pale walls contrasting with one or two strong shades. Some of the many facilities available to guests include a restaurant and on-site parking.

🏨 €185–€265
🛏 500
💲 🏊 Indoor and outdoor 🛗
🚇 María Cristina

PRINCIPAL
Map 239 G8
Carrer de la Junta de Comerç 8, 08001
Tel 93 318 89 70
www.hotelprincipal.es
Simple, functional accommodation for those on a budget. Rooms have red or yellow themed furnishings, as well as telephone, satellite TV and deposit box. The Principal is under the same management as the Joventut hotel, which is next door, in a very quiet street in the heart of El Raval. Other facilities include a bar, meeting rooms and a restaurant that caters for both hotels.

🏨 €90–€100
🛏 126
💲
🚇 Liceu

REGENCIA COLÓN
Map 237 G11
Carrer de Sagristans 13–17, 08002
Tel 93 318 98 58
www.hotelregenciacolon.com
This hotel exudes a pleasant and relaxing atmosphere after a hard day's sightseeing. The rooms are spacious and well

kept, and there's a range of facilities such as TV, room service and minibar. A bar and two lounges are available, and you are free to use the restaurant at the nearby Hotel Colón (see pages 244–245).

🏨 €130–€148
🛏 50
💲
🚇 Jaume I

RELAIS D'ORSÀ
Off map 238 E6
Carrer del Mont d'Orsa 35, 08017
Tel 93 406 94 11
www.relaisdorsa.com
Nestled at the foot of Mount Tibidabo, this is more than just a hotel with a view. The beautiful 19th-century palace is an ideal choice for getting away from it all. There are only six rooms so expect impeccable service. Each room is luxurious and equipped with minibar, safe, satellite TV and radio. Relax in the tranquil surroundings, stroll in the garden, take a dip in the swimming pool or simply gaze at the magnificent city panorama.

🏨 €215–€230, excluding breakfast
🛏 6
💲 🏊 Outdoor
🚆 Take FGC train from Plaça de Catalunya to Peu del Funicular (lines S2 or S55), then funicular to Vallvidrera Superior

REY JUAN CARLOS I
Off map 238 C6
Avinguda Diagonal 661–671, 08028
Tel 93 364 42 23
www.hrjuancarlos.com
This elegant hotel was opened for the 1992 Olympic Games. View the spacious foyer from the stylish glass elevators or

admire the beautiful garden with its own lake and restaurant. Facilities include two restaurants and two bars, spa facilities and a shopping area. Rooms all have satellite TV, minibar, climate control,

24-hour room service and laundry service.

🏨 €280–€420, excluding breakfast
🛏 412
💲 🏊 Indoor and outdoor 🛗
🚇 Palau Reial

RIALTO
Map 236 G11
Carrer de Ferran 40–42, 08002
Tel 93 318 52 12
www.gargallo-hotels.com
This three-star hotel is in the house where Joan Miró was born, and it provides good service at fair prices. Rooms are soundproofed and have telephone, TV and room service; you can also have your laundry done. The restaurant serves a selection of Catalan dishes, as well as international fare, and there's also a snack bar and breakfast room.

🏨 €131–€140, excluding breakfast
🛏 197
💲
🚇 Liceu

RITZ
Map 239 G9
Gran Vía de les Corts Catalanes 668, 08010
Tel 93 318 52 00
www.ritzbcn.com
Opened in 1919, this hotel embodies the essence of the Catalan bourgeoisie. It is internationally known for its understated style and elegance. The opulence is carried through the design, using blues, reds and golds. Relax by the indoor garden or visit the restaurant to sample delicious

Mediterranean cuisine. It is ideal for meetings or business conventions, as a range of rooms come equipped with the latest technology.

🏨 €350–€400
🛏 122 (60 non-smoking)
💲 🛗
🚇 Urquinaona

STAYING

RITZ ROGER DE LLÚRIA
Map 239 G9
Carrer de Roger de Llúria 28, 08010
Tel 93 343 60 80
www.rogerdelluria.com
The Roger de Llúria provides the quality of service expected of the Ritz chain but with an intimate feel. Although the building has been renovated, it still retains elements typical of houses in the Eixample, such as the façade. All the rooms are spacious and tastefully decorated, and seven of them have sun terraces. The restaurant serves Catalan cuisine with an exotic touch, as well as international dishes.
💶 €194–€210
🛏 48 (4 non-smoking)
♿
Ⓜ Urquinaona

RUBENS
Off map 239 G6
Carrer de Mare de Déu del Coll 10, 08023
Tel 93 219 12 04
www.hoteles-catalonia.es
The Rubens is off the beaten track, on a hilly street near to Gaudí's Park Güell. It's a relaxing alternative to the noisy main town and often has vacancies—many prefer it for the area's panoramic views and cleaner air. The rooms are slightly on the spartan side but the 1970s building is very appealing. Fifteen of the rooms have a private terrace.
💶 €93–€136, excluding breakfast
🛏 141
♿
Ⓜ Vallcarca

SANT AGUSTÍ
Map 236 F11
Plaça de Sant Agustí 3, 08001
Tel 93 318 16 58
www.hotelsa.com
Built in the first half of the 19th century in the old convent of St. Augustine, this hotel claims to be the oldest in the city, and has been run by the

Tura-Monistrol family for over a century. Rooms are comfortable, of a reasonable size and have telephone, TV and safe. There is also a coffee shop and access to the free internet and email. Rooms on the top floor, complete with sloping roof, have great views.
💶 €126–€158
🛏 77
♿
Ⓜ Liceu

SPLENDID
Map 236 F9
Carrer de Muntaner 2, 08011
Tel 93 451 21 42
www.hotel-splendid.com
This welcoming hotel, built in 1998, was designed for the business person who still likes a bit of family-type hospitality. It is just around the corner from the Plaça de Universitat and has medium-sized rooms and spacious suites, as well as a separate lounge area. All are decked out in soothing blues and yellows.
💶 €150–€190
🛏 43
♿
Ⓜ Universitat

SUIZO
Map 237 G11
Plaça de l'Angel 12, 08002
Tel 93 310 61 08
www.gargallo-hotels.com
This is a good-value three-star hotel, which is part of the Gargallo group. Don't be put off by the slightly shabby exterior as the inside is a pleasant surprise. There's a coffee shop, snack bar and lounge. Rooms are spacious and modern, and all have safety box, telephone, TV and minibar; a laundry service is also offered. Pets are permitted to stay.
💶 €122–€130, excluding breakfast
🛏 59
♿
Ⓜ Urquinaona

TOLEDANO/HOSTAL RESIDENCIA CAPITOL
Map 236 F10
La Rambla 138, 08002
Tel 93 301 08 72
www.hoteltoledano.com
These two hotels are on separate floors of the same building, but they are jointly run with the reception for both on the fourth floor. If you get one of the rooms that have a

balcony then you can enjoy a panoramic view of the city. They are inexpensive and central, but not necessarily spotlessly clean. The rooms have satellite TV, heating and a telephone. Most of the staff speak English and are happy to advise on places to visit or where to eat.
💶 €38–€56, excluding breakfast
🛏 11
♿ Some
Ⓜ Catalunya

TURÍN
Map 236 F10
Carrer del Pintor Fortuny 9, 08001
Tel 93 302 48 12
This three-star hotel, set in a peaceful street in the heart of the city, opened in 1989. The comfortable rooms are clean and functional with browns

and pastels dominating the palette. All have balconies, and there's a restaurant, conference rooms, a cafeteria and parking.
💶 €102–€135, excluding breakfast
🛏 59
♿
Ⓜ Catalunya

TURÓ DE VILANA
Off map 238 F6
Carrer de Vilana 7, 08017
Tel 93 434 03 63
www.turodevilana.com
The small Turó de Vilana, one of the few hotels in the suburb of Sarría, is for those who appreciate comfort and functionality. From its unfussy rooms in beige and white to the black marble bar, the Turó de Vilana is tasteful through and through. Try and secure one of the five rooms that have a private terrace. Off-street parking is also available.
💶 €115–€140, excluding breakfast
🛏 20
♿
🚇 FGC Sarría

HOTEL GROUPS

Group	Description	Number in the city	Contact number and website
AC-Hoteles	Stylish, four-star hotels, with more opening up all the time, both in the city and across the country	4	902 292 295 www.ac-hoteles.com
Best Western (España)	The world's largest hotel chain, aimed at those on business. This chain has one of the few hotels near the airport (Best Western Alfa)	6	900 993 900 www.bestwestern.com
Catalonia	This chain currently has 48 hotels in Spain. It has a good range of three- and four-star hotels across the city	16	900 301 078 www.hoteles-catalonia.es
Derby Hotels Collection	Smart range of hotels that includes the luxury Claris (see page 244)	5	93 366 88 05 www.derbyhotels.es
Gargallo	This chain has been in business for more than 40 years and its hotels in the city range from one- to four-stars	7	93 268 90 70 www.gargallo-hotels.com
H10	The chain has 37 hotels in 12 countries providing comfort in its three- and four-star hotels	6	902 100 906 www.h10.es
HCC Hotels	Providing more than 530 rooms spread across its five hotels	5	902 102 120 www.hcchotels.com
Hoteles Hesperia	Thirty-one hotels in Spain providing a high comfort factor in its four-star hotels	5	902 397 398 www.hoteles-hesperis.es
Husa	This group has more than 150 hotels in Spain, including the five-star Ritz and Rey Juan Carlos I	15	902 100 710 www.husa.com
Medium	These mainly two-star hotels aim to provide a high level of service and comfort at an affordable price	6	93 209 66 40 www.mediumhoteles.com
Minotel	This company has 700 hotels worldwide in more than 30 countries	8	900 401 402 www.minotel.com
NH	More than 206 hotels in Europe, with mostly three-star hotels in Barcelona	11	91 398 44 00 www.nh-hoteles.com
Nuñez i Navarro (NN)	This group has two-, three- and four-star hotels in the city, all in and around the heart of the city	5	www.nnhotels.es
Silken Hotels	This company has a range of hotels across Spain and its philosophy is attention to detail and service	2	902 363 600 www.hoteles-silken.com
Sol Melià	The third largest hotel company in Europe and includes TRYP Hotels, Sol Hotels and Paradisus Resorts	4	902 144 444 www.solmelia.es

STAYING

CLIMATE

Barcelona has a fairly stable climate and is not given to vast extremes. There may be a few unexpected down-pours, and winter can be cold, but there is also plenty of sunshine and blue skies to enjoy.

WHEN TO GO

The city has become a year-round destination, and it doesn't really have a peak season. Your choice will most likely depend on what sort of weather you want.

● Spring, especially March and April, is an unpredictable season. It can be cloudy and rainy or bright and sunny, depending on your luck.

● The best months to visit the city are May, June and September, when the weather is warm and pleasant and you will find lots of events taking place. Visiting at this time has the added bonus of missing the school summer holiday period, when prices tend to be more expensive.

● The real heat of summer takes hold during late July and August. It can be very hot and humid, leading to the occasional thunderstorm, and local residents often escape the city at this time. During the height of summer, many restaurants, shops and museums close or reduce their opening hours.

● September and October are officially the city's wettest months, but October in particular still benefits from the odd bright sunny day.

● Between November and Christmas is a lovely time to visit the city, with seasonal markets and religious pageantry.

● The winter, December through to the end of February, is cool rather than very cold, but it has been known to snow.

● Other times that you might want to consider avoiding are national holidays (see page 265) when many of the major attractions are closed.

● If you want to try and ensure a quiet city, check out if Barcelona is holding one of its huge trade fairs. The large number of delegates increases traffic and crowds at the major attractions, and pushes up the price of accommodation.

WEATHER REPORTS

● For information on the current weather picture, check the website of your local news network station, such as the BBC (www.bbc.co.uk) or CNN (www.CNN.com).

● There are a several dedicated weather websites including www.weather.com, www.idealspain.com, www.wunderground.com and www.onlineweather.com.

● English-language newspapers such as *Spain Daily News* (www.SpainDailyNews.com) have good weather coverage.

WHAT TO TAKE

● If you forget to take anything, you will be able to buy it in Barcelona, unless it is a very specialized item.

● The clothing you pack will depend on the time of year you visit, but you should bring a range of clothes for different weather conditions, even if you are visiting in summer. Bring an umbrella, a rain coat, comfortable walking shoes and at least one warm top for the evenings.

● You should also bring suitable clothing for visiting churches, although the rules about length of skirt, casualness of shoes or bare arms are quite relaxed.

● Residents generally like to dress well and appreciate it when others pay attention to their appearance. It is usual to dress up when going out for the evening, so remember to bring something smart.

● If you are on any prescribed medication, bring enough with you for the period of your visit.

● If you are going to decant tablets out of their original

Cafés on the Passeig de Gràcia are a good place for enjoying the Barcelona sunshine

packaging to reduce the amount you need to carry, or have a serious illness, you might consider getting a letter from your doctor stating your medical condition and what medication you are on. This will help you if you are stopped by customs or if you need to get emergency treatment while you are away.

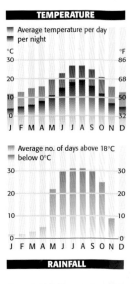

TEMPERATURE

■ Average temperature per day
■ per night

Average no. of days above 18°C
■ below 0°C

RAINFALL

Average rainfall

PLANNING

Before You Go   256–257
Practicalities   258–259
Money Matters   260–261
Health   262–263
Finding Help   264
Opening Times and Tickets   265
Communication   266–267
Media   268
Books, Maps and Films   269
Tourist Offices/Useful Websites   270
Words and Phrases   271–276

Planning

Barcelona is on CET (Central European Time), one hour ahead of GMT (Greenwich Mean Time).

City	Time difference	Time at 12 noon in Barcelona
Amsterdam	0	noon
Berlin	0	noon
Brussels	0	noon
Chicago	-7	5am
Dublin	-1	11am
Johannesburg*	+1	1pm
London	-1	11am
Montréal	-6	6am
New York	-6	6am
Perth*	+7	7pm
Rome	0	noon
San Francisco	-9	3am
Sydney*	+9	9pm
Tokyo*	+8	8pm

Summer Time begins on the last Sunday in March and ends on the last Sunday in October. For starred countries, which do not have daylight saving, take off one hour in during Summer Time.

CUSTOMS

Goods you buy in the EU
These are in line with other EU countries. There is no limit on the amount of foreign currency or euros that you can bring into Spain. Tax-paid goods for personal use (such as video cameras) can be brought in from other EU countries without customs charges being incurred. Guidance levels for tax-paid goods bought in the EU are as follows:

- 800 cigarettes; or
- 400 cigarillos; or
- 200 cigars; or
- 1kg of smoking tobacco

- 110 litres of beer
- 10 litres of spirits
- 90 litres of wine (of which only 60 litres can be sparkling wine)
- 20 litres of fortified wine (such as port or sherry)

Visiting Spain from outside the EU
You are entitled to the allowances shown below only if you travel with the goods and do not plan to sell them.

- 200 cigarettes; or
- 100 cigarillos; or
- 50 cigars; or
- 250g of smoking tobacco

- 1 litre of spirits or strong liqueurs
- 2 litres of still table wine
- 2 litres of fortified wine, sparkling wine or other liqueurs
- 50g of perfume
- 250cc/ml of eau de toilette

• Take photocopies of any important documents, such as passport and travel insurance. You should also keep a separate note of the serial numbers as well as the numbers of traveller's cheques in case of loss or theft.
• Make sure you have addresses and telephone numbers of any emergency contacts, and who to call if you need to cancel your credit cards.

PASSPORTS AND VISAS
• All visitors must carry a valid passport, or in the case of EU nationals, a national ID card may be used. You are required by law to keep one of these documents on you at all times, but in practice it is rare to be stopped and asked.

• EU visitors do not require a visa for entry. Visitors from the US, Canada Japan, Australia and New Zealand require a visa for stays exceeding 90 days.
• Always check with the consulate about visa requirements and entry regulations as they are liable to change, often at short notice. Visit www.tourspain.es, www.gospain.org, www.fco.gov.uk or www.travel.state.gov. For addresses of consulates and embassies, see page 264.
• Always keep a separate note of your passport number and a photocopy of the page that carries your details.

TRAVEL INSURANCE
• Make sure you have adequate travel insurance including medical cover, repatriation, baggage and money loss. And if your insurer has a 24-hour helpline remember to bring the number with you.
• If you rely on your credit card insurance, check exactly what's covered.
• Report losses or theft to the police and obtain a signed statement (una denuncia) from a police station (comisaría) to help with insurance claims.

CUSTOMS
The import of wildlife souvenirs from rare and endangered species may be either illegal or require a special permit. Before purchase you should check customs regulations. See above for more details on what can be brought through customs.

SPANISH EMBASSIES ABROAD

Country	Address	Telephone
Australia and New Zealand	15 Arkana Street, Yarralumla, ACT 2600, Canberra	06 273 3555
Canada	74 Stanley Avenue, Ottawa, Ontario K1M 1P4	613/747-2252
The Netherlands	Lange Voorhout 50, NL - 2514 EG The Hague	70/364 3814
Republic of Ireland	17a Merlyn Park, Ballsbridge, Dublin 4	(01) 269 1640/269 1854
UK	20 Draycott Place, London SW3 2RZ	0207 589 8989 visa information 0906 550 8970
	Suite 1a, Brook House, 70 Spring Gardens, Manchester, M2 2BQ	0161 236 1233
	63 North Castle Street, Edinburgh, EH2 3LJ	0131 220 1843
USA	150 East 58th Street, New York, NY 10155	212/355-4090
	5055 Wilshire Blvd., Suite 960, Los Angeles, CA 90036	323/938-0158

PLANNING

PRACTICALITIES

ELECTRICITY
- The power supply is 220 volts.
- Plugs have two round pins. It is a good idea to bring an adaptor with you, although these are readily available in the city.
- Visitors from North America should also bring a transformer for appliances operating on 110/120 volts; these can be hard to find.

LAUNDRY
- Use your hotel's laundry service as this will be the most convenient, and probably least expensive, way to have your clothes cleaned.
- Self-service launderettes (*lavanderías automáticas*) are difficult to find and tend to be in the older parts of town. Lavanderia Tigre (Carrer de Rauric 20) in the Barri Gòtic has coin-operated machines, and Lavamax (Junta de Comerç 14) is both a modern self-service laundry and dry-cleaners.
- There are a few more dry-cleaners (*tintorería*) around, such as Tintorería Ferrán (Carrer de Ferrán 11) with prices from €3 for a shirt and €7.50 for a dress.

LAVATORIES
- Public lavatories are rare around the city, and when you do find them, they might not be too pleasant. It is best to make use of the ones in large department stores, museums, galleries and places of interest, where standards are likely to be much higher.
- You can also use the facilities in cafés, bars and restaurants, but as these are usually for customers only, it is polite to buy something before doing so.
- Words to look out for are *aseos* or *servicios* in Castilian or *lavabos* in Catalan.

MEASUREMENTS
Spain uses the metric system. Distances are measured in metres and kilometres, fuel is sold by the litre and food is weighed in grams and kilograms.

SMOKING
- Smoking is banned on the metro and on buses, and you will be given a monetary fine if you are caught.

CONVERSION CHART

From	To	Multiply by
Inches	Centimetres	2.54
Centimetres	Inches	0.3937
Feet	Metres	0.3048
Metres	Feet	3.2810
Yards	Metres	0.9144
Metres	Yards	1.0940
Miles	Kilometres	1.6090
Kilometres	Miles	0.6214
Acres	Hectares	0.4047
Hectares	Acres	2.4710
Gallons	Litres	4.5460
Litres	Gallons	0.2200
Ounces	Grams	28.35
Grams	Ounces	0.0353
Pounds	Grams	453.6
Grams	Pounds	0.0022
Pounds	Kilograms	0.4536
Kilograms	Pounds	2.205
Tons	Tonnes	1.0160
Tonnes	Tons	0.9842

- It is not allowed in art galleries, museums, theatres and cinemas.
- Smoking is common in bars and restaurants and there are few non-smoking sections.

LOCAL WAYS
- The continental kiss (one kiss on each cheek) is used among friends only, so you won't be expected to kiss people you don't know. But always offer to shake hands when you meet people, even if it's not for the first time.

CLOTHING SIZES
Clothing sizes in Spain are in metric. Use the chart below to convert the size you use at home.

UK	Metric	USA	
36	46	36	SUITS
38	48	38	
40	50	40	
42	52	42	
44	54	44	
46	56	46	
48	58	48	
7	41	8	SHOES
7.5	42	8.5	
8.5	43	9.5	
9.5	44	10.5	
10.5	45	11.5	
11	46	12	
14.5	37	14.5	SHIRTS
15	38	15	
15.5	39/40	15.5	
16	41	16	
16.5	42	16.5	
17	43	17	
8	36	6	DRESSES
10	38	8	
12	40	10	
14	42	12	
16	44	14	
18	46	16	
20	46	18	
4.5	37.5	6	SHOES
5	38	6.5	
5.5	38.5	7	
6	39	7.5	
6.5	40	8	
7	41	8.5	

One kiss on each cheek is used among friends

- Follow the custom of having a siesta at lunchtime or be prepared to have a long lunch.

The siesta isn't as widespread as it once was and the entire city doesn't shut down. But you will find a number of shops and some museums close, many not reopening until 4 or 5pm. It's also a good way of avoiding the worst of the summer heat.
- Late lunches push evening meal times to past 9pm; it may be difficult to get dinner before this time.
- You should show respect and dress accordingly when visiting the cathedral and other religious places. Most, if not all, are still active places of worship. You should check before taking any photographs inside a church, but this is not acceptable when a service is taking place.
- Residents will warm to you if you try even just a few words of Spanish, but will love you all the more if you use Catalan, with

words such as *si us plau*
(please) and *gràcies* (thank you).
● Don't be tempted to refer to
Catalan as a dialect.
● Most hotel, museum and
tourist office staff speak at least
a few words of a number of
languages, and many speak
one or two languages very well,
so you should be able to get
your message across. Don't be
surprised if they want to try out
their language skills on you,
rather than vice versa.

VISITING WITH CHILDREN

● Children are welcome just
about anywhere in the city. Don't
be afraid that your children will
be regarded with hostility if you
want to sample the nightlife,
as they are routinely taken out
with the family at night and are
allowed to stay up late.
● Children's menus are not
widely available, but most
restaurants will provide you with
a smaller portion if you ask.
● Barcelona has a varied range
of attractions for children (see
pages 177–178), and the city's
parks are a good place for them
to let off steam. As many places
have that Modernista touch, the
unusual shapes and textures will
interest most children as you
walk around the city.
● For something a bit different,
and for tired feet, use the cable
cars rides around Montjuïc (see
pages 86–87) and the tour
buses (see page 204).
● Some of the squares in
the city, such as the Plaça de
Universitat, have small, fenced-
off playgrounds in them. They
are free and open to everyone.
● Many museums and
attractions have lower admission
charges for children, and those

younger than 5 often get in free.
● Travel on public transport can
be a headache with a pushchair
(stroller), where steps, escalators
and crowded services can hinder
your movement. Avoid travel
at rush hour, or during the busy
lunchtime period.
● Public transport is free for
children under 4.
● Baby changing facilities are not
easy to find, but more modern
museums and department stores
are the best option. You can buy
baby food and other items from
supermarkets and pharmacies.
● The tourist office keeps a list
of recommended child-minding
services.

*Children will love the Parc
d'Atracciones at Tibidabo*

PLACES OF WORSHIP

Worshippers of any religion should be able to find the appropriate church, temple
or synagogue, but Catholics obviously get the biggest choice, with services at the
cathedral and other churches listed in The Sights (see pages 62–130).

Anglican
St. George's Church, Carrer de Horaci
38, tel 93 417 88 67

Jewish
Synagogue de Barcelona, Carrer
d'Avenir 24, tel 93 200 61 48

Muslim
Centre Islàmic, Avinguda Meridiana 326,
tel 93 351 49 01

Protestant/Evangelist
Plaça Major del Rectoret 1–2,
tel 93 204 99 10

Roman Catholic
Parròquia María Reina,
Carretera d'Esplugues 103,
tel 93 203 41 15, for Mass in English

*The illuminated altar in the
Santa Maria del Pi church. The
single wide nave and shallow
arch of the choir are pure
Catalan Gothic (see page 130)*

VISITORS WITH A
DISABILITY

● The newer museums, such as
the MACBA (see pages 90–91),
have good access for those
with a disability, but many places
can still prove a problem. The
majority of buildings date from
either the Gothic period or are
Modernista and so have stairs,
but no elevators.
● The narrow, cobbled streets
of the Barri Gòtic are difficult
to negotiate, especially when
it is crowded, but at least it is
pedestrianized.
● Certain sections of the public
transport system have been
adapted, with elevators at metro
stations, and buses that can
lower ramps to enable access.
But this is by no means across
the board. For more information,
see page 52, or visit one of
the TMB offices for advice (see
page 43).
● Finding a place to stay that
suits your needs should be
easier, as many hotels are easily
accessible. Call ahead if you have
specific requirements.
● The Taxi Amic service has
minivans, but it is a very popular
service and you will need to
book ahead (*tel 93 420 80 88*).

PLANNING

MONEY MATTERS

Spain is one of 12 European countries that have adopted the euro as their official currency. Euro notes and coins were introduced in January 2002, replacing the former currency, the peseta.

BEFORE YOU GO
● It is advisable to use a combination of cash, traveller's cheques and credit cards rather than relying on any one means of payment during your trip.
● Check with your credit card company that you can withdraw cash from ATMs. You should also check what fee will be charged for this, and what number you should ring if your card is stolen (see below).
● Traveller's cheques are a relatively safe way of carrying money as you are insured if they are stolen. Remember to keep a note of their numbers separate from the traveller's cheques themselves.

Caixa Cash Caja

An ATM sign in Catalan, English and Spanish

EXCHANGE RATES
The exchange rate per euro for visitors from the UK, US and Canada is subject to daily fluctuation. At the time of printing €1 is worth approximately £0.70, US$1.10 and C$1.50.

CREDIT CARDS
Most restaurants, hotels and shops accept credit cards, but some may have a minimum spend. Smaller shops and cafés will still require cash. Ticket machines at metro stations also accept credit cards.

ATMS
These are widespread throughout the city, known as *telebanco*, and have instructions in a choice of languages, including French, Italian and German. If your card has the Maestro or Cirrus facilities (look for the red, white and blue logos) you will be able to pay for goods and services as well as withdraw cash.

BANKS
There is no shortage of banks, which tend to be open Monday to Friday 8.30–2, Saturday 8.30–1, but close Saturdays in summer. Most have a foreign exchange desk (*cambio* or

LOST/STOLEN CREDIT CARDS
Ring one of the following contact numbers in case of loss or theft:
American Express/cards
tel 902 375 637
American Express/ traveller's cheques
tel 900 994 426
Diners Club
tel 902 401 112
MasterCard
tel 900 971 231
Visa
tel 900 991 124/ 91 519 21 00

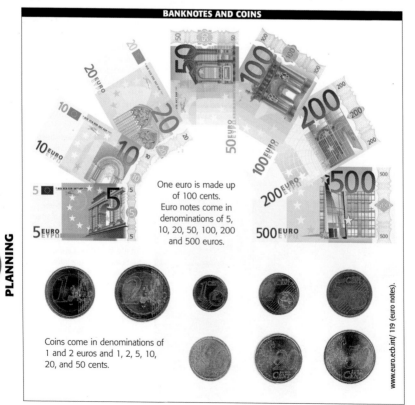

BANKNOTES AND COINS

One euro is made up of 100 cents. Euro notes come in denominations of 5, 10, 20, 50, 100, 200 and 500 euros.

Coins come in denominations of 1 and 2 euros and 1, 2, 5, 10, 20, and 50 cents.

www.euro.ecb.int/ 119 (euro notes).

PLANNING

FOREIGN BANKS

Name	Address	Telephone
Citibank	Plaça Francesc Macía 3	93 240 50 26
ABN AMRO	Avinguda Diagonal 662	93 280 52 00
HSBC	Avinguda Diagonal 605	93 322 22 23
Barclays	Passeig de Gràcia 45	93 481 20 00
Deutsche Bank	Plaça de Catalunya 19	93 318 47 00
Lloyds TSB	Rambla de Catalunya 123	93 236 33 00
The Bank of Tokyo/Mitsubishi	Avinguda Diagonal 605	93 494 74 50
The Chase Manhattan Bank	Josep Irla i Bosch 5-7	93 203 03 12
Banca Nazionale del Lavoro	Avinguda Diagonal 468	93 416 00 33

You'll find a number of banks across Barcelona

canvi), and remember to bring your passport if you want to change traveller's cheques.

CHANGING MONEY

You can change money at bureaux de change, which are dotted around the city and open until very late. The exchange rate won't be good, but commission is generally not charged. You can change money at the following places:
● American Express, Passeig de Gràcia 101, tel 93 415 23 71, Mon–Fri 9am–8.30pm, Sat 10am–noon.
● La Rambla 74, tel 93 301 11 66, daily 9am–midnight, Apr–end Sep; Mon–Fri 9am–8.30pm, Sat 10am–7pm, rest of year.
● Maccorp Exact Change, La Rambla 130, tel 93 268 11 09, daily 8am–2am.

WIRING MONEY

In an emergency you can have money wired from your home country, but this can be very expensive and time-consuming. You can send and receive money via agents such as Western Union (www.westernunion.com) or MoneyGram (www.moneygram.com).

DISCOUNTS

● Seniors can get reductions on some museum entry charges on production of an identity document.
● An International Student Identity Card (ISIC; www.isic.org) may help obtain free or reduced entry to museums and attractions as well as other discounts.
● There are a number of other discount passes available (see pages 43 and 265).

TAXES

● Sales tax, at 7 per cent and known as IVA, is added to everything, including all services such as hotel accommodation and meals in restaurants. This is non-refundable. For all other goods and services 16 per cent is added.
● Visitors from non–EU countries are entitled to a reimbursement of the 16 per cent tax paid on purchases to the value of more than €90.15, which needs to be spent in the same store.
● The store must provide a properly completed invoice itemizing all goods, the price paid for them, and the tax charged, as well as full address details of both the vendor and purchaser. The goods must then be brought out of the EU within three months.
● The goods and the invoice(s) should be taken to the booth provided at Spanish customs on your departure from the EU, prior to checking in your baggage. This is where your claim will be processed.
● Alternatively, tax can also be reclaimed through Global Refund Tax Free Shopping, a service offered by major retailers worldwide; visit www.globalrefund.com.

TIPPING

● Tipping is still a relavtively new culture in Spain, so high sums of money for a tip will not be expected.
● There will be no service charge added to your bill when you are in the city, so you should be prepared to leave a tip (see table below).

TIPPING

Tipping is usually expected for services. As a general guide, the following applies:

Restaurants	5–10 per cent*
Bar service	change*
Cafés	5 per cent*
Tour guides	optional
Hairdressers	change–5 per cent
Taxis	3–5 per cent, more if carried luggage
Chambermaids	€1–€2
Porters	€1–€2
Toilet attendants	€1

*Or more if you are impressed with the level of service

10 EVERYDAY ITEMS AND HOW MUCH THEY COST

Takeout sandwich		€2.20–€3.20
Bottle of mineral water	(from a shop, half a litre)	€0.40–€0.80
Cup of coffee	(from a café, espresso)	€1–€1.85
Beer	(half a litre)	€1.85–€2.60
Glass of house wine		€1.85–€2.15
Spanish national newspaper		€1–€1.20
International newspaper		€1.50–€2.30
Litre of petrol	(98 unleaded)	€0.86
	(diesel)	€0.66
Metro ticket	(single)	€1.10
Camera film	(36 pictures)	€4–€5

PLANNING

HEALTH

Spain's national health service works alongside the private sector, and its hospitals are generally of a high standard.

USEFUL NUMBERS

Emergencies (across EU)
112

Ambulance
061

Information Line
010

The Catalan Institute of Health
902 111 444

BEFORE YOU GO

● No inoculations are required, but it is a good idea to check when you last had a tetanus jab and, if more than 10 years ago, have a booster before you travel.
● Spain has a standard agreement with other EU countries entitling EU citizens to a certain amount of free health care, including hospital treatment. You must complete all the necessary paperwork before you travel. In the UK, ask for an E111 form at main post offices.
● If you will need treatment for a pre-existing condition while you are away, such as injections, you should apply to your department of health for an E112. You should only apply if it's necessary and not on a just in case basis.
● You are strongly advised to take out full health insurance, despite this arrangement. For non-EU visitors it's a must.
● US visitors are likely to find that their existing health policy stays effective when they travel abroad, but it is wise to check this before leaving home.
● If you think you will need to renew a prescription, ask your doctor to provide you with the chemical name of the drug before you travel, as it may be marketed under another name in Spain.

IF YOU NEED TREATMENT

● You will need to confirm that the doctor you visit works within the Spanish State Health Service in order to use your E111. Make

it clear that you want to be treated under this system.
● In some clinics there are separate surgery times for private patients and those treated under the health service. Again, make sure you are being treated at the appropriate surgery.
● If you are treated as a private patient, or go to a private health clinic, you will not be entitled to your money back.

HEALTHY FLYING

● Visitors to Spain from as far as the US, Australia or New Zealand may be concerned about the effect of long-haul flights on their health. The most widely publicized concern is Deep Vein Thrombosis, or DVT. Misleadingly called 'economy class syndrome', DVT is the forming of a blood clot in the body's deep veins, particularly in the legs. The clot can move around the bloodstream and could be fatal.
● Those most at risk include the elderly, pregnant women and those using the contraceptive pill, smokers and the overweight. If you are at increased risk of DVT see your doctor before departing. Flying increases the likelihood of DVT because passengers are often seated in a cramped position for long periods of time and may become dehydrated.

To minimize risk:
Drink water (not alcohol)
Don't stay immobile for hours at a time
Stretch and exercise your legs periodically
Do wear elastic flight socks, which support veins and reduce the chances of a clot forming
A small dose of aspirin may be recommended; this thins the blood before the flight.

EXERCISES

1 ANKLE ROTATIONS   **2 CALF STRETCHES**   **3 KNEE LIFTS**

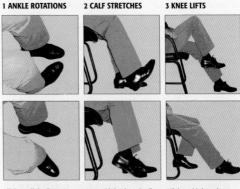

Lift feet off the floor. Draw a circle with the toes, moving one foot clockwise and the other counterclockwise

Start with heel on the floor and point foot upward as high as you can. Then lift heels high keeping balls of feet on the floor

Lift leg with knee bent while contracting your thigh muscle. Then straighten leg pressing foot flat to the floor

Other health hazards for flyers are airborne diseases and bugs spread by the plane's air-conditioning system. These are largely unavoidable but if you have a serious medical condition seek advice from a doctor before flying.

EMERGENCY TREATMENT

The telephone number 061 is for the ambulance service. The number 112 is for help when you are anywhere in Europe.

FINDING A DOCTOR

● A doctor (*médico*) can be found by asking at the local pharmacy (*farmacia*), at your hotel, by calling the city information line on 010 or by

HOSPITALS WITH EMERGENCY DEPARTMENTS (URGÈNCIES)		
Hospital	**Address**	**Telephone**
Centre d'Urgències Perecamps	Avinguda de las Drassanes 13–15	93 441 06 00
Hospital Clínic i Provincial	Carrer de València 184	93 227 54 00
Hospital del Mar	Passeig Marítim Barceloneta 23–31	93 248 30 00
Hospital de la Santa Creu i Sant Pau	Sant Antoni Maria Claret 167	93 291 91 91

Detail of the ornate gates of Hospital de la Santa Creu i Sant Pau

looking in the phone book (*Páginas Amarillas*).

● If you need to see an English-speaking doctor, contact the Centre Mèdic Assistencial de Catalonia, Carrer de Provença 281, tel 93 215 37 93. This is a private clinic and charges apply.

PHARMACIES

● Pharmacies (*farmàcia*) usually have a flashing green cross outside and are found across the city. A pharmacy displays a red or green cross when it is open at night.

● Staff will normally provide excellent over-the-counter advice, often in English. For minor ailments it is usually worth consulting a pharmacist before trying to find a doctor, because of the quality of this advice.

● Many drugs that can only be obtained on prescription in other countries are available without one in Spain, so again, check at a pharmacy.

● A rota system operates so there is always one pharmacy open 24 hours a day. These can be found by checking the pharmacy window for details. Farmàcia Alvarez, Passeig de Gràcia 26 and Farmàcia Clapés, La Rambla 98 are always open 24 hours.

DENTAL TREATMENT

● Dental treatment is expensive in Spain, so it makes sense to have a dental check-up before you depart.

● Check your medical insurance before you go to see if it covers emergency dental treatment.

There is no reciprocal arrangement using an E111.

● A walk-in clinic can be found at Centre Odontològic de Barcelona, Carrer de Calàbria 251, tel 93 439 45 00.

OPTICIANS

● It is a good idea to pack a spare pair of glasses or contact lenses in case you lose or break what you usually wear.

● Opticians can be found in the phone book under *Óptico*, or ask at the nearest pharmacy.

WATER

It is generally safe to drink the tap water (unless it is marked *no potable*), although it may have a strong taste of chlorine. Mineral water (*agua mineral*) is widely available and not expensive. It is sold carbonated (*con gas*) or still (*sin gas*).

SUNSHINE

● The city can get very hot and sunny, and not just in summer. Always protect against sunburn and dehydration by dressing

There are several pharmacies around the city that have Modernista façades

suitably in loose clothing, covering your head, applying high-factor sunscreen (particularly important for children and fair-skinned people) and drinking about 2 litres of water a day in really hot weather.

● During the hottest part of the day you will see few locals about on the streets. The most sensible thing is to go local and have a siesta, or at least stay in the shade between 1pm and 4pm if your itinerary allows it.

COMPLEMENTARY MEDICAL TREATMENT

● Alternative medicine, such as homeopathy and reflexology, is becoming increasingly more popular. It is not offered as part of the Health Service and has no legislation covering it. You should therefore be very careful in your choice.

● You can find a list of homeopathic doctors at the Académia Médica Homeopática de Barcelona, Carrer d'Aragó, tel 93 323 48 36, www.amhb.net.

● CENAC (naturopathy, homeopathy, acupuncture) Rambla de Catalunya 7, tel 93 412 64 10.

● Centro Quiropráctico Gracia-Diagonal (chiropractor) Paseo de Gràcia 106, tel 93 415 11 89, www.quirobarcelona.com.

● Yasumi (reflexology), Via Laietana 38, tel 93 310 41 22.

OPTICIANS			
Optician	**Address**	**Telephone**	**Opening hours**
Arense	Ronda Sant Pere 16	93 301 82 90	Mon–Sat 10–9
Cottet	Carrer de Muntaner 277	93 209 95 55	Mon 10–1, 4.30–8, Tue–Fri 9.30–1.30, 4.30–8, Sat 10–1.30
Cottet	Passieg de Gràcia 47	93 488 35 22	Mon–Sat 10–8.30
Glamoor	Carrer de Calders 10	93 310 39 92	Mon–Sat 11–2, 5–8.30
Grand Optical	El Triangle, Plaça de Catalunya 4	93 304 16 40	Mon–Sat 10–10

PLANNING

FINDING HELP

PERSONAL SAFETY

Barcelona is much like any other Western city when it comes to crime. You should be safe against personal attack, but petty crime, especially pick-pocketing, is fairly common. Visitors who are not on their guard are main targets, so take some sensible precautions:

● Never carry more cash than you need.

● Wear bags slung diagonally across your chest rather than hanging from a shoulder or in a rucksack-type bag. If you use a bag around your waist, don't assume that it's safe, as thieves know that you will be keeping valuables in it. Back pockets are also prone.

● Keep belongings close by in crowded areas and on the metro.

● Be aware of ploys to distract your attention by thieves working in pairs.

● Stick to brightly lit, main thoroughfares at night.

● Never leave belongings on view in a parked car.

● Keep any valuables in the hotel safe.

● Las Ramblas is becoming one of the areas to be most on your guard for pick-pockets, as well as the hustles to separate you from your money. These are ploys like asking which cup the ball is under or card tricks.

WOMEN VISITORS

You should not feel uneasy about visiting Barcelona. You are unlikely to receive any unwanted attention of the clichéd Spanish waiter kind, and if you use the guidelines above, your trip should be a safe one.

POLICE

There are three different types of police force in Spain, each dealing with different aspects of public order.

● *Guardia Urbana*, whose main responsibility is urban traffic, are the local police. They are identifiable by their blue uniforms and the white-checked bands on their vehicles.

● *Policía Nacional*, who wear brown uniforms and berets, deal with law and order and national security.

● *Guardia Civil*, who are responsible for border posts, policing country areas, highways and the coast, wear olive green.

● Catalonia has its own police force, the Mossos d'Escuadra, identifiable by their red berets.

● If you need help, the best option might be at the Turisme-Atenció station, La Rambla 43 (*tel 93 344 13 00*), which is open 24 hours. This is a service especially for visitors to the city, manned by police and with multilingual staff.

● Take the time to report thefts to the police, especially if you intend to make a claim for the loss. You will need a police report to pass on to your insurance company.

The Guardia Urbana *have a strong presence on the street*

LOSS OF PASSPORT

● Always keep a separate note of your passport number and photocopy of the page that carries your details, in case of loss or theft.

● You can also scan the most important pages of your passport and email them to yourself at an email account which you can access anywhere, such as www.hotmail.com.

● If you lose your passport or it is stolen, report it to the police and then contact your nearest embassy or consulate for assistance.

LOST PROPERTY

● If you lose an item around the city, visit the Servei de Troballes at the Ajuntament, Carrer de Cuitat 9, tel 010.

● If you lose something on public transport, you can contact one of the TMB offices (see page 43) to see if it's been handed in. It will then be sent to the Plaça de la Universitat branch for collection.

● If ithe item is not claimed, TMB will send it on to the Servei de Troballes.

LANGUAGE ASSISTANCE

● If you are worried about language barriers, you could buy yourself an Interpreter Card. This is a privately-run operation that originated in Barcelona and was intended to target the business market.

● You buy the card, which is similar to a phone card, for €30 from the tourist office, and follow the printed instructions to activate it. For as long as you have credit, you can call this translation service, which provides translations from Spanish to English, French and German and vice versa. The service is open Mon–Sat 9–9.

PLANNING

OPENING TIMES AND TICKETS

OPENING TIMES

The traditional shutdown at lunchtime and over the weekend is less observed in this city than it is in more rural areas of Spain. However, there are still times when places are shut when you might not expect them to be. The heat of summer means that many places will reduce their opening times or close altogether during August.

BANKS

These are open Monday to Friday 8.30–2, Saturday 8.30–1, but close Saturdays in summer. It is unusual for banks to be open in the afternoon, although savings banks, such as LaCaixa, are open all day Thursday.

MUSEUMS

There is a lot of variation in the opening times for museums and other attractions, so check before you go. Generally, places are closed on Mondays or Tuesdays. It's also likely that small museums will close for lunch.

RESTAURANTS

Lunch is served from around 1pm to 3.30pm, with dinner starting at 9pm onwards. Some will open earlier in the evening to cater for visitors who haven't yet adjusted to Mediterranean time.

SHOPS

Most shops close at around 1.30–2pm and do not reopen until 4–5pm. They are open much later into the evening, often until around 9pm. You will find a number of smaller places close on Saturday afternoons and Sundays. This does happen less often and the larger stores don't observe these times, opening instead throughout the day and on Saturdays.

Nearly all shops close on Sundays, except in the popular La Ribera area and on the two Sundays before Christmas.

PASSES

● If you want to immerse yourself in the city's art, buy the Articket pass, which gives free admission to six art galleries: the Museu National d'Art de Catalunya (MNAC), the Fundació Joan Miró, the Fundació Antoni Tàpies, the Centre de Cultura Contemporània de Barcelona (CCCB), the Centre Cultural Caixa Catalunya (at Casa Milà) and the MACBA. The pass can be bought from any of the museums' ticket offices or the tourist office at Plaça de Catalunya. It is valid for three months and costs €15.
● Ruta del Modernisme is a walk around the city's major Modernista buildings, including Casa Milà, Palau Güell, Palau de la Música and the Sagrada Família. The free route map is available from the Centre del Modernisme in the Casa Amatller (see pages 82–83).
● The Centre del Modernisme also sells a discount ticket, which gives you 50 per cent off entry to a small number of sights and costs €3.
● When you buy either the Barcelona Card or a Bus Turístic ticket (see page 43) you will also get discounted entry to a whole host of places.

DISCOUNTS

● Seniors can get reductions on some museum entry charges on production of an identity document.
● An International Student Identity Card (ISIC; www.isic.org) may help obtain free or reduced entry to many museums and attractions as well as other discounts at stores.
● Many museums and attractions have lower admission charges for children, and those under 5 often get in free.

NATIONAL HOLIDAYS

● If you find you are in the city on one of the days in the table (right) and you want to visit a particular sight, you should phone ahead to check if it's open.

Opening times vary from establishment to establishment, so check before you go

● If a national holiday falls on a Thursday or Friday, it's possible that celebrations will extend over the weekend, particularly if it's one of the more important days.
● The National Day of Spain on 12 October is not widely celebrated in Barcelona, but is marked by residents with a day off. The date commemorates the discovery of America.

NATIONAL HOLIDAYS
1 January
New Year's Day*
6 January
Epiphany*
March/April
Good Friday and Easter weekend*
1 May
Labour Day
May/June
Monday after Pentecost (Whit Monday)
24 June
St. John's Day*
15 August
Feast of the Assumption
11 September
National Day of Catalonia*
25 September
Feast of La Mercè*
12 October
National Day of Spain
1 November
All Saints' Day*
6 December
Constitution Day
8 December
Feast of the Immaculate Conception
25 December
Christmas Day*
26 December
St. Stephen's Day*
*Denotes a holiday that is most respected and observed.

PLANNING

COMMUNICATION

TELEPHONES

National numbers: All telephone numbers in Spain have a nine-digit number, which includes the area code—all area codes start with a 9. You must include the area code even when making a local call. Some provinces have two-digit codes, others have three digits. In Barcelona it is 93. The state telephone company is Telefónica.

Staying in touch with home

International calls: To call Spain from the US, prefix the area code and number with 011 34; from the UK prefix with 00 34. To call the US from Spain prefix the area code and number with 001; to call the UK, dial 00 44, then drop the first 0 from the area code. See the table opposite for more country codes.

CALL CHARGES

- Cheap international calls can be made between 8pm and 8am during the week and throughout the weekends.
- Using the telephone in your hotel room is bound to be more expensive than using a pay phone out on the street, whatever time you call.
- A small additional charge is made for connecting to some countries, which varies between €0.15–€0.20.

PUBLIC TELEPHONES

- Public phone boxes are blue and you won't have to go far to find one. Look out for the *telefono* signs.
- They operate with both coins

and phone cards (*tarjeta telefonica* or *credifone*), available from newsstands, post offices and tobacconists, and have instructions printed in English. Phones will accept 1 and 2 euro coins as well as 5, 10, 20 and 50 cents or phone cards of €6, €12 and €30.
- The international operator number is 1008 for Europe, 1005 for the rest of the world. For national directory enquiries, ring 11818.
- There are a number of phone rooms (*locutorios*) across the

city, where you pay the attendant at the end of your call. These can be the cheapest way to make calls to countries outside Europe and the US, such as Australia or Asiatic countries. But for national, European and US calls, the charges are the same.

USING A COIN OPERATED PHONE

1 Lift the receiver and listen for the dialing tone.

3 Dial or press the number.

2 Insert the required coin or coins. The coin drops as soon as you insert it.

4 If you want to cancel the call before it is answered, or if the call does not connect, press the coin release lever or hang up and take the coins from the coin return.

5 The call is answered.

AREA CODES WITHIN SPAIN

Madrid	91
Barcelona	93
Seville	95
Bilbao, Vizcaya	94
Valencia	96
Santander	942
Navarra	948
Granada	958

INTERNATIONAL DIALLING CODES

Australia	00 61
Belgium	00 32
Canada	00 1
France	00 33
Germany	00 49
Greece	00 30
Ireland	00 353
Italy	00 39
Netherlands	00 31
New Zealand	00 64
Spain	00 34
Sweden	00 46
UK	00 44
USA	00 1

CALL CHARGES FROM PUBLIC PAY PHONES (PER MINUTE)

	Peak rate	Reduced rate
Local	€0.06	€0.04
National	€0.10	€0.06
Western Europe	€0.18	€0.18
Eastern Europe	€0.40	€0.40
USA	€0.18	€0.18
North Africa	€0.40	€0.40
Australia	€0.96	€0.96
India	€0.96	€0.96
Japan	€0.96	€0.96
China	€0.96	€0.96

Street	Telephone	Opening hours
Carrer de Sant Pau 32–38	93 318 40 58	Daily 10–midnight
Carrer de Canvis Vells 11	–	Daily 10–midnight
Plaça de Catalunya (in RENFE rail station below the Plaça)	–	Daily 9–9
Avinguda de Roma 79–81	–	Daily 10am–11pm

A Spanish SIM card in your mobile will cut call charges

MOBILE PHONES

● Check with your phone company before leaving home that you can use your phone abroad and what the call charges will be.

● You will be charged for picking up calls when not in your home country.

● If your mobile phone SIM card is removable, it makes sense to replace it with a Spanish card on arrival. You will then be able to use the Spanish mobile system at local rates.

● You can rent mobile phones in Barcelona from Rent a Phone, Carrer de Numància 212, tel 93 280 21 31, or Maremagnum, Moll d'Espanya s/n, tel 93 225 81 06, www.rphone.es. But this is likely to be an expensive option.

ADDRESSES IN SPAIN

● The abbreviation s/n stands for *sin número* and signifies a building that has no street number. This is mostly used by businesses, shops and museums.

● The abbreviation o, as in 1o, stands for *primero piso* (first floor) and signifies the floor of a building in an address.

● The letter a, as in 1a, stands for *primera puerta* (first door) and signifies the number of an apartment.

SENDING AND RECEIVING POST

● Stamps (*sellos* in Castilian; *segells* in Catalan) are available from tobacconists (*estancos*), where you will see a brown and yellow symbol. Some hotels also sell them and have a post box you can use.

● Post boxes are bright yellow. Red post boxes are for urgent mail which is collected more often, but there are few of these.

● The postal service is not fast. Letters and postcards to other EU countries will take up to a week to arrive and up to two weeks to the US.

Post boxes, in distinctive yellow, are easy to find in Barcelona

● Use the address Lista de Correos, 08070 Barcelona, Spain if you want to be able to collect mail while on holiday. You will need to take your passport with you to collect it.

● Say something is *urgente* if you want to send it express.

● Use the Postal Exprés system if you want to send a parcel within Spain. It guarantees next-day delivery to main cities or

POST OFFICE BRANCHES
Avinguda Paral.lel 86
Avinguda Pedralbes 22
Carrer de Balmes 76
Carrer de València 231
Gran de Gràcia 118
Plaça Bonsuccès s/n
Plaça Urquinaona 6
El Prat Airport, terminal B
Ronda de Universitat 23

within 48 hours to the rest of the country.

● The current rates for sending a letter (up to 20g) are: within Spain €0.25, within Europe €0.50, rest of the world €1.30.

POST OFFICES

● The city's main post office (*correos*) is at Plaça d'Antoni López, open Mon–Sat 8.30am–9.30pm, Sun 9–2, www.correos.es.

● There are lots of branches around the city (see table below). Opening times for these branches are generally 8.30am–8.30pm.

INTERNET ACCESS

● This is becoming common across the city and there is a growing range of internet and cyber cafés (see table below). Internet access is also available at some libraries.

Cyber Mundo
Carrer de Bergara 3
www.cybermundobcn.com

Cyber Mundo
Carrer de Balmes 8
www.cybermundobcn.com

Easy Everything
Ronda Universitat 35
www.easyeverything.com

Easy Everything
La Rambla 41
www.easyeverything.com

Inetcorner
Carrer Sardenya 306
www.inetcorner.net

Interlight C@fe
Carrer de Pau Claris 106
interlight@bcn.servicom.es

● Set up an email account with a provider such as Hotmail (www.hotmail.com) or Yahoo (www.yahoo.com). Do this before you leave home and you will be able to send and receive emails while you are away.

PLANNING

MEDIA

TELEVISION

Television is loved in Spain and you will find that many local bars have a TV set tuned into a news or sports channel. There are lots of channels, but the ones that you are likely to come across are listed below.

● The two national state-run channels are TVE1, which shows Hollywood films, reality TV and music shows, and TVE2, which is dedicated to culture with documentaries, interviews and European films.

● TV3 is a Catalan station with a wide-ranging schedule entirely in Catalan: a good place to practise your language skills.

● Canal 33 is another Catalan station that shows films and documentaries.

● Most hotels have satellite, cable or digital television that will allow you to view international channels such as BBC World, CNN and Sky.

RADIO

Most stations in Barcelona are on the FM frequency and the majority of these tend to be music based.

● The state-run public radio company is Radio Nacional de Espana (RNE), which has a current affairs station (RNE 1, 738AM), a classical music station (Radio Clásica 99FM), a pop music station (Radio 3, 98.7FM) and a sports and entertainment station (RNE 5, 576AM).

● You can get the BBC World Service on 15485, 12095,

NEWSPAPERS	
ABC	A national, conservative daily
Avui	A Catalan nationalist daily
El Mundo	A national, centre-right daily
El Pais	A national daily with a Catalonian edition that leans to the left
El Periodico de Catalunya	A Catalan, centre-left daily
La Razon	A right-wing national daily
La Vanguardia	A Catalan daily that is more conservative with excellent listings sections

9410 and 6195 short wave, depending on the time of day.

NEWSPAPERS AND MAGAZINES

Newspaper readership in Spain is not as high as in other European countries, with TV and radio regarded as more entertaining purveyors of information. However, there is a still a very wide choice available.

● Spain's most popular national newspapers are *El Pais* and *El Mundo*, both of which have very informative events listings, particularly in the weekend editions.

● The biggest selling newspaper in the city is Barcelona's own *La Vanguardia*.

● Popular English-language newspapers and magazines are on sale at stands along Las Ramblas and at newsagents in Gràcia. US publications such as the *International Herald Tribune*, *USA Today* and the *Wall Street Journal* are also readily available. They tend to appear in the afternoon of the day of publication, if not the next day.

● An English language version of *El Pais* is available inside *The Herald Tribune*, Mon–Sat.

● The magazine market is dominated by TV weeklies and celebrity gossip glossies, with the queen of them all, *¡Hola!*, continuing to thrive.

La Vanguardia, *the city's own newspaper, is widely read (left); stands on Las Ramblas sell a range of newspapers (below)*

BOOKS, MAPS AND FILMS

BOOKS

● *Homage to Catalonia* (Penguin Modern Classics) is George Orwell's bittersweet memoir of his experiences as a member of the International Brigade during the Spanish Civil War and is a moving account of a time in Barcelona's history that was inspirational to the young writer.

● *Gaudí: a Biography* (Harper Collins, 2002) by Gijs van Hensbergen is the most complete critical biography of the great architect, a man who gave his life to his art and was cut down by a tram outside his beloved Sagrada Família to die later in a pauper's hospital.

● The first volume of John Richardson's definitive *A Life of Picasso* (Pimlico, 1997) is a fascinating account of the artist's early life in the city that was to shape his artistic sensibility for the rest of his life. This story of Picasso's formative years spent with the great Catalan artists of the age is a vivid account of turn-of-the-20th-century Barcelona, an artistic hothouse that moved to a distinctly bohemian beat.

● *Barcelona* (Harvill, 2001) by Robert Hughes provides a complete overview of Catalan art and the Catalan character, and attempts to get closer to the reasons why this corner of the Iberian peninsula has always stood out for its distinctive traditions and attention to detail. The book wasn't well received among many Catalans who objected to an outsider's perspective of their beloved city, but remains to this day the most complete and accessible account of Barcelona available in English.

● It is hard to find English translations of the many Catalan writers who chronicle life in their hometown, one exception being Eduardo Mendoza, who has written a number of novels set in the city. *City of Marvels* (Harvill, 1988) is his account of the difficulties of life in turn-of-the-20th-century Barcelona.

● Another is *The Soldiers of Salamis* (*Soldados de Salamina*) by the Catalan writer Javier Cercas. It was published in May 2003 by Bloomsbury and was one of Spain's most impressive best-sellers for three years. The

Hunt around in local shops for a book bargain, or try the larger stores for the latest release

novel tells the story of the last days of the Spanish Civil War in Catalonia and the retreat of the republican army to the Pyrenees.

● *Homage to Barcelona* (Picador, 2002) by Colm Toibin is an informative, visitor abroad account of the history of Barcelona and life in the Catalan capital today.

MAPS
There is a street map at the back of this guide (see pages 278–291) and a metro map in the inside back cover. All the tourist offices have free street maps if you want to pick up something else while you are out there. Free metro and pocket bus maps are available from stations and the TBM offices (see page 43).

FILMS
Barcelona has great locations for directors looking to give their films historical detail or to use as a spectacular backdrop to tell their stories.

● Pedro Almodóvar won an Oscar for his direction of *All About My Mother* (1999), which he considered a tribute to Barcelona, a city he has always admired for its sense of freedom. The film captures Barcelona's essence in its melodramatic portrayal of a place of larger than life characters.

● Catalonia's best-known director is probably Bigas Luna, whose

films are always controversial in their treatment of quintessentially Spanish obsessions. His film *La Teta y La Luna* (1994), which was shot in and around Barcelona, is the story of a young boy who falls in love with a breast.

● Veteran director Carlos Saura's *Marathon* (1993), the official film of the 1992 Olympic Games, is a beautifully shot record of one of the proudest moments in Barcelona's more recent history.

● Ken Loach's *Land and Freedom* (1994), loosely based on Orwell's book, charts the adventures of a young English communist in Spain during the Spanish Civil War.

● *Gaudí Afternoon* (2001) is the American director Susan Seidelman's film, based on a novel of the same name by Barbara Wilson. It uses Gaudí's buildings as a backdrop to this comedy.

● Whit Stillman's *Barcelona* (1994) deals with one specific moment in Spain's history. The year of 1989 was a time when Spain was opening itself up to the world and political tensions simmered beneath the surface. Again, the film uses the city as its backdrop.

TOURIST OFFICES

Tourist offices are identified by the use of the letter i and have a number of diamonds over the top of it. They don't have their own telephone numbers, as one central number serves all of them.

● The largest of the city's tourist offices is at Plaça de Catalunya. Here you will find the biggest selection of services: information on places of interest, transport and culture, a booking service for last-minute accommodation, an excellent gift shop and a branch of Caixa de Catalunya, which will change money for you and allow you to buy tickets from its Tel-entrada system (see page 155).

● Plaça de Sant Jaume has information, an accommodation booking service and a branch of Caixa de Catalunya; Estació de Sants has information and a branch of Caixa de Catalunya; and the airport has visitor information and an accommodation booking service.

● An army of people in red jackets take to the city streets in summer (Jun–end Sep), ready to assist visitors. They are known as Casaques Vermelles (red jackets) and work in pairs.

TOURIST OFFICES

Plaça de Catalunya
Open: daily 9–9
National calls: tel 807 117 222 (€0.40 per minute)
International calls: +34 93 368 97 30
www.barcelonaturisme.com

Plaça Sant Jaume
(inside the Town Hall, Carrer Ciutat 2)
Open: Mon–Fri 9–8, Sat 10–8, Sun and holidays 10–2

Estacio de Sants, Plaça dels Països Catalans
Open: daily 8–8, Jul–end Aug; Mon–Fri 8–8, Sat–Sun and holidays 8–2, rest of year

Airport terminals A and B Open: daily 9–9

SPANISH TOURIST OFFICES ABROAD

Australia
1st Floor, 178 Collins Street, Melbourne, VIC
tel 03/9650 7377

Canada
34th Floor, 2 Bloor Street West, Toronto, Ontario M4W 3E2
tel 416/961-3131
www.tourspain.toronto.on.ca

Germany
Myliusstrasse 14, 60325 Frankfurt Main, Frankfurt
tel 69 72 50 33

UK and Republic of Ireland
22–23 Manchester Square, London W1U 3PX
tel 0207 486 8077
www.tourspain.co.uk

USA
Los Angeles: 8383 Wilshire Boulevard, Suite 960, Beverley Hills, CA 90211
tel 323/658-7188
New York: 666 Fifth Avenue, 35th Floor, New York 10103
tel 212/265-8822
www.okspain.org

CATALAN TOURIST BOARDS OPEN TO THE PUBLIC
France
4-6-8 Cour du Commerce, St. André, 75006 Paris, tel 33 140 468 614

Spain
Punt d'Informació Turística, Serrano 1, 28001 Madrid, tel 91 431 00 70 or 91 431 00 22

USEFUL WEBSITES

www.barcelonaturisme.com
This is the official tourist site and it covers a vast range of topics and has lots of helpful information. It's biggest drawback is that you have to dig around for the information, which is hidden under some very broad headings (in Castilian, Catalan, English and French).

www.bestbarcelonahotels.com
This site has a good selection of mid-priced hotels, with on-line booking (in English).

www.bcn.es
Run by the city council, this site is aimed at local residents. But it does have a good section on tourism with information on opening times, plus practical information, such as where the nearest hospital is (in Castilian, Catalan and English).

www.fodors.com
A comprehensive travel-planning site that lets you research prices and book air tickets, aimed at the American market (in English).

www.renfe.es
Make use of the official site of the national railway company for information on arriving by train, and for trips out into Catalonia and beyond (see page 51 and 194–203; in Castilian and English).

www.theaa.com
If you are planning to drive to the city or rent a car when you are there, visit this site for up-to-date travel advice (in English).

www.tmb.net
This is the very useful website of Barcelona's local transport company, with route options and advice on fares (in Castilian, Catalan and English).

www.webarcelona.com
A good site with lots of general information and an excellent section that translates dishes on restaurant menus into English (in English, Dutch, Spanish and French).

PLANNING

WORDS AND PHRASES

Catalan pronunciation differs considerably from Castilian (Spanish). It is more closed and less staccato than Castilian, but is likewise nearly always phonetic, with a few rules. When a word ends in a vowel, an n or an s, the stress is usually on the penultimate syllable; otherwise, it falls on the last syllable. If a word has an accent, this is where the stress falls. Both languages are summarized below.

Catalan

au	ow as in wow
c	ss or k (never th)
ç	ss
eu	ay-oo
g	g or j (never h)
gu	(sometimes) w
h	silent
j	j (never h)
ig	ch at the end of a word: *vaig* sounds like batch
ll	lli as in million
l.l	ll as in silly
ny	as in canyon
r/rr	heavily rolled
s	z or ss
tg/tj	dge as in lodge
tx	ch as in cheque
v	b (*vi*, wine, sounds like 'bee')
x	sh as in shake

Spanish

a	as in pat	ai, ay	as i in side
e	as in set	au	as ou in out
i	as e in be	ei, ey	as ey in they
o	as in hot	oi, oy	as oy in boy
u	as in flute		

Consonants as in English except:

c	before i and e as th
ch	as ch in church
d	at the end of a word becomes th
g	before i or e becomes ch as in loch
h	is silent
j	as ch in loch
ll	as lli in million
ñ	as ny in canyon
qu	is hard like a k
r	usually rolled
v	is a b
z	is a th, *but s in parts of Andalucía*

The words and phrases are given in Catalan, then the *Spanish*.

Is there a bank/bureau de change nearby?
Hi ha un banc/una oficina de canvi a prop?
Hay un banco/una oficina de cambio cerca?

Can I cash this here?
Puc cobrar això aquí?
¿Puedo cobrar esto aquí?

I'd like to change sterling/ dollars into euros
Vull canviar lliures/dòlars a euros
Quiero cambiar libras/ dólares a euros

Can I use my credit card to withdraw cash?
Puc fer servir la targeta de crèdit per a treure diners?
¿Puedo usar la tarjeta de crédito para sacar dinero?

What is the exchange rate?
Com està el canvi?
¿Cómo está el cambio?

COLOURS

black	grey
negre	gris
negro	*gris*
blue	red
blau	vermell
azul	*rojo*
brown	white
marró	blanc
marrón	*blanco*
green	yellow
verd	groc
verde	*amarillo*

USEFUL WORDS

yes/no	there	when	who	large	bad
sí/no	allà	quan	qui	gran	dolent
sí/no	*allí*	*cuándo*	*quién*	*grande*	*malo*
please	where	why	I'm sorry	small	open
si us plau	on	per què	Em sap greu	petit	obert
por favor	*dónde*	*por qué*	*Lo siento*	*pequeño*	*abierto*
thank you	here	how	excuse me	good	closed
gràcies	aquí	com	perdoni	bo	tancat
gracias	*aquí*	*cómo*	*perdone*	*bueno*	*cerrado*

When does the shop open/close?
A quina hora obre/tanca la botiga?
¿A qué hora abre/cierra la tienda?

Could you help me, please?
Que em pot atendre, si us plau?
¿Me atiende, por favor?

How much is this?
Quant costa això?
¿Cuánto cuesta esto?

I'm looking for…
Busco…
Busco…

I'm just looking
Només miro
Sólo estoy mirando

I'd like…
Voldria…
Quisiera…

I'll take this
M'enduc això
Me llevo esto

Do you have anything smaller/larger
Té alguna cosa més petita/gran?
¿Tiene algo más pequeño/grande?

Please can I have a receipt?
Em dóna un rebut, si us plau?
¿Me da un recibo, por favor?

Do you accept credit cards?
Accepten targetes de crèdit?
¿Aceptan tarjetas de crédito?

bakery
el forn
la panadería

bookshop
la llibreria
la librería

butcher's shop
la carnisseria
la carnicería

fishmonger's
la peixateria
la pescadería

jewellers
la joieria
la joyería

pharmacy
la farmàcia
la farmacia

market
el mercat
el mercado

shoeshop
la sabateria
la zapatería

supermarket
el supermercat
el supermercado

Do you have a room?
Té una habitació?
¿Tiene una habitación?

I have a reservation for … nights
Tinc una reserva per a … nits
Tengo una reserva para … noches

How much per night?
Quant és per nit?
¿Cuánto por noche?

May I see the room?
Que puc veure l'habitació?
¿Puedo ver la habitación?

Single room
Habitació individual
Habitación individual

Twin room
Habitació doble amb dos llits
Habitación doble con dos camas

Double room
Habitació doble amb llit de matrmoni
Habitación doble con cama de matrimonio

With bath/shower/lavatory
Amb banyera/dutxa/vàter
Con bañera/ducha/váter

Is the room air-conditioned/heated?
Té aire condicionat/calefacció l'habitacío?
¿Tiene aire acondicionado/calefacción la habitación?

The room is too hot/cold
Fa massa calor/fred a l'habitació
Hace demasiado calor/frío en la habitación

non smoking
no fumeu
se prohibe fumar

I'll take this room
Em quedo l'habitació
Me quedo con la habitación

Is there a lift in the hotel?
Hi ha ascensor a l'hotel?
¿Hay ascensor en el hotel?

Is breakfast/lunch/dinner included in the price?
S'inclou el desdejuni/el dinar/el sopar en el preu?
¿Está el desayuno/la comida/la cena incluido/-a en el precio?

When is breakfast served?
A quina hora se serveix el desdejuni?
¿A qué hora se sirve el desayuno?

I am leaving this morning
Me'n vaig aquest matí
Me voy esta mañana

Please can I pay my bill?
El compte, si us plau
La cuenta, por favor

Will you look after my luggage until I leave?
Em pot guardar l'equipatge fins que me'n vagi?
¿Me puede guardar el equipaje hasta que me vaya?

Could you please order a taxi for me?
Em demana un taxi, si us plau?
¿Me pide un taxi, por favor?

swimming pool
la piscina
la piscina

See also the menu reader on pages 212–213.

What time does the restaurant open?
A quina hora obre el restaurant?
¿A qué hora abre el restaurante?

I'd like to reserve a table for …. people at …
Voldria reservar una taula per a … persones per a les …
Quiero reservar una mesa para … personas para las…

We'd like to wait for a table
Ens volem esperar fins que hi hagi una taula
Queremos esperar a que haya una mesa

A table for …, please
Una taula per a …, si us plau
Una mesa para … por favor

Could we sit here?
Que podem seure aquí?
¿Nos podemos sentar aquí?

Is this table free?
Està lliure aquesta taula?
¿Está libre esta mesa?

Could we see the menu/wine list?
Podem veure la carta/carta de vins?
¿Podemos ver la carta/carta de vinos?

What do you recommend?
Què ens recomana?
¿Qué nos recomienda?

Is there a dish of the day?
Té un plat del dia?
¿Tiene un plato del día?

How much is this dish?
Què costa aquest plat?
¿Cuánto cuesta este plato?

I am a vegetarian
Sóc vegetarià
Soy vegetariano

The food is cold
El menjar és fred
La comida está fría

The food was excellent
El menjar ha estat excel.lent
La comida ha sido excelente

I ordered …
He demanat …
Yo pedí …

This is not what I ordered
Això no és el que jo he demanat
Esto no es lo que yo he pedido

Can I have the bill, please?
Em duu el compte, si us plau?
¿Me trae la cuenta, por favor?

Is service included?
Que hi ha inclòs el servei?
¿Está incluido el servicio?

The bill is not right
El compte no està bé
La cuenta no está bien

waiter/waitress
el cambrer/la cambrera
el camarero/la camarera

Where is the information desk?
On hi ha el taulell d'informació?
¿Dónde está el mostrador de información?

Where is the train/bus station?
On hi ha l'estació de trens/autobusos?
¿Dónde está la estación de trenes/autobuses?

Where is the timetable?
On hi ha l'horari?
¿Dónde está el horario?

Does this train/bus go to…?
Va aquest tren/autobús a…?
¿Va este tren/autobús a…?

Does this train/bus stop at…?
S'atura aquest tren/aoutobús a…?
¿Para este tren/autobús en…?

Do I have to get off here?
He de baixar aquí?
¿Me tengo que bajar aquí?

Do you have a subway/bus map?
Té un mapa del metro/dels autobusos?
¿Tiene un mapa del metro/de los autobuses?

Can I have a single/return ticket to…
Em dóna un bitllet senzill/d'anada i tornada a…?
¿Me da un billete sencillo/de ida y vuelta para…?

How much is a ticket?
Quant costa un bitllet?
¿Cuánto vale un boleto?

Is this the way to…?
Aquest és el camí per a anar a…?
¿Es éste el camino para ir a…?

Where can I find a taxi?
On puc trobar un taxi?
¿Dónde puedo encontrar un taxi?

Please take me to…
A…, si us plau
A…, por favor

I'd like to get out here, please
Parí aquí, si us plau
Pare aquí, por favor

Go straight on
Continuï de dret
Siga recto

Turn left
Tombi a l'esquerra
Tuerza a la izquierda

Turn right
Tombi a la dreta
Tuerza a la derecha

Cross over
Passi a l'altre costat
Cruce al otro lado

ferry
el transbordador
el ferry

smoking/non smoking
fumadors/no fumadors
fumadores/no fumadores

Train/bus station
L'estació de trens/autobusos
La estación de trenes/autobuses

What is the time?
Quina hora és?
¿Qué hora es?

Write that down for me, please
Què m'ho pot escriure?
¿Me lo puede escribir?

Good morning/afternoon
Bon dia/Bona tarda
Buenos días/Buenas tardes

I don't speak Catalán/Spanish
No parlo català/espanyol
No hablo catalán/español

My name is…
Em dic…
Me llamo…

Good evening/night
Bona nit
Buenas noches

Do you speak English?
Parla anglès?
¿Habla inglés?

What's your name?
Com es diu?
¿Cómo se llama?

Goodbye
Adéu-siau
Adiós

I don't understand
No ho entenc
No entiendo

Hello, pleased to meet you
Hola, molt de gust
Hola, encantado/a

See you later
Fins després
Hasta luego

Please repeat that
Si us plau, repeteixi això
Por favor, repita eso

I'm from…
Sóc de…
Soy de…

I don't know
No ho sé
No lo sé

Please speak more slowly
Si us plau, parlimés a poc a poc
Por favor, hable más despacio

This is my wife/daughter/husband/son
Aquesta és la meva dona/filla/Aquest és el meu marit/fill
Esta es mi mujer/hija/marido/hijo

You're welcome
De res
De nada

What does this mean?
Què significa això?
¿Qué significa esto?

How are you?
Com estàs?
¿Cómo estás?

This is my friend
Aquest és el meu amic
Este es mi amigo

May I/Can I?
Puc?
Puedo?

Excuse me, I think I'm lost
Perdoni, em sembla que m'he perdut
Perdone, creo que me he perdido

I live in…
Visc a…
Vivo en…

That's all right
D'acord
Está bien

English	Catalan	Spanish	English	Catalan	Spanish	English	Catalan	Spanish
morning **el matí** *la mañana*	tomorrow **demà** *mañana*	Monday **dilluns** *lunes*	week **la setmana** *la semana*	May **maig** *mayo*	December **desembre** *diciembre*			
afternoon **la tarda** *la tarde*	now **ara** *alora*	Tuesday **dimarts** *martes*	month **el mes** *el mes*	June **juny** *junio*	Easter **Pàsqua** *Semana Santa*			
evening **el vespre** *la tarde*	later **més tard** *más tarde*	Wednesday **dimecres** *miércoles*	year **l'any** *el año*	July **juliol** *julio*	Christmas **Nadal** *Navidad*			
day **el dia** *el día*	spring **primavera** *primavera*	Thursday **dijous** *jueves*	January **gener** *enero*	August **agost** *agosto*	pilgrimage **romeria** *romería*			
night **la nit** *la noche*	summer **estiu** *verano*	Friday **divendres** *viernes*	February **febrer** *febrero*	September **setembre** *septiembre*	holiday (vacation) **vacances** *vacaciones*			
today **avui** *hoy*	autumn **tardor** *otoño*	Saturday **dissabte** *sábado*	March **març** *marzo*	October **octubre** *octubre*				
yesterday **ahir** *ayer*	winter **hivern** *invierno*	Sunday **diumenge** *domingo*	April **abril** *abril*	November **novembre** *noviembre*				

Where is the tourist information office, please?
On hi ha l'oficinal d'informació, si us plau?
¿Dónde está la oficina de información, por favor?

Do you have a city map?
Té un plànol de la ciutat?
¿Tiene un plano de la ciudad?

Can you give me some information about…?
Té cap informació sobre…?
¿Tiene alguna información sobre…?

I am interested in…
M'interessen…
Me interesan

What time does it open/close?
A quina hora obre/tanca?
¿A qué hora abre/cierra?

Are there organized excursions?
Hi ha excursions organitzades?
¿Tiene alguna excursións organizada?

Are there boat trips?
Hi ha excursions amb vaixell?
¿Hay paseos en barco?

Are there guided tours?
Hi ha visites amb guia?
¿Hay visitas con guía?

Where do they go?
On van?
¿Dónde vamos?

Is there an English-speaking guide?
Hi ha cap guia que parli anglès?
¿Hay algún guía que hable inglés?

Is photography allowed?
S'hi poden fer fotos?
¿Se pueden hacer fotos?

What is the admission price?
Quant costa l'entrada?
¿Cuánto cuesta la entrada?

Where is the museum?
On hi ha el museu?
¿Dónde está la museo?

Can we make reservations here?
Podem fer-ne les reserves aquí?
¿Podemos hacer las reservas aquí?

Could you reserve tickets for me?
Em pot reservar les entrades?
¿Me puede reservar las entradas?

Could I book … tickets for the … performance?
Podria reservar … entrades per a la funció de …?
¿Podría reservar … entradas para la función de …?

Is there a discount for senior citizens/students?
Fan descompte per a la tercera edat/els estudiants?
¿Hacen descuento para la tercera edad/los estudiantes?

What time does the show start?
A quina hora comença la funció?
¿A qué hora empieza la función?

I don't feel well
No em trobo bé
No me encuentro bien

Could you call a doctor?
Pot cridar un metge?
¿Puede llamar a un médico?

I feel nauseous
Estic marejat/Tinc ganes de vomitar
Tengo ganas de vomitar

I have a headache
Em fa mal el cap
Me duele la cabeza

I am allergic to…
Sóc al.lèrgic a…
Soy alérgico a…

I am on medication
Estic amb medicació
Estoy con medicación

How many tablets a day should I take?
Quantes pastilles m'he de prendre al dia?
¿Cuántas pastillas tengo que tomar al día?

I need to see a doctor/dentist
Necessito un metge/dentista
Necesito un médico/dentista

I have a bad toothache
Tinc un mal de queixals horrible
Tengo un dolor de muelas horrible

Can you recommend a dentist?
Que em pot recomanar un dentista?
¿Me puede recomendar un dentista?

Where is the hospital?
On hi ha l'hospital?
¿Dónde esta el hospital?

Call the fire brigade/police/ambulance
Truqui als bombers/la policia/una ambulància
Llame a los bomberos/la policía/una ambulancia

I have had an accident
He tingut un accident
He tenido un accidente

I have been robbed
M'han robat
Me han robado

I have lost my passport/wallet/purse/handbag
He perdut el passaport/la cartera/el moneder/la bossa
He perdido el pasaporte/la cartera/el monedero/el bolso

Is there a lost property office?
Que hi ha una oficina d'objectes perduts?
¿Hay una oficina de objetos perdidos?

Where is the police station?
On hi ha la comissaria?
¿Dónde está la comisaría?

Help!
Auxili
Socorro

Stop thief!
Al lladre
Al ladrón

1 u (un, una)/ *uno*	7 set/*siete*	13 tretze/*trece*	18 divuit/ *dieciocho*	40 quaranta/ *cuarenta*	90 noranta/ *noventa*
2 dos/*dos*	8 vuit/*ocho* 9 nou/*nueve*	14 catorze/ *catorce* 15 quinze/ *quince*	19 dinou/ *diecinueve* 20 vint/*veinte*	50 cinquanta/ *cincuenta* 60 seixanta/ *sesenta*	100 cent/*cien* 200 dos-cents/ *doscientos*
3 tres/*tres* 4 quatre/*cuatro*	10 deu/*diez* 11 onze/*once*	16 setze/ *dieciséis*	21 vint-i-u/ *veintiuno*	70 setanta/ *setenta*	1,000 mil/*mil*
5 cinc/*cinco* 6 sis/*seis*	12 dotze/ *doce*	17 disset/ *diecisiete*	30 trenta/ *treinta*	80 vuitanta/ *ochenta*	million milió/*millón*

bridge
el pont
el puente

castle
el castell
el castillo

cathedral
la catedral
la catedral

church
l'església
la iglesia

gallery
la galeria d'art
la galería de arte

lavatories
els lavabos
los aseos

monument
el monument
el monumento

museum
el museu
el museo

palace
el palau
el palacio

old town
la ciutat vella
la ciudad vieja

park
el parc
el parque

river
el riu
el río

town
la ciutat
la ciudad

town hall
el ajuntament
el ayuntamiento

corner
la cantonada
la esquina

entrance
entrada
entrada

exit
sortida
salida

intersection
l'encreuament
el cruce

traffic lights
el semàfor
el semáforo

no parking
prohibit aparcar
prohibido aparcar

pedestrian zone
zona per a vianants
zona peatonal

Can you direct me to...?
Com es va a...?
¿Cómo se va a...?

Where is the nearest post office/mail box?
On hi ha l'oficina de correus més pròxima/la bústia més pròxima?
¿Dónde está la oficina de correos más cercana/el buzón más cercano?

What is the postage to...
Quant costa enviar-ho a...?
¿Cuánto vale mandarlo a...?

I'd like to send this by air mail
Vull enviar això correu aeri
Quiero mandar esto por correo aéreo

Where can I buy a phone card?
On puc omprar una targeta telefònica?
¿Dónde puedo comprar una tarjeta de teléfono?

I'd like to speak to...
Voldria parlar amb...?
¿Me puede poner con...?

Who is this speaking, please?
Amb qui parlo, si us plau?
¿Con quién hablo, por favor?

Have there been any calls for me?
Que hi ha hagut cap telefonada per a mi?
¿Ha habido alguna llamada para mi?

Please ask him/her to call back
Li pot dir que em telefoni
Le puede decir que me llame

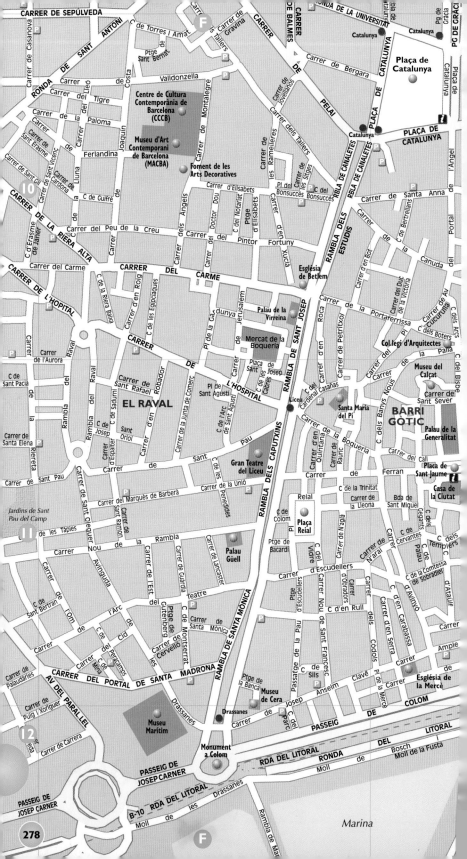

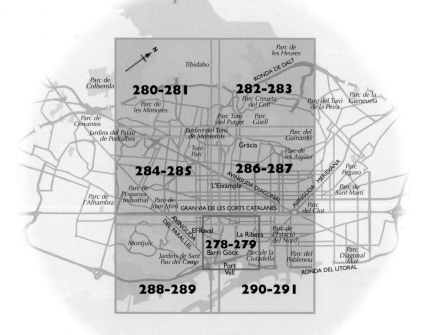

Parc de
les Heures

Tibidabo

RONDA DE DALT

Parc de
Collserola

280-281

282-283

Parc Creueta
del Coll

Parc del Turó
de la Peira

Parc de la
Guineueta

Parc de
les Mimoses

Parc de
Cervantes

Parc Turó
del Putget

Parc
Güell

Jardins del Palau
de Pedralbes

Jardins del Turó
de Monterols

Parc del
Guinardó

Turó
Parc

Gràcia

284-285

286-287

Parc de
les Aigües

AVINGUDA DIAGONAL

Parc
Pegaso

AVINGUDA MERIDIANA

L'Eixample

Parc de
l'Espanya
Industrial

Parc de
Joan Miró

GRAN VIA DE LES CORTS CATALANES

Parc de
Sant Martí

Parc de
l'Alhambra

Parc
del Clot

AVINGUDA DEL PARAL·LEL

El Raval

La Ribera

Parc de
l'Estació
del Nord

Montjuïc

278-279

Barri Gòtic

Parc de la
Ciutadella

Parc del
Poblenou

Parc
Diagonal
Mar

Jardins de Sant
Pau del Camp

Port
Vell

RONDA DEL LITORAL

288-289

290-291

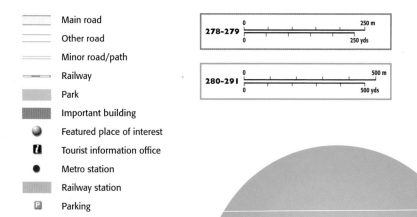

	Main road
	Other road
	Minor road/path
	Railway
	Park
	Important building
	Featured place of interest
	Tourist information office
	Metro station
	Railway station
	Parking

278-279

0 _____ 250 m
0 _____ 250 yds

280-291

0 _____ 500 m
0 _____ 500 yds

Maps

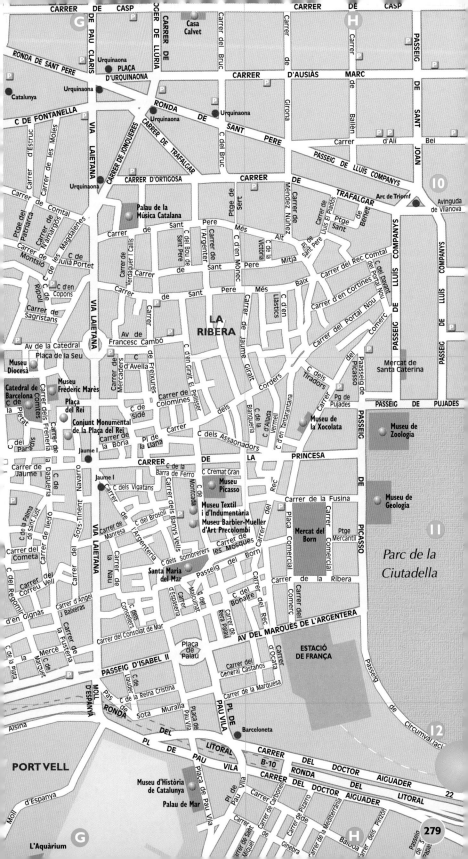

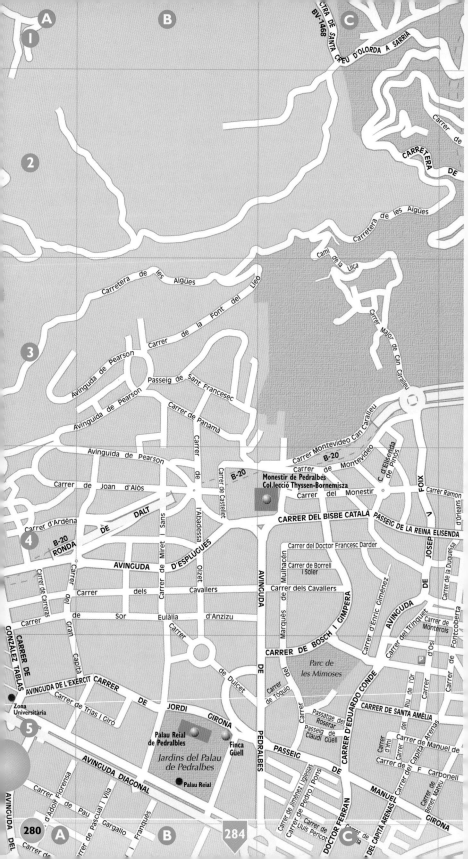

BV-1468

CTRA. DE SANTA CREU D'OLORDA A SARRIÀ

Carrer de

CARRETERA DE

Carretera de les Aigües

Camí de la Llica

Carrer Major de Can Caralleu

Carretera de les Aigües

Carrer de la Font del Lleó

Avinguda de Pearson

Avinguda de Pearson

Carrer de Panamà

Passeig de Sant Francesc

Avinguda de Pearson

Carrer de Joan d'Alòs

Carrer de Castellet

Carrer de

B-20

Carrer Montevideo Can Caralleu

B-20

Carrer de Montevideo

C. d'Eusebi de Pinós

Carrer del Monestir

Monestir de Pedralbes
Col·lecció Thyssen-Bornemisza

Carrer d'Ardèna

DE DALT

B-20 RONDA

AVINGUDA D'ESPLUGUES

Carrer de Miret i Sans

L'Abadessa Olzet

Carrer de Castellet

AVINGUDA DE

CARRER DEL BISBE CATALÀ

PASSEIG DE LA REINA ELISENDA

FOIX

Carrer Ramon

d'Orléans

Carrer del Doctor Francesc Darder

Carrer de Borrell i Soler

Marquès de Mulhacén

Carrer dels Cavallers

Carrer d'Enric Giménez

JOSEP

Carrer de la Duquessa

DE

Carrer de Carreras

Carrer del Gran Capità

Carrer de Sor Eulàlia d'Anzizu

Cavallers

CARRER DE BOSCH I GIMPERA

AVINGUDA

Carrer del Trinquet

Carrer de Montérols

Carrer de Fontcoberta

CARRER DE GONZÁLEZ TABLAS

AVINGUDA DE L'EXÈRCIT CARRER

DE JORDI GIRONA

Carrer de Trias i Giró

Carrer de Dulcet

PEDRALBES

Carrer de Tòquio

Parc de les Mimoses

CARRER D'EDUARDO CONDE

Carrer del Riu de l'Or

CARRER DE SANTA AMÈLIA

Carrer d'Ifni

Carrer Arenas

Carrer de Manuel de

Zona Universitària

Palau Reial de Pedralbes

Finca Güell

Passatge del Roserar

Passeig de Claudi Güell

PASSEIG

DE

MANUEL

Carrer d'Ifni

Carrer

Carrer del Capità

Carrer F. Carbonell

GIRONA

Jardins del Palau de Pedralbes

● **Palau Reial**

AVINGUDA DIAGONAL

AVINGUDA DE GONZÁLEZ TABLAS

Carrer d'Adolf Florensa

Carrer de Pau

Carrer de Pascual i Vila

Gargallo

Franquès

DOCTOR FERRAN

Carrer de Jiménez i Iglesias

Carrer de Pedro i Pons

Carrer de Lluís Pericot

Carrer de Benet Mateu

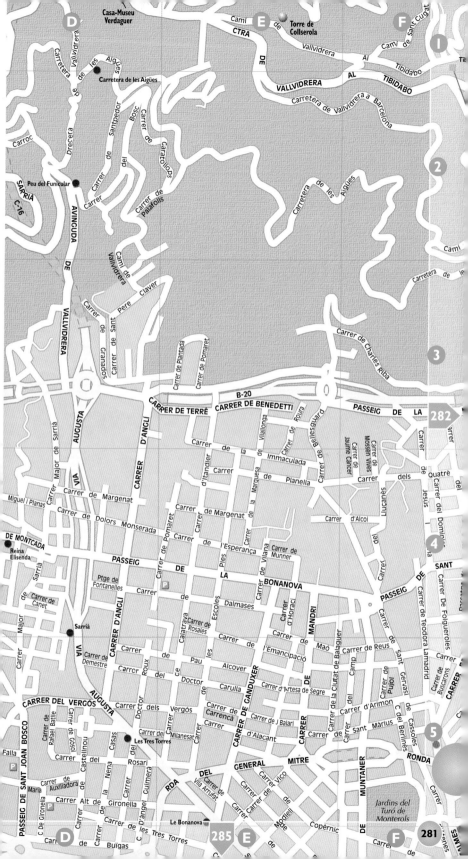

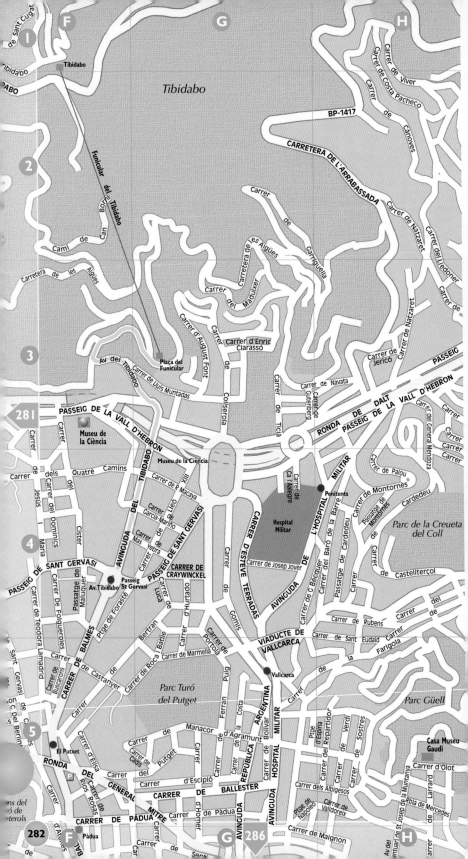

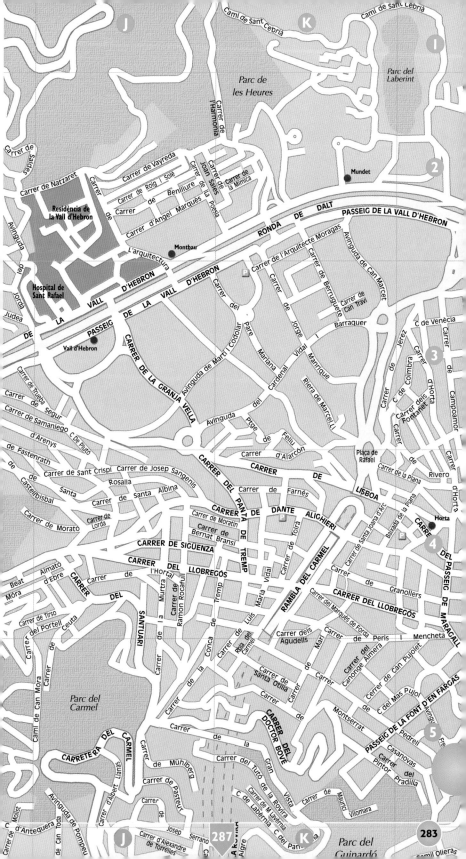

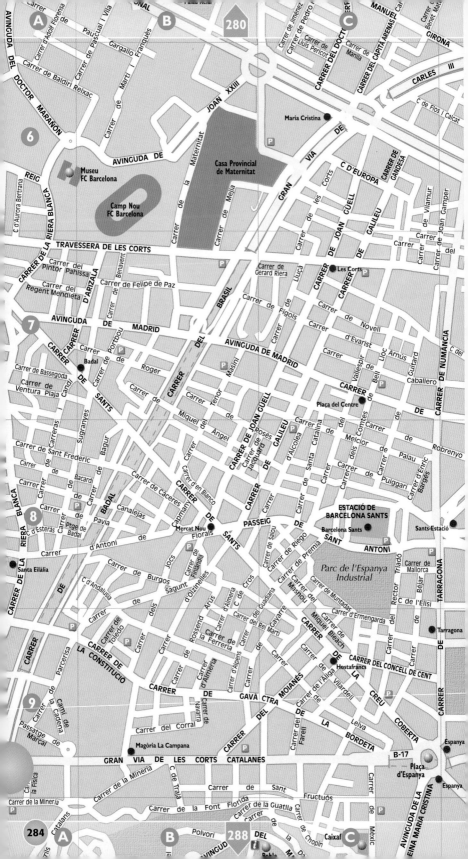

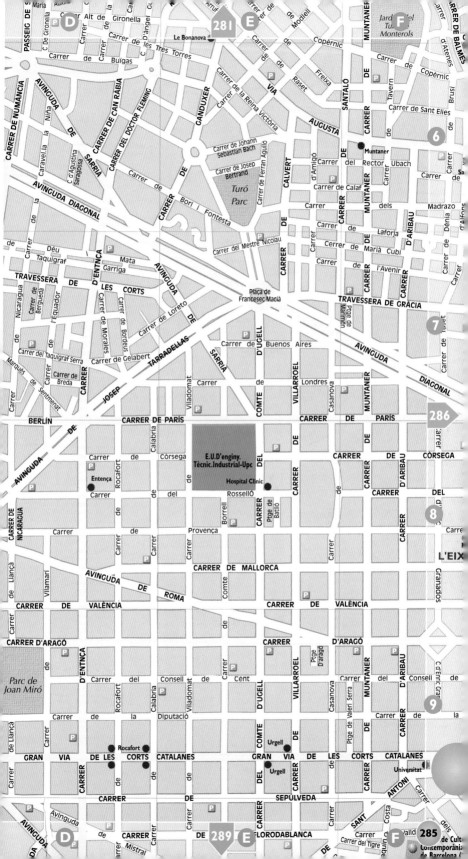

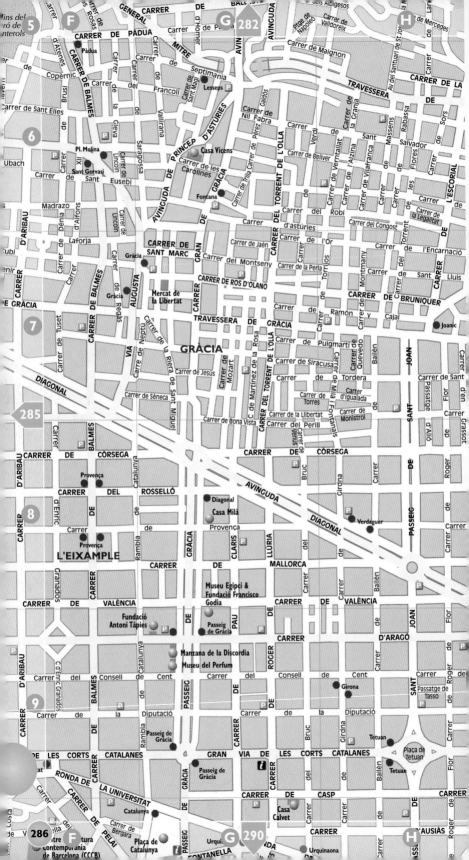

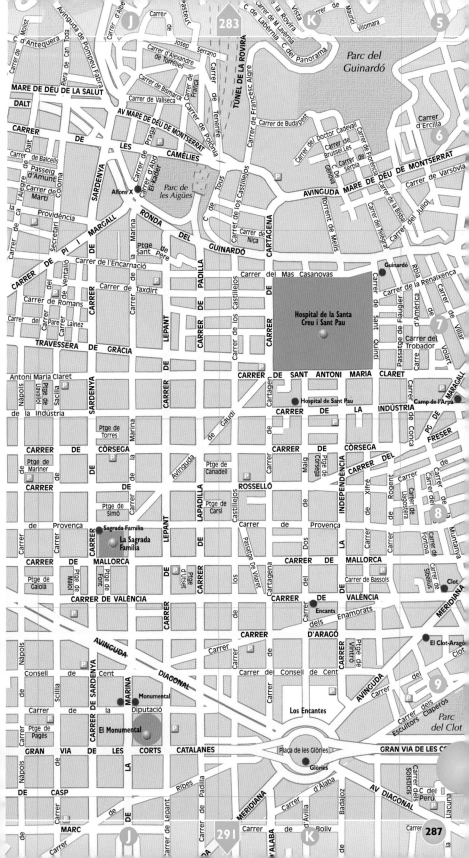

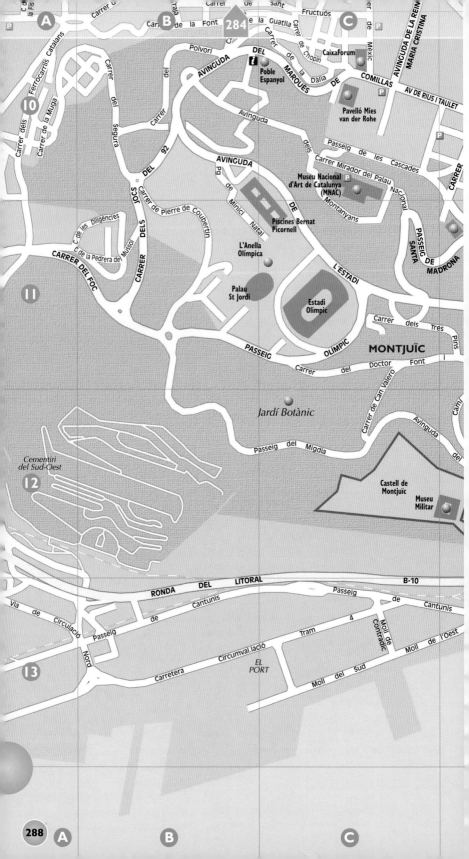

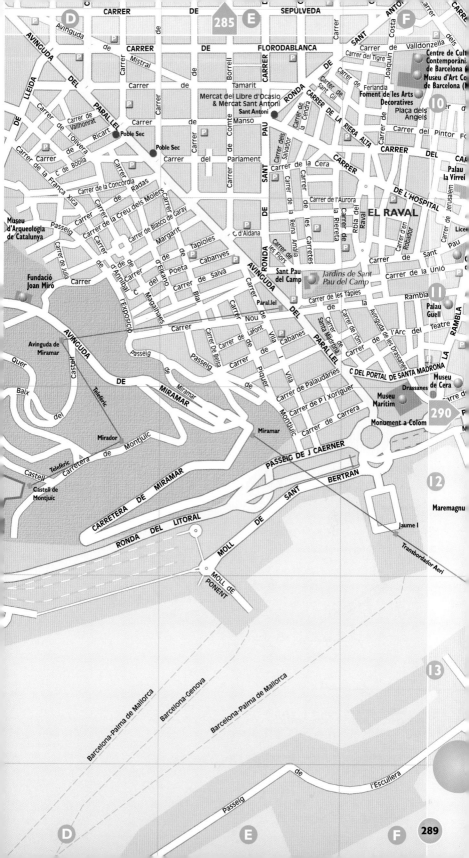

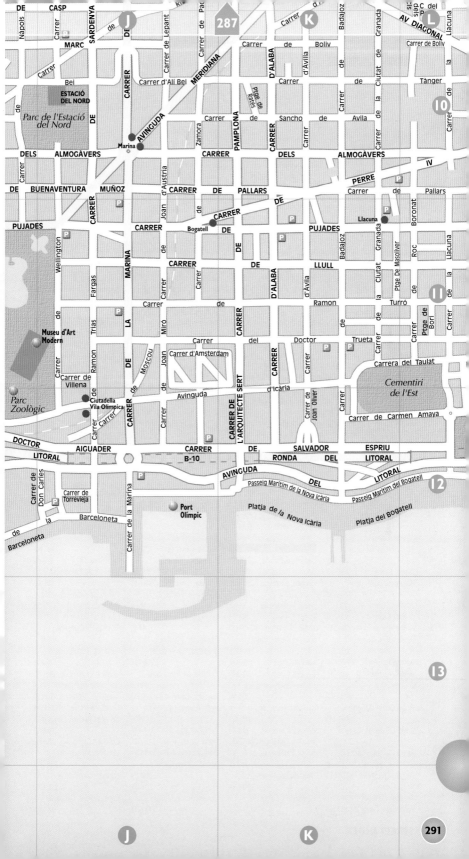

A

Aalegre, Carrer de ca l' 282 G4
Abadessa Olzet, Carrer de l' 280 B4
Abd El-Kader, Carrer d' 287 J6
Adolf Florensa, Carrer d' 284 A6
Aglà, Carrer de n' 278 F11
Agudells, Carrer dels 283 K4
Agustina Saragossa, Carrer d' 285 D6
Aigües, Carretera de les 280 C2
Àlaba, Carrer d' 287 K9
Alacant, Carrer d' 281 E5
Alarcón, Carrer d' 283 K4
Albareda, Carrer d' 278 E12
Albert Llanas, Carrer d' 283 J5
Albigesos, Carrer dels 282 G5
Alcoi, Carrer d' 281 F4
Alcolea, Carrer d' 284 C8
Aldana, Carrer d' 289 E11
Alegre de Dalt, Carrer de ca l' 287 H6
Alexandre de Torrelles, Carrer d' 287 J6
Alfons XII, Carrer d' 286 F6
Alí Bei, Carrer d' 279 H10
Àliga, Carrer de l' 284 C9
Alió, Passatge d' 286 H7
Allada Vermell, Carrer d' 279 H11
Almeria, Carrer d' 284 B9
Almirall Cervera, Carrer de l' 290 G12
Almogàvers, Carrer dels 291 K10
Alpens, Carrer d' 284 B9
Alt de Gironella, Carrer 281 D5
Alzina, Carrer de l' 286 H6
Amargós, Carrer de n' 279 G10
Amèrica, Carrer d' 287 L7
Amigó, Carrer d' 285 E6
Ample, Carrer 278 G11
Amsterdam, Carrer d' 291 J11
Amunt, Passeig d' 287 J6
Andalusia, Carrer d' 284 B8
Andrea Dòria, Carrer d' 290 H12
Àngel Guimerà, Carrer d' 281 D5
àngel J. Baixeras, Carrer d' 279 G11
Angel Marquès, Carrer d' 283 J2
Àngels, Carrer dels 278 F10
Anglí, Carrer d' 281 D4
Anníbal, Carrer d' 289 D11
Antequera, Carrer d' 287 H6

Antoni de Capmany, Carrer d' 284 B8
Aragó, Carrer d' 286 H9
Aragó, Passatge d' 285 E9
Arai, Carrer de n' 278 G11
Arc del Teatre, Carrer de l' 278 F11
Arcs, Carrer dels 278 G10
Ardéna, Carrer d' 280 A4
Arenys, Carrer d' 282 H3
Argenteria, Carrer de l' 279 G11
Aribau, Carrer d' 285 F8
Arimon, Carrer d' 281 F5
Arizala, Carrer d' 284 B7
Arquitecte Moragas, Carrer de l' 283 K2
Arquitecte Sert, Carrer de l' 291 K12
Arquitectura, Carrer de l' 283 J2
Arrabassada, Carretera de l' 282 H2
Artesa de Segre, Carrer d' 281 E5
Assaonadors, Carrer dels 279 G11
Astúries, Carrer d' 286 G6
Ataülf, Carrer d' 278 G11
Atenes, Carrer d' 286 F6
August Font, Carrer d' 282 G3
Augusta, Via 281 D5
Aurora Bertrana, Carrer d' 284 A6
Aurora, Carrer de l' 278 F11
Ausiàs Marc, Carrer d' 279 H10
Avella, Carrer d' 279 G11
Avenir, Carrer de l' 285 F7
Àvila, Carrer d' 291 K11
Avinyó, Carrer d' 278 G11

B

Bacardí, Carrer de 284 A8
Bacardí, Passatge de 278 F11
Badajoz, Carrer de 291 K11
Badal, Carrer de 284 A8
Badal, Passatge de 284 A8
Bagur, Carrer de 284 B8
Bailèn, Carrer de 279 H10
Baix del Castell, Camí 289 D12
Balboa, Carrer de 279 H12
Balcells, Carrer de 287 H6
Baldiri Reixac, Carrer de 284 A6
Ballester, Carrer de 282 G5
Balmes, Carrer de 286 F9
Baluard, Carrer del 290 G12
Banca, Passatge de la 278 F11
Banys Nous, Carrer dels 278 G11
Banys Vells, Carrer dels 279 G11

Baró de la Barre, Carrer del 282 H4
Barra de Ferro, Carrer de la 279 G11
Bassegoda, Carrer de 284 A7
Bassols, Carrer de 287 K8
Batlló, Passatge de 285 E8
Beat Almató, Carrer del 282 H4
Béjar, Carrer de 284 C8
Beliver, Carrer de 286 G6
Bellesguard, Carrer de 281 E4
Belsa, Carrer de 289 E11
Benavent, Carrer de 284 B7
Benedett, Carrer de 281 E3
Benet Mateu, Carrer de 280 C5
Benlliure, Carrer de 283 J2
Bergara, Carrer de 278 F10
Berguedà, Carrer de 285 D7
Berlín, Carrer de 284 C7
Berlinès, Carrer del 281 F5
Bernat Bransi, Carrer de 283 K4
Berruguete, Carrer de 283 K3
Bertran, Carrer de 282 F5
Bertrellans, Carrer de 278 G10
Bianco, Carrer d'en 284 B8
Bisbal, Carrer de la 287 K6
Bisbe Català, Carrer del 280 C4
Bisbe, Carrer del 278 G11
Bismarck, Carrer de 287 J6
Blai, Carrer de 289 E11
Blanqueria, Carrer de la 279 H11
Blasco de Garay, Carrer de 289 D11
Bòbila, Carrer de 289 D10
Boliv, Carrer de 291 K10
Bolívar, Carrer de 282 G5
Bona Vista, Carrer de 286 G8
Bonaire, Carrer del 279 G11
Bonanova, Passeig de la 281 E4
Bonsuccés, Carrer del 278 F10
Bonsuccés, Plaça del 278 F10
Boqueria, Carrer de la 278 F11
Bordeta, Carretera de la 284 C9
Bordeus, Carrer de 285 D7
Bori i Fontesta, Carrer de 285 D6
Bori, Passatge de 291 L11
Bòria, Carrer de la 279 G11
Born, Passeig del 279 G11
Borrell I Soler, Carrer de 280 C4
Bosc, Carrer del 281 D2
Bosch i Alsina, Moll de 278 G12

Bosch i Gimpera, Carrer de 280 C4
Bot, Carrer d'en 278 F10
Boters, Carrer dels 278 G10
Bou de Sant Pere, Carrer del 279 G10
Brasil, Carrer del 284 B7
Breda, Carrer de 285 D7
Brosolí Comtes, Carrer del 279 G11
Bruc, Carrer del 279 G10
Bruniquer, Carrer de 286 H7
Brusi, Carrer de 286 F6
Brussel.les, Carrer de 287 K6
Budapest, Carrer de 287 K6
Buenaventura Muñoz, Carrer de 291 J10
Buenos Aires, Carrer de 285 E7
Buïgas, Carrer de 285 D6
Burgos, Carrer de 284 B8
Buscarons, Carrer de 282 F5

C

Caballero, Carrer de 284 C7
Cabanes, Carrer de 289 E11
Cabres, Carrer de les 278 F11
Càceres, Carrer de 284 B8
Cadena, Camí de la 284 A9
Cadis, Carrer de 282 G5
Calabria, Carrer de 285 D8
Caldes, Carrer de 285 E6
Calatrava, Carrer de 281 E5
Call, Carrer del 278 G11
Calvert, Carrer de 285 E6
Camèlies, Carrer de les 287 J6
Camp, Carrer del 281 F5
Campoamor, Carrer de 283 L3
Can Borni, Camí de 282 F2
Can Marcet, Avinguda de 283 K2
Can Mora, Camí de 283 J5
Can Pujolet, Carrer de 283 K5
Can Ràbia, Carrer de 285 D6
Can Toda, Riera de 287 J6
Can Travi, Carrer de 283 K3
Can Valero, Carrer de 288 C12
Canadell, Passatge de 287 J8
Canalejas, Carrer de 284 A8
Canaletes, Rambla de 278 F10
Canet, Carrer de 281 D4
Canonge Almera, Carrer del 283 K5
Cànoves, Carrer de 282 H2
Cantunis, Passeig de 288 B13
Canuda, Carrer de la 278 G10
Capità Arenas, Carrer del 284 C6

Carabassa, Carrer d'en 278 G11
Caravel.la la Niña, Carrer de la 285 D6
Carbonell, Carrer de 279 H12
Cardedeu, Carrer de 282 H4
Cardedeu, Passatge de 282 H4
Cardenal Casañas, Carrer del 278 F11
Cardenal Vidal i Barraquer, Avinguda del 283 K3
Cardona, Carrer de 278 F10
Carles III, Gran Via de 284 C6
Carme, Carrer del 278 F10
Carmel, Carretera del 283 J5
Carmel, Rambla del 283 K4
Carmen Amaya, Carrer de 291 K12
Carrencà, Carrer de 281 E5
Carrera, Carrer de 278 F12
Carreras i Candi, Carrer de 284 A7
Carreras, Carrer de 280 A4
Carretes, Carrer de les 289 E11
Carroc, Carrer de 280 D2
Carsi, Passatge de 287 J8
Cartagena, Carrer de 287 K7
Casanova, Carrer de 278 F10
Cascades, Passeig de les 288 C10
Casp, Carrer de 279 G10
Castanyer, Carrer de 282 F5
Castell, Avinguda del 288 C12
Castellbisbal, Carrer de 283 H4
Castellet, Carrer de 280 B4
Castellnou, Carrer de 281 D5
Castellterçol, Carrer de 282 H4
Castillejos, Carrer de los 287 K7
Catalunya, Plaça de 278 G10
Catalunya, Rambla de 286 G8
Catedral, Avinguda de la 279 G10
Cavallers, Carrer dels 280 B4
Cendra, Carrer de la 289 E10
Cera, Carrer de la 289 E10
Cervantes, Carrer de 278 G11
Cervelló, Carrer de 278 F11
Ceuta, Carrer de 283 J4
Charles Riba, Carrer de 281 F3
Chopin, Carrer de 288 C10
Cid, Carrer del 278 F11
Circulació Nord, Via de 288 A13
Circumval.lació Tram 4, Carretera 288 B13
Circumval.lació, Passeig de 279 H11

Císter, Carrer del 282 F4
Ciutat de Balaguer, Carrer de la 281 E5
Ciutat de Granada, Carrer de la 291 K10
Claudi Güell, Passeig de 280 C5
Clot, Carrer del 287 K9
Ciutat Granada, Carrer de la 291 K11
Còdols, Carrer dels 278 G11
Coïmbra, Carrer de 283 L3
Collserola, Carrer de 282 G3
Colom, Carrer de 278 F11
Colom, Passeig de 278 F12
Colomines, Carrer de 279 G11
Comerç, Carrer del 279 H10
Comercial, Carrer 279 H11
Comercial, Plaça 279 H11
Comtal, Carrer 279 G10
Comte Borrell, Carrer de 285 E8
Comte d'Ugell, Carrer del 285 E7
Comtes de Bell-Lloc, Carrer dels 284 C7
Comtessa de Sobradiel, Carrer de la 278 G11
Conca de Tremp, Carrer de la 283 J5
Conca, Carrer de 287 L8
Concell de Cent, Carrer del 284 C9
Concòrdia, Carrer de la 289 D10
Congost, Carrer del 286 H6
Consell de Cent, Carrer del 285 E9
Consellers, Carrer dels 279 G11
Consolat de Mar, Carrer del 279 G11
Constitució, Carrer de la 284 B9
Contradic, Moll de 288 C13
Copèrnic, Carrer de 285 F6
Copons, Carrer d'en 279 G10
Corral, Carrer del 284 B9
Correu Vell, Carrer del 279 G11
Còrsega, Carrer de 287 J8
Còrsega, Passatge de 287 K8
Cortines, Carrer d'en 279 H10
Corts Catalanes, Gran Via de les 287 J9
Corts, Carrer de les 284 C6
Corts, Travessera de les 285 D7
Costa Pacheco, Carrer de 282 H2
Costa, Carrer de la 282 G5
Craywinckel, Carrer de 282 G4
Cremat Gran, Carrer 279 G11
Creu Coberta, Carrer de la 284 C9

Creu dels Molers, Carrer de la 289 D11
Cros, Carrer de 284 B8
Cucurulla, Carrer de 278 G10

D

Dagueria Manresa, Carrer de la 279 G11
Dàlia, Carrer de la 288 C10
Dalmases, Carrer de 281 E4
Dalt, Ronda de 282 H3
Dalt, Travessera de 286 H6
Dante Alighieri, Carrer de 283 K4
Davant del Portal Nou, Carrer del 279 H10
Deferlandina, Carrer 278 F10
Delparadís, Carrer 279 G11
Demestre, Carrer de 281 D5
Dénia, Carrer de 286 F7
Déu i Mata, Carrer de 285 D7
Diagonal, Avinguda 287 J9
Diligències, Carrer de les 288 B11
Diputacio, Carrer de la 287 J9
Doctor Aiguader, Carrer del 279 H12
Doctor Bové, Carrer del 283 K5
Doctor Cadevall, Carrer del 287 K6
Doctor Carulla, Carrer del 281 D5
Doctor Dou, Carrer del 278 F10
Doctor Ferran, Carrer del 284 C6
Doctor Fleming, Carrer del 285 D6
Doctor Font i Quer, Carrer del 288 C11
Doctor Francesc Darder, Carrer del 280 C4
Doctor Marañón, Avinguda del 284 A6
Doctor Roux, Carrer del 281 D5
Doctor Trueta, Carrer del 291 K11
Dolors Monserada, Carrer de 281 D4
Dominics, Carrer del 282 F4
Don Carles, Carrer de 291 J12
Dos de Maig, Carrer del 287 K8
Drassanes, Avinguda de les 278 F1
Drassanes, Moll de les 278 F12
Duc de la Victòria, Carrer del 278 G10
Dulcet, Carrer de 280 B5
Duquessa d'Orleans, Carrer de la 280 D4

E

Eduardo Conde, Carrer d' 280 C5
Egipcíaques, Carrer de les 278 F10
Elisa, Carrer d' 282 F5
Elisabets, Carrer d' 278 F10
Elisabets, Passatge d' 278 F10
Elisenda de Pinós, Carrer d' 280 C4
Elisi, Carrer de l' 284 C8
Elkano, Carrer d' 289 D10
Emancipació, Carrer de l' 281 E5
Enamorats, Carrer dels 287 K9
Encarnació, Carrer de l' 286 H7
Enric Bargés, Carrer d' 284 C8
Enric Clarassó, Carrer d' 282 G3
Enric Giménez, Carrer d' 280 C4
Enric Granados, Carrer d' 286 F8
Entença, Carrer d' 285 D9
Equador, Carrer de l' 285 D7
Erasme de Janer, Carrer d' 278 F10
Ercilla, Carrer d' 287 L6
Ermengarda, Carrer d' 284 C9
Escar, Carrer de l' 290 G13
Escipió, Carrer d' 282 G5
Escoles Pies, Carrer de les 281 E5
Escorial, Carrer de l' 286 H6
Escudellers, Carrer d' 278 F11
Escudellers, Passatge d' 278 F11
Escullera, Passeig de l' 290 G13
Escultors Claperós, Carrer dels 287 L9
Espalter, Carrer d' 278 F11
Espanya, Moll d' 279 G12
Espanya, Plaça d' 284 C9
Espaseria, Carrer d' 279 G11
Esperança, Carrer de l' 281 E4
Espíria, Passatge d' 282 H5
Esplugues, Avinguda d' 280 B4
Est, Carrer de l' 278 F11
Estadi, Avinguda de l' 288 B10
Esteràs, Carrer d' 284 A8
Esteve Terradas, Carrer d' 282 G4
Estruc, Carrer d' 79 G10
Estudis, Rambla dels 278 F10
Europa, Carrer d' 284 C6
Evarist Arnús, Carrer d' 284 C7
Exèrcit, Avinguda de l' 280 A5
Exposició, Passeig de l' 289 D11

F

Farigola, Carrer de la 282 H5
Farnés, Carrer de 283 K4
Fastenrath, Carrer de 283 J4
Felipe de Paz, Carrer de
284 B7
Feliu, Passatge de 283 K3
Ferlandia, Carrer de 289 F10
Ferran Agulló, Carrer de
285 E6
Ferran Puig, Carrer de
282 G5
Ferran, Carrer de 278 F11
Ferreria, Carrer de la
284 B9
Ferrocarrils Catalans,
Carrer dels 288 A10
Fígols, Carrer de 284 C7
Finlàndia, Carrer de 284 B8
Física, Carrer de la 284 A9
Flaugier, Passatge de
287 K7
Florència, Carrer de 287 K6
Floridablanca, Carrer de
289 D10
Flors, Carrer de les 289 E11
Flos i Calcat, Carrer de
284 C6
Foc, Carrer del 288 B11
Folgueroles, Carrer de
282 F4
Font del Lleó, Carrer de la
280 B3
Font d'en Fargas,
Passeig de la 283 K5
Font Florida, Carrer de la
284 B10
Font, Passatge de 287 J8
Fontanella, Carrer de
279 G10
Fontanelles, Passatge de
281 D4
Fontanet, Carrer dels
283 L3
Fontcoberta, Carrer de
280 D5
Fontova, Carrer de 287 L8
Forasté, Passatge de 282 F4
França Xica, Carrer de la
289 D10
França, Carrer de 287 J6
Francesc Algre, Carrer de
287 K6
Francesc Cambó,
Avinguda de 279 G10
Francesec Macià, Plaça de
285 E7
Francolí, Carrer del 286 F6
Frederic Rahola,
Avinguda de 283 L5
Freixa, Carrer de 285 E6
Freixures, Carrer de
279 G10
Freneria, Carrer de 279 G11
Freser, Carrer del 287 K8
Fusina, Carrer de la 279 H11
Fusta, Moll de la 278 G12
Fusteria, Carrer de la
279 G11

G

G Bécquer, Carrer de 282 G4
Gaiolà, Passatge de 287 J8
Galileu, Carrer de 284 C8
Gandesa, Carrer de 284 C6
Ganduxer, Carrer de 281 E5
Garatollops, Carrer de
281 D2
García-Mariño, Carrer de
282 G4
Gardunya, Plaça de la
278 F10
Garriguella, Carrer de
282 G2
Gaudí, Passatge de 287 J8
Gavà, Carrer de 284 B9
Gayarre, Carrer de 284 C9
Gegants, Carrer dels 278 G11
Gelabert, Carrer de 285 D7
General Castaños, Carrer del
279 G11
General Mendoza, Carrer del
282 H3
General Mitre, Ronda del
281 E5
Gènova, Carrer de 287 K6
Gerard Riera, Carrer de
284 C7
Gignàs, Carrer d'en 279 G11
Ginebra, Carrer de 279 H12
Giralt El Pellisser, Carrer d'en
279 G11
Girdna, Carrer de 286 H8
Gleva, Carrer de la 286 F6
Glòries, Plaça de les 287 K9
Gomis, Carrer de 282 G4
González Tablas, Carrer de
280 A5
Gósol, Carrer de 281 D5
Gràcia, Passeig de 286 G9
Gràcia, Travessera de 286 G7
Gran Capità, Carrer del
280 A4
Gran de Gràcia, Carrer
286 G6
Gran Vista, Carrer de la
283 J5
Granados, Carrer de 281 D3
Granja Vella, Carrer de la
283 J3
Granja, Carrer de la 286 H6
Granollers, Carrer de 283 K4
Grassot, Carrer d'en 286 H7
Gravina, Carrer de 278 F10
Guadiana, Carrer del 284 B9
Guàrdia, Carrer de 278 F11
Guatlla, Carrer de la 284 B10
Guifré, Carrer de 278 F10
Guinardó, Ronda del 287 J6
Guitard, Carrer de 284 C8
Gutenberg, Carrer de
282 G3
Gutenberg, Passatge de 278
F11

H

Harmonia, Carrer de l'
283 K2
Homer, Carrer d' 282 G5

Horaci, Carrer d' 281 E4
Horta, Carrer d' 283 L3
Hortal, Carrer de l' 283 J4
Hospital Militar,
Avinguda de l' 282 G5
Hospital, Carrer de l' 278 F10
Hurtado, Carrer d' 282 G4

I

Icària, Avinguda d' 291 J12
Ifni, Carrer d' 280 C5
Igualada, Carrer d' 286 H7
Immaculada, Carrer de la
281 E4
Independència, Carrer de la
287 K8
Indústria, Carrer de la
287 K7
Isabel II, Passeig d' 279 G11
Itandier, Carrer d' 281 E4

J

J Balari, Carrer de 281 E5
J Caerner, Passeig de
289 E12
Jacquard, Carrer de 284 B8
Jaén, Carrer de 286 G7
Jaume Càncer, Carrer de
281 F4
Jaume Giralt, Carrer de
279 H10
Jaume I, Carrer de la
279 G11
Jerez, Carrer de 283 L3
Jericó, Carrer de 282 H3
Jerusalem, Carrer de 278 F10
Jesús i Maria, Carrer de
281 F4
Jesús, Carrer de 286 G7
Jiménez i Iglesias, Carrer de
280 C5
Joan d'Alòs, Carrer de
280 B4
Joan d'Austria, Carrer de
291 J10
Joan de Borbó, Passeig
290 G12
Joan Gamper, Carrer de
284 C6
Joan Güell, Carrer de 284 B8
Joan Miró, Carrer de 291 J11
Joan Oliver, Carrer de
291 K12
Joan Sales, Carrer de 283 J2
Joan XXIII, Avinguda de
284 B6
Joaquín Costa, Carrer de
278 F10
Jocs del 92, Carrer dels
288 B11
Jocs Florals, Carrer dels
284 B8
Johann Sebastian Bach,
Carrer de 285 E6
Jonqueres, Carrer de
279 G10
Jordà, Avinguda del 283 H3
Jordi Girona, Carrer de
280 B5

Jorge Manrique, Carrer de
283 K3
Josep Anselm Clavé,
Carrer de 278 F11
Josep Bertrand, Carrer de
285 E6
Josep Carner, Passeig de
278 F12
Josep Jover, Carrer de
282 G4
Josep Sangenis, Carrer de
283 J4
Josep Serrano, Carrer de
287 J6
Josep Tarradellas,
Avinguda de 285 E7
Josep V Foix, Avinguda de
280 C4
Jovellanos, Carrer de
278 F10
Judea, Carrer de 282 H3
Judid, Carrer del 290 G13
Julià Portet, Carrer de
279 G10
Julià, Carrer de 289 D11
Juliol, Carrer del 287 L6
Junta de Comerç,
Carrer de la 278 F11

L

Labèrnia, Carrer de 283 K5
Lafont, Carrer de 289 E11
Laforja, Carrer de 285 F6
Laietana, Via 279 G10
Lancaster, Carrer de 278 F11
Larrard, Carrer de 282 H5
Legalitat, Carrer de la
286 H6
Leiva, Carrer de 284 C9
Lepant, Carrer de 287 J8
Lincoln, Carrer de 286 F6
Lisboa, Carrer de 283 K4
Litoral, Avinguda del 291 K12
Litoral, Ronda del 278 G12
Llacuna, Carrer de la 291 L10
Llagostera, Carrer de 287 L8
Llana, Plaça de la 279 G11
Llançà, Carrer de 285 D9
Llàstics, Carrer d'en 279 H10
Llavallol, Passatge de 287 J7
Lledó, Carrer de 279 G11
Lledoner, Carrer del 282 H2
Lleida, Carrer de 289 D10
Lleó XIII, Carrer de 282 G4
Lleó, Carrer del 278 F10
Lleona, Carrer de la 278 F11
Llibertat, Carrer de la 286 G7
Lliça, Cami de la 280 C3
Llobregós, Carrer del 283 J4
Lluçà, Carrer de 84 C7
Lluçanès, Carrer del 281 F4
Lluís Companys, Passeig de
279 H10
Lluís El Piadós, Carrer de
279 H10
Lluís Muntadas, Carrer de
282 G3
Lluís Pericot, Carrer de
284 C6

Llull, Carrer de 291 K11
Lluna, Carrer de la 278 F10
Londres, Carrer de 285 E7
Lorda, Carrer de 283 J4
Loreto, Carrer de 285 E7
Lucà, Carrer de 282 G4
Luis Marià Vidal, Carrer de
283 K4

M

M Lavèrnia, Carrer de
283 K5
Madrazo, Carrer dels
285 F6
Madrid, Avinguda de 284 B7
Maduixer, Carrer del 282 G3
Magalhaes, Carrer de
289 D11
Magdalenes, Carrer de les
279 G10
Maignon, Carrer de 286 G6
Maiol, Passatge de 287 J8
Major de Can Caralleu,
Carrer 280 C3
Major de Sarrià, Carrer
281 D4
Malcuinat, Carrer del
279 G11
Mallorca, Carrer de 286 G8
Maluquer, Passatge de
282 F4
Manacor, Carrer de 282 G5
Mandri, Carrer de 281 E5
Manila, Carrer de 284 C6
Manso, Carrer de 289 D10
Manuel de Falla, Carrer de
280 C5
Manuel Girona, Passeig de
280 C5
Maó, Carrer de 281 E5
Maquinista, Carrer de la
290 H12
Mar, Rambla de 278 F12
Maragall, Passatge de 287 L8
Maragall, Passeig de 83 L4
Marçal, Passatge de 284 A9
Marcel.li, Riera de 283 K3
Mare de Déu de la Salut,
Carrer de la 286 H6
Mare de Déu de Montserrat,
Avinguda 287 J6
Margarit, Carrer de 289 D11
Margenat, Carrer de 281 D4
Marí, Carrer de 283 K5
Maria Auxiliadora, Carrer de
281 D5
Marià Cubi, Carrer de 285 F7
Marimon, Passsatge de
285 F7
Marina, Carrer de la 291 J11
Mariner, Passatge de 287 J8
Marítim de la Barceloneta,
Passeig 290 H12
Marítim del Bogatell,
Passeig 291 K12
Marmellà d'Agramunt,
Carrer de 282 G5
Marquès de Barberà,
Carrer del 278 F11

Marquès de Comillas,
Avinguda del 288 B10
Marquès de Forda,
Carrer del 283 K4
Marquès de l'Argentera,
Avinguda del 279 H11
Marquès de Mulhacén,
Carrer del 280 C4
Marquès de Sentmenat,
Carrer del 285 D7
Marquesa de Vilallonga,
Carrer de la 281 E4
Marquesa, Carrer de la
279 H11
Marquet, Carrer de 279 G11
Martí i Codolar,
Avinguda de 283 K3
Martí i Franquès,
Carrer de 284 B6
Martí, Carrer de 287 H6
Martínez de la Rosa,
Carrer de 286 G7
Mas Casanovas,
Carrer del 287 K7
Mas Pujol, Carrer del 283 K5
Mas Yebra, Carrer de 282 G4
Masnou, Carrer del 284 C8
Masoliver, Passatge de
291 K11
Massens, Carrer de 286 H6
Maternitat, Carrer de la
284 B6
Maurici Vilomara, Carrer de
283 K5
Mediterrània, Carrer de la
279 H12
Mejía, Carrer de 284 B6
Melcior de Palau, Carrer de
284 C8
Melis, Torrent de 287 K6
Méndez Núñez, Carrer de
279 H10
Mercaders, Carrer de
279 G11
Mercantil, Passatge 279 H11
Mercè, Carrer de la 278 G11
Mercè, Plaça de la 278 G11
Mercedes, Rambla de
282 H5
Meridiana, Avinguda
291 J10
Mestre Nicolau, Carrer del
285 E7
Mèxic, Carrer de 284 C9
Migdia, Passeig del 288 C12
Milà i Fontanals, Carrer de
286 H7
Milanesat, Carrer del 281 D5
Mímica, Carrer de la 283 K2
Mina, Carrer de 278 F11
Mineria, Carrer de la 284 B9
Minici Natal, Passeig de
288 B10
Miquel Àngel, Carrer de
284 B7
Miquel Bleach, Carrer de
284 C9
Mirador del Palau Nacional,
Carrer 288 C10

Miramar, Avinguda de
289 D11
Miramar, Carretera de
289 D12
Miramar, Passeig de
289 D11
Miret i Sans, Carrer de
280 B4
Mistral, Avinguda de
289 D10
Modlell, Carrer de 285 E6
Moianés, Carrer del 284 B9
Moles, Carrer de les 279 G10
Molist, Carrer de 287 H6
Mònec l'Argenter,
Carrer d'en 279 G10
Monestir, Carrer del 280 C4
Monistrol, Carrer de 286 H7
Montalegre, Carrer de
278 F10
Montanyans, Avinguda dels
288 B10
Montcada, Carrer de
279 G11
Monterols, Carrer de 280 C4
Montevideo Can Caralleu,
Carrer 280 C3
Montevideo, Carrer de
280 B4
Montjuïc, Carrer de 289 E11
Montjuïc, Carretera de
289 D12
Montmany, Carrer de
286 H7
Montornès, Carrer de
282 H4
Montornès, Passatge de
282 H4
Montseny, Carrer del 286 G7
Montserrat Casanovas,
Carrer de 283 K5
Montserrat, Carrer de
278 F11
Montsió, Carrer de 279 G10
Móra d'Ebre, Carrer de
282 H4
Morales, Carrer de 285 D7
Moratín, Carrer de 283 K4
Morató, Carrer de 283 J4
Moscou, Carrer de 291 J12
Mosques, Carrer de les
279 G11
Mossèn Vives, Carrer de
281 F4
Mozart, Carrer de 286 G7
Muga, Carrer de la 288 A10
Mühlberg, Carrer de 283 J5
Munner, Carrer de 281 E4
Muntadas, Carrer de 284 C8
Muntaner, Carrer de 285 F7
Muntanya, Carrer de la
287 L8
Murtra, Carrer de la 283 J4

N

Napoleó, Passatge de
282 G5
Nàpols, Carrer de 291 J10
Natzaret, Carrer de 282 H3

Nau, Carrer de la 279 G11
Navarra, Carrer de 284 B9
Navata, Carrer de 282 H3
Nena Casas, Carrer de la
281 D5
Neptú, Carre de 286 G7
Niça, Carrer de 287 K7
Nicaragua, Carrer de 285 D7
Nil Fabra, Carrer de 286 G6
Notariat, Carrer del 278 F10
Nou de la Rambla,
Carrer 278 F11
Nou de Sant Francesc,
Carrer 278 F11
Nova Icària, Platja de la
291 K12
Novell, Carrer de 284 C7
Numància, Carrer de 285 D6

O

Obradors, Carrer d' 278 F11
Ocata, Carrer del d' 279 H11
Oest, Moll de l' 288 C13
Olímpic, Passeig 288 C11
Olivera, Carrer de l' 289 D10
Olot, Carrer d' 282 H5
Olzinelles, Carrer d' 284 B8
Om, Carrer de l' 278 F11
Or, Carrer de l' 286 G7
Ortigosa, Carrer d' 279 G10
Osi, Carrer d' 280 C5

P

Padilla, Carrer de 287 J8
Pàdua, Carrer de 282 G5
Pagès, Passatge de 287 J9
Palafolls, Carrer de 281 D2
Palau Cometa, Plaça de
279 G11
Palau, Carrer de 278 G11
Palau, Plaça de 279 G11
Palaudàries, Carrer de
289 E11
Palla, Carrer de la 278 G10
Pallars, Carrer de 291 K10
Palma de Sant Just,
Carrer de la 279 G11
Paloma, Carrer de la 278 F10
Palou, Carrer de 282 H4
Pamplona, Carrer de
291 K11
Panamà, Carrer de 280 B3
Panorama, Carrer del 287 K6
Pantà de Tremp, Carrer del
283 K4
Paral.lel, Avinguda del
289 E11
Parc, Carrer del 278 F12
Parcerisa, Carrer de 284 A9
Pare Laínez, Carrer del
287 J7
Pare Mariana, Carrer del
283 K3
París, Carrer de 285 E7
Parlament, Carrer del
289 E10
Pascual i Víla, Carrer de
284 B6
Pasteur, Carrer de 283 J5

Patriarca, Passatge del
    279 G10
Pau Alcover, Carrer de
    281 D5
Pau Claris, Carrer de 279 G10
Pau Gargallo, Carrer de
    284 B6
Pau Vila, Plaça de 279 G12
Pau, Passatge de la 278 F11
Pavia, Carrer de 284 A8
Pearson, Avinguda de
    280 B3
Pedralbes, Carrer de 280 C5
Pedrell, Carrer de 283 K5
Pedrera del Mussol,
    Carrer de la 288 B11
Pedro i Pons, Carrer de
    280 C5
Pelai, Carrer de 78 F10
Penedides, Carrer de les
    278 F11
Peracamps, Carrer de
    278 F11
Pérez Galdós, Carrer de
    286 G6
Perill, Carrer del 286 G8
Peris i Mencheta, Carrer de
    283 K4
Perla, Carrer de la 286 G7
Perre IV, Carrer de 291 K10
Perú, Carrer del 287 L9
Petritxol, Carrer de 278 F10
Peu de la Creu, Carrer del
    278 F10
Pi i Margall, Carrer de 287 J7
Pi, Carrer del 278 G10
Picasso, Passeig de 279 H11
Pierre de Coubertin,
    Carrer de 288 B11
Pietat, Carrer de la 279 G11
Pintor Fortuny, Carrer del
    278 F10
Pintor Pahissa, Carrer del
    284 A7
Pintor Pradilla, Carrer del
    283 K5
Pinzón, Carrer dels 279 H12
Piquer, Carrer de 289 E11
Pistó, Carrer del 287 L8
Pizarro, Carrer de 279 H12
Plana, Baixada de la 283 L4
Plana, Carrer de la 283 L4
Planella, Carrer de 281 E4
Plantada, Carrer de 281 E3
Plata, Carrer de 279 G11
Plutó, Carrer de 283 J3
Poesia, Carrer de la 283 J2
Poeta Cabanyes, Carrer del
    289 E11
Polònia, Carrer de 287 J6
Polvorí, Carrer del 288 B10
Pomaret, Carrer de 281 E4
Pompeu Fabra, Avinguda de
    287 J6
Ponent, Moll de 289 E13
Portaferrissa, Carrer de la
    278 F10
Portal de l'Angel,
    Avinguda del 278 G10

Portal de Santa Madrona,
    Carrer del 278 F11
Portal Nou, Carrer del
    279 H10
Portbou, Carrer de 284 B7
Portell, Carrer del 283 J4
Portolà, Carrer de 282 G5
Praga, Carrer de 287 J6
Premià, Carrer de 284 C8
Príncep d'Astúries,
    Avinguda de 286 G6
Princesa, Carrer de la
    279 H11
Provença, Carrer de 286 G8
Providència, Carrer de la
    286 H6
Puig i Xoriguer,
    Carrer de 289 E12
Puiggarí, Carrer de 284 C8
Puigmartí, Carrer de 286 G7
Pujades, Carrer de 291 K11
Pujades, Passeig de 279 H11
Pujol, Carrer de 281 F5
Putget, Carrer del 282 G5

Q

Quatrè Camins, Carrer dels
    282 F4
Quevedo, Carrer de 286 H7

R

R Macaya, Carrer de 282 G4
Rabassa, Carrer de 286 H6
Radas, Carrer de 289 D11
Rafael Batlle, Carrer de
    281 D5
Rambla, La 278 F11
Ramelleres, Carrer de les
    278 F10
Ramon Miguel i Planas,
    Carrer 281 D4
Ramon Rocafull,
    Carrer de 283 J4
Ramon Trias Fargas,
    Carrer de 291 J11
Ramon Turró, Carrer de
    291 K11
Ramón y Cajal, Carrer de
    286 H7
Raset, Carrer de 285 E6
Ratés, Passatge de 291 K10
Rauric, Carrer de 278 F11
Raval, Rambla del 278 F11
Rec Comtal, Carrer del
    279 H10
Rec, Carrer de 279 H11
Rector Triadó, Carrer del
    284 C8
Rector Ubach, Carrer del
    285 F6
Regàs, Carrer de 286 F7
Regent Mendieta, Carrer del
    284 A7
Regomir Llauder, Carrer del
    279 G11
Rei Martí, Carrer del 284 B9
Reial, Plaça 278 F11
Reina Amàlia, Carrer de la
    289 E11

Reina Cristina, Carrer de la
    279 G11
Reina Elisenda de Montcada,
    Passeig de la 280 C4
Reina Victòria, Carrer de la
    285 E6
Renaixença, Carrer de la
    287 L7
Repartidor, Carrer del
    282 H5
República Argentina,
    Avinguda 282 G5
Rera Palau, Carrer de
    279 G11
Reus, Carrer de 281 F5
Ribera, Carrer de la 279 H11
Ricart, Carrer de 289 D10
Riego, Carrer de 284 C8
Riera Alta, Carrer de la
    278 F10
Riera Baixa, Carrer de la
    278 F10
Riera Blanca, Carrer de la
    284 A7
Riera de Sant Miguel,
    Carrer de la 286 G7
Riereta, Carrer de la 289 F11
Ríos Rosas, Carrer de
    282 F5
Ripoll, Carrer de 279 G10
Riu de l'Or, Carrer del
    280 C5
Rius i Taule, Avinguda de
    288 C10
Rivero, Carrer de 283 L4
Robador, Carrer d'en
    278 F11
Robí, Carrer del 286 G6
Robrenyo, Carrer de 84 C8
Roc Boronat, Carrer de
    291 L11
Roca i Batlle, Carrer de
    282 G5
Roca, Carrer d'en 278 F10
Rocafort, Carrer de 285 D8
Rogent, Carrer de la 287 K8
Roger de Flor, Carrer de
    286 H9
Roger de Llúria, Carrer de
    279 G10
Roger, Carrer de 284 B7
Roig i Solé, Carrer de
    283 J2
Roig, Carrer d'en 278 F10
Roma, Avinguda de 285 E8
Romans, Carrer de 287 J7
Ros d'Olano, Carrer de
    286 G7
Rosales, Carrer de 281 E4
Rosari, Carrer del 281 D5
Roserar, Passatge del 280 C5
Rosés, Carrer de 284 B7
Rosselló, Carrer del 286 G8
Rossend Arús, Carrer de
    284 B9
Roura, Carrer de 281 E3
Rovira, Túnel de la 287 K6
Rubens, Carrer de 282 H4
Rull, Carrer d'en 78 F11

S

Sacilla, Carrer de 287 J8
Sadurní, Carrer de 278 F11
Sagristans, Carrer de 279 G10
Sagunt, Carrer de 284 B8
Saldes, Carrer de 283 H2
Salou, Carrer de 284 C8
Salvà, Carrer de 289 E11
Salvador Espriu, Carrer de
    291 K12
Salvador, Carrer dels
    289 E10
Salvat Papasseit, Passeig de
    290 H12
Samaniego, Carrer de 283 J3
Sancho de Avila, Carrer de
    291 K10
Sant Agustí, Plaça de 278 F11
Sant Antoni Maria Claret,
    Carrer de 287 K7
Sant Antoni, Passeig de
    284 C8
Sant Antoni, Ronda de
    278 F10
Sant Benet, Passatge de
    279 H10
Sant Bernat, Passatge de
    278 F10
Sant Bertran, Carrer de
    278 F11
Sant Bertran, Moll de
    289 E12
Sant Carles, Carrer des
    290 H12
Sant Cebrià, Camí de
    283 K1
Sant Crispí, Carrer de 283 J4
Sant Cugat, Camí de 281 F1
Sant Elies, Carrer de 285 F6
Sant Erasme, Carrer de
    278 F10
Sant Eudald, Carrer de
    282 H5
Sant Eusebi, Carrer de
    286 F6
Sant Francesc, Passeig de
    280 B3
Sant Frederic, Carrer de
    284 A8
Sant Fructuós, Carrer de
    284 C9
Sant Gervasi de Cassoles,
    Carrer de 281 F5
Sant Gervasi, Passeig de
    282 G4
Sant Gil, Carrer de 289 E10
Sant Joan Bosco, Passeig de
    281 D5
Sant Joan, Passeig de
    279 H10
Sant Josep Oriol, Carrer de
    278 F1
Sant Josep Rauric Quintana,
    Plaça de 278 F11
Sant Lluís, Carrer de 286 H7
Sant Magí, Carrer de 286 G6
Sant Marc, Carrer de 286 G7
Sant Màrius, Carrer de
    281 F5

Sant Miquel, Baixada de 278 G11
Sant Miquel, Carrer de 290 G12
Sant Oleguer, Carrer de 278 F11
Sant Pacià, Carrer de 278 E11
Sant Pau, Carrer de 278 F11
Sant Pau, Ronda de 289 E10
Sant Pere Claver, Carrer de 281 D3
Sant Pere Més Alt, Carrer de 279 G10
Sant Pere Més Baix, Carrer de 279 G10
Sant Pere Mitjà, Carrer de 279 G10
Sant Pere, Passatge de 287 J7
Sant Pere, Plaça de 279 H10
Sant Pere, Ronda de 279 G10
Sant Quintí, Carrer de 287 K7
Sant Rafael, Carrer de 278 F11
Sant Ramon, Carrer de 278 F11
Sant Salvador, Carrer de 286 H6
Sant Sever, Carrer de 278 G11
Sant Vicenç, Carrer de 278 F10
Santa Albina, Carrer de 283 J4
Santa Amèlia, Carrer de 280 C5
Santa Anna, Carrer de 278 G10
Santa Catalina, Carrer de 284 C8
Santa Creu d'Olorda a Sarrià, Carretera de 280 C1
Santa Elena, Carrer de 278 E11
Santa Joana d'Arc, Carrer de 283 K4
Santa Madrona, Carrer de 289 E11
Santa Madrona, Passeig de 288 C11
Santa Mònica, Carrer de 278 F11
Santa Otília, Carrer de 283 K5
Santa Rosalia, Carrer de 283 J4
Santaló, Carrer de 285 F6
Santpedor, Carrer de 281 D2
Sants, Carrer de 84 B8
Santuari de St Josep de la Muntanya, Avinguda del 286 H6
Santuari, Carrer del 283 J4
Saragossa, Carrer de 286 G6
Sardenya, Carrer de 287 J9
Sarrià, Avinguda de 285 D6

Sarrià, Carretera de 280 C2
Scillia, Carrer de 287 J9
Secretari Coloma, Carrer del 287 J6
Segur, Carrer de 283 J3
Segura, Carrer del 288 B10
Sèneca, Carrer de 286 G7
Septimania, Carrer de 286 G6
Sepúlveda, Carrer de 285 E9
Sèrbia, Carrer de 287 K6
Serra, Carrer d'en 279 G11
Sert, Passatge de 279 G10
Sibelius, Carrer de 287 L8
Sidé, Carrer de 279 G11
Sigüenza, Carrer de 283 J4
Sils, Carrer de 278 F11
Simó, Passatge de 287 J8
Siracusa, Carrer de 286 G7
Sitges, Carrer de les 278 F10
Solsticis, Carrer dels 287 L9
Sombrerers, Carrer dels 279 G11
Sor Eulàlia d'Anzizu, Carrer de 280 B4
Sòria, Carrer de 290 H12
Sors, Carrer de 2 86 H6
Sostres, Carrer de 282 H5
Sota Muralla, Passatge de 279 G12
Sots-Tinent Navarro, Carrer del 279 G11
St Ramon St Oleger, Carrer 289 E11
Sud, Moll del 288 C13
Sugranyes, Carrer de 284 A8

T

Tallers, Carrer dels 278 F10
Tamarit, Carrer de 289 D10
Tànger, Carrer de 291 K10
Tantarantana, Carrer d'en 279 H11
Tàpies, Carrer de les 278 F11
Tapioles, Carrer de 289 E11
Taquígraf Garriga, Carrer del 284 C7
Taquígraf Serra, Carrer del 285 D7
Tarragona, Carrer de 284 C9
Tasso, Passatge de 286 H9
Taulat, Carrer del 291 L11
Tavern, Carrer de 285 F6
Taxdirt, Carrer de 287 J7
Telègraf, Carrer del 287 K6
Templers, Carrer dels 278 G11
Tenerife, Carrer de 287 J6
Tenor Masini, Carrer del 284 B7
Teodora Lamadrid, Carrer de 281 F4
Terrê, Carrer de 281 E3
Tetuan, Plaça de 286 H9
Tibidabo, Avinguda del 282 G4
Ticià, Carrer de 282 G3
Tigre, Carrer del 278 F10

Tiradors Corders, Carrer dels 279 H11
Tirso, Carrer de 283 J4
Toledo, Carrer de 284 B9
Tolrà, Carrer de 283 K4
Tòquio, Carrer de 280 C5
Tordera, Carrer de 286 H7
Torrent de les Flores, Carrer del 286 H6
Torrent de l'Olla, Carrer del 286 G6
Torres i Amat, Carrer de 278 F10
Torres, Carrer de 286 G7
Torres, Passatge de 287 J8
Torrevieja, Carrer de 291 J12
Torrijos, Carrer de 286 H7
Tous, Carrer de 287 J6
Trafalgar, Carrer de 279 H10
Trajà, Carrer de 284 B9
Tres Pins, Carrer dels 288 C11
Tres Torres, Carrer de les 285 D6
Trias i Giró, Carrer de 280 A5
Trilla, Carrer de 286 G6
Trinitat, Carrer de la 278 F11
Trinquet, Carrer del 280 C4
Trobador, Carrer del 287 L7
Trueba, Carrer de 282 H3
Tuset, Carrer de 286 F7
Tutó de la Rovíra, Carrer del 283 K5

U

Unió, Carrer de la 278 F11
Universitat, Ronda de la 278 F10
Urquinaona, Plaça d' 279 G10
Utset, Passatge d' 287 J8

V

València, Carrer de 287 J8
Valeri Serra, Passatge de 285 F9
Vall d'Hebron, Passeig de la 283 J3
Vallcarca, Viaducte de 282 G5
Valldonzella, Carrer de 278 F10
Valldoreix, Carrer de 282 H5
Vallespir, Carrer del 284 C7
Vallhonrat, Carrer de 289 D10
Vallirana, Carrer de 286 G6
Vallseca, Carrer de 287 J6
Vallvidrera a Barcelona, Carretera de 281 E2
Vallvidrera Al Tibidabo, Camí de 281 F1
Vallvidrera Al Tibidabo, Carretera de 281 E2
Vallvidrera, Avinguda de 281 D3
Vallvidrera, Camí de 281 D3
Vallvidrera, Drecera de 281 D2

Varsòvia, Carrer de 287 L6
Vayreda, Carrer de 283 J2
Venècia, Carrer de 283 L3
Ventalló, Carrer de 287 J7
Ventura Plaja, Carrer de 284 A7
Venus, Carrer de 286 G8
Verdaguer i Callís, Carrer de 279 G10
Verdi, Carrer de 286 G6
Vergós, Carrer del 281 D5
Verntallat, Carrer de 286 H6
Vico, Carrer de 281 E5
Victòria, Carrer de la 279 H10
Vidre, Carrer del 278 F11
Vigatans, Carrer dels 279 G11
Vila Arrufat, Carrer de 81 E5
Vila i Vilà, Carrer de 289 E11
Viladomat, Carrer de 285 E9
Vilafranca, Carrer de 286 H6
Vilamarí, Carrer de 285 D8
Vilamur, Carrer de 284 C6
Vilana, Carrer de 281 E4
Vilanova, Avinguda de 279 H10
Vilardell, Carrer de 284 C9
Vilaret, Passatge de 287 K8
Villar, Carrer de 287 L7
Villarroel, Carrer de 285 E9
Villena, Carrer de 291 J11
Vintró, Passatge de 287 K9
Viver, Carrer de 282 H1
Volart, Rambla de 287 L7

W

Wellington, Carrer de 291 J11

X

Xifré, Carrer de 287 K8
Xuclà, Carrer d'en 278 F10
Zamora, Carrer de 291 J11

Barcelona's main attractions, described in The Sights and Out and About sections, are highlighted in **bold type**.

A

Academia de les Bones Lletrès 183
accommodation 9, 235–254
children 241
disabilities, visitors with 259
hostals 240, 248–249
hotels 9, 240
locator maps 236–239
private house rentals 240
self-catering 240
tips 241
useful words and phrases 272
websites 270
acupuncture 263
adaptors 258
air travel 40–41
airport 40
airport to city transport 40–41
disabilities, visitors with 52
health hazards for flyers 262
Ajuntament 60, 116, 117
Al-Mansur 27
amusement and theme parks
Parc d'Atraccions 130, 178, 259
Port Aventura 177
L'Anella Olímpica 58, **62**
Angelico, Fra 85
Angel Jobal 192, 193
Anglada, Lola 197
Antic Hospital de la Santa Creu 119
antiques markets 154
antiques shops 142
L'Aquàrium de Barcelona 59, **62**, 184
Arabic Bathhouse, Girona 203
Archaeological Museum 58, 88
Archaeological Museum, Girona 203
Archaeological Museum, Tarragona 199
architects
Aulenti, Gae 99
Bargués, Arnau 70
Berenguer, Francesc 112, 186
Bofill, Ricardo 62
Bohigas, Oriol 17, 114
Domènech i Roura Pere 62
Fosteré, Josep 192
Foster, Norman 130

architects (cont.)
Isozaki, Arata 62, 65
Meier, Richard 90
Mies van der Rohe, Ludwig 65, 114
Molina, Daniel 115
Moneo, Rafael 161
Nabot, Francesc 115
Nouvel, Jean 14, 15
Rogers, Richard 14, 15
Rovira i Trias, Antonio 92
Villar, Francesc de 128
see also Domènech i Montaner, Lluís; Gaudí, Antoni; Puig i Cadafalch, Josep
architecture 14–15
art nouveau 144, 163, 164
Catalan Gothic 14, 84, 123, 130
Col.legi d'Arquitectes 74
International style 114
Noucentista 190
Romanesque 130
see also Modernisme
areas of the city see Barceloneta; Barri Gòtic; L'Eixample; Gràcia; Montjuïc; El Raval; La Ribera
Las Arenas 88, 115
Arnau, Eusebi 82, 83, 106
art and crafts markets 119, 137, 154
art and design 16–17
art galleries, commercial 139
Articket pass 265
art museums see museums and galleries
art nouveau 144, 163, 164
Ateneu Barcelonès 190
athletics 173
ATMs 260
L'Auditori 161
Aulenti, Gae 99
Avinguda de Pau Casals 140
Avinguda de la Reina Maria Cristina 58, 87

B

baby changing facilities 259
Balcó del Mediterrani, Tarragona 198
Balenciaga, Cristóbal 102
ballet and modern dance 155
ballroom dancing 10, 173
banks 260–261, 265
Banys Àrabs, Girona 203
Barcelona Card 43
Barcelona Chair 114
Barcelona Football Club Museum 92

Barcelona Head (sculpture) 8, 17, 119, 184
Barcelona Museum of Contemporary Art (MACBA) 8, 16, **90–91**
Barcelona society
business sector 21
cultural diversity 20, 21
economy 5, 21
housing 13
language 4–5, 37
politics and government 12, 13, 38
population 4
seny and rauxa 18
social problems 5
Barceloneta 4, 5, 32, **63**
Bargués, Arnau 70
Barri Chino 119
Barri Gòtic 4, 5, **60**, **64**, 137, **182–183**
Catedral de la Seu 60, **70–73**
Conjunt Monumental de la Plaça del Rei 60, **75**, 182
Museu del Calçat 60, **89**
Museu Diocesà 60, **92**
Museu Frederic Marès 60, **92**, 182
Plaça del Pí 60, 64, 137, 154, 190
Plaça del Rei 60, **115**, 182
Plaça de Sant Felip Neri 60, 64, 182
Plaça de Sant Jaume 13, 60, **116–117**, 182
Santa Maria del Pí 15, 60, **130**, 259
bars 9, 166–169
Basílica de Santa Maria del Mar 23, 61, **123**, 192
basketball 171, 172
Bassa, Ferrer 84
beaches
Mar Bella 173
Nova Icària 118
Platja de la Barceloneta 59, 63, 173
Sant Sebastià 173
beer, wines and spirits 211
Berenguer, Francesc 112, 186
Best of Barcelona 8–10
Beuys, Joseph 65
bicycling 173
bicycle routes 49
bicycle tours 204
bike rental 49
La Bisbal 12
Black Virgin 200, 201
Block of Discord 76, **82–83**, 188
boat trips 174–175

Bofill, Ricardo 62
Bohigas, Oriol 17, 114
Bonaparte, Joseph 32, 33
books
bookshops 141
further reading 269
market 154
La Boqueria 8, 153, 190
El Born see **La Ribera**
El Bosque de les Fades 89, 167, 190
bridges
Bridge of Sighs 60, 64, 116
Rambla del Mar 59, 119, 121, 190
Brossa, Joan 90
bullfighting 171, 172
Bullfighting Museum 88
bullrings
Las Arenas 88, 115
El Monumental 88, 172
Burial of the Sardine 179
buses
airport buses 41
bus tours 204
Bus Turístic 46–47
disabilities, visitors with 52
long-distance buses 42, 51
night buses 47
Shopping Line 47
tourist routes 47, 48
urban buses 46–47, 52
business sector 21

C

cable car 49, 59, 86
Café de l'Opera 9, 121, 166, 190, 191
Café Zurich 115, 167
cafés 9, 166–169
internet cafés 267
listings 166–169
CaixaForum 58, **65**, 161
Caldes de Montbui 175
El Call 64, 182
Camino de la Santa Cova 201
Camp Nou 92, 172
Cap d'Any 180
Capella de Sant Jordi 116
Carnestoltes 179, 197
Carnival 179, 197
car rental 41
Carrer d'Aragó 188
Carrer d'Avinyó 137
Carrer dels Banys Nous 137
Carrer dels Canvis Vells 122, 193
Carrer de les Carolines 187
Carrer del Consell de Cent 139
Carrer de l'Espaseria 138
Carrer de Montcada 29, 61, 192

Carrer de les Mosques 192
Carrer de Muntaner 140
Carrer d'Olot 110
Carrer de Pescateria 192
Carrer de Petritxol 64, 137, 190
Carrer de Portaferrisa 190
Carrer de la Princesa 192
Carrer de Verdi 80, 186
Carrer de Vidreria 138
car tours 204
Casa Amatller 15, **82–83**, 188
Casa Antiga Figueres 122, 190, 191
Casa de l'Ardiaca 182, 183
Casa Batlló 14, 15, **82**, 83, 188
Casa Calvet 65
Casa dels Canonges 116
Casa Castellarnau, Tarragona 199
Casa de la Ciutat 13, 116, **117**
Casa Francesc Cama Escurra 186
Casa Fuster 80, 186, 187
Casa Lleó Morera 82, **83**, 188
La Casa de la Marina 184
Casa Milà 8, 14, **66–69**
Casa dels Paraigües 121
Casa Pedellas 75
Casa de les Punxes 76, 188, 189
Casa Quadros 34
Casaques Vermelles (Red Jackets) 270
Casa Terrades see Casa de les Punxes
Casa Tomas 76, 188, 189
Casa Vicens 15, **74**, 80, 187
Casals, Pau (Pablo) 89
Casa-Museu Gaudí 110, 112
Casa-Museu Verdaguer 74
Casaramona 65
Casas, Ramón 16, 88, 144, 196
The Cascade 10, 108
Castell de Montjuïc 177
castellers (human towers) 10, 13, 116, 179, 194
Castilian language 4
Castle of Three Dragons 102
Catalan Gothic 14, 84, 123, 130
Catalan History Museum 59, 93
Catalan language 4, 5, 12, 37, 258–259
Catalan Museum of Jewish Culture, Girona 203

Catalan National Library 119
Catalan Renaixença (Renaissance) 5, 14, 15, 34, 74, 107
Catalonia 12–13, 18, 36, 38
Catedral de la Seu 60, **70–73**
cava 195
Cavalcava dels Reis 179
Centre d'Art Santa Mònica 190, 191
Centre Català d'Artesania 139, 143
Centre de Cultura Contemporània de Barcelona (CCCB) 74
Centre Islàmic 259
Centre del Modernisme 76, 83, 265
Ceramics Museum 108
Cerdà, Ildefons 15, 76
Cereria Subira 182, 183
chain stores 152–153
Chapel of St. Christopher 182
child-minding services 259
children 259
  accommodation 241
  baby changing facilities 259
  child-minding services 259
  eating out with 210, 259
  public transport 43, 51, 259
Children's Barcelona 177–178, 259
L'Aquàrium de Barcelona 59, **62**, 184
Casa Milà 8, 14, **66–69**
Castell de Montjuïc 177
Egyptian Museum 98
Fundacío Joan Miró 8, 58, **78–79**
IMAX cinema 59, 160
Jove Teatre Regina 178
Museu de Cera 59, **89**
Museu de la Ciencia 89
Museu FC Barcelona 92
Museu Marítim 8, 59, **94–95**
Parc d'Atraccions 130, 178
Parc de la Ciutadella 10, 61, **108**, 178
Parc de la Creueta del Col 109
Park Güell 8, **110–113**
Parc del Laberint 114, 178
Parc Zoològic 114
playgrounds 259
Poble Espanyol 58, **118**, 178
Port Aventura 177
Chillida, Eduardo 109, 115
chiropractic 263
Chocolate Museum 102

churches
  Basilica de Santa Maria, Vilafranca 194
  Capella de Sant Jordi 116
  Catedral de la Seu 60, **70–73**
  Chapel of St. Christopher 182
  Eglesia de Sant Miquel del Port 63
  Església de Betlem 76
  Església de La Mercè 59, **76**
  Església de Sant Joan 186, 187
  Girona cathedral 202, 203
  Parròquia Maria Reina 259
  La Sagrada Família 8, 10, 14, 34, **124–129**
  Sagrado Corazón 130
  St. George's Anglican Church 259
  Sant Bartomeu i Santa Tecla, Sitges 196
  Santa Maria de Gràcia 186, 187
  Santa Maria del Mar 23, 61, **123**, 192
  Santa Maria del Pí 15, 60, **130**, 259
  Sant Nicolau, Girona 203
  Sant Pau del Camp 130
  Sant Pere del Castell, Gelida 195
  Tarragona cathedral 198–199
churches, visiting 256, 258
cinema 155
  film festival 197
  Film Museum, Girona 203
  IMAX cinema 59, 160
  listings 160
  Verdi Cinema Complex 80, 160
city areas see Barceloneta; Barri Gòtic; L'Eixample; Gràcia; Montjuïc; El Raval; La Ribera
city layout 4
Clarà, Josep 8
Clavé, Josep Anselm 106
climate 256
clothing sizes 258
Cloud and Chair sculpture 77
clubs 165, 169–170
Codorníu 194–195
coffee and tea 211
Cofradía de Sant Marc 89
coin and stamp market 154
Col.legi d'Arquitectes 74
Collserola National Park 130
Colmados Murria 8, 144, 188, 189

Columbus, Christopher 15, 30, 31, 75, 88
Columbus Monument 31, 59, **88**, 184, 190
communications 266–267
  internet access 267
  post offices and postal services 267, 273
  telephones 266–267, 273
Companys, Lluís 36
complementary medical treatment 263
concert halls
  L'Auditori 161
  Palau de la Música Catalana 8, 10, **104–107**, 161
concessions 43, 51, 261, 265
Conjunt Monumental de la Plaça del Rei 60, **75**, 182
Consell de Cent 28, 117
continental kiss 258
conversion chart 258
cork industry 32
Corpus Christi 18, 72, 197
correfoc (fire-running) 10, 19, 179
El Corte Inglés 8, 115, 139, 151
crafts 136, 142–143
credit cards 210, 260
crime and personal safety 120, 264
cruise ships 23
cultural diversity 20, 21
currency exchange 260, 261
Custo Barcelona 16, 17, 138
customs regulations 257
cycling see bicycling

D

Dalí, Salvador 199
dance
  ballet and modern dance 155
  flamenco 155, 162
  line dancing 21
  sardana 10, 19, 116, 117, 173
Dau Al Set 90, 91
Decorative Arts Museum 108
Deessa sculpture 8
dental treatment 263
department stores and shopping centres 151–152
Design Guide 17
Diada de Catalunya 180
Diadeta 63
La Diagonal 38, 140
Diocesan Museum 60, **92**
Diocesan Museum, Tarragona 199

disabilities, visitors with 52, 259
discount passes 43, 261, 265
doctors 262–263
Domènech i Montaner, Lluís 14, 76, 77, 161
  Casa Fuster 80, 186, 187
  Casa Lleó Morera 82, **83**, 188
  Casa Tomas 76, 188, 189
  Castle of Three Dragons 102
  Hospital de la Santa Creu i Sant Pau 81
  Palau de la Música Catalana 8, 10, **104–107**, 161
Domènech i Roura, Pere 62
Dona i Ocell (Woman and Bird) 8, 16, 17, 109
Don John of Austria 31, 70, 94
Drassanos Reials 28, 94–95
dress code 256
drinking water 263
driving 50
  car ferry services 42
  car rental 41
  drink-driving laws 50
  motor rail 42
  parking 50
  park and ride 50
  regulations 50
  road signs 50
  seat belts 50
  speed limits 50
  to Barcelona 42
  vintage and classic car rental 49
duty-free allowances 257

E

eating out 19, 205–234
  breakfast 210
  with children 210, 259
  credit cards 210
  dinner 210
  fast food 211
  granjas 64, 190, 211
  horchaterias 211
  lunch 210
  menu reader 212–213
  smoking etiquette 210
  tipping 210, 211
  useful words and phrases 273
  vegetarian food 210
  see also restaurants
economy 5, 12, 21
Eglesia de Sant Miquel del Port 63
Egyptian Museum 178
L'Eixample 4, 5, 15, **76**, 139, **188–189**

electricity 258
Elogio del Agua sculpture 109
embassies and consulates
  abroad 257
  in Barcelona 264
emergencies 264
  emergency telephone numbers 262, 264
  useful words and phrases 275
Empúries 88
Els Encants 153
Enterrament de la Sardina 179
entertainment *see* nightlife; performance; sports and activities
entry requirements 257
La Escolania (boys' choir, Montserrat) 201
Església de Betlem 76
Església de La Mercè 59, **76**
Església de Sant Joan 186, 187
Espai Gaudí 67
Estació de França 42, 122, 192
Estació del Nord 109
Estadi Olímpic de Montjuïc 172
ETA (Basque separatist group) 37
Exchange 61, 192
excursions 194–203
  Girona 202–203
  Montserrat 200–201
  Penedès 194–195
  Sitges 196–197
  Tarragona 198–199

F

Fairy Forest 89, 167, 190
Fallen Sky sculpture 109
Farmàcia Bolós 188
Farmàcia Nadal 190
fashion and design 17, 136
fashion shopping 145–147
fast food 211
FC Barcelona 4, 10, 24, 35, 92
Ferdinand and Isabella (Catholic Monarchs) 30, 31, 75, 115
Feria de Abril 180
La Ferralla sculpture 23
ferry services 42
Festa de la Diversitat 180
Festa Major de Barceloneta 63
Festa Major de Gràcia 180
Festes de La Mercè 19, 108, 180
Festival International de Jazz de Barcelona 180

festivals and events 10, 12, 18, 179–180
  Cap d'Any 180
  Carnestoltes 179, 197
  Cavalcava dels Reis 179
  Diada de Catalunya 180
  Diadeta 63
  Feria de Abril 180
  Festa de la Diversitat 180
  Festa Major de Barceloneta 63
  Festa Major de Gràcia 180
  Festes de La Mercè 19, 108, 180
  Festival International de Jazz de Barcelona 180
  Festival de Música Antiga 180
  Fiestas de la Barceloneta 63
  Fiestas de Gràcia 80, 180
  Fira de Santa Llúcia 180
  Grec Festival 118, 180
  Mostra de Vins i Caves de Catalunya 180
  Primavera Sound 118
  Sant Joan 180
  Sant Jordi (St. George's Day) 179
  Sant Medir de Gràcia 179
  Setmana Santa 179
  Sitges Festival International de Cinema 197
  Sónar 74, 180
  Tots Sants 180
Fiestas de la Barceloneta 63
Fiestas de Gràcia 80, 180
Film Museum, Girona 203
Finca Güell 77
Fira de Barcelona 58
Fira de Santa Llúcia 180
fireworks displays 115, 180
fishing industry 23
Fish sculpture 8, 118, 184, 185
flea market 153
La Font del Gat 87
Font Màgica 58, 115, 173
Fontsere, Josep 108
food and drink
  beer, wines and spirits 211
  Catalan cuisine 210, 211
  cava 195
  coffee and tea 211
  drinking water 263
  food shopping 136, 143–145
  food and wine tours 175
  soft drinks 211
  tapas 10, 211
  vegetarian food 210
  wine festival 180
  winery tours 195
  see also eating out

Forment de les Arts Decoratives 77
Fornells-Pla, Francesc 185
Forum 2004 13, 38
Fossar de les Moreres 192
Fosteré, Josep 192
Foster, Norman 130
fountains
  Canaletes 120, 121, 191
  The Cascade 10, 108
  La Font del Gat 87
  Font Màgica 58, 115, 173
  Plaça Reial 115
  Plaça dels Voluntaris 184–185
Franco, General 13, 17, 34, 35, 36, 89
Freixenet 195
Fuente de Santa Maria 192
Fundació Antoni Tàpies 16, **77**, 188
Fundacio Caixa Catalunya 67, 69
Fundacío Joan Miró 8, 16, 58, **78–79**
funicular 49, 86

G

Galeria Olímpica 62
gardens
  Jardí Botànic 58, 81
  Jardins d'Atlanta 185
  Jardins de Mossèn Costa i Llobera 86, 87
  Jardins del Terramar, Sithes 197
Garriga 176
Gaudí, Antoni 14, 34, 88, 128–129, 201, 269
Gaudí buildings
  Casa Batlló 14, 15, **82**, 83, 188
  Casa Calvet 65
  Casa Milà 8, 14, **66–69**
  Casa Vicens 15, **74**, 80, 187
  Finca Güell 77
  Palau Güell 103
  Park Güell 8, **110–113**
  La Sagrada Família 8, 10, 14, 34, **124–129**
gay and lesbian scene 165
gegants and *capsgrossos* (giants and bigheads) 18, 108, 179
Gehry, Frank 8, 118
Gelida 195
  Sant Pere del Castell 195
Generalitat 12, 34, 36, 37, 60, 116
Geology Museum 61, **92**
gifts and souvenirs 136, 142–143

Girona 202–203
  Arabic Bathhouse 203
  Catalan Museum of Jewish
    Culture 203
  cathedral 202, 203
  Centre Bonastruc Ca Porta
    203
  Institute for Sephardic and
    Kabalistic Studies 203
  Jewish community
    202–203
  Monastery of Sant Pere de
    Galligants 203
  Museu d'Arqueològic 203
  Museu d'Art 203
  Museu Capitular 202
  Museu del Cinema 203
  Museu d'Història 203
  Palau Episcopal 203
  Sant Nicolau 203
Golden Square 76, 114, 188
golf 173–174
Gothic Quarter see Barri Gòtic
Gràcia 5, 80, 186–187
granjas 64, 190, 211
Gran Teatre del Liceu 36,
  37, 80, 161, 190
Grec Festival 118, 180
greeting people 258
Guardia Civil 264
Guardia Urbana 264
Güell, Eusebi 15, 77, 103, 113
Guerra dels Segadors
  (Reapers' War) 30, 31
Guifré Borrell 130
Guifré el Pélos
  (Wilfred the Hairy) 26, 27
guilds 64
guiris 21

H

health 262–263
  complementary medical
    treatment 263
  dental treatment 263
  doctors 262–263
  drinking water 263
  emergency telephone
    numbers 262
  health hazards for flyers
    262
  hospitals 263
  inoculations 262
  insurance 262
  medical treatment 262–263
  opticians 263
  pharmacies (farmàcia) 263
  prescription medicines
    256–257, 262, 263
  sun safety 263
  useful words and phrases
    275
health and beauty 175–176

helicopter tours 204
herbalist 144
history 25–38
  anti-clerical riots 33, 35, 69
  Basque terrorism 37
  Catalan nationalism 34, 38
  Catalan Renaixença
    (Renaissance) 5, 14, 15,
    34, 74, 107
  colonialism 32, 33
  Consell de Cent 28, 117
  Counts of Barcelona 26, 28
  Frankish rule 26
  Guerra dels Segadors
    (Reapers' War) 30, 31
  Inquisition 30
  Jewish community 29,
    30, 64
  medieval Barcelona 28–29
  Moorish Spain 26, 27
  Olympics (1992) 5, 36, 37,
    58, 62
  Reconquista 30
  Roman city 26
  Spanish Civil War 13, 34,
    35, 269
  Spanish-American War 33
  Twenty-first century 38
  Usatges de Barcelona 27
  War of the Spanish
    Succession 31, 192
Homage to Barceloneta 8,
  36, 63
Homar, Gaspar 68, 88
Homenage a Picasso 192
homeopathy 263
horchaterias 211
Horn, Rebecca 8
horse riding 174, 195
Hospital de la Santa Creu
  i Sant Pau 81
L'Hospitalet 13
hospitals 263
Hostalric 203
hostals 240, 248–249
hotels 9, 240, 241, 242–253
  booking 240, 241
  by area 241
  facilities 240
  grading 240
  hotel groups 254
  listings 242–253
  locator maps 236–239
  main hotel areas 241
  prices 240
  useful words and phrases
    272
House of Umbrellas 121

I

ice-skating 174
Ictineo (submarine) 33, 119,
  184

IMAX cinema 59, 160
immigration 20
inoculations 262
Inquisition 30
Institute for Sephardic and
  Kabalistic Studies, Girona
  203
Institut del Teatre 162
insurance
  health insurance 262
  travel insurance 257
interior design and home
  furnishings 149–151
International Exhibition
  (1929) 118
internet access 267
Interpreter Card 264
Isozaki, Arata 62, 65
IVA (sales tax) 261

J

Jardí Botànic 58, 81
Jardins d'Atlanta 185
Jardins de Mossèn Costa i
  Llobera 86, 87
Jardins de Salvador Espríu
  186
Jardins del Terramar, Sithes
  197
Jaume I 15, 28, 76
jazz 161, 162, 168, 180
jewellery and accessories
  147–148
Jewish community 29, 30, 64,
  202–203
Jove Teatre Regina 178
Juan Carlos, King 36, 37
Jujol, Josep Maria 67, 112, 115
Julius II, Pope 201

L

Lady with the Parasol (Pepita)
  108
language
  Castilian 4
  Catalan 4, 5, 12, 37,
    258–259
  language assistance 264
  menu reader 212–213
  useful words and phrases
    271–275
laundry and dry-cleaning 258
lavatories 258
leather goods 136, 148–149
Lepanto, battle of 31, 94
LeWitt, Sol 65
libraries
  Catalan National Library
    119
  Fundació Antoni Tàpies 77
  Reial Càtedra Gaudí 77
El Liceu 36, 37, 80, 161, 190
Lichtenstein, Roy 8, 17, 119

Little Barcelona see
  Barceloneta
living statues 120, 121
La Llibertat 153, 186
Llibre d'Ocasió 154
Lloret de Mar 175
La Llotja 61, 192
Lluch, Ernest 37
Llull, Ramon 29
local etiquette 258–259
lost property 264
Louis the Pious 26, 27

M

Macià, Francesc 115
Magic Fountain 58, 115, 173
Mallol, Tomàs 203
Manzana de la Discordia
  8, 76, 82–83
  Casa Amatller 15, 82–83,
    188
  Casa Batlló 14, 15, 82, 83,
    188
  Casa Lleó Morera 83, 188
maps
  accommodation locator
    236–239
  city district 6–7
  free maps 269
  performance arts locator
    156–159
  restaurant locator 206–209
  shopping locator 132–135
  sights locator 54–57
  street map 278–291
Maragall, Pascual 12, 36, 38
Marathon 171, 173
Mar Bella 173
Maremagnum 22, 59, 119,
  152
Marès i Deuloval, Frederic
  92, 130
Maritime Museum 8, 59,
  94–95
markets 153–154
  antiques markets 154
  art and crafts markets 119,
    137, 154
  book market 154
  Christmas market 180
  coin and stamp market
    154
  Els Encantes 153
  flea market 153
  La Llibertat 153, 186
  Llibre d'Ocasió 154
  Mercat Abaceria 186
  Mercat La Barceloneta
    152–153
  Mercat de la Boqueria 8,
    153, 190
  Plaça del Pí 137, 154
  Plaça Reial 154

markets *(cont.)*
Plaça de Sant Josep Oriol
137, 154
Plaça de Sant Just 182–183
Plaça de la Seu 154
Poble Nou 154
Port Vell 154
Sant Antoni 154
Santa Caterina 154
Santa Llúcia 154
Mas, Artur 12, 38
Maugham, Somerset 120
measurements and sizes 258
media 268
newspapers and magazines
268
radio 268
television 268
medical treatment 262–263
Meier, Richard 90
Mercat Abaceria 186
Mercat la Barceloneta
152–153
Mercat de la Boqueria 8, 153,
190
Mercat del Born 61, 122, 192
Mercat de les Flors 163
Mercat de la Llibertat 153,
186
Mercat de Sant Josep *see*
Mercat de la Boqueria
MerkaFad 77
metro 44–45
Mies van der Rohe, Ludwig
65, 114
Military Museum 86–87
Mirador del Rei 75, 115
Miró, Joan 8, 16, 17, 19,
78–79, 109, 121, 199
Miró Foundation 8, 16, 58,
78–79
mobile phones 267
Modern Art Museum 30,
61, **88**
Modernisme 5, 14, 15, 16,
34
Modernista architecture
Ateneu Barcelonès 190
Casa Amatller 15, **82–83**,
188
Casa Antiga Figueres 122,
190, 191
Casa Batlló 14, 15, **82**, 83,
188
Casa Calvet 65
Casa Fuster 80, 186, 187
Casa Lleó Morera 82, **83**,
188
Casa Milà 8, 14, **66–69**
Casa de les Punxes 76, 188,
189
Casa Quadros 34
Casa Terrades 76

Modernista architecture
(cont.)
Casa Tomas 76, 188, 189
Casa Vicens 15, **74**, 80,
187
Casaramona 65
Centre del Modernisme 76,
83
Colmados Murria 8, 144,
188, 189
Farmàcia Bolós 188
Finca Güell 77
Fundacío La Caixa 89
**Hospital de la Santa
Creu i Sant Pau 81**
**Manzana de la
Discordia** 8, 76, **82–83**,
188
Palau Güell 103
**Palau de la Música
Catalana** 8, 10,
104–107, 161
Park Güell 8, **110–113**
Quadrat d'Or 76, 114, 188
Ruta del Modernisme 265
La Sagrada Família 8, 10,
34, **124–129**
Molina, Daniel 115
Moll de Barcelona 59, 119
Moll d'Espanya 119
Moll de la Fusta 184
monasteries
Monastery of Sant Pere de
Galligants, Girona 203
**Monestir de Pedralbes
84–85**
Montserrat 200–201
Moneo, Rafael 161
**Monestir de Pedralbes
84–85**
money 260–261
ATMs 260
banknotes and coins 260
banks 260–261, 265
concessions 43, 51, 261,
265
credit cards 210, 260
currency exchange 260,
261
everyday items and prices
261
exchange rates 260
taxes 261
tipping 210, 211, 261
traveller's cheques 257,
260
useful words and phrases
271
wiring money 261
Montjuïc 5, 58, **86–87**
L'Anella Olímpica 58, **62**
CaixaForum 58, **65**, 161
La Font del Gat 87

Montjuïc *(cont.)*
Font Màgica 58, 115, 173
Fundacío Joan Miró 8,
16, 58, **78–79**
funicular 49, 86
Jardí Botànic 58, **81**
**Museu d'Arqueologia
de Catalunya** 58, **88**
**Museu Nacíonal d'Art
de Catalunya (MNAC)**
9, 58, 96, **96–99**
**Pavelló Mies van der
Rohe** 58, **114**
Poble Espanyol 58,
118
Teatre Grec 87, 163, 180
Telefèric do Montjuïc 49,
86, 87
Mont Pelat 110
Montserrat 200–201
Monturiol, Narcís 33, 119
El Monumental 88, 172
Monument a Colom 31, 59,
88, 184, 190
La Moreneta 200, 201
Mostra de Vins i Caves de
Catalunya 180
motorcycle rental 49
motor rail 42
motorsport 172
Mulberry Graveyard 192
museum and gallery opening
times 265
museum and gallery passes
265
museums and galleries
Archaeological Museum
58, **88**
Archaeological Museum,
Girona 203
Archaeological Museum,
Tarragona 199
**Barcelona Football Club
Museum 92**
**Barcelona Museum of
Contemporary Art
(MACBA)** 8, 16, **90–91**
Bullfighting Museum 88
CaixaForum 58, **65**
Casa-Museu Gaudí 110, 112
**Casa-Museu Verdaguer
74**
**Catalan History
Museum** 59, **93**
Catalan Museum of Jewish
Culture, Girona 203
**Centre de Cultura
Contemporània de
Barcelona (CCCB)** 74
Ceramics Museum 108
Chocolate Museum 102
**Conjunt Monumental de
la Plaça del Rei** 60, **75**

museums and galleries
(cont.)
**Decorative Arts
Museum 108**
Diocesan Museum 60,
92
Diocesan Museum,
Tarragona 199
Egyptian Museum 178
Film Museum, Girona 203
Fundació Antoni Tàpies
16, **77**, 188
Fundació Joan Miró 8,
16, 58, **78–79**
Geology Museum 61, **92**
Maritime Museum 8, 59,
94–95
Military Museum 86–87
Modern Art Museum 30,
61, **88**
**Museu d'Arqueologia
de Catalunya** 58, **88**
Museu d'Arqueològic,
Girona 203
Museu d'Art, Girona 203
**Museu d'Art
Contemporani de
Barcelona (MACBA)** 8,
16, **90–91**
Museu d'Art Modern 30,
61, **88**
**Museu de les Arts
Decoratives 108**
**Museu Barbier-Mueller
d'Art Precolombi 89**
Museu del Calçat 60,
89
Museu Capitular, Girona
202
Museu Cau Ferrat, Sitges
196
Museu de Cera 59, **89**
Museu de Ceramica 108
Museu de la Ciencia 89
Museu del Cinema, Girona
203
Museu Diocesà 60, **92**
Museu Diocesà, Tarragona
199
Museu Egipci de Barcelona
178
**Museu FC Barcelona
92**
Museu Frederic Marès
60, **92**, 182
Museu de Geologia 61,
92
**Museu d'Història de
Catalunya** 59, **93**
Museu d'Història de la
Ciutat *see* **Conjunt
Monumental de la
Plaça del Rei**

Museu d'Historia, Girona 203
Museu d'Historia, Tarragona 199
Museu Maricel, Sitges 197
Museu Marítim 8, 59, **94–95**
Museu Militar 86–87
Museu Nacíonal d'Art de Catalunya (MNAC) 8, 58, **96–99**
Museu del Perfum 102
Museu Picasso 8, 61, **100–101**
Museu de la Romanitat, Tarragona 199
Museu Romàntic, Sitges 197
Museu Tèxtil i d'Indumentària 61, **102**
Museu de Vilafranca 194
Museu del Ví, Vilafranca 194, 195
Museu de la Xocolata 102
Museu de Zoologia 61, **102**
National Museum of Catalan Art 8, 58, **96–99**
Perfume Museum 102
Picasso Museum 8, 61, **100–101**
Science Museum 89
Shoe Museum 60, **89**
Textile and Clothing Museum 61, **102**
Thyssen Collection, Monestir de Pedralbes 84–85
Waxworks Museum 59, **89**
Wine Museum, Vilafranca 194
Zoological Museum 102
music
classical music 155, 161
contemporary live music 155, 161–162
country music 21
jazz 161, 162, 168, 180
music stores 141–142
opera 155, 161

N

Nabot, Francesc 115
national holidays 265
National Museum of Catalan Art 8, 58, **96–99**
naturopathy 263
Nesjar, Carl 74
New Cemetery 22

newspapers and magazines 268
New Year's Eve 180
nightlife 165–170
bars and cafés 9, 166–169
clubs 165, 169–170
gay and lesbian nightlife 165
listings magazines 165
Nou Camp 24
Noucentista 190
Nouvel, Jean 14, 15
Nova Icària 23, 118

O

Olèrdola 195
Olot School 88, 203
Olympic Port and Village 4, 22, 23, **118**, 184–185
Olympic Ring 58, **62**
Olympics (1992) 5, 36, 37, 58, 62
opening times 265
opera 155, 161
opticians 263
Orfeó Català (Catalan Choral Society) 105, 107
Orwell, George 35, 121, 129, 269

P

packing tips 256–257
Palace of Catalan Music 8, 10, **104–107**
Palau Berenguer d'Aguilar 100
Palau Dalmases 192, 193
Palau Episcopal, Girona 203
Palau de la Generalitat 13, **116–117**
Palau Güell 103
Palau de Llotinent 115, 182
Palau del Mar 93, 184, 185
Palau Maricel, Sitges 197
Palau de la Música Catalana 8, 10, **104–107**, 161
Palau Nacional 97, 99
Palau Nadal 89
Palau Reial 60, 115
Palau Reial de Pedralbes 108
Palau Sant Jordi 36–37, 62
Palau de la Virreina 108
La Paloma 10, 162, 173
Parc d'Atraccions 130, 178, 259
Parc de la Barceloneta 184, 185
Parc de les Cascades 185
Parc de la Ciutadella 10, 61, **108**, 178
Parc del Clot 108

Parc de la Creueta del Col 109
Parc de l'Espanya Industriel 109
Parc de l'Estació del Nord 109
Park Güell 8, **110–113**
Parc de Joan Miró 17, **109**
Parc del Laberint 114, 178
Parc Zoològic 114
parking 50
park and ride 42, 50
Parlement de Catalunya 61
Parròquia Maria Reina 259
Pasarela Gaudí fashion show 17
Passeig del Born 29, 122, 138
Passeig de Colom 5
Passeig de Gràcia 4, 10, 15, 80, **114**, 139, 256
Passeig Joan de Borbó 59, 63, 119, 184
Passeig Marítim de la Barceloneta 184
Passeig Marítim del Port Olímpic 184
passports 257
lost passport 264
Pati Llimona 182
Pavelló Mies van der Rohe 58, **114**
Penedès 194–195
Codorníu 194–195
Gelida 195
Olèrdola 195
Sant Qunití de Mediona 195
Vilafranca 194
Pepper, Beverly 109
performance 155–164
cinema 155, 160
classical music, dance and opera 155, 161
contemporary live music 155, 161–162
flamenco 155, 162
locator maps 156–159
theatre 155, 162–164
tickets 155
Perfume Museum 102
pessebres (Christmas nativity dioramas) 76
pharmacies (farmàcia) 263
Picasso, Pablo 16, 35, 74, 100–101, 192, 201, 269
Picasso Museum 8, 61, **100–101**
pickpockets 120, 264
Picornell swimming pools 62, 174
Plaça dels Àngels 90, 119
Plaça de la Barceloneta 63
Plaça de la Boqueria 121

Plaça de Catalunya 15, **115**, 139
Plaça d'Espanya 5, 14, 15, 58, **115**
Plaça de Glòries 15
Plaça John Lennon 80
Plaça de la Llibertat 186
Plaça del Mar 184
Plaça Martorell 119
Plaça de les Olles 192, 193
Plaça del Pí 60, 64, 137, 154, 190
Plaça del Rei 60, **115**, 182
Plaça Reial 115, 154, 190
Plaça de Ruis i Taulet 80, 186
Plaça de Sant Felip Neri 60, 64, 182
Plaça de Sant Jaume 13, 60, **116–117**, 182
Plaça de Sant Josep Oriol 137, 154
Plaça de Sant Just 182–183
Plaça de Santa Maria del Mar 122, 138
Plaça de la Seu 60, 154
Plaça del Sol 80, 186, 187
Plaça de Universitat 259
Plaça Víla de Madrid 190
Plaça de la Virreina 80, 186
Plaça dels Voluntaris 184–185
places of worship 259
Platja de la Barceloneta 59, 63, 173
playgrounds 259
Plaza de Toros Monumental 88, 172
Poble Espanyol 58, **118**, 178
Poble Nou 22, 38, 154
police 264
Policía Nacional 264
politics and government 12, 13, 38
Pont del Diable, Tarragona 198
Pontius Pilate 199
population 4
Port Aventura 177
Port Olímpic 4, 22, 23, **118**, 184
Port Vell 4, 22, **59**, **118–119**, 154, 184
L'Aquàrium de Barcelona 59, **62**, 184
Eglésia de La Mercè 59, **76**
Maremagnum 22, 59, 119, 152
Monument a Colom 31, 59, **88**, 184, 190
Museu de Cera 59, **89**
Museu d'Història de Catalunya 59, **93**

Port Vell *(cont.)*
Museu Marítim 8, 59,
    94–95
Platja de la Barceloneta 59,
    63, 173
Porxes de Fosteré 192
post offices and postal
    services 267, 273
prescription medicines
    256–257, 262, 263
Primavera Sound 118
private house rentals 240
public transport 43–50
    Barcelona Card 43
    buses 46
    children 43, 51, 259
    disabilities, visitors with 52,
        259
    discount passes 43
    funicular 49, 59, 86
    horse-drawn carriages 49
    local and regional trains 42,
        49, 51
    maps and information 43
    metro 44–45
    smoking etiquette 43
    taxis 41, 49
    Telefèric de Montjuïc 49,
        86, 87
    Tramvia Blau 49, 130
    Transports Metropolitans
        de Barcelona (TMB) 43
    useful words and phrases
        273
    website 270
Puig i Cadafalch, Josep 14, 76,
    87, 88, 97, 195, 200, 201
    Casa Amatller 15, **82–83**,
        188
    Casa Terrades (Casa de les
        Punxes) 76, 188, 189
    Casaramona 65
    Fundació La Caixa 89
    Quatre Gats 16
Pujol, Jordi 12, 36, 38, 89
puppet shows 178

Q

Quadrat d'Or 76, 114, 188
Els Quatre Gats (Four Cats)
    16, 229

R

radio 268
rail travel 40–41, 42, 51
    airport to city transport
        40–41
    concessions 51
    disabilities, visitors with 52
    international trains 42
    journey times 51
    local and regional trains 42,
        49, 51

rail travel *(cont.)*
    overnight trains 42, 51
    tickets 51
rainfall 256
Rambla del Mar 59, 119, 121,
    190
Las Ramblas 4, 10, 32, 33,
    120–121, **190–191**, 264
    La Rambla dels Caputxins
        121
    La Rambla de Canaletes
        120–121, 190
    La Rambla dels Estudis 121
    La Rambla de les Flors 121,
        190
    La Rambla dels Ocells 121
    La Rambla de Santa
        Mònica 121
    self-guided walk 190–191
El Raval 4, 5, 20, 21, 38,
    91, **119**
RCD Espanyol 171
Real Madrid 4, 24, 35
reflexology 263
Reial Càtedra Gaudí 77
religious celebrations 18, 179
restaurants 9
    by cuisine 214–215
    listings 216–234
    locator maps 206–209
    menú del dia 210
    menu reader 212–213
    opening times 265
    reservations 210
    tipping 210
    useful words and phrases
        273
La Ribera 5, 29, 61, **122**, 138,
    192–193
    Carrer de Montcada 29, 61,
        192
    La Llotja 61, 192
    Mercat del Born 61, 122,
        192
    Museu d'Art Modern 30,
        61, **88**
    Museu de Geologia 61,
        92
    Museu Picasso 8, 61,
        100–101
    **Museu Tèxtil i
        d'Indumentària** 61,
        102
    Museu de Zoologia 61,
        102
    Parc de la Ciutadella 10,
        61, **108**, 178
    Santa Maria del Mar 23,
        123, 192
Rogers, Richard 14, 15
Roig i Soler 108
Roman Barcelona 27, 75,
    182, 190

Romanesque architecture
    130
Romeu, Pere 16, 89
Route of the Holy Cave 201
Rovira i Trias, Antonio 92
Royal Palace 60, 115
royal shipyards 28, 94–95
Royo, Josep 78
Rusiñyol, Santiago 16, 69, 196
Ruta del Modernisme 265

S

La Sagrada Família 8, 10,
    14, 34, **124–129**
Sagrado Corazón 130
St. George's Anglican Church
    259
sales tax 261
Saló de les Croniques 117
Saló de Sant Jordi 116–117
Saló del Tinell 60, 75, 115
Sant Antoni 154
Sant Bartomeu i Santa Tecla,
    Sitges 196
Santa Caterina 154
Santa Eulàlia 26, 27, 70, 72,
    123
Santa Eulàlia (schooner) 95
Sant Joan de les Abadesses
    26
Sant Joan, feast of 180
Sant Jordi (St. George) 15, 69,
    82, 188
Sant Jordi (St. George's Day)
    179
Santa Llúcia 154
Santa Maria de Gràcia 186,
    187
Santa Maria del Mar 23,
    123, 192
Santa Maria del Pí 15, 60,
    130, 259
Sant Medir de Gràcia 179
Sant Nicolau, Girona 203
Sant Pau del Camp 130
Sant Pere del Castell, Gelida
    195
Sant Qunití de Mediona 195
Sant Sadorni d'Anoia 195
Sant Sebastià 173
sardana 10, 19, 116, 117, 173
Sardana sculpture 34, 87
Saura, Antonio 90–91
scatalogical traditions 19
Science Museum 89
sculptures, outdoor
    Barcelona Head 8, 17, 119,
        184
    The Cascade 108
    Cloud and Chair 77
    Deessa 8
    Dona i Ocell (Woman and
        Bird) 8, 16, 17, 109

sculptures, outdoor *(cont.)*
    Elogio del Agua 109
    Fallen Sky 109
    La Ferralla 23
    Fish 8, 118, 184, 185
    Homage to Barceloneta 8,
        36, 63
    Homenage a Picasso 192
    Lady with the Parasol
        (*Pepita*) 108
    Sardana 34, 87
    Tallavents (Windbreaker)
        185
    Topo 115
    Wooded Spiral 109
seasons 256
self-catering accommodation
    240
seniors 261
Serra, Richard 17
Sert, Josep Lluís 79, 117
Setmana Santa 179
Setmana Tràgica 35, 69
Shoe Museum 60, **89**
shopping 8, 136–154
    antiques 142
    arts, crafts and gifts 136,
        142–143
    bookshops 141
    chain stores 152–153
    department stores and
        shopping centres
        151–152
    fashion and design 136,
        145–147
    food shopping 136,
        143–145
    interior design and home
        furnishings 149–151
    jewellery and accessories
        147–148
    leather goods 136,
        148–149
    locator maps 132–135
    music stores 141–142
    opening times 265
    sales tax 261
    Shopping Line (bus route)
        47
    useful words and phrases
        272
    see also markets
shopping areas
    Barri Gòtic 137
    La Diagonal 140
    L'Eixample 139
    La Ribera 138
siesta 258, 263
sightseeing areas
    Barri Gòtic 60
    Montjuïc 58
    the Port 59
    La Ribera 61

Sitges 196–197
  Hotel Terramar 197
  Jardins del Terramar 197
  Museu Cau Ferrat 196
  Museu Maricel 197
  Museu Romàntic 197
  Palau Maricel 197
  Sant Bartomeu i Santa
    Tecla 196
  Sitges Festival International
    de Cinema 197
smoking etiquette 43, 155,
  210, 258
soccer 4, 10, 24, 35, 92,
  171, 172
social problems 5
soft drinks 211
sombreros 137
Sónar 74, 180
Spanish Civil War 13, 34, 35,
  269
Spanish Village 58, **118**, 178
Spanish–American War 33
spas and salons 175–176
sports and activities 171–176
  athletics 173
  ballroom dancing 10, 173
  basketball 171, 172
  beaches 173
  bullfighting 171, 172
  cycling 173
  dancing 173
  golf 173–174
  health and beauty 175–176
  horse riding 174, 195
  ice-skating 174
  Marathon 171, 173
  motorsport 172
  soccer 4, 10, 24, 35, 92,
    171, 172
  sports complexes 171, 174
  swimming 62, 174
  tennis 171, 174
  tenpin bowling 174
  watersports 175
student and young visitors
  261, 265
Subirachs, Josep M. 17, 125,
  200
sun safety 263
Sunyol, Josep 24
swimming 62, 174
Synagogue de Barcelona 259

T

Tallavents (Windbreaker) 185
Tallers Oberts (Open
  Workshops) 77
tapas 10, 211
Tàpies, Antoni 16, 17, 77, 91,
  192
Tàpies Foundation 16, **77**,
  188

Taradellas, Josep 36, 93
Tarragona 26, 27, 198–199
  amphitheatre 198
  aqueduct 26, 198
  Archaeological Museum
    199
  Balcó del Mediterrani 198
  Casa Castellarnau 199
  cathedral 198–199
  Museu Diocesà 199
  Museu d'Historia 199
  Museu de la Romanitat 199
  Passeig Arqueològic 198
  Pont del Diable 198
taxes 261
taxis 41, 49
Teatre Grec 87, 163, 180
Teatre Musical 161
Teatre Nacional de Catalunya
  163
Teatre Principal 121, 164
Teatro Poliorama 121, 164
telebanco 260
Telefèric de Montjuïc 49, 86,
  87
telephones 266–267, 273
  charges 266
  international calls 266
  mobile phones 267
  national numbers 266
  public telephones 266, 267
television 268
Temple d'Augustus 182, 183
tennis 171, 174
tenpin bowling 174
**Textile and Clothing
  Museum** 61, **102**
theatre 155, 162–164
**Thyssen Collection,
  Monestir de Pedralbes
  84–85**
Tibidabo 10, **130**
time zones 257
tipping 210, 211, 261
toilets 258
Topo sculpture 115
La Torre Agbor 15
Torre de Collserola 130
Torres 195
Tots Sants 180
tourism 5, 13
tourist offices
  abroad 270
  Barcelona 270
  useful words and phrases
    275
  websites 270
tours of Barcelona 204
  bicycle tours 204
  bus tours 204
  car tours 204
  helicopter tours 204
  see also walks

Town Hall 13, 60, **116–117**
trade fairs 256
Tramvia Blau 49, 130
travel
  air travel 40–41, 52
  buses, long-distance 42, 51
  disabilities, visitors with 52
  ferry services 42
  rail travel 40–41, 42, 49,
    51, 52
  websites 270
  see also driving; public
    transport
travel insurance 257
traveller's cheques 257, 260
trencadís 82, 103, 107, 113

U

Universal Exhibition (1888)
  32, 108
Universal Forum of Cultures
  (2004) 13, 38
Utrillo, Miquel 16

V

vegetarian food 210
Verdaguer, Jacint 74, 77
Verdi Cinema Complex 80,
  160
Vía Laietana 61
Vilafranca 194
  Basilica de Santa Maria 194
  Museu del Vi 194, 195
  Museu de Vilafranca 194
Vila Olímpica 23, 118
Villar, Francesc de 128
vintage and classic car rental
  49
visas 257

W

walks 182–193
  Barri Gòtic 182–183
  L'Eixample 188–189
  Gràcia 186–187
  guided walks 204
  Las Ramblas 190–191
  La Ribera 192–193
  Ruta del Modernisme 265
  waterfront 184–185
War of the Spanish
  Succession 31
waterfront 22–23, 184–185
  cruise and container traffic
    23
  Port Olímpic 4, 22, 23,
    118, 184
  Port Vell 4, 22, **118–119**,
    154, 184
watersports 175
Waxworks Museum 59, **89**
weather reports 256
websites 270

wildlife attractions
  **L'Aquàrium de
    Barcelona** 59, **62**, 184
  Parc Zoològic 114
Wine Museum, Vilafranca
  194
winery tours 195
women visitors 264
Wooded Spiral sculpture 109
World Trade Center 119

Z

Zoological Museum 102

The following indexes list individual perfomance and nightlife venues, hotels, restaurants and stores.

BARS AND CAFÉS

Al Limón Negro 166
L'Ascensor 166
El Bar del Majestic 166
Bar del Pí 166
BCN Rouge 166
Benidorm 166
Berimbau 166
Boadas Cocktail Bar 166
El Bosque de les Fades 167
Buda Barcelona 167
Café d'Estiu
Café de l'Opera 166
Café Royale 167
Café Zurich 167
Caputxes 167
Espai Barroc 167
La Fira 167
Les Gens Que J'aime 167
Glaciar 168
Granja de Gavà 168
Harlem Jazz Club 168
Hivernacle 168
Hotel Ritz 167
Ideal 168
Los Juanele 168
Kentucky 168
London Bar 168
Marsella 168
Mirablau 168
Miramelindo 168
Mond 168
Muebles Navarro 169
Pilé 43 169
Punto BCN 169
Schilling 169
El Taco de Margarita 169
Tetería Jazmín 169
Els Tres Tombs 169

CINEMAS

Coliseum 160
Comedia 160
FilmaTeca de Catalunya 160
IMAX 160
Maldà 160
Mèlies 160
Renoir les Cortes 160
Renoir Floridablanca 160
Verdi 160
Verdi Park 160
Yelmo Cineplex Icaria 160

CLUBS

Arena 169
Danzatoria 169
Dietrich 169
Discothèque 169

Dostrece 170
Dot 170
Lekasbah 170
Metro 170
Moog 170
Otto Zutz 170
República 170
Sweet Café 170
La Terraza 170
VIP 170

CLASSICAL MUSIC AND DANCE VENUES

L'Auditori 161
Gran Teatre del Liceu 161
Palau de la Música Catalana 161
Teatre Musical 161

CONTEMPORARY MUSIC VENUES

Bikini 161
La Boîte 161
CaixaForum 161
La Cova del Drac 162
L'Espai 162
Jamboree 162
Luz de Gas 162
La Paloma 162
Razzmatazz 162
Los Tarantos 162

HOTELS

Abalon 242
AC Diplomatic 242
Actual 242
Alexandra 242
Ambassador 242
Amrey Diagonal 242–243
Arts Hotel 243
Banys Orientals 243
Barcelona House 243
Barcelona Plaza 243
California 243
Catalonia Duques de Bergara 243–244
Catalonia Roma 244
Cataluña 244
Center Ramblas 244
Citadines Barcelona Ramblas 244
Claris 244
Colón 244–245
Comercio 245
Condado 245
Condestable 245
Confort 245
Continental 245
Continental Palacete 245–246
Cortes 246
De l'Arc 246
España 246
Gallery 246

Gat-Raval 246
Gaudí 247
Gòtico 247
Grand Marina 247
Gran Hotel Havana 247
Gran Hotel La Florida 247
Granvia 247–248
Hesperia Metropol 248
Hilton Barcelona 248
Hostal Central 248
Hostal Goya 248
Hostal Ítaca 248
Hostal Nilo 248–249
Hostal Nuevo Colón 249
Hostal Oasis 249
Hostal Oliva 249
Husa Oriente 249
Lleó 249
Lyon 250
Majestic 250
Marina Folch 250
Le Meridien Barcelona 230
Mesón Castilla 250
Millennium 250–251
Monegal 251
Ònix 251
Paral.lel 251
Park Hotel 251
Peninsular 251
Pensión Segre 251
Princesa Sofía 251–252
Principal 252
Regencia Colón 252
Relais d'Orsà 252
Rey Juan Carlos I 252
Rialto 252
Ritz 252
Ritz Roger de Llúria 253
Rubens 253
Sant Agustí 253
Splendid 253
Suizo 253
Toledano/Hostal Residencia Capitol 253
Turín 253
Turó de Vilana 253

RESTAURANTS

Àbac 216
El Abrevadero 216
Agua 216
Agullers 216
Agut 216
Altamar 216
Anfiteatro 216–217
Anima 217
Antiga Casa Solé 217
Arc Café 217
Asador de Aranda 217
Bar Canigó 187
Barceloneta 218
Bar Central 217
Bar del Pí 137

Bar Ra 217
Bar Raval 217–218
La Barra del Botafumeiro 218
Bestial 218
Biblioteca 218
Bio-Center 218
Blues Café 218
Bodega Manolo 219
La Bodegueta 189
El Boix de la Cerdanya 219
La Bombeta 219
Buenas Migas 219
La Buena Tierra 219
Ca l'Isidre 219
Cal Pep 220
El Cangrejo Loco 220
Can Culleretes 220
Can Juanito 220
Can Majó 220
Can Ramonet 220
La Carassa 220–221
Casa Leopoldo 221
Casa Madrid 221
Cerveceria Catalana 139, 221
Comerç 24
La Cova Fumada 221
Cros Diagonal 140
Damasco 221
Daps 140
De Tapa Madre 222
Don Marisco 222
Emperador 222
Estrella de Plata 222
Flash Flash 222
La Flauta Mágica 222
Fragile 222
El Foro 222
La Gavina (Barceloneta) 223
La Gavina (Gràcia) 222
Ginger 223
Hello Sushi 223
Hoffmann 223
El Huevo de Colón 223
Ikastola 223
L'Illa de Gràcia 224
Julius 224
Julivert Meu 224
Limbo 224
Little Italy 138, 224
Living 224
El Lobito 224–225
Lupino 224
El Magatzem del Port 225
Mama Café 225
Mastroqué 225
Melitón 225
Ménage à Trois 225–226
Il Mercante di Venezia 226
Merendero de la Mari 226
Mesón David 226
Mesopotamia 226
El Moncho's 226
La Mundial 226

Negro 226
Nervión 226–227
Norbaltic 227
Noti 227
Nou Can Tipa 227
Oolong 227
Orígenes 99,9% 138, 227
Organic 227
Ot 228
Oven 228
Els Pescadors 228
El Petit Miau 228
Pitarra 228
Pla 228
Plats 229
Polenta 229
Pop's 229
Pou Dolç 229
Pucca 229
Els Quatre Gats 229
Quim 229
Quimet, Quimet 230
Quo Vadis 230
El Racó d'en Freixa 230
Racó de la Vila 230
Reial Club Maritim de
   Barcelona 230
El Rey de la Gamba 230
Rías de Galicia 230
Rita Blue 230–231
Rúccula 231
Salamanca 231
Salambó 231
Salero 231
El Salón 231
Salsitas 231
San Telmo 231
Sésamo 232
Set Portes 232
Shunka 232
Silenus 232
Slokai 232
Sol Soler 232
Tábata 233
Taixdermista 233
Talaia 233
Teresa 233
El Tragaluz 233
El Túnel del Port 233
Umita 233–234
El Vell de Sarriá 234
La Venta 234
Venus Delicatessen 234
La Verónica 137, 234
Vía Veneto 234
Vinatería del Call 234
Zoo 234

STORES
37ºC 138
Adolfo Domínquez 140, 145
Against 149
Agatha 147

Agua del Carmen 138, 145
Altaïr 141
Angel Batlle 142
Anna Povo 138
Antiga Casa Sala 137
Antiga Pasamaneria J. Soler
   137
Antonio Miró 145
Antonio Pernas 145
L'Arca de L'Àvia 137
Armand Basi 145
Arte & Objeto 149
Bagués Joieria 139
BD Ediciones de Diseño 149
La Botifarreria de Santa Maria
   138
Botiga del Te i Cafès 143
El Bulevard dels Antiquaris
   142
Bulevard Rosa 139, 151
La Caixa de Fang 142–143
Calpa 148
Calvin Klein 140
Camisería Pons 145
Camper 139, 148
Candela con Burundanga 138
Carles Galindo 147
Casa Colomina 137
Casa del Libro 141
Casas 148–149
Casa Usher 142
Castelló Discos 141
Celestial 137
Celler de Gelida 144
Centre Català d'Artesania
   139, 143
Colmado Afro-Latino 144
Colmado Murria 144
La Comercial Woman 138
Cómplices 141
Conti 140
Coriumcasa 149
El Corte Inglés 139, 151
Custo 138
Czar 149
Daaz 138
D Barcelona 149
Diagonal Mar 151
Diesel 139
Dom 150
Emporio Armani 140
Escribá 144
Espai Ras 141
Farga 140
FNAC 139, 141–142
Gabriel Torres 145–146
Gala 149
Galeria d'Art 139
Galeria F. Cervera 137
Galeria de Santa Novella 138
Gastón y Daniela 150
Gemma Pichot 147
Gemma Povo 137, 150

Germanes Garcia 137
The Gift 147
Giménez & Zuazo 138
Glamoor 148
Gotham 150
Gucci 140
Habitat 140, 150
Herbolari 144
Hipótesis 148
Ici et Là 138, 150
Iranzo 139
Jamonísimo 144
Joaquín Berao 148
Jordi Barnadas 139
Josep Font 139
Kitsch 143
Laie 141
L'Illa 151–152
Llibreria Quera 137
Loewe 145
Loring Art 141
M69 146
MACBA 143
Mango 139, 146
MDM 140, 150
La Manual Alpargatera 148
Maremagnum 152
Mar Franc 149
Massimo Dutti 146
Mechén Tomàs 138
El Mercadillo 137
Mil Barrets i Gorres 148
MTX 138
Natura Casa 140
Neck and Neck 140
Nunoya 143
On Land 146
Otranto 142
Overales & Bluyines 146
Papirum 143
Pascual Miró 142
Pepa Paper 143
Pilma 140, 150–151
Quilez 144
Rafa 149
Rafa Teja Atelier 138
Re-Born 139
Regia 139
Riera 140, 151
Roberto Verino 139
Sala Parés 137
Sarri 140
Señor 146
Sephora 139
Sita Murt 137
SO_DA 137
Sombreria Obach 137
Them 146
Toscana 140
El Triangle 152
Tribu 146–147
Urbana 142
Vialis 138

Victor Caparros 140
Vientos del Sur 151
Vina Viniteca 144–145
Vinçon 139, 151
Vitra 138
Zara 139, 147
[Z]ink 137, 147
Zona Eleven 147
Zsu Zsa 147

THEATRES
Artenbrut 162
Club Capitol 162
Espai Joan Brossa 162
Institut del Teatre 162
Mercat de les Flors 163
Sala Beckett 163
Sala Muntaner 163
Teatre Borràs 163
Teatre Goya 163
Teatre Grec 163
Teatre Lliure 163
Teatre Lliure de Gràcia 163
Teatre Malic 163
Teatre Nacional de Catalunya
   163
Teatreneu Teatre 164
Teatre Principal 164
Teatre Romea 164
Teatro Apolo 164
Teatro Poliorama 164
Teatro Tívoli 164
Teatro Víctoria 164
Teatro Villarroel 164
Versus Teatre 164

ACKNOWLEDGMENTS

Abbreviations for the credits are as follows:
AA = AA World Travel Library, t (top), b (bottom), c (centre), l (left), r (right), bg (background)

UNDERSTANDING BARCELONA

5cl AA/S Day; 5cc AA/S Day; 5cr AA/M Chaplow; 8tl AA/S Day; 8tr AA/M Jourdan; 8cr Clare Garcia; 8bcr AA/M Chaplow; 8br AA/S McBride; 9tl AA/M Chaplow; 9cr AA/M Chaplow; 9cl AA/S McBride; 9bl AA/A Molyneux; 9br AA/S McBride; 10tl AA/M Jourdan; 10tr AA/S Day; 10cl Clare Garcia; 10cr AA/J Edmanson; 10bcl AA/S Day; 10br AA/M Jourdan

LIVING BARCELONA

11 AA/M Jourdan; 12/13bg AA/M Jourdan; 12tl AA/M Jourdan; 12ctl AA/P Enticknap; 12cl AA/M Chaplow; 12bl AA/P Wilson; 12tr AA/M Chaplow; 12ctr S Day; 13l © Archivo Iconografico, S.A./CORBIS; 13tr AA/M Chaplow; 13cr Forum 2004; 14/15bg AA/S Day; 14tl Richard Rogers Partnership and Alonso Balaguer; 14bc AA/S Day; 14tr AA/S Day; 14c AA/S Day; 14ctr AA/S McBride; 14cbr AA/S Day; 15tl AA/S Day; 15tr AA/ M Jourdan; 15cr AA/M Jourdan; 15cl AA/S Day; 16/17bg AA/S Day; 16tl AA/M Jourdan; 16tr AA/M Chaplow; 16cr AA/M Chaplow; 16cct Illustrated London News; 16tc AA/M Chaplow; 16cbc Custo; 16cl AA/M Jourdan; 17tr Vincon; 17cl AA/S Day; 17cc Paserela Gaudi; 17cr Vincon; 18/19bg AA/M Chaplow; 18tc Pictures Colour Library; 18tl Forum 2004; 18tr Eye Ubiquitous; 18b World Pictures; 18/19t AA/M Jourdan; 19tr AA/P Enticknap; 19cc AA/M Jourdan; 18/19b AA/M Jourdan; 19cr AA/M Chaplow; 20/21bg AA/M Chaplow; 20tl AA/S McBride; 20ctl AA/ M Chaplow; 20tr AA/S McBride; 20ctr AA/M Chaplow; 20b Forum 2004; 20r AA/S McBride; 20/21 AA/C Sawyer; 21tcc AA/M Chaplow; 21tcl AA/M Chaplow; 21cc AA/D Miterdiri; 21tcr AA/M Chaplow; 21tr © Kevin Fleming/CORBIS; 22/23bg AA/M Chaplow; 22tl AA/M Jourdan; 22tr AA/M Jourdan; 22ctl AA/M Chaplow; 22bl AA/M Jourdan; 23tl AA/M Jourdan; 23tc AA/M Jourdan; 23tr AA/M Chaplow; 23ctr AA/M Chaplow; 23cl Forum 2004; 24bg FC Barcelona; 24tr AA/M Chaplow; 24c AA/M Chaplow; 24tl Clare Garcia; 24tc FC Barcelona

THE STORY OF BARCELONA

25 AA/S Day; 26/7 AA; 26c Mary Evans Picture Library; 26bl AA; 26bc AA; 26/7 AA; 27cl AA; 27cr AA; 27br AA; 27bl Index/Bridgeman Art Library; 28/9 b/g AA/K Paterson; 28c K Paterson; 28bl Index/Bridgeman Art Library; 28bc AA/M Jourdan; 28/9t AA/W Voysey; 28/9b AA/M Jourdan; 29cc Bridgeman Art Library; 29cr AA/P Wilson; 29br AA/P Baker; 29bc AA/M Jourdan; 30/1 b/g AA/P Bennett; 30cl Index/Bridgeman Art Library; 30bl AA/S Day; 30/1b AA; 31l AA/P Wilson; 31cc AA/M Jourdan; 31cr Index/Bridgeman Art Library; 31br Mary Evans Picture Library; 32/3 b/g AA; 32cl AA/M Chaplow; 32bl AA/M Jourdan; 32b AA/M Chaplow; 32/3 AA/S Day; 33b AA/J A Tims; 33cr Lauros / Giraudon / Bridgeman Art Library; 33br Mary Evans Picture Library; 34/5 b/g AA/S Day; 34c AA/S Day; 34bl AA/S Day; 34/5 AA/S Day; 35cl AA/M Chaplow; 35ccl AA/M Chaplow; 35ccr Illustrated London News; 35cr Bridgeman Art Library; 35br AA/M Chaplow; 36/7 b/g AA/M Chaplow; 36cl AA/M Jourdan; 36cr AA/M Chaplow; 36bc AA/M Chaplow; 36/7 AA/S Day; 37cl AA/M Chaplow; 37cr AFP/Getty Images; 37br Getty Images; 38 b/g Forum 2004; 38cl Forum 2004; 38cr Forum 2004; 38bl Rex Features; 38cbr Forum 2004; 38br Forum 2004

ON THE MOVE

39 AA/S Day; 40t Digitalvision; 41t Digitalvision; 41cl AA/S Day; 42t Digitalvision; 42bl AA/S Day; 43t AA/B Smith; 44t AA/B Smith; 44cl AA/S Day; 44cc AA/M Jourdan; 45t AA/B Smith; 46 AA/B Smith; 46bl AA/S Day; 47t AA/B Smith; 48t AA/B Smith; 48cl AA/P Enticknap; 49t AA/B Smith; 49cr AA/S Day; 50t Digitalvision; 51t AA/M Chaplow; 51cr AA/M Chaplow; 52t Digitalvision; 52l AA/S Watkins; 52b Transports Metropolitans de Barcelona

THE SIGHTS

53 AA/S Day; 58 AA/S Day; 59cr AA/S Day; 59bl AA/M Jourdan; 60l AA/S Day; 60r AA/M Jourdan; 61 AA/M Chaplow; 62tl AA/S Day; 62tr AA/ M Jourdan; 62br AA/M Jourdan; 63t AA/M Jourdan; 63br AA/M Chaplow; 63cr AA/M Chaplow; 64t AA/M Chaplow; 64b AA/P Wilson; 65tl AA/M Chaplow; 65br Forum 2004; 66 AA/S Day; 67t AA/M Jourdan; 67cl AA/S Day; 67c AA/S Day; 67cr AA/S Day; 68/69t Forum 2004; 68cr AA/M Jourdan; 69cl AA/M Jourdan; 69cr AA/M Jourdan; 70t AA/M Chaplow; 70cl AA/S Day; 70c AA/M Jourdan; 71 AA/S Day; 72t AA/M Jourdan; 72cl AA/M Jourdan; 73cl AA/S Day; 73c AA/M Jourdan; 73cr AA/M Chaplow; 74tl AA/M Jourdan; 74tr AA/M Chaplow; 75t AA/S Day; 75cr AA/S Day; 76tl AA/M Chaplow; 76cr AA/M Chaplow; 76bc AA/M Chaplow; 76br AA/M Chaplow; 77tl AA/S Day; 77tr AA/M Jourdan/© Fundacio Antoni Tapies/DACS, London, 2004; 77b AA/S Day; 78t AA/P Wilson/© Succession Miro, DACS, 2004; 78cl AA/S Day; 78cr AA/m Jourdan; 79bl AA/M Jourdan/© Succession Miro, DACS, 2004; 79br AA/P Wilson/© Succession Miro, DACS, 2004, "detail"; 80tr AA/M Jourdan; 80cl AA/S Day; 80bl AA/S Day; 81tl AA/C Sawyer; 81tr AA/M Jourdan; 81bl AA/J Tims; 82t AA/M Chaplow; 82cl AA/S Day; 82c AA/S Day; 82cr AA/M Chaplow; 83t AA/M Chaplow; 83b AA/M Chaplow; 84t AA/M Jourdan; 84cl AA/S Day; 85t AA/M Jourdan; 85cl AA/S Day; 86t AA/M Jourdan; 86cl AA/S Day; 86/7 AA/M Jourdan; 86bl AA/M Chaplow; 87cr AA/M Chaplow; 87br AA/M Chaplow; 88tl AA/S Day; 88tr AA/P Wilson; 88bl AA/P Wilson; 89tl AA/P Wilson; 89tr AA/M Chaplow; 90t MACBA; 90cl MACBA; 90cr AA/M Jourdan; 91t AA/M Jourdan/© Fundacio Antoni Tapies/DACS, 2004; 91b AA/P Wilson; 92tl AA/S Day; 92tc AA/S Day; 92tr AA/MChaplow; 92bl AA/M Chaplow; 93t Museu d'historia de Catalunya; 92br AA/M Chaplow; 94t Museu Maritim; 94cl AA/M Jourdan; 94c Museu Maritim; 94cr AA/P Wilson; 95t Museu Maritim; 95cl Museu Maritim; 96 © Museu Nacional d'Art de Catalunya (Barcelona); 97t AA/M Jourdan; 97cl © Museu Nacional d'Art de Catalunya (Barcelona); 97c AA/M Jourdan; 97cr/98tl/tr/c/99t © Museu Nacional d'Art de Catalunya (Barcelona); 99bl AA/M Jourdan; 99br AA/M Jourdan; 100t AA/P Wilson; 100cl Illustrated London News; 101c Giraudon/Bridgeman Art Library/© Succession Picasso/DACS 2004; 101br Giraudon/Bridgeman Art Library/© Succession Picasso/DACS 2004; 102tl Museu de la Xocolata; 102tr AA/M Chaplow; 103bl AA/M Jourdan; 103br AA/M Jourdan; 104 Palau de la Musica Catalunya; 105t Palau de la Musica Catalunya; 105ccl Palau de la Musica Catalunya; 105cl Palau de la Musica Catalunya; 105cr Palau de la Musica Catalunya; 105ccr AA/P Wilson; 106c Palau de la Musica Catalunya; 106b Palau de la Musica Catalunya; 107 Palau de la Musica Catalunya; 108tl AA/S Day; 108tc AA/S Day; 108tr AA/M Chaplow; 109tl AA/S Day; 109tr AA/M Chaplow; 109br AA/S Day; 110t AA/S Day; 110cl AA/M Jourdan; 110c AA/S Day; 110cr AA/S Day; 111 AA/M Jourdan; 112/113 AA/M Jourdan; 112bl AA/M Jourdan; 113c AA/S Day; 113br AA/S Day; 114tl AA/M Chaplow; 114tc AA/M Jourdan; 114tr AA/M Jourdan; 115tl AA/P Wilson; 115tc AA/M Jourdan; 115tr AA/M Jourdan; 116t AA/M Chaplow; 116cl AA/P Wilson; 117t AA/S Day; 117cl © Maury Christian/Corbis Sygma; 117br AA/S Day; 118tl AA/S Day; 118tr AA/M Jourdan; 118b AA/M Chaplow; 119tl AA/M Jourdan; 119tr AA/M Chaplow; 119cr AA/M Chaplow; 119br AA/M Chaplow; 120t AA/S Day; 120cl AA/M Chaplow; 120c AA/S Day; 120cr AA/M Jourdan; 120br AA/ M Chaplow; 121c AA/M Chaplow; 121cl AA/S Day; 121cr AA/P Wilson; 121br AA/M Jourdan; 122cl AA/M Chaplow; 122cr AA/M Chaplow; 122b AA/M Chaplow; 123tl AA/M Jourdan; 123tr AA/P Wilson; 124 AA/S Day; 125t AA/M Chaplow; 125cl AA/S Day; 125c AA/S Day; 125cr AA/M Chaplow; 125b AA/ M Jourdan; 126t AA/M Chaplow; 126cr AA/S Day; 127tr AA/M Chaplow; 127bl AA/M Chaplow; 127br AA/P Wilson; 128t AA/M Chaplow; 128cl AA/M Chaplow; 129cl AA/S Day; 129cr AA/M Chaplow; 130tl AA/S Day; 130tc AA/M Chaplow; 130tr AA/S Day

WHAT TO DO

131 AA/M Chaplow; 136t AA/M Chaplow; 136cl AA/M Chaplow; 136cr AA/S McBride; 137cl AA/S McBride; 137cr AA/S McBride; 138cl AA/S McBride; 138cr AA/S McBride; 139cl AA/S McBride; 139cr AA/S McBride; 140cl AA/S Day; 140cr AA/S McBride; 141t AA/M Chaplow; 141bc Laie llibreria; 142t AA/M Chaplow; 142tcl AA/S McBride; 142tcc AA/S McBride; 142bcc AA/S McBride; 143t AA/M Chaplow; 143tcc AA/M Chaplow; 143tcr AA/S McBride; 143cr AA/S McBride; 144t AA/M Chaplow; 144cl AA/S McBride; 144cc AA/S McBride; 145t AA/M Chaplow; 145cl AA/S McBride; 145c AA/S McBride; 146t AA/M Chaplow; 146cl AA/S McBride; 146bl AA/S McBride; 147t AA/M Chaplow; 147cl AA/S McBride; 147tcc AA/S McBride; 148t AA/M Chaplow; 148tcc AA/M Chaplow; 148bc AA/S McBride; 148tcr AA/M Chaplow; 149t AA/M Chaplow; 149c AA/S McBride; 150t AA/M Chaplow; 150bl AA/S McBride; 150bc AA/S McBride; 150cr AA/S McBride; 151t AA/MChaplow; 151tcl Vincon; 151tcc AA/S McBride; 151cr AA/M Chaplow; 152t AA/M Chaplow; 152c Clare Garcia; 153t AA/M Chaplow; 154t AA/M Chaplow; 154cl AA/S Day; 154cr AA/S McBride; 155t Bikini Club; 155cl La Paloma; 160t Bikini Club; 160cl Clare Garcia; 161t Bikini Club; 161cl AA/M Jourdan; 161tcc AA/P Wilson; 161bc Bikini Club; 161cr AA/M Chaplow; 162t Bikini Club; 162c La Paloma; 163t Bikini Club; 163br Presma Teatre Nacional de Catalunya; 164t Bikini Club; 164bc Teatro Tivoli/Grup Balaria; 164br Versus Teatre; 165t Bikini Club; 165cl Brand X Pics; 166t Bikini Club; 166tcl Photodisc; 166c BCN Rouge; 166tcr AA/M Chaplow; 167t Bikini Club: 167c Clare Garcia; 167cr AA/S McBride; 168t Bikini Club; 169t Bikini Club; 169bc Brand X Pics; 170t Bikini Club; 170cr Sweet Café; 171t AA/ S Day; 171c Clare Garcia; 171cr Photodisc; 171br Photodisc; 172t AA/S Day; 172tcl Photodisc; 172bl AA/S Day; 172c AA/S Day; 172tcr AA/S Day; 172br AA/P Wilson; 173t AA/S Day; 173cl AA/M Jourdan; 173bc AA/S Day; 173cr AA/M Jourdan; 174t AA/S Day; 174bl Pista de Gel; 174bc Piscines Bernat; 174tcr Photodisc; 175t AA/S Day; 175cl AA/E Meacher; 175tcc Image 100; 176t AA/ S Day; 176cl Koré; 177t AA/M Jourdan; 177cl AA/S Day; 177tcr AA/M Jourdan; 177bcr AA/ S Day; 178t AA/M Jourdan; 178bl AA/M Jourdan; 178bc AA/ P Wilson; 178tcr AA/P Enticknap; 178bcr AA/M Chaplow; 179t La Paloma; 179br AA/M Jourdan; 180t La Paloma; 180tcl AA/M Jourdan; 180bl Brand X Pics; 180cr Digitalvision

OUT AND ABOUT

181 AA/M Jourdan; 182t AA/M Chaplow; 183tl AA/M Chaplow; 183tr AA/M Chaplow; 183cr AA/M Chaplow; 183b AA/M Chaplow; 184b AA/M Chaplow; 185t AA/M Jourdan; 185cl AA/M Jourdan; 185cr AA/M Chaplow; 186b AA/M Chaplow; 187tl AA/M Chaplow; 187tr AA/M Chaplow; 187bl AA/M Chaplow; 187bc AA/M Jourdan; 188t AA/M Chaplow; 188b AA/M Chaplow; 189t AA/M Chaplow; 189cl AA/M Chaplow; 189bl AA/M Chaplow; 189br AA/M Chaplow; 190t AA/S Day; 191tr AA/M Chaplow; 191cr AA/S Day; 191bl AA/S Day; 191br AA/M Chaplow; 192b AA/M Chaplow; 193t AA/M Chaplow; 193b AA/M Chaplow; 194c AA/A Baker; 195tr AA/P Wilson; 195cr AA/P Wilson; 196t AA/S Watkins; 196c AA/ P Wilson; 197c AA/S Watkins; 197b AA/P Wilson; 198t AA/P Enticknap; 198b AA/P Enticknap; 199t AA/P Enticknap; 199c AA/S Watkins; 200c AA/ S Watkins; 200bl AA/S Watkins; 201t AA/P Wilson; 201b AA/P Enticknap; 202t AA/M Chaplow; 202c AA/M Chaplow; 203cl AA/M Chaplow; 203c AA/M Chaplow; 203cr AA/M Chaplow; 204tl AA/M Chaplow; 204tr AA/S Day

EATING AND STAYING

205 AA/E Meacher; 216cl AA/S McBride; 216bl AA/S McBride; 216bc AA/S McBride; 217bl Antiga Casa Solé/Can Solé; 217cc ARCCAFÉ; 217br AA/S McBride; 218bl AA/S McBride; 218cc AA/S McBride; 218cr AA/S McBride; 218bc AA/S McBride; 219cl AA/S McBride; 219tc AA/S

McBride; 219bl AA/S McBride; 219cr Buenas Migas; 220tc AA/S McBride; 220bc AA/S McBride; 220cr Can Ramonet; 220br AA/S McBride; 221cl Restaurant Casa Calvet; 221cc AA/S McBride; 221bl AA/S McBride; 222bc AA/S McBride; 223tcl AA/S McBride; 223tc AA/S McBride; 223cc AA/S McBride; 223tcr AA/S McBride; 223bcr AA/S McBride; 224tl AA/S McBride; 224cl AA/S McBride; 224cc AA/S McBride; 224tr AA/S McBride; 224cr Living; 225tl AA/S McBride; 225cl AA/S McBride; 225tc AA/S McBride; 225bc AA/S McBride; 225cr AA/S McBride; 226tl AA/S McBride; 226cl AA/S McBride; 226cr AA/S McBride; 227ct AA/S McBride; 227cc Oriol Tarridas; 227tr AA/S McBride; 227br AA/S McBride; 228tl Ot Restaurant; 228tc Restaurant Els Pescadors; 228tr Pitarra Restaurant; 228bl AA/S McBride; 228br AA/S McBride; 229cl Polenta Restaurant; 229cr AA/S McBride; 229br AA/S Day; 230tl AA/S McBride; 230cc AA/S McBride; 230cr AA/S McBride; 231tl AA/S McBride; 231bl AA/S McBride; 231cc AA/S McBride; 231bc AA/S McBride; 232cl 7 Portes; 232bl Sesamo bar y comida sin bestias; 232bc AA/S McBride; 232tr AA/S McBride; 233cl AA/S McBride; 233tc Taxidermista; 233tr AA/S McBride; 233bl AA/S McBride; 233br Umita; 234tc AA/S McBride; 234cr AA/S McBride; 234br AA/S McBride; 235 AA/S McBride; 242cl AA/S McBride; 242bl AA/S McBride; 242cc AA/S McBride; 242tr Alexandra Hotel; 242cr AA/S Day; 243tl AA/S McBride; 243bl AA/S McBride; 243tc AA/M Chaplow; 243cr AA/S McBride; 244tl AA/S McBride; 244cl AA/S McBride; 244cc AA/S McBride; 244tr AA/S McBride; 245tl AA/S McBride; 245tc AA/S McBride; 245cl AA/S McBride; 245cc AA/S McBride; 245cr Hotel Continental; 245bc AA/S McBride; 246tl Hotel Continental Palacete; 246cl AA/S McBride; 246tc AA/S McBride; 246bc AA/S McBride; 246cr AA/S McBride; 246br AA/S McBride; 247cl AA/S McBride; 247bl AA/S McBride; 247cc AA/S McBride; 247cr AA/M Chaplow; 248tl AA/S McBride; 248tc AA/S McBride; 248tr AA/S McBride; 248cl AA/S McBride; 248cc AA/S McBride; 248cr AA/S McBride; 249tl AA/S McBride; 249tc AA/S McBride; 249tr AA/S McBride; 249cl AA/S McBride; 249cc AA/S McBride; 249cr AA/S McBride; 250tcl AA/S McBride; 250bl Hotel Majestic; 250bc AA/M Chaplow; 250br AA/S McBride; 251cl AA/S McBride; 251tc AA/S McBride; 251tr AA/S McBride; 251bc AA/S McBride; 252tl AA/S McBride; 252bl AA/S McBride; 252bc Hotel Rey Juan Carlos I; 252br Hotel Ritz; 253bl AA/S McBride; 252cr AA/S McBride

PLANNING

255 AA/S Day; 256t AA/M Chaplow; 258b AA/C Sawyer; 259tr AA/S Day; 259bl AA/M Chaplow; 260t AA/S Day; 260b European Central Bank Press and Information Division; 261tl AA/S Watkins; 261cr AA/S McBride; 263tl AA/M Jourdan; 263c AA/S McBride; 264 AA/M Jourdan; 265 AA/S McBride; 266tl AA/P Wilson; 266tr AA/M Chaplow; 267tl Photodisc; 267c AA/M Chaplow; 267crt Stockbyte; 267crb AA/B Rieger; 268c AA/M Jourdan; 268b AA/S Day; 269t AA/S McBride; 269cr AA/M Chaplow; 270 AA/ S Day

Project editor
Clare Garcia

AA Travel Guides design team
David Austin, Glyn Barlow, Alan Gooch, Kate Harling, Bob Johnson,
Nick Otway, Carole Philp, Keith Russell

Picture research
Liz Allen, Serena Mellish, Caroline Thomas

Internal repro work
Susan Crowhurst, Ian Little, Michael Moody

Production
Lyn Kirby, Caroline Nyman

Mapping
Maps produced by the Cartography Department of AA Publishing

Main contributors
Sarah Andrews, Daniel Campi, Paula Canal, The Content Works, Tony Kelly,
Sally Roy, Damien Simonis, Suzanne Wales

Copy editors
Jenni Davis, Julia Sandford

Published by AA Publishing, a trading name of Automobile Association Developments Limited,
whose registered office is Millstream, Maidenhead Road, Windsor, Berkshire SL4 5GD. Registered
number 1878835.

A CIP catalogue record for this book is available from the British Library.

ISBN 0 7495 4001 X

Binding style with plastic section dividers by permission of AA Publishing.

Colour separation by Keenes
Printed and bound by Leo, China

Find out more about AA Publishing and the wide range of travel publications and services the AA
provides by visiting our website at www.theAA.com

A01522

Mapping in this title produced from:
Map data © 1998–2003 Navigation Technologies BV. All rights reserved.
Mapping © GEOnext (Gruppo De Agostini) Novara

Relief map images supplied by Mountain High Maps ® Copyright © 1993 Digital Wisdom, Inc

Weather chart statistics supplied by Weatherbase © Copyright 2003 Canty and Associates, LLC

We believe the contents of this book are correct at the time of printing.
However, some details, particularly prices, opening times and telephone numbers
do change. We do not accept responsibility for any consequences arising from the use
of this book. This does not affect your statutory rights. We would be grateful if readers would
advise us of any inaccuracies they may encounter, or any suggestions they might like to make
to improve the book. There is a form provided at the back of the book for this purpose, or you
can email us at Keyguides@theaa.com

Dear Key Guide Reader

•

Thank you for buying Key Guide Barcelona.
Your comments and opinions are very important to us, so please help us to
improve our travel guides by taking a few minutes to complete this
questionnaire.

You do not need a stamp (unless posted outside the UK). If you do not want to
cut this page from your guide, then photocopy it or write your answers on a plain
sheet of paper.

Send to: **Key Guide Editor, AA World Travel Guides**
FREEPOST SCE 4598, Basingstoke RG21 4GY

ABOUT THIS GUIDE Where did you buy it?_____

_____

When? _ _ month/ _ _ year

Why did you choose AA Key Guide Barcelona?
❏ Price
❏ AA Publication
❏ Used this series before; title_____
❏ Cover
❏ Other_____

_____

Please rate how helpful the following features of the guide
are to you: very helpful (**VH**), helpful (**H**) or little help (**LH**)

Size	**VH**	**H**	**LH**
Layout	**VH**	**H**	**LH**
Photos	**VH**	**H**	**LH**
Excursions	**VH**	**H**	**LH**
Entertainment	**VH**	**H**	**LH**
Hotels	**VH**	**H**	**LH**
Maps	**VH**	**H**	**LH**
Practical info	**VH**	**H**	**LH**
Restaurants	**VH**	**H**	**LH**
Shopping	**VH**	**H**	**LH**
Walks	**VH**	**H**	**LH**
Sights	**VH**	**H**	**LH**
Transport info	**VH**	**H**	**LH**

continued on next page

What was your favourite sight, attraction or feature listed in the guide?

Page _____

Please give your reason _____

_____

Which features in the guide could be changed or improved, or any other comment you would like to make:

_____

_____

ABOUT YOU Name (*Mr/Mrs/Ms*) _____

Address _____

_____

_____ Postcode _____

Daytime tel nos _____

Which age group are you in?

Under 25 ❑ 25–34 ❑ 35–44 ❑ 45–54 ❑ 55+ ❑

How many trips do you make a year?

Less than one ❑ One ❑ Two ❑ Three or more ❑

Are you an AA member? Yes ❑ No ❑

ABOUT YOUR TRIP When did you book? _ _ month/_ _ year

When did you travel? _ _ month/_ _ year

Were you travelling for business or leisure? _____

How many nights did you stay? _____

How did you travel?

Individual ❑ Couple ❑ Family ❑ Group ❑

Did you buy any other travel guides for your trip? _____

If yes, which ones? _____

_____

_____

Thank you for taking the time to complete this questionnaire. Please send it to us as soon as possible, and remember, you do not need a stamp (*unless posted outside the UK*).